ENGLISH / SPANISH
INGLÉS / ESPAÑOL

OXFORD
PICTURE
DICTIONARY

SECOND EDITION

Jayme Adelson-Goldstein

Norma Shapiro

OXFORD
UNIVERSITY PRESS

198 Madison Avenue
New York, NY 10016 USA

Great Clarendon Street, Oxford OX2 6DP UK

Oxford University Press is a department of the University of Oxford.
It furthers the University's objective of excellence in research, scholarship,
and education by publishing worldwide in

Oxford New York

Auckland Cape Town Dar es Salaam Hong Kong Karachi
Kuala Lumpur Madrid Melbourne Mexico City Nairobi
New Delhi Shanghai Taipei Toronto

With offices in

Argentina Austria Brazil Chile Czech Republic France Greece
Guatemala Hungary Italy Japan Poland Portugal Singapore
South Korea Switzerland Thailand Turkey Ukraine Vietnam

OXFORD and OXFORD ENGLISH are registered trademarks of
Oxford University Press.

© Oxford University Press 2009

Library of Congress Cataloging-in-Publication Data

Adelson-Goldstein, Jayme.
    The Oxford picture dictionary. Monolingual /
Jayme Adelson-Goldstein and Norma Shapiro.– 2nd ed.
        p. cm.
    Includes index.
    ISBN: 978 0 19 474009 8

    1. Picture dictionaries, English. 2. English
language–Textbooks for foreign speakers.
I. Shapiro, Norma. II. Title.
PE1629.S52 2008
423'.1–dc22

                        2007041017

Database right Oxford University Press (maker)

Executive Publishing Manager: Stephanie Karras
Managing Editor: Sharon Sargent
Development Editors: Glenn Mathes II, Bruce Myint, Katie La Storia
Associate Development Editors: Olga Christopoulos, Hannah Ryu, Meredith Stoll
Design Manager: Maj-Britt Hagsted
Project Manager: Allison Harm
Senior Designers: Stacy Merlin, Michael Steinhofer
Designer: Jaclyn Smith
Senior Production Artist: Julie Armstrong
Production Layout Artist: Colleen Ho
Cover Design: Stacy Merlin
Senior Image Editor: Justine Eun
Image Editors: Robin Fadool, Fran Newman, Jenny Vainisi
Manufacturing Manager: Shanta Persaud
Manufacturing Controller: Eve Wong
Translated by: Techno-Graphics & Translations, Inc.

ISBN: 978 0 19 474009 8

Printed in China

10 9 8 7 6

This book is printed on paper from certified and well-managed sources.

The OPD team thanks the following artists for their storyboarding and sketches:
Cecilia Aranovich, Chris Brandt, Giacomo Ghiazza, Gary Goldstein, Gordan Kljucec,
Vincent Lucido, and Glenn Urieta

Illustrations by: Lori Anzalone: 13, 70-71, 76-77; Joe "Fearless" Arenella/Will Sumpter:
178; Argosy Publishing: 66-67 (call-outs), 98-99, 108-109, 112-113 (call-outs), 152, 178,
193, 194-195, 196, 197, 205; Barbara Bastian: 4, 15, 17, 20-21, 162 (map), 198, 216-217
(map), 220-221; Philip Batini/AA Reps: 50; Thomas Bayley/Sparks Literary Agency:
158-159; Sally Bensusen: 211, 214; Annie Bissett: 112; Peter Bollinger/Shannon
Associates: 14-15; Higgens Bond/Anita Grien: 226; Molly Borman-Pullman: 116,
117; Jim Fanning/Ravenhill Represents: 80-81; Mike Gardner: 10, 12, 17, 22, 132,
114-115, 142-143, 174, 219, 228-229; Garth Glazier/AA Reps: 106, 118-119; Dennis
Godfrey/Mike Wepplo: 204; Steve Graham: 124-125, 224; Graphic Map & Chart Co.:
200-201, 202-203; Julia Green/Mendola Art: 225; Glenn Gustafson: 9, 27, 48, 76,
100, 101, 117, 132, 133, 136, 155, 161, 179, 196; Barbara Harmon: 212-213, 215; Ben
Hasler/NB Illustration: 94-95, 101, 148-149, 172, 182, 186-187; Betsy Hayes: 134,
138-139; Matthew Holmes: 75; Stewart Holmes/Illustration Ltd.: 192; Janos Jantner/
Beehive Illustration: 5, 13, 82-83, 122-123, 130-131, 146-147, 164-165, 184, 185; Ken
Joudrey/Munro Campagna: 52, 68-69, 177, 208-209; Bob Kaganich/Deborah Wolfe:
10, 40-41, 121; Steve Karp: 230, 231; Mike Kasun/Munro Campagna: 218; Graham
Kennedy: 27; Marcel Laverdet/AA Reps: 23; Jeffrey Lindberg: 33, 42-43, 92-93, 133,
160-161, 170-171, 176; Dennis Lyall/Artworks: 198; Chris Lyons:/Lindgren & Smith:
173, 191; Alan Male/Artworks: 210, 211; Jeff Mangiat/Mendola Art: 53, 54, 55, 56, 57,
58, 59, 66-67; Adrian Mateescu/The Studio: 188-189, 232-233; Karen Minot: 28-29;
Paul Mirocha/The Wiley Group: 194, 216-217; Peter Miserendino/P.T. Pie Illustrations
198; Lee Montgomery/Illustration Ltd.: 4; Roger Motzkus: 229; Laurie O'Keefe: 111,
216-217; Daniel O'Leary/Illustration Ltd.: 8-9, 26, 34-35, 78, 135, 136-137, 238; Vilma
Ortiz-Dillon: 16, 20-21, 60, 98-99, 100, 211; Terry Pazcko: 46-47, 144-145, 152, 180,
227; David Preiss/Munro Campagna: 5; Pronk & Associates: 192-193; Tony Randazzo/
AA Reps: 156, 234-235; Mike Renwick/Creative Eye: 126-127; Mark Riedy/Scott Hull
Associates: 48-49, 79, 140, 153; Jon Rogers/AA Reps: 112; Jeff Sanson/Schumann &
Co.: 84-85, 240-241; David Schweitzer/Munro Campagna: 162-163; Ben Shannon/
Magnet Reps: 11, 64-65, 90, 91, 96, 97, 166-167, 168-169, 179, 239; Reed Sprunger/
Jae Wagoner Artists Rep.: 18-19, 232-233; Studio Liddell/AA Reps: 27; Angelo Tillary:
108-109; Ralph Voltz/Deborah Wolfe: 50-51, 128-129, 141, 154, 175, 236-237;
Jeff Wack/Mendola Art: 24, 25, 86-87, 102-103, 134-135, 231; Brad Walker: 104-105,
150-151, 157, 206-207; Wendy Wassink: 110-111; John White/The Neis Group: 199;
Eric Wilkerson: 32, 138; Simon Williams/Illustration Ltd.: 2-3, 6-7, 30-31, 36, 38-39,
44-45, 72-73; Lee Woodgate/Eye Candy Illustration: 222-223; Andy Zito: 62-23; Craig
Zuckerman: 14, 88-89, 112-113, 120-121, 194-195.

Chapter icons designed by Von Glitschka/Scott Hull Associates

Cover Art by CUBE/Illustration Ltd (hummingbird, branch); Paul Mirocha/The Wiley
Group (cherry); Mark Riedy/Scott Hull Associates (stamp); 9 Surf Studios (lettering).

Studio photography for Oxford University Press done by Dennis Kitchen Studio: 37,
61, 72, 73, 74, 75, 95, 96, 100, 180, 181, 183, 226.

Stock Photography: Age FotoStock: 238 (flute; clarinet; bassoon; saxophone; violin; cello;
bass; guitar; trombone; trumpet; xylophone; harmonica); Comstock, 61 (window);
Morales, 221 (bat); Franco Pizzochero, 98 (cashmere); Thinkstock, 61 (sink); Alamy:
Corbis, 61 (table); Gary Crabbe, 220 (park ranger); The Associated Press: 198 (strike;
soldiers in trench); Joe Rosenthal, 198 (Iwo Jima); Neil Armstrong, 198 (Buzz Aldrin
on Moon); CORBIS: Philip Gould, 198 (Civil War); Photo Library, 220 (Yosemite Falls);
Danita Delimont: Greg Johnston, 220 (snorkeling); Jamie & Judy Wild, 220 (El Capitan);
Getty Images: 198 (Martin Luther King, Jr.); Amana Images, 61 (soapy plates), The
Granger Collection: 198 (Jazz Age); The Image Works: Kelly Spranger, 220 (sea turtle);
Inmagine: 238 (oboe; tuba; French horn; piano; drums; tambourine; accordion);
istockphoto: 61 (oven), 98 (silk), 99 (suede; lace; velvet); Jupiter Images: 61 (tiles); 98
(wool); 99 (corduroy); Foodpix, 98 (linen); Rob Melnychuk/Brand X Pictures, 61 (glass
shower door); Jupiter Unlimited: 220 (seagulls); 238 (electric keyboard); Comstock, 99
(denim); Mary Evans Picture Library: 198 (women in factory); NPS Photo: Peter Jones, 221
(Carlsbad Cavern entrance; tour; cavern; spelunker); OceanwideImages.com: Gary Bell,
220 (coral); Photo Edit, Inc: David Young-Wolff, 220 (trail); Picture History: 198 (Hiram
Rhodes); Robertstock: 198 (Great Depression); Punchstock: 98 (t-shirt), Robert Glusic,
31 (Monument Valley); Roland Corporation: 238 (organ); SuperStock: 99 (leather); 198
(Daniel Boone); Shutterstock: Marek Szumlas, 94 (watch); United States Mint: 126;
Veer: Brand X Pictures, 220 (deer); Photodisc, 220 (black bear); Yankee Fleet, Inc.: 220
(Fort Jefferson; Yankee Freedom Ferry), Emil von Maltitz/Lime Photo, 37 (baby carrier).

This second edition of
the Oxford Picture Dictionary
is lovingly dedicated to
the memory of Norma Shapiro.

Her ideas, her pictures, and
her stories continue to teach,
inspire, and delight.

Acknowledgments

The publisher and authors would like to acknowledge the following individuals for their invaluable feedback during the development of this program:

Dr. Macarena Aguilar, Cy-Fair College, Houston, TX

Joseph F. Anselme, Atlantic Technical Center, Coconut Creek, FL

Stacy Antonopoulos, Monterey Trail High School, Elk Grove, CA

Carol Antunano, The English Center, Miami, FL

Irma Arencibia, Thomas A. Edison School, Union City, NJ

Suzi Austin, Alexandria City Public School Adult Program, Alexandria, FL

Patricia S. Bell, Lake Technical Center, Eustis, FL

Jim Brice, San Diego Community College District, San Diego, CA

Phil Cackley, Arlington Education and Employment Program (REEP), Arlington, VA

Frieda Caldwell, Metropolitan Adult Education Program, San Jose, CA

Sandra Cancel, Robert Waters School, Union City, NJ

Anne Marie Caney, Chula Vista Adult School, Chula Vista, CA

Patricia Castro, Harvest English Institute, Newark, NJ

Paohui Lola Chen, Milpitas Adult School, Milpitas, CA

Lori Cisneros, Atlantic Vo-Tech, Ft. Lauderdale, FL

Joyce Clapp, Hayward Adult School, Hayward, CA

Stacy Clark, Arlington Education and Employment Program (REEP), Arlington, VA

Nancy B. Crowell, Southside Programs for Adults in Continuing Education, Prince George, VA

Doroti da Cunha, Hialeah-Miami Lakes Adult Education Center, Miami, FL

Paula Da Silva-Michelin, La Guardia Community College, Long Island City, NY

Cynthia L. Davies, Humble I.S.D., Humble, TX

Christopher Davis, Overfelt Adult Center, San Jose, CA

Beverly De Nicola, Capistrano Unified School District, San Juan Capistrano, CA

Beatriz Diaz, Miami-Dade County Public Schools, Miami, FL

Druci J. Diaz, Hillsborough County Public Schools, Tampa, FL

Marion Donahue, San Dieguito Adult School, Encinitas, CA

Nick Doorn, International Education Services, South Lyon, MI

Mercedes Douglass, Seminole Community College, Sanford, FL

Jenny Elliott, Montgomery College, Rockville, MD

Paige Endo, Mt. Diablo Adult Education, Concord, CA

Megan Ernst, Glendale Community College, Glendale, CA

Elizabeth Escobar, Robert Waters School, Union City, NJ

Joanne Everett, Dave Thomas Education Center, Pompano Beach, FL

Jennifer Fadden, Arlington Education and Employment Program (REEP), Arlington, VA

Judy Farron, Fort Myers Language Center, Fort Myers, FL

Sharyl Ferguson, Montwood High School, El Paso, TX

Dr. Monica Fishkin, University of Central Florida, Orlando, FL

Nancy Frampton, Reedley College, Reedley, CA

Lynn A. Freeland, San Dieguito Union High School District, Encinitas, CA

Cathy Gample, San Leandro Adult School, San Leandro, CA

Hillary Gardner, Center for Immigrant Education and Training, Long Island City, NY

Martha C. Giffen, Alhambra Unified School District, Alhambra, CA

Jill Gluck, Hollywood Community Adult School, Los Angeles, CA

Carolyn Grimaldi, LaGuardia Community College, Long Island City, NY

William Gruenholz, USD Adult School, Concord, CA

Sandra G. Gutierrez, Hialeah-Miami Lakes Adult Education Center, Miami, FL

Conte Gúzman-Hoffman, Triton College, River Grove, IL

Amanda Harllee, Palmetto High School, Palmetto, FL

Mercedes Hearn, Tampa Bay Technical Center, Tampa, FL

Robert Hearst, Truman College, Chicago, IL

Patty Heiser, University of Washington, Seattle, WA

Joyce Hettiger, Metropolitan Education District, San Jose, CA

Karen Hirsimaki, Napa Valley Adult School, Napa, CA

Marvina Hooper, Lake Technical Center, Eustis, FL

Katie Hurter, North Harris College, Houston, TX

Nuchamon James, Miami Dade College, Miami, FL

Linda Jennings, Montgomery College, Rockville, MD

Bonnie Boyd Johnson, Chapman Education Center, Garden Grove, CA

Fayne B. Johnson, Broward County Public Schools, Fort Lauderdale, FL

Stavroula Katseyeanis, Robert Waters School, Union City, NJ

Dale Keith, Broadbase Consulting, Inc. at Kidworks USA, Miami, FL

Blanche Kellawon, Bronx Community College, Bronx, NY

Mary Kernel, Migrant Education Regional Office, Northwest Educational Service District, Anacortes, WA

Karen Kipke, Antioch High School Freshman Academy, Antioch, TN

Jody Kirkwood, ABC Adult School, Cerritos, CA

Matthew Kogan, Evans Community Adult School, Los Angeles, CA

Ineza Kuceba, Renton Technical College, Renton, WA

John Kuntz, California State University, San Bernadino, San Bernadino, CA

Claudia Kupiec, DePaul University, Chicago, IL

E.C. Land, Southside Programs for Adult Continuing Education, Prince George, VA

Betty Lau, Franklin High School, Seattle, WA

Patt Lemonie, Thomas A. Edison School, Union City, NJ

Lia Lerner, Burbank Adult School, Burbank, CA

Krystyna Lett, Metropolitan Education District, San Jose, CA

Renata Lima, TALK International School of Languages, Fort Lauderdale, FL

Luz M. Lopez, Sweetwater Union High School District, Chula Vista, CA

Osmara Lopez, Bronx Community College, Bronx, NY

Heather Lozano, North Lake College, Irving, TX

Betty Lynch, Arlington Education and Employment Program (REEP), Arlington, VA

Meera Madan, REID Park Elementary School, Charlotte, NC

Ivanna Mann Thrower, Charlotte Mecklenburg Schools, Charlotte, NC

Michael R. Mason, Loma Vista Adult Center, Concord, CA

Holley Mayville, Charlotte Mecklenburg Schools, Charlotte, NC

Margaret McCabe, United Methodist Cooperative Ministries, Clearwater, FL

Todd McDonald, Hillsborough Adult Education, Tampa, FL

Nancy A. McKeand, ESL Consultant, St. Benedict, LA

Rebecca L. McLain, Gaston College, Dallas, NC

John M. Mendoza, Redlands Adult School, Redlands, CA

Bet Messmer, Santa Clara Adult Education Center, Santa Clara, CA

Christina Morales, BEGIN Managed Programs, New York, NY

Lisa Munoz, Metropolitan Education District, San Jose, CA

Mary Murphy-Clagett, Sweetwater Union High School District, Chula Vista, CA

Jonetta Myles, Rockdale County High School, Conyers, GA

Marwan Nabi, Troy High School, Fullerton, CA

Dr. Christine L. Nelsen, Salvation Army Community Center, Tampa, FL

Michael W. Newman, Arlington Education and Employment Program (REEP), Arlington, VA

Rehana Nusrat, Huntington Beach Adult School, Huntington Beach, CA

Cindy Oakley-Paulik, Embry-Riddle Aeronautical University, Daytona Beach, FL

Acknowledgments

Janet Ochi-Fontanott, Sweetwater Union High School District, Chula Vista, CA

Lorraine Pedretti, Metropolitan Education District, San Jose, CA

Isabel Pena, BE/ESL Programs, Garland, TX

Margaret Perry, Everett Public Schools, Everett, WA

Dale Pesmen, PhD, Chicago, IL

Cathleen Petersen, Chapman Education Center, Garden Grove, CA

Allison Pickering, Escondido Adult School, Escondido, CA

Ellen Quish, LaGuardia Community College, Long Island City, NY

Teresa Reen, Independence Adult Center, San Jose, CA

Kathleen Reynolds, Albany Park Community Center, Chicago, IL

Melba I. Rillen, Palmetto High School, Palmetto, FL

Lorraine Romero, Houston Community College, Houston, TX

Eric Rosenbaum, BEGIN Managed Programs, New York, NY

Blair Roy, Chapman Education Center, Garden Grove, CA

Arlene R. Schwartz, Broward Community Schools, Fort Lauderdale, FL

Geraldyne Blake Scott, Truman College, Chicago, IL

Sharada Sekar, Antioch High School Freshman Academy, Antioch, TN

Dr. Cheryl J. Serrano, Lynn University, Boca Raton, FL

Janet Setzekorn, United Methodist Cooperative Ministries, Clearwater, FL

Terry Shearer, EDUCALL Learning Services, Houston, TX

Elisabeth Sklar, Township High School District 113, Highland Park, IL

Robert Stein, BEGIN Managed Programs, New York, NY

Ruth Sutton, Township High School District 113, Highland Park, IL

Alisa Takeuchi, Chapman Education Center, Garden Grove, CA

Grace Tanaka, Santa Ana College School of Continuing Education, Santa Ana, CA

Annalisa Te, Overfelt Adult Center, San Jose, CA

Don Torluemke, South Bay Adult School, Redondo Beach, CA

Maliheh Vafai, Overfelt Adult Center, San Jose, CA

Tara Vasquez, Robert Waters School, Union City, NJ

Nina Velasco, Naples Language Center, Naples, FL

Theresa Warren, East Side Adult Center, San Jose, CA

Lucie Gates Watel, Truman College, Chicago, IL

Wendy Weil, Arnold Middle School, Cypress, TX

Patricia Weist, TALK International School of Languages, Fort Lauderdale, FL

Dr. Carole Lynn Weisz, Lehman College, Bronx, NY

Desiree Wesner, Robert Waters School, Union City, NJ

David Wexler, Napa Valley Adult School, Napa, CA

Cynthia Wiseman, Borough of Manhattan Community College, New York, NY

Debbie Cullinane Wood, Lincoln Education Center, Garden Grove, CA

Banu Yaylali, Miami Dade College, Miami, FL

Hongyan Zheng, Milpitas Adult Education, Milpitas, CA

Arlene Zivitz, ESOL Teacher, Jupiter, FL

The publisher, authors, and editors would like to thank the following people for their expertise in reviewing specific content areas:

Ross Feldberg, Tufts University, Medford, MA

William J. Hall, M.D. FACP/FRSM (UK), Cumberland Foreside, ME

Jill A. Horohoe, Arizona State University, Tempe, AZ

Phoebe B. Rouse, Louisiana State University, Baton Rouge, LA

Dr. Susan Rouse, Southern Wesleyan University, Central, SC

Dr. Ira M. Sheskin, University of Miami, Coral Gables, FL

Maiko Tomizawa, D.D.S., New York, NY

Table of Contents Índice Temático

Introduction Introducción . . . . .ix–xi

1. Everyday Language Lenguaje cotidiano

Meeting and Greeting Reunirse y saludar 2–3
Personal Information Información personal. 4
School La escuela. 5
A Classroom Un salón de clase .6–7
Studying Estudiar 8–9
Succeeding in School Cómo tener éxito en la escuela. 10
A Day at School Un día en la escuela 11
Everyday Conversation La conversación diaria 12
Weather El tiempo 13
The Telephone El teléfono 14–15
Numbers Números 16
Measurements Medidas 17
Time La hora 18–19
The Calendar El calendario .20–21
Calendar Events Calendario de eventos. 22
Describing Things Descripción de los objetos. 23
Colors Colores 24
Prepositions Las preposiciones .25
Money El dinero 26
Shopping Ir de compras 27
Same and Different Igual y diferente 28–29

2. People Gente

Adults and Children Adultos y niños 30–31
Describing People Descripción de las personas 32
Describing Hair Descripción del cabello. 33
Families Las familias 34–35
Childcare and Parenting Crianza y cuidado de los niños 36–37
Daily Routines Rutinas diarias 38–39
Life Events and Documents Sucesos de la vida y documentos 40–41
Feelings Estados de ánimo y sentimientos. 42–43
A Family Reunion Una reunión familiar 44–45

3. Housing Vivienda

The Home El hogar. 46–47
Finding a Home Búsqueda de casa 48–49
Apartments Los apartamentos 50–51
Different Places to Live Lugares diferentes para vivir 52
A House and Yard La casa y el jardín 53
A Kitchen Una cocina. 54
A Dining Area Un comedor. 55
A Living Room Una sala de estar 56
A Bathroom Un baño. 57
A Bedroom Un dormitorio 58
The Kids' Bedroom El dormitorio de los niños. 59
Housework Quehaceres domésticos 60
Cleaning Supplies Los artículos de limpieza. 61
Household Problems and Repairs Problemas y reparaciones domésticas 62–63
The Tenant Meeting La reunión de los inquilinos 64–65

Contents Contenido

4. Food Alimentos

Back from the Market De vuelta del mercado. 66–67
Fruit Las frutas 68
Vegetables Las verduras y hortalizas 69
Meat and Poultry Carne y aves de corral 70
Seafood and Deli Mariscos y comestibles preparados 71
A Grocery Store Una tienda de comestibles 72–73
Containers and Packaging Contenedores y envases 74
Weights and Measurements Pesos y medidas 75
Food Preparation and Safety Preparación y seguridad de los alimentos 76–77
Kitchen Utensils Utensilios de cocina 78
Fast Food Restaurant Restaurante de comida rápida 79
A Coffee Shop Menu El menú de un café 80–81
A Restaurant Un restaurante 82–83
The Farmers' Market El mercado de agricultores 84–85

5. Clothing Ropa

Everyday Clothes La ropa diaria 86–87
Casual, Work, and Formal Clothes Ropa casual, de trabajo y formal 88–89
Seasonal Clothing Ropa de temporada 90
Underwear and Sleepwear Ropa interior y ropa de dormir 91
Workplace Clothing Ropa de trabajo 92–93
Shoes and Accessories Zapatos y accesorios 94–95
Describing Clothes Descripción de la ropa 96–97
Making Clothes Confección de ropa 98–99
Making Alterations Alteraciones 100
Doing the Laundry Lavar la ropa / Hacer la colada 101
A Garage Sale Una venta de garaje 102–103

6. Health Salud

The Body El cuerpo. 104–105
Inside and Outside the Body Dentro y fuera del cuerpo 106–107
Personal Hygiene La higiene personal 108–109
Symptoms and Injuries Los síntomas y las lesiones 110
Illnesses and Medical Conditions Las enfermedades y los padecimientos 111
A Pharmacy Una farmacia 112–113
Taking Care of Your Health El cuidado de su salud 114–115
Medical Emergencies Las emergencias médicas 116
First Aid Los primeros auxilios. 117
Medical Care La atención médica 118
Dental Care La atención dental 119
Hospital El hospital 120–121
A Health Fair Una feria de salud. 122–123

7. **Community** La comunidad

Downtown El centro de la ciudad 124–125
City Streets Las calles de la ciudad 126–127
An Intersection Una intersección 128–129
A Mall Un centro comercial 130–131
The Bank El banco 132
The Library La biblioteca 133
The Post Office La oficina de correos 134–135
Department of Motor Vehicles (DMV) El Departamento de
   Vehículos Motorizados (DMV) 136–137
Government and Military Service El gobierno y el servicio militar 138–139
Civic Rights and Responsibilities Derechos y responsabilidades cívicas 140
The Legal System El sistema legal 141
Crime La delincuencia 142
Public Safety La seguridad pública 143
Emergencies and Natural Disasters Emergencias y desastres naturales 144–145
Emergency Procedures Procedimientos de emergencia 146–147
Community Cleanup Limpieza comunitaria 148–149

8. **Transportation** Transporte

Basic Transportation El transporte básico 150–151
Public Transportation El transporte público 152
Prepositions of Motion Preposiciones de movimiento 153
Traffic Signs Señales de tráfico 154
Directions and Maps Direcciones y mapas 155
Cars and Trucks Automóviles y camiones 156
Buying and Maintaining a Car Compra y mantenimiento de un automóvil 157
Parts of a Car Partes de un automóvil 158–159
An Airport Un aeropuerto 160–161
Taking a Trip Hacer un viaje 162–163

9. **Work** Trabajo

The Workplace El lugar de trabajo 164–165
Jobs and Occupations A-C Empleos y profesiones A-C 166
Jobs and Occupations C-H Empleos y profesiones C-H 167
Jobs and Occupations H-P Empleos y profesiones H-P 168
Jobs and Occupations P-W Empleos y profesiones P-W 169
Job Skills Destrezas laborales 170
Office Skills Destrezas de oficina 171
Career Planning Planificación de carreras 172
Job Search En busca de trabajo 173
Interview Skills Destrezas de entrevista 174
A Factory Una fábrica 175
Landscaping and Gardening Paisajismo y jardinería 176
Farming and Ranching La agricultura y la ganadería 177
Construction La construcción 178
Job Safety La seguridad en el lugar de trabajo 179
Tools and Building Supplies Herramientas y materiales de construcción . . . 180–181
An Office Una oficina 182–183
A Hotel Un hotel 184
Food Service Servicio de comidas 185
A Bad Day at Work Un mal día en el trabajo 186–187

Contents Contenido

10. Areas of Study Áreas de estudio

Schools and Subjects Las escuelas y materias 188–189
English Composition La composición en inglés 190–191
Mathematics Las matemáticas 192–193
Science Las ciencias 194–195
Computers Las computadoras 196
The Internet La red Internet 197
U.S. History La historia de EE.UU. 198
World History La historia universal 199
North America and Central America Norte América y Centro América 200–201
World Map El mapa del mundo 202–203
Geography and Habitats La geografía y los hábitats 204
The Universe El universo 205
A Graduation Una graduación 206–207

11. Plants and Animals Plantas y animales

Nature Center El centro ecológico 208–209
Trees and Plants Árboles y plantas 210
Flowers Flores 211
Marine Life, Amphibians, and Reptiles Vida marina, anfibios y reptiles . . . 212–213
Birds, Insects, and Arachnids Pájaros, insectos y arácnidos 214
Domestic Animals and Rodents Animales domésticos y roedores 215
Mammals Mamíferos 216–217
Energy and Conservation Energía y conservación 218–219
U.S. National Parks Parques nacionales de EE.UU. 220–221

12. Recreation Recreación

Places to Go Lugares a donde ir 222–223
The Park and Playground El parque y el patio de recreo 224
The Beach La playa 225
Outdoor Recreation Recreación al aire libre 226
Winter and Water Sports Deportes de invierno y acuáticos 227
Individual Sports Deportes individuales 228
Team Sports Deportes en equipo 229
Sports Verbs Verbos utilizados en los deportes 230
Sports Equipment Equipo deportivo 231
Hobbies and Games Pasatiempos y juegos 232–233
Electronics and Photography Electrónica y fotografía 234–235
Entertainment Entretenimiento 236–237
Music Música 238
Holidays Días feriados 239
A Birthday Party Una fiesta de cumpleaños 240–241

Verb Guide Guía de verbos 242–244
How to Use the Index Cómo usar el Índice 245
English Index Índice en Inglés 246–281
Geographical Index Índice geográfico 282–284
Spanish Index Índice en Español 285–304
Research Bibliography Bibliografía de investigación 305

Teaching with the *Oxford Picture Dictionary* Program

The following general guidelines will help you prepare single and multilevel lessons using the OPD program. For step-by-step, topic-specific lesson plans, see *OPD Lesson Plans*.

1. Use Students' Needs to Identify Lesson Objectives

- Create communicative objectives based on your learners' needs assessments (*see OPD 2e Assessment Program*).

- Make sure objectives state what students will be able to do at the end of the lesson. For example: *Students will be able to respond to basic classroom commands and requests for classroom objects.* (pp. 6–7, A Classroom)

- For multilevel classes, identify a low-beginning, high-beginning, and low-intermediate objective for each topic.

2. Preview the Topic

Identify what your students already know about the topic.

- Ask general questions related to the topic.
- Have students list words they know from the topic.
- Ask questions about the picture(s) on the page.

3. Present the New Vocabulary

Research shows that it is best to present no more than 5–7 new words at a time. Here are a few presentation techniques:

- Say each new word and describe it within the context of the picture. Have volunteers act out verbs and verb sequences.

- Use Total Physical Response commands to build vocabulary comprehension.

- For long or unfamiliar word lists, introduce words by categories or select the words your students need most.

- Ask a series of questions to build comprehension and give students an opportunity to say the new words. Begin with *yes/no* questions: *Is #16 chalk?* Progress to *or* questions: *Is #16 chalk or a marker?* Finally, ask *Wh-* questions: *What can I use to write on this paper?*

- Focus on the words that students want to learn. Have them write 3–5 new words from each topic, along with meaning clues such as a drawing, translation, or sentence.

More vocabulary and **Grammar Point** sections provide additional presentation opportunities (see p. 5, School). For multilevel presentation ideas, see *OPD Lesson Plans*.

4. Check Comprehension

Make sure that students understand the target vocabulary. Here are two activities you can try:

- Say vocabulary words, and have students point to the correct items in their books. Walk around the room, checking if students are pointing to the correct pictures.

- Make true/false statements about the target vocabulary. Have students hold up two fingers for true, three for false.

5. Provide Guided and Communicative Practice

The exercise bands at the bottom of the topic pages provide a variety of guided and communicative practice opportunities and engage students' higher-level thinking.

6. Provide More Practice

OPD Second Edition offers a variety of components to facilitate vocabulary acquisition. Each of the print and electronic materials listed below offers suggestions and support for single and multilevel instruction.

OPD Lesson Plans Step-by-step multilevel lesson plans feature 3 CDs with multilevel listening, context-based pronunciation practice, and leveled reading practice. Includes multilevel teaching notes for *The OPD Reading Library*.

OPD Audio CDs or Audio Cassettes Each word in *OPD's* word list is recorded by topic.

Low-Beginning, High-Beginning, and Low-Intermediate Workbooks Guided practice for each page in *OPD* features linked visual contexts, realia, and listening practice.

Classic Classroom Activities A photocopiable resource of interactive multilevel activities, grammar practice, and communicative tasks.

The OPD Reading Library Readers include civics, academic content, and workplace themes.

Overhead Transparencies Vibrant transparencies help to focus students on the lesson.

OPD Presentation Software A multilevel interactive teaching tool using interactive whiteboard and LCD technology. Audio, animation, and video instructional support bring each dictionary topic to life.

The OPD CD-ROM An interactive learning tool featuring four-skill practice based on *OPD* topics.

Bilingual Editions *OPD* is available in numerous bilingual editions including Spanish, Chinese, Vietnamese, Arabic, Korean, and many more.

My hope is that OPD makes it easier for you to take your learners from comprehension to communication. Please share your thoughts with us as you make the book your own.

Jayme Adelson-Goldstein

OPDteam.us@oup.com

Welcome to the
OPD SECOND EDITION

The second edition of the *Oxford Picture Dictionary* expands on the best aspects of the 1998 edition with:

- New artwork presenting words within meaningful, real-life contexts
- An updated word list to meet the needs of today's English language learners
- 4,000 English words and phrases, including 285 verbs
- 40 new topics with 12 intro pages and 12 story pages
- Unparalleled support for vocabulary teaching

Subtopics present the words in easy-to-learn "chunks."

Color coding and icons make it easy to navigate through *OPD*.

New art and rich contexts improve vocabulary acquisition.

Revised practice activities help students from low-beginning through low-intermediate levels.

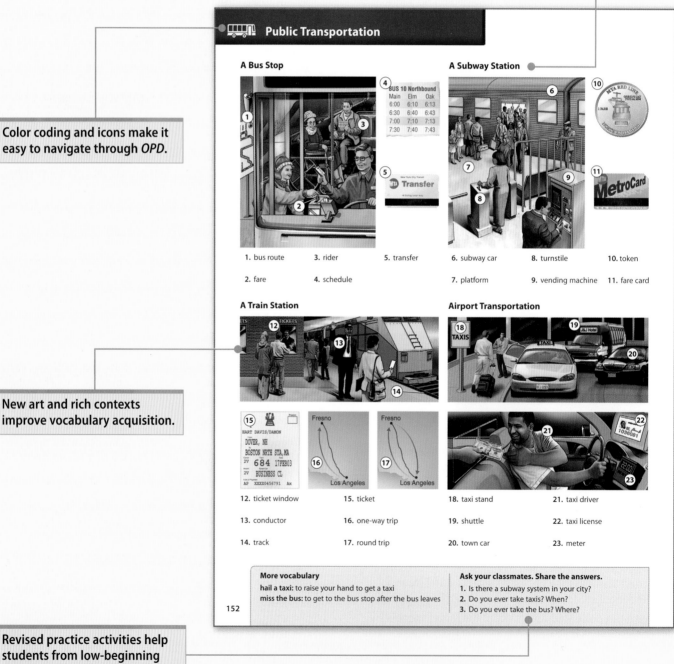

Public Transportation

A Bus Stop

BUS 10 Northbound
Main	Elm	Oak
6:00	6:10	6:13
6:30	6:40	6:43
7:00	7:10	7:13
7:30	7:40	7:43

1. bus route
2. fare
3. rider
4. schedule
5. transfer

A Subway Station

6. subway car
7. platform
8. turnstile
9. vending machine
10. token
11. fare card

A Train Station

12. ticket window
13. conductor
14. track
15. ticket
16. one-way trip
17. round trip

Airport Transportation

18. taxi stand
19. shuttle
20. town car
21. taxi driver
22. taxi license
23. meter

More vocabulary

hail a taxi: to raise your hand to get a taxi
miss the bus: to get to the bus stop after the bus leaves

Ask your classmates. Share the answers.

1. Is there a subway system in your city?
2. Do you ever take taxis? When?
3. Do you ever take the bus? Where?

152

x

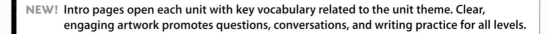

NEW! Intro pages open each unit with key vocabulary related to the unit theme. Clear, engaging artwork promotes questions, conversations, and writing practice for all levels.

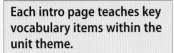

Each intro page teaches key vocabulary items within the unit theme.

Practice activities make it easy to manage multilevel classrooms.

NEW! Story pages close each unit with a lively scene for reviewing vocabulary and teaching additional language. Meanwhile, rich visual contexts recycle words from the unit.

Pre-reading questions build students' previewing and predicting skills.

High-interest readings promote literacy skills.

Post-reading questions and role-play activities support critical thinking and encourage students to use the language they have learned.

The thematic word list previews words that students will encounter in the story.

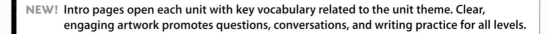

A. **Say**, "Hello."
   Diga, "Hola."

B. **Ask**, "How are you?"
   Pregunte, "¿Cómo está usted?"

C. **Introduce** yourself.
   Preséntese.

D. **Smile**.
   Sonría.

E. **Hug**.
   Abrace.

F. **Wave**.
   Salude con la mano.

Tell your partner what to do. Take turns.

1. *Say*, "Hello."   4. *Shake hands*.
2. *Bow*.   5. *Wave*.
3. *Smile*.   6. *Say*, "Goodbye."

Dictate to your partner. Take turns.

A: *Write smile*.
B: *Is it spelled s-m-i-l-e?*
A: *Yes, that's right.*

G. **Greet** people.
   Salude a la gente.

H. **Bow.**
   Haga una reverencia.

I. **Introduce** a friend.
   Presente a un amigo.

J. **Shake** hands.
   Dé un apretón de manos.

K. **Kiss.**
   Bese.

L. **Say,** "Goodbye."
   Diga, "Hasta luego."

Ways to greet people

Good morning.
Good afternoon.
Good evening.

Ways to introduce yourself

I'm <u>Tom</u>.
My name is <u>Tom</u>.

Pair practice. Make new conversations.

A: *Good morning. My name is* <u>Tom</u>.
B: *Nice to meet you,* <u>Tom</u>. *I'm* <u>Sara</u>.
A: *Nice to meet you,* <u>Sara</u>.

3

A

Carlos

B

C-a-r-l-o-s

C

CARLOS R. SOTO

D

Carlos R. Soto

A. **Say** your name.
Diga su nombre.

B. **Spell** your name.
Deletree su nombre.

C. **Print** your name.
Imprima su nombre.

D. **Sign** your name.
Firme su nombre.

Filling Out a Form Cómo llenar un formulario

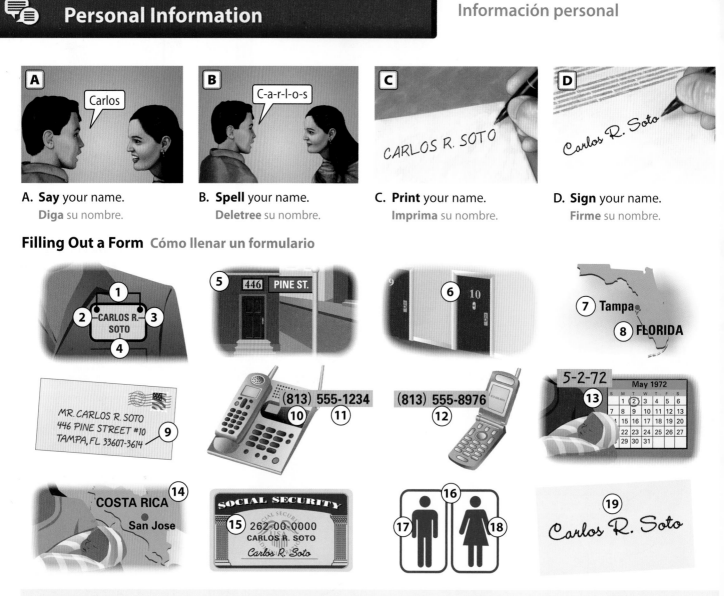

School Registration Form Formulario de inscripción escolar

1. name:
   nombre:

2. first name
   primer nombre

3. middle initial
   inicial del segundo nombre

4. last name
   apellido

5. address
   dirección

6. apartment number
   número de apartamento

7. city
   ciudad

8. state
   estado

9. ZIP code
   código postal

10. area code
    código de área

11. phone number
    número de teléfono

12. cell phone number
    número de teléfono celular

13. date of birth (DOB)
    fecha de nacimiento

14. place of birth
    lugar de nacimiento

15. Social Security number
    Número de Seguro Social

16. sex:
    sexo:

17. male
    masculino

18. female
    femenino

19. signature
    firma

Pair practice. Make new conversations.

A: *My first name is Carlos.*
B: *Please spell Carlos for me.*
A: *C-a-r-l-o-s*

Ask your classmates. Share the answers.

1. Do you like your first name?
2. Is your last name from your mother? father? husband?
3. What is your middle name?

Campus El campus

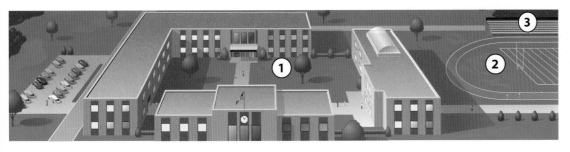

1. quad
   el patio interior
2. field
   el campo
3. bleachers
   las gradas
4. principal
   el director / la directora
5. assistant principal
   el asistente de director
6. counselor
   el consejero / la consejera
7. classroom
   el salón de clase
8. teacher
   el profesor / el maestro
9. restrooms
   los baños
10. hallway
    el pasillo
11. locker
    el armario
12. main office
    la oficina principal
13. clerk
    el empleado / la empleada
14. cafeteria
    la cafetería
15. computer lab
    el laboratorio de computadoras
16. teacher's aide
    el asistente del profesor o maestro
17. library
    la biblioteca
18. auditorium
    el auditorio
19. gym
    el gimnasio
20. coach
    el entrenador
21. track
    la pista

Administrators Los administradores

Around Campus Alrededor del campus

More vocabulary

Students do not pay to go to a **public school**.
Students pay to go to a **private school**.
A church, mosque, or temple school is a **parochial school**.

Grammar Point: contractions of the verb *be*

He + is = He's   *He's a teacher.*
She + is = She's   *She's a counselor.*
They + are = They're *They're students.*

5

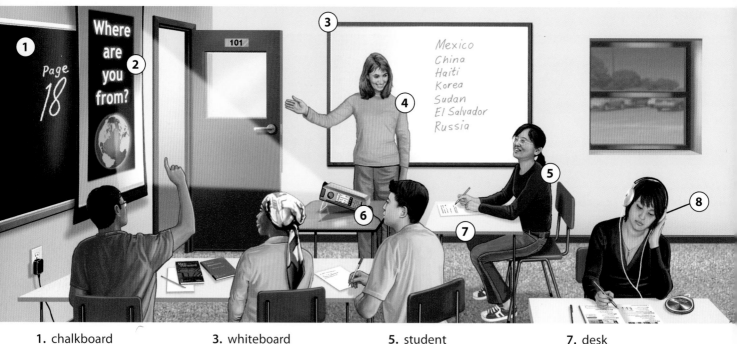

1. **chalkboard**
   la pizarra

2. **screen**
   la pantalla

3. **whiteboard**
   la pizarra para rotuladores

4. **teacher / instructor**
   la maestra / la profesora / la instructora

5. **student**
   el estudiante

6. **LCD projector**
   el proyector LCD

7. **desk**
   el escritorio

8. **headphones**
   los audífonos

A. **Raise** your hand.
   Levante la mano.

B. **Talk** to the teacher.
   Hable con la maestra.

C. **Listen** to a CD.
   Escuche un CD.

D. **Stand up**.
   Póngase de pie.

E. **Write** on the board.
   Escriba en la pizarra.

F. **Sit down. / Take** a seat.
   Siéntese. / Tome asiento.

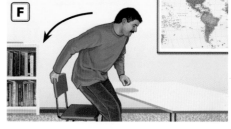

G. **Open** your book.
   Abra el libro.

H. **Close** your book.
   Cierre el libro.

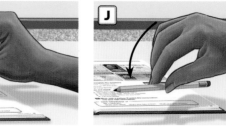

I. **Pick up** the pencil.
   Coja el lápiz.

J. **Put down** the pencil.
   Suelte el lápiz.

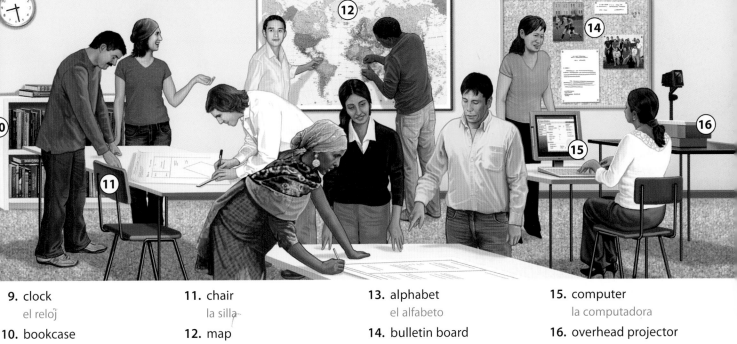

9. clock
el reloj

10. bookcase
el librero

11. chair
la silla

12. map
el mapa

13. alphabet
el alfabeto

14. bulletin board
la cartelera

15. computer
la computadora

16. overhead projector
el retroproyector

17. dry erase marker
el marcador borrable en seco

18. chalk
la tiza / el gis

19. eraser
el borrador

20. pencil
el lápiz

21. (pencil) eraser
la goma de borrar

22. pen
el bolígrafo / la pluma

23. pencil sharpener
el sacapuntas

24. marker
el marcador

25. textbook
el libro de texto

26. workbook
el cuaderno de trabajo

27. 3-ring binder / notebook
la carpeta de 3 anillos /
la libreta

28. notebook paper
el papel para libreta

29. spiral notebook
la libreta de espiral

30. dictionary
el diccionario

31. picture dictionary
el diccionario gráfico

Look at the picture.
Describe the classroom.

A: There's a chalkboard.
B: There are fifteen students.

Ask your classmates. Share the answers.

1. Do you like to raise your hand in class?
2. Do you like to listen to CDs in class?
3. Do you ever talk to the teacher?

7

Learning New Words Aprender palabras nuevas

A. **Look up** the word.
Busque la palabra.

B. **Read** the definition.
Lea la definición.

C. **Translate** the word.
Traduzca la palabra.

D. **Check** the pronunciation.
Verifique la pronunciación.

E. **Copy** the word.
Copie la palabra.

F. **Draw** a picture.
Haga un dibujo.

Working with Your Classmates Trabajar con sus compañeros de clase

G. **Discuss** a problem.
Discuta un problema.

H. **Brainstorm** solutions / answers.
Elabore soluciones / respuestas.

I. **Work** in a group.
Trabaje en grupo.

J. **Help** a classmate.
Ayude a un compañero.

Working with a Partner Trabajar con un compañero

K. **Ask** a question.
Haga una pregunta.

L. **Answer** a question.
Conteste una pregunta.

M. **Share** a book.
Comparta un libro.

N. **Dictate** a sentence.
Dicte una oración.

Following Directions Seguir las instrucciones

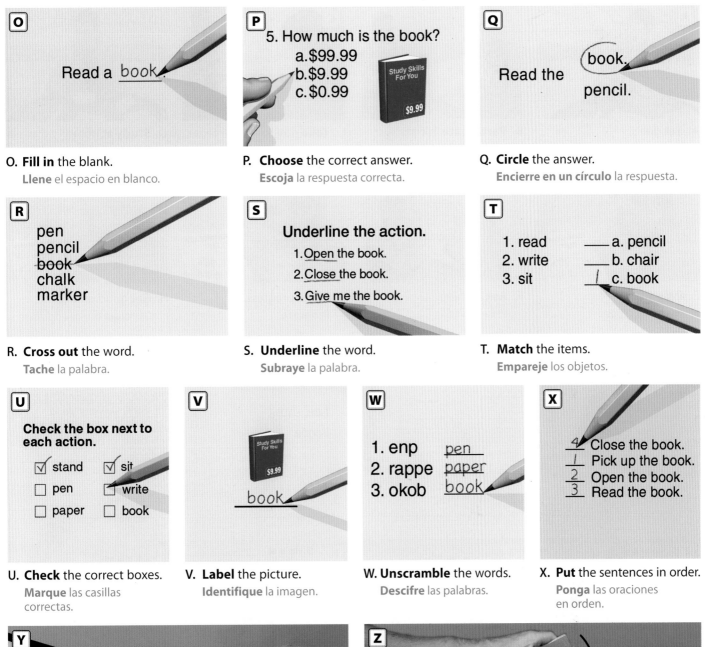

O. | **Fill in** the blank.
Llene el espacio en blanco.

P. | **Choose** the correct answer.
Escoja la respuesta correcta.

Q. | **Circle** the answer.
Encierre en un círculo la respuesta.

R. | **Cross out** the word.
Tache la palabra.

S. | **Underline** the word.
Subraye la palabra.

T. | **Match** the items.
Empareje los objetos.

U. | **Check** the correct boxes.
Marque las casillas correctas.

V. | **Label** the picture.
Identifique la imagen.

W. | **Unscramble** the words.
Descifre las palabras.

X. | **Put** the sentences in order.
Ponga las oraciones en orden.

Y. | **Take out** a piece of paper.
Saque una hoja de papel.

Z. | **Put away** your books.
Guarde sus libros.

Ask your classmates. Share the answers.
1. Do you like to work in a group?
2. Do you ever share a book?
3. Do you like to answer questions?

Think about it. Discuss.
1. How can classmates help each other?
2. Why is it important to ask questions in class?
3. How can students check their pronunciation? Explain.

Ways to Succeed Formas para tener éxito

A. Set goals.
Fije metas.

B. Participate in class.
Participe en la clase.

C. Take notes.
Tome notas.

D. Study at home.
Estudie en la casa.

E. Pass a test.
Pase una prueba.

F. Ask for help.
Pida ayuda.

G. Make progress.
Progrese.

H. Get good grades.
Obtenga buenas notas.

Taking a Test Cómo tomar una prueba

1. test booklet
el folleto de prueba

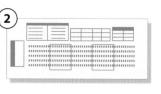

2. answer sheet
la hoja de respuestas

Lee, Jung
Score 35/40

3. score
el puntaje

A	90%-100%	Outstanding
B	80%-89%	Very good
C	70%-79%	Satisfactory
D	60%-69%	Barely passing
F	0%-59%	Fail

4. grades
las calificaciones

I. Clear off your desk.
Limpie su escritorio.

J. Work on your own.
Trabaje por sí solo.

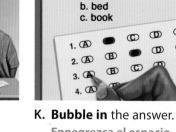

K. Bubble in the answer.
Ennegrezca el espacio correspondiente a la respuesta.

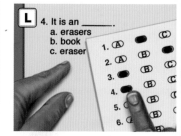

L. Check your work.
Revise su trabajo.

M. Erase the mistake.
Borre el error.

N. Correct the mistake.
Corrija el error.

O. Hand in your test.
Entregue la prueba.

A Day at School

A. **Enter** the room.
Ingrese al salón.

B. **Turn on** the lights.
Encienda las luces.

C. **Walk** to class.
Camine a la clase.

D. **Run** to class.
Corra a la clase.

E. **Lift / Pick up** the books.
Levante / Recoja los libros.

F. **Carry** the books.
Lleve los libros.

G. **Deliver** the books.
Entregue los libros.

H. **Take** a break.
Tome un descanso.

I. **Eat**.
Coma.

J. **Drink**.
Beba.

K. **Buy** a snack.
Cómprese un bocadito.

L. **Have** a conversation.
Converse con alguien.

M. **Go back** to class.
Regrese a la clase.

N. **Throw away** trash.
Tire la basura.

O. **Leave** the room.
Salga del salón.

P. **Turn off** the lights.
Apague las luces.

Grammar Point: present continuous

Use **be** + verb + *ing*
He **is** walk**ing**. They **are** enter**ing**.
Note: He is runn**ing**. They are leav**ing**.

Look at the pictures.
Describe what is happening.

A: They are <u>entering the room</u>.
B: He is <u>walking</u>.

11

A. **start** a conversation
inicie una conversación

B. **make** small talk
charle

C. **compliment** someone
elogie a alguien

D. **offer** something
ofrezca algo

E. **thank** someone
agradézcale a alguien

F. **apologize**
discúlpese

G. **accept** an apology
acepte una disculpa

H. **invite** someone
invite a alguien

I. **accept** an invitation
acepte una invitación

J. **decline** an invitation
rechace una invitación

K. **agree**
asiente

L. **disagree**
disiente

M. **explain** something
explique algo

N. **check** your understanding
verifique lo que oye

More vocabulary

request: to ask for something
accept a compliment: to thank someone for a compliment

Pair practice. Follow the directions.

1. Start a conversation with your partner.
2. Make small talk with your partner.
3. Compliment each other.

Temperature Temperatura

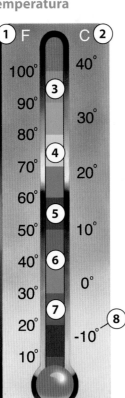

1. Fahrenheit
   Fahrenheit
2. Celsius
   Centígrados
3. hot
   caliente /
   cálido
4. warm
   tibio
5. cool
   fresco /
   templado
6. cold
   frío
7. freezing
   bajo cero /
   muy frío
8. degrees
   grados

A Weather Map Un mapa del tiempo

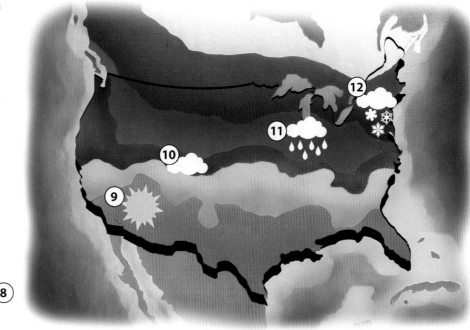

9. sunny / clear
   soleado / despejado
10. cloudy
    nublado
11. raining
    lluvioso
12. snowing
    nevoso

Weather Conditions Condiciones del tiempo

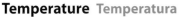

13. heat wave
    ola de calor
14. smoggy
    con smog
15. humid
    húmedo

16. thunderstorm
    tormenta
17. lightning
    relámpagos
18. windy
    con viento

19. dust storm
    tormenta de polvo
20. foggy
    neblinoso
21. hailstorm
    granizada

22. icy
    helado
23. snowstorm / blizzard
    tormenta / ventisca
    de nieve

Ways to talk about the weather

It's <u>sunny</u> in <u>Dallas</u>.
What's the temperature?
It's <u>108</u>. They're having <u>a heat wave</u>.

Pair practice. Make new conversations.

A: *What's the weather like in <u>Chicago</u>?*
B: *It's <u>raining</u> and it's <u>cold</u>. It's <u>30</u> degrees.*

13

PARTS OF A PHONE

1. receiver / handset
   el receptor / el auricular manual
2. cord
   el cable
3. phone jack
   el enchufe del teléfono

4. phone line
   la línea de teléfono
5. key pad
   el teclado del teléfono
6. star key
   la tecla estrella

7. pound key
   la tecla numérica
8. cellular phone
   el teléfono celular
9. antenna
   la antena

10. charger
    el cargador
11. strong signal
    una señal fuerte
12. weak signal
    una señal débil

13. headset
    el audífono
14. wireless headset
    el audífono inalámbrico

15. calling card
    la tarjeta de llamada
16. access number
    el número de acceso

17. answering machine
    la contestadora
18. voice message
    el mensaje de voz

19. text message
    el mensaje de texto

20. Internet phone call
    la llamada telefónica por Internet

21. operator
    el operador

22. directory assistance
    el servicio de directorio

23. automated phone system
    el sistema telefónico automatizado

24. cordless phone
el teléfono inalámbrico

25. pay phone
el teléfono público

26. TDD*
el TDD

27. smart phone
el teléfono inteligente

Reading a Phone Bill Lectura de la factura telefónica

28. phone bill
la factura telefónica

29. area code
el código de área

30. phone number
el número de
teléfono

31. local call
la llamada local

rtr

Page 1 of 2

Your Phone Company Statement
October 8-November 8, 2010

Customer ID 505-555-6090

Linda Lopez
1212 Marble Lane
Roswell, NM 88203

LOCAL CALLS

DATE	NUMBER CALLED	TIME	RATE
OCT 12	505-555-2346	2:15 p.m.	day
OCT 17	505-555-7890	7:30 p.m.	night
NOV 1	505-555-6176	7:00 a.m	day
NOV 8	505-555-7890	6:30 p.m	night

rtr

Customer ID 505-555-6090
Linda Lopez

LONG DISTANCE CALLS

DATE	NUMBER CALLED	WHERE	TIME	RATE
OCT 10	212-555-1234	New York, NY	3:00 p.m	day
OCT 31	415-555-6874	Marin, CA	9:45 p.m.	eve

INTERNATIONAL CALLS

| OCT 30 | 56-2-555-1394 | Chile |
| OCT 30 | 81-3-555-2086 | Japan |

32. long distance call
la llamada a
larga distancia

33. country code
el código del país

34. city code
el código de
la ciudad

35. international call
la llamada
internacional

Making a Phone Call Para llamar por teléfono

A. Dial the phone number.
Marque el número de
teléfono.

B. Press "send".
Oprima "enviar".

Hi!

Hi!

C. Talk on the phone.
Hable por teléfono.

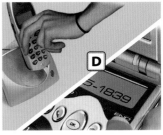

D. Hang up. / **Press** "end".
Cuelgue. / **Oprima**
"finalizar".

Making an Emergency Call Para hacer una llamada de emergencia

E. Dial 911.
Marque 911.

This is
Roy Chu.

F. Give your name.
Dé su nombre.

There's a fire on
5th and Oak.

G. State the emergency.
Diga cuál es la emergencia.

Please stay
on the line.

H. Stay on the line.
Permanezca en la línea.

*telecommunication device for the deaf

Cardinal Numbers Números cardinales

0	zero / cero	20	twenty / veinte
1	one / uno	21	twenty-one / veintiuno
2	two / dos	22	twenty-two / veintidós
3	three / tres	23	twenty-three / veintitrés
4	four / cuatro	24	twenty-four / veinticuatro
5	five / cinco	25	twenty-five / veinticinco
6	six / seis	30	thirty / treinta
7	seven / siete	40	forty / cuarenta
8	eight / ocho	50	fifty / cincuenta
9	nine / nueve	60	sixty / sesenta
10	ten / diez	70	seventy / setenta
11	eleven / once	80	eighty / ochenta
12	twelve / doce	90	ninety / noventa
13	thirteen / trece	100	one hundred / cien
14	fourteen / catorce	101	one hundred one / ciento uno
15	fifteen / quince	1,000	one thousand / mil
16	sixteen / dieciséis	10,000	ten thousand / diez mil
17	seventeen / diecisiete	100,000	one hundred thousand / cien mil
18	eighteen / dieciocho	1,000,000	one million / un millón
19	nineteen / diecinueve	1,000,000,000	one billion / mil millones

Ordinal Numbers Números ordinales

1st / 1°	first / primero	16th / 16°	sixteenth / decimosexto
2nd / 2°	second / segundo	17th / 17°	seventeenth / decimoséptimo
3rd / 3°	third / tercero	18th / 18°	eighteenth / decimooctavo
4th / 4°	fourth / cuarto	19th / 19°	nineteenth / decimonoveno
5th / 5°	fifth / quinto	20th / 20°	twentieth / vigésimo
6th / 6°	sixth / sexto	21st / 21°	twenty-first / vigésimoprimero
7th / 7°	seventh / séptimo	30th / 30°	thirtieth / trigésimo
8th / 8°	eighth / octavo	40th / 40°	fortieth / cuadragésimo
9th / 9°	ninth / noveno	50th / 50°	fiftieth / quincuagésimo
10th / 10°	tenth / décimo	60th / 60°	sixtieth / sexagésimo
11th / 11°	eleventh / undécimo	70th / 70°	seventieth / septuagésimo
12th / 12°	twelfth / duodécimo	80th / 80°	eightieth / octogésimo
13th / 13°	thirteenth / decimotercero	90th / 90°	ninetieth / nonagésimo
14th / 14°	fourteenth / decimocuarto	100th / 100°	one hundredth / centésimo
15th / 15°	fifteenth / decimoquinto	1,000th / 1,000°	one thousandth / milésimo

Roman Numerals Números romanos

I = 1	VII = 7	XXX = 30
II = 2	VIII = 8	XL = 40
III = 3	IX = 9	L = 50
IV = 4	X = 10	C = 100
V = 5	XV = 15	D = 500
VI = 6	XX = 20	M = 1,000

Measurements

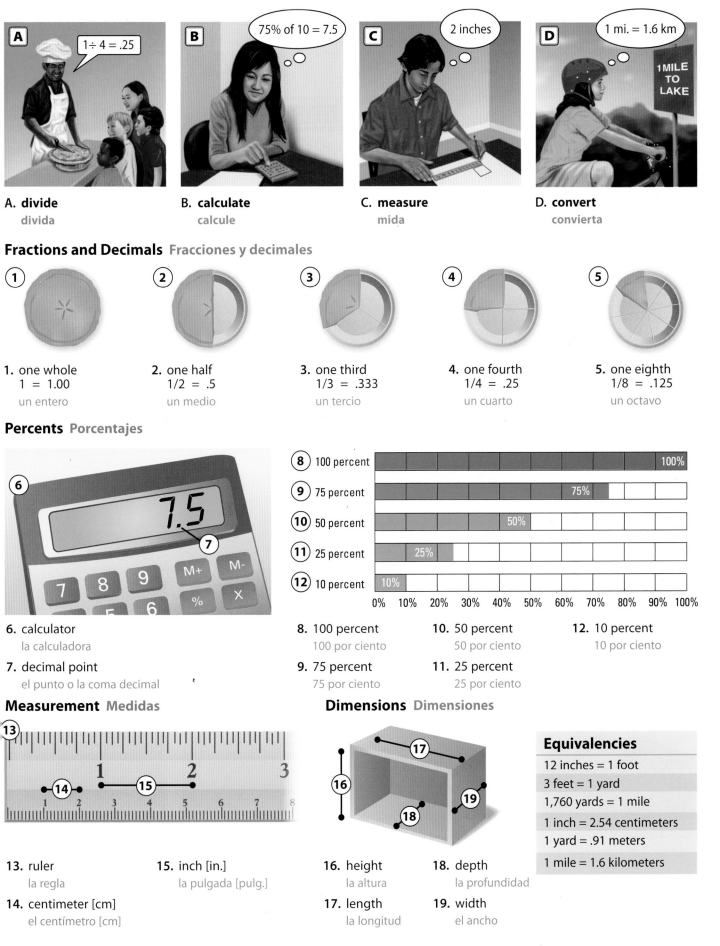

A 1 ÷ 4 = .25

B 75% of 10 = 7.5

C 2 inches

D 1 mi. = 1.6 km

1 MILE TO LAKE

A. **divide**
divida

B. **calculate**
calcule

C. **measure**
mida

D. **convert**
convierta

Fractions and Decimals Fracciones y decimales

1. one whole
1 = 1.00
un entero

2. one half
1/2 = .5
un medio

3. one third
1/3 = .333
un tercio

4. one fourth
1/4 = .25
un cuarto

5. one eighth
1/8 = .125
un octavo

Percents Porcentajes

6 7.5 **7**

8 100 percent — 100%
9 75 percent — 75%
10 50 percent — 50%
11 25 percent — 25%
12 10 percent — 10%

0% 10% 20% 30% 40% 50% 60% 70% 80% 90% 100%

6. calculator
la calculadora

7. decimal point
el punto o la coma decimal

8. 100 percent
100 por ciento

9. 75 percent
75 por ciento

10. 50 percent
50 por ciento

11. 25 percent
25 por ciento

12. 10 percent
10 por ciento

Measurement Medidas

13 **14** **15**
1 2 3

Dimensions Dimensiones

16 **17** **18** **19**

13. ruler
la regla

14. centimeter [cm]
el centímetro [cm]

15. inch [in.]
la pulgada [pulg.]

16. height
la altura

17. length
la longitud

18. depth
la profundidad

19. width
el ancho

Equivalencies

12 inches = 1 foot
3 feet = 1 yard
1,760 yards = 1 mile
1 inch = 2.54 centimeters
1 yard = .91 meters
1 mile = 1.6 kilometers

 # Time — La hora

Telling Time Saber la hora

1. **hour**
   la hora

2. **minutes**
   los minutos

3. **seconds**
   los segundos

4. **a.m.**
   a.m.

5. **p.m.**
   p.m.

6. **1:00**
   one o'clock
   la una en punto

7. **1:05**
   one-oh-five
   five after one
   la una y cinco

8. **1:10**
   one-ten
   ten after one
   la una y diez

9. **1:15**
   one-fifteen
   a quarter after one
   la una y quince
   la una y cuarto

10. **1:20**
    one-twenty
    twenty after one
    la una y veinte

11. **1:30**
    one-thirty
    half past one
    la una y treinta
    la una y media

12. **1:40**
    one-forty
    twenty to two
    la una y cuarenta
    veinte para las dos

13. **1:45**
    one-forty-five
    a quarter to two
    la una y cuarenta y cinco
    un cuarto para las dos

Times of Day Las horas del día

14. **sunrise**
    la salida del sol /
    el amanecer

15. **morning**
    la mañana

16. **noon**
    el mediodía

17. **afternoon**
    la tarde

18. **sunset**
    la puesta del sol /
    el atardecer

19. **evening**
    el anochecer

20. **night**
    la noche

21. **midnight**
    la medianoche

Ways to talk about time
I wake up at 6:30 a.m.
I wake up at 6:30 in the morning.
I wake up at 6:30.

Pair practice. Make new conversations.
A: *What time do you wake up on weekdays?*
B: *At 6:30 a.m. How about you?*
A: *I wake up at 7:00.*

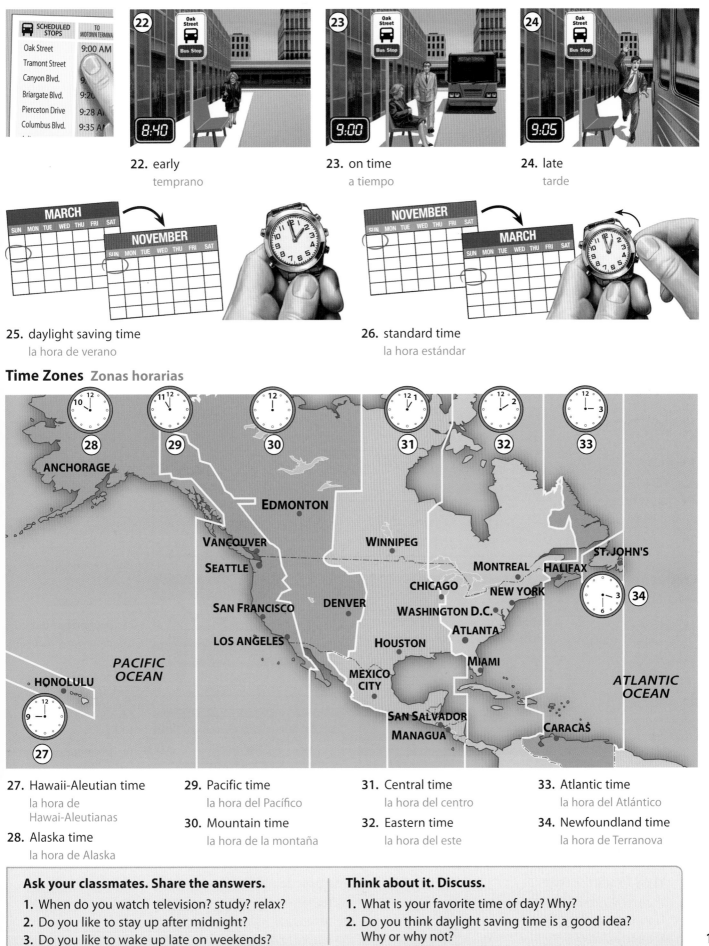

SCHEDULED STOPS	TO MIDTOWN TERMINAL
Oak Street	9:00 AM
Tramont Street	
Canyon Blvd.	9
Briargate Blvd.	9:2
Pierceton Drive	9:28 A
Columbus Blvd.	9:35 A

22. early
temprano

23. on time
a tiempo

24. late
tarde

25. daylight saving time
la hora de verano

26. standard time
la hora estándar

Time Zones Zonas horarias

ANCHORAGE

EDMONTON

VANCOUVER   WINNIPEG

SEATTLE   MONTREAL HALIFAX   ST. JOHN'S

CHICAGO   NEW YORK

SAN FRANCISCO   DENVER
WASHINGTON D.C.

LOS ANGELES   ATLANTA

HOUSTON

PACIFIC   MIAMI
OCEAN

HONOLULU   MEXICO
CITY   ATLANTIC
OCEAN

SAN SALVADOR
CARACAS
MANAGUA

27. Hawaii-Aleutian time
la hora de
Hawai-Aleutianas

28. Alaska time
la hora de Alaska

29. Pacific time
la hora del Pacífico

30. Mountain time
la hora de la montaña

31. Central time
la hora del centro

32. Eastern time
la hora del este

33. Atlantic time
la hora del Atlántico

34. Newfoundland time
la hora de Terranova

Ask your classmates. Share the answers.

1. When do you watch television? study? relax?
2. Do you like to stay up after midnight?
3. Do you like to wake up late on weekends?

Think about it. Discuss.

1. What is your favorite time of day? Why?
2. Do you think daylight saving time is a good idea? Why or why not?

1. date
   la fecha

2. day
   el día

3. month
   el mes

4. year
   el año

5. today
   hoy

6. tomorrow
   mañana

7. yesterday
   ayer

Days of the Week
Los días de la semana

8. Sunday
   domingo

9. Monday
   lunes

10. Tuesday
    martes

11. Wednesday
    miércoles

12. Thursday
    jueves

13. Friday
    viernes

14. Saturday
    sábado

15. week
    la semana

16. weekdays
    los días de la semana

17. weekend
    el fin de semana

MAY

⑧ SUN	⑨ MON	⑩ TUE	⑪ WED	⑫ THU	⑬ FRI	⑭ SAT
1	2	3	4	5	6	7
8	9	10	11	12	13	14
15	16	17	18	19	20	21
22	23	24	25	26	27	28
29	30	31				

Frequency
Frecuencia

18. last week
    la semana pasada

19. this week
    esta semana

20. next week
    la semana próxima

21. every day / daily
    todos los días /
    diariamente

22. once a week
    una vez por semana

23. twice a week
    dos veces por semana

24. three times a week
    tres veces por semana

Ways to say the date

Today is <u>May 10th</u>. It's the <u>tenth</u>.
Yesterday was <u>May 9th</u>.
The party is on <u>May 21st</u>.

Pair practice. Make new conversations.

A: *The <u>test</u> is on <u>Friday</u>, <u>June 14th</u>.*
B: *Did you say <u>Friday</u>, the <u>fourteenth</u>?*
A: *Yes, the <u>fourteenth</u>.*

㉕ JAN

SUN	MON	TUE	WED	THU	FRI	SAT
					1	2
3	4	5	6	7	8	9
10	11	12	13	14	15	16
17	18	19	20	21	22	23
24/31	25	26	27	28	29	30

㉖ FEB

SUN	MON	TUE	WED	THU	FRI	SAT
	1	2	3	4	5	6
7	8	9	10	11	12	13
14	15	16	17	18	19	20
21	22	23	24	25	26	27
28						

㉗ MAR

SUN	MON	TUE	WED	THU	FRI	SAT
	1	2	3	4	5	6
7	8	9	10	11	12	13
14	15	16	17	18	19	20
21	22	23	24	25	26	27
28	29	30	31			

㉘ APR

SUN	MON	TUE	WED	THU	FRI	SAT
				1	2	3
4	5	6	7	8	9	10
11	12	13	14	15	16	17
18	19	20	21	22	23	24
25	26	27	28	29	30	

㉙ MAY

SUN	MON	TUE	WED	THU	FRI	SAT
						1
2	3	4	5	6	7	8
9	10	11	12	13	14	15
16	17	18	19	20	21	22
23/30	24/31	25	26	27	28	29

㉚ JUN

SUN	MON	TUE	WED	THU	FRI	SAT
		1	2	3	4	5
6	7	8	9	10	11	12
13	14	15	16	17	18	19
20	21	22	23	24	25	26
27	28	29	30			

㉛ JUL

SUN	MON	TUE	WED	THU	FRI	SAT
				1	2	3
4	5	6	7	8	9	10
11	12	13	14	15	16	17
18	19	20	21	22	23	24
25	26	27	28	29	30	31

㉜ AUG

SUN	MON	TUE	WED	THU	FRI	SAT
1	2	3	4	5	6	7
8	9	10	11	12	13	14
15	16	17	18	19	20	21
22	23	24	25	26	27	28
29	30	31				

㉝ SEP

SUN	MON	TUE	WED	THU	FRI	SAT
			1	2	3	4
5	6	7	8	9	10	11
12	13	14	15	16	17	18
19	20	21	22	23	24	25
26	27	28	29	30		

㉞ OCT

SUN	MON	TUE	WED	THU	FRI	SAT
					1	2
3	4	5	6	7	8	9
10	11	12	13	14	15	16
17	18	19	20	21	22	23
24/31	25	26	27	28	29	30

㉟ NOV

SUN	MON	TUE	WED	THU	FRI	SAT
	1	2	3	4	5	6
7	8	9	10	11	12	13
14	15	16	17	18	19	20
21	22	23	24	25	26	27
28	29	30				

㊱ DEC

SUN	MON	TUE	WED	THU	FRI	SAT
			1	2	3	4
5	6	7	8	9	10	11
12	13	14	15	16	17	18
19	20	21	22	23	24	25
26	27	28	29	30	31	

Months of the Year
Los meses del año

25. January
   enero
26. February
   febrero
27. March
   marzo
28. April
   abril
29. May
   mayo
30. June
   junio
31. July
   julio
32. August
   agosto
33. September
   septiembre
34. October
   octubre
35. November
   noviembre
36. December
   diciembre

Seasons
Las estaciones

37. spring
   la primavera
38. summer
   el verano
39. fall / autumn
   el otoño
40. winter
   el invierno

Dictate to your partner. Take turns.

A: *Write <u>Monday</u>.*
B: *Is it spelled <u>M-o-n-d-a-y</u>?*
A: *Yes, that's right.*

Ask your classmates. Share the answers.

1. What is your favorite day of the week? Why?
2. What is your busiest day of the week? Why?
3. What is your favorite season of the year? Why?

1. birthday
el cumpleaños

2. wedding
la boda

3. anniversary
el aniversario

4. appointment
la cita

5. parent-teacher conference
la conferencia de padres
y maestros

6. vacation
las vacaciones

7. religious holiday
la fiesta religiosa

8. legal holiday
el día de fiesta oficial /
el día feriado legal

Legal Holidays   Los días feriados legales

9. New Year's Day
el Día de año nuevo

10. Martin Luther King Jr. Day
el Día de Martin Luther King Jr.

11. Presidents' Day
el Día de los presidentes

12. Memorial Day
el Día de la recordación

**13. Fourth of July /
Independence Day**
el Cuatro de julio /
el Día de la independencia

14. Labor Day
el Día del trabajo

15. Columbus Day
el Día de Colón

16. Veterans Day
el Día de los veteranos

17. Thanksgiving
el Día de acción de gracias

18. Christmas
la Navidad

Pair practice. Make new conversations.

A: *When is your <u>birthday</u>?*
B: *It's on <u>January 31st</u>. How about you?*
A: *It's on <u>December 22nd</u>.*

Ask your classmates. Share the answers.

1. What are the legal holidays in your native country?
2. When is Labor Day in your native country?
3. When do you celebrate the New Year in your native country?

1. **little** hand
   la mano **pequeña**
2. **big** hand
   la mano **grande**

3. **fast** driver
   el chofer **rápido**
4. **slow** driver
   el chofer **lento**

5. **hard** chair
   la silla **dura**
6. **soft** chair
   la silla **blanda**

7. **thick** book
   el libro **grueso**
8. **thin** book
   el libro **delgado**

9. **full** glass
   el vaso **lleno**
10. **empty** glass
    el vaso **vacío**

11. **noisy** children /
    loud children
    los niños **ruidosos**
12. **quiet** children
    los niños **tranquilos**

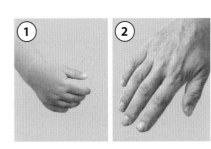

13. **heavy** box
    la caja **pesada**
14. **light** box
    la caja **liviana**

15. **same** color
    el **mismo** color
16. **different** colors
    colores **diferentes**

17. **good** dog
    el perro **bueno**
18. **bad** dog
    el perro **malo**

19. **expensive** ring
    el anillo **caro**
20. **cheap** ring
    el anillo **barato**

21. **beautiful** view
    la vista **hermosa**
22. **ugly** view
    la vista **fea**

23. **easy** problem
    el problema **fácil**
24. **difficult** problem /
    hard problem
    el problema **difícil**

Ask your classmates. Share the answers.

1. Are you a slow driver or a fast driver?
2. Do you prefer a hard bed or a soft bed?
3. Do you like loud parties or quiet parties?

Use the new words.
Look at page 150–151. Describe the things you see.

A: *The street* is *hard*.
B: *The truck* is *heavy*.

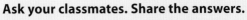

Basic Colors Los colores básicos

1. red
rojo

2. yellow
amarillo

3. blue
azul

4. orange
anaranjado

5. green
verde

6. purple
morado

7. pink
rosado

8. violet
violeta

9. turquoise
azul turquesa

10. dark blue
azul oscuro

11. light blue
azul claro

12. bright blue
azul brillante

Neutral Colors Los colores neutros

13. black
negro

14. white
blanco

15. gray
gris

16. cream / ivory
color crema / color marfil

17. brown
marrón / café

18. beige / tan
beige / moreno

Ask your classmates. Share the answers.

1. What colors are you wearing today?

2. What colors do you like?

3. Is there a color you don't like? What is it?

Use the new words. Look at pages 86–87.

Take turns naming the colors you see.

A: *His shirt is <u>blue</u>.*

B: *Her shoes are <u>white</u>.*

Prepositions

1. The yellow sweaters are **on the left**.
   Los suéteres amarillos están **a la izquierda**.

2. The purple sweaters are **in the middle**.
   Los suéteres morados están **en medio**.

3. The brown sweaters are **on the right**.
   Los suéteres marrones están **a la derecha**.

4. The red sweaters are **above** the blue sweaters.
   Los suéteres rojos están **encima** de los suéteres azules.

5. The blue sweaters are **below** the red sweaters.
   Los suéteres azules están **debajo** de los suéteres rojos.

6. The turquoise sweater is **in** the box.
   El suéter azul turquesa está **dentro de** la caja.

7. The white sweater is **in front of** the black sweater.
   El suéter blanco está **en frente del** suéter negro.

8. The black sweater is **behind** the white sweater.
   El suéter negro está **detrás** del suéter blanco.

9. The orange sweater is **on** the gray sweater.
   El suéter anaranjado está **sobre** el suéter gris.

10. The violet sweater is **next to** the gray sweater.
    El suéter violeta está **al lado del** suéter gris.

11. The gray sweater is **under** the orange sweater.
    El suéter gris está **debajo** del suéter anaranjado.

12. The green sweater is **between** the pink sweaters.
    El suéter verde está **entre** los suéteres rosados.

More vocabulary

near: in the same area
far from: not near

Role play. Make new conversations.

A: *Excuse me. Where are the <u>red</u> sweaters?*
B: *They're <u>on the left</u>, <u>above</u> the <u>blue</u> sweaters.*
A: *Thanks very much.*

25

Coins Las monedas

 1
 2
 3
 4
 5
 6

1. $.01 = 1¢
   a penny / 1 cent
   un centavo

2. $.05 = 5¢
   a nickel / 5 cents
   cinco centavos

3. $.10 = 10¢
   a dime / 10 cents
   diez centavos

4. $.25 = 25¢
   a quarter / 25 cents
   veinticinco centavos

5. $.50 = 50¢
   a half dollar
   medio dólar

6. $1.00
   a dollar coin
   una moneda de un dólar

Bills Los billetes

7. $1.00
   a dollar
   un dólar

8. $5.00
   five dollars
   cinco dólares

9. $10.00
   ten dollars
   diez dólares

10. $20.00
    twenty dollars
    veinte dólares

11. $50.00
    fifty dollars
    cincuenta dólares

12. $100.00
    one hundred dollars
    cien dólares

Do you have change for a dollar?
Yes, I do.
A

A. **Get** change.
   Obtener cambio.

Can I borrow a dollar?
Sure. Here you go.
B
C

B. **Borrow** money.
   Prestarse dinero.

C. **Lend** money.
   Prestar dinero.

Thanks.
D

D. **Pay back** the money.
   Pagar el dinero prestado.

Pair practice. Make new conversations.

A: *Do you have change for <u>a dollar</u>?*
B: *Sure. How about <u>two quarters</u> and <u>five dimes</u>?*
A: *Perfect!*

Think about it. Discuss.

1. Is it a good idea to lend money to a friend? Why or why not?
2. Is it better to carry a dollar or four quarters? Why?
3. Do you prefer dollar coins or dollar bills? Why?

Ways to Pay Formas de pagar

A. pay cash
   pagar en efectivo

B. use a credit card
   usar una tarjeta de crédito

C. use a debit card
   usar una tarjeta de débito

D. write a (personal) check
   escribir un cheque (personal)

E. use a gift card
   usar una tarjeta de regalo

F. cash a traveler's check
   cambiar un cheque de viajero

1. price tag
   la etiqueta del precio

2. regular price
   el precio normal

3. sale price
   el precio de oferta

4. bar code
   el código de barras

5. SKU number
   el número SKU

6. receipt
   el recibo

7. price / cost
   el precio / el costo

8. sales tax
   el impuesto de ventas

9. total
   el total

10. cash register
   la caja registradora

G. buy / pay for
   comprar / pagar

H. return
   devolver

I. exchange
   cambiar

27

1. twins
   las mellizas

2. sweater
   el suéter

3. matching
   iguales

4. disappointed
   desilusionada

5. navy blue
   azul marino

6. happy
   feliz

A. **shop**
   buscando para
   comprar

B. **keep**
   quedarse con

Look at the pictures. What do you see?

Answer the questions.

1. Who is the woman shopping for?
2. Does she buy matching sweaters or different sweaters?
3. How does Anya feel about her green sweater? What does she do?
4. What does Manda do with her sweater?

📖 Read the story.

Same and Different

Mrs. Kumar likes to <u>shop</u> for her <u>twins</u>. Today she's looking at <u>sweaters</u>. There are many different colors on sale. Mrs. Kumar chooses two <u>matching</u> green sweaters.

The next day, Manda and Anya open their gifts. Manda likes the green sweater, but Anya is <u>disappointed</u>. Mrs. Kumar understands the problem. Anya wants to be different.

Manda <u>keeps</u> her sweater. But Anya goes to the store. She exchanges her green sweater for a <u>navy blue</u> sweater. It's an easy answer to Anya's problem. Now the twins can be warm, <u>happy</u>, and different.

Think about it.

1. Do you like to shop for other people? Why or why not?
2. Imagine you are Anya. Would you keep the sweater or exchange it? Why?

1. **man**
   el hombre

2. **woman**
   la mujer

3. **women**
   las mujeres

4. **men**
   los hombres

5. **senior citizen**
   la anciana

Listen and point. Take turns.

A: *Point to a <u>woman</u>.*
B: *Point to a <u>senior citizen</u>.*
A: *Point to an <u>infant</u>.*

Dictate to your partner. Take turns.

A: *Write <u>woman</u>.*
B: *Is that spelled <u>w-o-m-a-n</u>?*
A: *Yes, that's right, <u>woman</u>.*

6. infant
el bebé

7. baby
el niño

8. toddler
la niña pequeña

9. 6-year-old boy
el niño de 6 años

10. 10-year-old girl
la niña de 10 años

11. teenager / teen
el adolescente

Ways to talk about age

1 month – 3 months old = **infant**

18 months – 3 years old = **toddler**

3 years old – 12 years old = **child**

13 – 19 years old = **teenager**

18+ years old = **adult**

62+ years old = **senior citizen**

Pair practice. Make new conversations.

A: *How old is Sandra?*

B: *She's thirteen years old.*

A: *Wow, she's a teenager now!*

31

Age Edad

1. young
   joven
2. middle-aged
   de mediana edad
3. elderly
   anciano(a)

Height Estatura

4. tall
   alto(a)
5. average height
   de estatura promedio
6. short
   bajo(a)

Weight Peso

7. heavy / fat
   pesado(a) / obeso(a)
8. average weight
   de peso promedio
9. thin / slender
   flaco(a) / delgado(a)

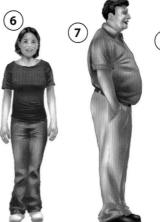

Disabilities
Discapacidades

10. physically challenged
    impedido(a) físico
11. sight impaired / blind
    impedido(a) visual / ciego(a)
12. hearing impaired / deaf
    con problemas auditivos /
    sordo(a)

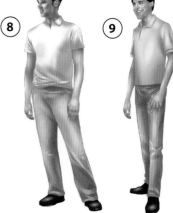

Prepositions of Motion p.153

Appearance Aspecto

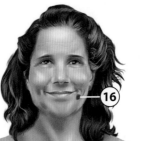

13. attractive
    atractivo(a)
14. cute
    bonito(a)
15. pregnant
    embarazada
16. mole
    lunar
17. pierced ear
    oreja perforada
18. tattoo
    tatuaje

Ways to describe people

He's a <u>heavy</u>, <u>young</u> man.
She's a <u>pregnant</u> woman with <u>a mole</u>.
He's <u>sight impaired</u>.

Use the new words. Look at pages 2–3.
Describe the people and point. Take turns.

A: *He's a <u>tall</u>, <u>thin</u>, <u>middle-aged</u> man.*
B: *She's a <u>short</u>, <u>average-weight</u> <u>young</u> woman.*

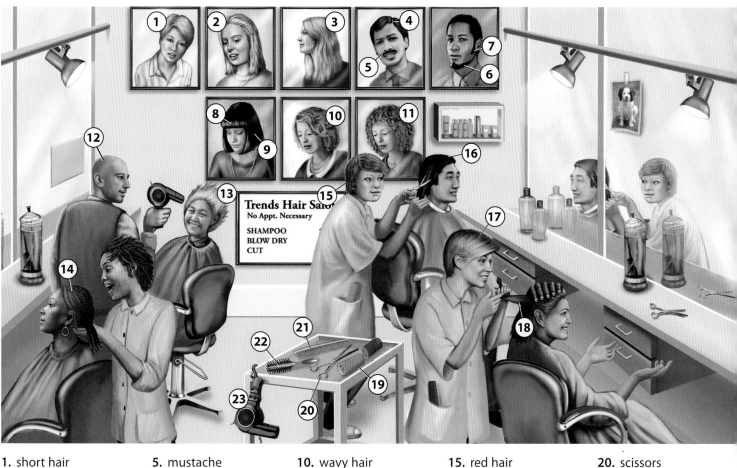

1. **short hair**
   el cabello corto

2. **shoulder-length hair**
   el cabello a la altura
   de los hombros

3. **long hair**
   el cabello largo

4. **part**
   la raya

5. **mustache**
   el bigote

6. **beard**
   la barba

7. **sideburns**
   las patillas

8. **bangs**
   el flequillo / el fleco

9. **straight hair**
   el cabello liso

10. **wavy hair**
    el cabello ondulado

11. **curly hair**
    el cabello rizado

12. **bald**
    calvo

13. **gray hair**
    las canas

14. **corn rows**
    con trenzas tejidas
    en el cabello

15. **red hair**
    pelirrojo(a)

16. **black hair**
    el cabello negro

17. **blond hair**
    el cabello rubio

18. **brown hair**
    el cabello castaño

19. **rollers**
    los rizadores

20. **scissors**
    las tijeras

21. **comb**
    el peine / la peinilla

22. **brush**
    el cepillo

23. **blow dryer**
    el secador

Style Hair Arreglo del cabello

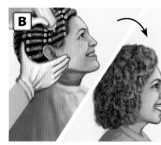

A. **cut** hair
cortar el cabello

B. **perm** hair
hacer la **permanente**

C. **set** hair
rizar el cabello

D. **color** hair / **dye** hair
teñir el cabello

Ways to talk about hair

Describe hair in this order: length, style, and then color.
She has <u>long</u>, <u>straight</u>, <u>brown</u> hair.

Role play. Talk to a stylist.

A: *I need a new hairstyle.*
B: *How about <u>short</u> and <u>straight</u>?*
A: *Great. Do you think I should <u>dye</u> it?*

33

1. grandmother
   la abuela
2. grandfather
   el abuelo
3. mother
   la madre
4. father
   el padre
5. sister
   la hermana
6. brother
   el hermano
7. aunt
   la tía
8. uncle
   el tío
9. cousin
   el primo / la prima

10. mother-in-law
    la suegra
11. father-in-law
    el suegro
12. wife
    la esposa
13. husband
    el esposo
14. daughter
    la hija
15. son
    el hijo
16. sister-in-law
    la cuñada
17. brother-in-law
    el cuñado
18. niece
    la sobrina
19. nephew
    el sobrino

Tim Lee's Family

GRANDPARENTS

1 Min 2 Lu

Immediate Family

PARENTS

3 Rose 4 Ken 7 Lynn 8 Dan

CHILDREN

Tim 5 Lily 6 Alex 9 Emily

Ana Garcia's Family

10 Eva 11 Sam

Extended Family

12 Ana 13 Tito 16 Marta 17 Carlos

14 Sara 15 Felix 18 Alice 19 Eddie

More vocabulary

Tim is Min and Lu's **grandson**.
Lily and Emily are Min and Lu's **granddaughters**.
Alex is Min's youngest **grandchild**.

Ana is Tito's **wife**.
Ana is Eva and Sam's **daughter-in-law**.
Carlos is Eva and Sam's **son-in-law**.

20. married couple
la pareja casada

21. divorced couple
la pareja divorciada

22. single mother
la madre soltera

23. single father
el padre soltero

Carol, Bruce, and Lisa

Lisa, Age 4

Lisa Green's Family

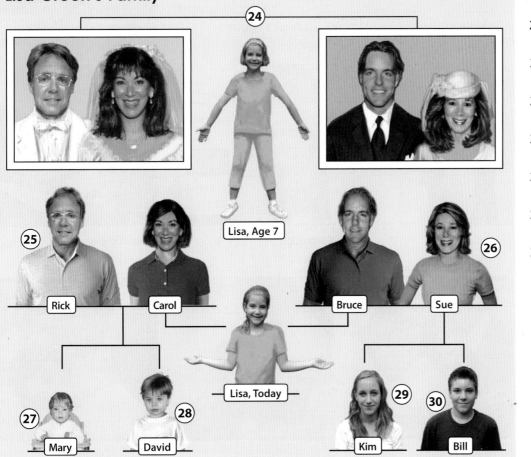

24. remarried
casados nuevamente

25. stepfather
el padrastro

26. stepmother
la madrastra

27. half sister
la media hermana

28. half brother
el medio hermano

29. stepsister
la hermanastra

30. stepbrother
el hermanastro

Lisa, Age 7

Rick

Carol

Bruce

Sue

Lisa, Today

Mary

David

Kim

Bill

More vocabulary

Bruce is Carol's **former husband** or **ex-husband**.
Carol is Bruce's **former wife** or **ex-wife**.
Lisa is the **stepdaughter** of both Rick and Sue.

Look at the pictures.
Name the people.

A: *Who is Lisa's half sister?*
B: *Mary is. Who is Lisa's stepsister?*

35

A. **hold**
sostenerlo

B. **nurse**
amamantarlo

C. **feed**
alimentarlo

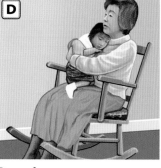

D. **rock**
mecerlo

E. **undress**
desvestirlo

F. **bathe**
bañarlo

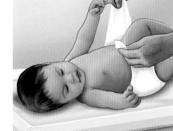

G. **change** a diaper
cambiarle el pañal

H. **dress**
vestirlo

I. **comfort**
consolarlo

Good job!

J. **praise**
elogiarlo

No!

K. **discipline**
disciplinarlo

L. **buckle up**
abrocharle el cinturón

M. **play** with
jugar con él

N. **read** to
leerle

O. **sing** a lullaby
cantarle una canción
de cuna

P. **kiss** goodnight
besarlo en la noche

Look at the pictures.
Describe what is happening.

A: *She's changing her baby's diaper*.
B: *He's kissing his son goodnight*.

Ask your classmates. Share the answers.

1. Do you like to take care of children?
2. Do you prefer to read to children or play with them?
3. Can you sing a lullaby? Which one?

1. bottle
   la botella

2. nipple
   la mamadera / el chupón

3. formula
   la fórmula

4. baby food
   el alimento para bebé

5. bib
   el babero

6. high chair
   la silla alta

7. diaper pail
   el cesto para pañales

8. cloth diaper
   el pañal de tela

9. safety pins
   los prendedores
   de seguridad

10. disposable diaper
    el pañal desechable

11. training pants
    los calzoncitos de
    entrenamiento

12. potty seat
    la bacinilla

13. baby lotion
    la loción para bebé

14. baby powder
    el talco para bebé

15. wipes
    las toallitas húmedas

16. baby bag
    la bolsa para bebé

17. baby carrier
    el cargador para bebé

18. stroller
    el carrito

19. car safety seat
    el asiento de seguridad
    para el automóvil

20. carriage
    el cochecito

21. rocking chair
    la silla mecedora

22. nursery rhymes
    las canciones de cuna

23. teddy bear
    el osito de peluche

24. pacifier
    el chupete / el chupón

25. teething ring
    el anillo de dentición

26. rattle
    la sonaja / el sonajero

27. night light
    la luz de noche

Dictate to your partner. Take turns.

A: *Write pacifier.*
B: *Was that pacifier, p-a-c-i-f-i-e-r?*
A: *Yes, that's right.*

Think about it. Discuss.

1. How can parents discipline toddlers? teens?
2. What are some things you can say to praise a child?
3. Why are nursery rhymes important for young children?

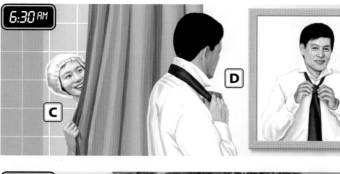

A. wake up
despertarse

B. get up
levantarse

C. take a shower
tomar una ducha

D. get dressed
vestirse

E. eat breakfast
desayunar

F. make lunch
preparar el almuerzo

G. take the children to school /
drop off the kids
llevar a los niños al colegio /
dejar a los niños

H. take the bus to school
tomar el autobús para ir al colegio

I. drive to work / **go** to work
conducir al trabajo / ir al trabajo

J. go to class
ir a la clase

K. work
trabajar

L. go to the grocery store
ir a la tienda de comestibles

M. pick up the kids
recoger a los niños

N. leave work
salir del trabajo

Grammar Point: third person singular

For *he* and *she*, add -s or -es to the verb:

He wakes up.   *He watches TV.*

He gets up.   *She goes to the store.*

These verbs are different (irregular):

*Be: She **is** in school at 10:00 a.m.*

*Have: He **has** dinner at 6:30 p.m.*

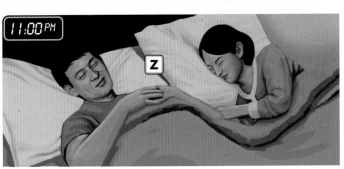

O. **clean** the house
   limpiar la casa

P. **exercise**
   hacer ejercicios

Q. **cook** dinner / **make** dinner
   preparar la cena / **hacer** la cena

R. **come** home / **get** home
   venir a la casa / **llegar** a la casa

S. **have** dinner / **eat** dinner
   cenar / **comer** la cena

T. **do** homework
   hacer la tarea

U. **relax**
   descansar

V. **read** the paper
   leer el periódico

W. **check** email
   revisar los correos electrónicos

X. **watch** TV
   ver televisión

Y. **go** to bed
   acostarse

Z. **go** to sleep
   dormirse

Pair practice. Make new conversations.

A: *When does he go to work?*
B: *He goes to work at 8:00 a.m. When does she go to class?*
A: *She goes to class at 10:00 a.m.*

Ask your classmates. Share the answers.

1. Who cooks dinner in your family?
2. Who goes to the grocery store?
3. Who goes to work?

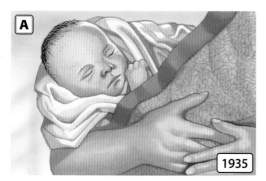

A. be born
nacer

1935

B. start school
empezar a ir al colegio

1940

C. immigrate
inmigrar

1950

D. graduate
graduarse

1953

E. learn to drive
aprender a conducir

1953

F. get a job
conseguir empleo

1954

G. become a citizen
convertirse en ciudadano

1954

H. fall in love
enamorarse

1955

1. birth certificate
la partida / el acta / el certificado de nacimiento

2. Resident Alien card / green card
la tarjeta de residente permanente

3. diploma
el diploma

4. driver's license
la licencia de conducir

5. Social Security card
la tarjeta del seguro social

6. Certificate of Naturalization
el certificado de naturalización

Grammar Point: past tense

start		immigrate	retire	
learn	+ed	graduate	die	+d
travel				

These verbs are different (irregular):

be – was	go – went	buy – bought
get – got	have – had	
become – became	fall – fell	

I. **go** to college
ir *a la universidad*

1956

J. **get** engaged
comprometerse *para casarse*

1958

7. college degree
el diploma universitario

K. **get** married
casarse

1959

L. **have** a baby
tener *un bebé*

1961

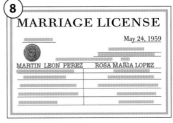

MARRIAGE LICENSE
May 24, 1959
MARTIN LEON PEREZ   ROSA MARIA LOPEZ

8. marriage license
la licencia de matrimonio

M. **buy** a home
comprar *una casa*

1965

FOR SALE
SOLD

N. **become** a grandparent
convertirse *en abuelo(a)*

1986

LAND DEED   6/7/1965
MARTIN LEON PEREZ
ROSA MARIA LOPEZ

9. deed
la escritura del terreno

GOODBYE MARTIN AND GOOD LUCK!

2000

O. **retire**
jubilarse

2005

P. **travel**
viajar

PASSPORT
United States of America

10. passport
el pasaporte

2006

Q. **volunteer**
trabajar como voluntario

2008

R. **die**
morir

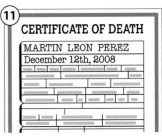

CERTIFICATE OF DEATH
MARTIN LEON PEREZ
December 12th, 2008

11. death certificate
el certificado de defunción

More vocabulary

When a husband dies, his wife becomes a **widow**.
When a wife dies, her husband becomes a **widower**.

Ask your classmates. Share the answers.

1. When did you start school?
2. When did you get your first job?
3. Do you want to travel?

41

1. hot
   tener calor
2. thirsty
   tener sed
3. sleepy
   tener sueño
4. cold
   tener frío
5. hungry
   tener hambre
6. full / satisfied
   sentirse satisfecho(a)

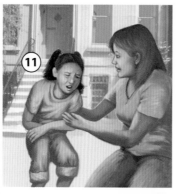

7. disgusted
   sentir disgusto
8. calm
   tranquilo(a)
9. uncomfortable
   incómodo(a)
10. nervous
    nervioso(a)

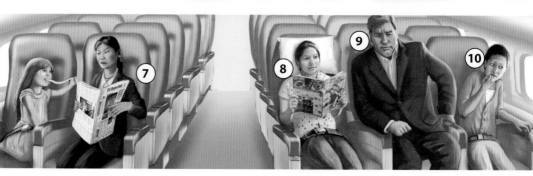

11. in pain
    sentir dolor
12. sick
    enfermo(a)
13. worried
    preocupado(a)
14. well
    bien
15. relieved
    aliviado(a)

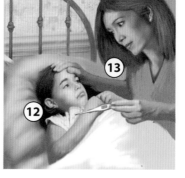

16. hurt
    lastimado(a)
17. lonely
    solo(a)
18. in love
    enamorado(a)

Pair practice. Make new conversations.

A: *How are you doing?*
B: *I'm <u>hungry</u>. How about you?*
A: *I'm <u>hungry</u> and <u>thirsty</u>, too!*

Use the new words.
Look at pages 40–41. Describe what each person is feeling.

A: *Martin is <u>excited</u>.*
B: *Martin's mother is <u>proud</u>.*

19. sad
   triste

20. homesick
   nostálgico(a)

21. proud
   orgulloso(a)

22. excited
   emocionado(a)

23. scared / afraid
   asustado(a) /
   temeroso(a)

24. embarrassed
   avergonzado(a)

25. bored
   aburrido(a)

26. confused
   confundido(a)

27. frustrated
   frustrado(a)

28. upset
   molesto(a)

29. angry
   enojado(a)

30. surprised
   sorprendido(a)

31. happy
   contento(a)

32. tired
   cansado(a)

Ask your classmates. Share the answers.

1. Do you ever feel homesick?
2. What makes you feel frustrated?
3. Describe a time when you were very happy.

More vocabulary

exhausted: very tired

furious: very angry

humiliated: very embarrassed

overjoyed: very happy

starving: very hungry

terrified: very scared

1. banner
   el anuncio de pancarta
2. baseball game
   el juego de béisbol
3. opinion
   la opinión
4. balloons
   los globos
5. glad
   alegre
6. relatives
   los parientes

A. **laugh**
   reír
B. **misbehave**
   comportarse mal

I think large families are best.

Look at the picture. What do you see?

Answer the questions.

1. How many relatives are there at this reunion?

2. How many children are there? Which children are misbehaving?

3. What are people doing at this reunion?

📖 Read the story.

A Family Reunion

Ben Lu has a lot of <u>relatives</u> and they're all at his house. Today is the Lu family reunion.

There is a lot of good food. There are also <u>balloons</u> and a <u>banner</u>. And this year there are four new babies!

People are having a good time at the reunion. Ben's grandfather and his aunt are talking about the <u>baseball game</u>. His cousins <u>are laughing</u>. His mother-in-law is giving her <u>opinion</u>. And many of the children <u>are misbehaving</u>.

Ben looks at his family and smiles. He loves his relatives, but he's <u>glad</u> the reunion is once a year.

Think about it.

1. Do you like to have large parties? Why or why not?

2. Imagine you see a little girl at a party. She's misbehaving. What do you do? What do you say?

The Home El hogar

1. roof
   el techo
2. bedroom
   el dormitorio
3. door
   la puerta
4. bathroom
   el baño
5. kitchen
   la cocina
6. floor
   el piso
7. dining area
   el área del comedor

Listen and point. Take turns.

A: *Point to the kitchen.*
B: *Point to the living room.*
A: *Point to the basement.*

Dictate to your partner. Take turns.

A: *Write kitchen.*
B: *Was that k-i-t-c-h-e-n?*
A: *Yes, that's right, kitchen.*

8. attic
el desván

9. kids' bedroom
el dormitorio
de los niños

10. baby's room
la habitación
del bebé

11. window
la ventana

12. living room
la sala

13. basement
el sótano

14. garage
el garaje

Ways to give locations

I'm home.

I'm in the kitchen.

I'm on the roof.

Pair practice. Make new conversations.

A: *Where's the man?*

B: *He's in the attic. Where's the teenager?*

A: *She's in the laundry room.*

47

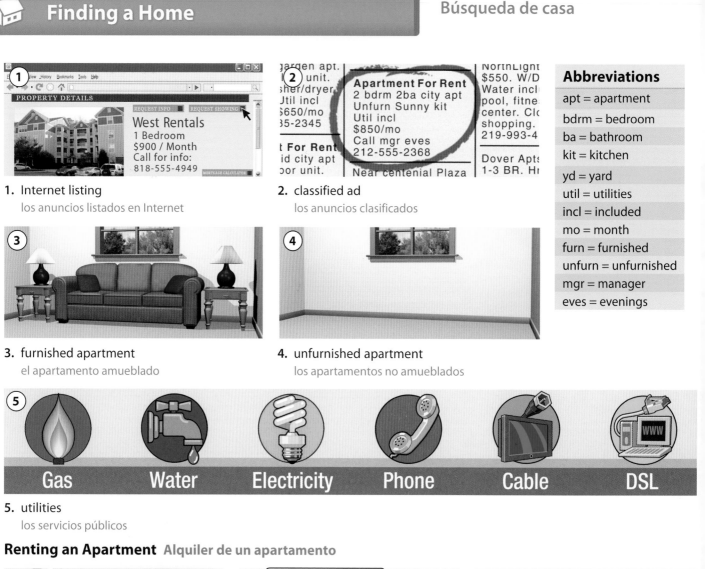

1. Internet listing
los anuncios listados en Internet

2. classified ad
los anuncios clasificados

Abbreviations

apt = apartment
bdrm = bedroom
ba = bathroom
kit = kitchen
yd = yard
util = utilities
incl = included
mo = month
furn = furnished
unfurn = unfurnished
mgr = manager
eves = evenings

3. furnished apartment
el apartamento amueblado

4. unfurnished apartment
los apartamentos no amueblados

Gas | **Water** | **Electricity** | **Phone** | **Cable** | **DSL**

5. utilities
los servicios públicos

Renting an Apartment Alquiler de un apartamento

A. **Call** the manager.
Llame al administrador.

B. **Ask** about the features.
Pregúntele sobre las características.

Are utilities included?

No, they aren't.

C. **Submit** an application.
Presente su solicitud.

D. **Sign** the rental agreement.
Firme el contrato de alquiler / renta.

E. **Pay** the first and last month's rent.
Pague el alquiler / la renta del primer y del último mes.

F. **Move in**.
Múdese al apartamento.

More vocabulary

lease: a monthly or yearly rental agreement
redecorate: to change the paint and furniture in a home
move out: to pack and leave a home

Ask your classmates. Share the answers.

1. How did you find your home?
2. Do you like to paint or arrange furniture?
3. Does gas or electricity cost more for you?

Buying a House La compra de una casa

G. Meet with a realtor.
Reúnase con un agente inmobiliario.

H. Look at houses.
Vea casas.

I. Make an offer.
Haga una oferta.

Congratulations!

J. Get a loan.
Obtenga un préstamo.

K. Take ownership.
Tome posesión.

Mr. Young Chang
4445 2nd Street
Pixaville, CA 00543
Pay to the order of *Towne Bank* $ *2000.00*
Two Thousand and 00/100 Dollars
Y

L. Make a mortgage payment.
Haga un pago de hipoteca.

Moving In La mudanza

M. Pack.
Empaque.

N. Unpack.
Desempaque.

We have a new address.

PHONE✓
DWP✓
GAS
CABLE✓

GAS

O. Put the utilities in your name.
Cambie los servicios públicos a su nombre.

P. Paint.
Pinte.

Q. Arrange the furniture.
Acomode los muebles.

Welcome!

R. Meet the neighbors.
Conozca a sus vecinos.

Ways to ask about a home's features

Are <u>utilities</u> included?
Is <u>the kitchen</u> large and sunny?
Are <u>the neighbors</u> quiet?

Role play. Talk to an apartment manager.

A: *Hi. I'm calling about <u>the apartment</u>.*
B: *OK. It's <u>unfurnished</u> and rent is $<u>800</u> a month.*
A: *<u>Are utilities included</u>?*

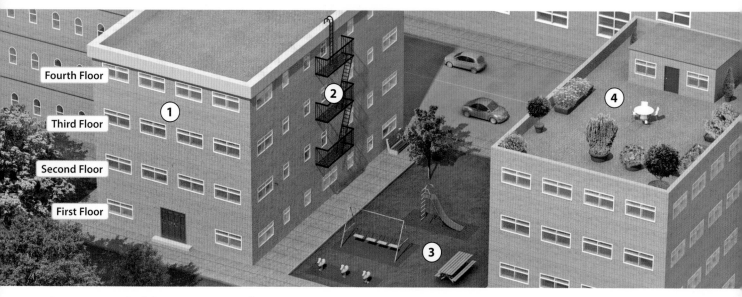

Fourth Floor — 1
Third Floor
Second Floor
First Floor — 2, 3

1. **apartment building**
   el edificio de apartamentos

2. **fire escape**
   la salida de incendios

3. **playground**
   el parque

4. **roof garden**
   el jardín aéreo

Entrance La entrada

Apartment Available
2BD + 2BA
555-4263

5. **intercom / speaker**
   el intercomunicador

6. **tenant**
   el inquilino / el arrendatario

7. **vacancy sign**
   el aviso de "se alquila"

8. **manager / superintendent**
   el administrador / el superintendente

Lobby El vestíbulo

9. **elevator**
   el elevador / el ascensor

10. **stairs / stairway**
    las escaleras

11. **mailboxes**
    los buzones

Basement El sótano

LAUNDRY ROOM

RECREATION ROOM

GARAGE

12. **washer**
    la lavadora

13. **dryer**
    la secadora

14. **big-screen TV**
    el televisor de pantalla grande

15. **pool table**
    la mesa de billar

16. **security gate**
    la puerta / la reja de seguridad

17. **storage locker**
    el armario / el depósito de almacenamiento

18. **parking space**
    el espacio de estacionamiento

19. **security camera**
    la cámara de seguridad

Grammar Point: *there is / there are*

singular: there is   **plural:** there are
***There is** a recreation room in the basement.*
***There are** mailboxes in the lobby.*

Look at the pictures.
Describe the apartment building.

A: *There's <u>a pool table</u> in the recreation room.*
B: *There are <u>parking spaces</u> in the garage.*

APARTMENT COMPLEX

20. balcony
el balcón

21. courtyard
el patio

22. swimming pool
la piscina / la alberca

23. trash bin
el depósito de basura

24. alley
el callejón

Hallway El pasillo

FIRE EXIT

25. emergency exit
la salida de emergencia

26. trash chute
el conducto para basura

Rental Office La oficina de alquiler

Rental Agreement

27. landlord
el arrendador / el dueño

28. lease / rental agreement
el contrato de alquiler /
alquiler a largo plazo

An Apartment Entryway La entrada al apartamento

It's Joe.

Come up.

29. smoke detector
el detector de humo

30. key
la llave

31. buzzer
el timbre

32. peephole
el ojo mágico / la mirilla

33. door chain
la cadena para puerta

34. dead-bolt lock
el cerrojo de seguridad

More vocabulary

upstairs: the floor(s) above you
downstairs: the floor(s) below you
fire exit: another name for emergency exit

Role play. Talk to a landlord.

A: *Is there a swimming pool in this complex?*
B: *Yes, there is. It's near the courtyard.*
A: *Is there…?*

51

1. the city / an urban area
la ciudad / un área urbana

2. the suburbs
los suburbios / las afueras

3. a small town / a village
un pueblo pequeño /
una aldea

4. the country / a rural area
el campo / un área rural

5. condominium / condo
el condominio / un condo

6. townhouse
la residencia urbana

7. mobile home
la casa rodante / la casa móvil

8. college dormitory / dorm
la residencia universitaria

9. farm
la granja

10. ranch
la hacienda / el rancho

11. senior housing
las viviendas para ancianos

12. nursing home
el hogar de ancianos

13. shelter
el refugio

More vocabulary

co-op: an apartment building owned by residents
duplex: a house divided into two homes
two-story house: a house with two floors

Think about it. Discuss.

1. What's good and bad about these places to live?
2. How are small towns different from cities?
3. How do shelters help people in need?

Front Yard and House El jardín delantero y la casa

Front Porch El porche frontal

1. **mailbox**
   el buzón

2. **front walk**
   la vereda / el caminito

3. **steps**
   los escalones /
   los peldaños

4. **gutter**
   el canal / el canalón

5. **chimney**
   la chimenea

6. **satellite dish**
   la antena parabólica

7. **garage door**
   la puerta del garaje

8. **driveway**
   la entrada del garaje

9. **gate**
   la puerta

10. **storm door**
    la contrapuerta

11. **front door**
    la puerta principal

12. **doorknob**
    la perilla de la puerta

13. **porch light**
    la luz del porche

14. **doorbell**
    el timbre

15. **screen door**
    la puerta mosquitero

Backyard El jardín posterior

16. **patio**
    el patio

17. **grill**
    la parrilla

18. **sliding glass door**
    la puerta de
    vidrio deslizante

19. **patio furniture**
    los muebles del patio

20. **flower bed**
    el lecho de flores

21. **hose**
    la manguera

22. **sprinkler**
    el rociador

23. **hammock**
    la hamaca

24. **garbage can**
    el tacho de basura

25. **compost pile**
    la pila de abono

26. **lawn**
    el césped

27. **vegetable garden**
    el jardín de verduras y
    hortalizas / la huerta /
    el huerto

A. **take** a nap
   tomar una siesta

B. **garden**
   trabajar en el jardín

53

1. **cabinet**
   el gabinete

2. **shelf**
   el estante

3. **paper towels**
   las toallas de papel

4. **sink**
   el fregadero

5. **dish rack**
   el secaplatos / el secador de vajilla

6. **toaster**
   la tostadora

7. **garbage disposal**
   el triturador de desperdicios

8. **dishwasher**
   el lavaplatos

9. **refrigerator**
   el refrigerador / la nevera

10. **freezer**
    el congelador

11. **coffeemaker**
    la cafetera

12. **blender**
    la licuadora

13. **microwave**
    el horno microondas

14. **electric can opener**
    el abrelatas eléctrico

15. **toaster oven**
    el horno tostador

16. **pot**
    la olla / la cacerola

17. **teakettle**
    la tetera

18. **stove**
    la estufa / la cocina

19. **burner**
    la hornilla

20. **oven**
    el horno

21. **broiler**
    la parrilla

22. **counter**
    el tope / el mostrador

23. **drawer**
    el cajón / la gaveta

24. **pan**
    la sartén

25. **electric mixer**
    la batidora eléctrica

26. **food processor**
    el procesador de alimentos

27. **cutting board**
    la tabla de cortar / picar

28. **mixing bowl**
    el tazón para mezclar / batir

Ways to talk about location using *on* and *in*

Use *on* for the counter, shelf, burner, stove, and cutting board. *It's on the counter.* Use *in* for the dishwasher, oven, sink, and drawer. *Put it in the sink.*

Pair practice. Make new conversations.

A: *Please move <u>the blender</u>.*
B: *Sure. Do you want it <u>in the cabinet</u>?*
A: *No, put it <u>on the counter</u>.*

1. dish / plate
   el plato

2. bowl
   el tazón / el plato hondo

3. fork
   el tenedor

4. knife
   el cuchillo

5. spoon
   la cuchara

6. teacup
   la taza de té

7. coffee mug
   la taza grande de café

8. dining room chair
   la silla del comedor

9. dining room table
   la mesa del comedor

10. napkin
    la servilleta

11. placemat
    el mantel individual

12. tablecloth
    el mantel

13. salt and pepper shakers
    el salero y el pimentero

14. sugar bowl
    la taza de azúcar /
    la azucarera

15. creamer
    la lechera

16. teapot
    la tetera

17. tray
    la bandeja / la charola

18. light fixture
    la lámpara

19. fan
    el ventilador

20. platter
    el platón / el plato grande

21. serving bowl
    el plato hondo de servir

22. hutch
    el aparador con vitrina

23. vase
    el florero

24. buffet
    el aparador

Ways to make requests at the table

May I have the sugar bowl?

Would you pass the creamer, please?

Could I have a coffee mug?

Role play. Request items at the table.

A: *What do you need?*

B: *Could I have a coffee mug?*

A: *Certainly. And would you...*

55

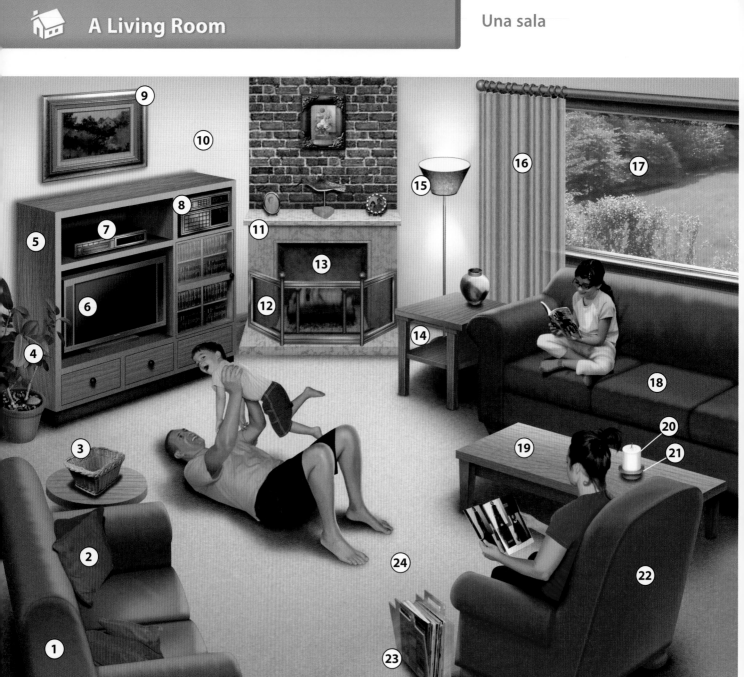

1. love seat
el sofá para dos

2. throw pillow
el cojín

3. basket
la cesta

4. houseplant
la planta interior

5. entertainment center
el centro de entretenimiento

6. TV (television)
el televisor / el TV

7. DVD player
el reproductor de DVD

8. stereo system
el sistema estereofónico

9. painting
el cuadro

10. wall
la pared

11. mantle
la repisa de la chimenea

12. fire screen
la pantalla de protección

13. fireplace
el hogar / la chimenea

14. end table
la mesita

15. floor lamp
la lámpara de pie

16. drapes
las cortinas

17. window
la ventana

18. sofa / couch
el sofá

19. coffee table
la mesa de centro

20. candle
la vela

21. candle holder
el portavela

22. armchair / easy chair
la butaca / el sillón

23. magazine holder
el revistero

24. carpet
la alfombra

Use the new words.
Look at pages 44–45. Name the things in the room.

A: *There's a TV.*
B: *There's a carpet.*

More vocabulary

light bulb: the light inside a lamp

lampshade: the part of the lamp that covers the light bulb

sofa cushions: the pillows that are part of the sofa

1. hamper
   la cesta para la ropa

2. bathtub
   la bañera

3. soap dish
   la jabonera

4. soap
   el jabón

5. rubber mat
   la alfombra de goma /
   el tapete de hule

6. washcloth
   la toalla para frotarse

7. drain
   el desagüe

8. faucet
   el grifo / la llave

9. hot water
   el agua caliente

10. cold water
    el agua fría

11. grab bar
    la barra de sujeción

12. tile
    la losa / la baldosa /
    el azulejo

13. showerhead
    el cabezal de la ducha

14. shower curtain
    la cortina de la ducha

15. towel rack
    el toallero

16. bath towel
    la toalla de baño

17. hand towel
    la toalla de manos

18. mirror
    el espejo

19. toilet paper
    el papel higiénico

20. toilet brush
    el cepillo para el inodoro

21. toilet
    el inodoro

22. medicine cabinet
    el gabinete de baño /
    el botiquín

23. toothbrush
    el cepillo de dientes

24. toothbrush holder
    el portacepillos

25. sink
    el lavamanos

26. wastebasket
    la papelera

27. scale
    la balanza

28. bath mat
    la alfombrilla para baño

More vocabulary

stall shower: a shower without a bathtub
half bath: a bathroom with no shower or tub
linen closet: a closet for towels and sheets

Ask your classmates. Share the answers.

1. Is your toothbrush on the sink or in the medicine cabinet?
2. Do you have a bathtub or a shower?
3. Do you have a shower curtain or a shower door?

1. dresser / bureau
la cómoda

2. drawer
la gaveta / el cajón

3. photos
las fotografías / las fotos

4. picture frame
el marco de foto

5. closet
el clóset

6. full-length mirror
el espejo largo

7. curtains
las cortinas

8. mini-blinds
las minipersianas

9. bed
la cama

10. headboard
la cabecera

11. pillow
la almohada

12. fitted sheet
la sábana esquinera

13. flat sheet
la sábana

14. pillowcase
la funda de la almohada

15. blanket
la cobija / la manta

16. quilt
la colcha / el cubrecama

17. dust ruffle
el volante

18. bed frame
el marco de la cama

19. box spring
la caja de resortes / el muelle

20. mattress
el colchón

21. wood floor
el piso de madera

22. rug
la alfombra

23. night table / nightstand
la mesita de noche

24. alarm clock
el reloj de alarma

25. lamp
la lámpara

26. lampshade
la pantalla de la lámpara

27. light switch
el interruptor de la luz

28. outlet
el enchufe / el tomacorrientes

Look at the pictures.
Describe the bedroom.

A: *There's a lamp on the nightstand.*
B: *There's a mirror in the closet.*

Ask your classmates. Share the answers.

1. Do you prefer a hard or a soft mattress?
2. Do you prefer mini-blinds or curtains?
3. How many pillows do you like on your bed?

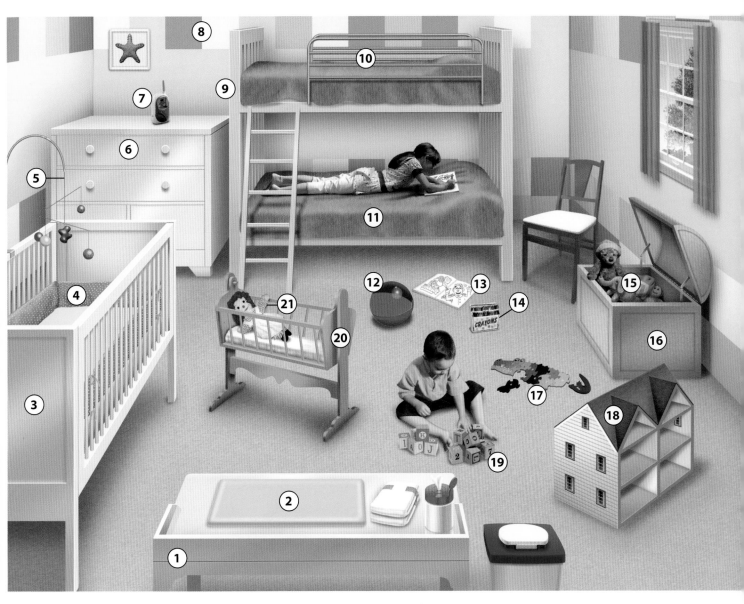

Furniture and Accessories Muebles y accesorios

1. **changing table**
   la mesa para cambiar pañales

2. **changing pad**
   la almohadilla para cambiar pañales

3. **crib**
   la cuna

4. **bumper pad**
   el protector

5. **mobile**
   el móvil

6. **chest of drawers**
   el gavetero / la cómoda

7. **baby monitor**
   el monitor para bebés

8. **wallpaper**
   el papel tapiz

9. **bunk beds**
   la litera

10. **safety rail**
    el riel de seguridad

11. **bedspread**
    el cubrecama / la colcha

Toys and Games Juguetes y juegos

12. **ball**
    la bola

13. **coloring book**
    el libro de pintar

14. **crayons**
    los creyones

15. **stuffed animals**
    los animales de peluche

16. **toy chest**
    el baúl para juguetes

17. **puzzle**
    el rompecabezas

18. **dollhouse**
    la casa de muñecas

19. **blocks**
    los bloques

20. **cradle**
    la cuna mecedora

21. **doll**
    la muñeca

Pair practice. Make conversations.

A: *Where's the changing pad?*
B: *It's on the changing table.*

Think about it. Discuss.

1. Which toys help children learn? How?
2. Which toys are good for older and younger children?
3. What safety features does this room need? Why?

59

A. **dust** the furniture
   sacudir los muebles

B. **recycle** the newspapers
   reciclar los periódicos

C. **clean** the oven
   limpiar el horno

D. **mop** the floor
   trapear / limpiar el piso

E. **polish** the furniture
   pulir los muebles

F. **make** the bed
   hacer la cama

G. **put away** the toys
   guardar los juguetes

H. **vacuum** the carpet
   aspirar la alfombra

I. **wash** the windows
   lavar las ventanas

J. **sweep** the floor
   barrer el piso

K. **scrub** the sink
   refregar / fregar
   el fregadero

L. **empty** the trash
   vaciar la basura

M. **wash** the dishes
   lavar los platos

N. **dry** the dishes
   secar los platos

O. **wipe** the counter
   limpiar el mostrador /
   la barra

P. **change** the sheets
   cambiar las sábanas

Q. **take out** the garbage
   sacar la basura

Pair practice. Make new conversations.

A: *Let's clean this place. First, I'll <u>sweep the floor</u>.*
B: *I'll <u>mop the floor</u> when you finish.*

Ask your classmates. Share the answers.

1. Who does the housework in your home?
2. How often do you wash the windows?
3. When should kids start to do housework?

1
2
3
4
5
6

7
8
9
10
11
12

13
14
15
16
17
18

19
20
21
22
23
24

1. feather duster
el plumero

2. recycling bin
el recipiente de reciclaje

3. oven cleaner
el limpiador de hornos

4. rubber gloves
los guantes de goma

5. steel-wool soap pads
las esponjas de lana de acero

6. sponge mop
la fregona con esponja

7. bucket / pail
el cubo / el balde / la cubeta

8. furniture polish
la cera para muebles

9. rags
los trapos

10. vacuum cleaner
la aspiradora

11. vacuum cleaner attachments
los accesorios para aspiradora

12. vacuum cleaner bag
la bolsa para aspiradora

13. stepladder
la escalerilla

14. glass cleaner
el limpiador de vidrios

15. squeegee
el escurridor

16. broom
la escoba

17. dustpan
el recogedor / la pala

18. cleanser
el limpiador

19. sponge
la esponja

20. scrub brush
el cepillo de frotar / de fregar

21. dishwashing liquid
el líquido lavaplatos

22. dish towel
la toalla para platos

23. disinfectant wipes
las toallitas húmedas desinfectantes

24. trash bags
las bolsas para basura

Ways to ask for something
Please hand me the squeegee.
Can you get me the broom?
I need the sponge mop.

Pair practice. Make new conversations.
A: *Please hand me the sponge mop.*
B: *Here you go. Do you need the bucket?*
A: *Yes, please. Can you get me the rubber gloves, too?*

61

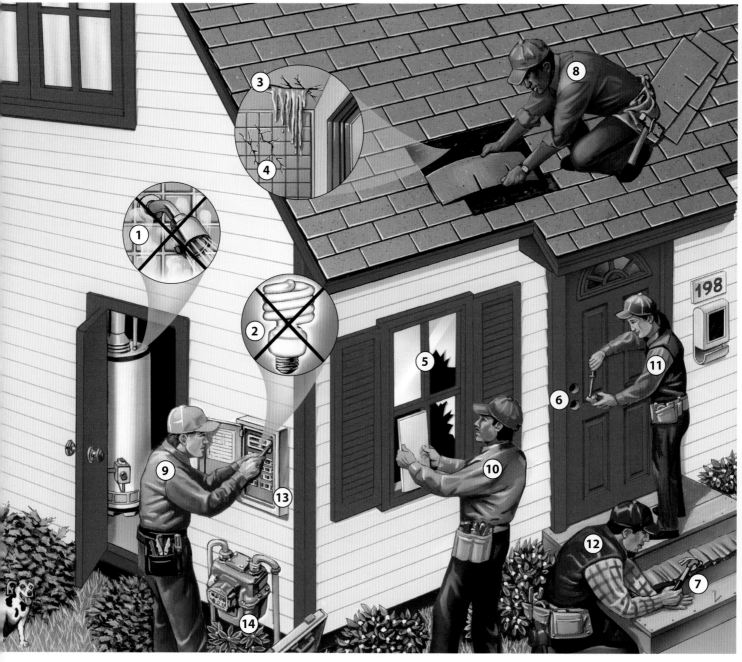

1. The water heater is **not working**.
   El calentador de agua **no funciona**.

2. The power is **out**.
   No hay electricidad.

3. The roof is **leaking**.
   El techo **gotea**.

4. The tile is **cracked**.
   La losa está **rota**.

5. The window is **broken**.
   La ventana está **rota**.

6. The lock is **broken**.
   La cerradura está **estropeada**.

7. The steps are **broken**.
   Los escalones están **rotos**.

8. roofer
   el reparador de techos

9. electrician
   el electricista

10. repair person
    el reparador

11. locksmith
    el cerrajero

12. carpenter
    el carpintero

13. fuse box
    la caja de fusibles

14. gas meter
    el medidor de gas

More vocabulary

fix: to repair something that is broken

pests: termites, fleas, rats, etc.

exterminate: to kill household pests

Pair practice. Make new conversations.

A: The faucet is <u>leaking</u>.

B: Let's call <u>the plumber</u>. He can fix it.

15. The furnace is **broken**.
La caldera está **estropeada**.

16. The pipes are **frozen**.
Las tuberías están **congeladas**.

17. The faucet is **dripping**.
El grifo / la llave **gotea**.

18. The sink is **overflowing**.
El lavamanos / el lavaplatos se **desborda**.

19. The toilet is **stopped up**.
El inodoro está **atorado**.

20. plumber
el plomero

21. exterminator
el fumigador / el exterminador

22. termites
las termitas / los comejenes

23. ants
las hormigas

24. bedbugs
los chinches

25. fleas
las pulgas

26. cockroaches / roaches
las cucarachas

27. rats
las ratas

28. mice*
los ratones

*Note: one mouse, two mice

Ways to ask about repairs

How much will this repair cost?
When can you begin?
How long will the repair take?

Role play. Talk to a repair person.

A: *Can you fix <u>the roof</u>?*
B: *Yes, but it will take <u>two weeks</u>.*
A: *How much will the repair cost?*

63

The Tenant Meeting / La reunión de los inquilinos

THE NEXT DAY…

LATER THAT EVENING…

Use rec room for large parties

No loud music on weeknights

Come to Our "We're Sorry!" Party SAT 8pm REC ROOM

1. roommates
   los compañeros / las compañeras de habitación

2. party
   la fiesta

3. music
   la música

4. DJ
   el disc-jockey

5. noise
   el ruido

6. irritated
   está irritado

7. rules
   las normas

8. mess
   el desorden

9. invitation
   la invitación

A. **dance**
   baile / bailar

THE NEXT SATURDAY...

Look at the pictures. What do you see?

Answer the questions.

1. What happened in apartment 2B? How many people were there?

2. How did the neighbor feel? Why?

3. What rules did they write at the tenant meeting?

4. What did the roommates do after the tenant meeting?

Read the story.

The Tenant Meeting

Sally Lopez and Tina Green are <u>roommates</u>. They live in apartment 2B. One night they had a big <u>party</u> with <u>music</u> and a <u>DJ</u>. There was a <u>mess</u> in the hallway. Their neighbors were very unhappy. Mr. Clark in 2A was very <u>irritated</u>. He hates <u>noise</u>!

The next day there was a tenant meeting. Everyone wanted <u>rules</u> about parties and loud music. The girls were very embarrassed.

After the meeting, the girls cleaned the mess in the hallway. Then they gave each neighbor an <u>invitation</u> to a new party. Everyone had a good time at the rec room party. Now the tenants have two new rules and a new place to <u>dance</u>.

Think about it.

1. What are the most important rules in an apartment building? Why?

2. Imagine you are the neighbor in 2A. What do you say to Tina and Sally?

65

1. **fish**
   el pescado

2. **meat**
   la carne

3. **chicken**
   el pollo

4. **cheese**
   el queso

5. **milk**
   la leche

6. **butter**
   la mantequilla

7. **eggs**
   los huevos

8. **vegetables**
   las verduras y
   hortalizas

Listen and point. Take turns.

A: *Point to the <u>vegetables</u>.*
B: *Point to the <u>bread</u>.*
A: *Point to the <u>fruit</u>.*

Pair Dictation

A: *Write <u>vegetables</u>.*
B: *Please spell <u>vegetables</u> for me.*
A: *V-e-g-e-t-a-b-l-e-s.*

9. fruit
   las frutas

10. rice
    el arroz

11. bread
    el pan

12. pasta
    la pasta

13. grocery bag
    la bolsa de comestibles

14. shopping list
    la lista de compra

15. coupons
    los cupones / los vales

Ways to talk about food.

Do we need <u>eggs</u>?
Do we have any <u>pasta</u>?
We have some <u>vegetables</u>, but we need <u>fruit</u>.

Role play. Talk about your shopping list.

A: *Do we need eggs?*
B: *No, we have some.*
A: *Do we have any...*

67

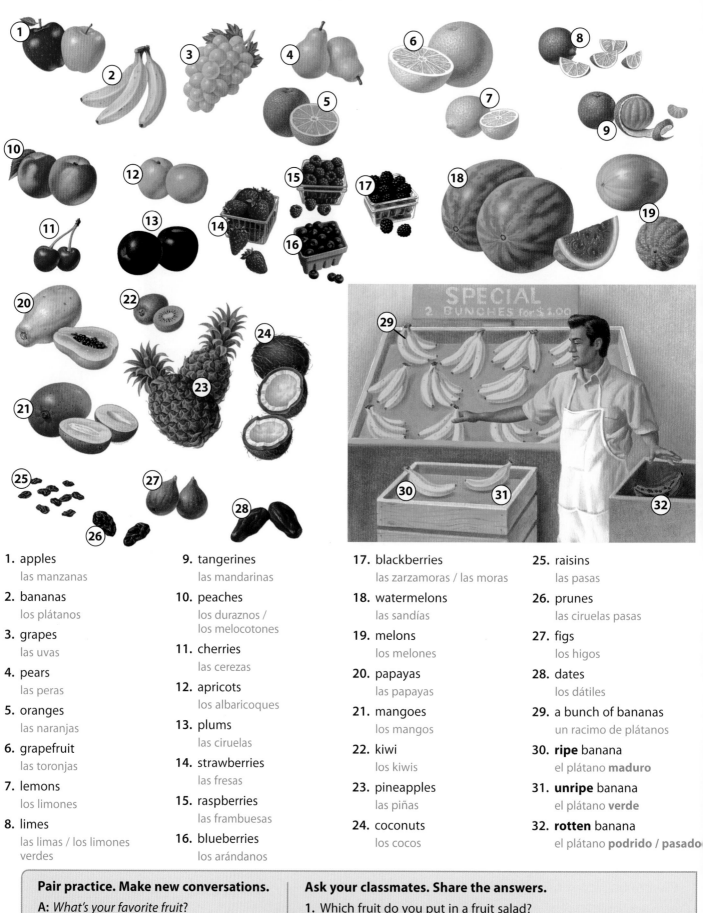

1. apples
   las manzanas
2. bananas
   los plátanos
3. grapes
   las uvas
4. pears
   las peras
5. oranges
   las naranjas
6. grapefruit
   las toronjas
7. lemons
   los limones
8. limes
   las limas / los limones
   verdes

9. tangerines
   las mandarinas
10. peaches
    los duraznos /
    los melocotones
11. cherries
    las cerezas
12. apricots
    los albaricoques
13. plums
    las ciruelas
14. strawberries
    las fresas
15. raspberries
    las frambuesas
16. blueberries
    los arándanos

17. blackberries
    las zarzamoras / las moras
18. watermelons
    las sandías
19. melons
    los melones
20. papayas
    las papayas
21. mangoes
    los mangos
22. kiwi
    los kiwis
23. pineapples
    las piñas
24. coconuts
    los cocos

25. raisins
    las pasas
26. prunes
    las ciruelas pasas
27. figs
    los higos
28. dates
    los dátiles
29. a bunch of bananas
    un racimo de plátanos
30. **ripe** banana
    el plátano **maduro**
31. **unripe** banana
    el plátano **verde**
32. **rotten** banana
    el plátano **podrido / pasado**

Pair practice. Make new conversations.

A: *What's your favorite fruit?*
B: *I like <u>apples</u>. Do you?*
A: *I prefer <u>bananas</u>.*

Ask your classmates. Share the answers.

1. Which fruit do you put in a fruit salad?
2. What kinds of fruit are common in your native country?
3. What kinds of fruit are in your kitchen right now?

1. lettuce
   la lechuga

2. cabbage
   la col

3. carrots
   las zanahorias

4. radishes
   los rábanos

5. beets
   las remolachas / los betabeles

6. tomatoes
   los tomates

7. bell peppers
   los pimientos / los pimentones

8. string beans
   las judías verdes / los ejotes

9. celery
   el apio

10. cucumbers
    los pepinos

11. spinach
    la espinaca

12. corn
    el maíz

13. broccoli
    el brócoli

14. cauliflower
    la coliflor

15. bok choy
    el repollo chino

16. turnips
    los nabos

17. potatoes
    las papas

18. sweet potatoes
    los camotes

19. onions
    las cebollas

20. green onions / scallions
    las cebollas verdes /
    las cebollitas

21. peas
    los guisantes / los chícharos

22. artichokes
    las alcachofas

23. eggplants
    las berenjenas

24. squash
    la calabaza

25. zucchini
    el calabacín / la calabacita

26. asparagus
    los espárragos

27. mushrooms
    los hongos / las setas

28. parsley
    el perejil

29. chili peppers
    los chiles / los ajíes

30. garlic
    el ajo

31. a **bag of** lettuce
    una **bolsa de** lechuga

32. a **head of** lettuce
    una **cabeza de** lechuga

Pair practice. Make new conversations.

A: *Do you eat <u>broccoli</u>?*
B: *Yes. I like most vegetables, but not <u>peppers</u>.*
A: *Really? Well, I don't like <u>cauliflower</u>.*

Ask your classmates. Share the answers.

1. Which vegetables do you eat raw? cooked?
2. Which vegetables do you put in a green salad?
3. Which vegetables are in your refrigerator right now?

69

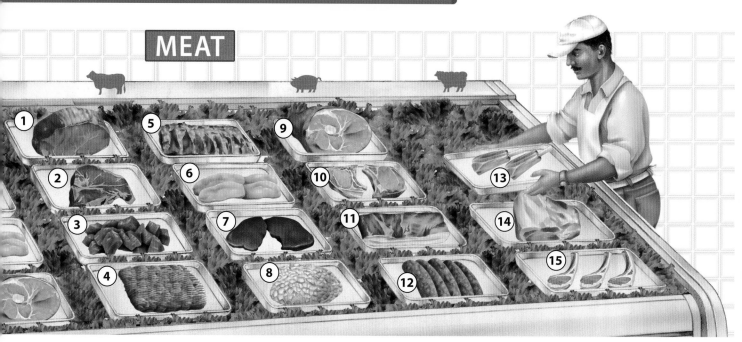

MEAT

POULTRY

Beef Carne de res

1. roast
   el asado / el rosbif
2. steak
   el filete / el bistec
3. stewing beef
   la carne para guisar
4. ground beef
   la carne molida
5. beef ribs
   las costillas de res
6. veal cutlets
   las chuletas de ternera
7. liver
   el hígado
8. tripe
   la tripa / el mondongo

Pork Carne de cerdo

9. ham
   el jamón
10. pork chops
    las chuletas de cerdo
11. bacon
    el tocino
12. sausage
    la salchicha

Lamb Carne de cordero

13. lamb shanks
    los jarretes de cordero
14. leg of lamb
    la pata de cordero
15. lamb chops
    las chuletas de cordero

Poultry Carne de aves de corral

16. chicken
    el pollo
17. turkey
    el pavo
18. duck
    el pato
19. breasts
    las pechugas
20. wings
    las alas
21. legs
    las patas
22. thighs
    los muslos
23. drumsticks
    las patas
24. **raw** chicken
    el pollo **crudo**
25. **cooked** chicken
    el pollo **cocido**

More vocabulary

vegetarian: a person who doesn't eat meat
boneless: meat and poultry without bones
skinless: poultry without skin

Ask your classmates. Share the answers.

1. What kind of meat do you eat most often?
2. What kind of meat do you use in soups?
3. What part of the chicken do you like the most?

SEAFOOD

Fish Pescado

1. trout
   la trucha
2. catfish
   el bagre
3. whole salmon
   el salmón entero
4. salmon steak
   el filete de salmón
5. swordfish
   el pez espada
6. halibut steak
   el filete de halibut
7. tuna
   el atún
8. cod
   el bacalao

Shellfish Moluscos y crustáceos

9. crab
   el cangrejo
10. lobster
    la langosta
11. shrimp
    el langostino / el camarón
12. scallops
    los escalopes
13. mussels
    los mejillones
14. oysters
    las ostras
15. clams
    las almejas
16. **fresh** fish
    el pescado **fresco**
17. **frozen** fish
    el pescado **congelado**

DELI

18. white bread
    el pan blanco
19. wheat bread
    el pan de trigo
20. rye bread
    el pan de centeno

21. roast beef
    el rosbif
22. corned beef
    la cecina / la carne en conserva
23. pastrami
    el pastrami

24. salami
    el salami
25. smoked turkey
    el pavo ahumado
26. American cheese
    el queso americano

27. Swiss cheese
    el queso suizo
28. cheddar cheese
    el queso cheddar
29. mozzarella cheese
    el queso mozzarella

Ways to order at the counter

I'd like some <u>roast beef</u>.
I'll have <u>a halibut steak</u> and some <u>shrimp</u>.
Could I get some <u>Swiss cheese</u>?

Pair practice. Make new conversations.

A: *What can I get for you?*
B: *I'd like some <u>roast beef</u>. How about a pound?*
A: *A pound of <u>roast beef</u> coming up!*

71

SEAFOOD

DAIRY

2A 2B

FROZEN FOODS

POULTRY

MEAT

1. customer	**3. scale**	**5. pet food**	**7. cart**
el cliente	la balanza	la comida para mascotas	el carrito
2. produce section	**4. grocery clerk**	**6. aisle**	**8. manager**
la sección de verduras, hortalizas y frutas	el ayudante de la tienda	el pasillo	el gerente

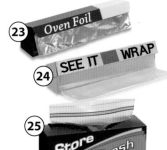

Canned Foods
Alimentos envasados

17. beans
los frijoles / las habichuelas

18. soup
la sopa

19. tuna
el atún

Dairy
Productos lácteos

20. margarine
la margarina

21. sour cream
la crema agria

22. yogurt
el yogurt

Grocery Products
Otros productos

23. aluminum foil
el papel de aluminio

24. plastic wrap
el plástico para envolver

25. plastic storage bags
las bolsas de plástico para almacenar

Frozen Foods
Alimentos congelados

26. ice cream
el helado

27. frozen vegetables
las verduras congeladas

28. frozen dinner
las comidas congeladas

Ways to ask for information in a grocery store

Excuse me, where are the carrots?
Can you please tell me where to find the dog food?
Do you have any lamb chops today?

Pair practice. Make conversations.

A: *Can you please tell me where to find the dog food?*
B: *Sure. It's in aisle 1B. Do you need anything else?*
A: *Yes, where are the carrots?*

BAKERY

15 items or less

Best Baked Goods

Cash for Bottles | Cash for Bottle

3A | 3B

SNACKS

IN | OUT

9. shopping basket	11. line	13. cashier	15. cash register
la canasta	la línea	el cajero / la cajera	la caja registradora
10. self-checkout	12. checkstand	14. bagger	16. bottle return
el autopago	la caja	la persona que empaca la compra	la devolución de botellas

WHOLE WHEAT

J&G

Franco's

Baking Products
Productos para pastelerías

29. flour
   la harina

30. sugar
   el azúcar

31. oil
   el aceite

Italian Roast

Tasty Cola

Beverages
Bebidas

32. apple juice
   el jugo de manzana

33. coffee
   el café

34. soda / pop
   las bebidas gaseosas

Baked not Fried!

YUM! CHOCOLATE

Snack Foods
Botanas / Meriendas

35. potato chips
   las papas fritas de bolsa

36. nuts
   los frutos secos

37. candy bar
   las barras de chocolate

Baked Goods
Productos de pastelería

38. cookies
   las galletas dulces

39. cake
   la torta

40. bagels
   los bollos con forma de rosquilla

Ask your classmates. Share the answers.

1. What is your favorite grocery store?
2. Do you prefer to shop alone or with friends?
3. Which foods from your country are hard to find?

Think about it. Discuss.

1. Is it better to shop every day or once a week? Why?
2. Why do grocery stores put snacks near the checkstands?
3. What's good and what's bad about small grocery stores?

73

 **1.** bottles
las botellas

2. jars
los frascos

 **3.** cans
las latas

 **4.** cartons
las cajas
de cartón

5. containers
los contenedores

 **6.** boxes
las cajas

 **7.** bags
las bolsas

 **8.** packages
los paquetes

 **9.** six-packs
los paquetes
de seis

10. loaves
las hogazas

 **11.** rolls
los rollos

 **12.** tubes
los tubos

 **13.** a bottle of water
una botella de agua

14. a jar of jam
un frasco de mermelada

15. a can of beans
una lata de frijoles

 **16.** a carton of eggs
un cartón de huevos

 17. a container of cottage cheese
un contenedor de queso fresco

18. a box of cereal
una caja de cereal

 **19.** a bag of flour
una bolsa de harina

 **20.** a package of cookies
un paquete de galletas dulces

 **21.** a six-pack of soda (pop)
media docena de bebidas gaseosas

 **22.** a loaf of bread
una hogaza de pan

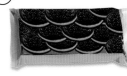 **23.** a roll of paper towels
un rollo de toallas de papel

 **24.** a tube of toothpaste
un tubo de pasta de dientes

Grammar Point: count and non-count

Some foods can be counted: *an apple, two apples*.

Some foods can't be counted: *some rice, some water*.

For non-count foods, count containers: *two bags of rice*.

Pair practice. Make conversations.

A: How many <u>boxes of cereal</u> do we need?

B: We need <u>two boxes</u>.

A. Measure the ingredients.
Mida los ingredientes.

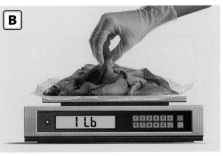

B. Weigh the food.
Pese la comida.

1 cup = 237 milliliters

C. Convert the measurements.
Convierta las medidas.

Liquid Measures Medidas para líquidos

1
1 fl. oz.

2
1 c.

3
1 pt.

4
1 qt.

5
1 gal.

Dry Measures Medidas secas

6
1 tsp.

7
1 TBS.

8
1/4 c.

9
1/2 c.

10
1 c.

Weight Peso

11

12

1. a fluid ounce of milk
una onza líquida de leche

2. a cup of oil
una taza de aceite

3. a pint of frozen yogurt
una pinta de yogurt congelado

4. a quart of milk
un cuarto de galón de leche

5. a gallon of water
un galón de agua

6. a teaspoon of salt
una cucharadita de sal

7. a tablespoon of sugar
una cucharada de azúcar

8. a quarter cup of brown sugar
un cuarto de taza de azúcar morena

9. a half cup of raisins
media taza de pasas

10. a cup of flour
una taza de harina

11. an ounce of cheese
una onza de queso

12. a pound of roast beef
una libra de rosbif

Equivalencies	
3 tsp. = 1 TBS.	2 c. = 1 pt.
2 TBS. = 1 fl. oz.	2 pt. = 1 qt.
8 fl. oz. = 1 c.	4 qt. = 1 gal.

Volume
1 fl. oz. = 30 ml
1 c. = 237 ml
1 pt. = .47 L
1 qt. = .95 L
1 gal. = 3.79 L

Weight
1 oz. = 28.35 grams (g)
1 lb. = 453.6 g
2.205 lbs. = 1 kilogram (kg)
1 lb. = 16 oz.

Food Safety Seguridad de los alimentos

A. clean
limpiar

B. separate
separar

C. cook
cocinar

D. chill
refrigerar

A. Clean counters! 20 SECONDS Wash your hands!

B. Use separate cutting boards for vegetables and meat!

C. 165 160 Cook to the right temperature!

D. Refrigerate leftovers quickly!

Ways to Serve Meat and Poultry Maneras de servir las carnes de res y de ave

1. fried chicken
pollo frito

2. barbecued / grilled ribs
costillas a la parrilla

3. broiled steak
filete de res asado a la brasa

4. roasted turkey
pavo al horno

5. boiled ham
jamón hervido

6. stir-fried beef
carne de res sofrita

Ways to Serve Eggs Maneras de servir los huevos

7. scrambled eggs
huevos revueltos

8. hardboiled eggs
huevos duros

9. poached eggs
huevos escalfados

10. eggs sunny-side up
huevos fritos

11. eggs over easy
huevos fritos, con una vuelta

12. omelet
tortilla de huevos

Role play. Make new conversations.

A: *How do you like your eggs?*
B: *I like them <u>scrambled</u>. And you?*
A: *I like them <u>hardboiled</u>.*

Ask your classmates. Share the answers.

1. Do you use separate cutting boards?
2. What is your favorite way to serve meat? poultry?
3. What are healthy ways of preparing meat? poultry?

Cheesy Tofu Vegetable Casserole Estofado de verduras, hortalizas y tofú con queso

A. Preheat the oven.
Precaliente el horno.

B. Grease a baking pan.
Engrase una cazuela para hornear.

C. Slice the tofu.
Rebane el tofú.

D. Steam the broccoli.
Cocine el brócoli al vapor.

E. Saute the mushrooms.
Saltee los hongos / las setas.

F. Spoon sauce on top.
Échele salsa encima con una cuchara.

G. Grate the cheese.
Ralle el queso.

H. Bake.
Hornee.

Easy Chicken Soup Sopa de pollo fácil

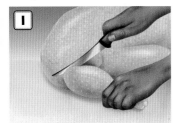

I. Cut up the chicken.
Corte el pollo.

J. Dice the celery.
Corte el apio en trocitos.

K. Peel the carrots.
Pele las zanahorias.

L. Chop the onions.
Corte las cebollas.

M. Boil the chicken.
Hierva el pollo.

N. Add the vegetables.
Añada las legumbres y hortalizas.

O. Stir.
Revuelva.

P. Simmer.
Cocine a fuego lento.

Quick and Easy Cake Torta fácil y rápida

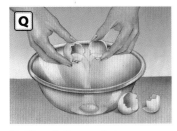

Q. Break 2 eggs into a microwave-safe bowl.
Rompa 2 huevos en un tazón para horno microonda.

R. Mix the ingredients.
Mezcle los ingredientes.

S. Beat the mixture.
Bata la mezcla.

T. Microwave for 5 minutes.
Hornee la mezcla en el horno microondas durante 5 minutos.

1. can opener
   el abrelatas

2. grater
   el rallador

3. steamer
   la olla / la cacerola a vapor

4. plastic storage container
   el recipiente de plástico

5. frying pan
   la sartén

6. pot
   la olla / la cacerola

7. ladle
   el cucharón / el cazo

8. double boiler
   la cacerola doble

9. wooden spoon
   la cuchara de madera

10. casserole dish
    el molde refractario /
    el recipiente refractario

11. garlic press
    la prensa para ajo

12. carving knife
    el cuchillo de trinchar

13. roasting pan
    la bandeja para asar

14. roasting rack
    la parrilla para asar

15. vegetable peeler
    el pelador de verduras
    y hortalizas

16. paring knife
    el cuchillo de pelar

17. colander
    el escurridor

18. kitchen timer
    el cronómetro de cocina

19. spatula
    la espátula

20. eggbeater
    el batidor de huevos

21. whisk
    el batidor

22. strainer
    la coladera

23. tongs
    las pinzas / las tenazas

24. lid
    la tapa

25. saucepan
    el cacillo / la olla

26. cake pan
    el molde para torta

27. cookie sheet
    la bandeja para
    galletas dulces

28. pie pan
    el molde para pastel

29. pot holders
    los agarraollas

30. rolling pin
    el rodillo

31. mixing bowl
    el tazón para mezclar

Pair practice. Make new conversations.

A: *Please hand me the whisk.*

B: *Here's the whisk. Do you need anything else?*

A: *Yes, pass me the casserole dish.*

Use the new words.

Look at page 77. Name the kitchen utensils you see.

A: *Here's a grater.*

B: *This is a mixing bowl.*

1. hamburger
   la hamburguesa

2. french fries
   las papas fritas

3. cheeseburger
   la hamburguesa con queso

4. onion rings
   los anillos de cebolla

5. chicken sandwich
   el sándwich de pollo

6. hot dog
   el perro caliente / la salchicha

7. nachos
   los nachos

8. taco
   el taco

9. burrito
   el burrito

10. pizza
    la pizza

11. soda
    el refresco

12. iced tea
    el té helado

13. ice-cream cone
    el barquillo de helado

14. milkshake
    la malteada

15. donut
    la rosquilla

16. muffin
    el mollete / el bollo dulce

17. counterperson
    el atendiente en el mostrador

18. straw
    la caña / el sorbeto

19. plastic utensils
    los utensilios de plástico

20. sugar substitute
    el endulzante artificial

21. ketchup
    la salsa catsup

22. mustard
    la mostaza

23. mayonnaise
    la mayonesa

24. salad bar
    la barra de ensaladas

Grammar Point: yes/no questions (do)

Do you like hamburgers? Yes, I do.
Do you like nachos? No, I don't.

Think about it. Discuss.

1. Do you think that fast food is bad for people? Why or why not?
2. What fast foods do you have in your country?
3. Do you have a favorite fast food restaurant? Which one?

79

1. bacon
   el tocino

2. sausage
   la salchicha

3. hash browns
   las papitas doradas

4. toast
   la tostada

5. English muffin
   el bollo dulce Inglés

6. biscuits
   los panecillos

7. pancakes
   los panqueques

8. waffles
   los wafles

9. hot cereal
   el cereal caliente

10. grilled cheese sandwich
    el sándwich de queso
    a la plancha

11. pickle
    el pepinillo en vinagre

12. club sandwich
    el sándwich club

13. spinach salad
    la ensalada de espinaca

14. chef's salad
    la ensalada del chef

15. dinner salad
    la ensalada de cena

16. soup
    la sopa

17. rolls
    los panecillos

18. coleslaw
    la ensalada de col

19. potato salad
    la ensalada de papas

20. pasta salad
    la ensalada de pasta

21. fruit salad
    la ensalada de frutas

BREAKFAST SPECIAL
Served 6 a.m. to 11 a.m.

Two egg omelet with one side

JELLY

HONEY

SYRUP

LUNCH
Served 11 a.m. to 2 p.m.
All sandwiches come with soup or salad

CRACKERS

SIDE SALADS

SALAD DRESSINGS

Thousand Island   Ranch

Italian   Blue Cheese

Ways to order from a menu

I'd like a grilled cheese sandwich.
I'll have a bowl of tomato soup.
Could I get the chef's salad with ranch dressing?

Pair practice. Make conversations.

A: *I'd like a grilled cheese sandwich, please.*
B: *Anything else for you?*
A: *Yes, I'll have a bowl of tomato soup with that.*

A Coffee Shop Menu 🍽

DINNER

DESSERTS

BEVERAGES

22. **roast chicken**
    el pollo asado
23. **mashed potatoes**
    el puré de papas
24. **steak**
    el filete / el bistec
25. **baked potato**
    la papa asada /
    la papa al horno
26. **spaghetti**
    el spaghetti
27. **meatballs**
    las bolas de carne
28. **garlic bread**
    el pan con ajo
29. **grilled fish**
    el pescado a la parrilla
30. **rice**
    el arroz
31. **meatloaf**
    el molde de carne
32. **steamed vegetables**
    las verduras y hortalizas
    al vapor
33. **layer cake**
    la torta de capas
34. **cheesecake**
    la torta de queso
35. **pie**
    el pastel
36. **mixed berries**
    las bayas mixtas
37. **coffee**
    el café
38. **decaf coffee**
    el café descafeinado
39. **tea**
    el té
40. **herbal tea**
    el té de hierbas
41. **cream**
    la crema
42. **low-fat milk**
    la leche baja en grasa

Ask your classmates. Share the answers.

1. Do you prefer vegetable soup or chicken soup?
2. Do you prefer tea or coffee?
3. Which desserts on the menu do you like?

Role play. Order a dinner from the menu.

A: *Are you ready to order?*
B: *I think so. I'll have <u>the roast chicken</u>.*
A: *Would you also like…?*

81

1. dining room
   el comedor

2. hostess
   la anfitriona / el jefe
   de comedor

3. high chair
   la silla alta

4. booth
   el compartimiento

5. to-go box
   la caja para llevar

6. patron / diner
   el cliente

7. menu
   el menú

8. server / waiter
   el mesero / el camarero

A. **set** the table
   poner la mesa

B. **seat** the customer
   sentar al cliente

C. **pour** the water
   servir el agua

D. **order** from the menu
   pedir del menú

E. **take** the order
   tomar la orden

F. **serve** the meal
   servir la comida

G. **clear** / **bus** the dishes
   recoger los platos

H. **carry** the tray
   llevar la bandeja

I. **pay** the check
   pagar la cuenta

J. **leave** a tip
   dejar una propina

More vocabulary

eat out: to go to a restaurant to eat

take out: to buy food at a restaurant and take it
home to eat

Look at the pictures.
Describe what is happening.

A: *She's seating the customer*.
B: *He's taking the order*.

82

9. server / waitress
la mesera / la camarera

10. dessert tray
la bandeja de los postres

11. bread basket
la cesta para el pan

12. busser
el ayudante del camarero

13. dish room
el cuarto de lavado

14. dishwasher
el lavaplatos

15. kitchen
la cocina

16. chef
el chef

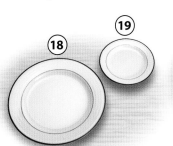

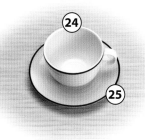
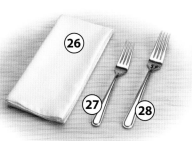

17. place setting
la distribución de los
cubiertos y vajillas

18. dinner plate
el plato

19. bread-and-butter plate
el plato para el pan
y la mantequilla

20. salad plate
el plato para ensalada

21. soup bowl
el tazón de sopa

22. water glass
el vaso de agua

23. wine glass
la copa de vino

24. cup
la taza

25. saucer
el platito / el platillo

26. napkin
la servilleta

27. salad fork
el tenedor para ensalada

28. dinner fork
el tenedor

29. steak knife
el cuchillo para carne

30. knife
el cuchillo

31. teaspoon
la cucharita

32. soupspoon
la cuchara para sopa

Pair practice. Make new conversations.

A: *Excuse me, this* <u>spoon</u> *is dirty.*
B: *I'm so sorry. I'll get you a clean* <u>spoon</u> *right away.*
A: *Thanks.*

Role play. Talk to a new busser.

A: *Do the* <u>salad forks</u> *go on* <u>the left</u>?
B: *Yes. They go* <u>next to the dinner forks</u>.
A: *What about the…?*

1. **live music**
   la música en vivo

2. **organic**
   los productos
   orgánicos

3. **lemonade**
   la limonada

4. **sour**
   agria

5. **samples**
   las muestras

6. **avocados**
   los avocados /
   las paltas

7. **vendors**
   los vendedores

8. **sweets**
   los dulces

9. **herbs**
   las hierbas

A. **count**
   contar

Look at the pictures.
What do you see?

Answer the questions.

1. How many vendors are at the market today?

2. Which vegetables are organic?

3. What are the children eating?

4. What is the woman counting? Why?

Read the story.

The Farmers' Market

On Saturdays, the Novaks go to the farmers' market. They like to visit the <u>vendors</u>. Alex Novak always goes to the hot food stand for lunch. His children love to eat the fruit <u>samples</u>. Alex's father usually buys some <u>sweets</u> and <u>lemonade</u>. The lemonade is very <u>sour</u>.

Nina Novak likes to buy <u>organic</u> <u>herbs</u> and vegetables. Today, she is buying <u>avocados</u>. The market worker <u>counts</u> eight avocados. She gives Nina one more for free.

There are other things to do at the market. The Novaks like to listen to the <u>live music</u>. Sometimes they meet friends there. The farmers' market is a great place for families on a Saturday afternoon.

Think about it.

1. What's good or bad about shopping at a farmers' market?

2. Imagine you are at the farmers' market. What will you buy?

Everyday Clothes · La ropa diaria

1. shirt
   la camisa
2. jeans
   los pantalones jeans /
   los vaqueros
3. dress
   el vestido
4. T-shirt
   la camiseta
5. baseball cap
   la gorra de béisbol
6. socks
   los calcetines / las medias
7. athletic shoes
   el calzado atlético /
   las zapatillas
A. **tie**
   amarrar

BEST OF JAZZ CONCERT

TICKETS

BEST OF JAZZ

Listen and point. Take turns.

A: *Point to the dress.*
B: *Point to the T-shirt.*
A: *Point to the baseball cap.*

Dictate to your partner. Take turns.

A: *Write dress.*
B: *Is that spelled d-r-e-s-s?*
A: *Yes. That's right.*

ONE NIGHT ONLY

DOORS OPEN AT 8:00

8. blouse
la blusa

9. handbag
el bolso

10. skirt
la falda

11. suit
el terno / el traje

12. slacks / pants
los pantalones

13. shoes
los zapatos

14. sweater
el abrigo / el suéter

B. **put on**
ponérselo

Ways to compliment clothes

That's a pretty dress!
Those are great shoes!
I really like your baseball cap!

Role play. Compliment a friend.

A: *That's a pretty dress! Green is a great color on you.*
B: *Thanks! I really like your…*

Casual Clothes Ropa casual

1. cap
   el gorrito

2. cardigan sweater
   el abrigo de lana tejida / el cardigan

3. pullover sweater
   el abrigo cerrado / pulóver

4. sports shirt
   la camisa deportiva

5. maternity dress
   el vestido de maternidad

6. overalls
   el overol

7. knit top
   la blusa bordada

8. capris
   el pantalón Capri

9. sandals
   las sandalias

Work Clothes Ropa de trabajo

10. uniform
    el uniforme

11. business suit
    el terno / el traje

12. tie
    la corbata

13. briefcase
    el maletín

More vocabulary

three piece suit: matching jacket, vest, and slacks
outfit: clothes that look nice together
in fashion / in style: clothes that are popular now

Describe the people. Take turns.

A: *She's wearing a maternity dress.*
B: *He's wearing a uniform.*

Casual, Work, and Formal Clothes

Formal Clothes   Ropa formal

14. sports jacket / sports coat
    la chaqueta deportiva

15. vest
    el chaleco

16. bow tie
    la corbata de moño / lazo

17. tuxedo
    el esmoquin

18. evening gown
    el vestido de noche

19. clutch bag
    el bolso de mano

20. cocktail dress
    el vestido de cóctel

21. high heels
    los tacones altos

Exercise Wear   Ropa para hacer ejercicio

22. sweatshirt / hoodie
    la sudadera

23. sweatpants
    los pantalones de ejercicio

24. tank top
    la camiseta

25. shorts
    los pantalones cortos

Ask your classmates. Share the answers.

1. What's your favorite outfit?
2. Do you like to wear formal clothes? Why or why not?
3. Do you prefer to exercise in shorts or sweatpants?

Think about it. Discuss.

1. What jobs require formal clothes? Uniforms?
2. What's good and bad about wearing school uniforms?
3. What is your opinion of today's popular clothing?

89

1. hat
   el gorro
2. (over)coat
   el abrigo
3. headband
   la banda de cabeza
4. leather jacket
   la chaqueta de cuero
5. winter scarf
   la bufanda para el invierno
6. gloves
   los guantes
7. headwrap
   el pañuelo de cabeza
8. jacket
   la chaqueta

9. parka
   la parka
10. mittens
    los mitones
11. ski hat
    el gorro para esquiar
12. leggings
    los leggings / pantalones
13. earmuffs
    las orejeras
14. down vest
    el chaleco relleno con plumas
15. ski mask
    la máscara de esquí
16. down jacket
    la chaqueta rellena con plumas

17. umbrella
    el paraguas
18. raincoat
    la gabardina / el impermeable
19. poncho
    el poncho
20. rain boots
    las botas para la lluvia
21. trench coat
    la trinchera

22. swimming trunks
    el traje de baño
23. straw hat
    el sombrero de paja
24. windbreaker
    el cortaviento
25. cover-up
    el albornoz / la bata de playa
26. swimsuit / bathing suit
    el traje de baño
27. sunglasses
    las gafas de sol

Grammar Point: should

It's raining. You **should** take an umbrella.
It's snowing. You **should** wear a scarf.
It's sunny. You **should** wear a straw hat.

Pair practice. Make new conversations.

A: It's <u>snowing</u>. You should wear <u>a scarf</u>.
B: Don't worry. I'm wearing my <u>parka</u>.
A: Good, and don't forget your <u>mittens</u>.

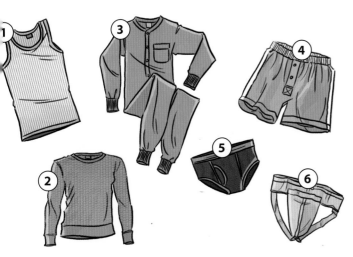

Unisex Underwear
Ropa interior unisex

1. undershirt
   la camiseta
2. thermal undershirt
   la camiseta térmica
3. long underwear
   la ropa interior de invierno

Men's Underwear
Ropa interior de hombre

4. boxer shorts
   los calzoncillos tipo bóxer
5. briefs
   los calzoncillos
6. athletic supporter /
   jockstrap
   el suspensor /
   el soporte atlético

Unisex Socks
Calcetines unisex

7. ankle socks
   los calcetines al tobillo
8. crew socks
   los calcetines de trabajo
9. dress socks
   los calcetines de vestir

Women's Socks
Calcetines de mujer

10. low-cut socks
    los calcetines de tobillo
11. anklets
    los calcetines cortos
12. knee highs
    los calcetines hasta
    la rodilla

Women's Underwear Ropa interior de mujer

13. (bikini) panties
    los panties (bikinis)
14. briefs /
    underpants
    las pantaletas /
    los calzones
15. body shaper /
    girdle
    la faja

16. garter belt
    el liguero
17. stockings
    las medias largas
18. panty hose
    las medias panti /
    las pantimedias
19. tights
    las medias de malla

20. bra
    el sostén
21. camisole
    la camisola
22. full slip
    la enagua entera
23. half slip
    la media enagua

Sleepwear Ropa de dormir

24. pajamas
    la pijama / el pijama
25. nightgown
    el camisón
26. slippers
    las pantuflas

27. blanket sleeper
    la cobija
28. nightshirt
    la camisa de dormir
29. robe
    la bata

More vocabulary

lingerie: underwear or sleepwear for women
loungewear: very casual clothing for relaxing around
the home

Ask your classmates. Share the answers.

1. What kind of socks are you wearing today?
2. What kind of sleepwear do you prefer?
3. Do you wear slippers at home?

Construction Worker

Road Worker

Automotive Painter

Food Processor

1. **hard hat**
   el casco de protección
   para la cabeza

2. **work shirt**
   la camisa de trabajo

3. **tool belt**
   la correa de herramientas

4. **Hi-Visibility safety vest**
   el chaleco de seguridad
   de alta visibilidad

5. **work pants**
   los pantalones de trabajo

6. **steel toe boots**
   las botas con punta de acero

7. **ventilation mask**
   la máscara de ventilación

8. **coveralls**
   el overol / el mono
   de trabajo

9. **bump cap**
   el casco de protección

10. **safety glasses**
    las gafas / los anteojos
    de seguridad

11. **apron**
    el mandil

Manager

Salesperson

Farmworker

Ranch Hand

12. **blazer**
    el blazier

13. **tie**
    la corbata

14. **polo shirt**
    la camisa tipo polo

15. **name tag**
    la etiqueta de
    identificación

16. **bandana**
    el pañuelo de cabeza

17. **work gloves**
    los guantes de trabajo

18. **cowboy hat**
    el gorro de vaquero

19. **jeans**
    los pantalones jeans /
    vaqueros

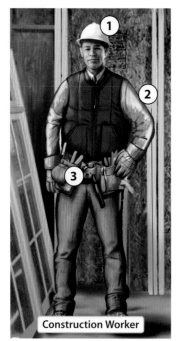

Pair practice. Make new conversations.

A: *What do <u>construction workers</u> wear to work?*

B: *They wear <u>hard hats</u> and <u>tool belts</u>.*

A: *What do <u>road workers</u> wear to work?*

Use the new words.

Look at pages 166–169. Name the workplace clothing you see.

A: *He's wearing <u>a hard hat</u>.*

B: *She's wearing <u>scrubs</u>.*

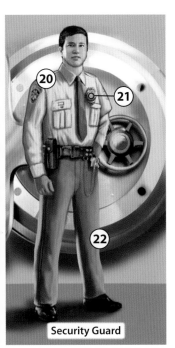

Security Guard

Emergency Worker

Counterperson

Chef

Line Cook

20. security shirt
la camisa de seguridad

21. badge
la insignia

22. security pants
los pantalones
de seguridad

23. helmet
el casco

24. jumpsuit
el mono / el enterito

25. hairnet
la malla para el cabello

26. smock
el blusón

27. disposable gloves
los guantes desechables

28. chef's hat
el gorro del chef

29. chef's jacket
la chaqueta del chef

30. waist apron
el mandil de cintura

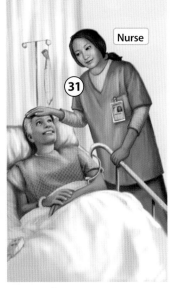

Nurse

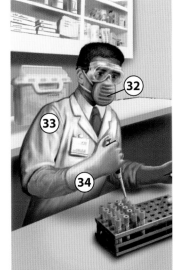

Medical Technician

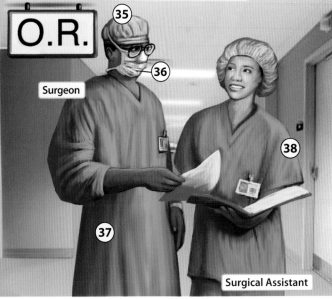

O.R.

Surgeon

Surgical Assistant

31. scrubs
la ropa de la enfermera

32. face mask
la máscara facial

33. lab coat
el delantal de laboratorio

34. latex gloves
los guantes de látex

35. surgical scrub cap
el gorro / la gorra de cirugía

36. surgical mask
la máscara de cirugía

37. surgical gown
el camisón de cirugía

38. surgical scrubs
el delantal / el camisón

Ask your classmates. Share the answers.

1. Which of these outfits would you like to wear?

2. Which of these items are in your closet?

3. Do you wear safety clothing at work? What kinds?

Think about it. Discuss.

1. What other jobs require helmets? disposable gloves?

2. Is it better to have a uniform or wear your own
clothes at work? Why?

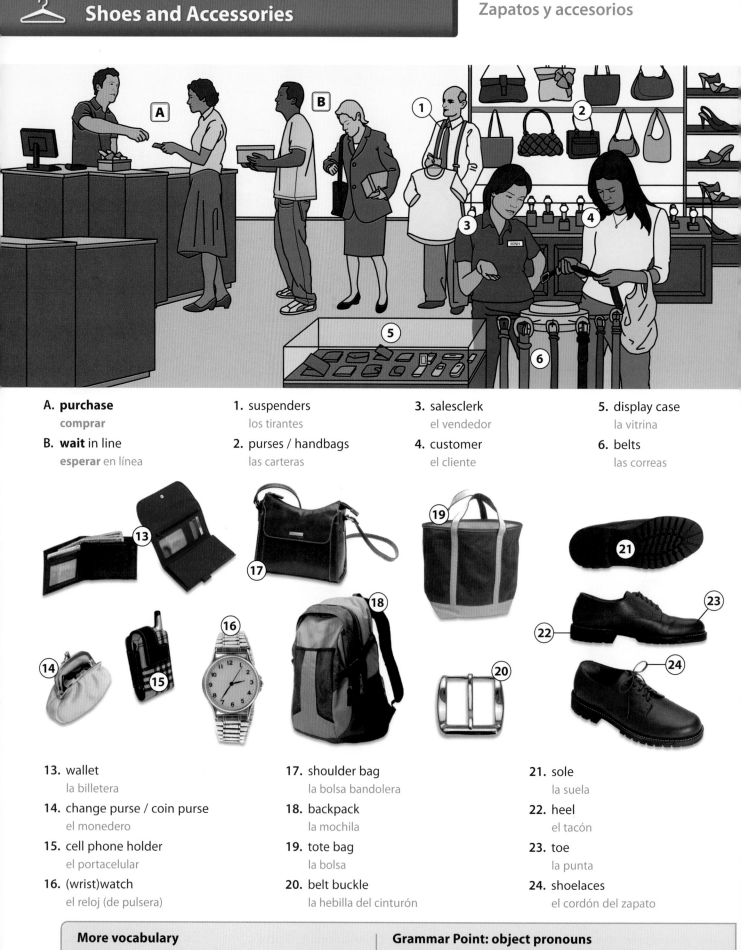

A. purchase
comprar

B. wait in line
esperar en línea

1. suspenders
los tirantes

2. purses / handbags
las carteras

3. salesclerk
el vendedor

4. customer
el cliente

5. display case
la vitrina

6. belts
las correas

13. wallet
la billetera

14. change purse / coin purse
el monedero

15. cell phone holder
el portacelular

16. (wrist)watch
el reloj (de pulsera)

17. shoulder bag
la bolsa bandolera

18. backpack
la mochila

19. tote bag
la bolsa

20. belt buckle
la hebilla del cinturón

21. sole
la suela

22. heel
el tacón

23. toe
la punta

24. shoelaces
el cordón del zapato

More vocabulary

gift: something you give or receive from friends or
family for a special occasion
present: a gift

Grammar Point: object pronouns

*My **sister** loves jewelry. I'll buy **her** a necklace.*
*My **dad** likes belts. I'll buy **him** a belt buckle.*
*My **friends** love scarves. I'll buy **them** scarves.*

7. shoe department
el departamento de zapatos

8. jewelry department
el departamento de joyería

9. bracelets
los brazaletes

10. necklaces
los collares

11. hats
los gorros

12. scarves
las bufandas

C. try on shoes
probarse zapatos

D. assist a customer
asistir a un cliente

25. high heels
los tacones altos

26. pumps
los zapatos de salón

27. flats
los zapatos de taco bajo

28. boots
las botas

29. oxfords
los zapatos Oxford

30. loafers
los mocasines

31. hiking boots
las botas para excursión

32. tennis shoes
las zapatillas de tenis

33. chain
la cadena

34. beads
las cuentas / los abalorios

35. locket
el relicario

36. pierced earrings
los aretes de colgar

37. clip-on earrings
los aretes de presilla

38. pin
el prendedor

39. string of pearls
el collar de perlas

40. ring
el anillo

Ways to talk about accessories

I need *a hat* to wear with *this scarf*.
I'd like *earrings* to go with *the necklace*.
Do you have *a belt* that would go with my *shoes*?

Role play. Talk to a salesperson.

A: *Do you have* boots *that would go with* this skirt?
B: *Let me see. How about* these brown ones?
A: *Perfect. I also need…*

95

Sizes Tallas

1. extra small
   extra pequeño

2. small
   pequeño

3. medium
   mediano

4. large
   grande

5. extra large
   extra grande

6. one-size-fits-all
   talla universal

Styles Estilos

Sweaters 50% off

7. **crewneck** sweater
   el suéter con **cuello de cisne**

8. **V-neck** sweater
   el suéter con **cuello en V**

9. **turtleneck** sweater
   el suéter con **cuello de tortuga**

10. **scoop neck** sweater
    el suéter con **cuello redondo**

11. **sleeveless** shirt
    la camisa **sin mangas**

12. **short-sleeved** shirt
    la camisa **con mangas cortas**

13. **3/4-sleeved** shirt
    la camisa de **manga de 3/4**

14. **long-sleeved** shirt
    la camisa de **manga larga**

15. **mini**-skirt
    la **mini**-falda

16. **short** skirt
    la falda **corta**

17. **mid-length / calf-length** skirt
    la falda de **media pierna**

18. **long** skirt
    la falda **larga**

Patterns Patrones

19. solid
    sólido

20. striped
    con rayas

21. polka-dotted
    con lunares

22. plaid
    con cuadros

23. print
    estampado

24. checked
    a cuadros

25. floral
    con flores

26. paisley
    estampado de cachemira /
    estampado búlgaro

Ask your classmates. Share the answers.

1. Do you prefer crewneck or V-neck sweaters?
2. Do you prefer checked or striped shirts?
3. Do you prefer short-sleeved or sleeveless shirts?

Role play. Talk to a salesperson.

A: *Excuse me. I'm looking for this V-neck sweater in large.*
B: *Here's a large. It's on sale for $19.99.*
A: *Wonderful! I'll take it. I'm also looking for…*

Comparing Clothing Comparación de la ropa

27. heavy jacket
la chaqueta **gruesa**

28. light jacket
la chaqueta **liviana**

29. tight pants
los pantalones
apretados / ceñidos

30. loose / baggy pants
los pantalones
flojos / holgados

31. low heels
los tacones /
los tacos **bajos**

32. high heels
los tacones /
los tacos **altos**

33. plain blouse
la blusa **lisa**

34. fancy blouse
la blusa **vistosa**

35. narrow tie
la corbata **estrecha**

36. wide tie
la corbata **ancha**

Clothing Problems Problemas con la ropa

37. It's **too small**.
Es **demasiado pequeña**.

38. It's **too big**.
Es **demasiado grande**.

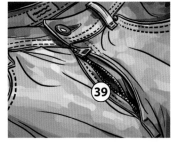

39. The zipper is **broken**.
El cierre está **estropeado**.

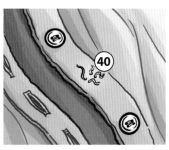

40. A button is **missing**.
Falta un botón.

41. It's **ripped / torn**.
Está **rasgado / descosido**.

42. It's **stained**.
Está **manchado**.

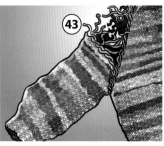

43. It's **unraveling**.
Se está **descosiendo**.

44. It's **too expensive**.
Es **demasiado caro**.

More vocabulary

refund: money you get back when you return an item to the store
complaint: a statement that something is not right
customer service: the place customers go with their complaints

Role play. Return an item to a salesperson.

A: *Welcome to Shopmart. How may I help you?*
B: *This sweater is new, but it's unraveling*.
A: *I'm sorry. Would you like a refund?*

Types of Material Tipos de material

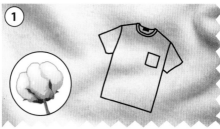

1. cotton
algodón

2. linen
hilo

3. wool
lana

4. cashmere
cachemir

5. silk
seda

6. leather
cuero

A Garment Factory Una fábrica de ropa

Parts of a Sewing Machine
Partes de una máquina de coser

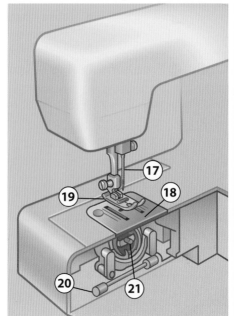

A. sew by machine
coser a máquina

B. sew by hand
coser a mano

13. sewing machine
la máquina de coser

14. sewing machine operator
la operadora de la máquina de coser

15. bolt of fabric
el rollo de tela

16. rack
el bastidor

17. needle
la aguja

18. needle plate
la placa de la aguja

19. presser foot
el pie prensatelas

20. feed dog / feed bar
el alimentador

21. bobbin
la bobina

More vocabulary

fashion designer: a person who makes original clothes
natural materials: cloth made from things that grow in nature
synthetic materials: cloth made by people, such as nylon

Use the new words.
Look at pages 86–87. Name the materials you see.

A: *That's denim.*
B: *That's leather.*

Types of Material Tipos de material

7. denim
tela de jeans / tela vaquera

8. suede
gamuza

9. lace
encaje

10. velvet
terciopelo

11. corduroy
corduroy / pana

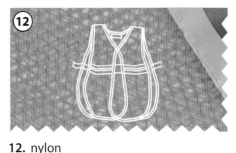

12. nylon
nilón

A Fabric Store Una tienda de telas

Closures Cierres

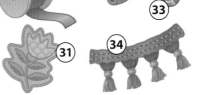

Trim Adornos

22. pattern el modelo / el patrón	**25.** zipper el cierre
23. thread los hilos	**26.** snap la presilla
24. button el botón	**27.** hook and eye el gancho y ojal

28. buckle la hebilla	**31.** appliqué las decoraciones / los apliques
29. hook and loop fastener la cinta de enganche	**32.** beads las cuentas
30. ribbon la cinta	**33.** sequins las decoraciones
	34. fringe el fleco

Ask your classmates. Share the answers.

1. Can you sew?
2. What's your favorite type of material?
3. How many types of material are you wearing today?

Think about it. Discuss.

1. Do most people make or buy clothes in your country?
2. Is it better to make or buy clothes? Why?
3. Which materials are best for formal clothes?

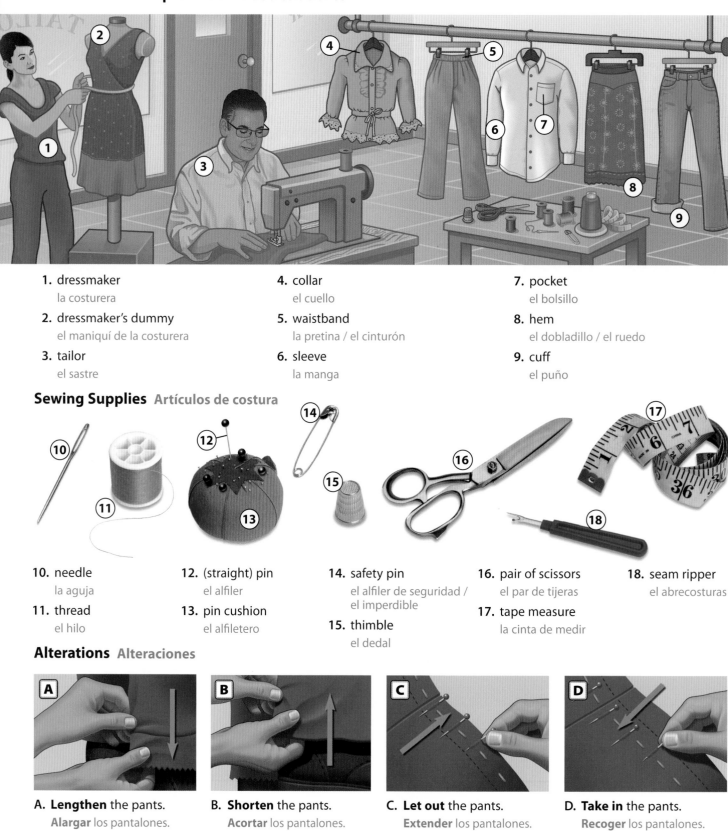

An Alterations Shop Una tienda de alteraciones

1. **dressmaker**
   la costurera
2. **dressmaker's dummy**
   el maniquí de la costurera
3. **tailor**
   el sastre

4. **collar**
   el cuello
5. **waistband**
   la pretina / el cinturón
6. **sleeve**
   la manga

7. **pocket**
   el bolsillo
8. **hem**
   el dobladillo / el ruedo
9. **cuff**
   el puño

Sewing Supplies Artículos de costura

10. **needle**
    la aguja
11. **thread**
    el hilo

12. **(straight) pin**
    el alfiler
13. **pin cushion**
    el alfiletero

14. **safety pin**
    el alfiler de seguridad /
    el imperdible
15. **thimble**
    el dedal

16. **pair of scissors**
    el par de tijeras
17. **tape measure**
    la cinta de medir

18. **seam ripper**
    el abrecosturas

Alterations Alteraciones

A. **Lengthen** the pants.
   Alargar los pantalones.

B. **Shorten** the pants.
   Acortar los pantalones.

C. **Let out** the pants.
   Extender los pantalones.

D. **Take in** the pants.
   Recoger los pantalones.

Pair practice. Make new conversations.

A: *Would you hand me the thread?*
B: *OK. What are you going to do?*
A: *I'm going to take in these pants.*

Ask your classmates. Share the answers.

1. Is there an alterations shop near your home?
2. Do you ever go to a tailor or a dressmaker?
3. What sewing supplies do you have at home?

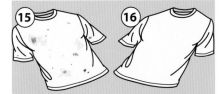

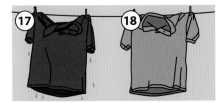

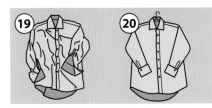

1. laundry
   la ropa sucia

2. laundry basket
   el cesto para la ropa sucia

3. washer
   la lavadora

4. dryer
   la secadora

5. dryer sheets
   las toallitas para la secadora

6. fabric softener
   el suavizante / el suavizador

7. bleach
   el cloro / la lejía /
   el blanqueador

8. laundry detergent
   el detergente para ropa

9. clothesline
   el tendedero / la cuerda

10. clothespin
    la pinza para colgar la ropa

11. hanger
    el gancho / la percha

12. spray starch
    el almidón para rociar

13. iron
    la plancha

14. ironing board
    la tabla para planchar

15. **dirty** T-shirt
    la camiseta **sucia**

16. **clean** T-shirt
    la camiseta **limpia**

17. **wet** shirt
    la camisa **húmeda**

18. **dry** shirt
    la camisa **seca**

19. **wrinkled** shirt
    la camisa **arrugada**

20. **ironed** shirt
    la camisa **planchada**

A. **Sort** the laundry.
   Separar la ropa.

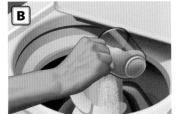

B. **Add** the detergent.
   Añadir el detergente.

C. **Load** the washer.
   Llenar/Cargar la lavadora.

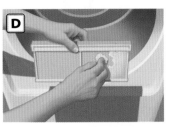

D. **Clean** the lint trap.
   Limpiar el filtro de pelusas.

E. **Unload** the dryer.
   Vaciar/Descargar
   la secadora.

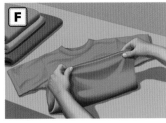

F. **Fold** the laundry.
   Doblar la ropa.

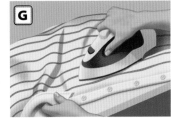

G. **Iron** the clothes.
   Planchar la ropa.

H. **Hang up** the clothes.
   Colgar la ropa.

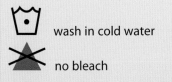

	wash in cold water		line dry
	no bleach		dry clean only, do not wash

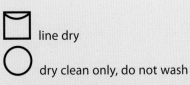

Pair practice. Make new conversations.

A: *I have to sort the laundry. Can you help?*
B: *Sure. Here's the laundry basket.*
A: *Thanks a lot!*

101

1. flyer
   el aviso / el volante
2. used clothing
   la ropa usada
3. sticker
   la etiqueta / la pegatina
4. folding card table
   la mesa plegable
5. folding chair
   la silla plegable
6. clock radio
   la radio-reloj
7. VCR
   la VCR
A. **bargain**
   regatear
B. **browse**
   mirar

Look at the pictures. What do you see?

Answer the questions.

1. What kind of used clothing do you see?
2. What information is on the flyer?
3. Why are the stickers different colors?
4. How much is the clock radio? the VCR?

📖 Read the story.

A Garage Sale

Last Sunday, I had a garage sale. At 5:00 a.m., I put up <u>flyers</u> in my neighborhood. Next, I put price <u>stickers</u> on my <u>used clothing</u>, my <u>VCR</u>, and some other old things. At 7:00 a.m., I opened my <u>folding card table</u> and <u>folding chair</u>. Then I waited.

At 7:05 a.m., my first customer arrived. She asked, "How much is the sweatshirt?"

"Two dollars," I said.

She said, "It's stained. I can give you seventy-five cents." We <u>bargained</u> for a minute and she paid $1.00.

All day people came to <u>browse</u>, bargain, and buy. At 7:00 p.m., I had $85.00.

Now I know two things: Garage sales are hard work and nobody wants to buy an old <u>clock radio</u>!

Think about it.

1. Do you like to buy things at garage sales? Why or why not?
2. Imagine you want the VCR. How will you bargain for it?

103

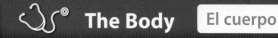

1. **head**
   la cabeza

2. **hair**
   el cabello / el pelo

3. **neck**
   el cuello

4. **chest**
   el pecho

5. **back**
   la espalda

6. **nose**
   la nariz

7. **mouth**
   la boca

8. **foot**
   el pie

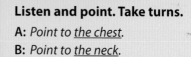

Listen and point. Take turns.

A: *Point to the chest.*
B: *Point to the neck.*
A: *Point to the mouth.*

Dictate to your partner. Take turns.

A: *Write hair.*
B: *Did you say hair?*
A: *That's right, h-a-i-r.*

9. leg
la pierna

10. toe
el dedo del pie

11. eye
el ojo

12. ear
la oreja

13. shoulder
el hombro

14. arm
el brazo

15. hand
la mano

16. finger
el dedo

Grammar Point: imperatives

Please touch your right foot.
Put your hands on your feet.
Don't put your hands on your shoulders.

Pair practice. Take turns giving commands.

A: *Raise* your *arms*.
B: *Touch* your *feet*.
A: *Put* your *hand* on your *shoulder*.

105

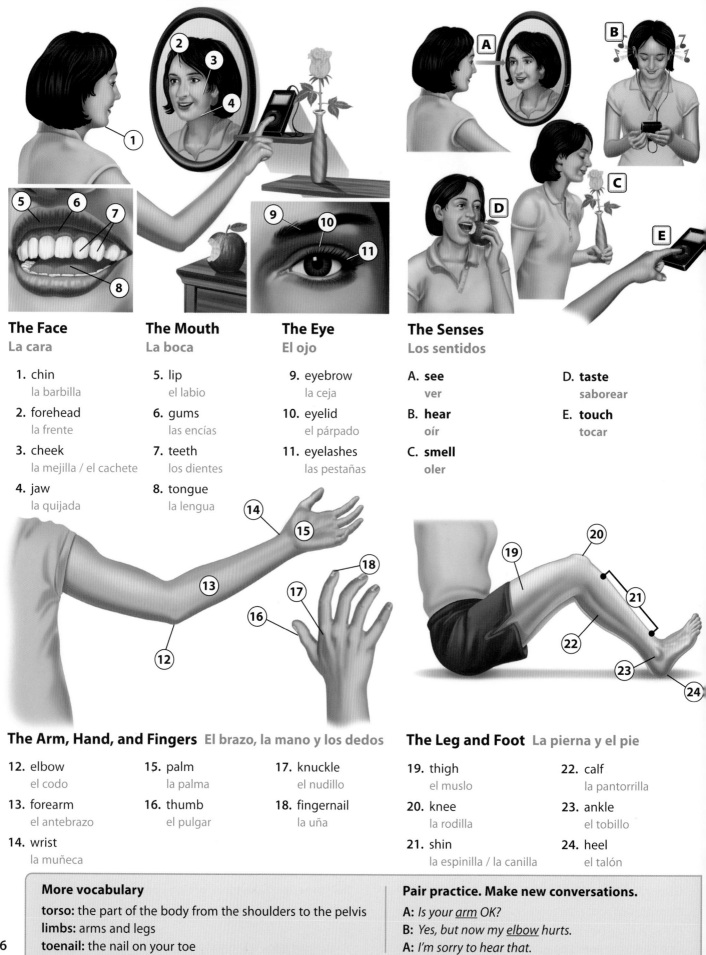

The Face
La cara

1. chin
   la barbilla
2. forehead
   la frente
3. cheek
   la mejilla / el cachete
4. jaw
   la quijada

The Mouth
La boca

5. lip
   el labio
6. gums
   las encías
7. teeth
   los dientes
8. tongue
   la lengua

The Eye
El ojo

9. eyebrow
   la ceja
10. eyelid
   el párpado
11. eyelashes
   las pestañas

The Senses
Los sentidos

A. **see**
   ver
B. **hear**
   oír
C. **smell**
   oler

D. **taste**
   saborear
E. **touch**
   tocar

The Arm, Hand, and Fingers El brazo, la mano y los dedos

12. elbow
   el codo
13. forearm
   el antebrazo
14. wrist
   la muñeca

15. palm
   la palma
16. thumb
   el pulgar

17. knuckle
   el nudillo
18. fingernail
   la uña

The Leg and Foot La pierna y el pie

19. thigh
   el muslo
20. knee
   la rodilla
21. shin
   la espinilla / la canilla

22. calf
   la pantorrilla
23. ankle
   el tobillo
24. heel
   el talón

More vocabulary

torso: the part of the body from the shoulders to the pelvis
limbs: arms and legs
toenail: the nail on your toe

Pair practice. Make new conversations.

A: *Is your <u>arm</u> OK?*
B: *Yes, but now my <u>elbow</u> hurts.*
A: *I'm sorry to hear that.*

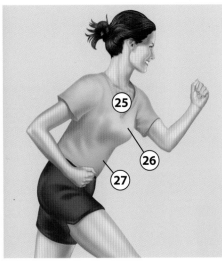

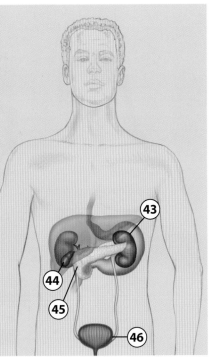

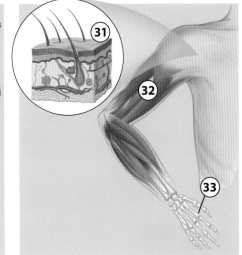

25. chest
el pecho

26. breast
el seno / el pecho

27. abdomen
el abdomen

28. shoulder blade
el omóplato

29. lower back
la parte inferior de la espalda

30. buttocks
las nalgas

31. skin
la piel

32. muscle
el músculo

33. bone
el hueso

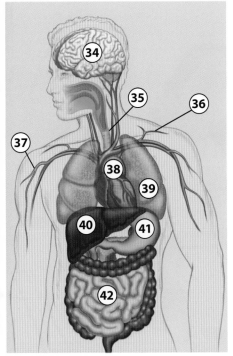

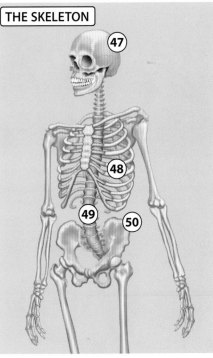

THE SKELETON

34. brain
el cerebro

35. throat
la garganta

36. artery
la arteria

37. vein
la vena

38. heart
el corazón

39. lung
el pulmón

40. liver
el hígado

41. stomach
el estómago

42. intestines
los intestinos

43. kidney
el riñón

44. gallbladder
la vesícula biliar

45. pancreas
el páncreas

46. bladder
la vejiga

47. skull
el cráneo

48. rib cage
la caja toráxica

49. spinal column
la columna vertebral

50. pelvis
la pelvis

A

A. take a shower
darse una ducha /
ducharse

B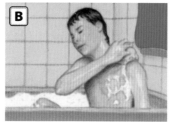

B. take a bath / **bathe**
tomar un baño / **bañarse**

C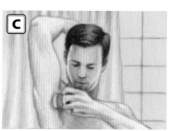

C. use deodorant
usar desodorante

D

D. put on sunscreen
ponerse protector solar

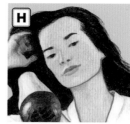

1. **shower cap**
la gorra de baño

2. **shower gel**
el gel de ducha

3. **soap**
el jabón

4. **bath powder**
el talco

5. **deodorant / antiperspirant**
el desodorante / el antiperspirante

6. **perfume / cologne**
el perfume / la colonia

7. **sunscreen**
el protector solar

8. **sunblock**
el bloqueador solar

9. **body lotion / moisturizer**
la crema para el cuerpo /
la crema humectante

E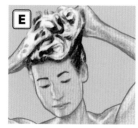

E. wash…hair
lavarse…el cabello

F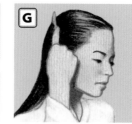

F. rinse…hair
enjuagarse…
el cabello

G

G. comb…hair
peinarse…el cabello

H

H. dry…hair
secarse…el cabello

I

I. brush…hair
cepillarse…
el cabello

10. **shampoo**
el champú

11. **conditioner**
el acondicionador

12. **hair spray**
la laca

13. **comb**
el peine / la peinilla

14. **brush**
el cepillo

15. **pick**
la peineta

16. **hair gel**
el gel de cabello

17. **curling iron**
el rizador

18. **blow dryer**
el secador de cabello

19. **hair clip**
la pinza / el gancho
para el cabello

20. **barrette**
el broche

21. **bobby pins**
los pasadores / las horquillas

More vocabulary

unscented: a product without perfume or scent
hypoallergenic: a product that is better for people
with allergies

Think about it. Discuss.

1. Which personal hygiene products should someone use
before a job interview?
2. What is the right age to start wearing makeup? Why?

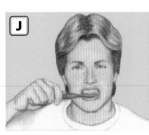

J. brush…teeth
cepillarse…los dientes

K. floss…teeth
usar hilo dental

L. gargle
hacer gárgara

M. shave
afeitarse

22. toothbrush
el cepillo de dientes

23. toothpaste
la pasta de dientes

24. dental floss
el hilo dental

25. mouthwash
el enjuague bucal

26. electric shaver
la rasuradora eléctrica

27. razor
el rastrillo

28. razorblade
la hoja / la cuchilla de afeitar / la navaja

29. shaving cream
la crema de afeitar

30. aftershave
la loción para después de afeitarse

N. cut…nails
cortarse…las uñas

O. polish…nails
pulirse / pintarse…las uñas

P. put on / apply
ponerse / aplicarse

Q. take off / remove
quitarse / limpiarse

Makeup Maquillaje

31. nail clipper
el cortauñas

32. emery board
la lima

33. nail polish
la pintura / el esmalte
de uñas

34. eyebrow pencil
el lápiz de cejas

35. eye shadow
la sombra

36. eyeliner
el delineador (de ojos)

37. blush
el rubor

38. lipstick
el lápiz de labios

39. mascara
el rímel

40. foundation
la base

41. face powder
el polvo facial

42. makeup remover
el desmaquillador

1. headache
   el dolor de cabeza
2. toothache
   el dolor de muelas
3. earache
   el dolor de oído
4. stomachache
   el dolor de estómago
5. backache
   el dolor de espalda

6. sore throat
   el dolor de garganta
7. nasal congestion
   la congestión nasal
8. fever / temperature
   la fiebre
9. chills
   los escalofríos
10. rash
   la erupción / el sarpullido

A. **cough**
   toser
B. **sneeze**
   estornudar
C. **feel** dizzy
   sentirse mareado
D. **feel** nauseous
   sentir / tener náuseas
E. **throw up / vomit**
   vomitar

11. insect bite
   la picadura de insecto
12. bruise
   el moretón / el morado /
   el cardenal
13. cut
   el corte
14. sunburn
   la quemadura de sol
15. blister
   la ampolla
16. swollen finger
   el dedo hinchado
17. bloody nose
   la hemorragia nasal
18. sprained ankle
   el tobillo torcido

Look at the pictures.
Describe the symptoms and injuries.

A: He has <u>a backache</u>.
B: She has <u>a toothache</u>.

Think about it. Discuss.
1. What are some common cold symptoms?
2. What do you recommend for a stomachache?
3. What is the best way to stop a bloody nose?

Illnesses and Medical Conditions

Common Illnesses and Childhood Diseases Enfermedades comunes y de la infancia

1. cold
el resfrío

2. flu
la gripe

3. ear infection
la infección de oído

4. strep throat
la infección de la garganta

5. measles
el sarampión

6. chicken pox
la varicela

7. mumps
las paperas

8. allergies
las alergias

Serious Medical Conditions and Diseases Enfermedades y padecimientos graves

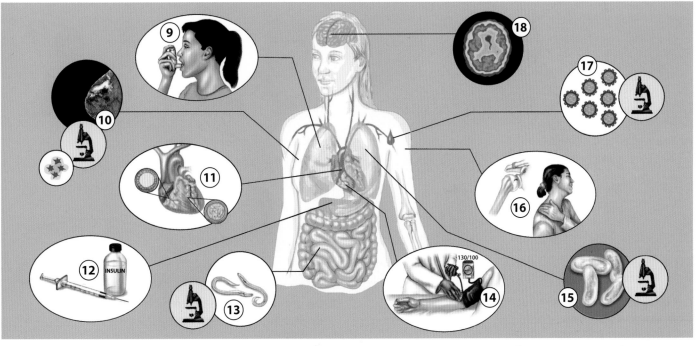

9. asthma
el asma

10. cancer
el cáncer

11. heart disease
las enfermedades cardíacas

12. diabetes
la diabetes

13. intestinal parasites
los parásitos intestinales

14. high blood pressure / hypertension
la presión arterial alta / la hipertensión

15. TB (tuberculosis)
la tuberculosis

16. arthritis
la artritis

17. HIV (human immunodeficiency virus)
el VIH / el virus de inmunodeficiencia humana

18. dementia
la demencia

More vocabulary

AIDS (acquired immune deficiency syndrome): a medical condition that results from contracting the HIV virus

Alzheimer's disease: a disease that causes dementia

coronary disease: heart disease

infectious disease: a disease that is spread through air or water

influenza: flu

111

DROP-OFF PICK-UP

Smallgreen Pharmacy
1818 Oak Ave
Rosemead, CA 91770
Dr. L. Luther PHONE **555-5522**

NO **00859023–57988** DATE **03/07/10**

Alki Elmi
345 First Street Rosemead, CA 91770

TAKE ONE TABLET BY MOUTH 2 TIMES A DAY AS NEEDED FOR PAIN.

NAPROXEN 500 MG

REFILLS: 2

Discard after 03/07/12

👁 May cause drowsiness.

Family Physician Medical Group Inc.
1515 Elm Court Suite 100, Rosemead CA 91770
TEL: (800) 555-3999
CAL LIC. #54POI5U170   183098WUFCSDJE

PATIENT NAME: Bruce Kent
DOB: 02/29/88
DATE: 03/07/10

℞

Diclofenac 50 MG Refill: 0

Laura Lane, MD

1. **pharmacist**
   el farmaceuta / el farmacéutico

2. **prescription**
   la prescripción / la receta

3. **prescription medication**
   el medicamento prescrito

4. **prescription label**
   la etiqueta de la receta

5. **prescription number**
   el número de la receta

6. **dosage**
   la dosis

7. **expiration date**
   la fecha de vencimiento

8. **warning label**
   la etiqueta de advertencia

Medical Warnings Advertencias médicas

A. **Take** with food or milk.
Tómelo con alimentos o leche.

B. **Take** one hour before eating.
Tómelo una hora antes de comer.

C. **Finish** all medication.
Acabe todo el medicamento.

D. **Do not take** with dairy products.
No se debe tomar con productos lácteos.

E. **Do not drive or operate** heavy machinery.
No maneje ni opere maquinaria pesada.

F. **Do not drink** alcohol.
No beba alcohol.

More Vocabulary

prescribe medication: to write a prescription
fill prescriptions: to prepare medication for patients
pick up a prescription: to get prescription medication

Role play. Talk to the pharmacist.

A: *Hi. I need to pick up a prescription for Jones.*
B: *Here's your medication, Mr. Jones. Take these once a day with milk or food.*

A Pharmacy

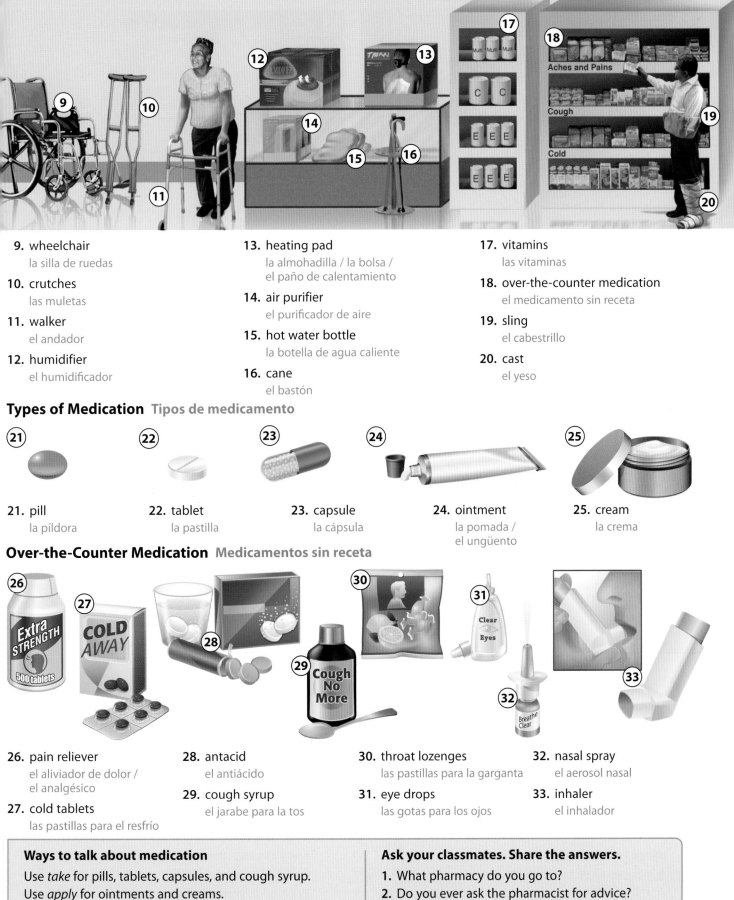

9. wheelchair
la silla de ruedas

10. crutches
las muletas

11. walker
el andador

12. humidifier
el humidificador

13. heating pad
la almohadilla / la bolsa /
el paño de calentamiento

14. air purifier
el purificador de aire

15. hot water bottle
la botella de agua caliente

16. cane
el bastón

17. vitamins
las vitaminas

18. over-the-counter medication
el medicamento sin receta

19. sling
el cabestrillo

20. cast
el yeso

Types of Medication Tipos de medicamento

21. pill
la píldora

22. tablet
la pastilla

23. capsule
la cápsula

24. ointment
la pomada /
el ungüento

25. cream
la crema

Over-the-Counter Medication Medicamentos sin receta

26. pain reliever
el aliviador de dolor /
el analgésico

27. cold tablets
las pastillas para el resfrío

28. antacid
el antiácido

29. cough syrup
el jarabe para la tos

30. throat lozenges
las pastillas para la garganta

31. eye drops
las gotas para los ojos

32. nasal spray
el aerosol nasal

33. inhaler
el inhalador

Ways to talk about medication

Use *take* for pills, tablets, capsules, and cough syrup.
Use *apply* for ointments and creams.
Use *use* for drops, nasal sprays, and inhalers.

Ask your classmates. Share the answers.

1. What pharmacy do you go to?
2. Do you ever ask the pharmacist for advice?
3. Do you take any vitamins? Which ones?

113

Ways to Get Well Maneras para sanarse

A. Seek medical attention.
   Obtenga atención médica.

B. Get bed rest.
   Descanse en la cama.

C. Drink fluids.
   Beba líquidos.

D. Take medicine.
   Tome un medicamento.

Ways to Stay Well Maneras para mantenerse sano

E. Stay fit.
   Manténgase en buena condición física.

F. Eat a healthy diet.
   Coma una dieta saludable.

G. Don't smoke.
   No fume.

Ms. Jones, you must stop smoking!

H. Have regular checkups.
   Hágase exámenes médicos regularmente.

IMMUNIZATION SCHEDULE
Tetanus - Every 10 years
Flu Shot - Every year

I. Get immunized.
   Hágase inmunizar.

J. Follow medical advice.
   Cumpla con las indicaciones médicas.

More vocabulary

injection: medicine in a syringe that is put into the body
immunization / vaccination: an injection that stops
serious diseases

Ask your classmates. Share the answers.

1. How do you stay fit?
2. What do you do when you're sick?
3. Which two foods are a part of your healthy diet?

Types of Health Problems Tipos de problemas de salud

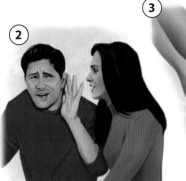

1. vision problems
   los problemas de visión

2. hearing loss
   la pérdida de la audición

3. pain
   el dolor

4. stress
   el estrés

5. depression
   la depresión

Help with Health Problems Ayuda para los problemas de salud

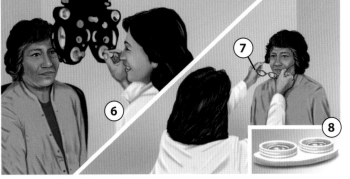
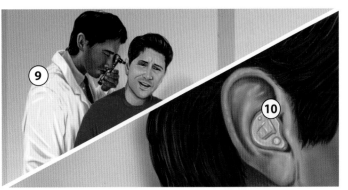

6. optometrist
   el optometrista /
   el optómetra

7. glasses
   los anteojos

8. contact lenses
   los lentes de contacto

9. audiologist
   el audiólogo

10. hearing aid
    el audífono

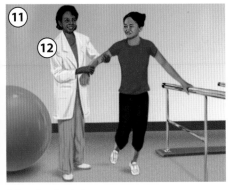

11. physical therapy
    la terapia física

12. physical therapist
    el fisioterapeuta

13. talk therapy
    la terapia del habla

14. therapist
    el terapeuta

15. support group
    el grupo de apoyo

Ways to ask about health problems

Are you in pain?
Are you having vision problems?
Are you experiencing depression?

Pair practice. Make new conversations.

A: *Do you know a good optometrist?*
B: *Why? Are you having vision problems?*
A: *Yes, I might need glasses.*

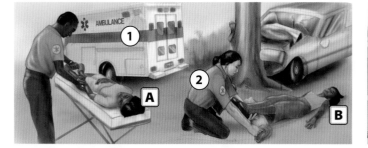

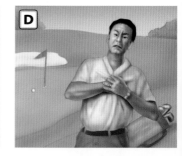

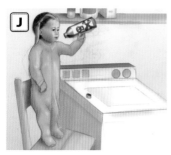

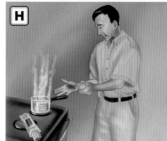

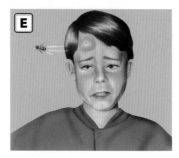

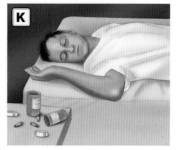
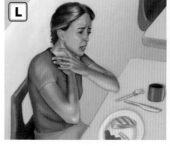

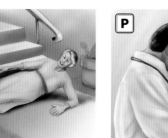

1. ambulance
   la ambulancia

2. paramedic
   el paramédico / el enfermero de urgencias

A. **be** unconscious
   estar inconsciente

B. **be** in shock
   estar en shock / choque

C. **be** injured / **be** hurt
   estar lesionado / **estar** herido

D. **have** a heart attack
   tener un ataque al corazón

E. **have** an allergic reaction
   tener una reacción alérgica

F. **get** an electric shock
   recibir una descarga eléctrica

G. **get** frostbite
   quemarse por el frío

H. **burn** (your)self
   quemar(se)

I. **drown**
   ahogarse

J. **swallow** poison
   envenenarse

K. **overdose** on drugs
   tomar una sobredosis de drogas

L. **choke**
   atragantarse / asfixiarse

M. **bleed**
   sangrar

N. **can't breathe**
   asfixiarse / no poder respirar

O. **fall**
   caerse

P. **break** a bone
   fracturarse un hueso

Grammar Point: past tense

For past tense add –ed:
burned, drowned, swallowed,
overdosed, choked

These verbs are different (irregular):

be – was, were	bleed – bled	fall – fell
have – had	can't – couldn't	
get – got	break – broke	

First Aid Los primeros auxilios

1. first aid kit
el botiquín de primeros auxilios

2. first aid manual
el manual de primeros auxilios

3. medical emergency bracelet
la pulsera / el brazalete de
emergencia médica

Inside the Kit Dentro del botiquín

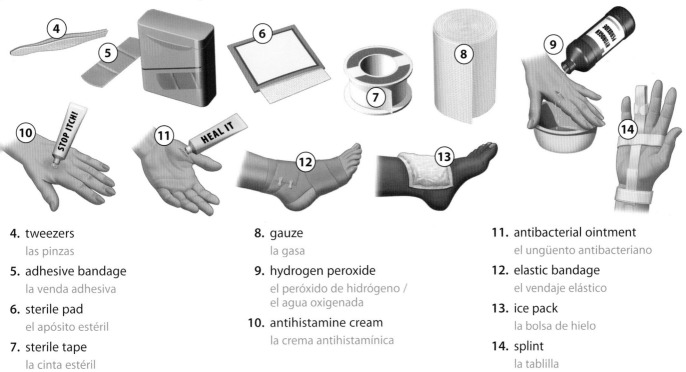

4. tweezers
las pinzas

5. adhesive bandage
la venda adhesiva

6. sterile pad
el apósito estéril

7. sterile tape
la cinta estéril

8. gauze
la gasa

9. hydrogen peroxide
el peróxido de hidrógeno /
el agua oxigenada

10. antihistamine cream
la crema antihistamínica

11. antibacterial ointment
el ungüento antibacteriano

12. elastic bandage
el vendaje elástico

13. ice pack
la bolsa de hielo

14. splint
la tablilla

First Aid Procedures Los procedimientos de primeros auxilios

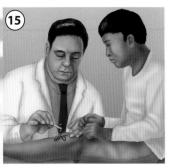

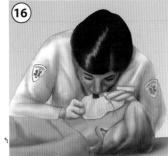

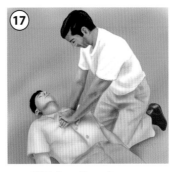

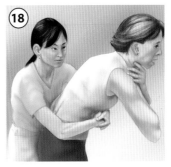

15. stitches
los puntos

16. rescue breathing
la respiración de
boca a boca

**17. CPR (cardiopulmonary
resuscitation)**
CPR (la resucitación
cardiopulmonar)

18. Heimlich maneuver
la maniobra de Heimlich

Pair practice. Make new conversations.

A: *What do we need in the first aid kit?*
B: *We need __tweezers__ and __gauze__.*
A: *I think we need __sterile tape__, too.*

Think about it. Discuss.

1. What are the three most important first aid items? Why?
2. Which first aid procedures should everyone know? Why?
3. What are some good places to keep a first aid kit?

In the Waiting Room En la sala de espera

Health Form

Name: Andre Zolmar
Date of birth: July 8, 1973
Current symptoms: stomachache

Health History:

Childhood Diseases:
- ☑ chicken pox
- ☑ diphtheria
- ☑ rubella
- ☑ measles
- ☐ mumps
- ☐ other

Description of symptoms:

1. appointment
la cita

2. receptionist
el / la recepcionista

3. health insurance card
la tarjeta de seguro médico

4. health history form
el formulario de historial médico

In the Examining Room En la sala de examen

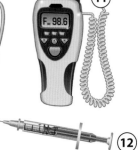

5. doctor
el médico / el doctor / la doctora

6. patient
el paciente

7. examination table
la mesa de examen

8. nurse
la enfermera / el enfermero

9. blood pressure gauge
el medidor de presión sanguínea

10. stethoscope
el estetoscopio

11. thermometer
el termómetro

12. syringe
la jeringa

Medical Procedures Los procedimientos médicos

A. check...blood pressure
revisarle...la presión sanguínea

B. take...temperature
tomarle...la temperatura

C. listen to...heart
escucharle el corazón

D. examine...eyes
examinarle...los ojos

E. examine...throat
examinarle...la garganta

F. draw...blood
sacarle...sangre

Grammar Point: future tense with *will* + verb

To show a future action, use ***will*** + verb.
The subject pronoun contraction of ***will*** is ***-'ll.***
*She **will draw** your blood. = She**'ll draw** your blood.*

Role play. Talk to a medical receptionist.

A: *Will the nurse <u>examine my eyes</u>?*
B: *No, but she'll <u>draw your blood</u>.*
A: *What will the doctor do?*

Dental Care

Dentistry La odontología

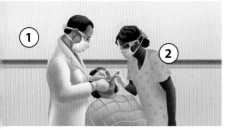
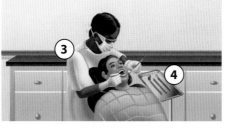

Orthodontics La ortodoncia

1. dentist
   el dentista

2. dental assistant
   el asistente dental / el ayudante
   del dentista

3. dental hygienist
   el higienista dental

4. dental instruments
   los instrumentos dentales

5. orthodontist
   el ortodoncista

6. braces
   los frenos / los frenillos

Dental Problems Los problemas dentales

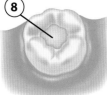

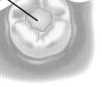

7. cavity / decay
   las caries / las picaduras

8. filling
   la amalgama

9. crown
   la corona

10. dentures
    la dentadura postiza

11. gum disease
    la enfermedad de las encías

12. plaque
    el sarro

An Office Visit Una visita a la oficina del dentista

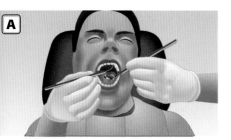

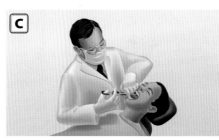

A. **clean**…teeth
   limpiar…los dientes

B. **take** x-rays
   tomar una radiografía

C. **numb** the mouth
   anestesiar la boca

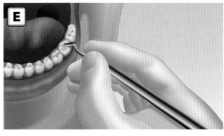

D. **drill** a tooth
   taladrar un diente / una muela

E. **fill** a cavity
   arreglar una caries

F. **pull** a tooth
   sacar / extraer un diente / una muela

Ask your classmates. Share the answers.

1. Do you know someone with braces? Who?
2. Do dentists make you nervous? Why or why not?
3. How often do you go to the dentist?

Role play. Talk to a dentist.

A: *I think I have a cavity.*
B: *Let me take a look.*
A: *Will I need a filling?*

119

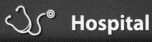

Medical Specialists Los especialistas médicos

1. internist
el internista

2. obstetrician
el obstetra

3. cardiologist
el cardiólogo

4. pediatrician
el pediatra

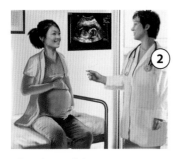

5. oncologist
el oncólogo

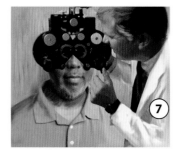

6. radiologist
el radiólogo

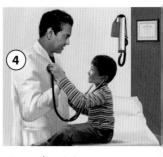

7. ophthalmologist
el oftalmólogo

8. psychiatrist
el siquiatra

Nursing Staff El personal de enfermería

9. surgical nurse
la enfermera quirúrgica

10. registered nurse (RN)
la enfermera registrada

11. licensed practical nurse (LPN)
la enfermera con licencia práctica

12. certified nursing assistant (CNA)
la asistente certificada de enfermería

Hospital Staff El personal del hospital

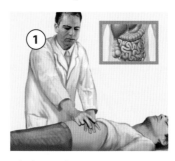

13. administrator
el administrador

14. admissions clerk
el encargado de admisiones

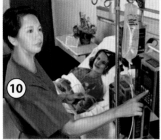

15. dietician
el / la dietista

16. orderly
el camillero / el asistente

More vocabulary

Gynecologists examine and treat women.
Nurse practitioners can give medical exams.
Nurse midwives deliver babies.

Chiropractors move the spine to improve health.
Orthopedists treat bone and joint problems.

A Hospital Room Una habitación en el hospital

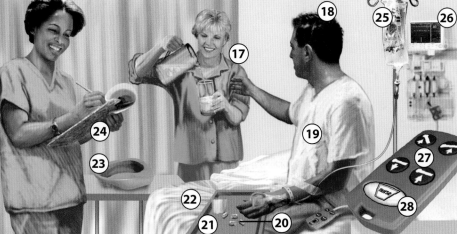

17. volunteer
la voluntaria /
el voluntario
18. patient
el paciente
19. hospital gown
la bata de hospital
20. medication
el medicamento

21. bed table
la mesa de cama
22. hospital bed
cama de hospital
23. bed pan
la bacinilla
24. medical chart
el expediente médico

25. IV (intravenous drip)
el goteo intravenoso
26. vital signs monitor
el monitor de signos
vitales
27. bed control
el control de la cama
28. call button
el botón para llamar

Lab El laboratorio

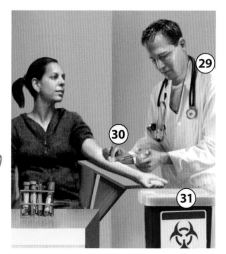

29. phlebotomist
el flebótomo
30. blood work / blood test
el examen de sangre / sanguíneo
31. medical waste disposal
el recipiente para desechos médicos

Emergency Room Entrance
La entrada de la sala de emergencias

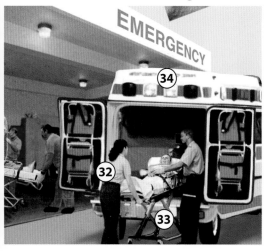

32. emergency medical technician (EMT)
el técnico médico de emergencias
33. stretcher / gurney
la camilla
34. ambulance
la ambulancia

Operating Room
La sala de operaciones / el quirófano

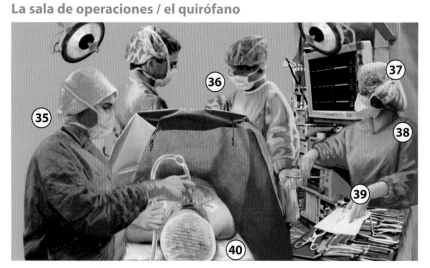

35. anesthesiologist
el anestesiólogo
36. surgeon
el cirujano

37. surgical cap
el gorro quirúrgico
38. surgical gown
la bata quirúrgica

39. surgical gloves
los guantes
quirúrgicos
40. operating table
la mesa quirúrgica

Dictate to your partner. Take turns.

A: *Write this sentence. She's a volunteer.*
B: *She's a what?*
A: *Volunteer. That's v-o-l-u-n-t-e-e-r.*

Role play. Ask about a doctor.

A: *I need to find a good surgeon.*
B: *Dr. Jones is a great surgeon. You should call him.*
A: *I will! Please give me his number.*

121

A Health Fair Una feria de salud

FADOOL HEALTH CLINIC

HEALTH FAIR — SATURDAY 9-4

GOOD FOODS MARKET — Vitamins

TREATMENT $5.00

FREE EYE EXAM

MEDICAL SCREENING $2

HATHA 2-3

FUN AND FIT 10-11

1. low-cost exam
un examen de bajo costo

2. acupuncture
la acupuntura

3. booth
el quiosco

4. yoga
el yoga

5. aerobic exercise
el ejercicio aeróbico

6. demonstration
una demostración

7. sugar-free
sin azúcar

8. nutrition label
la etiqueta de nutrición

A. **check**...pulse
verificar...el pulso

B. **give** a lecture
dar una clase

122

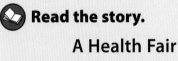

Look at the picture. What do you see?

Answer the questions.

1. How many different booths are there at the health fair?

2. What kinds of exams and treatments can you get at the fair?

3. What kinds of lectures and demonstrations are there?

4. How much is an acupuncture treatment? a medical screening?

Read the story.

A Health Fair

Once a month the Fadool Health Clinic has a health fair. You can get a <u>low-cost</u> medical <u>exam</u> at one <u>booth</u>. The nurses check your blood pressure and <u>check your pulse</u>. At another booth you can get a free eye exam. And an <u>acupuncture</u> treatment is only $5.00.

You can learn a lot at the fair. This month a doctor <u>is giving a lecture</u> on <u>nutrition labels</u>. There is also a <u>demonstration</u> on <u>sugar-free</u> cooking. You can learn to do <u>aerobic exercise</u> and <u>yoga</u>, too.

Do you want to get healthy and stay healthy? Then come to the Fadool Clinic Health Fair!

Think about it.

1. Which booths at this fair look interesting to you? Why?

2. Do you read nutrition labels? Why or why not?

 **Downtown** | El centro de la ciudad

1. **parking garage**
   el estacionamiento / la cochera

2. **office building**
   el edificio de oficinas

3. **hotel**
   el hotel

4. **Department of Motor Vehicles**
   el Departamento de Vehículos Motorizados

5. **bank**
   el banco

6. **police station**
   la comisaría / la estación de policía

7. **bus station**
   la estación de autobuses / la estación de camiones

THE SHELTON

Grand Avenue

Elm Street

RED LINE BUS CO.

FIRST U.S.

DOWNTOWN DIVISION

Grand Avenue

Listen and point. Take turns.

A: *Point to the bank.*
B: *Point to the hotel.*
A: *Point to the restaurant.*

Dictate to your partner. Take turns.

A: *Write bank.*
B: *Is that spelled b-a-n-k?*
A: *Yes, that's right.*

8. city hall
   el palacio municipal /
   la alcaldía
9. hospital
   el hospital
10. gas station
    la gasolinera
11. post office
    la oficina de correos
12. fire station
    la estación de
    bomberos
13. courthouse
    el tribunal
14. restaurant
    el restaurante
15. library
    la biblioteca

Grammar Point: *in* and *at* with locations

Use *in* when you are inside the building. *I am in
(inside) the bank.* Use *at* to describe your general
location. *I am at the bank.*

Pair practice. Make new conversations.

A: *I'm in the <u>bank</u>. Where are you?*
B: *I'm at the <u>bank</u>, too, but I'm outside.*
A: *OK. I'll meet you there.*

125

1. **stadium**
   el estadio

2. **construction site**
   la obra

3. **factory**
   la fábrica

4. **car dealership**
   el lote de autos / la concesionaria de autos

5. **mosque**
   la mezquita

6. **movie theater**
   el cine

7. **shopping mall**
   el centro comercial

8. **furniture store**
   la mueblería

9. **school**
   la escuela

10. **gym**
    el gimnasio

11. **coffee shop**
    la cafetería

12. **motel**
    el motel

Ways to state your destination using *to* and *to the*

Use *to* for schools, churches, and synagogues.
*I'm going **to** school.*
Use ***to the*** for all other locations. *I have to go **to the** bakery.*

Pair practice. Make new conversations.

A: *Where are you going today?*
B: *I'm going to school. How about you?*
A: *I have to go to the bakery.*

THIRD

13. skyscraper / high-rise
    el rascacielos

14. church
    la iglesia

15. cemetery
    el cementerio

16. synagogue
    la sinagoga

17. community college
    el instituto de enseñanza superior

18. supermarket
    el supermercado

19. bakery
    la panadería

20. home improvement store
    la tienda de mejoras para el hogar

21. office supply store
    la tienda de artículos de oficina

22. garbage truck
    el camión de la basura

23. theater
    el teatro

24. convention center
    el centro de convenciones

Ways to give locations

The mall is on 2nd Street.
The mall is on the corner of 2nd and Elm.
The mall is next to the movie theater.

Ask your classmates. Share the answers.

1. Where's your favorite coffee shop?
2. Where's your favorite supermarket?
3. Where's your favorite movie theater?

127

1. laundromat
   la lavandería
2. dry cleaners
   la tintorería
3. convenience store
   la tienda de conveniencia
4. pharmacy
   la farmacia
5. parking space
   el lugar para estacionar
6. handicapped parking
   el estacionamiento para minusválidos

7. corner
   la esquina
8. traffic light
   el semáforo
9. bus
   el autobús / el camión
10. fast food restaurant
    el restaurante de comida rápida
11. drive-thru window
    el servicio para automovilistas
12. newsstand
    el puesto de periódicos

13. mailbox
    el buzón
14. pedestrian
    el peatón
15. crosswalk
    el cruce peatonal
A. **cross** the street
   cruzar la calle
B. **wait for** the light
   esperar a que cambie el semáforo
C. **jaywalk**
   cruzar imprudentemente una calle

Pair practice. Make new conversations.

A: *I have a lot of errands to do today.*
B: *Me, too. First, I'm going to the laundromat.*
A: *I'll see you there after I stop at the copy center.*

Think about it. Discuss.

1. Which businesses are good to have in a neighborhood? Why?
2. Would you like to own a small business? If yes, what kind? If no, why not?

16. bus stop
    la parada de autobús

17. donut shop
    la tienda de donas

18. copy center
    el centro de fotocopiado

19. barbershop
    la barbería

20. video store
    la tienda de videos

21. curb
    el borde de la acera / de la banqueta

22. bike
    la bicicleta

23. pay phone
    el teléfono público

24. sidewalk
    la acera / la banqueta

25. parking meter
    el parquímetro

26. street sign
    el letrero

27. fire hydrant
    la boca de incendio

28. cart
    el carrito

29. street vendor
    el vendedor ambulante

30. childcare center
    la guardería infantil

D. **ride** a bike
    andar en bicicleta

E. **park** the car
    estacionar el auto / el coche

F. **walk** a dog
    pasear el perro

More vocabulary

neighborhood: the area close to your home
do errands: to make a short trip from your home to
buy or pick up things

Ask your classmates. Share the answers.

1. What errands do you do every week?
2. What stores do you go to in your neighborhood?
3. What things can you buy from a street vendor?

129

1. music store
   la tienda de música

2. jewelry store
   la joyería

3. nail salon
   el salón de uñas

4. bookstore
   la librería

5. toy store
   la juguetería

6. pet store
   la tienda de mascotas

7. card store
   la tienda de tarjetas

8. florist
   la florería / la floristería

9. optician
   la óptica

10. shoe store
    la zapatería

11. play area
    el área de juegos

12. guest services
    el módulo de información

More vocabulary

beauty shop: hair salon

men's store: men's clothing store

gift shop: a store that sells t-shirts, mugs, and other small gifts

Pair practice. Make new conversations.

A: *Where is the florist?*

B: *It's on the first floor, next to the optician.*

130

13. department store la tienda por departamentos	**17.** candy store la dulcería	**21.** elevator el elevador / el ascensor
14. travel agency la agencia de viajes	**18.** hair salon la peluquería	**22.** cell phone kiosk el quiosco de teléfonos celulares
15. food court la feria de comida rápida	**19.** maternity store la tienda de ropa de maternidad	**23.** escalator la escalera automática
16. ice cream shop la heladería	**20.** electronics store la tienda de aparatos electrónicos	**24.** directory el directorio

Ways to talk about plans

Let's go to the card store.
I have to go to the card store.
I want to go to the card store.

Role play. Talk to a friend at the mall.

A: *Let's go to the card store. I need to buy a card for Maggie's birthday.*
B: *OK, but can we go to the shoe store next?*

131

1. teller
el cajero

2. customer
el cliente

3. deposit
el depósito

4. deposit slip
el comprobante de depósito /
la hoja de ingreso

5. security guard
el guardia

6. vault
la bóveda

7. safety deposit box
la caja de seguridad

8. valuables
los objetos valiosos

Opening an Account Apertura de una cuenta

9. account manager
el gerente de cuentas

10. passbook
la libreta de banco

11. savings account number
el número de cuenta de ahorro

12. check book
la chequera

13. check
el cheque

14. checking account number
el número de cuenta corriente

15. ATM card
la tarjeta de cajero automático

16. bank statement
el estado de cuenta

17. balance
el saldo

A. Cash a check.
Cobre un cheque.

B. Make a deposit.
Haga un depósito.

C. Bank online.
Haga una transacción bancaria en línea.

The ATM (Automated Teller Machine) El cajero automático

D. Insert your ATM card.
Inserte su tarjeta de
cajero automático.

E. Enter your PIN.*
Introduzca su clave
en el teclado.

F. Withdraw cash.
Retire el efectivo.

G. Remove your card.
Retire la tarjeta.

*PIN = personal identification number

A. **get** a library card
obtener una tarjeta
para uso de la biblioteca

B. **look for** a book
buscar un libro

C. **check out** a book
sacar un libro
en préstamo

D. **return** a book
devolver un libro

E. **pay** a late fine
pagar una multa

1. library clerk
el bibliotecario

2. circulation desk
el escritorio de distribución

3. library patron
el usuario de la biblioteca

4. periodicals
las publicaciones
periódicas

5. magazine
la revista

6. newspaper
el periódico

7. headline
el titular

8. atlas
el atlas

9. reference librarian
el bibliotecario
de información

10. self-checkout
el autoservicio

11. online catalog
el catálogo en línea

12. picture book
el libro de dibujos

13. biography
la biografía

14. title
el título

15. author
el autor

16. novel
la novela

17. audiobook
el audiolibro /
el libro hablado

18. videocassette
el video / la cinta de video

19. DVD
el DVD (disco de
video digital)

The Post Office

La oficina de correos

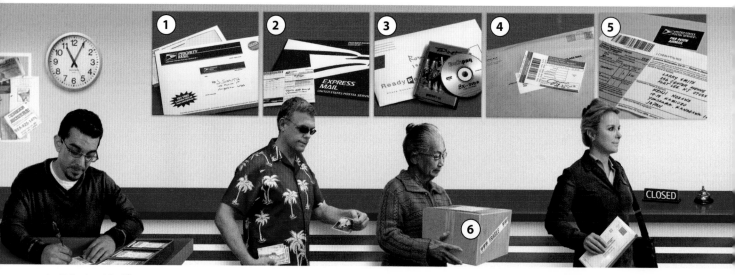

1. Priority Mail®
   Priority Mail® (el correo prioritario)
2. Express Mail®
   Express Mail® (el correo expreso)
3. media mail
   el correo de otros medios de información
4. Certified Mail™
   Certified Mail™ (el correo certificado)
5. airmail
   el correo aéreo
6. ground post / parcel post
   el envío por vía terrestre

13. letter
    la carta
14. envelope
    el sobre
15. greeting card
    la tarjeta de felicitación
16. post card
    la postal
17. package
    el paquete
18. book of stamps
    el libro de estampillas
19. postal forms
    los formularios de correo
20. letter carrier
    el cartero

21. return address
    el remitente
22. mailing address
    la dirección del destinatario
23. stamp
    la estampilla
24. postmark
    el matasellos

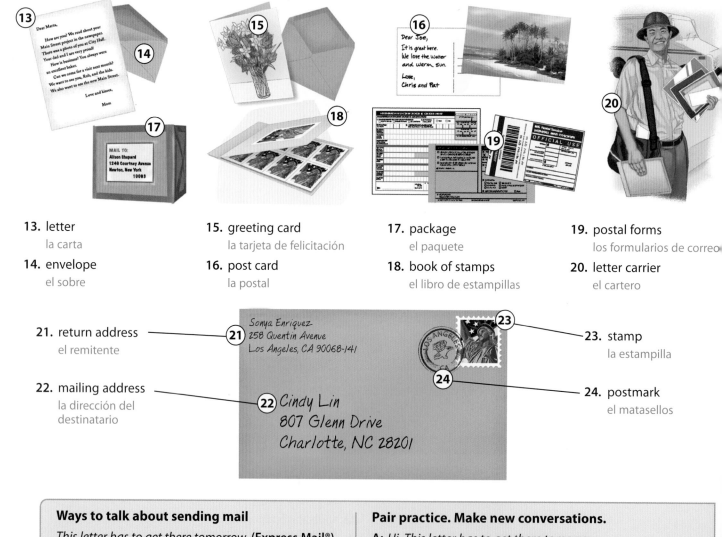

Ways to talk about sending mail

This letter has to <u>get there tomorrow</u>. (Express Mail®)
This letter has to <u>arrive in two days</u>. (Priority Mail®)
This letter can go in <u>regular mail</u>. (First Class)

Pair practice. Make new conversations.

A: Hi. <u>This letter has to get there tomorrow.</u>
B: You can send it by <u>Express Mail®</u>.
A: OK. I need <u>a book of stamps</u>, too.

7. postal clerk
el empleado de correos

8. scale
la máquina franqueadora

9. post office box (PO box)
el apartado postal (PO box)

10. automated postal center (APC)
el centro postal automático (CPA)

11. stamp machine
la máquina expendedora de estampillas

12. mailbox
el buzón

Sending a Card El envío de una tarjeta

A. Write a note in a card.
Escriba un mensaje
en la tarjeta.

B. Address the envelope.
Escriba la dirección
en el sobre.

C. Put on a stamp.
Póngale la estampilla.

D. Mail the card.
Envíe la tarjeta.

E. Deliver the card.
Entregue la tarjeta.

F. Receive the card.
Reciba la tarjeta.

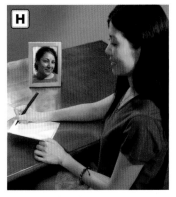

G. Read the card.
Lea la tarjeta.

H. Write back.
Responda.

More vocabulary

overnight / next day mail: Express Mail®
postage: the cost to send mail
junk mail: mail you don't want

Think about it. Discuss.

1. What kind of mail do you send overnight?
2. Do you want to be a letter carrier? Why or why not?
3. Do you get junk mail? What do you do with it?

135

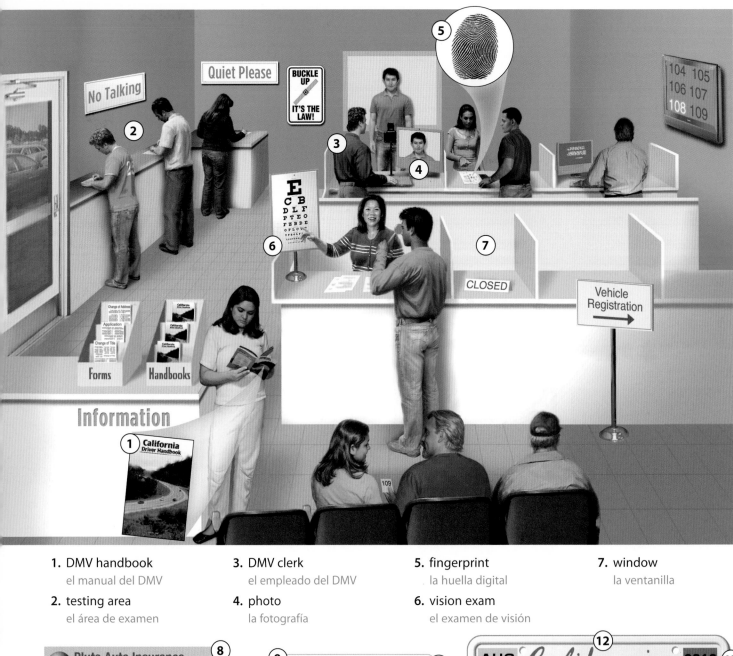

Department of Motor Vehicles (DMV)

El Departamento de Vehículos Motorizados (DMV)

1. DMV handbook
   el manual del DMV

2. testing area
   el área de examen

3. DMV clerk
   el empleado del DMV

4. photo
   la fotografía

5. fingerprint
   la huella digital

6. vision exam
   el examen de visión

7. window
   la ventanilla

8. proof of insurance
   la prueba de seguro

9. driver's license
   la licencia de manejar

10. expiration date
    la fecha de vencimiento

11. driver's license number
    el número de licencia de conductor

12. license plate
    la placa / la tablilla

13. registration sticker / tag
    el marbete / la etiqueta de registro

More vocabulary

expire: a license is no good, or **expires**, after the expiration date
renew a license: to apply to keep a license before it expires
vanity plate: a more expensive, personal license plate

Ask your classmates. Share the answers.

1. How far is the DMV from your home?
2. Do you have a driver's license? If yes, when does it expire? If not, do you want one?

Getting Your First License Obteniendo su primera licencia

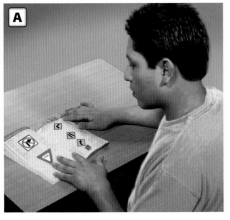

A. Study the handbook.
Estudie el manual.

B. Take a driver education course.*
Tome un curso de manejo.

C. Show your identification.
Muestre su identificación.

D. Pay the application fee.
Pague los costos de solicitud.

E. Take a written test.
Tome una prueba escrita.

F. Get a learner's permit.
Obtenga un permiso de aprendiz.

G. Take a driver's training course.*
Tome un curso de capacitación
para conductores.

H. Pass a driving test.
Pase una prueba de manejo.

I. Get your license.
Obtenga su licencia.

***Note:** This is not required for drivers 18 and older.

Ways to request more information

What do I do next?
What's the next step?
Where do I go from here?

Role play. Talk to a DMV clerk.

A: *I want to apply for <u>a driver's license</u>.*
B: *Did you <u>study the handbook</u>?*
A: *Yes, I did. <u>What do I do next</u>?*

137

Federal Government El gobierno federal

Legislative Branch
La rama legislativa

1. U.S. Capitol
   El capitolio
   de EE.UU.

2. Congress
   el Congreso

3. House of
   Representatives
   la Cámara de
   Representantes

4. congressperson
   el/la congresista

5. Senate
   el Senado

6. senator
   el senador

435   100

Executive Branch
La rama ejecutiva

7. White House
   la Casa Blanca

8. president
   el presidente

9. vice president
   el vicepresidente

10. Cabinet
    el Gabinete

STATE   DEFENSE   LABOR

Judicial Branch
La rama judicial

11. Supreme Court
    la Corte Suprema

12. justices
    los jueces

13. chief justice
    el presidente de
    la Corte Suprema

The Military La rama militar

14. Army
    el Ejército

15. Navy
    la Marina

16. Air Force
    la Fuerza Aérea

17. Marines
    los Infantes
    de Marina

18. Coast Guard
    la Guardia
    Costera

19. National Guard
    la Guardia
    Nacional

Government and Military Service

State Government El gobierno estatal

20. governor
el gobernador

21. lieutenant governor
el vicegobernador

22. state capital
la capital del estado

23. Legislature
la legislatura

24. assemblyperson
el asambleísta

25. state senator
el senador del estado

City Government El gobierno municipal

26. mayor
el alcalde

27. city council
el consejo municipal

28. councilperson
el concejal

An Election Una elección

A. run for office
postularse para un cargo

29. political campaign
la campaña política

B. debate
debatir

30. opponent
el oponente

C. get elected
ser electo

31. election results
los resultados de
las elecciones

D. serve
servir

32. elected official
el funcionario electo

More vocabulary

term: the period of time an elected official serves
political party: a group of people with the same
political goals

Think about it. Discuss.

1. Should everyone have to serve in the military? Why or
why not?
2. Would you prefer to run for city council or mayor? Why?

Responsibilities Responsabilidades

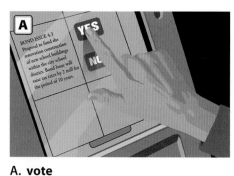

A. **vote**
   votar

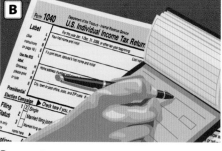

B. **pay** taxes
   pagar impuestos

C. **obey** the law
   obedecer / acatar las leyes

D. **register** with Selective Service*
   inscribirse en el servicio selectivo del ejército

E. **serve** on a jury
   servir en un jurado

F. **be** informed
   estar informado

Citizenship Requirements Requisitos de ciudadanía

G. **be** 18 or older
   tener 18 o más años de edad

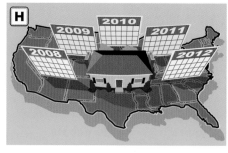

H. **live** in the U.S. for 5 years
   vivir en EE.UU. por cinco años

I. **take** a citizenship test
   tomar un examen de ciudadanía

Rights Derechos

1. peaceful assembly
   la reunión pacífica

2. free speech
   la libertad de expresión

3. freedom of religion
   la libertad de religión

4. freedom of the press
   la libertad de prensa

5. fair trial
   el juicio justo

*Note: All males 18 to 26 who live in the U.S. are required to register with Selective Service.

A. **arrest** a suspect
   arrestar a un sospechoso
1. police officer
   el oficial de policía / el policía
2. handcuffs
   las esposas

B. **hire** a lawyer / **hire** an attorney
   contratar a un abogado
3. guard
   el guardia
4. defense attorney
   el abogado defensor

C. **appear** in court
   comparecer ante el tribunal
5. defendant
   el acusado
6. judge
   el juez

D. **stand** trial
   ser juzgado
7. courtroom
   la sala del tribunal

8. jury
   el jurado
9. evidence
   la evidencia / las pruebas

10. prosecuting attorney
    el fiscal
11. witness
    el testigo

12. court reporter
    el escribiente / el secretario
13. bailiff
    el alguacil

E. **convict** the defendant
   condenar al acusado
14. verdict*
    el veredicto

F. **sentence** the defendant
   sentenciar al acusado

G. **go** to jail / **go** to prison
   ir a la cárcel / ir a prisión
15. convict / prisoner
    el condenado / el preso

H. **be** released
   salir en libertad

*Note: There are two possible verdicts, "guilty" and "not guilty."

Look at the pictures.
Describe what happened.

A: *The police officer arrested a suspect*.
B: *He put handcuffs on him.*

Think about it. Discuss.

1. Would you want to serve on a jury? Why or why not?
2. Look at the crimes on page 142. What sentence would you give for each crime? Why?

1. vandalism
   el vandalismo
2. burglary
   el robo

3. assault
   la agresión
4. gang violence
   el pandillismo

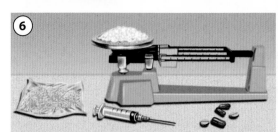

5. drunk driving
   manejar en estado
   de embriaguez
6. illegal drugs
   las sustancias /
   las drogas ilegales

7. arson
   el incendio provocado
8. shoplifting
   los hurtos en
   comercios

9. identity theft
   la usurpación
   de identidad
10. victim
    la víctima

Town Bank Online
Town Bank Customer:
Jane Montes
Withdrawal Amount:
$ 10,000.00

Jane Montes
Town Bank Statement
Account
Balance:
$0.00

11. mugging
    el ataque
12. murder
    el asesinato
13. gun
    la pistola

More vocabulary

steal: to take money or things from someone illegally
commit a crime: to do something illegal
criminal: someone who does something illegal

Think about it. Discuss.

1. Is there too much crime on TV or in the movies? Explain.
2. How can communities help stop crime?

A. **Walk** with a friend.
   Camine con un amigo.

B. **Stay** on well-lit streets.
   Permanezca en calles bien iluminadas.

C. **Conceal** your PIN number.
   Resguarde su clave.

D. **Protect** your purse or wallet.
   Proteja el bolso o la cartera / billetera.

E. **Lock** your doors.
   Cierre las puertas con llave.

F. Don't **open** your door to strangers.
   No **abra** la puerta a extraños.

G. Don't **drink** and **drive**.
   No **maneje en estado de embriaguez**.

H. **Shop** on secure websites.
   Haga compras en sitios Web seguros.

I. **Be** aware of your surroundings.
   Esté pendiente de sus alrededores.

J. **Report** suspicious packages.
   Denuncie los paquetes sospechosos.

K. **Report** crimes to the police.
   Denuncie los delitos a la policía.

L. **Join** a Neighborhood Watch.
   Únase al grupo de vigilancia del vecindario.

More vocabulary

sober: not drunk
designated drivers: sober drivers who drive drunk people home safely

Ask your classmates. Share the answers.

1. Do you feel safe in your neighborhood?
2. Look at the pictures. Which of these things do you do?
3. What other things do you do to stay safe?

143

1. lost child
el niño perdido

2. car accident
el accidente automovilístico

3. airplane crash
el accidente aéreo

4. explosion
la explosión

5. earthquake
el terremoto

6. mudslide
el derrumbe

7. forest fire
el incendio forestal

8. fire
el incendio

9. firefighter
el bombero

10. fire truck
el camión de bomberos

Ways to report an emergency

First, give your name. *My name is <u>Tim Johnson</u>.*
Then, state the emergency and give the address.
There was <u>a car accident</u> at <u>219 Elm Street</u>.

Role play. Call 911.

A: *911 Emergency Operator.*
B: *My name is <u>Lisa Diaz</u>. There is <u>a fire</u> at <u>323 Oak Street</u>.*
   Please hurry!

11. drought
la sequía

12. famine
el hambre epidémica

13. blizzard
la ventisca

14. hurricane
el huracán

15. tornado
el tornado

16. volcanic eruption
la erupción volcánica

17. tidal wave / tsunami
el maremoto

18. avalanche
la avalancha

19. flood
la inundación

20. search and rescue team
las brigadas de búsqueda y rescate

Ask your classmates. Share the answers.

1. Which natural disaster worries you the most?
2. Which natural disaster worries you the least?
3. Which disasters are common in your local area?

Think about it. Discuss.

1. What organizations can help you in an emergency?
2. What are some ways to prepare for natural disasters?
3. Where would you go in an emergency?

Before an Emergency Antes de una emergencia

A. **Plan** for an emergency.
   Planifique para una emergencia.

1. meeting place
   el lugar de encuentro

2. out-of-state contact
   los contactos fuera del estado

3. escape route
   la ruta de escape

4. gas shut-off valve
   la válvula de cierre del gas

5. evacuation route
   la ruta de evacuación

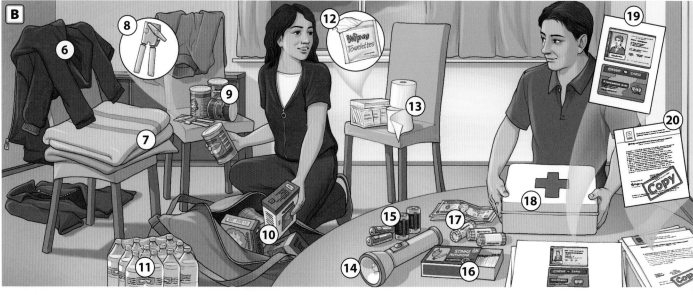

B. **Make** a disaster kit.
   Prepare un equipo de suministros en caso de desastres.

6. warm clothes
   las vestimentas calientes

7. blankets
   las cobijas / las mantas

8. can opener
   el abrelatas

9. canned food
   la comida enlatada

10. packaged food
    la comida envasada

11. bottled water
    el agua en botella

12. moist towelettes
    las toallitas húmedas

13. toilet paper
    el papel higiénico

14. flashlight
    la linterna / la lámpara de mano

15. batteries
    las pilas

16. matches
    los cerillos / los fósforos

17. cash and coins
    el efectivo y las monedas

18. first aid kit
    el botiquín de primeros auxilios

19. copies of ID and credit cards
    las copias de las tarjetas de identificación y de crédito

20. copies of important papers
    las copias de documentos importantes

Pair practice. Make new conversations.

A: *What do we need for our disaster kit?*
B: *We need blankets and matches.*
A: *I think we also need batteries.*

Ask your classmates. Share the answers.

1. Who would you call first after an emergency?
2. Do you have escape and evacuation routes planned?
3. Are you a calm person in case of an emergency?

Emergency Procedures

During an Emergency Durante una emergencia

C. **Watch** the weather.
Esté pendiente de los informes del tiempo.

D. **Pay attention** to warnings.
Preste atención a las advertencias.

E. **Remain** calm.
Permanezca tranquilo.

F. **Follow** directions.
Siga las instrucciones.

G. **Help** people with disabilities.
Ayude a las personas discapacitadas.

H. **Seek** shelter.
Busque refugio.

I. **Stay away** from windows.
Manténgase alejado de las ventanas.

J. **Take** cover.
Busque resguardo.

K. **Evacuate** the area.
Evacue el área.

After an Emergency Luego de una emergencia

L. **Call** out-of-state contacts.
Llame a sus contactos fuera del estado.

M. **Clean up** debris.
Limpie los escombros.

N. **Inspect** utilities.
Revise los servicios básicos.

Ways to say you're OK	**Ways to say you need help**	**Role play. Prepare for an emergency.**
I'm fine.	*We need help.*	A: *They just issued a hurricane warning.*
We're OK here.	*Someone is hurt.*	B: *OK. We need to stay calm and follow directions.*
Everything's under control.	*I'm injured. Please get help.*	A: *What do we need to do first?*

Community Cleanup   Limpieza comunitaria

1. graffiti	**3.** streetlight	**5.** petition	**B. applaud**
el graffiti	la luz de la calle	la petición	**aplaudir**
2. litter	**4.** hardware store	**A. give** a speech	**C. change**
la basura	la ferretería	**dar** un discurso	**cambiar**

Look at the pictures. What do you see?

Answer the questions.

1. What were the problems on Main Street?
2. What was the petition for?
3. Why did the city council applaud?
4. How did the people change the street?

📖 Read the story.

Community Cleanup

Marta Lopez has a donut shop on Main Street. One day she looked at her street and was very upset. She saw <u>graffiti</u> on her donut shop and the other stores. <u>Litter</u> was everywhere. All the <u>streetlights</u> were broken. Marta wanted to fix the lights and clean up the street.

Marta started a <u>petition</u> about the streetlights. Five hundred people signed it. Then she <u>gave a speech</u> to the city council. The council members voted to repair the streetlights. Everyone <u>applauded</u>. Marta was happy, but her work wasn't finished.

Next, Marta asked for volunteers to clean up Main Street. The <u>hardware store</u> manager gave the volunteers free paint. Marta gave them free donuts and coffee. The volunteers painted and cleaned. They <u>changed</u> Main Street. Now Main Street is beautiful and Marta is proud.

Think about it.

1. What are some problems in your community? How can people help?
2. Imagine you are Marta. What do you say in your speech to the city council?

1. car
   el automóvil
2. passenger
   el pasajero
3. taxi
   el taxi
4. motorcycle
   la motocicleta
5. street
   la calle
6. truck
   la camioneta
7. train
   el tren
8. (air)plane
   el avión

Listen and point. Take turns.

A: *Point to the motorcycle.*
B: *Point to the truck.*
A: *Point to the train.*

Dictate to your partner. Take turns.

A: *Write motorcycle.*
B: *Could you repeat that for me?*
A: *Motorcycle. M-o-t-o-r-c-y-c-l-e.*

9. helicopter
el helicóptero

10. airport
el aeropuerto

11. subway station
la estación del metro /
el tren subterráneo

12. subway
el metro / el tren
subterráneo

13. bus stop
la parada de autobús

14. bus
el autobús

15. bicycle
la bicicleta

Ways to talk about using transportation
Use **take** for buses, trains, subways, taxis, planes,
and helicopters. Use **drive** for cars and trucks.
Use **ride** for bicycles and motorcycles.

Pair practice. Make new conversations.
A: *How do you get to school?*
B: *I take the bus. How about you?*
A: *I ride a bicycle to school.*

151

A Bus Stop
Una parada de autobús

BUS 10 Northbound		
Main	Elm	Oak
6:00	6:10	6:13
6:30	6:40	6:43
7:00	7:10	7:13
7:30	7:40	7:43

New York City Transit
MTA **Transfer**
◄ Going your way

1. bus route
la ruta de autobús

2. fare
el pasaje

3. rider
el pasajero

4. schedule
el horario

5. transfer
el billete de transbordo

A Subway Station
Una estación de metro / de tren subterráneo

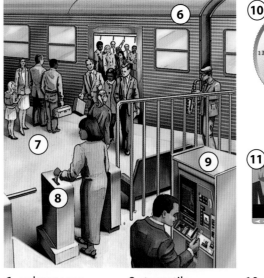

MTA RED LINE
OPENING DAY
JUNE 24, 2000
1 FARE
NORTH HOLLYWOOD

MTA **MetroCard**
◄ ◄ Insert this way/This side facing you

6. subway car
el vagón del tren subterráneo

7. platform
la plataforma

8. turnstile
el molinete

9. vending machine
la máquina expendedora

10. token
la ficha / el vale

11. fare card
el boleto / el billete

A Train Station
Una estación de tren

HART DAVIS/DAMON
From
DOVER, NH
To
BOSTON NRTH STA,MA
Carrier Train   Date
2V   **684** 17FEB03
Accom   Space/Car
2V **BUSINESS CL**
Form of Payment
AP XXXX0456791 Ax

Fresno
Los Angeles

Fresno
Los Angeles

12. ticket window
la ventanilla de boletos / billetes

13. conductor
el conductor

14. track
la vía férrea

15. ticket
el boleto / el billete

16. one-way trip
el viaje de ida

17. round trip
el viaje de ida y vuelta

Airport Transportation
Transporte al o del aeropuerto

TAXIS

TAXI

J&J Hotel

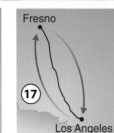
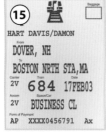

1036081

18. taxi stand
la parada de taxis

19. shuttle
el autobús de servicio regular / el autobús puente

20. town car
el automóvil urbano

21. taxi driver
el chofer de taxi

22. taxi license
la licencia del taxi

23. meter
el taxímetro

More vocabulary

hail a taxi: to raise your hand to get a taxi
miss the bus: to get to the bus stop after the bus leaves

Ask your classmates. Share the answers.

1. Is there a subway system in your city?
2. Do you ever take taxis? When?
3. Do you ever take the bus? Where?

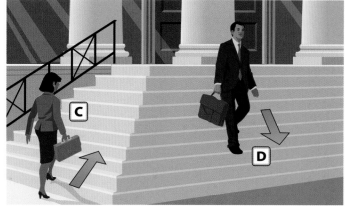

A. go under the bridge
ir debajo del puente

B. go over the bridge
ir sobre el puente

C. walk up the steps
ascender los peldaños

D. walk down the steps
descender los peldaños

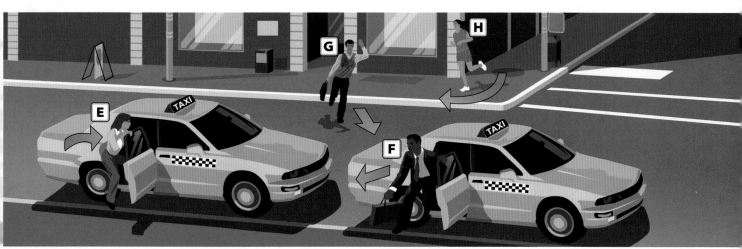

E. get into the taxi
subirse al taxi

F. get out of the taxi
bajarse del taxi

G. run across the street
cruzar corriendo la calle

H. run around the corner
correr alrededor de la esquina

I. get on the highway
entrar en la autopista

J. get off the highway
salir de la autopista

K. drive through the tunnel
conducir a través del túnel

Grammar Point: *into, out of, on, off*

Use *get into* for taxis and cars.
Use *get on* for buses, trains, planes, and highways.

Use *get out of* for taxis and cars.
Use *get off* for buses, trains, planes, and highways.

153

1. stop
detenerse / pararse

2. do not enter / wrong way
no entrar / sentido contrario

3. one way
un solo sentido

4. speed limit
el límite de velocidad

5. U-turn OK
la vuelta en U permitida

6. no outlet / dead end
el callejón sin salida /
la calle sin salida

7. right turn only
sólo giro a la derecha

8. no left turn
no se permite girar
a la izquierda

9. yield
ceder el paso

10. merge
convergir

11. no parking
no estacionarse

12. handicapped parking
el estacionamiento
para minusválidos

13. pedestrian crossing
el cruce peatonal

14. railroad crossing
el cruce del ferrocarril

15. school crossing
el cruce escolar

16. road work
trabajos en carretera

17. U.S. route / highway marker
la ruta de EE.UU. / el marcador
de autopista

18. hospital
el hospital

Pair practice. Make new conversations.

A: *Watch out! The sign says <u>no left turn</u>.*
B: *Sorry, I was looking at the <u>stop</u> sign.*
A: *That's OK. Just be careful!*

Ask your classmates. Share the answers.

1. How many traffic signs are on your street?
2. What's the speed limit on your street?
3. What traffic signs are the same in your native country?

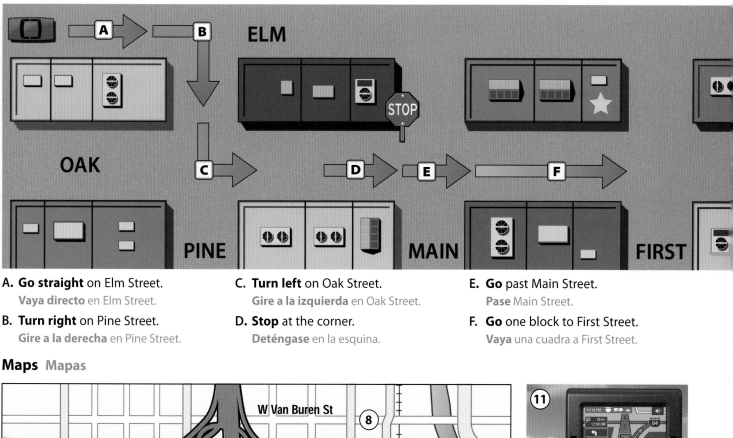

Directions Direcciones

A. **Go straight** on Elm Street.
   Vaya directo en Elm Street.

B. **Turn right** on Pine Street.
   Gire a la derecha en Pine Street.

C. **Turn left** on Oak Street.
   Gire a la izquierda en Oak Street.

D. **Stop** at the corner.
   Deténgase en la esquina.

E. **Go** past Main Street.
   Pase Main Street.

F. **Go** one block to First Street.
   Vaya una cuadra a First Street.

Maps Mapas

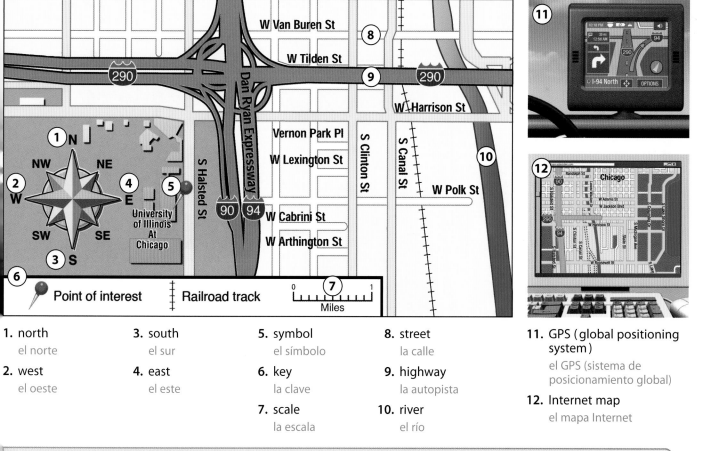

1. north
   el norte

2. west
   el oeste

3. south
   el sur

4. east
   el este

5. symbol
   el símbolo

6. key
   la clave

7. scale
   la escala

8. street
   la calle

9. highway
   la autopista

10. river
    el río

11. GPS (global positioning system)
    el GPS (sistema de posicionamiento global)

12. Internet map
    el mapa Internet

Role play. Ask for directions.

A: *I'm lost. I need to get to Elm and Pine.*
B: *Go straight on Oak and make a right on Pine.*
A: *Thanks so much.*

Ask your classmates. Share the answers.

1. How often do you use Internet maps? GPS? paper maps?
2. What was the last map you used? Why?

1. 4-door car / sedan
   el automóvil de 4 puertas / el sedán

2. 2-door car / coupe
   el automóvil de 2 puertas / el coupe

3. hybrid
   el híbrido

4. sports car
   el automóvil deportivo

5. convertible
   el convertible

6. station wagon
   la camioneta

7. SUV (sport–utility vehicle)
   el SUV (vehículo deportivo utilitario) /
   el vehículo de doble tracción

8. minivan
   la miniván

9. camper
   el cámper

10. RV (recreational vehicle)
    el RV (vehículo recreacional)

11. limousine / limo
    la limusina

12. pickup truck
    el pickup /
    la camioneta

13. cargo van
    el furgón de carga

14. tow truck
    la grúa

15. tractor trailer / semi
    el camión
    semirremolque /
    el trailer

16. cab
    la cabina

17. trailer
    el remolque

18. moving van
    el camión de
    mudanza

19. dump truck
    el camión volquete

20. tank truck
    el camión tanque

21. school bus
    el ómnibus escolar

Pair practice. Make new conversations.

A: *I have a new car!*
B: *Did you get a hybrid?*
A: *Yes, but I really wanted a sports car.*

More vocabulary

make: the name of the company that makes the car
model: the style of the car

Buying a Used Car Compra de un automóvil usado

'04 Compact. Only $3,000.

'05 Sedan. Must sell. Great deal!

A. Look at car ads.
Mire los anuncios de automóviles.

B

How many miles does it have?

B. Ask the seller about the car.
Pregúntele al vendedor sobre el automóvil.

It's in good condition.

C

C. Take the car to a mechanic.
Lleve el automóvil a un mecánico.

D

It's $2,500.

I can give you $2,000.

D. Negotiate a price.
Negocie un precio.

E

E. Get the title from the seller.
Obtenga el título del vendedor.

F

F. Register the car.
Registre el automóvil.

Taking Care of Your Car El cuidado de su automóvil

G

G. Fill the tank with gas.
Llene el tanque con gasolina.

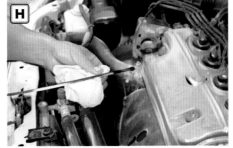

H

H. Check the oil.
Revise el aceite.

I

I. Put in coolant.
Póngale refrigerante.

J

J. Go for a smog check.*
Llévelo para que le hagan una prueba de esmog.

K

K. Replace the windshield wipers.
Reemplace los limpiaparabrisas.

L

L. Fill the tires with air.
Infle los neumáticos.

*smog check = emissions test

Ways to request service

Please check the oil.
Could you fill the tank?
Put in coolant, please.

Think about it. Discuss.

1. What's good and bad about a used car?
2. Do you like to negotiate car prices? Why?
3. Do you know any good mechanics? Why are they good?

157

At the Dealer
En el lugar del concesionario

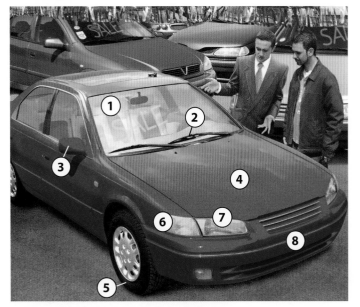

At the Mechanic
En el taller del mecánico

1. windshield
el parabrisas

2. windshield wipers
los limpiaparabrisas

3. sideview mirror
el espejo lateral

4. hood
el capó / la capota

5. tire
el neumático / la llanta

6. turn signal
la luz direccional

7. headlight
la luz delantera

8. bumper
el parachoques / la defensa

9. hubcap / wheel cover
el tapacubos / la tapa de rueda

10. gas tank
el tanque de gasolina

11. trunk
la maletera / el baúl

12. license plate
la placa / la tablilla

13. tail light
la luz trasera

14. brake light
la luz de freno

15. tail pipe
el escape

16. muffler
el silenciador

Under the Hood Debajo del capó

Inside the Trunk Dentro de la maletera

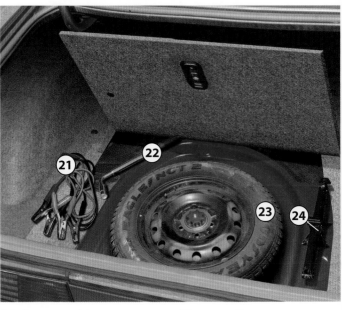

17. fuel injection system
el sistema inyector de combustible

18. engine
el motor

19. radiator
el radiador

20. battery
la batería

21. jumper cables
los cables puente / los cables para pasar corriente

22. lug wrench
la llave de tuerca

23. spare tire
el neumático / la llanta de repuesto

24. jack
el gato hidráulico

The Dashboard and Instrument Panel
El tablero y el panel de instrumentos

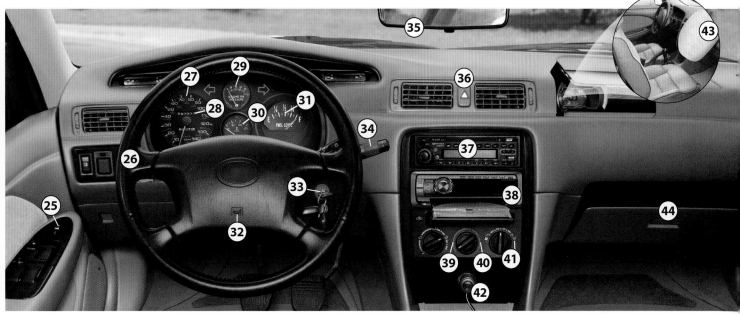

25. door lock
el seguro de puerta

26. steering wheel
el volante / el timón

27. speedometer
el velocímetro

28. odometer
el odómetro

29. oil gauge
el indicador / medidor
de aceite

30. temperature gauge
el indicador / medidor
de temperatura

31. gas gauge
el indicador / medidor
de gasolina

32. horn
el claxon / la bocina

33. ignition
el arranque / la ignición

34. turn signal
la palanca de luz direccional

35. rearview mirror
el espejo retrovisor

36. hazard lights
las luces de peligro

37. radio
la radio

38. CD player
el reproductor de CD

39. air conditioner
el aire acondicionado

40. heater
el calentador

41. defroster
el descongelador

42. power outlet
la toma de corriente

43. air bag
la bolsa de aire

44. glove compartment
el compartimiento de
guantes / la guantera

An Automatic Transmission
Una transmisión automática

A Manual Transmission
Una transmisión manual

Inside the Car
Dentro del automóvil

45. brake pedal
el pedal de freno

**46. gas pedal /
accelerator**
el pedal de gasolina /
el acelerador

47. gear shift
la palanca de cambio
de velocidad

48. hand brake
el freno de mano

49. clutch
el embrague

50. stick shift
la palanca de
velocidades

51. front seat
el asiento delantero

52. seat belt
la correa de
seguridad

53. child safety seat
el asiento para niños

54. backseat
el asiento trasero

In the Airline Terminal En la terminal de la línea aérea

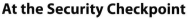

At the Security Checkpoint
En el punto de inspección de seguridad

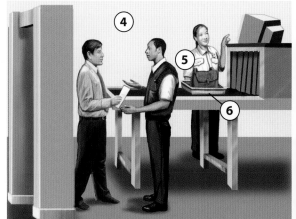

1. skycap
el maletero

2. check-in kiosk
el quiosco para registrarse

3. ticket agent
el agente de pasajes

4. screening area
el área de control de seguridad

5. TSA* agent / security screener
el agente de la TSA / el inspector de
seguridad / el revisor de seguridad

6. bin
la caja

Taking a Flight Para tomar un vuelo

A. Check in electronically.
Regístrese
electrónicamente.

B. Check your bags.
Registre su equipaje.

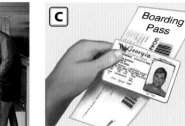

C. Show your boarding pass
and ID.
Muestre su billete de
abordaje y su identificación.

D. Go through security.
Pase por el área de
seguridad.

E. Board the plane.
Aborde el avión.

F. Find your seat.
Encuentre su asiento.

G. Stow your carry-on bag.
Guarde su equipaje
de mano.

H. Fasten your seat belt.
Abróchese el cinturón
de seguridad.

I. Turn off your cell phone.
Apague su teléfono celular.

J. Take off. / Leave.
Despega. / Se va.

K. Land. / Arrive.
Aterriza. / Llega.

L. Claim your baggage.
Reclame su equipaje.

* Transportation Security Administration

At the Gate En la puerta

On the Airplane En el avión

At Customs En la aduana

7. arrival and departure monitors
los monitores de salidas y llegadas

8. gate
la puerta

9. boarding area
la zona de abordaje

10. cockpit
la cabina del piloto

11. pilot
el piloto

12. flight attendant
la aeromoza / la azafata

13. overhead compartment
el compartimiento para el equipaje de mano

14. emergency exit
la salida de emergencia

15. passenger
el pasajero

16. declaration form
la declaración de aduana

17. customs officer
el agente de aduana

18. luggage / bag
el equipaje

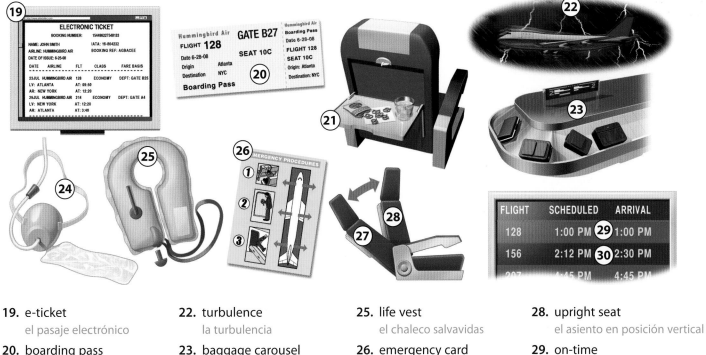

19. e-ticket
el pasaje electrónico

20. boarding pass
el billete de abordaje

21. tray table
la mesita

22. turbulence
la turbulencia

23. baggage carousel
el carrusel de equipajes

24. oxygen mask
la máscara de oxígeno

25. life vest
el chaleco salvavidas

26. emergency card
la tarjeta de emergencia

27. reclined seat
el asiento reclinado

28. upright seat
el asiento en posición vertical

29. on-time
a tiempo

30. delayed flight
el vuelo retrasado

More vocabulary

departure time: the time the plane takes off
arrival time: the time the plane lands
direct flight: a trip with no stops

Pair practice. Make new conversations.

A: *Excuse me. Where do I check in?*
B: *At the check-in kiosk.*
A: *Thanks.*

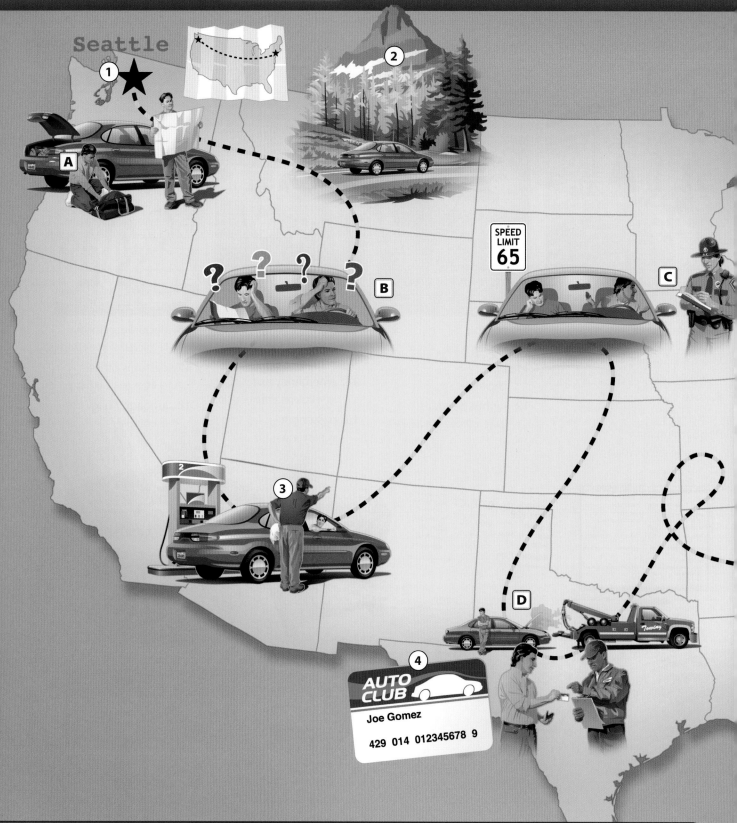

1. starting point
   el punto de partida

2. scenery
   el paisaje

3. gas station attendant
   el dependiente de
   la gasolinera

4. auto club card
   la tarjeta del club
   de conductores

5. destination
   el destino

A. **pack**
   empacar

B. **get** lost
   perderse

C. **get** a speeding ticket
   ser multado por exceso
   de velocidad

D. **break down**
   avería del auto

E. **run out** of gas
   quedarse sin gasolina

F. **have** a flat tire
   tener un neumático
   reventado

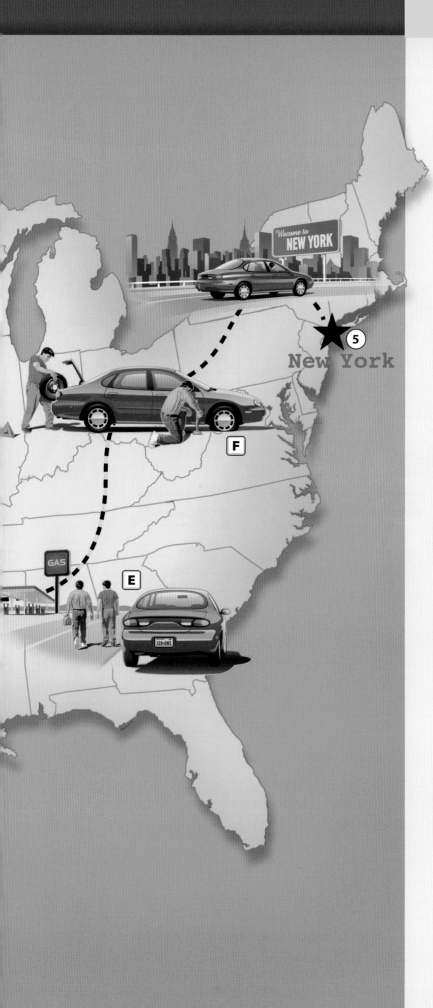

**Look at the pictures.
What do you see?**

Answer the questions.

1. What are the young men's starting point and destination?

2. What do they see on their trip?

3. What kinds of problems do they have?

📖 Read the story.

A Road Trip

On July 7th Joe and Rob <u>packed</u> their bags for a road trip. Their <u>starting point</u> was Seattle. Their <u>destination</u> was New York City.

The young men saw beautiful <u>scenery</u> on their trip. But there were also problems. They <u>got lost</u>. Then, a <u>gas station attendant</u> gave them bad directions. Next, they <u>got a speeding ticket</u>. Joe was very upset. After that, their car <u>broke down</u>. Joe called a tow truck and used his <u>auto club card</u>.

The end of their trip was difficult, too. They <u>ran out of gas</u> and then they had a <u>flat tire</u>.

After 7,000 miles of problems, Joe and Rob arrived in New York City. They were happy, but tired. Next time, they're going to take the train.

Think about it.

1. What is the best way to travel across the U.S.? by car? by plane? by train? Why?

2. Imagine your car breaks down on the road. Who can you call?
   What can you do?

1. **entrance**
   la entrada
2. **customer**
   el cliente
3. **office**
   la oficina
4. **employer /
   boss**
   el empleador /
   el jefe
5. **receptionist**
   la recepcionista
6. **safety regulations**
   los reglamentos
   de seguridad

IRINA'S COMPUTER SERVICE

OSHA

HAZARDS

SPILLS

CALL 911

SAFETY FIRST

COMPUTER NEWS

Irina Sarkov Owner

Listen and point. Take turns.

A: Point to <u>the front entrance</u>.
B: Point to <u>the receptionist</u>.
A: Point to <u>the time clock</u>.

Dictate to your partner. Take turns.

A: *Can you spell employer?*
B: *I'm not sure. Is it e-m-p-l-o-y-e-r?*
A: *Yes, that's right.*

7. time clock
el reloj registrador /
el marcador de tiempo

8. supervisor
el supervisor

9. employee
el empleado

10. payroll clerk
el encargado
de nómina

11. pay stub
el talón de pago

12. wages
los sueldos

13. deductions
las deducciones

14. paycheck
el cheque de pago

Ways to talk about wages

I **earn** $250 a week.
He **makes** $7 an hour.
I'm **paid** $1,000 a month.

Role play. Talk to an employer.

A: *Is everything correct on your paycheck?*
B: *No, it isn't. I make $250 a week, not $200.*
A: *Let's talk to the payroll clerk. Where is she?*

165

1. accountant
el contador / la contadora

2. actor
el actor / la actriz

3. administrative assistant
el asistente administrativo /
la asistente administrativa

4. appliance repair person
el técnico de reparación de
aparatos electrodomésticos

5. architect
el arquitecto / la arquitecta

6. artist
el artista / la artista

7. assembler
el ensamblador /
la ensambladora

8. auto mechanic
el mecánico de automóviles

9. babysitter
la niñera

10. baker
el panadero / la panadera

11. business owner
el dueño / la dueña
de negocios

12. businessperson
la persona de negocios

13. butcher
el carnicero

14. carpenter
el carpintero

15. cashier
el cajero / la cajera

16. childcare worker
la trabajadora de
cuidado de niños

Ways to ask about someone's job

What's her job?
What does he do?
What kind of work do they do?

Pair practice. Make new conversations.

A: *What kind of work <u>does she</u> do?*
B: <u>*She's an accountant*</u>. *What <u>do they</u> do?*
A: <u>*They're actors*</u>.

17. commercial fisher
el pescador comercial

18. computer software engineer
el ingeniero de software de computadoras

19. computer technician
el técnico de computadoras

We have that shirt in red.

20. customer service representative
el representante de servicio al cliente

21. delivery person
el repartidor

22. dental assistant
el / la asistente dental

23. dockworker
el trabajador portuario / el estibador

24. electronics repair person
el técnico de reparación electrónica

25. engineer
el ingeniero

26. firefighter
el bombero

27. florist
la florista

28. gardener
el jardinero

29. garment worker
el empleado / la empleada de una fábrica de ropa

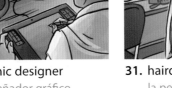

30. graphic designer
el diseñador gráfico

31. hairdresser / hair stylist
la peluquera

32. home health care aide
la asistenta de atención de la salud a domicilio

Ways to talk about jobs and occupations

Sue's a _garment worker_. She works **in** a factory.
Tom's _an engineer_. He works **for** _a large company_.
Ann's a _dental assistant_. She works **with** _a dentist_.

Role play. Talk about a friend's new job.

A: Does your friend like _his_ new job?
B: Yes, _he_ does. _He's a graphic designer_.
A: Does _he_ work _in an office_?

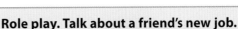

167

33. homemaker
el ama de casa

34. housekeeper
el ama de llaves

35. interpreter / translator
el intérprete / el traductor

36. lawyer
el abogado

37. machine operator
el operador / la operadora
de maquinaria

38. manicurist
la manicurista

39. medical records
technician
la técnica de registros
médicos

40. messenger / courier
el mensajero

41. model
la modelo

42. mover
el empleado de una
casa de mudanzas

43. musician
el músico

44. nurse
la enfermera

45. occupational therapist
el / la terapista ocupacional

46. (house) painter
el pintor (de casas)

47. physician assistant
el / la asistente del médico

48. police officer
el / la oficial de la policía

Grammar Point: past tense of *be*

I **was** a machine operator for 5 years.
She **was** a nurse for a year.
They **were** movers from 2003–2007.

Pair practice. Make new conversations.

A: *What was your first job?*
B: *I was a musician. How about you?*
A: *I was a messenger for a small company.*

49. postal worker
el empleado / la empleada
de correos

50. printer
el impresor

51. receptionist
la recepcionista

52. reporter
el reportero / la reportera

53. retail clerk
el dependiente de la
tienda minorista

54. sanitation worker
el empleado de servicios
de la higiene pública

55. security guard
el / la guardia de seguridad

56. server
la camarera

Here are some programs
that will help you.

HELPING
HEART
AGENCY

57. social worker
la trabajadora social

58. soldier
el soldado

59. stock clerk
el empleado de almacén

Hello. I'm
calling with a
very special
offer.

60. telemarketer
la persona que realiza
ventas por teléfono

61. truck driver
el camionero

62. veterinarian
el doctor / la doctora
en veterinaria

63. welder
el soldador

Norma's
Story

64. writer / author
el escritor / la escritora /
el autor / la autora

Ask your classmates. Share the answers.

1. Which of these jobs could you do now?
2. What is one job you don't want to have?
3. Which jobs do you want to have?

Think about it. Discuss.

1. Which jobs need special training?
2. What kind of person makes a good interpreter? A
   good nurse? A good reporter? Why?

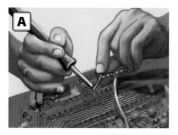

A. assemble components
ensamblar componentes

B. assist medical patients
ayudar a los pacientes

C. cook
cocinar

D. do manual labor
hacer labores manuales

E. drive a truck
conducir un camión

F. fly a plane
volar un avión

G. make furniture
hacer muebles

H. operate heavy machinery
operar maquinaria pesada

I. program computers
programar computadoras

J. repair appliances
reparar electrodomésticos

K. sell cars
vender automóviles

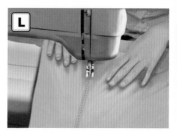

L. sew clothes
coser ropa

M. solve math problems
resolver problemas matemáticos

N. speak another language
hablar otro idioma

O. supervise people
supervisar a las personas

P. take care of children
cuidar niños

Q. teach
enseñar

R. type
escribir a máquina

S. use a cash register
usar una caja registradora

T. wait on customers
atender a los clientes

Grammar Point: can, can't

I am a chef. I **can** cook.
I'm not a pilot. I **can't** fly a plane.
I **can't** speak French, but I **can** speak Spanish.

Role play. Talk to a job counselor.

A: Tell me about your skills. Can you type?
B: No, I can't, but I can use a cash register.
A: OK. What other skills do you have?

Customers need better service…

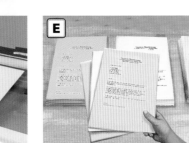

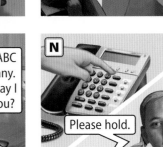

Let's meet at 2:00.

Sure.

Dear Mr. Smith…

Hello. ABC Company. How may I help you?

Please hold.

Mr. Perez, I'm transferring you.

Hello. This is Sue Jones. Please call me.

This is Lee Tran. Please call me back.

Message Pad
Call From: Ana Puerta
Tel: 555-1234
Message:
Please Call

Office Skills
Destrezas de oficina

A. **type** a letter
   escribir una carta a máquina

B. **enter** data
   introducir datos

C. **transcribe** notes
   transcribir notas

D. **make** copies
   hacer copias

E. **collate** papers
   compaginar papeles

F. **staple**
   engrapar

G. **fax** a document
   enviar un documento por fax

H. **scan** a document
   escanear un documento

I. **print** a document
   imprimir un documento

J. **schedule** a meeting
   programar una reunión

K. **take** dictation
   tomar dictado

L. **organize** materials
   organizar materiales

Telephone Skills
Destrezas telefónicas

M. **greet** the caller
   saludar al que llama

N. **put** the caller on hold
   poner en espera al llamante

O. **transfer** the call
   transferir la llamada

P. **leave** a message
   dejar un mensaje

Q. **take** a message
   tomar un mensaje

R. **check** messages
   revisar los mensajes

Career Path Trayectoria de carrera

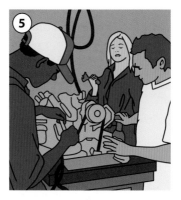

1. entry-level job
el trabajo de nivel de entrada

2. training
la capacitación

3. new job
el trabajo nuevo

4. promotion
el ascenso

Types of Job Training Tipos de capacitación laboral

Enter the number here.

Medical Transcription 101
Log In
Password

5. vocational training
la capacitación vocacional

6. internship
el internado

7. on-the-job training
la capacitación en el trabajo

8. online course
el curso en línea

Planning a Career Planificación de la carrera

JOB BOARD

We offer training here.

Interests
Click on your interests. I like to work:
☐ Outside   ☐ With Children
☑ Inside   ☐ By Myself
☑ On a team

Skills
Click on your skills:
☐ Drive
☐ Speak Spanish
☑ Type

Work for Go-Mart

Why work for Go-Mart?

9. resource center
el centro de recursos

10. career counselor
el orientador de carreras

11. interest inventory
el inventario de interés

12. skill inventory
el inventario de destrezas

13. job fair
la feria de empleos

14. recruiter
el reclutador

Ways to talk about job training

I'm looking into an online course.
I'm interested in on-the-job training.
I want to sign up for an internship.

Ask your classmates. Share the answers.

1. What kind of job training are you interested in?
2. Would your rather learn English in an online course or in a classroom?

A. **talk** to friends / **network**
hablar con los amigos / relacionarse con otros

B. **look in** the classifieds
buscar en los anuncios clasificados

C. **look for** help wanted signs
buscar avisos de "se solicita ayuda"

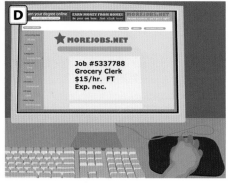

D. **check** Internet job sites
buscar en los sitios de empleos de Internet

E. **go** to an employment agency
ir a una agencia de empleos

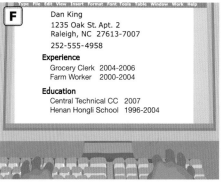

F. **write** a resume
escribir un resumé

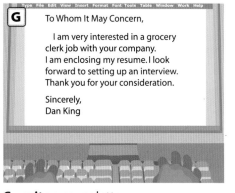

G. **write** a cover letter
escribir una carta de presentación

H. **send in** your resume and cover letter
enviar su resumé y su carta de presentación

I. **set up** an interview
concertar una entrevista

J. **fill out** an application
llenar una solicitud

K. **go on** an interview
ir a una entrevista

L. **get** hired
ser contratado

A. Prepare for the interview.
Prepárese para la entrevista.

B. Dress appropriately.
Vístase con ropa adecuada.

C. Be neat.
Esté bien arreglado.

D. Bring your resume and ID.
Lleve su resumé y su identificación.

E. Don't be late.
No llegue tarde.

F. Be on time.
Sea puntual.

G. Turn off your cell phone.
Apague su teléfono celular.

H. Greet the interviewer.
Salude al entrevistador.

I. Shake hands.
Estréchense las manos.

J. Make eye contact.
Haga contacto visual.

K. Listen carefully.
Escuche cuidadosamente.

L. Talk about your experience.
Hable sobre su experiencia.

M. Ask questions.
Hágale preguntas.

N. Thank the interviewer.
Agradézcale al entrevistador.

O. Write a thank-you note.
Escríbale una nota de agradecimiento.

More vocabulary

benefits: health insurance, vacation pay, or other things the employer can offer an employee
inquire about benefits: ask about benefits

Think about it. Discuss.

1. How can you prepare for an interview?
2. Why is it important to make eye contact?
3. What kinds of questions should you ask?

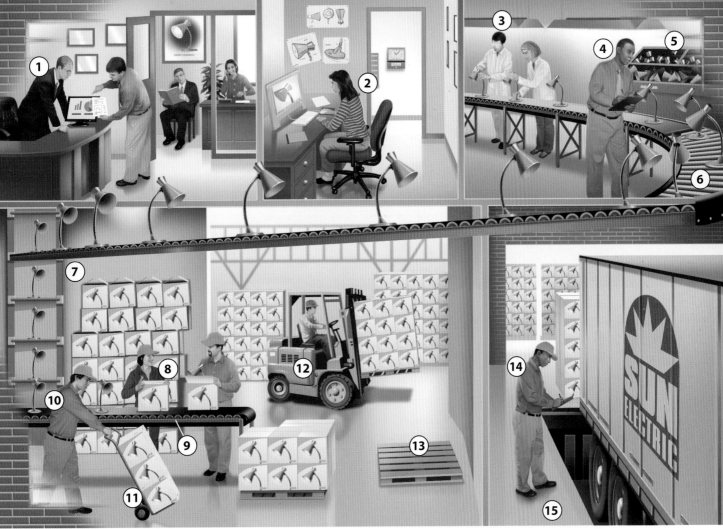

1. factory owner
   el dueño de la fábrica

2. designer
   el diseñador / la diseñadora

3. factory worker
   el obrero

4. line supervisor
   el supervisor de línea /
   de la cadena

5. parts
   las piezas

6. assembly line
   la línea de montaje /
   la línea de ensamblaje

7. warehouse
   la bodega / el almacén

8. packer
   el empacador /
   la empacadora

9. conveyer belt
   la cinta transportadora

10. order puller
    el encargado de pedidos

11. hand truck
    la carretilla de mano

12. forklift
    el elevador de carga

13. pallet
    la paleta

14. shipping clerk
    el dependiente encargado
    del despacho de
    mercadería

15. loading dock
    el muelle de carga

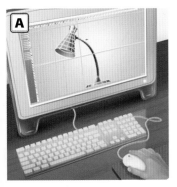

A. design
diseñar

B. manufacture
fabricar

C. assemble
ensamblar / montar / armar

D. ship
despachar

175

Bloom Nursery

1. **gardening crew**
   el personal de jardinería

2. **leaf blower**
   el soplador de hojas

3. **wheelbarrow**
   la carretilla

4. **gardening crew leader**
   el jefe del personal de jardinería

5. **landscape designer**
   el diseñador de paisajes

6. **lawn mower**
   la cortadora de césped

7. **shovel**
   la pala

8. **rake**
   el rastrillo

9. **pruning shears**
   las tijeras de podar

10. **trowel**
    el desplantador

11. **hedge clippers**
    las tijeras para setos

12. **weed whacker / weed eater**
    el recortador / el cortador

A. **mow** the lawn
   cortar el césped

B. **trim** the hedges
   podar los setos

C. **rake** the leaves
   rastrillar las hojas

D. **fertilize / feed** the plants
   fertilizar / alimentar
   las plantas

E. **plant** a tree
   plantar un árbol

F. **water** the plants
   regar las plantas

G. **weed** the flower beds
   quitar la maleza de las flores

H. **install** a sprinkler system
   instalar un sistema de rociador

Use the new words.
Look at page 53. Name what you can do in the yard.

A: I can <u>mow the lawn</u>.
B: I can <u>weed the flower bed</u>.

Ask your classmates. Share the answers.

1. Do you know someone who does landscaping? Who?
2. Do you enjoy gardening? Why or why not?
3. Which gardening activity is the hardest to do? Why?

Crops Las siembras

1. rice
el arroz

2. wheat
el trigo

3. soybeans
los frijoles de soya

4. corn
el maíz

5. alfalfa
la alfalfa

6. cotton
el algodón

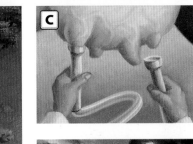

7. field
el campo

8. farmworker
el trabajador agrícola

9. tractor
el tractor

10. orchard
la huerta

11. barn
la granja

12. farm equipment
el equipo para trabajar
en el campo

13. farmer / grower
el agricultor / el cultivador

14. vegetable garden
el huerto / la huerta de
verduras y hortalizas

15. livestock
el ganado

16. vineyard
la viña

17. corral
el corral

18. hay
el heno

19. fence
la cerca

20. hired hand
el mozo de campo /
el peón de labranza

21. cattle
el ganado

22. rancher
el ganadero

A. plant
sembrar

B. harvest
cosechar

C. milk
ordeñar

D. feed
alimentar

177

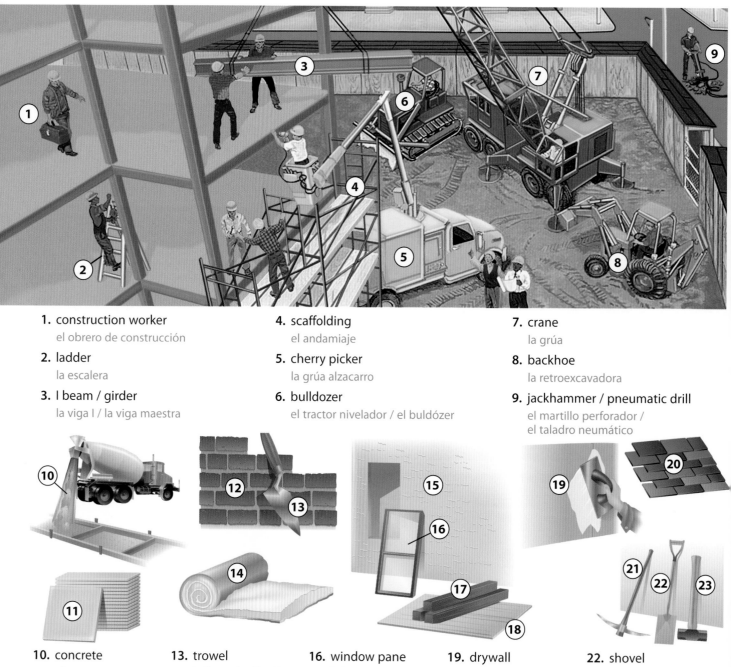

1. construction worker
el obrero de construcción

2. ladder
la escalera

3. I beam / girder
la viga I / la viga maestra

4. scaffolding
el andamiaje

5. cherry picker
la grúa alzacarro

6. bulldozer
el tractor nivelador / el buldózer

7. crane
la grúa

8. backhoe
la retroexcavadora

9. jackhammer / pneumatic drill
el martillo perforador /
el taladro neumático

10. concrete
el cemento

11. tile
las losas / las baldosas

12. bricks
los ladrillos

13. trowel
la llana de albañil

14. insulation
el aislamiento

15. stucco
el estuco

16. window pane
la hoja de vidrio

17. wood / lumber
la madera / el madero

18. plywood
la madera terciada /
contrachapada

19. drywall
la pared de yeso

20. shingles
las tejas de madera

21. pickax
el azadón de pico

22. shovel
la pala

23. sledgehammer
el mazo

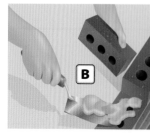

A. paint
pintar

B. lay bricks
colocar ladrillos

C. install tile
instalar losas

D. hammer
martillar

Safety Hazards and Hazardous Materials Peligros de seguridad y materiales peligrosos

1. **careless worker**
   el trabajador descuidado

2. **careful worker**
   el trabajador cuidadoso

3. **poisonous fumes**
   los humos venenosos

4. **broken equipment**
   el equipo averiado o roto

5. **frayed cord**
   el cable desgastado

6. **slippery floor**
   el piso resbaloso

7. **radioactive materials**
   los materiales radioactivos

8. **flammable liquids**
   los líquidos inflamables

Safety Equipment Equipo de seguridad

9. **hard hat**
   el casco protector

10. **safety glasses**
    las gafas de seguridad /
    las antiparras

11. **safety goggles**
    las gafas protectoras

12. **safety visor**
    la visera de seguridad

13. **respirator**
    el respirador

14. **particle mask**
    la máscara para partículas

15. **ear plugs**
    los tapones para el oído

16. **earmuffs**
    las orejeras

17. **work gloves**
    los guantes de trabajo

18. **back support belt**
    la correa de soporte
    para la espalda

19. **knee pads**
    las rodilleras

20. **safety boots**
    las botas de seguridad

21. **fire extinguisher**
    el extintor / extinguidor
    de incendios

22. **two-way radio**
    el / la radio bidireccional

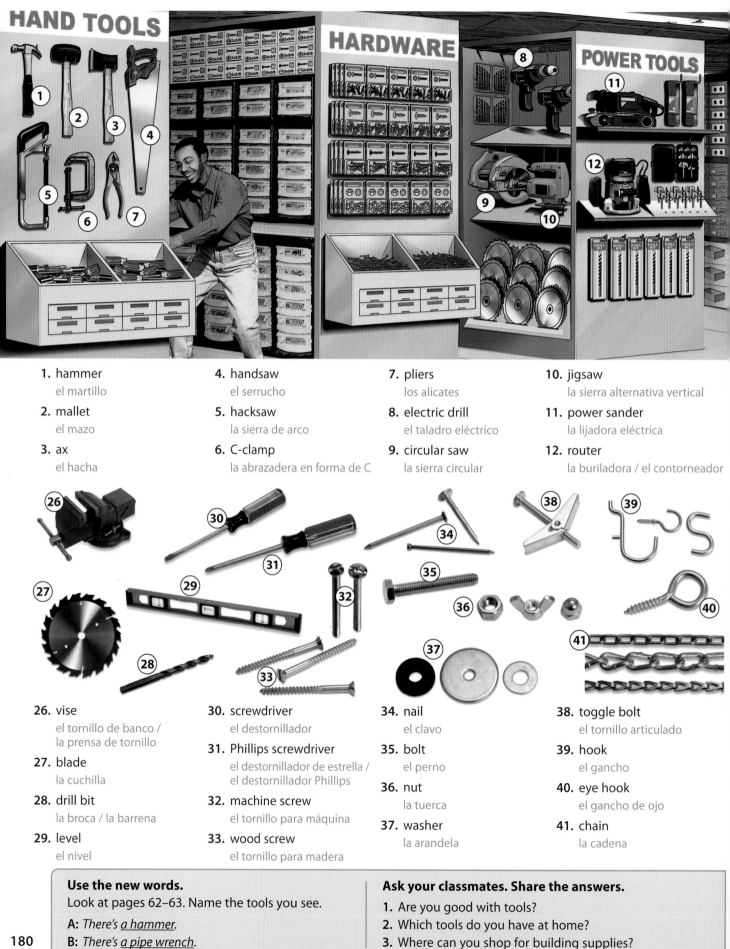

HAND TOOLS

HARDWARE

POWER TOOLS

1. hammer
el martillo

2. mallet
el mazo

3. ax
el hacha

4. handsaw
el serrucho

5. hacksaw
la sierra de arco

6. C-clamp
la abrazadera en forma de C

7. pliers
los alicates

8. electric drill
el taladro eléctrico

9. circular saw
la sierra circular

10. jigsaw
la sierra alternativa vertical

11. power sander
la lijadora eléctrica

12. router
la buriladora / el contorneador

26. vise
el tornillo de banco /
la prensa de tornillo

27. blade
la cuchilla

28. drill bit
la broca / la barrena

29. level
el nivel

30. screwdriver
el destornillador

31. Phillips screwdriver
el destornillador de estrella /
el destornillador Phillips

32. machine screw
el tornillo para máquina

33. wood screw
el tornillo para madera

34. nail
el clavo

35. bolt
el perno

36. nut
la tuerca

37. washer
la arandela

38. toggle bolt
el tornillo articulado

39. hook
el gancho

40. eye hook
el gancho de ojo

41. chain
la cadena

Use the new words.
Look at pages 62–63. Name the tools you see.

A: *There's a hammer.*
B: *There's a pipe wrench.*

Ask your classmates. Share the answers.

1. Are you good with tools?
2. Which tools do you have at home?
3. Where can you shop for building supplies?

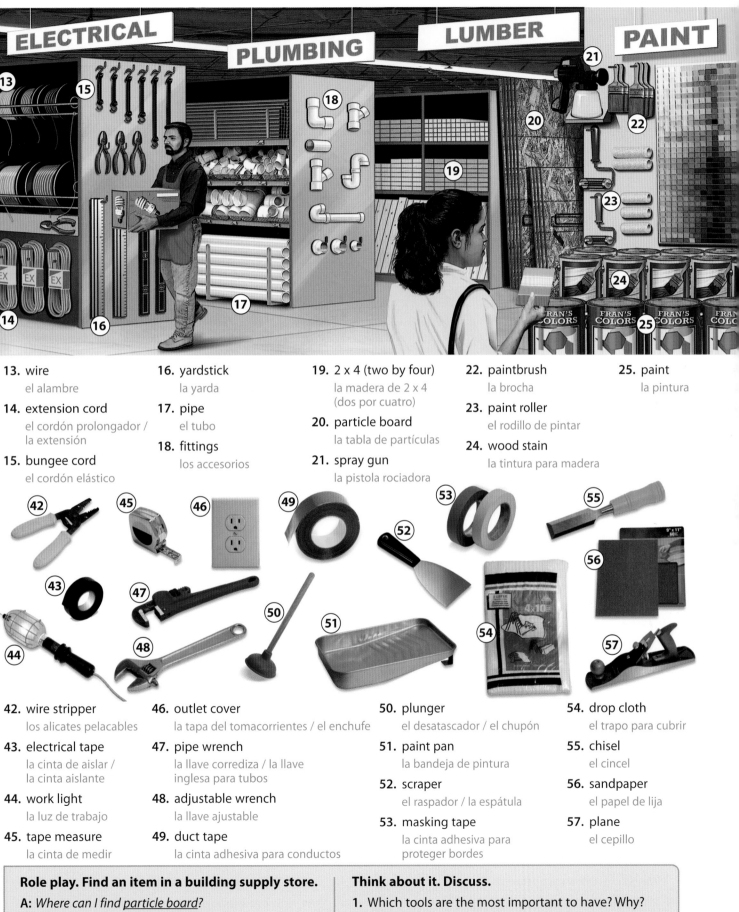

ELECTRICAL

PLUMBING

LUMBER

PAINT

FRAN'S COLORS

13. wire
el alambre

14. extension cord
el cordón prolongador /
la extensión

15. bungee cord
el cordón elástico

16. yardstick
la yarda

17. pipe
el tubo

18. fittings
los accesorios

19. 2 x 4 (two by four)
la madera de 2 x 4
(dos por cuatro)

20. particle board
la tabla de partículas

21. spray gun
la pistola rociadora

22. paintbrush
la brocha

23. paint roller
el rodillo de pintar

24. wood stain
la tintura para madera

25. paint
la pintura

42. wire stripper
los alicates pelacables

43. electrical tape
la cinta de aislar /
la cinta aislante

44. work light
la luz de trabajo

45. tape measure
la cinta de medir

46. outlet cover
la tapa del tomacorrientes / el enchufe

47. pipe wrench
la llave corrediza / la llave
inglesa para tubos

48. adjustable wrench
la llave ajustable

49. duct tape
la cinta adhesiva para conductos

50. plunger
el desatascador / el chupón

51. paint pan
la bandeja de pintura

52. scraper
el raspador / la espátula

53. masking tape
la cinta adhesiva para
proteger bordes

54. drop cloth
el trapo para cubrir

55. chisel
el cincel

56. sandpaper
el papel de lija

57. plane
el cepillo

Role play. Find an item in a building supply store.

A: *Where can I find particle board?*
B: *It's on the back wall, in the lumber section.*
A: *Great. And where are the nails?*

Think about it. Discuss.

1. Which tools are the most important to have? Why?
2. Which tools can be dangerous? Why?
3. Do you borrow tools from friends? Why or why not?

181

1. **supply cabinet**
   el gabinete de artículos
   de oficina
2. **clerk**
   el empleado
3. **janitor**
   el limpiador
4. **conference room**
   la sala de conferencias

5. **executive**
   el ejecutivo / la ejecutiva
6. **presentation**
   la presentación
7. **cubicle**
   el cubículo
8. **office manager**
   el gerente de oficina

9. **desk**
   el escritorio
10. **file clerk**
    el archivista
11. **file cabinet**
    el archivero / el fichero
12. **computer technician**
    el técnico de computadoras

13. **PBX**
    la centralita PBX
14. **receptionist**
    la recepcionista
15. **reception area**
    el área de recepción
16. **waiting area**
    área de espera

Ways to greet a receptionist

I'm here for a job interview.
I have a 9:00 a.m. appointment with Mr. Lee.
I'd like to leave a message for Mr. Lee.

Role play. Talk to a receptionist.

A: *Hello. How can I help you?*
B: *I'm here for a job interview with Mr. Lee.*
A: *OK. What is your name?*

An Office

Office Equipment Equipos de oficina

17. computer
el computador

18. inkjet printer
la impresora de chorro
de tinta

19. laser printer
la impresora láser

20. scanner
el escáner

21. fax machine
la máquina de fax / el fax

22. paper cutter
la cortadora de papel /
la guillotina

23. photocopier
la fotocopiadora

24. paper shredder
la trituradora de papel

25. calculator
la calculadora

26. electric pencil sharpener
el sacapuntas eléctrico

27. postal scale
la máquina franqueadora

Office Supplies Artículos de oficina

28. stapler
la engrapadora / la grapadora

29. staples
las grapas

30. clear tape
la cinta adhesiva transparente

31. paper clip
el clip / el sujetapapeles

32. packing tape
la cinta adhesiva para
empacar

33. glue
la goma / la pega

34. rubber band
la liga elástica

35. pushpin
la tachuela

36. correction fluid
el líquido corrector

37. correction tape
la cinta correctora

38. legal pad
el cuaderno de papel de
tamaño legal

39. sticky notes
el papel de notas adhesivo

40. mailer
el envase especial para remitir
objetos por correo

41. mailing label
la etiqueta engomada
de dirección postal

42. letterhead / stationery
el papel membreteado /
el papel de escribir

43. envelope
el sobre

44. rotary card file
el archivo de tarjetas giratorio

45. ink cartridge
el cartucho de tinta

46. ink pad
la almohadilla de tinta

47. stamp
el sello

48. appointment book
la libreta de citas

49. organizer
el organizador

50. file folder
la carpeta de archivo

183

VALET PARKING

1. doorman
el portero

2. revolving door
la puerta giratoria

3. parking attendant
el auxiliar de estacionamiento

4. concierge
el conserje

5. gift shop
la tienda de regalos

6. bell captain
el capitán de botones

7. bellhop
el botones

8. luggage cart
el carrito de maletas

9. elevator
el elevador / el ascensor

10. guest
el huésped

11. desk clerk
el recepcionista

12. front desk
la recepción

13. guest room
la habitación para huésped

14. double bed
doble cama

15. king-size bed
la cama doble amplia

16. suite
la suite

17. room service
el servicio en la habitación

18. hallway
el pasillo

19. housekeeping cart
el carrito de la limpieza

20. housekeeper
el ama de llaves

21. pool service
el servicio en la alberca / piscina

22. pool
la alberca / piscina

23. maintenance
el mantenimiento

24. gym
el gimnasio

25. meeting room
la sala de conferencias

26. ballroom
el salón de bailes

Food Service

A Restaurant Kitchen Una cocina de restaurante

1. short-order cook
el cocinero de platos rápidos

2. dishwasher
el lavaplatos

3. walk-in freezer
la cámara congeladora /
el almacén-congelador

4. food preparation worker
el preparador de comidas

5. storeroom
el almacén / la bodega

6. sous chef
el chef de partida /
el subchef

7. head chef / executive chef
el chef principal /
el chef ejecutivo

Restaurant Dining Comer en un restaurante

8. server
la mesera / la camarera

9. diner
el cliente

10. buffet
el buffet

11. maitre d'
el jefe de comedor

12. headwaiter
el capitán de meseros

13. bus person
el ayudante de meseros

14. banquet room
la sala de banquetes

15. runner
el servidor de comida

16. caterer
la encargada del servicio de
comida y bebidas

More vocabulary

line cook: short-order cook
wait staff: servers, headwaiters, and runners

Ask your classmates. Share the answers.

1. Have you ever worked in a hotel? What did you do?
2. What is the hardest job in a hotel?
3. Would you prefer to stay at a hotel in the city or in the country?

185

1. dangerous
   peligroso
2. clinic
   la clínica
3. budget
   el presupuesto
4. floor plan
   el plan del piso
5. contractor
   el contratista
6. electrical hazard
   el peligro eléctrico
7. wiring
   el cableado
8. bricklayer
   el albañil
A. **call in** sick
   ausentarse por enfermedad

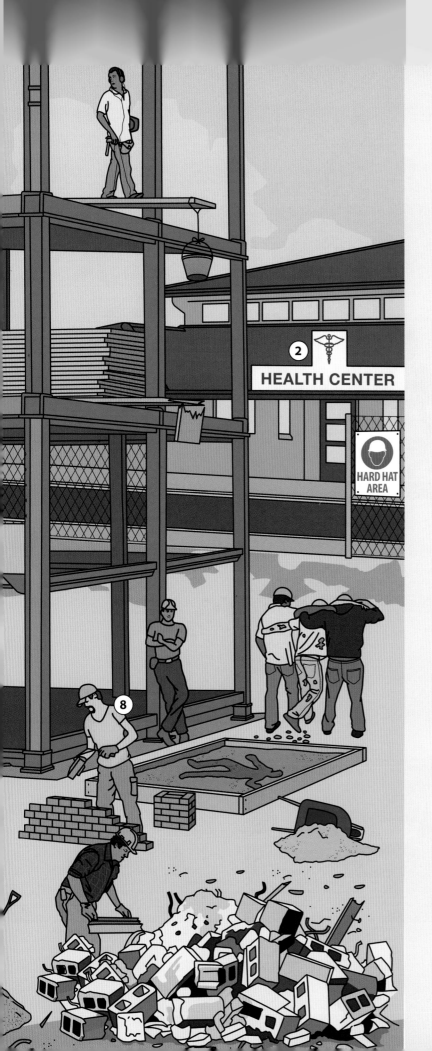

HEALTH CENTER

HARD HAT AREA

Look at the picture. What do you see?

Answer the questions.

1. How many workers are there? How many are working?

2. Why did two workers call in sick?

3. What is dangerous at the construction site?

📖 Read the story.

A Bad Day at Work

Sam Lopez is the <u>contractor</u> for a new building. He makes the schedule and supervises the <u>budget</u>. He also solves problems. Today there are a lot of problems.

Two <u>bricklayers</u> <u>called in sick</u> this morning. Now Sam has only one bricklayer at work. One hour later, a construction worker fell. Now he has to go to the <u>clinic</u>. Sam always tells his workers to be careful. Construction work is <u>dangerous</u>. Sam's also worried because the new <u>wiring</u> is an <u>electrical hazard</u>.

Right now, the building owner is in Sam's office. Her new <u>floor plan</u> has 25 more offices. Sam has a headache. Maybe he needs to call in sick tomorrow.

Think about it.

1. What do you say when you can't come in to work? to school?

2. Imagine you are Sam. What do you tell the building owner? Why?

1. preschool /
   nursery school
   la escuela de párvulos /
   el centro de enseñanza
   preescolar

2. elementary school
   la escuela primaria

3. middle school /
   junior high school
   la escuela intermedia

4. high school
   la escuela secundaria

5. vocational school /
   technical school
   la escuela vocacional /
   la escuela técnica

6. community college
   el instituto de
   enseñanza superior

7. college / university
   la universidad

8. adult school
   la escuela para adultos

1, 2, 3, 4

$3 + 3 = ?$

Name the 13 colonies.

Massachusetts   New Jersey
Rhode Island   Pennsylvania
Connecticut   Virginia
New Hampshire   Maryland
New York   Georgia
Delaware   North Carolina
South Carolina

Reasons for the Civil War

GED

Early Childhood Education

Listen and point. Take turns.

A: *Point to the preschool.*
B: *Point to the high school.*
A: *Point to the adult school.*

Dictate to your partner. Take turns.

A: *Write preschool.*
B: *Is that p-r-e-s-c-h-o-o-l?*
A: *Yes. That's right.*

9. language arts
   las artes del lenguaje
10. math
    las matemáticas
11. science
    las ciencias
12. history
    la historia
13. world languages
    los idiomas del mundo
14. ESL / ESOL
    el inglés como segundo idioma (ESL) / el inglés para hablantes de otros idiomas (ESOL)
15. arts
    las artes
16. music
    la música
17. physical education
    la educación física

More vocabulary

core course: a subject students have to take. Math is a core course.

elective: a subject students choose to take. Art is an elective.

Pair practice. Make new conversations.

A: *I go to community college.*

B: *What subjects are you taking?*

A: *I'm taking history and science.*

189

1. word
la palabra

2. sentence
la oración

3. paragraph
el párrafo

4. essay
el ensayo / la composición

(1) factory

(2) I worked in a factory.

(3) Little by little, work and success came to me. My first job wasn't good. I worked in a small factory. Now, I help manage two factories.

(4) *[essay card: Carlos Lopez, Eng. Comp. 10/21/10 — Success in the U.S.]*

Parts of an Essay
Las partes de un ensayo

5. title
el título

6. introduction
la introducción

7. body
el cuerpo

8. conclusion
la conclusión

9. quotation
la cita

10. footnote
la nota al pie
de la página

> Carlos Lopez
> Eng. Comp.
> 10/21/10
>
> (5) Success in the U.S.
>
> (6) I came to Los Angeles from Mexico in 2006. I had no job, no friends, and no family here. I was homesick and scared, but I did not go home. I took English classes (always at night) and I studied hard. I believed in my future success!
>
> (7) More than 400,000 new immigrants come to the U.S every year.[1] Most of us need to find work. During my first year here, my routine was the same: get up; look for work; go to class; go to bed. I had to take jobs with long hours and low pay. Often I had two or three jobs.
>
> Little by little, work and success came to me. My first job wasn't good. I worked in a small factory. Now, I help manage two factories.
>
> (8) Hard work makes success possible. Henry David Thoreau said, (9) "Men are born to succeed, not fail." My story shows that he was right.
>
> (10) [1] U.S. Census

Punctuation
La puntuación

11. period
el punto

12. question mark
el signo de interrogación

13. exclamation mark
el signo de exclamación

14. comma
la coma

15. quotation marks
las comillas

16. apostrophe
el apóstrofe

17. colon
los dos puntos

18. semicolon
el punto y coma

19. parentheses
los paréntesis

20. hyphen
el guión

Writing Rules Las reglas de escritura

A
Carlos
Mexico
Los Angeles

B
Hard work makes success possible.

C
I was homesick and scared, but I did not go home.

D
I came to Los Angeles from Mexico in 2006. I had no job, no friends, and no family here. I was homesick and scared, but I did not go home. I took English classes (always at night) and I studied hard. I believed in my future success!

A. Capitalize names.
Capitalizar los nombres.

B. Capitalize the first letter in a sentence.
Capitalizar la primera letra de una oración.

C. Use punctuation.
Usar la puntuación.

D. Indent the first sentence in a paragraph.
Indentar la primera oración de un párrafo.

Ways to ask for suggestions on your compositions

What do you think of this title?

Is this paragraph OK? Is the punctuation correct?

Do you have any suggestions for the conclusion?

Pair practice. Make new conversations.

A: What do you think of this *title*?

B: I think you need to *revise* it.

A: Thanks. Do you have any more suggestions?

The Writing Process El proceso de escritura

PREWRITING

E. **Think about** the assignment.
Piense sobre la tarea.

F. **Brainstorm** ideas.
Fórmese ideas.

G. **Organize** your ideas.
Organice las ideas.

WRITING AND REVISING

H. **Write** a first draft.
Escriba un primer borrador.

I. **Edit**. / **Proofread**.
Edítelo. / Corríjalo.

J. **Revise**. / **Rewrite**.
Revíselo. / Reescríbalo.

SHARING AND RESPONDING

K. **Get** feedback.
Reciba comentarios.

L. **Write** a final draft.
Escriba el borrador final.

M. **Turn in** your paper.
Entregue su papel.

Ask your classmates. Share the answers.

1. Do you like to write essays?
2. Which part of the writing process do you like best? least?

Think about it. Discuss.

1. In which jobs are writing skills important?
2. What tools can help you edit your writing?
3. What are some good subjects for essays?

Mathematics
Las matemáticas

Integers Los números enteros

$$...-4\ -3\ -2\ -1\ 0\ 1\ 2\ 3\ 4...$$

① ②

1. negative integers
los números enteros negativos

2. positive integers
los números enteros positivos

Fractions Las fracciones

③ 1, 3, 5, 7, 9, 11...

④ 2, 4, 6, 8, 10 ...

$\dfrac{3}{8}$ ⑤ ⑥ $\dfrac{3}{8}$

3. odd numbers
los números impares

4. even numbers
los números pares

5. numerator
el numerador

6. denominator
el denominador

Math Operations Las operaciones matemáticas

A. add
sumar

B. subtract
restar

C. multiply
multiplicar

D. divide
dividir

A $8 + 4 = 12$ ⑦

B $8 - 4 = 4$ ⑧

C $8 \times 4 = 32$ ⑨

D $8 \div 4 = 2$ ⑩

7. sum
la suma

8. difference
la diferencia

9. product
el producto

10. quotient
el cociente

A Math Problem Un problema matemático

⑪
Tom is 10 years older than Kim. Next year he will be twice as old as Kim. How old is Tom this year?

⑫ — x = Kim's age now
$x + 10$ = Tom's age now
$x + 1$ = Kim's age next year
$2(x + 1)$ = Tom's age next year

$x + 10 + 1 = 2(x + 1)$
$x + 11 = 2x + 2$
$11 - 2 = 2x - x$
⑬

$x = 9$, Kim is 9, Tom is 19 ⑭

⑮

horizontal axis

vertical axis

11. word problem
un problema expresado con palabras

12. variable
la variable

13. equation
la ecuación

14. solution
la solución

15. graph
la gráfica

Types of Math Los tipos de matemática

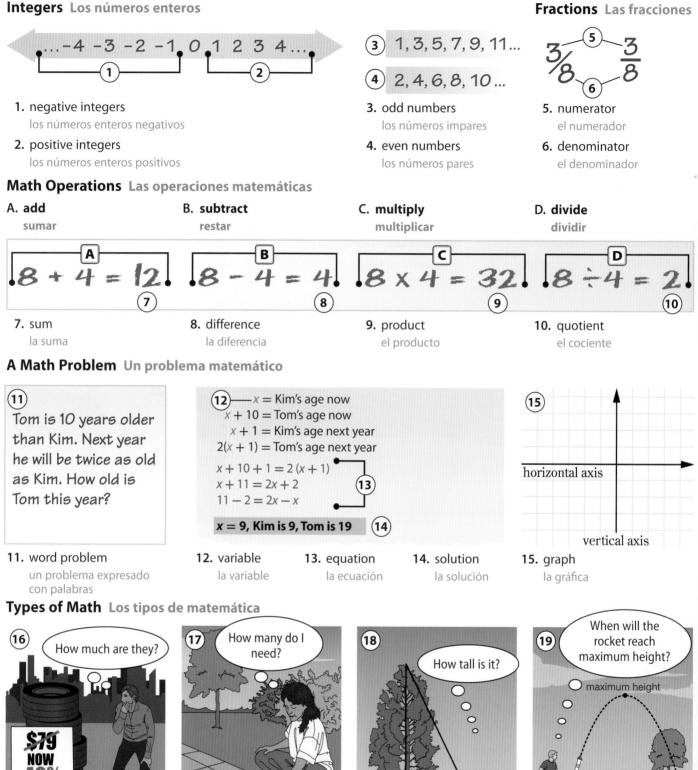

⑯ How much are they?

\$79 NOW **40% OFF!**

x = the sale price
$x = 79.00 - .40\,(79.00)$
$x = \$47.40$

⑰ How many do I need?

area of path = 24 square ft.
area of brick = 2 square ft.
$24 / 2 = 12$ bricks

⑱ How tall is it?

14 ft.

$\tan 63° = $ height $/ 14$ feet
height = 14 feet $(\tan 63°)$
height $\simeq 27.48$ feet

⑲ When will the rocket reach maximum height?

maximum height

$s(t) = -\frac{1}{2}\,gt^2 + V_0\,t + h$
$s^{l}(t) = -gt + V_0 = 0$
$t = V_0 / g$

16. algebra
el álgebra

17. geometry
la geometría

18. trigonometry
la trigonometría

19. calculus
el cálculo

Mathematics

Lines
Las líneas

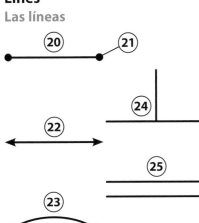

Angles
Los ángulos

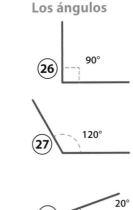

Shapes
Las formas

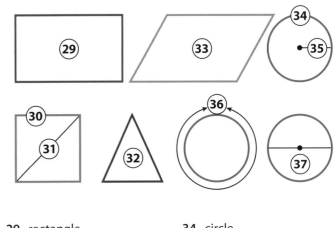

20. line segment
    el segmento de línea

21. endpoint
    el punto extremo

22. straight line
    la línea recta

23. curved line
    la línea curva

24. perpendicular lines
    las líneas perpendiculares

25. parallel lines
    las líneas paralelas

26. right angle / 90° angle
    el ángulo recto /
    el ángulo de 90°

27. obtuse angle
    el ángulo obtuso

28. acute angle
    el ángulo agudo

29. rectangle
    el rectángulo

30. square
    el cuadrado

31. diagonal
    la diagonal

32. triangle
    el triángulo

33. parallelogram
    el paralelogramo

34. circle
    el círculo

35. radius
    el radio

36. circumference
    la circunferencia

37. diameter
    el diámetro

Geometric Solids
Los sólidos geométricos

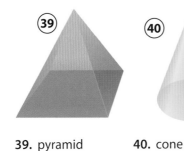

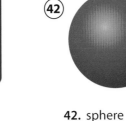

Measuring Area and Volume
La medición de área y volumen

$\ell \times w =$ area

$6 \times f =$ surface area

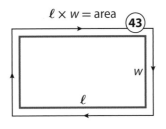
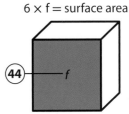

38. cube
    el cubo

39. pyramid
    la pirámide

40. cone
    el cono

41. cylinder
    el cilindro

42. sphere
    la esfera

43. perimeter
    el perímetro

44. face
    la cara

$\pi \times r^2 \times h =$ volume

$\frac{4}{3} \times \pi \times r^3 =$ volume

$\pi \approx 3.14$

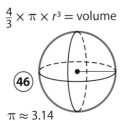

45. base
    la base

46. pi
    pi

Ask your classmates. Share the answers.

1. Are you good at math?
2. Which types of math are easy for you?
3. Which types of math are difficult for you?

Think about it. Discuss.

1. What's the best way to learn mathematics?
2. How can you find the area of your classroom?
3. Which jobs use math? Which don't?

Science

Biology La biología

1. organisms
   los organismos
2. biologist
   el biólogo
3. slide
   la platina
4. cell
   la célula
5. cell wall
   la pared de la célula
6. cell membrane
   la membrana de
   la célula
7. nucleus
   el núcleo
8. chromosome
   el cromosoma
9. cytoplasm
   el citoplasma

THE DESERT

THE OCEAN

10. photosynthesis
    la fotosíntesis
11. habitat
    el hábitat
12. vertebrates
    los vertebrados
13. invertebrates
    los invertebrados

A Microscope Un microscopio

14. eyepiece
    el ocular
15. revolving nosepiece
    el portaobjetivo rotatorio
16. objective
    el objetivo
17. stage
    el portaobjetos
18. diaphragm
    el diafragma
19. light source
    la fuente de luz
20. base
    la base
21. stage clips
    las presillas del portaobjetos
22. fine adjustment knob
    la perilla de ajuste fino
23. arm
    el brazo
24. coarse adjustment knob
    la perilla de ajuste grueso

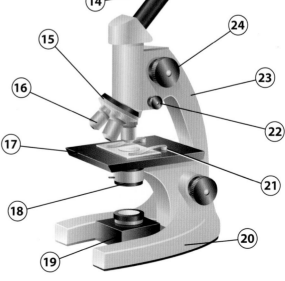

194

Chemistry La química

Physics La física

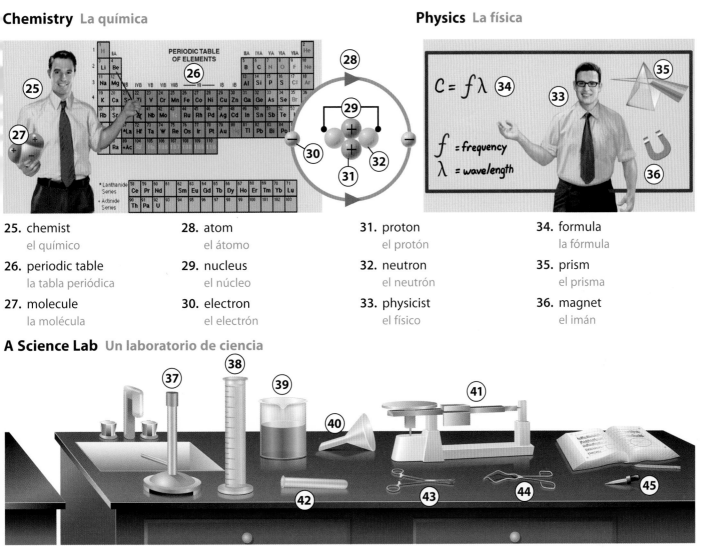

25. chemist
el químico

26. periodic table
la tabla periódica

27. molecule
la molécula

28. atom
el átomo

29. nucleus
el núcleo

30. electron
el electrón

31. proton
el protón

32. neutron
el neutrón

33. physicist
el físico

34. formula
la fórmula

35. prism
el prisma

36. magnet
el imán

A Science Lab Un laboratorio de ciencia

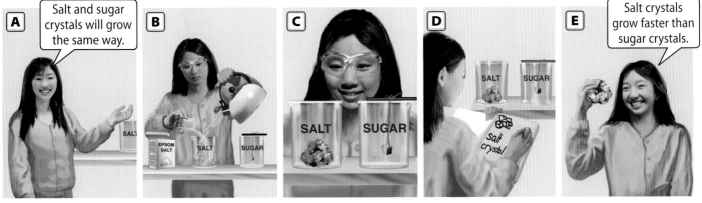

37. Bunsen burner
el quemador Bunsen

38. graduated cylinder
el cilindro graduado

39. beaker
el vaso de laboratorio

40. funnel
el embudo

41. balance / scale
la balanza / la escala

42. test tube
el tubo de pruebas

43. forceps
las tenazas

44. crucible tongs
las tenazas para crisol

45. dropper
el gotero

An Experiment Un experimento

A. **State** a hypothesis.
Establezca una hipótesis.

B. **Do** an experiment.
Haga un experimento.

C. **Observe.**
Observe.

D. **Record** the results.
Anote los resultados.

E. **Draw** a conclusion.
Saque una conclusión.

195

Desktop Computer Los computadores de escritorio

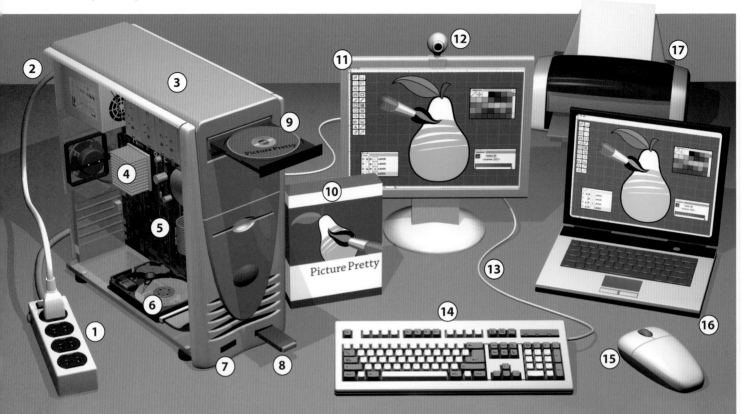

1. surge protector
   el protector de sobretensiones

2. power cord
   el cordón de alimentación

3. tower
   la torre / la caja

4. microprocessor / CPU
   el microprocesador / la CPU

5. motherboard
   la tarjeta principal / la tarjeta madre

6. hard drive
   el disco duro

7. USB port
   el puerto USB

8. flash drive
   la unidad flash

9. DVD and CD-ROM drive
   la unidad para discos DVD y CD-ROM

10. software
    el software / los programas

11. monitor / screen
    el monitor / la pantalla

12. webcam
    la cámara Web

13. cable
    el cable

14. keyboard
    el teclado

15. mouse
    el ratón

16. laptop
    la computadora portátil

17. printer
    la impresora

Keyboarding Uso del teclado

A. **type**
escriba con el teclado

B. **select**
seleccione

C. **delete**
borre

D. **go to** the next line
pase a la siguiente línea

Navigating a Webpage Cómo navegar por una página Web

1. **menu bar**
   la barra de menús
2. **back button**
   el botón de retroceso
3. **forward button**
   el botón de avance

4. **URL / website address**
   el URL / la dirección
   de un sitio Web
5. **search box**
   el campo de búsqueda
6. **search engine**
   el motor de búsqueda

7. **tab**
   la pestaña
8. **drop-down menu**
   el menú desplegable
9. **pop-up ad**
   el aviso emergente

10. **links**
    los enlaces
11. **video player**
    el reproductor de video
12. **pointer**
    el puntero

13. **text box**
    el campo
    de texto
14. **cursor**
    el cursor
15. **scroll bar**
    la barra de
    avance

Logging on and Sending Email Cómo abrir sesión y enviar un correo electrónico

A. **type** your password
   introduzca su contraseña
B. **click** "sign in"
   haga clic en "registrar entrada"

C. **address** the email
   **ponga o escriba la dirección de correo
   electrónico** del destinatario del correo
   electrónico

D. **type** the subject
   escriba el tema
E. **type** the message
   escriba el mensaje

F. **check** your spelling
   revise su ortografía

G. **attach** a picture
   adjunte una foto

H. **attach** a file
   adjunte un archivo

I. **send** the email
   envíe el correo electrónico   **197**

U.S. History

La historia de EE.UU.

Colonial Period El período colonial

New Hampshire
Massachusetts
Connecticut
New York
Rhode Island
Pennsylvania
New Jersey
Delaware
Virginia Maryland
North Carolina
South Carolina
Georgia

1. thirteen colonies
las trece colonias

2. colonists
los colonos

3. Native Americans
los americanos nativos

4. slave
el esclavo

5. Declaration of Independence
la declaración de la independencia

6. First Continental Congress
el primer congreso continental

7. founders
los fundadores

8. Revolutionary War
la guerra revolucionaria

9. redcoat
los casaca roja

10. minuteman
los milicianos

11. first president
el primer presidente

12. Constitution
la constitución

13. Bill of Rights
la declaración de derechos

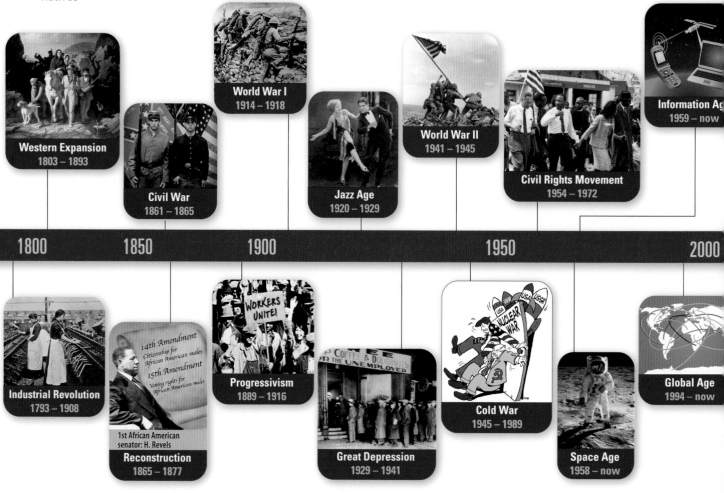

Western Expansion
1803 – 1893

Civil War
1861 – 1865

World War I
1914 – 1918

Jazz Age
1920 – 1929

World War II
1941 – 1945

Civil Rights Movement
1954 – 1972

Information Age
1959 – now

1800 1850 1900 1950 2000

Industrial Revolution
1793 – 1908

1st African American senator: H. Revels
Reconstruction
1865 – 1877

Progressivism
1889 – 1916

Great Depression
1929 – 1941

Cold War
1945 – 1989

Space Age
1958 – now

Global Age
1994 – now

Civilizations Las civilizaciones

Pyramids **1** Parthenon

2

Times Square

Caesar

3

Qin Shi Huang

King Henry VIII

4

Queen Elizabeth I

5

Juarez

6

Mussolini

7

Churchill

1. ancient
   antiguas
2. modern
   modernas

3. emperor
   el emperador
4. monarch
   el monarca

5. president
   el presidente
6. dictator
   el dictador

7. prime minister
   el primer ministro

Historical Terms Los términos históricos

8

9

Vikings Astronauts

10

11

12

13

8. exploration
   la exploración
9. explorer
   el explorador

10. war
    la guerra
11. army
    el ejército

12. immigration
    la inmigración
13. immigrant
    el inmigrante

14

15

Mozart Duke Ellington

16

17

Susan B. Anthony César Chávez

18

19

Edison Camarena

14. composer
    el compositor
15. composition
    la composición

16. political movement
    el movimiento político
17. activist
    el activista

18. inventor
    el inventor
19. invention
    la invención

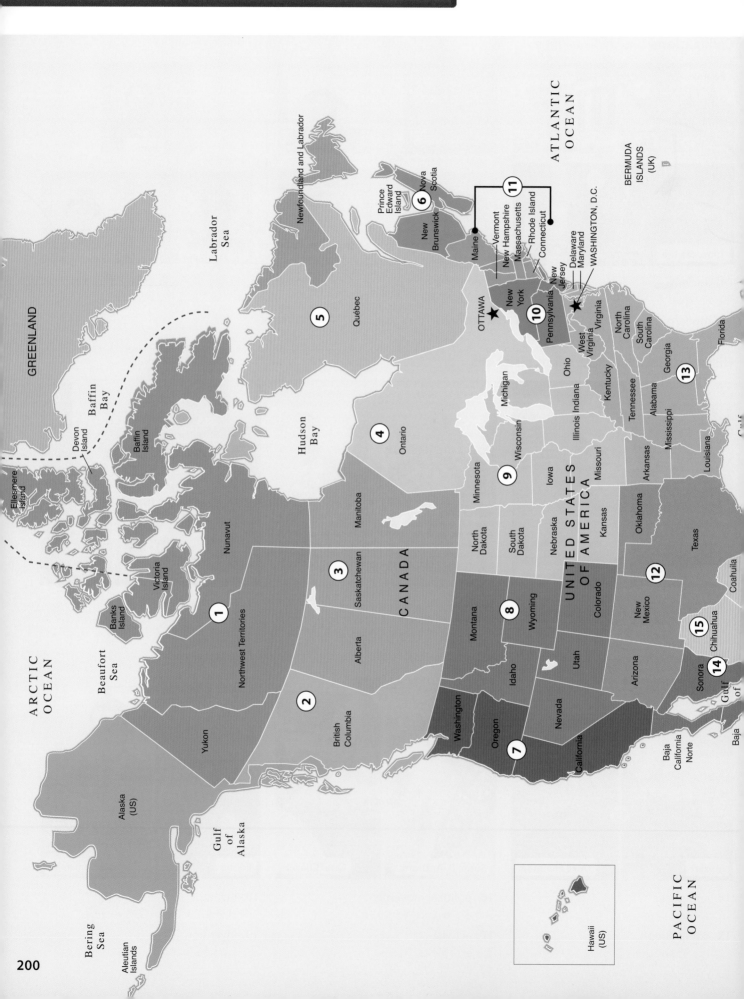

ATLANTIC OCEAN

BERMUDA ISLANDS (UK)

GREENLAND

Baffin Bay

Labrador Sea

Newfoundland and Labrador

Prince Edward Island

Nova Scotia

New Brunswick

(6)

(11)

Maine

Vermont
New Hampshire
Massachusetts
Rhode Island
Connecticut

Delaware
Maryland
WASHINGTON, D.C.

New Jersey

Devon Island

Baffin Island

Ellesmere Island

Hudson Bay

Québec

(5)

New York

OTTAWA

Pennsylvania

(10)

West Virginia

Virginia

North Carolina

South Carolina

Florida

Ohio

Michigan

Indiana

Kentucky

Tennessee

Georgia

(13)

Alabama

Victoria Island

Banks Island

Nunavut

Ontario

(4)

Wisconsin

(9)

Illinois

Missouri

Arkansas

Mississippi

Louisiana

Gulf

Minnesota

Iowa

Saskatchewan

(3)

Manitoba

CANADA

North Dakota

South Dakota

Nebraska

Kansas

Oklahoma

(12)

Texas

Coahuila

ARCTIC OCEAN

Beaufort Sea

Northwest Territories

(1)

Alberta

British Columbia

(2)

Montana

(8)

Wyoming

UNITED STATES OF AMERICA

Colorado

New Mexico

Arizona

Chihuahua

(15)

Sonora

(14)

Gulf of

Yukon

Idaho

Utah

Nevada

Washington

Oregon

(7)

California

Baja California Norte

Baja

Alaska (US)

Gulf of Alaska

Bering Sea

Aleutian Islands

PACIFIC OCEAN

Hawaii (US)

Lesser Antilles

Puerto Rico (US)

HAITI
DOMINICAN REPUBLIC

Hispaniola

JAMAICA

Greater Antilles

Caribbean Sea

NICARAGUA

PANAMA

BELIZE

HONDURAS

COSTA RICA

EL SALVADOR

GUATEMALA

Quintana Roo

Yucatán

Campeche

Chiapas

Tabasco

Veracruz

Oaxaca

Morelos

Guerrero

Puebla

DISTRITO FEDERAL

Michoacán

Colima

Jalisco

Guanajuato

Nayarit

Aguascalientes

Potosí

Querétaro
Hidalgo
México
Tlaxcala

⑰

⑱

⑲

EAST

NORTH

SOUTH

WEST

Regions of Canada
Las regiones de Canadá

1. Northern Canada
   Canadá del Norte

2. British Columbia
   Columbia Británica

3. The Prairie Provinces
   Las Provincias de las praderas

4. Ontario
   Ontario

5. Québec
   Québec

6. The Maritime Provinces
   Las Provincias marítimas

Regions of the United States
Las regiones de Estados Unidos

7. The Pacific States / the West Coast
   Los estados del Pacífico / la costa oeste

8. The Rocky Mountain States
   Los estados de las Montañas Rocosas

9. The Midwest
   El medio oeste

10. The Mid-Atlantic States
    Los estados del centro del Atlántico

11. New England
    Nueva Inglaterra

12. The Southwest
    El suroeste

13. The Southeast / the South
    El sureste / El sur

Regions of Mexico
Las regiones de México

14. The Pacific Northwest
    El noroeste del Pacífico

15. The Plateau of Mexico
    El altiplano de México

16. The Gulf Coastal Plain
    La planicie de la costa del Golfo

17. The Southern Uplands
    Las mesetas del sur

18. The Chiapas Highlands
    Las regiones montañosas de Chiapas

19. The Yucatan Peninsula
    La península de Yucatán

Continents
Los continentes

1. **North America**
   Norte América
2. **South America**
   Sur América
3. **Europe**
   Europa
4. **Asia**
   Asia
5. **Africa**
   África
6. **Australia**
   Australia
7. **Antarctica**
   Antártica

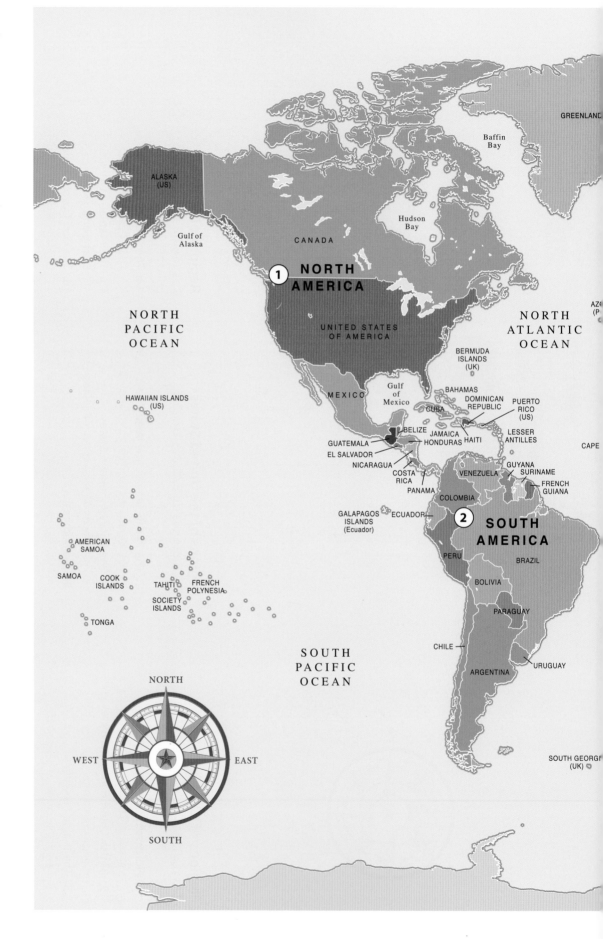

1. rain forest
el bosque húmedo /
la selva tropical
húmeda

2. waterfall
la cascada / el salto
de agua / la catarata

3. river
el río

4. desert
el desierto

5. sand dune
la duna

6. ocean
el océano

7. peninsula
la península

8. island
la isla

9. bay
la bahía

10. beach
la playa

11. forest
el bosque

12. shore
la orilla

13. lake
el lago

14. mountain peak
el pico / la cima
de la montaña

15. mountain range
la cordillera /
la sierra

16. hills
las colinas

17. canyon
el cañón

18. valley
el valle

19. plains
el llano / la llanura

20. meadow
la pradera / el prado

21. pond
el estanque /
la charca / la laguna

More vocabulary

a body of water: a river, lake, or ocean
stream / creek: a very small river

Ask your classmates. Share the answers.

1. Would you rather live near a river or a lake?
2. Would you rather travel through a forest or a desert?
3. How often do you go to the beach or the shore?

The Universe

The Solar System and the Planets El sistema solar y los planetas

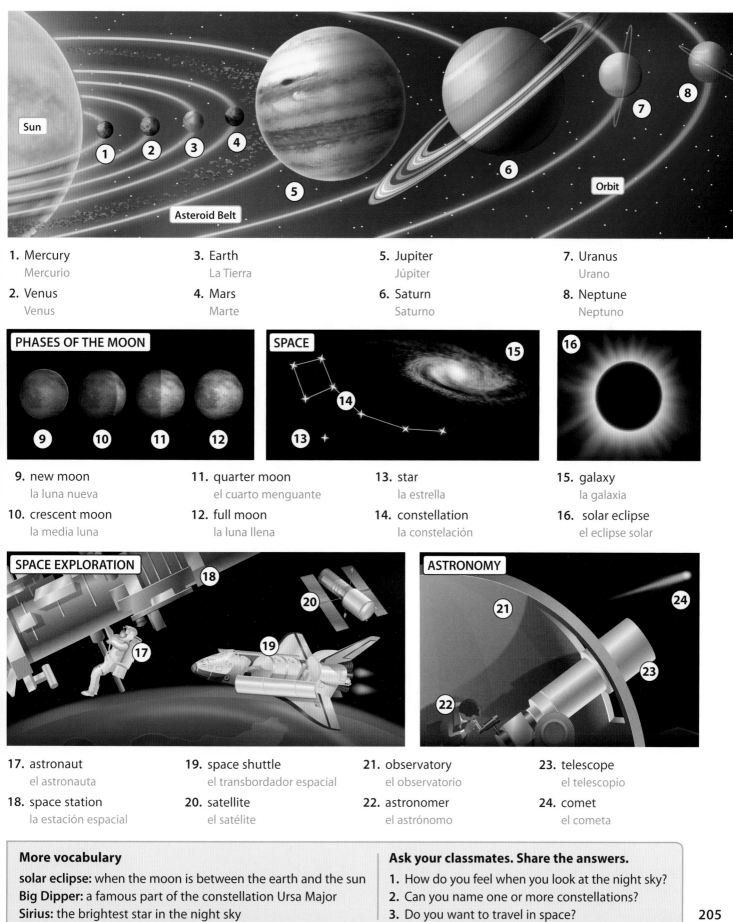

1. Mercury
   Mercurio
2. Venus
   Venus

3. Earth
   La Tierra
4. Mars
   Marte

5. Jupiter
   Júpiter
6. Saturn
   Saturno

7. Uranus
   Urano
8. Neptune
   Neptuno

PHASES OF THE MOON

SPACE

9. new moon
   la luna nueva
10. crescent moon
    la media luna

11. quarter moon
    el cuarto menguante
12. full moon
    la luna llena

13. star
    la estrella
14. constellation
    la constelación

15. galaxy
    la galaxia
16. solar eclipse
    el eclipse solar

SPACE EXPLORATION

ASTRONOMY

17. astronaut
    el astronauta
18. space station
    la estación espacial

19. space shuttle
    el transbordador espacial
20. satellite
    el satélite

21. observatory
    el observatorio
22. astronomer
    el astrónomo

23. telescope
    el telescopio
24. comet
    el cometa

More vocabulary

solar eclipse: when the moon is between the earth and the sun
Big Dipper: a famous part of the constellation Ursa Major
Sirius: the brightest star in the night sky

Ask your classmates. Share the answers.

1. How do you feel when you look at the night sky?
2. Can you name one or more constellations?
3. Do you want to travel in space?

205

MySpot.Edu | Help | SignOut

Home | **Search** | **Invite** | **Mail** |

All Adelia's photos

I loved Art History.

My last economics lesson

Marching Band is great!

The photographer was upset.

We look good!

I get my diploma.

Dad and his digital camera

1. photographer el fotógrafo	3. serious photo la foto seria	5. podium el podio	7. cap el birrete	A. **take** a picture **tomar** una foto	C. **celebrate** **celebrar**
2. funny photo la foto chistosa	4. guest speaker el orador invitado	6. ceremony la ceremonia	8. gown la toga	B. **cry** **llorar**	

Videos | Music | Classifieds |

People	Comments	
Sara	**June 29th 8:19 p.m.**	
	Great pictures! What a day!	Delete
Zannie baby	**June 30th 10 a.m.**	
	Love the funny photo.	Delete

I'm behind the mayor.

We're all very happy.

Look at the pictures. What do you see?

Answer the questions.

1. How many people are wearing caps and gowns?

2. How many people are being funny? How many are being serious?

3. Who is standing at the podium?

4. Why are the graduates throwing their caps in the air?

📖 Read the story.

A Graduation

Look at these great photos on my web page! The first three are from my favorite classes, but the other pictures are from graduation day.

There are two pictures of my classmates in <u>caps</u> and <u>gowns</u>. In the first picture, we're laughing and the <u>photographer</u> is upset. In the second photo, we're serious. I like the <u>serious photo</u>, but I love the <u>funny photo</u>!

There's also a picture of our <u>guest speaker</u>, the mayor. She is standing at the <u>podium</u>. Next, you can see me at the graduation <u>ceremony</u>. My dad wanted to <u>take a picture</u> of me with my diploma. That's my mom next to him. She <u>cries</u> when she's happy.

After the ceremony, everyone was happy, but no one cried. We wanted to <u>celebrate</u> and we did!

Think about it.

1. What kinds of ceremonies are important for children? for teens? for adults?

2. Imagine you are the guest speaker at a graduation. What will you say to the graduates?

207

Nature Center — El centro ecológico

1. trees
   los árboles
2. soil
   la tierra
3. path
   el sendero
4. bird
   el pájaro
5. plants
   las plantas
6. rock
   la roca
7. flowers
   las flores

Listen and point. Take turns.

A: *Point to the trees.*
B: *Point to a bird.*
A: *Point to the flowers.*

Dictate to your partner. Take turns.

A: *Write it's a tree.*
B: *Let me check that. I-t-'s -a- t-r-e-e?*
A: *Yes, that's right.*

208

8. sun
   el sol

9. sky
   el cielo

10. mammals
    los mamíferos

11. insects
    los insectos

12. nest
    el nido

13. water
    el agua

14. fish
    los peces

Ways to talk about nature

Look at the sky! Isn't it beautiful?
Did you see the fish / insects?
It's / They're so interesting.

Pair practice. Make new conversations.

A: *Do you know the name of that yellow flower?*
B: *I think it's a sunflower.*
A: *Oh, and what about that blue bird?*

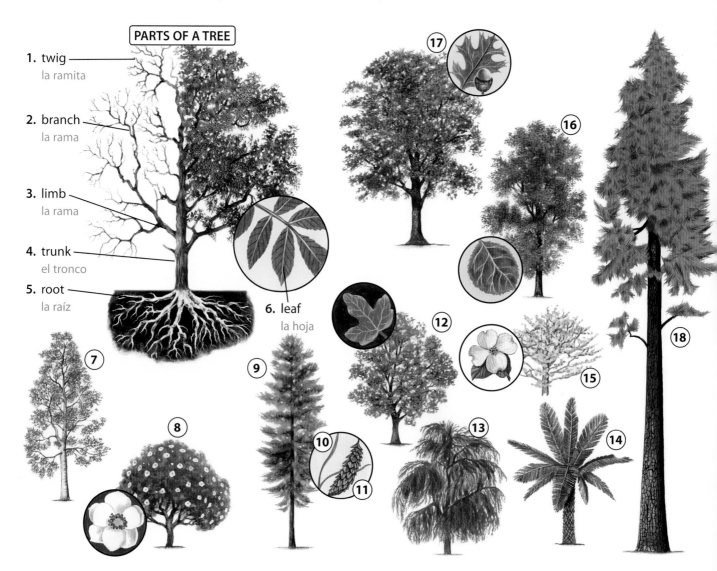

PARTS OF A TREE

1. twig
   la ramita

2. branch
   la rama

3. limb
   la rama

4. trunk
   el tronco

5. root
   la raíz

6. leaf
   la hoja

7. birch
   el abedul

8. magnolia
   la magnolia

9. pine
   el pino

10. needle
    la aguja

11. pinecone
    la piña / el cono

12. maple
    el arce

13. willow
    el sauce

14. palm
    la palma

15. dogwood
    el cornejo / el cerezo silvestre

16. elm
    el olmo

17. oak
    el roble

18. redwood
    la secoya

Plants Plantas

19. holly
    el acebo

20. berries
    las bayas

21. cactus
    el cactus

22. vine
    la enredadera

23. poison sumac
    el zumaque venenoso

24. poison oak
    el árbol de las pulgas

25. poison ivy
    la hiedra venenosa

210

Parts of a Flower Partes de una flor

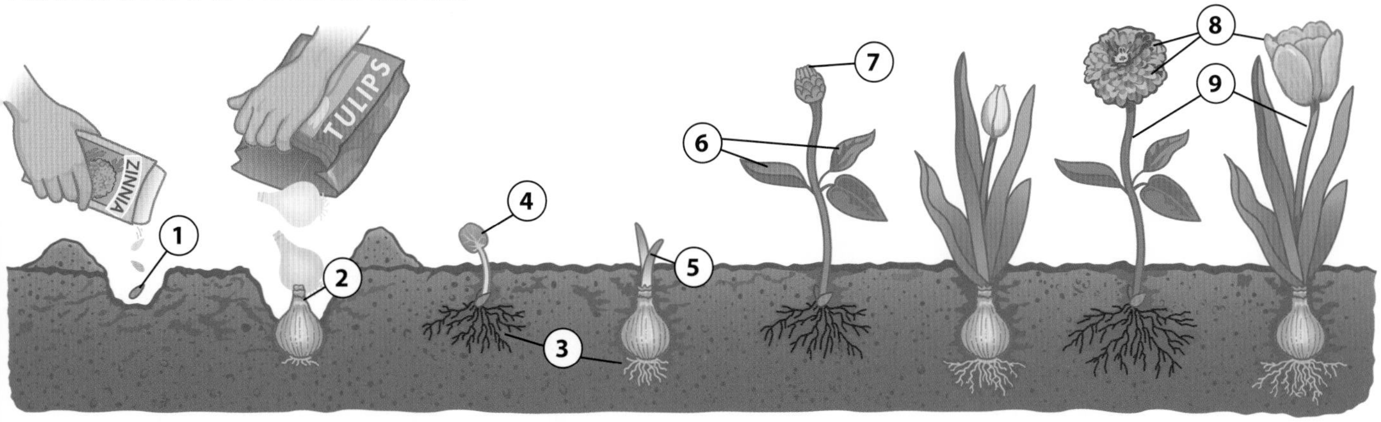

1. seed
   la semilla

2. bulb
   el bulbo

3. roots
   las raíces

4. seedling
   la plántula / el pimpollo

5. shoot
   el brote

6. leaves
   las hojas

7. bud
   el capullo

8. petals
   los pétalos

9. stems
   los tallos

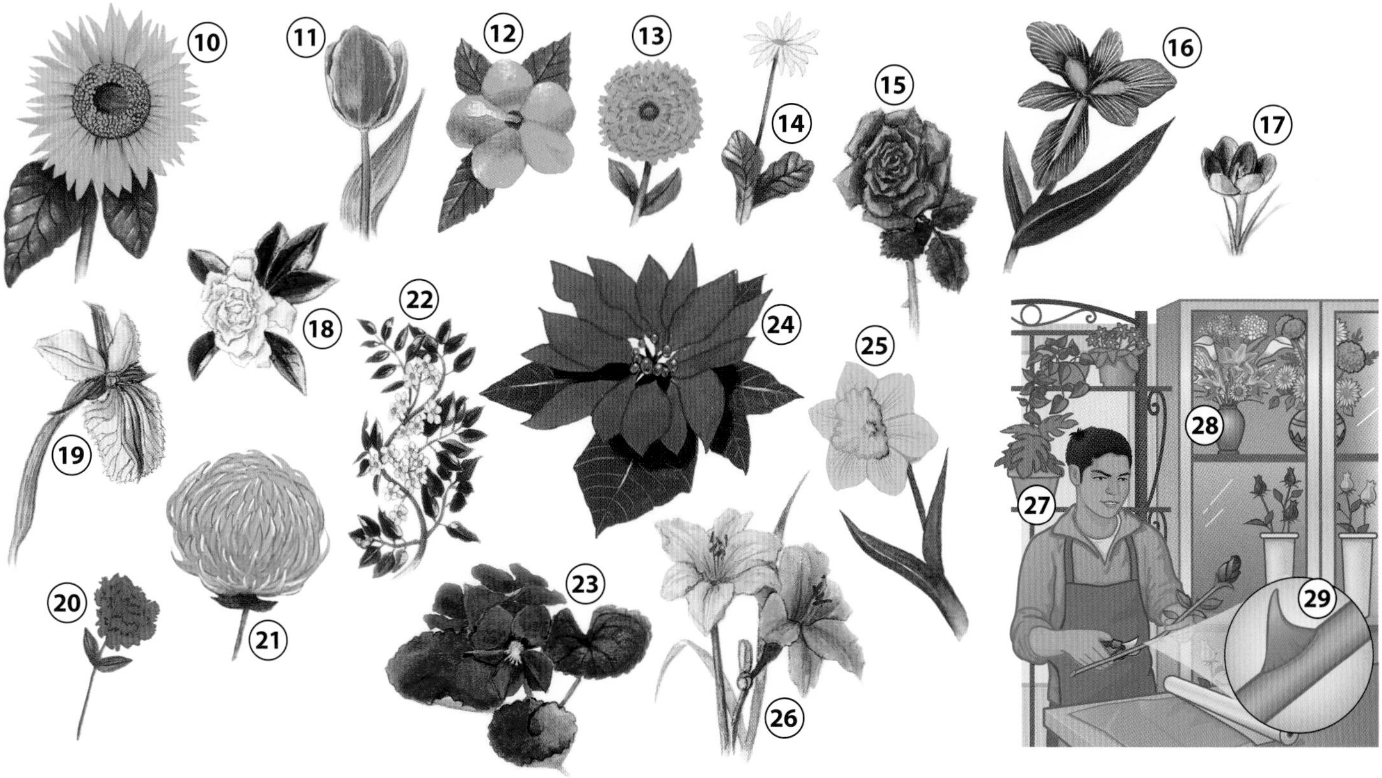

10. sunflower
    el girasol

11. tulip
    el tulipán

12. hibiscus
    el hibisco

13. marigold
    la maravilla / el clavelón

14. daisy
    la margarita

15. rose
    la rosa

16. iris
    el lirio

17. crocus
    el azafrán

18. gardenia
    la gardenia

19. orchid
    la orquídea

20. carnation
    el clavel

21. chrysanthemum
    el crisantemo

22. jasmine
    el jazmín

23. violet
    la violeta

24. poinsettia
    la flor de Nochebuena /
    la pascua

25. daffodil
    el narciso atrompetado /
    el trompón

26. lily
    la azucena / el lirio

27. houseplant
    la planta para interiores

28. bouquet
    el ramo / el ramillete

29. thorn
    la espina

211

Sea Animals Fauna marina

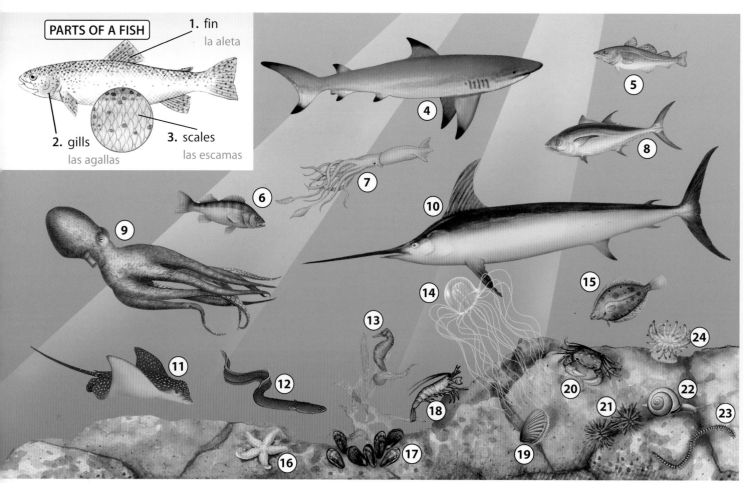

PARTS OF A FISH

1. fin
   la aleta

2. gills
   las agallas

3. scales
   las escamas

4. shark
   el tiburón

5. cod
   el bacalao / el abadejo

6. bass
   el róbalo / la percha

7. squid
   el calamar

8. tuna
   el atún

9. octopus
   el pulpo

10. swordfish
    el pez espada

11. ray
    la raya

12. eel
    la anguila

13. seahorse
    el caballo de mar

14. jellyfish
    la medusa

15. flounder
    el lenguado

16. starfish
    la estrella de mar

17. mussel
    el mejillón

18. shrimp
    el camarón

19. scallop
    la venera / el escalope

20. crab
    el cangrejo

21. sea urchin
    el erizo de mar

22. snail
    el caracol

23. worm
    la lombriz / el gusano

24. sea anemone
    la anémona
    de mar

Amphibians Anfibios

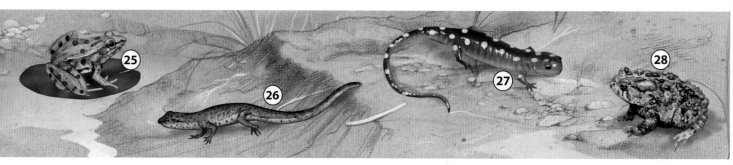

25. frog
    la rana

26. newt
    la salamandra acuática /
    el tritón

27. salamander
    la salamandra

28. toad
    el sapo

Sea Mammals Mamíferos marinos

29. whale la ballena	**31.** dolphin el delfín	**33.** sea lion el león marino	**35.** sea otter la nutria marina
30. porpoise la marsopa	**32.** walrus la morsa	**34.** seal la foca	

Reptiles Reptiles

36. alligator el caimán	**38.** rattlesnake la serpiente de cascabel	**40.** lizard la lagartija	**42.** tortoise la tortuga
37. crocodile el cocodrilo	**39.** garter snake la culebra americana no venenosa	**41.** cobra la cobra	**43.** turtle la tortuga

213

PARTS OF A BIRD

1. wing
   el ala

2. claw
   la garra

3. beak / bill
   el pico

4. feather
   la pluma

5. owl
   el búho / la lechuza

6. blue jay
   el arrendajo azul /
   el grajo azul

7. sparrow
   el gorrión

8. woodpecker
   el pájaro carpintero

9. eagle
   el águila

10. hummingbird
    el colibrí / el picaflor

11. penguin
    el pingüino

12. duck
    el pato

13. goose
    el ganso

14. peacock
    el pavo real

15. pigeon
    la paloma

16. robin
    el petirrojo

Insects and Arachnids Insectos y arácnidos

17. wasp
    la avispa

18. beetle
    el escarabajo

19. butterfly
    la mariposa

20. caterpillar
    la oruga

21. moth
    la mariposa nocturna /
    la polilla

22. mosquito
    el mosquito

23. cricket
    el grillo

24. grasshopper
    el saltamontes

25. honeybee
    la abeja melífera

26. ladybug
    la mariquita / la catarinita

27. tick
    la garrapata

28. fly
    la mosca

29. spider
    la araña

30. scorpion
    el escorpión

Domestic Animals and Rodents

Farm Animals Animales de la granja

1. cow
   la vaca
2. pig
   el cerdo / el puerco / el cochino
3. donkey
   el burro
4. horse
   el caballo
5. goat
   la cabra
6. sheep
   la oveja
7. rooster
   el gallo
8. hen
   la gallina

Pets Mascotas

9. cat
   el gato
10. kitten
    el gatito
11. dog
    el perro
12. puppy
    el perrito
13. rabbit
    el conejo
14. guinea pig
    el conejillo de Indias / el cuy
15. parakeet
    el periquito
16. goldfish
    la carpa dorada

Rodents Roedores

17. rat
    la rata
18. mouse
    el ratón
19. gopher
    la tuza
20. chipmunk
    la ardilla listada
21. squirrel
    la ardilla
22. prairie dog
    la marmota de las praderas

More vocabulary

domesticated: animals that work for and / or live with people

wild: animals that live away from people

Ask your classmates. Share the answers.

1. Have you worked with farm animals? Which ones?
2. Are you afraid of rodents? Which ones?
3. Do you have a pet? What kind?

215

1. moose
el alce

2. mountain lion
el puma

3. coyote
el coyote

4. opossum
el oposum / la zarigüeya

5. wolf
el lobo

6. buffalo / bison
el búfalo / el bisonte

7. bat
el murciélago

8. armadillo
el armadillo

9. beaver
el castor

10. porcupine
el puerco espín

11. bear
el oso

12. skunk
el zorrillo / la mofeta

13. raccoon
el mapache

14. deer
el venado

15. fox
el zorro

16. antlers
la cornamenta del ciervo

17. hooves
las pezuñas

18. whiskers
los bigotes

19. coat / fur
el pelaje / la piel

20. paw
la garra / la pata

21. horn
el cuerno

22. tail
la cola

23. quill
la púa

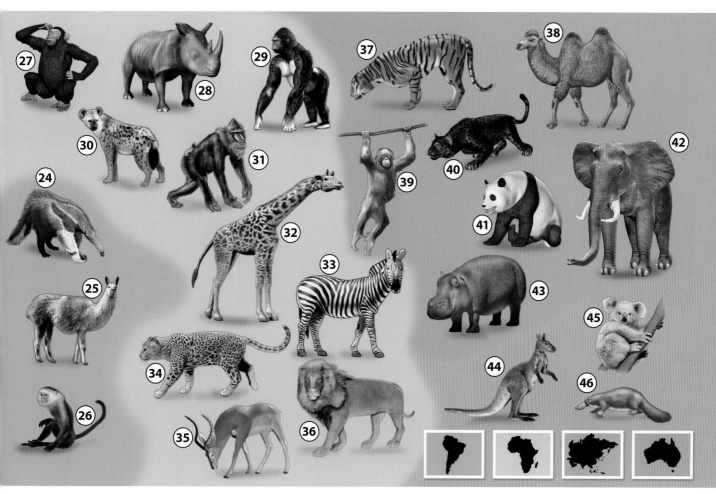

24. anteater el oso hormiguero	**29.** gorilla el gorila	**34.** leopard el leopardo	**39.** orangutan el orangután	**44.** kangaroo el canguro
25. llama la llama	**30.** hyena la hiena	**35.** antelope el antílope	**40.** panther la pantera	**45.** koala el koala
26. monkey el mono	**31.** baboon el mandril	**36.** lion el león	**41.** panda el panda	**46.** platypus el ornitorrinco
27. chimpanzee el chimpancé	**32.** giraffe la jirafa	**37.** tiger el tigre	**42.** elephant el elefante	
28. rhinoceros el rinoceronte	**33.** zebra la cebra	**38.** camel el camello	**43.** hippopotamus el hipopótamo	

47. trunk la trompa	**48.** tusk el colmillo	**49.** mane la melena / la crin	**50.** pouch la bolsa	**51.** hump la joroba

217

Energy Sources Fuentes de energía

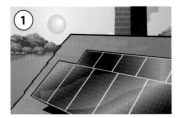

1. solar energy
la energía solar

2. wind power
la energía eólica

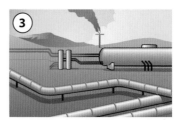

3. natural gas
el gas natural

4. coal
el carbón

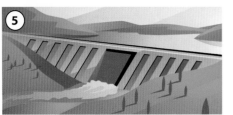

5. hydroelectric power
la energía hidroeléctrica

6. oil / petroleum
el petróleo

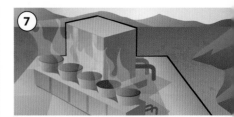

7. geothermal energy
la energía geotérmica

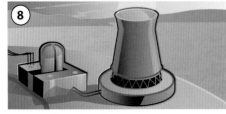

8. nuclear energy
la energía nuclear

9. biomass / bioenergy
la energía de biomasas / la bioenergía

10. fusion
la energía de fusión

Pollution La contaminación

11. air pollution / smog
la contaminación del aire / el esmog

12. hazardous waste
los desechos peligrosos

13. acid rain
la lluvia ácida

14. water pollution
la contaminación del agua

15. radiation
la radiación

16. pesticide poisoning
el envenenamiento
con insecticidas

17. oil spill
el derrame de petróleo

Ask your classmates. Share the answers.

1. What types of things do you recycle?
2. What types of energy sources are in your area?
3. What types of pollution do you worry about?

Think about it. Discuss.

1. How can you save energy in the summer? winter?
2. What are some other ways that people can conserve energy or prevent pollution?

Ways to Conserve Energy and Resources Formas de conservar la energía y los recursos

A. reduce trash
reducir la basura

B. reuse shopping bags
volver a usar las bolsas de compra

C. recycle
reciclar

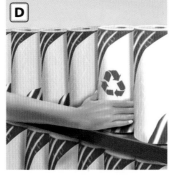

D. buy recycled products
comprar productos reciclados

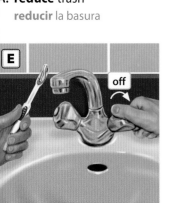

E. save water
ahorrar agua

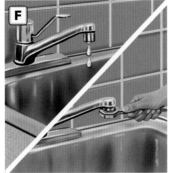

F. fix leaky faucets
reparar los grifos goteantes

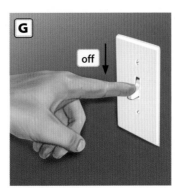

G. turn off lights
apagar las luces

H. use energy-efficient bulbs
usar bulbos de bajo consumo energético

I. carpool
participar en un plan de viaje compartido en auto **(carpool)**

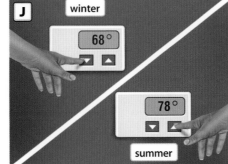

J. adjust the thermostat
ajustar el termostato

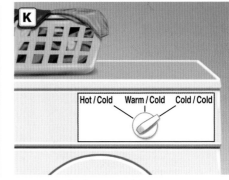

K. wash clothes in cold water
lavar la ropa en agua fría

L. don't litter
no tirar basura

M. compost food scraps
convertir en abono las sobras de alimentos

N. plant a tree
plantar un árbol

219

Yosemite
NATIONAL PARK

Dry Tortugas
NATIONAL PARK

1 Half Dome

1 Fort Jefferson

2

4

3

5

1. **landmarks**
   los lugares más famosos
2. **park ranger**
   el guardabosques de parque

3. **wildlife**
   la fauna y flora natural
4. **ferry**
   el transbordador

5. **coral**
   el coral
6. **cave**
   la cueva

7. **caverns**
   las cavernas
A. **take** a tour
   haga una gira

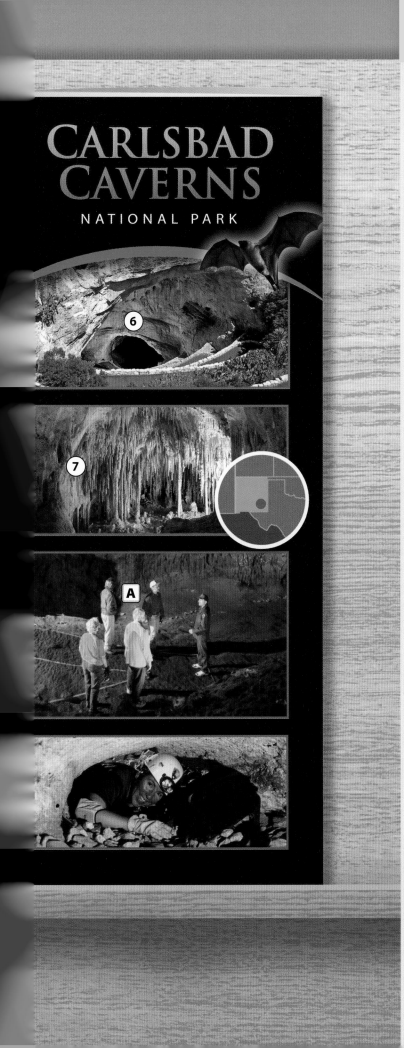

CARLSBAD
CAVERNS
NATIONAL PARK

6

7

A

Answer the questions.

1. How many U.S. landmarks are in the pictures?

2. What kinds of wildlife do you see?

3. What can you do at Carlsbad Caverns?

Read the story.

U.S. National Parks

More than 200 million people visit U.S. National Parks every year. These parks protect the <u>wildlife</u> and <u>landmarks</u> of the United States. Each park is different, and each one is beautiful.

At Yosemite, in California, you can take a nature walk with a <u>park ranger</u>. You'll see waterfalls, redwoods, and deer there.

In south Florida, you can take a <u>ferry</u> to Dry Tortugas. It's great to snorkel around the park's <u>coral</u> islands.

There are 113 <u>caves</u> at Carlsbad <u>Caverns</u> in New Mexico. The deepest cave is 830 feet below the desert! You can <u>take a tour</u> of these beautiful caverns.

There are 391 national parks to see. Go online for information about a park near you.

Think about it.

1. Why are national parks important?

2. Imagine you are a park ranger at a national park. Give your classmates a tour of the landmarks and wildlife.

1. zoo
   el zoológico

2. movies
   el cine

3. botanical garden
   el jardín botánico

4. bowling alley
   la pista de boliche

5. rock concert
   el concierto de música rock

6. swap meet / flea market
   el bazar / el mercado de pulgas

7. aquarium
   el acuario

File Edit View History Bookmarks Tools

Places to Go in Our City

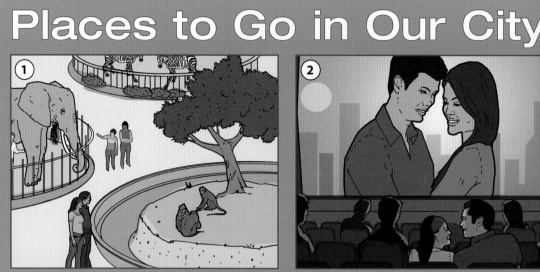

T-SHIRTS $3 2 FOR $5

SUNGLASSES $10

ANTIQU

Listen and point. Take turns.

A: *Point to the zoo.*
B: *Point to the flea market.*
A: *Point to the rock concert.*

Dictate to your partner. Take turns.

A: *Write these words: zoo, movies, aquarium.*
B: *Zoo, movies, and what?*
A: *Aquarium.*

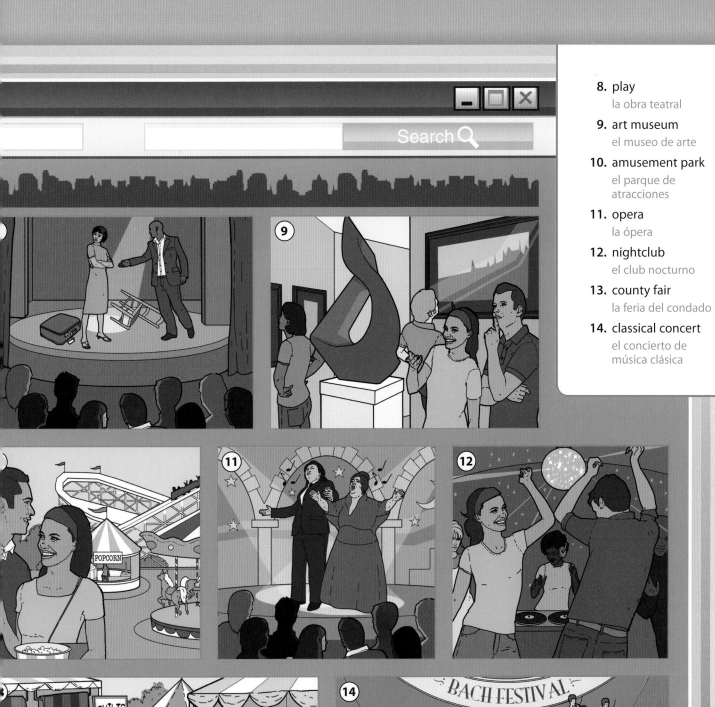

8. play
   la obra teatral

9. art museum
   el museo de arte

10. amusement park
    el parque de atracciones

11. opera
    la ópera

12. nightclub
    el club nocturno

13. county fair
    la feria del condado

14. classical concert
    el concierto de música clásica

Ways to make plans using *Let's go*

Let's go to <u>the amusement park</u> tomorrow.
Let's go to <u>the opera</u> on Saturday.
Let's go to <u>the movies</u> tonight.

Pair practice. Make new conversations.

A: <u>*Let's go to the zoo this afternoon*</u>.
B: *OK. And let's go to* <u>*the movies tonight*</u>.
A: *That sounds like a good plan.*

The Park and Playground

El parque y el patio de recreo

1. **ball field**
   el campo de béisbol

2. **cyclist**
   el ciclista

3. **bike path**
   el camino para bicicletas

4. **jump rope**
   la cuerda para saltar

5. **fountain**
   la fuente

6. **tennis court**
   la cancha de tenis

7. **skateboard**
   el monopatín

8. **picnic table**
   la mesa para comidas campestres

9. **water fountain**
   la fuente de agua para beber / el bebedero

10. **bench**
    la banca

11. **swings**
    los columpios

12. **tricycle**
    el triciclo

13. **slide**
    la resbaladilla / la chorrera

14. **climbing apparatus**
    el aparato para trepar

15. **sandbox**
    la caja de arena

16. **seesaw**
    el subibaja

A. **pull** the wagon
arrastrar el cochecito

B. **push** the swing
empujar el columpio

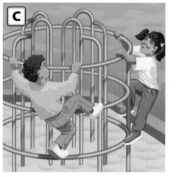

C. **climb** the bars
trepar las barras

D. **picnic / have** a picnic
hacer una comida campestre

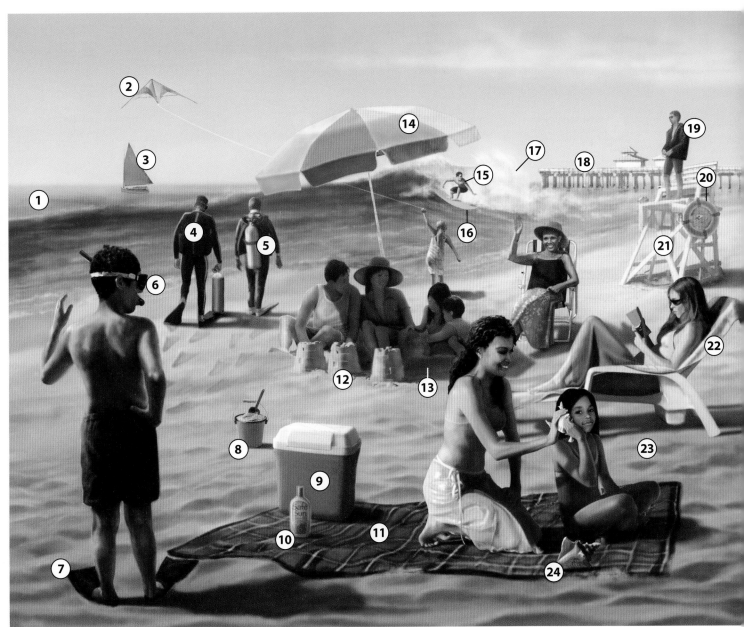

1. ocean / water
   el océano / el agua

2. kite
   la cometa

3. sailboat
   el velero

4. wet suit
   el traje de buzo

5. scuba tank
   el tanque de buceo

6. diving mask
   la careta de buzo

7. fins
   las aletas

8. pail / bucket
   la pala / el cubo

9. cooler
   la hielera / la nevera de playa

10. sunscreen / sunblock
    el protector solar

11. blanket
    la manta (o toalla) de playa

12. sand castle
    el castillo de arena

13. shade
    la sombra

14. beach umbrella
    la sombrilla de playa

15. surfer
    el tablista

16. surfboard
    la tabla hawaiana

17. wave
    la ola

18. pier
    el muelle

19. lifeguard
    el salvavidas

20. lifesaving device
    el dispositivo salvavidas

21. lifeguard station
    la estación del salvavidas

22. beach chair
    la silla de playa

23. sand
    la arena

24. seashell
    la concha (de mar)

More vocabulary

seaweed: a plant that grows in the ocean
tide: the level of the ocean. The tide goes in and out every 12 hours.

Ask your classmates. Share the answers.

1. Do you like to go to the beach?
2. Are there famous beaches in your native country?
3. Do you prefer to be on the sand or in the water?

225

1. **boating**
   el paseo en bote

2. **rafting**
   el paseo en balsa

3. **canoeing**
   el piragüismo

4. **fishing**
   la pesca

5. **camping**
   el campamento

6. **backpacking**
   ir de campamento

7. **hiking**
   la caminata / la excursión

8. **mountain biking**
   el ciclismo de montañas

9. **horseback riding**
   la equitación / el paseo a caballo

10. **tent**
    la carpa / la tienda de campaña

11. **campfire**
    la fogata / la hoguera

12. **sleeping bag**
    el saco para dormir

13. **foam pad**
    el relleno de espuma

14. **life vest**
    el chaleco salvavidas

15. **backpack**
    la mochila

16. **camping stove**
    la cocina de campamento

17. **fishing net**
    la red de pescar

18. **fishing pole**
    la caña de pescar

19. **rope**
    la cuerda

20. **multi-use knife**
    el cuchillo multiusos

21. **matches**
    los cerillos / los fósforos

22. **lantern**
    la linterna

23. **insect repellent**
    el repelente de insectos

24. **canteen**
    la cantimplora

1. downhill skiing
el esquí de descenso

2. snowboarding
el monopatinador de nieve

3. cross-country skiing
el esquí a campo traviesa /
la carrera de fondo

4. ice skating
el patinaje sobre hielo

5. figure skating
el patinaje artístico de figuras

6. sledding
el viajar en trineo

7. waterskiing
el esquí acuático

8. sailing
el velerismo

9. surfing
el deporte de la tabla hawaiana /
el surfing

10. windsurfing
el surfing a vela

11. snorkeling
el esnórquel

12. scuba diving
el buceo con escafandra

More vocabulary

speed skating: racing while ice skating
windsurfing: sailboarding

Ask your classmates. Share the Answers.

1. Which of these sports do you like?
2. Which of these sports would you like to learn?
3. Which of these sports is the most fun to watch?

227

1. archery
el tiro con arco

2. billiards / pool
el billar

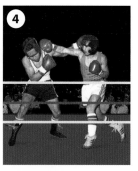

3. bowling
el boliche

4. boxing
el boxeo

5. cycling / biking
el ciclismo

6. badminton
el bádminton

7. fencing
la esgrima

8. golf
el golf

9. gymnastics
la gimnasia

10. inline skating
el patinaje sobre ruedas

11. martial arts
las artes marciales

12. racquetball
el juego de raqueta

13. skateboarding
el deporte de la patineta

14. table tennis
el tenis de mesa

15. tennis
el tenis

16. weightlifting
el levantamiento de pesas

17. wrestling
la lucha

18. track and field
el atletismo

19. horse racing
la carrera de caballos

Pair practice. Make new conversations.

A: *What sports do you like?*
B: *I like <u>bowling</u>. What do you like?*
A: *I like <u>gymnastics</u>.*

Think about it. Discuss.

1. Why do people like to watch sports?
2. Which sports can be dangerous?
3. Why do people do dangerous sports?

1. score
el tanteo / la puntuación

2. coach
el entrenador

3. team
el equipo

4. fan
el admirador / el entusiasta

5. player
el jugador

6. official / referee
el oficial / el árbitro

7. basketball court
la cancha de baloncesto

8. basketball
el baloncesto

9. baseball
el béisbol

10. softball
el sófbol

11. football
el fútbol americano

12. soccer
el fútbol / el balompié

13. ice hockey
el hockey sobre hielo

14. volleyball
el voleibol

15. water polo
el polo acuático

More Vocabulary

win: to have the best score
lose: the opposite of win
tie: to have the same score

captain: the team leader
umpire: the name of the referee in baseball
Little League: a baseball and softball program for children

A. **pitch**
   lanzar

B. **hit**
   pegar

C. **throw**
   arrojar / aventar

D. **catch**
   atrapar / agarrar

E. **kick**
   patear

F. **tackle**
   atajar / tumbar

G. **pass**
   pasar

H. **shoot**
   disparar / tirar

I. **jump**
   saltar

J. **dribble**
   driblar / regatear / rebotar

K. **dive**
   tirarse / aventarse

L. **swim**
   nadar

M. **stretch**
   estirarse

N. **exercise / work out**
   hacer ejercicios / entrenar

O. **bend**
   doblarse

P. **serve**
   servir

Q. **swing**
   girar

R. **start**
   comenzar

S. **race**
   competir en una carrera

T. **finish**
   terminar

U. **skate**
   patinar

V. **ski**
   esquiar

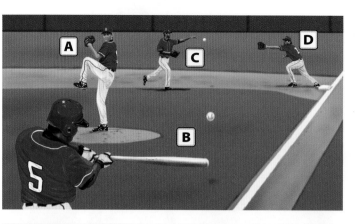

Use the new words.
Look on page 229. Name the actions you see.

A: *He's throwing.*
B: *She's jumping.*

Ways to talk about your sports skills

I can throw, but I can't catch.
I swim well, but I don't dive well.
I'm good at skating, but I'm terrible at skiing.

1. golf club el palo de golf	**8. arrow** la flecha	**15. catcher's mask** la careta del receptor	**22. weights** las pesas
2. tennis racket la raqueta de tenis	**9. ice skates** los patines de hielo	**16. uniform** el uniforme	**23. snowboard** el monopatinador de nieve
3. volleyball la bola de voleibol	**10. inline skates** los patines de rueda	**17. glove** el guante	**24. skis** los esquíes
4. basketball la bola de baloncesto	**11. hockey stick** el palo de hockey	**18. baseball** la pelota de béisbol	**25. ski poles** los bastones de esquí
5. bowling ball la bola de boliche	**12. soccer ball** la bola de fútbol	**19. football helmet** el casco de fútbol americano	**26. ski boots** las botas de esquí
6. bow el arco	**13. shin guards** las espinilleras	**20. shoulder pads** las hombreras	**27. flying disc*** el disco volador
7. target el blanco	**14. baseball bat** el bate de béisbol	**21. football** el balón de fútbol americano	*** Note:** one brand is Frisbee®, of Wham-O, Inc.

Use the new words.

Look at pages 228–229. Name the sports equipment you see.

A: *Those are ice skates.*

B: *That's a football.*

Ask your classmates. Share the answers.

1. Do you own any sports equipment? What kind?

2. What do you want to buy at this store?

3. Where is the best place to buy sports equipment?

A. collect things
coleccionar objetos

B. play games
participar en juegos

C. quilt
acolchar

D. do crafts
hacer artesanías

1. figurine
   la figurilla

2. baseball cards
   las tarjetas de béisbol

3. video game console
   el juego de video
   (el sistema)

4. video game control
   el control del juego
   de video

5. board game
   el juego de mesa

6. dice
   los dados

7. checkers
   las damas

8. chess
   el ajedrez

9. model kit
   el juego para construir
   modelos a escala

10. acrylic paint
    la pintura de acrílico

11. glue stick
    el pegamento

12. construction paper
    el papel de construcción

13. doll making kit
    el juego para hacer
    muñecas

14. woodworking kit
    el juego de artesanía
    en madera

15. quilt block
    el bloque de colcha

16. rotary cutter
    el cortador rotatorio

Grammar Point: *How often do you play cards?*

*I play **all the time**. (every day)*

*I play **sometimes**. (once a month)*

*I **never** play. (0 times)*

Pair practice. Make new conversations.

A: How often do you do your hobbies?

B: I play games all the time. I love chess.

A: Really? I never play chess.

232

E. paint
pintar

F. knit
tejer

G. pretend
hacer creer / actuar

H. play cards
jugar a los naipes

17. canvas
el lienzo

18. easel
el caballete

19. oil paint
la pintura de aceite /
al óleo

20. paintbrush
el pincel

21. watercolor
las acuarelas

22. yarn
el hilo

23. knitting needles
las agujas de tejer

24. embroidery
el bordado

25. crocheting
el tejido a gancho

26. action figure
el héroe de aventuras

27. model trains
los trenes a escala

28. paper dolls
las muñecas de papel

29. diamonds
diamantes

30. spades
espadas

31. hearts
corazones

32. clubs
tréboles

Ways to talk about hobbies and games

*This <u>board game</u> is **interesting**. It makes me think.*
*That <u>video game</u> is **boring**. Nothing happens.*
*I love to <u>play cards</u>. It's **fun** to play with my friends.*

Ask your classmates. Share the answers.

1. Do you collect anything? What?
2. Which games do you like to play?
3. What hobbies did you have as a child?

233

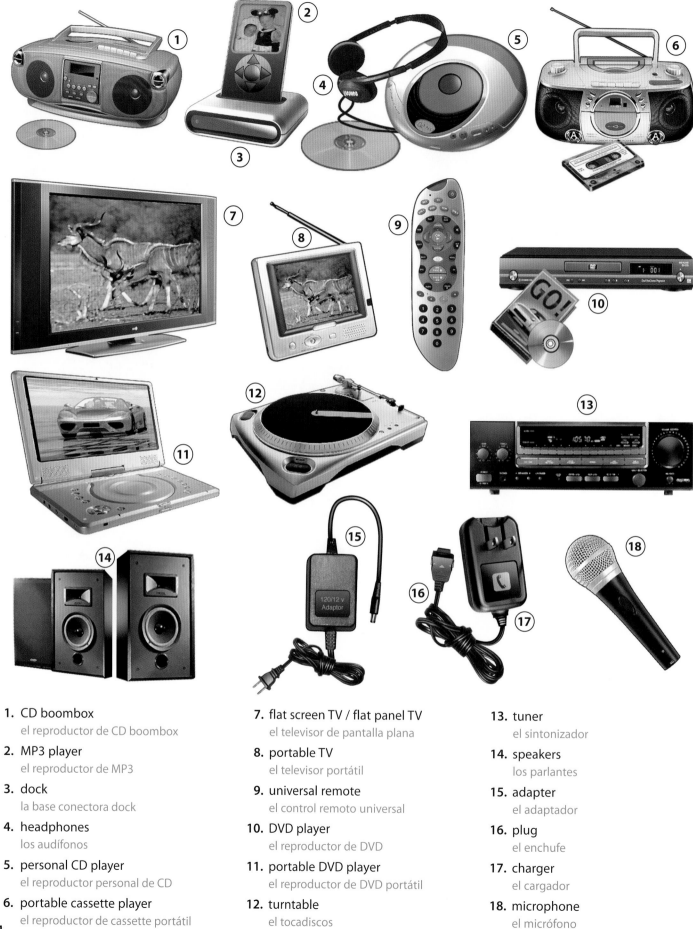

1. **CD boombox**
   el reproductor de CD boombox

2. **MP3 player**
   el reproductor de MP3

3. **dock**
   la base conectora dock

4. **headphones**
   los audífonos

5. **personal CD player**
   el reproductor personal de CD

6. **portable cassette player**
   el reproductor de cassette portátil

7. **flat screen TV / flat panel TV**
   el televisor de pantalla plana

8. **portable TV**
   el televisor portátil

9. **universal remote**
   el control remoto universal

10. **DVD player**
    el reproductor de DVD

11. **portable DVD player**
    el reproductor de DVD portátil

12. **turntable**
    el tocadiscos

13. **tuner**
    el sintonizador

14. **speakers**
    los parlantes

15. **adapter**
    el adaptador

16. **plug**
    el enchufe

17. **charger**
    el cargador

18. **microphone**
    el micrófono

19. digital camera
la cámara digital

20. memory card
la tarjeta de memoria

21. film camera / 35 mm camera
la cámara de película / la cámara de 35 mm

22. film
los rollos de película

23. zoom lens
el lente de zoom / el teleobjetivo

24. camcorder
la cámara de video y audio

25. tripod
el trípode

26. battery pack
el bloque de pilas secas

27. battery charger
el cargador de pilas

28. camera case
el estuche para la cámara

29. LCD projector
el proyector LCD

30. screen
la pantalla

31. photo album
el álbum de fotos

32. digital photo album
el álbum de fotos digital

33. out of focus
fuera de foco

34. overexposed
sobreexpuesta

35. underexposed
expuesta insuficientemente

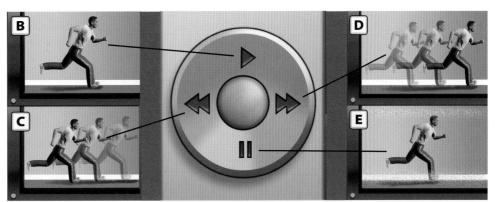

A. record
grabar

B. play
reproducir

C. rewind
rebobinar

D. fast forward
avanzar rápido

E. pause
pausar

Types of TV Programs Tipos de programas de televisión

1. news program
los programas de noticias

2. sitcom (situation comedy)
la comedia de situaciones

3. cartoon
el dibujo animado

4. talk show
los programas de entrevistas

5. soap opera
las telenovelas

6. reality show
los programas de realidad

7. nature program
los programas sobre la naturaleza

8. game show
los programas de juegos /
de preguntas

9. children's program
los programas para niños

10. shopping program
los programas de ventas por televisión

11. sports program
los programas deportivos

12. drama
los programas de drama

236

Types of Movies Tipos de películas

13. comedy
de comedia

14. tragedy
de tragedia

15. western
del oeste

16. romance
románticas

17. horror story
de horror

18. science fiction story
de ciencia-ficción

19. action story / adventure story
de acción / de aventuras

20. mystery / suspense
de misterio / de suspenso

Types of Music Tipos de música

21. classical
clásica

22. blues
blues

23. rock
rock

24. jazz
jazz

25. pop
pop

26. hip hop
hip hop

27. country
country

28. R&B / soul
R&B / soul

29. folk
folk

30. gospel
religiosa

31. reggae
reggae

32. world music
música del mundo

A. play an instrument
tocar un instrumento

B. sing a song
cantar una canción

C. conduct an orchestra
conducir una orquesta

D. be in a rock band
ser miembro de una banda de rock

Woodwinds
Instrumentos de viento de madera

1. flute
   la flauta
2. clarinet
   el clarinete
3. oboe
   el oboe
4. bassoon
   el fagot
5. saxophone
   el saxofón

Strings
Instrumentos de cuerda

6. violin
   el violín
7. cello
   el violoncelo
8. bass
   el bajo
9. guitar
   la guitarra

Brass
Instrumentos de bronce o metales

10. trombone
    el trombón
11. trumpet / horn
    la trompeta / el corno
12. tuba
    la tuba
13. French horn
    el corno francés

Percussion Instrumentos de percusión

14. piano
    el piano
15. xylophone
    el xilófono
16. drums
    los tambores
17. tambourine
    la pandereta / el pandero

Other Instruments Otros instrumentos

18. electric keyboard
    el teclado electrónico
19. accordion
    el acordeón
20. organ
    el órgano
21. harmonica
    la armónica

1. **parade**
   el desfile

2. **float**
   la carroza

3. **confetti**
   el confeti

4. **couple**
   la pareja

5. **card**
   la tarjeta

6. **heart**
   el corazón

7. **fireworks**
   los fuegos artificiales

8. **flag**
   la bandera

9. **mask**
   la máscara / la careta /
   el antifaz

10. **jack-o'-lantern**
    la linterna hecha de
    una calabaza

11. **costume**
    el disfraz

12. **candy**
    los dulces

13. **feast**
    la festividad

14. **turkey**
    el pavo / el guajolote

15. **ornament**
    el adorno

16. **Christmas tree**
    el árbol de Navidad

17. **candy cane**
    los bastones dulces

18. **string lights**
    las luces navideñas

*Thanksgiving is on the fourth Thursday in November.

HAPPY BIRTHDAY LOU and GANI

1. decorations
las decoraciones

2. deck
la terraza

3. present / gift
los regalos

A. **videotape**
grabar en video

B. **make** a wish
pedir un deseo

C. **blow out**
soplar las velas

D. **hide**
esconderse

E. **bring**
traer

F. **wrap**
envolver

Happy Birthday!

E

F

**Look at the picture.
What do you see?**

Answer the questions.

1. What kinds of decorations do you see?

2. What are people doing at this birthday party?

3. What wish did the teenager make?

4. How many presents did people bring?

📖 **Read the story.**

A Birthday Party

Today is Lou and Gani Bombata's birthday barbecue. There are <u>decorations</u> around the backyard, and food and drinks on the <u>deck</u>. There are also <u>presents</u>. Everyone in the Bombata family likes to <u>bring</u> presents.

Right now, it's time for cake. Gani <u>is blowing out</u> the candles, and Lou <u>is making a wish</u>. Lou's mom wants to <u>videotape</u> everyone, but she can't find Lou's brother, Todd. Todd hates to sing, so he always <u>hides</u> for the birthday song.

Lou's sister, Amaka, has to <u>wrap</u> some <u>gifts</u>. She doesn't want Lou to see. Amaka isn't worried. She knows her family loves to sing. She can put her gifts on the present table before they finish the first song.

Think about it.

1. What wish do you think Gani made?

2. What kinds of presents do you give to relatives? What kinds of presents can you give to friends or co-workers?

241

Verb Guide

Verbs in English are either regular or irregular in the past tense and past participle forms.

Regular Verbs

The regular verbs below are marked 1, 2, 3, or 4 according to four different spelling patterns.
(See page 244 for the irregular verbs which do not follow any of these patterns.)

Spelling Patterns for the Past and the Past Participle	Example	
1. Add -ed to the end of the verb.	ASK	ASKED
2. Add -d to the end of the verb.	LIVE	LIVED
3. Double the final consonant and add -ed to the end of the verb.	DROP	DROPPED
4. Drop the final y and add -ied to the end of the verb.	CRY	CRIED

The Oxford Picture Dictionary List of Regular Verbs

accept (1)
add (1)
address (1)
adjust (1)
agree (2)
answer (1)
apologize (2)
appear (1)
applaud (1)
apply (4)
arrange (2)
arrest (1)
arrive (2)
ask (1)
assemble (2)
assist (1)
attach (1)
bake (2)
bank (1)
bargain (1)
bathe (2)
board (1)
boil (1)
borrow (1)
bow (1)
brainstorm (1)
breathe (2)
browse (2)
brush (1)
bubble (2)
buckle (2)
burn (1)
bus (1)
calculate (2)
call (1)
capitalize (2)
carpool (1)

carry (4)
cash (1)
celebrate (2)
change (2)
check (1)
chill (1)
choke (2)
chop (3)
circle (2)
claim (1)
clean (1)
clear (1)
click (1)
climb (1)
close (2)
collate (2)
collect (1)
color (1)
comb (1)
comfort (1)
commit (3)
compliment (1)
compost (1)
conceal (1)
conduct (1)
convert (1)
convict (1)
cook (1)
copy (4)
correct (1)
cough (1)
count (1)
cross (1)
cry (4)
dance (2)
debate (2)
decline (2)

delete (2)
deliver (1)
design (1)
dial (1)
dice (2)
dictate (2)
die (2)
disagree (2)
discipline (2)
discuss (1)
dive (2)
divide (2)
dress (1)
dribble (2)
drill (1)
drop (3)
drown (1)
dry (4)
dust (1)
dye (2)
edit (1)
empty (4)
enter (1)
erase (2)
evacuate (2)
examine (2)
exchange (2)
exercise (2)
expire (2)
explain (1)
exterminate (2)
fasten (1)
fast forward (1)
fax (1)
fertilize (2)
fill (1)
finish (1)

fix (1)
floss (1)
fold (1)
follow (1)
garden (1)
gargle (2)
graduate (2)
grate (2)
grease (2)
greet (1)
hail (1)
hammer (1)
hand (1)
harvest (1)
help (1)
hire (2)
hug (3)
immigrate (2)
indent (1)
inquire (2)
insert (1)
inspect (1)
install (1)
introduce (2)
invite (2)
iron (1)
jaywalk (1)
join (1)
jump (1)
kick (1)
kiss (1)
knit (3)
label (1)
land (1)
laugh (1)
learn (1)
lengthen (1)

lift (1)
listen (1)
litter (1)
live (2)
load (1)
lock (1)
look (1)
mail (1)
manufacture (2)
match (1)
measure (2)
microwave (2)
milk (1)
misbehave (2)
miss (1)
mix (1)
mop (3)
move (2)
mow (1)
multiply (4)
negotiate (2)
network (1)
numb (1)
nurse (2)
obey (1)
observe (2)
offer (1)
open (1)
operate (2)
order (1)
organize (2)
overdose (2)
pack (1)
paint (1)
park (1)
participate (2)
pass (1)
pause (2)
peel (1)
perm (1)
pick (1)

pitch (1)
plan (3)
plant (1)
play (1)
polish (1)
pour (1)
praise (2)
preheat (1)
prepare (2)
prescribe (2)
press (1)
pretend (1)
print (1)
program (3)
protect (1)
pull (1)
purchase (2)
push (1)
quilt (1)
race (2)
raise (2)
rake (2)
receive (2)
record (1)
recycle (2)
redecorate (2)
reduce (2)
register (1)
relax (1)
remain (1)
remove (2)
renew (1)
repair (1)
replace (2)
report (1)
request (1)
retire (2)
return (1)
reuse (2)
revise (2)
rinse (2)

rock (1)
sauté (1)
save (2)
scan (3)
schedule (2)
scrub (3)
seat (1)
select (1)
sentence (2)
separate (2)
serve (2)
share (2)
shave (2)
ship (3)
shop (3)
shorten (1)
sign (1)
simmer (1)
skate (2)
ski (1)
slice (2)
smell (1)
smile (2)
smoke (2)
sneeze (2)
solve (2)
sort (1)
spell (1)
spoon (1)
staple (2)
start (1)
state (2)
stay (1)
steam (1)
stir (3)
stop (3)
stow (1)
stretch (1)
study (4)
submit (3)
subtract (1)

supervise (2)
swallow (1)
tackle (2)
talk (1)
taste (2)
thank (1)
tie (2)
touch (1)
transcribe (2)
transfer (3)
translate (2)
travel (1)
trim (3)
try (4)
turn (1)
type (2)
underline (2)
undress (1)
unload (1)
unpack (1)
unscramble (2)
use (2)
vacuum (1)
videotape (2)
volunteer (1)
vomit (1)
vote (2)
wait (1)
walk (1)
wash (1)
watch (1)
water (1)
wave (2)
weed (1)
weigh (1)
wipe (2)
work (1)
wrap (3)

243

Verb Guide

Irregular Verbs

These verbs have irregular endings in the past and/or the past participle.

The Oxford Picture Dictionary List of Irregular Verbs

simple	past	past participle	simple	past	past participle
be	was	been	make	made	made
beat	beat	beaten	meet	met	met
become	became	become	pay	paid	paid
bend	bent	bent	picnic	picnicked	picnicked
bleed	bled	bled	proofread	proofread	proofread
blow	blew	blown	put	put	put
break	broke	broken	read	read	read
bring	brought	brought	rewind	rewound	rewound
buy	bought	bought	rewrite	rewrote	rewritten
catch	caught	caught	ride	rode	ridden
choose	chose	chosen	run	ran	run
come	came	come	say	said	said
cut	cut	cut	see	saw	seen
do	did	done	seek	sought	sought
draw	drew	drawn	sell	sold	sold
drink	drank	drunk	send	sent	sent
drive	drove	driven	set	set	set
eat	ate	eaten	sew	sewed	sewn
fall	fell	fallen	shake	shook	shaken
feed	fed	fed	shoot	shot	shot
feel	felt	felt	show	showed	shown
find	found	found	sing	sang	sung
fly	flew	flown	sit	sat	sat
get	got	gotten	speak	spoke	spoken
give	gave	given	stand	stood	stood
go	went	gone	steal	stole	stolen
hang	hung	hung	sweep	swept	swept
have	had	had	swim	swam	swum
hear	heard	heard	swing	swung	swung
hide	hid	hidden	take	took	taken
hit	hit	hit	teach	taught	taught
hold	held	held	think	thought	thought
keep	kept	kept	throw	threw	thrown
lay	laid	laid	wake	woke	woken
leave	left	left	withdraw	withdrew	withdrawn
lend	lent	lent	write	wrote	written
let	let	let			

Index

Index Key

Font
bold type = verbs or verb phrases (example: **catch**)
ordinary type = all other parts of speech (example: baseball)
ALL CAPS = unit titles (example: MATHEMATICS)
Initial caps = subunit titles (example: Equivalencies)

Symbols
✦ = word found in exercise band at bottom of page

Numbers/Letters
first number in **bold** type = page on which word appears
second number, or letter, following number in **bold** type = item number on page
(examples: cool [ko͞ol] **13**-5 means that the word *cool* is item number 5 on page 13;
across [ə krös/] **153**–G means that the word *across* is item G on page 153).

Pronunciation Guide

The index includes a pronunciation guide for all the words and phrases illustrated in the book. This guide uses symbols commonly found in dictionaries for native speakers. These symbols, unlike those used in pronunciation systems such as the International Phonetic Alphabet, tend to use English spelling patterns and so should help you to become more aware of the connections between written English and spoken English.

Consonants

[b] as in back [băk]	[k] as in key [kē]	[sh] as in shoe [sho͞o]
[ch] as in cheek [chēk]	[l] as in leaf [lēf]	[t] as in tape [tāp]
[d] as in date [dāt]	[m] as in match [măch]	[th] as in three [thrē]
[dh] as in this [dhĭs]	[n] as in neck [nĕk]	[v] as in vine [vīn]
[f] as in face [fās]	[ng] as in ring [rĭng]	[w] as in wait [wāt]
[g] as in gas [găs]	[p] as in park [pärk]	[y] as in yams [yămz]
[h] as in half [hăf]	[r] as in rice [rīs]	[z] as in zoo [zo͞o]
[j] as in jam [jăm]	[s] as in sand [sănd]	[zh] as in measure [mĕzhər]

Vowels

[ā] as in bake [bāk]	[ī] as in line [līn]	[o͝o] as in cook [ko͝ok]
[ă] as in back [băk]	[ĭ] as in lip [lĭp]	[ow] as in cow [kow]
[ä] as in car [kär] or box [bäks]	[ï] as in near [nïr]	[oy] as in boy [boy]
[ē] as in beat [bēt]	[ō] as in cold [kōld]	[ŭ] as in cut [kŭt]
[ĕ] as in bed [bĕd]	[ö] as in short [shört] or claw [klö]	[ü] as in curb [kürb]
[ë] as in bear [bër]	[o͞o] as in cool [ko͞ol]	[ə] as in above [ə bŭv/]

All the pronunciation symbols used are alphabetical except for the schwa [ə]. The schwa is the most frequent vowel sound in English. If you use the schwa appropriately in unstressed syllables, your pronunciation will sound more natural.

Vowels before [r] are shown with the symbol [¨] to call attention to the special quality that vowels have before [r]. (Note that the symbols [ä] and [ö] are also used for vowels not followed by [r], as in *box* or *claw*.) You should listen carefully to native speakers to discover how these vowels actually sound.

Stress
This index follows the system for marking stress used in many dictionaries for native speakers.
1. Stress is not marked if a word consisting of a single syllable occurs by itself.
2. Where stress is marked, two levels are distinguished:
a bold accent [/] is placed after each syllable with primary (or strong) stress, a light accent [/] is placed after each syllable with secondary (or weaker) stress. In phrases and other combinations of words, stress is indicated for each word as it would be pronounced within the whole phrase.

Syllable Boundaries
Syllable boundaries are indicated by a single space or by a stress mark.

Note: The pronunciations shown in this index are based on patterns of American English. There has been no attempt to represent all of the varieties of American English. Students should listen to native speakers to hear how the language actually sounds in a particular region.

Abbreviations [ə brē/vē ā/shənz] **48**
abdomen [ăb/də mən] **107**–27
about [ə bowt/] **48**–B, **174**–L, **191**–E
above [ə bŭv/] **25**–4
accelerator [ĭk sĕl/ə rā/tər] **159**–46
accept [ĭk sĕpt/] **12**–G, **12**–I, **12** ✦
access number [ăk/sĕs/ nŭm/bər] **14**–16
Accessories [ĭk sĕs/ə rēz] **59**, **94**–95
accident [ăk/sə dənt] **144**–2
accordion [ə kör/dē ən] **238**–19
account [ə kownt/] **132**–11, **132**–14
    account manager [ə kownt/ măn/ə jər] **132**–9
Account [ə kownt/] **132**
accountant [ə kown/tənt] **166**–1
ache [āk]
    backache [băk/āk/] **110**–5
    earache [ïr/āk/] **110**–3
    headache [hĕd/āk/] **110**–1
    stomachache [stŭm/ək/ āk/] **110**–4
    toothache [tōōth/āk/] **110**–2
acid rain [ăs/əd rān/] **218**–13
across [ə krös] **153**–G
acrylic paint [ə krĭl/ĭk pānt] **232**–10
action [ăk/shən]
    action figure [ăk/shən fĭg/yər] **233**–26
    action story [ăk/shən stör/ē] **237**–19
activist [ăk/tə vĭst] **199**–17
actor [ăk/tər] **166**–2
acupuncture [ăk/yə pŭngk/chər] **122**–2
acute angle [ə kyōōt/ ăng/gəl] **193**–28
ad [ăd] **48**–2, **197**–9
adapter [ə dăp/tər] **234**–15
add [ăd] **77**–N, **101**–B, **192**–A
address [ə drĕs/, ă/drĕs] **4**–5
    mailing address [mā/lĭng ə drĕs/, –ă/drĕs] **134**–22
    return address [rĭ tŭrn/ ə drĕs/, –ă/drĕs] **134**–21
    website address [wĕb/sīt ə drĕs/, –ă/drĕs] **197**–4
address [ə drĕs/] **135**–B, **197**–C
adhesive bandage [əd hē/sïv băn/dĭj] **117**–5
adjust [ə jŭst/] **219**–J
    adjustable wrench [ə jŭs/tə bəl rĕnch/] **181**–48
    adjustment [ə jŭst/mənt] **194**–23, **194**–24
administrative assistant
    [əd mĭn/ə strā/tĭv ə sĭs/tənt] **166**–3
administrator [əd mĭn/ə strā/tər] **120**–13
Administrators [əd mĭn/ə strā/tərz] **5**
admissions clerk [əd mĭ/shənz klŭrk/] **120**–14
ADULTS AND CHILDREN [ə dŭlts/ en chĭl/ drən] **30**–31
adult school [ə dŭlt/ skōōl/, ăd/ŭlt–] **188**–8
adventure story [əd vĕn/chər stör/ē] **237**–19
aerobic exercise [ə rō/bĭk ĕk/sər sīz/] **122**–5
afraid [ə frād/] **43**–23
after [ăf/tər]
    afternoon [ăf/tər nōōn/] **18**–17
    aftershave [ăf/tər shāv/] **109**–30
    five after one [fïv/ ăf/tər wŭn/] **18**–7
    quarter after one [kwör/tər ăf/tər wŭn/] **18**–9
    ten after one [tĕn/ ăf/tər wŭn/] **18**–8
    twenty after one [twĕn/tē ăf/tər wŭn/] **18**–10
After an Emergency [ăf/tər ən ï mür/jən sē] **147**
Age [āj] **32**
    agency [ā/jən sē] **131**–14

agent [ā/jənt] **160**–3, **160**–5
agree [ə grē/] **12**–K
agreement [ə grē/mənt] **51**–28
aid [ād]
    first aid kit [fürst/ ād/ kĭt/] **117**–1, **146**–18
    first aid manual [fürst/ ād/ măn/yōō əl] **117**–2
    hearing aid [hïr/ïng ād/] **115**–10
aide [ād] **167**–32
AIDS (acquired immune deficiency syndrome) [ādz] /
    [ə kwī/rd ï myōōn/ də fĭ/shən sē sĭn/dröm] **111** ✦
air [ër]
    air bag [ër/ băg/] **159**–43
    air conditioner [ër/ kən dĭsh/ə nər] **159**–39
    Air Force [ër/ förs/] **138**–16
    airmail [ër/māl/] **134**–5
    airplane [ër/plān/] **150**–8
    airplane crash [ër/plān/ krăsh/] **144**–3
    air pollution [ër/ pə lōō/shən] **218**–11
    airport [ër/pört/] **151**–10
    air purifier [ër/ pyōōr/ə fī ər] **113**–14
Airline Terminal [ër/līn/ tür/mə nəl] **160**
Airplane [ër/plān/] **161**
AIRPORT [ër/pört/] **160**–161
Airport Transportation
    [ër/pört/ trăns/pər tā/shən] **152**
aisle [īl] **72**–6
alarm clock [ə lärm/ kläk/] **58**–24
Alaska time [ə lăs/kə tīm/] **19**–28
album [ăl/bəm] **235**–31, **235**–32
alfalfa [ăl făl/fə] **177**–5
algebra [ăl/jə brə] **192**–16
allergic reaction [ə lür/jĭk rē ăk/shən] **116**–E
allergies [ăl/ər jēz] **111**–8
alley [ăl/ē] **51**–24, **222**–4
alligator [ăl/ə gā/tər] **213**–36
alphabet [ăl/fə bĕt/] **7**–13
Alterations [öl/tə rā/shənz] **100**
ALTERATIONS [öl/tə rā/shənz] **100**
Alteration Shop [öl/tə rā/shən shäp/] **100**
aluminum foil [ə lōō/mə nəm foyl/] **72**–23
Alzheimer's disease [älts/hī mərz dī zēz/, älts–] **111** ✦
a.m. [ā/ĕm/] **18**–4
ambulance [ăm/byə ləns] **116**–1, **121**–34
AMERICA [ə mĕr/ə kə] **200**–201
American cheese [ə mĕr/ə kən chēz/] **71**–26
Americans [ə mĕr/ə kənz] **198**–3
Amphibians [ăm fĭb/ē ənz] **212**
AMPHIBIANS [ăm fĭb/ē ənz] **212**–213
amusement park [ə myōōz/mənt pärk/] **223**–10
ancient [ān/shənt] **199**–1
anemone [ə nĕ/mə nē] **212**–24
anesthesiologist [ă/nəs thē/zē ä/lə jïst] **121**–35
angle [ăng/gəl] **193**–26, **193**–27, **193**–28
Angles [ăng/gəlz] **193**
angry [ăng/grē] **43**–29
animals [ăn/ə məlz] **59**–15
Animals [ăn/ə məlz] **212**, **215**
ANIMALS [ăn/ə məlz] **215**
ankle [ăng/kəl] **106**–23, **110**–18
    ankle socks [ăng/kəl säks/] **91**–7
anklets [ăngk/ləts/] **91**–11
anniversary [ăn/ə vür/sə rē] **22**–3

answer [ăn/sər] **8**–L
answering machine [ăn/sə rĭng mə shēn/] **14**–17
answer sheet [ăn/sər shēt/] **10**–2
antacid [ănt ăs/əd] **113**–28
anteater [ănt/ē/tər] **217**–24
antelope [ăn/tə lōp/] **217**–35
antenna [ăn tĕ/nə] **14**–9
antibacterial ointment
    [ăn/tē băk tïr/ē əl oynt/mənt] **117**–10
antihistamine cream [ăn/tī hĭs/tə mēn krēm/] **117**–11
antiperspirant [ăn/tē pürs/pə rənt] **108**–5
antlers [ănt/lərz] **216**–16
ants [ănts] **63**–23
apartment [ə pärt/mənt] **48**–3, **48**–4
    apartment building [ə pärt/mənt bĭl/dĭng] **50**–1
    apartment number [ə pärt/mənt nüm/bər] **4**–6
Apartment [ə pärt/mənt] **48**
Apartment Complex [ə pärt/mənt käm/plĕx] **51**
Apartment Entryway [ə pärt/mənt ĕn/trē wā/] **51**
APARTMENTS [ə pärt/məntz] **50**–51
APC (automated postal center) [ā/pē/sē/] /
    [ö/tə mät ĭd pōs/təl–sĕn/tər] **135**–10
apologize [ə päl/ə jīz/] **12**–F
apostrophe [ə päs/trə fē] **190**–16
apparatus [ăp/ə rä/təs] **224**–14
appear [ə pïr/] **141**–C
Appearance [ə pïr/əns] **32**
applaud [ə plöd/] **148**–B
apples [ăp/əlz] **68**–1
    apple juice [ăp/əl jōōs/] **73**–32
appliance repair person
    [ə plī/əns rĭ përr/ pür/sən] **166**–4
appliqué [ăp/lə kā/] **99**–31
apply [ə plī/] **109**–P
appointment [ə poynt/mənt] **22**–4, **118**–1
    appointment book [ə poynt/mənt bŏŏk/] **183**–48
apricots [ăp/rə käts/] **68**–12
April [ā/prəl] **21**–28
apron [ā/prən] **92**–11, **93**–30
aquarium [ə kwër/ē əm] **222**–7
Arachnids [ə răk/nĭdz/] **214**
ARACHNIDS [ə răk/nĭdz/] **214**
archery [är/chə rē] **228**–1
architect [är/kə tĕkt/] **166**–5
area [ër/ē ə]
    area code [ër/ē ə kōd/] **4**–10, **15**–29
    boarding area [bör/dĭng ër/ē ə] **161**–9
    dining area [dī/nĭng ër/ē ə] **46**–7
    play area [plā/ ër/ē ə] **130**–11
    reception area [rĭ sĕp/shən ër/ē ə] **182**–5
    rural area [rŏŏr/əl ër/ē ə] **52**–4
    screening area [skrē/nĭng ër/ē ə] **160**–4
    testing area [tĕs/tĭng ër/ē ə] **136**–2
    urban area [ür/bən ër/ē ə] **52**–1
AREA [ër/ē ə] **55**
Area and Volume [ër/ē ə ən väl/yəm, –yōōm] **193**
arm [ärm] **105**–14, **194**–15
    armchair [ärm/chër/] **56**–22
armadillo [är/mə dĭl/ō] **216**–8
Arm, Hand, and Fingers [ärm/ hănd/ ən fĭng/gərz] **106**
Army [är/mē] **138**–14, **199**–11
around [ə rownd/] **153**–H

Around Campus [ə rownd/ kăm/pəs] **5**

arrange [ə rănj/] **49**–Q

arrest [ə rĕst/] **141**–A

arrival [ə rī/vəl] **161**–7, **161** ✦

arrive [ə rīv/] **160**–K

arrow [ăr/ō] **231**–8

arson [är/sən] **142**–7

artery [är/tə rē] **107**–36

arthritis [är thrī/təs] **111**–16

artichokes [är/tə chōks/] **69**–22

artist [är/tĭst] **166**–6

arts [ärts] **189**–9, **189**–15, **228**–11

art museum [ärt/ myŏŏ zē/əm] **223**–9

ask [ăsk] **2**–B

ask about [ăsk/ ə bowt/] **48**–B, **157**–B

ask for [ăsk/ för/] **10**–F

ask questions [ăsk/ kwĕs/chənz] **8**–K, **174**–M

asparagus [ə spĕr/ə gəs] **69**–26

assault [ə sölt/] **142**–3

assemble [ə sĕm/bəl] **170**–A, **175**–C

assembler [ə sĕm/blər] **166**–7

assembly [ə sĕm/blē] **140**–1

assembly line [ə sĕm/blē līn/] **175**–6

assemblyperson [ə sĕm/blē pür/sən] **139**–24

assist [ə sĭst/] **95**–D, **170**–B

assistance [ə sĭs/təns] **14**–22

assistant [ə sĭs/tənt]

administrative assistant
[əd mĭn/ ə strā/ tĭv ə sĭs/tənt] **166**–3

assistant principal [ə sĭs/tənt prĭn/sə pəl] **5**–5

certified nursing assistant (CNA) [sür/tə fīd/
nür/sĭng ə sĭs/tənt] / [sē/ĕn/ā/] **120**–12

dental assistant [dĕn/təl ə sĭs/tənt] **119**–2, **167**–22

physician assistant [fə zĭ/shən ə sĭs/tənt] **168**–47

Assistant [ə sĭs/tənt] **93**

asthma [ăz/mə] **111**–9

astronaut [ăs/trə nöt/] **205**–17

astronomer [ə strä/nə mər] **205**–22

Astronomy [ə strä/nə mē] **205**

At Customs [ăt/ kŭs/təmz] **161**

athletic [ăth lĕt/ĭk]

athletic shoes [ăth lĕt/ĭk shŏŏz/] **86**–7

athletic supporter [ăth lĕt/ĭk sə pör/tər] **91**–6

Atlantic time [ət lăn/tĭk tīm/] **19**–33

atlas [ăt/ləs] **133**–8

ATM (Automated Teller Machine) [ā/tē/ĕm/] /
[ö/tə māt ĭd tĕ/lər mə shēn/] **132**

ATM card [ā/tē/ĕm/ kärd/] **132**–15

atom [ăt/əm] **195**–28

attach [ə tăch/] **197**–G, **197**–H

attachments [ə tăch/mənts] **61**–11

attack [ə tăk/] **116**–D

attendant [ə tĕn/dənt] **161**–12, **162**–3, **184**–3

At the Dealer [ăt/ dhə dē/lər] **158**

At the Gate [ăt/ dhə gāt/] **161**

At the Mechanic [ăt/ dhə mə kăn/ĭk] **158**

At the Security Checkpoint
[ăt/ dhə sə kyŏŏ/ rə tē/ chĕk/ poynt/] **160**

attic [ăt/ĭk] **47**–7

attorney [ə tür/nē] **141**–4, **141**–10

attractive [ə trăk/tĭv] **32**–13

audiobook [ö/dē ō bŏŏk/] **133**–17

audiologist [ö dē ä/lə jĭst] **115**–9

auditorium [ö/də tör/ē əm] **5**–18

August [ö/gəst] **21**–32

aunt [ănt] **34**–7

author [ö/thər] **133**–15, **169**–64

auto [ö/tō]

auto club card [ö/tō klŭb/ kärd/] **162**–4

auto mechanic [ö/tō mə kăn/ĭk] **166**–8

automated [ö/tə māt ĭd]

automated phone system
[ö/tə māt ĭd fōn/ sĭs/təm] **14**–23

automated postal center (APC)
[ö/tə māt ĭd pōs/təl sĕn/tər] / [ā/pē/sē/] **135**–10

Automated Teller Machine
[ö/tə māt ĭd tĕl/ər mə shēn/] **132**

Automatic Transmission
[ö tə māt/ĭk trănz mĭ/shən] **159**

Automotive Painter [ö tə mōt/ĭv pān/tər] **92**

autumn [ö/təm] **21**–39

avalanche [ăv/ə lănch/] **145**–18

average [ăv/rĭj]

average height [ăv/rĭj hīt/] **32**–5

average weight [ăv/rĭj wāt/] **32**–8

avocados [ä/və kä/dōz, ăv/ə–] **84**–6

ax [ăks] **180**–3

baboon [bă bŏŏn/] **217**–31

baby [bā/bē] **31**–7

baby bag [bā/bē băg/] **37**–16

baby carrier [bā/bē kă/rē/ər] **37**–17

baby food [bā/bē fŏŏd/] **37**–4

baby lotion [bā/bē lō/shən] **37**–13

baby monitor [bā/bē män/ə tər] **59**–7

baby powder [bā/bē pow/dər] **37**–14

babysitter [bā/bē sĭt/ər] **166**–9

baby's room [bā/bēz/ rŏŏm/] **47**–10

back [băk] **104**–5

backache [băk/āk/] **110**–5

back button [băk/ bŭt/n] **197**–2

backhoe [băk/hō/] **178**–8

backpack [băk/păk/] **94**–18, **226**–15

backpacking [băk/păk/ĭng] **226**–6

backseat [băk/sēt/] **159**–54

back support belt [băk/ sə pört/ bĕlt/] **179**–18

go back [gō/ băk/] **11**–M

horseback riding [hörs/băk/ rī/dĭng] **226**–9

lower back [lō/ər băk/] **107**–29

pay back [pā/ băk/] **26**–D

Backyard [băk/yärd/] **53**

BACK FROM THE MARKET
[băk/ frəm dhə mär/kət] **66**–67

bacon [bā/kən] **70**–11, **80**–1

bad [băd] **23**–18

BAD DAY AT WORK [băd/ dā/ ăt würk/] **186**–187

badge [băj] **93**–21

badminton [băd/mĭn tən] **228**–6

bag [băg] **69**–31, **74**–7, **74**–19, **161**–18

air bag [ĕr/ băg/] **159**–43

baby bag [bā/bē băg/] **37**–16

clutch bag [klŭch/ băg/] **89**–19

grocery bag [grōs/rē băg/] **67**–13

handbag [hănd/ băg/] **87**–9, **94**–2

plastic storage bags [plăs/tĭk stör/ĭj băgz/] **72**–25

shoulder bag [shōl/dər băg/] **94**–17

sleeping bag [slē/pĭng băg/] **226**–12

totebag [tōt/ băg/] **94**–19

trash bags [trăsh/ băgz/] **61**–24

vacuum cleaner bag
[văk/yŏŏm klē/nər băg/] **61**–12

bagels [bā/gəlz] **73**–40

baggage [băg/ĭj]

baggage carousel [băg/ĭj kăr/ə sĕl/] **161**–23

bagger [băg/ər] **73**–14

baggy [băg/ē] **97**–30

bailiff [bā/lĭf] **141**–13

bake [bāk] **77**–H

Baked Goods [bākt/ gŏŏdz/] **73**

baked potato [bākt/ pə tā/tō] **81**–25

baker [bā/kər] **166**–10

bakery [bā/kə rē] **127**–19

Baking Products [bā/kĭng präd/ŭkts] **73**

balance [băl/əns] **132**–17, **195**–41

balcony [băl/kə nē] **51**–20

bald [böld] **33**–12

ball [böl] **59**–12, **231**–5, **231**–12

ball field [böl/ fēld/] **224**–1

ballroom [böl/rŏŏm/] **184**–26

baseball [bās/böl/] **231**–18, **231**–14

basketball [băs/kət böl/] **229**–8, **231**–4

basketball court [băs/kət böl/ kört/] **229**–7

football [fŏŏt/böl/] **229**–11, **231**–21

meatballs [mēt/bölz/] **81**–27

racquetball [răk/ət böl/] **228**–12

softball [söft/böl/] **229**–10

volleyball [väl/ē böl/] **229**–14, **231**–3

balloons [bə lŏŏnz/] **44**–4

bananas [bə năn/əz] **68**–2

band [bănd] **183**–34

headband [hĕd/bănd/] **90**–3

waistband [wāst/bănd/] **100**–5

bandage [băn/dĭj] **117**–5, **117**–12

bandana [băn dă/nə] **92**–16

bangs [băngz] **33**–8

bank [băngk] **124**–5

bank statement [băngk/ stāt/mənt] **132**–16

bank online [băngk/ än līn/] **132**–C

BANK [băngk] **132**

banner [băn/ər] **44**–1

banquet room [băng/kwət rŏŏm/] **185**–14

bar [bär]

bar code [bär/ kōd/] **27**–4

candy bar [kăn/dē bär/] **73**–37

grab bar [grăb/ bär/] **57**–9

menu bar [mĕn/yŏŏ bär/] **197**–1

salad bar [săl/əd bär/] **79**–24

scroll bar [skröl/ bär/] **197**–15

barbecued ribs [bär/bĭ kyŏŏd/ rĭbz/] **76**–2

barbershop [bär/bər shäp/] **129**–19

bargain [bär/gən] **102**–A

barn [bärn] **177**–11

barrette [bə rĕt/] **108**–20

base [bās] **193**–45, **194**–20

baseball [bās/böl/] **229**–9, **231**–18

baseball bat [bās/böl/ băt/] **231**–14

baseball cap [bās/böl/ kăp/] **86**–5

baseball cards [bās/bȯl/ kärds/] **232**–2
baseball game [bās/bȯl/ gām/] **44**–2
basement [bās/mənt] **47**–13
Basement [bās/mənt] **50**
Basic Colors [bā/sĭk kŭ/lərz] **24**
BASIC TRANSPORTATION
   [bā/sĭk tränz/pər tā/shən] **150**–151
basket [bās/kət] **56**–3
   basketball [bās/kət bȯl/] **229**–8, **231**–4
   basketball court [bās/kət bȯl kȯrt/] **229**–7
   bread basket [brĕd/ bās/kət] **83**–11
   laundry basket [lȯn/drē bās/kət] **101**–2
   shopping basket [shäp/ĭng bās/kət] **73**–9
   wastebasket [wāst/bās/kət] **57**–26
bass [bās] **212**–6, [bās] **238**–8
bassoon [bə sōōn/] **238**–4
bat [băt] **216**–7, **231**–14
bath [băth]
   bath mat [băth/ măt/] **57**–28
   bath powder [băth/ pow/dər] **108**–4
   bathroom [băth/rōōm/] **46**–4
   bath towel [băth/ tow/əl] **57**–13
   bathtub [băth/tŭb/] **57**–2
   half bath [hăf/ băth/] **57** ✦
bathe [bādh] **36**–F, **108**–B
bathing suit [bā/dhĭng sōōt/] **90**–26
BATHROOM [băth/rōōm/] **57**
battery / batteries [băt/ə rē] / [băt/ə rēz]
   146–15, **158**–20
   battery charger [băt/ə rē chär/jər] **235**–27
   battery pack [băt/ə rē păk/] **235**–26
bay [bā] **204**–9
be [bē]
   be aware [bē ə wër/] **143**–I
   be born [bē bȯrn/] **40**–A
   be 18 or older [bē ā/tēn/ ȯr ōld/ər] **140**–G
   be hurt [bē hürt/] **116**–C
   be in a rock band [bē ĭn ə räk/ bănd/] **238**–D
   be informed [bē ĭn fȯrmd/] **140**–F
   be injured [bē ĭn/jərd] **116**–C
   be in shock [bē ĭn shäk/] **116**–B
   be neat [bē nēt/] **174**–C
   be on time [bē ȯn tīm/] **174**–F
   be released [bē rĭ lēst/] **141**–H
   be unconscious [bē ŭn kän/shəs] **116**–A
   don't be late [dōnt/ bē lāt/] **174**–D
beach [bēch] **204**–10
   beach chair [bēch/ chër/] **225**–22
   beach umbrella [bēch/ ŭm brĕl/ə] **225**–14
BEACH [bēch] **225**
beads [bēdz] **95**–34, **99**–32
beak [bēk] **214**–3
beaker [bē/kər] **195**–39
beam [bēm] **178**–3
beans [bēnz] **69**–8, **72**–17
   soybeans [soy/bēnz/] **177**–3
bear [bër] **37**–23, **216**–11
beard [bërd] **33**–6
beat [bēt] **77**–S
beater [bē/tər]
   eggbeater [ĕg/bē/tər] **78**–20
beautiful [byōō/tə fəl] **23**–21

beauty shop [byōō/tē shäp/] **130** ✦
beaver [bē/vər] **216**–9
become [bē kŭm/] **40**–G, **41**–N
bed [bĕd] **58**–9
   bedbugs [bĕd/bŭgz/] **63**–24
   bed control [bĕd/ kən trōl/] **121**–27
   bed frame [bĕd/ frām/] **58**–18
   bed pan [bĕd/ păn/] **121**–23
   bedroom [bĕd/rōōm/] **46**–2
   bedspread [bĕd/sprĕd/] **59**–11
   bed table [bĕd/ tā/bəl] **121**–21
   bunk beds [bŭnk/ bĕdz/] **59**–9
   double bed [dŭb/əl bĕd/] **184**–14
   flower bed [flow/ər bĕd/] **53**–20
   hospital bed [häs/pĭ tl bĕd/] **121**–22
   kids' bedroom [kĭdz/ bĕd/rōōm/] **47**–9
   king-size bed [kĭng/sīz/ bĕd/] **184**–15
BEDROOM [bĕd/rōōm/] **58, 59**
bee [bē]
   honeybee [hŭn/ē bē/] **214**–25
beef [bēf]
   beef ribs [bēf/ rĭbz/] **70**–5
   corned beef [kȯrnd/ bēf/] **71**–22
   ground beef [grownd/ bēf/] **70**–4
   roast beef [rōst/ bēf/] **71**–21
   stewing beef [stōō/ĭng bēf/] **70**–3
   stir-fried beef [stür/frīd/ bēf/] **76**–6
Beef [bēf] **70**
beetle [bēt/l] **214**–18
beets [bēts] **69**–5
Before an Emergency [bĭ fȯr/ ən ĭ mür/jən sē] **146**
behind [bĭ hīnd/] **25**–8
beige [bāzh] **24**–18
bell [bĕl]
   bell captain [bĕl/ kăp/tən] **184**–6
   bellhop [bĕl/häp/] **184**–7
   bell peppers [bĕl/ pĕp/ərz] **69**–7
   doorbell [dȯr/bĕl/] **53**–14
below [bĭ lō/] **25**–5
belts [bĕlts] **94**–6
   back support belt [băk/ sə pȯrt/ bĕlt/] **179**–18
   belt buckle [bĕlt/ bŭk/əl] **94**–20
   conveyor belt [kən vā/ər bĕlt/] **175**–9
   garter belt [gär/tər bĕlt/] **91**–16
   seat belt [sēt/ bĕlt/] **159**–52
   tool belt [tōōl/ bĕlt/] **92**–3
bench [bĕnch] **224**–10
bend [bĕnd] **230**–O
benefits [bĕn/ə fĭts] **174** ✦
berries [bĕr/ēz] **210**–20
   blackberries [blăk/bĕr/ēz] **68**–17
   blueberries [blōō/bĕr/ēz] **68**–16
   mixed berries [mĭkst/ bĕr/ēz] **81**–36
   raspberries [răz/bĕr/ēz] **68**–15
   strawberries [strȯ/bĕr/ēz] **68**–14
between [bĭ twēn/] **25**–12
Beverages [bĕv/rə jəz] **73, 81**
bib [bĭb] **37**–5
bicycle / bike [bī/sĭ kəl] / [bīk] **129**–22, **151**–15
big [bĭg] **23**–2, **97**–38
   Big Dipper [bĭg/ dĭ/pər] **205** ✦
   big-screen TV [bĭg/skrēn/ tē/vē/] **50**–15

bike / bicycle [bīk] / [bī/sĭ kəl] **129**–22, **151**–15
   bike path [bīk/ păth/] **224**–3
biking [bī/kĭng] **226**–8, **228**–5
bikini panties [bə kē/nē păn/tēz] **91**–13
bill [bĭl] **214**–3
Bill [bĭl] **15**
billiards [bĭl/yərdz] **228**–2
Bill of Rights [bĭl/ əv rīts/] **198**–10
Bills [bĭlz] **26**
bin [bĭn] **51**–23, **61**–2, **160**–6
bioenergy [bī/ō ĕn/ər jē] **218**–9
biography [bī ä/grə fē] **133**–15
biologist [bī ä/lə jĭst] **194**–2
Biology [bī ä/lə jē] **194**
biomass [bī/ō măs/] **218**–9
birch [bürch] **210**–7
bird [bürd] **208**–4
Bird [bürd] **214**
BIRDS, INSECTS, AND ARACHNIDS
   [bürdz/ ĭn/sĕkts ən ə răk/nĭdz] **214**
birth [bürth]
   birth certificate [bürth/ sər tĭf/ə kət] **40**–1
   birthday [bürth/dā/] **22**–1
BIRTHDAY PARTY [bürth/dā/ pär/tē] **240**–241
biscuits [bĭs/kəts] **80**–6
bison [bī/sən] **216**–6
bit [bĭt] **180**–28
bite [bīt] **110**–11
black [blăk] **24**–13
   blackberries [blăk/bĕr/ēz] **68**–17
   black hair [blăk/ hër/] **33**–16
bladder [blăd/ər] **107**–46
blade [blād] **107**–28, **109**–28, **180**–27
blankets [blăng/kəts] **58**–15, **146**–7, **225**–11
   blanket sleeper [blăng/kət slē/pər] **91**–27
blazer [blā/zər] **92**–12
bleach [blēch] **101**–7
bleachers [blē/chərz] **5**–3
bleed [blēd] **116**–M
blender [blĕn/dər] **54**–12
blind [blīnd] **32**–11
blister [blĭs/tər] **110**–15
blizzard [blĭz/ərd] **13**–23, **145**–13
blocks [bläks] **59**–19
   quilt block [kwĭlt/ bläk/] **232**–15
   sunblock [sŭn/bläk/] **108**–8, **225**–10
blond hair [bländ/ hër/] **33**–17
blood [blŭd] **111**–14
   blood pressure gauge [blŭd/ prĕsh/ər gāj/] **118**–9
   blood test [blŭd/ tĕst/] **121**–30
   blood work [blŭd/ würk/] **121**–30
   bloody nose [blŭd/ē nōz/] **110**–17
blouse [blows] **87**–8
blow dryer [blō/ drī/ər] **33**–23, **108**–18
blower [blō/ər] **176**–2
blow out [blō/ owt/] **240**–C
blue [blōō] **24**–3
   blueberries [blōō/bĕr/ēz] **68**–16
   blue jay [blōō/ jā/] **214**–6
   bright blue [brīt/ blōō/] **24**–12
   dark blue [därk/ blōō/] **24**–10
   light blue [līt/ blōō/] **24**–11
   navy blue [nā/vē blōō/] **28**–5

blues [blōōz] **237**–22
blush [blŭsh] **109**–37
board [bôrd]
  board game [bôrd/ gām/] **232**–5
  bulletin board [bŏŏl/ə tn bôrd/] **7**–14
  chalkboard [chôk/bôrd/] **6**–1
  cutting board [kŭt/ĭng bôrd/] **54**–27
  emery board [ĕm/ə rē bôrd/, ĕm/rē–] **109**–32
  headboard [hĕd/bôrd/] **58**–10
  ironing board [ī/ər nĭng bôrd/] **101**–14
  motherboard [mŭdh/ər bôrd/] **196**–5
  particle board [pär/tə kəl bôrd/] **181**–20
  skateboard [skāt/bôrd/] **224**–7
  snowboard [snō/bôrd/] **231**–23
  surfboard [sürf/bôrd/] **225**–16
  whiteboard [wīt/bôrd/] **6**–3
board [bôrd] **160**–E
boarding [bôr/dĭng]
  boarding area [bôr/dĭng ër/ē ə] **161**–9
  boarding pass [bôr/dĭng păs/] **161**–20
  sailboarding [sāl/bôr/dĭng] **227** ✦
  skateboarding [skāt/bôr/dĭng] **228**–13
  snowboarding [snō/bôr/dĭng] **227**–2
boat [bōt]
  sailboat [sāl/bōt/] **225**–3
boating [bō/tĭng] **226**–1
bobbin [bä/bĭn] **98**–21
bobby pins [bäb/ē pĭnz/]**108**–21
body [bäd/ē] **190**–7
  body lotion [bäd/ē lō/shən] **108**–9
  body of water [bäd/ē əv wö/tər] **204** ✦
  body shaper [bäd/ē/ shā/pər] **91**–15
BODY [bäd/ē] **104–105, 106–107**
boil [boyl] **77**–M
boiled ham [boyld/ hăm/] **76**–5
boiler [boy/lər] **78**–8
bok choy [bäk/ choy/] **69**–15
bolt [bōlt] **51**–34, **180**–35, **180**–38
  bolt of fabric [bōlt/ əv făb/rĭk] **98**–15
bone [bōn] **107**–33, **116**–P
  boneless [bōn/ləs] **70** ✦
book [bŏŏk]
  appointment book [ə poynt/mənt bŏŏk/] **183**–48
  audiobook [ö/dē ō bŏŏk/] **133**–17
  bookkeeper [bŏŏk/ kē/pər] **175**–2
  book of stamps [bŏŏk/ əv stămps/] **134**–18
  bookcase [bŏŏk/ kās/] **7**–10
  bookstore [bŏŏk/ stör/] **130**–4
  check book [chĕk/ bŏŏk/] **132**–12
  coloring book [kŭl/ə rĭng bŏŏk/] **59**–13
  DMV handbook [dē/ĕm/vē/ hănd/bŏŏk/] **136**–1
  notebook [nōt/bŏŏk/] **7**–27
  passbook [păs/bŏŏk/] **132**–10
  picture book [pĭk/chər bŏŏk/] **133**–12
  spiral notebook [spī/rəl nōt/bŏŏk/] **7**–29
  test booklet [tĕst/ bŏŏk/lət] **10**–1
  textbook [tĕkst/bŏŏk/, tĕks–/] **7**–25
  workbook [würk/bŏŏk/] **7**–26
boombox [bōōm/bäks/] **234**–1
booth [bōōth] **82**–4, **122**–3

boots [bōōts] **95**–28
  hiking boots [hī/kĭng bōōts/] **95**–31
  rain boots [rān/ bōōts/] **90**–20
  safety boots [sāf/tē bōōts/] **179**–20
  ski boots [skē/ bōōts/] **231**–26
  steel toe boots [stēl/ tō/ bōōts/] **92**–6
bored [bôrd] **43**–25
borrow [bär/ō, bör/ō] **26**–B
boss [bäs] **164**–4
botanical garden [bə tăn/ĭ kəl gär/dn] **222**–3
bottle [bät/l] **37**–1, **74**–1, **74**–13
  bottle return [bät/l rĭ türn/] **73**–16
  hot water bottle [hät/ wö/tər bät/l] **113**–15
bottled water [bät/ld wö/tər] **146**–11
bouquet [bō kā/, bōō–] **211**–28
bow [bō] **231**–6
  bow tie [bō/ tī/] **89**–16
bow [bow] **3**–H
bowl [bōl] **55**–2
  mixing bowl [mĭks/ĭng bōl/] **54**–28, **78**–31
  serving bowl [sürv/ĭng bōl/] **55**–21
  soup bowl [sōōp/ bōl/] **83**–21
  sugar bowl [shŏŏg/ər bōl/] **55**–14
bowling [bō/lĭng] **228**–3
  bowling alley [bō/lĭng ăl/ē] **222**–4
  bowling ball [bō/lĭng bōl/] **231**–5
box / boxes [bäks/, bäks/ĭz] **74**–6, **74**–18
  box spring [bäks/ sprĭng/] **58**–19
  CD boombox [sē/dē/ bōōm/bäks/] **234**–1
  fuse box [fyōōz/ bäks/] **62**–13
  mailboxes [māl/bäk/səz] **50**–11, **128**–13
  post office box (PO box)
    [pōst/ ö/fəs bäks/] / [pē/ō bäks/] **135**–9
  safety deposit box [sāf/tē dĭ päz/ət bäks/] **132**–7
  sandbox [sănd/bäks/] **224**–15
  search box [sürch/ bäks/] **197**–5
  text box [tĕkst/ bäks/] **197**–13
  to-go box [tə gō/ bäks/] **82**–5
boxer shorts [bäk/sər shörts/] **91**–4
boxing [bäks/ĭng] **228**–4
boy [boy] **31**–9
bra [brä] **91**–20
bracelets [brās/ləts] **95**–9, **117**–3
braces [brā/səz] **119**–6
brain [brān] **107**–34
brainstorm [brān/störm/] **8**–H, **191**–F
brake [brāk] **159**–48
  brake light [brāk/ līt/] **158**–14
  brake pedal [brāk/ pĕd/l] **159**–45
branch [brănch] **210**–2
Branch [brănch] **138**
Brass [brăs] **238**
bread [brĕd] **67**–11
  bread-and-butter plate [brĕd/ n bŭt/ər plāt/] **83**–19
  bread basket [brĕd/ băs/kət] **83**–11
  garlic bread [gär/lĭk brĕd/] **81**–28
  rye bread [rī/ brĕd/] **71**–20
  wheat bread [wēt/ brĕd/] **71**–19
  white bread [wīt/ brĕd/] **71**–18
break [brāk] **77**–Q, **116**–P
  break down [brāk/ down/] **162**–D

Breakfast Special [brĕk/fəst spĕ/shəl] **80**
breasts [brĕsts] **70**–19, **107**–26
breathe [brēdh] **116**–N
breathing [brē/dhĭng] **117**–16
bricklayer [brĭk/lā/ər] **186**–8
bricks [brĭks] **178**–12, **178**–B
briefcase [brēf/kās/] **88**–13
briefs [brēfs] **91**–5, **91**–14
bright blue [brīt/ blōō/] **24**–12
bring [brĭng] **174**–D, **240**–E
broccoli [bräk/ə lē] **69**–13
broiled steak [broyld/ stāk/] **76**–3
broiler [broy/lər] **54**–21
broken [brō/kən] **62**–5, **62**–6, **62**–7, **63**–15, **97**–39
  broken equipment [brō/kən ĭ kwĭp/mənt] **179**–4
broom [brōōm] **61**–16
brother [brŭdh/ər] **34**–6, **35**–28
  brother-in-law [brŭdh/ər ĭn lö/] **34**–17
  stepbrother [stĕp/brŭdh/ər] **35**–30
brown [brown] **24**–17
  brown hair [brown/ hër/] **33**–18
  hash browns [hăsh/ brownz/] **80**–3
browse [browz] **102**–B
bruise [brōōz] **110**–12
brush [brŭsh] **33**–22, **108**–14
  paintbrush [pānt/brŭsh/] **181**–22, **233**–20
  scrub brush [skrŭb/ brŭsh/] **61**–20
  toilet brush [toy/lət brŭsh/] **57**–18
  toothbrush [tōōth/brŭsh/] **109**–22
brush [brŭsh] **108**–I, **109**–J
bubble in [bŭ/bəl ĭn/] **10**–K
bucket [bŭk/ət] **61**–7, **225**–8
buckle [bŭk/əl] **94**–20, **99**–28
buckle up [bŭk/əl ŭp/] **36**–L
bud [bŭd] **211**–7
budget [bŭ jĭt/] **186**–3
buffalo [bŭf/ə lō] **216**–6
buffet [bə fā/] **55**–24, **185**–10
bugs [bŭgz]
  bedbugs [bĕd/bŭgz/] **63**–24
building [bĭl/dĭng] **50**–1, **124**–2
BUILDING SUPPLIES [bĭl/dĭng sə plīz/] **180–181**
bulb [bŭlb] **56** ✦, **211**–2
bulldozer [bŏŏl/dō/zər] **178**–6
bulletin board [bŏŏl/ə tn bôrd/] **7**–14
bump cap [bŭmp/ kăp/] **92**–9
bumper [bŭm/pər] **158**–8
  bumper pad [bŭm/pər păd/] **59**–4
bunch [bŭnch] **68**–29
bunk beds [bŭngk/ bĕdz/] **59**–9
Bunsen burner [bŭn/sən bür/nər] **195**–37
bureau [byōōr/ō] **58**–1
burger [bür/gər]
  cheeseburger [chēz/bür/gər] **79**–3
  hamburger [hăm/bür/gər] **79**–1
burglary [bür/glə rē] **142**–2
burn [bürn]
  sunburn [sŭn/bürn/] **110**–14
burn [bürn] **116**–H
burner [bür/nər] **54**–19, **195**–37
burrito [bə rē/tō] **79**–9

bus [bŭs] **128**–9, **151**–14
    bus person [bŭs/ pür/sən] **185**–13
    bus route [bŭs/ rōōt/, –rowt/] **152**–1
    bus station [bŭs/ stā/shən] **124**–7
    bus stop [bŭs/ stäp/] **129**–16, **151**–13
    miss the bus [mĭs/ dhə bŭs/] **152** ✦
bus [bŭs] **82**–G
business [bĭz/nəs]
    business owner [bĭz/nəs ō/nər] **166**–11
    businessperson [bĭz/nəs pür/sən] **166**–12
    business suit [bĭz/nəs sōōt/] **88**–11
busser [bŭ/sər] **83**–12
Bus Stop [bŭs/ stäp/] **152**
butcher [bŏŏch/ər] **166**–13
butter [bŭt/ər] **66**–6, **83**–19
butterfly [bŭt/ər flī/] **214**–19
buttocks [bŭt/əks] **107**–30
button [bŭt/n] **99**–24
    back button [băk/ bŭt/n] **197**–2
    call button [köl/ bŭt/n] **121**–28
    forward button [för/wərd bŭt/n] **197**–3
buy [bī] **27**–G
    buy a home [bī/ ə hōm/] **41**–M
    buy a snack [bī/ ə snăk/] **11**–K
    buy recycled products
        [bī/ rē sī/kəld präd/ŭkts] **219**–D
Buying a House [bī/ĭng ə hows/] **49**
BUYING AND MAINTAINING A CAR
    [bī/ĭng ən mān tā/nĭng ə kär/] **157**
Buying a Used Car [bī/ĭng ə yōōzd/ kär/] **157**
buzzer [bŭz/ər] **51**–31
cab [kăb] **156**–16
cabbage [kăb/ĭj] **69**–2
Cabinet [kăb/ə nət] **138**–10
cabinet [kăb/ə nət] **54**–1
    file cabinet [fīl/ kăb/ə nət] **182**–11
    medicine cabinet [mĕd/ə sən käb/ə nət] **57**–20
    supply cabinet [sə plī/ käb/ə nət] **182**–1
cables [kā/bəlz] **158**–21, **196**–13
cactus [kăk/təs] **210**–21
cafeteria [kăf/ə tïr/ē ə] **5**–14
cage [kāj] **107**–48
cake [kāk] **73**–39, **81**–33
    cake pan [kāk/ pän/] **78**–26
    cheesecake [chēz/kāk/] **81**–34
    pancakes [pän/kāks/] **80**–7
Cake [kāk] **77**
calculate [kăl/kyə lāt/] **17**–B
calculator [kăl/kyə lā/tər] **17**–6, **183**–25
calculus [kăl/kyə ləs] **192**–19
CALENDAR [kăl/ən dər] **20**–21
CALENDAR EVENTS [kăl/ən dər ĭ vĕnts/] **22**
calf [kăf] **106**–22
    calf-length [kăf/ lĕnth/] **96**–17
call [köl]
    call button [köl/ bŭt/n] **121**–28
    international call [ĭn/tər năsh/ə nəl köl/] **15**–35
    Internet phone call [ĭn/tər nĕt/ fōn/ köl/] **14**–20
    local call [lō/kəl köl/] **15**–31
    long distance call [löng/ dĭs/təns köl/] **15**–32
call [köl] **48**–A, **147**–L
    call in [köl/ ĭn/] **186**–A

calling card [kö/lĭng kärd/] **14**–15
calm [köm] **42**–8
camcorder [kăm/kör dər] **235**–24
camel [kăm/əl] **217**–38
camera [kăm/rə]
    camera case [kăm/rə kās/] **235**–28
    digital camera [dĭ/jə təl kăm/rə] **235**–19
    film camera [fĭlm/ kăm/rə] **235**–21
    security camera [sĭ kyŏŏr/ə tē kăm/rə] **50**–19
    35 mm camera
        [thür/tē fīv/ mĭl/ə mē/tər kăm/rə] **235**–21
camisole [kăm/ə sōl/] **91**–21
campaign [kăm pān/] **139**–29
camper [kăm/pər] **156**–9
campfire [kămp/fïr/] **226**–11
camping [kăm/pĭng] **226**–5
    camping stove [kăm/pĭng stōv/] **226**–16
Campus [kăm/pəs] **5**
can [kăn] **74**–3, **74**–15
    can opener [kăn/ ō/pə nər] **78**–1, **146**–8
    electric can opener [ĭ lĕk/trĭk/ kăn/ ō/pə nər] **54**–14
    garbage can [gär/bĭj kăn/] **53**–24
cancer [kăn/sər] **111**–10
candle [kăn/dl] **56**–20
    candle holder [kăn/dl hōl/dər] **56**–21
candy [kăn/dē] **239**–12
    candy bar [kăn/dē bär/] **73**–37
    candy cane [kăn/dē kān/] **239**–17
    candy store [kăn/dē stör/] **131**–17
cane [kān] **113**–16, **239**–17
canned food [kănd/ fōōd/] **146**–9
Canned Foods [kănd/ fōōdz/] **72**
canoeing [kə nōō/ĭng] **226**–3
can't breathe [kănt/ brēdh/] **116**–N
canteen [kăn tēn/] **226**–24
canvas [kăn/vəs] **233**–17
canyon [kăn/yən] **204**–17
cap [kăp] **88**–1, **206**–7
    baseball cap [bās/böl/ kăp/] **86**–5
    bump cap [bŭmp/ kăp/] **92**–9
    shower cap [show/ər kăp/] **108**–1
    surgical cap [sür/jĭ kəl kăp/] **121**–37
    surgical scrub cap [sür/jĭ kəl skrŭb/ kăp/] **93**–35
capital [kä/pət əl] **139**–22
capitalize [kä/pət əl īz/] **190**–A, **190**–B
Capitol [kä/pət əl] **138**–1
capris [kə prēz/] **88**–8
capsule [kăp/səl] **113**–23
car [kär] **150**–1
    car accident [kär/ ăk/sə dənt] **144**–2
    car dealership [kär/ dē/lər shĭp/] **126**–4
    car safety seat [kär/ sāf/tē sēt/] **37**–19
    4-door car [för/dör/ kär/] **156**–1
    sports car [spörts/kär/] **156**–4
    subway car [sŭb/wā/ kär/] **152**–6
    town car [town/ kär/] **152**–20
    2-door car [tōō/dör/ kär/] **156**–2
Car [kär] **157**, **159**
CAR [kär] **156**, **157**, **158–159**
card [kärd] **239**–5
    ATM card [ā/tē/ĕm/ kärd/] **132**–15
    auto club card [ö tō/ klŭb/ kärd/] **162**–4

baseball cards [bās/böl/ kärdz/] **232**–2
card store [kärd/ stör/] **130**–7
copies of ID and credit cards
    [käp/ēz əv ī/dē/ ən krĕd/ət/ kärdz/] **146**–19
emergency card [ĭ mür/jən sē/ kärd/] **161**–23
fare card [fër/ kärd/] **152**–11
folding card table [fōl/dĭng/ kärd/ tā/bəl] **102**–4
green card [grēn/ kärd/] **40**–2
greeting card [grē/tĭng kärd/] **134**–15
health insurance card
    [hĕlth/ ĭn shŏŏr/əns kärd/] **118**–3
memory card [mĕm/ə rē kärd/] **235**–20
post card [pōst/ kärd/] **134**–16
Resident Alien card [rĕz/ə dənt ā/lē ən kärd/] **40**–2
rotary card file [rō/tə rē kärd/ fīl/] **183**–44
Social Security card
    [sō/shəl sĭ kyŏŏr/ə tē kärd/] **40**–5
Card [kärd] **135**
cardigan sweater [kär/də gən swĕt/ər] **88**–2
Cardinal Numbers [kärd/nəl nŭm/bərz] **16**
cardiologist [kär/dē äl/ə jĭst] **120**–3
cardiopulmonary resuscitation (CPR)
    [kär/dē ō pŏŏl mə nër/ē rĭ sŭs/ə tā/shən] /
    [sē/pē/är/] **117**–17
care [kër] **167**–32
careful worker [kër/fəl wür/kər] **179**–2
careless worker [kër/ləs wür/kər] **179**–1
childcare worker [chīld/kër wür/kər] **166**–16
CARE [kër] **114–115, 118, 119**
Care of Your Car [kër/ əv yər kär/] **157**
career counselor [kə rēr/ kown/slər] **172**–10
Career Path [kə rēr/ păth/] **172**
CAREER PLANNING [kə rēr/ plăn/ĭng] **172**
cargo van [kär/gō văn/] **156**–13
carnation [kär nā/shən] **211**–20
carousel [kär/ə sĕl/] **161**–23
carpenter [kär/pən tər] **62**–12, **166**–14
carpet [kär/pət] **56**–24
carpool [kär/pōōl/] **219**–I
carriage [kär/ĭj] **37**–20
carrier [kär/ē ər] **37**–17, **134**–20
carrots [kär/əts] **69**–3
carry [kär/ē] **11**–F, **82**–H
CARS AND TRUCKS [kärz/ ən trŭks/] **156**
cart [kärt] **72**–7, **129**–28
    housekeeping cart [hows/kē/pĭng kärt/] **184**–19
    luggage cart [lŭg/ĭj/ kärt/] **184**–8
carton [kär/tn] **74**–4, **74**–16
cartoon [kär/tōōn] **236**–3
cartridge [kär/trĭj] **183**–45
carving knife [kär/vĭng nīf/] **78**–12
case [kās] **94**–5, **235**–28
cash [kăsh]
    cash and coins [kăsh/ ən koynz/] **146**–17
    cash register [kăsh/ rĕj/ə stər] **27**–10, **73**–15
cash [kăsh] **27**–F, **132**–A
cashier [kă shïr/] **73**–13, **166**–15
cashmere [kăzh/mïr/] **98**–4
Casserole [kăs/ə rōl] **77**
casserole dish [kăs/ə rōl dĭsh/] **78**–10
cassette [kə sĕt/] **234**–6
    videocassette [vĭ/dē ō kə sĕt/] **133**–18

cast [kăst] **113**–20

castle [kă/səl] **225**–12

Casual Clothes [kăzh/ōō əl klōz/] **88**

CASUAL, WORK, AND FORMAL CLOTHES
[kăzh/ōō əl würk/ ən för/məl klōz/] **88**–**89**

cat [kăt] **215**–9

catfish [kăt/fĭsh/] **71**–2

catalog [kăt ə /lög] **133**–11

catch [kăch] **230**–D

catcher's mask [kăch/ərz măsk/] **231**–15

caterer [kā/tər ər] **185**–16

caterpillar [kăt/ə pĭl/ər, kăt/ər–] **214**–20

cattle [kăt/l] **177**–21

cauliflower [kö/lĭ flow/ər, kä/–] **69**–14

cave [kāv] **220**–6

caverns [kă/vərnz] **220**–7

cavity [kăv/ə tē] **119**–7

C-clamp [sē/klămp/] **180**–6

CD [sē/dē/] **196**–9, **234**–5

CD boombox [sē/dē/ bōōm/băks/] **234**–1

CD player [sē/dē/ plā/ər] **159**–38

celebrate [sĕl/ə brāt] **206**–C

celery [sĕl/ə rē] **69**–9

cell [sĕl] **194**–4

cell membrane [sĕl/ mĕm/brān] **194**–6

cell phone holder [sĕl/ fōn/ hōl/dər] **94**–15

cell phone kiosk [sĕl/ fōn/ kē/ösk] **131**–22

cell phone number [sĕl/ fōn/ nŭm/bər] **4**–12

cell wall [sĕl/ wäl/] **194**–5

cellular phone [sĕl/yə lər fōn/] **14**–8

cello [chĕl/ō] **238**–7

Celsius [sĕl/sē əs] **13**–2

cemetery [sĕ/mə tĕr/ē] **127**–15

cent [sĕnt] **26**–1, **26**–2, **26**–3, **26**–4

center [sĕn/tər]

automated postal center (APC)
[ö/tə măt ĭd pōs/təl sĕn/tər] / [ā/pē/sē/] **135**–10

childcare center [chĭld/kĕr/ sĕn/tər] **129**–30

convention center [kən vĕn/shən sĕn/tər] **127**–24

copy center [käp/ē sĕn/tər] **129**–18

entertainment center
[ĕn/tər tān/mənt sĕn/tər] **56**–5

resource center [rē/sörs sĕn/tər] **172**–9

CENTER [sĕn/tər] **208**–**209**

centimeter [cm] [sĕn/tə mē/tər] **17**–14

CENTRAL AMERICA [sĕn/trəl ə mĕr/ə kə] **200**–**201**

Central time [sĕn/trəl tīm/] **19**–31

cereal [sĭr/ē əl] **80**–9

ceremony [sĕr/ə mō/nē] **206**–6

certificate [sər tĭf/ə kət] **40**–1, **41**–11

Certificate of Naturalization
[sər tĭf/ə kət əv năch/rə lə zā/shən] **40**–6

certified [sür/tə fīd/]

Certified Mail® [sür/tə fīd/ māl/] **134**–4

certified nursing assistant (CNA)
[sür/tə fīd/ nür/sĭng ə sĭs/tənt] / [sē/ĕn/ā/]
120–12

chain [chān] **51**–33, **95**–33, **180**–41

chair [chër] **7**–11

armchair [ärm/chër/] **56**–22

beach chair [bēch/ chër/] **225**–22

dining room chair [dī/nĭng rōōm/chër/] **55**–8

easy chair [ē/zē/ chër] **56**–22

folding chair [fōld/ĭng chër/] **102**–5

high chair [hī/ chër/] **37**–6, **82**–3

rocking chair [räk/ĭng chër/] **37**–21

wheelchair [wēl/chër/] **113**–9

chalk [chök] **7**–18

chalkboard [chök/börd/] **6**–1

challenged [chăl/əngd] **32**–10

change [chānj] **36**–G, **60**–P, **148**–C

change purse [chānj/ pürs/] **94**–14

changing [chān/jĭng]

changing pad [chān/jĭng păd/] **59**–2

changing table [chān/jĭng tā/bəl] **59**–1

charger [chär/jər] **14**–10, **234**–17, **235**–27

chart [chärt] **121**–24

cheap [chēp] **23**–20

check [chĕk] **132**–13

check book [chĕk/ bŏŏk/] **132**–12

check-in kiosk [chĕk/ĭn kē/ösk] **160**–2

checkstand [chĕk/stănd/] **73**–12

paycheck [pā/chĕk/] **165**–14

check [chĕk]

check blood pressure [chĕk/ blŭd/ prĕsh/ər] **118**–A

check email [chĕk/ ē/ māl/] **39**–W

check in [chĕk/ ĭn/] **160**–A

check Internet job sites
[chĕk/ ĭn/tər nĕt/ jäb/ sīts/] **173**–D

check messages [chĕk/ mĕs/ə jĭz] **171**–R

check out [chĕk/ owt/] **133**–C

check the correct boxes
[chĕk/ dhə kə rĕkt/ bäk/səz] **9**–U

check the oil [chĕk/ dhə oyl/] **157**–H

check the pronunciation
[chĕk/ dhe prə nən sē ā/ shən] **8**–D

check your bags [chĕk/ yər băgz/] **160**–B

check pulse [chĕk/ püls/] **122**–A

check your spelling [chĕk/ yər spĕl/ĭng] **197**–F

check your understanding
[chĕk/ yər ŭn/dər stănd/ĭng] **12**–N

check your work [chĕk/ yər würk/] **10**–L

checked [chĕkt] **96**–24

checkers [chĕk/ərz] **232**–7

checking account number
[chĕk/ĭng ə kownt/ nŭm/bər] **132**–14

checkout [chĕk/owt/] **133**–10

Checkpoint [chĕk/poynt/] **160**

cheddar cheese [chĕd/ər chēz/] **71**–28

cheek [chēk] **106**–3

cheese [chēz] **66**–4

American cheese [ə mĕr/ə kən chēz/] **71**–26

cheddar cheese [chĕd/ər chēz/] **71**–28

cheeseburger [chēz/bür/gər] **79**–3

cheesecake [chēz/kāk/] **81**–34

grilled cheese sandwich
[grĭld/ chēz/ săn/wĭch, –sănd/–] **80**–10

Swiss cheese [swĭs/ chēz/] **71**–27

Cheesy Tofu Vegetable Casserole
[chē/zē tō/fōō vĕj/tə bəl kăs/ə rōl] **77**

chef [shĕf] **83**–16

chef's hat [shĕfs/ hăt/] **93**–28

chef's jacket [shĕfs/ jăk/ət] **93**–29

chef's salad [shĕfs/ săl/ əd] **80**–14

executive chef [ĭg zĕk/yə tĭv shĕf/] **185**–7

head chef [hĕd/ shĕf/] **185**–7

sous chef [sōō/ shĕf/] **185**–6

Chef [shĕf] **93**

chemist [kĕm/ĭst] **195**–25

Chemistry [kĕm/ə strē] **195**

cherries [chĕr/ēz] **68**–11

cherry picker [chĕr/ē pĭk/ər] **178**–5

chess [chĕs] **232**–8

chest [chĕst] **59**–16, **104**–4, **107**–25

chest of drawers [chĕst/ əv drörz/] **59**–6

chicken [chĭk/ən] **66**–3, **70**–16

chicken pox [chĭk/ən päks/] **111**–6

chicken sandwich [chĭk/ən săn/wĭch, –sănd–] **79**–5

fried chicken [frīd/ chĭk/ən] **76**–1

roast chicken [rōst/ chĭk/ən] **81**–22

Chicken [chĭk/ən] **77**

chief justice [chēf/ jŭs/təs] **138**–13

CHILDCARE AND PARENTING
[chĭld/kër ən për/ən tĭng] **36**–**37**

child / children [chĭld] / [chĭl/ drən]

childcare center [chĭld/kër sĕn/tər] **129**–30

childcare worker [chĭld/kër wür/kər] **166**–16

children's program [chĭl/drənz prō/grăm] **236**–9

child safety seat [chĭld/ săf/tē sēt/] **159**–53

grandchild [grăn/chĭld/, grănd/–] **34** ✦

lost child [löst/ chĭld/] **144**–1

Childhood Diseases [chĭld/hŏŏd dĭ zē/zəz] **111**

chili peppers [chĭl/ē pĕp/ərz] **69**–29

chill [chĭl] **76**–D

chills [chĭlz] **110**–9

chimney [chĭm/nē] **53**–5

chimpanzee [chĭm/păn zē/] **217**–27

chin [chĭn] **106**–1

chipmunk [chĭp/mŭngk] **215**–20

chips [chĭps] **73**–35

chiropractors [kī/rō prăk/tərz] **120**

chisel [chĭz/əl] **181**–55

choke [chōk] **116**–L

choose [chōōz] **9**–P

chop [chäp] **77**–L

chops [chäps] **70**–10, **70**–15

Christmas [krĭs/məs] **22**–18

Christmas tree [krĭs/məs trē/] **239**–16

chromosome [krō/mə zōm/] **194**–8

chrysanthemum [krĭ săn/thə məm] **211**–21

church [chürch] **127**–14

chute [shōōt] **51**–26

circle [sür/ kəl] **193**–34

circle [sür/ kəl] **9**–Q

circular saw [sür/kyə lər sö/] **180**–9

circulation desk [sür/kyə lā/shən dĕsk/] **133**–2

circumference [sər kŭm/frəns] **193**–36

citizen [sĭt/ə zən] **30**–5

Citizenship Requirements
[sĭt/ə zən shĭp/ rĭ kwīr/mənts] **140**

city [sĭt/ē] **4**–7, **52**–1

city code [sĭt/ē kōd/] **15**–34

city council [sĭt/ē kown/səl] **139**–27

city hall [sĭt/ē häl/] **124**–8

City Government [sĭt/ē gŭ/vərn mənt] **139**

CITY STREETS [sĭt/ē strēts/] **126**–**127**

Index

CIVIC RIGHTS AND RESPONSIBILITIES
[sǐ/vǐk rǐts n rǐ spän/sə bǐl/ə tēz] **140**

Civilizations [sǐ/və lə zā/shenz] **199**

claim [klām] **160**–L

clamp [klămp] **180**–6

clams [klămz] **71**–15

clarinet [klär/ə nĕt/] **238**–2

classical [kla/sǐ kəl] **237**–21

   classical concert [kla/sǐ kəl kän/sərt] **223**–14

classified ad [klăs/e fǐd] **48**–2

Classmates [klăs/māts/] **8**

classroom [klăs/rōōm/] **5**–7

CLASSROOM [klăs/rōōm/] **6**–7

claw [klö] **214**–2

clean [klēn] **101**–16

clean [klēn] **76**–A

   clean teeth [klēn/ tēth/] **119**–A

   clean the house [klēn/ dhə hows/] **39**–O

   clean the lint trap [klēn/ dhə lǐnt/ trăp/] **101**–D

   clean the oven [klēn/ dhə ŭv/ən] **60**–C

   clean up [klēn/ ŭp/] **147**–M

cleaner [klēn/ər]

   dry cleaners [drī/ klēn/ərz] **128**–2

   glass cleaner [glăs/ klēn/ər] **61**–14

   oven cleaner [ŭv/ən klēn/ər] **61**–3

   vacuum cleaner [văk/yōōm klēn/ər] **61**–10

   vacuum cleaner attachments
      [văk/yōōm klēn/ər ə tăch/mənts] **61**–11

   vacuum cleaner bag [văk/yəm klēn/ər băg/] **61**–12

CLEANING SUPPLIES [klē/nǐng sə plīz/] **61**

cleanser [klēn/zər] **61**–18

CLEANUP [klēn/ŭp/] **148**–149

clear [klǐr] **13**–9

   clear tape [klǐr/tāp/] **183**–30

clear [klǐr] **82**–G

   clear off [klǐr/ äf/] **10**–I

clerk [klürk] **5**–13, **182**–2

   admissions clerk [əd mǐsh/ənz klürk/] **120**–14

   desk clerk [dĕsk/ klürk/] **184**–11

   DMV clerk [dē/ĕm/vē/ klürk/] **136**–3

   file clerk [fīl/ klürk/] **182**–10

   grocery clerk [grōs/rē klürk/, grösh/–, grō/sə–] **72**–4

   library clerk [lī/brĕr ē klürk/] **133**–1

   payroll clerk [pā/rōl/ klürk/] **165**–10

   postal clerk [pō/stəl klürk/] **135**–7

   retail clerk [rē/tāl/ klürk/] **169**–53

   salesclerk [sālz/klürk/] **94**–3

   shipping clerk [shǐp/ǐng klürk/] **175**–16

   stock clerk [stäk/ klürk/] **169**–59

click [klǐk] **197**–B

climb [klīm] **224**–C

climbing apparatus [klīm/ǐng ă/pə ră/təs] **224**–14

clinic [klǐn/ǐk] **186**–2

clip-on earrings [klǐp/än ǐr/ǐngz, –ön–] **95**–37

clipper [klǐp/ər] **109**–31, **176**–11

clips [klǐps] **108**–19, **183**–31, **194**–24

clock [kläk] **7**–9, **58**–24, **165**–7

   clock radio [kläk/ rā/dē ō] **102**–6

close [klōz] **6**–H

closet [kläz/ət] **57** ✦, **58**–5

Closures [klō/zhərz] **99**

cloth [klöth] **181**–54

   cloth diaper [klöth/ dī/pərz] **37**–8

   tablecloth [tā/bəl klöth/] **55**–12

   washcloth [wäsh/klöth/] **57**–4

clothes [klōz] **146**–6

   clothesline [klōz/līn/] **101**–9

   clothespin [klōz/pǐn/] **101**–10

CLOTHES [klōz] **86**–87, **88**–89, **96**–97, **98**–99

clothing [klō/dhǐng] **102**–2

CLOTHING [klō/dhǐng] **90**, **92**–93

Clothing Problems [klō/dhǐng präb/ləmz] **97**

cloudy [klow/dē] **13**–10

club [klŭb] **162**–4, **223**–12, **231**–1

   club sandwich [klŭb săn/wǐch/, –sănd–] **80**–12

clubs [klŭbz] **233**–32

clutch [klŭch] **159**–49

   clutch bag [klŭch/ băg/] **89**–19

CNA (certified nursing assistant) [sē/ĕn/ā/] /
   [sür/tə tə fīd/ nür/sǐng ə sǐs/tənt] **120**–12

coach [kōch] **5**–20, **229**–2

coal [kōl] **218**–4

coarse adjustment knob
   [körs/ ə jüst/mənt näb/] **194**–22

Coast Guard [kōst/ gärd/] **138**–18

coat [kōt] **90**–2, **216**–19

   lab coat [lăb/ kōt/] **93**–33

   raincoat [rān/ kōt/] **90**–18

   sports coat [spörts/ kōt/] **89**–14

   trench coat [trĕnch/ kōt/] **90**–21

cobra [kō/brə] **213**–41

cockpit [käk/pǐt/] **161**–10

cockroaches [käk/rō/chəz] **63**–26

cocktail dress [käk/tāl/ drĕs/] **89**–20

coconuts [kō/kə nŭts/] **68**–24

cod [käd] **71**–8, **212**–5

code [kōd]

   area code [ĕr/ē ə kōd/] **15**–29

   bar code [bär/ kōd/] **27**–4

   city code [sǐt/ē kōd/] **15**–34

   country code [kŭn/trē kōd/] **15**–33

coffee [kö/fē] **73**–33, **81**–37, **81**–38

   coffeemaker [kö/fē mā/kər] **54**–11

   coffee mug [kö/fē mŭg/] **55**–7

   coffee shop [kö/fē shäp/] **126**–11

   coffee table [kö/fē tā/bəl] **56**–19

COFFEE SHOP MENU [kö/fē shäp/ mĕn/yōō] **80**–81

coins [koynz] **146**–17

   coin purse [koyn/ pürs/] **94**–14

Coins [koynz] **26**

colander [käl/ən dər] **78**–17

cold [kōld] **13**–6, **42**–4, **111**–1

   cold tablets [kōld tăb/ləts] **113**–27

   cold water [kōld wö/tər] **57**–7

coleslaw [kōl/slö/] **80**–18

collar [käl/ər] **100**–4

collate [kō/lāt/, kə lāt/] **171**–E

collect [kə lĕkt/] **232**–A

college [käl/ǐj] **127**–17, **188**–6, **188**–7

   college degree [käl/ǐj də grē/] **41**–7

   college dormitory [käl/ǐj dör/mə tör/ē] **52**–8

cologne [kə lōn/] **108**–6

colon [kō/lən] **190**–17

Colonial Period [kə lō/nē əl pǐr/ē əd] **198**

colonies [kä/lə nēz] **198**–1

colonists [kä/lə nǐsts] **198**–2

color [kŭl/ər]

   watercolor [wö/tər kŭl/ər] **233**–21

color [kŭl/ər] **33**–D

coloring book [kŭl/ə rǐng bōōk/] **59**–13

Colors [kŭl/ərs] **24**

COLORS [kŭl/ərs] **24**

Columbus Day [kə lŭm/bəs dā/] **22**–15

column [käl/ŭm] **107**–49

comb [kōm] **33**–21, **108**–13

comb [kōm] **108**–G

come [kŭm] **39**–R

comedy [kăm/ə dē] **236**–2, **237**–13

comet [kăm/ət] **205**–24

comfort [kŭm/fərt] **36**–I

comma [käm/ə] **190**–14

commercial fisher [kə mür/shəl fǐsh/ər] **167**–17

commit a crime [kə mǐt/ ə krīm/] **142** ✦

Common Illnesses and Childhood Diseases
   [käm/ən ǐl/nə səz ən chīld/hōōd-dǐ zē/zəz] **111**

COMMUNITY CLEANUP
   [kə myōō/nə tē klēn/ŭp] **148**–149

community college
   [kə myōō/nə tē käl/ǐj] **127**–17, **188**–6

Comparing Clothing [kəm për/ǐng klō/dhǐng] **97**

compartment [kəm pärt/mənt] **159**–44, **161**–13

complaint [kəm plānt/] **97** ✦

Complex [käm/plĕks] **51**

compliment [käm/plə mĕnt/] **12** ✦

compliment [käm/plə mĕnt/] **12**–C

composer [kəm pō/zər] **199**–15

composition [käm/pə zǐsh/ən] **199**–14

compost [käm/pōst/] **219**–M

   compost pile [käm/pōst pīl/] **53**–25

computer [kəm pyōō/tər] **7**–15, **183**–17

   computer lab [kəm pyōō/tər lăb/] **5**–15

   computer software engineer
      [kəm pyōō/tər söft/wër/ ĕn/jə nǐr/] **167**–18

   computer technician [kəm pyōō/tər tĕk nǐsh/ən]
      167–19, **182**–12

Computer [kəm pyōō/tər] **196**

COMPUTERS [kəm pyōō/tərz] **196**

conceal [kən sēl/] **143**–C

concert [kän/sərt] **222**–5, **223**–14

concierge [kän/sē ĕrzh/, kōn/–] **184**–4

conclusion [kən klōō/zhən] **190**–8

concrete [käng/krēt, kän krēt/] **178**–10

conditioner [kən dǐsh/ə nər] **108**–11, **159**–39

Conditions [kən dǐsh/ənz] **13**, **111**

CONDITIONS [kən dǐsh/ənz] **111**

condominium [kän/də mǐn/ē əm] **52**–5

conduct [kən dükt/] **238**–C

conductor [kən dük/tər] **152**–13

cone [kōn] **79**–13, **193**–40

   pinecone [pīn/kōn] **210**–11

conference room [kän/frəns rōōm/] **182**–4

confetti [kən fĕt/ē] **239**–3

confused [kən fyōōzd/] **43**–26

congestion [kən jĕs/chən] **110**–7

Congress [käng/grəs] **138**–2, **198**–6

congressperson [kän/grəs pür/sən] **138**–4
CONSERVATION [kän/sər vā/shən] **218**–**219**
Conserve Energy and Resources
[kən sürv/ ĕn/ər jē ən rē/sörs/əz] **219**
console [kän/sōl] **232**–3
constellation [kän/stə lā/shən] **205**–14
Constitution [kän/stə tōō/shən] **198**–19
construction [kən strŭk/shən]
construction paper [kən strŭk/shən pā/pər] **232**–12
construction site [kən strŭk/shən sīt/] **126**–2
construction worker
[kən strŭk/shən wür/kər] **178**–1
CONSTRUCTION [kən strŭk/shən] **178**
Construction Worker [kən strŭk/shən wür/kər] **92**
contact [kän/tăkt] **146**–2
contact lenses [kän/tăkt lĕn/zəz] **115**–8
container [kən tā/nər] **74**–5, **74**–17, **78**–4
CONTAINERS AND PACKAGING
[kən tā/nərz ən păk/ĭ jĭng] **74**
continental [kän/tə nĕnt/əl] **198**–6
contractor [kän/trăk tər] **186**–5
control [kən trōl/] **121**–27, **232**–4
convenience store [kən vēn/yəns stör/] **128**–3
convention center [kən vĕn/shən sĕn/tər] **127**–24
convert [kən vürt/] **17**–D, **75**–C
convertible [kən vür/tə bəl] **156**–5
conveyor belt [kən vā/ər bĕlt/] **175**–16
convict [kän/vĭkt] **141**–15
convict [kən vĭkt/] **141**–E
cook [kŏŏk] **185**–1, **185** ✦
cook [kŏŏk] **39**–Q, **76**–C, **170**–C
cooked [kŏŏkt] **70**–25
cookies [kŏŏk/ēz] **73**–38
cookie sheet [kŏŏk/ē shĕt/] **78**–27
cool [kōōl] **13**–5
cooler [kōō/lər] **225**–19
co-op [kō/äp/] **52** ✦
copier [kä/pē ər]
photocopier [fō/tō kä/pē ər]**183**–23
copies / copy [kä/pēz] / [kä/pē]
copies of ID and credit cards
[käp/ēz əv ī/dē ən krĕd/ət kärdz/] **146**–19
copies of important papers
[käp/ēz əv ĭm pört/ənt pā/pərz] **146**–20
copy center [käp/ē sĕn/tər] **129**–18
copy [käp/ē] **8**–E
coral [kör/əl] **220**–5
cord [körd] **14**–2
bungee cord [bŭn/jē körd/] **181**–15
cordless phone [körd/ləs fōn/] **15**–24
extension cord [ĭk stĕn/shən körd/] **181**–14
frayed cord [frād/ körd/] **179**–5
power cord [pow/ər körd/] **196**–2
corduroy [kör/də roy/] **99**–11
core course [kör/ körs/] **189** ✦
corn [körn] **69**–12, **177**–4
corn rows [körn/ rōz/] **33**–14
corned beef [körnd/ bēf/] **71**–22
corner [kör/nər] **128**–7
coronary disease [kör/ə nĕ/rē dĭ zēz/] **111** ✦
corral [kə răl/] **177**–17
correct [kə rĕkt/] **10**–N

correction [kə rĕk/shən]
correction fluid [kə rĕk/shən flōō/əd] **183**–36
correction tape [kə rĕk/shən tāp/] **183**–37
cost [köst] **27**–7, **122**–1
costume [käs/tōōm] **239**–11
cotton [kät/n] **98**–1, **177**–6
couch [kowch] **56**–18
cough [köf] **110**–A
cough syrup [köf/ sĭr/əp, –sür/–] **113**–29
council [kown/səl] **139**–27
councilperson [kown/səl pür/sən] **139**–28
counselor [kown/slər] **5**–6, **172**–10
count [kownt] **84**–A
counter [kown/tər] **54**–22, **113**–18
counterperson [kown/tər pür/sən] **79**–17
Counterperson [kown/tər pür/sən] **93**
country [kŭn/trē] **52**–4, **227**–3, **237**–27
country code [kŭn/trē kōd/] **15**–33
county fair [kown/tē fĕr/] **223**–13
coupe [kōōp] **156**–2
couple [kŭ/pəl] **35**–20, **35**–21, **239**–4
coupons [kōō/pönz] **67**–15
courier [kür/ē ər, kŏŏr/–] **168**–40
course [körs] **172**–8, **189** ✦
court [kört]
basketball court [băs/kət böl/ kört/] **229**–7
courthouse [kört/hows/] **125**–13
courtroom [kört/rōōm/] **141**–7
court reporter [kört/ rĭ pör/tər] **141**–12
courtyard [kört/yärd/] **51**–21
food court [fōōd/ kört/] **131**–15
Supreme Court [sə prēm/ kört/] **138**–11
tennis court [tĕ/nəs kört/] **224**–6
cousin [kŭz/ən] **34**–9
cover [kŭv/ər] **158**–9, **181**–46
coveralls [kŭv/ər ölz/] **92**–8
cover-up [kŭv/ər ŭp/] **90**–25
cow [kow] **215**–1
cowboy hat [kow/boy/ hăt/] **92**–18
coyote [kī ō/tē, kī/ōt/] **216**–3
CPR (cardiopulmonary resuscitation) [sē/pē/är/] /
[kär/dē ō pŏŏl/mə nër/ē-rē sŭs/ə tā/shən] **117**–17
CPU [sē/pē/yōō/] **196**–4
crab [krăb] **71**–9, **212**–20
cracked [krăkt] **62**–4
cradle [krād/l] **59**–20
crane [krān] **178**–7
crash [krăsh] **144**–3
crayons [krā/änz] **59**–14
cream [krēm] **24**–16, **81**–41, **113**–25
antihistamine cream
[ăn/tī hĭs/tə mēn krēm/] **117**–11
ice-cream [īs/ krēm/] **72**–26
ice-cream cone [īs/ krēm kōn/] **79**–13
ice cream shop [īs/ krēm shäp/] **131**–16
shaving cream [shā/vĭng krēm/] **109**–29
sour cream [sow/ər krēm/] **72**–21
creamer [krē/mər] **55**–15
credit [krĕd/ət] **146**–19
creek [krēk, krĭk] **204** ✦
crescent moon [krĕs/ənt mōōn/] **205**–10

crew [krōō] **176**–1, **176**–4
crewneck [krōō/nĕk] **96**–7
crew socks [krōō/säks/] **91**–8
crib [krĭb] **59**–3
cricket [krĭk/ət] **214**–23
crime [krīm] **142** ✦
CRIME [krīm] **142**
criminal [krĭm/ə nəl] **142** ✦
crocheting [krō shā/ĭng] **233**–25
crocodile [krăk/ə dīl/] **213**–37
crocus [krō/kəs] **211**–17
Crops [kräps] **177**
cross [krös]
cross-country skiing [krös/kŭn/trē skē/ĭng] **227**–3
crosswalk [krös/wök/] **128**–15
cross [krös] **128**–A
cross out [krös/ owt/] **9**–R
crossing [krö/sĭng] **154**–13, **154**–14, **154**–15
crown [krown] **119**–9
crucible tongs [krōō/sə bəl tängz/, –töngz/] **195**–44
crutches [krŭch/əz] **113**–10
cry [krī] **206**–B
cube [kyōōb] **193**–38
cubicle [kyōōb/ə kəl] **182**–7
cucumbers [kyōō/kŭm bərz] **69**–10
cuff [kŭf] **100**–9
cup [kŭp] **75**–2, **75**–10, **83**–24
1/2 cup [hăf/ kŭp/] **75**–9
1/4 cup [kwör/tər kŭp/] **75**–8
teacup [tē/kŭp/] **55**–6
curb [kürb] **129**–21
curling iron [kür/lĭng ī/ərn] **108**–17
curly hair [kür/lē hĕr/] **33**–11
cursor [kür/sər] **197**–14
curtains [kür/tnz] **57**–12, **58**–7
curved line [kürvd/ līn/] **193**–23
cushion [kŏŏ/shən] **56** ✦, **100**–13
customer [kŭs/tə mər] **72**–1, **94**–4, **132**–2, **164**–2
customer service [kŭs/tə mər sür/vəs] **97** ✦
customer service representative
[kŭs/tə mər-sür/vəs rĕ/prə zĕn/tə tĭv] **167**–20
Customs [kŭs/təmz] **161**
customs officer [kŭs/təmz ö/fə sər] **161**–17
cut [kŭt] **91**–10, **110**–13
cut [kŭt] **33**–A, **109**–N
cut up [kŭt/ ŭp/] **77**–I
cute [kyōōt] **32**–14
cutlets [kŭt/ləts] **70**–6
cutter [kut/ər] **183**–22, **232**–16
cutting board [kŭt/ĭng börd/] **54**–27
cycling [sī/klĭng] **228**–5
cyclist [sī/klĭst] **224**–2
cylinder [sĭl/ən dər] **193**–41, **195**–38
cytoplasm [sī/tə plăzm/] **194**–9
daffodil [dăf/ə dĭl/] **211**–25
daily [dā/lē] **20**–21
DAILY ROUTINES [dā/lē rōō tēnz/] **38**–**39**
Dairy [dĕr/ē] **72**
daisy [dā/zē] **211**–14
dance [dăns] **64**–A
dangerous [dān/jər əs] **186**–1
dark blue [därk/ blōō/] **24**–10

Index

Dashboard and Instrument Panel
[dăsh/ börd/ ən ĭn/strə mənt păn/əl] **159**
dates [dāts] **20**–1, **68**–28
  date of birth [dāt əv bürth/] **4**–13
  expiration date
    [ĕk/spə rā/shən dāt/] **112**–7, **136**–10
daughter [dö/tər] **34**–14
  daughter-in-law [dö/tər ĭn lö/] **34** ✦
  granddaughters [grăn/dö/tərz] **34** ✦
  stepdaughter [stĕp/dö/tər] **35** ✦
day [dā] **20**–2
  birthday [bürth/dā/] **22**–1
  Columbus Day [kə lŭm/bəs dā] **22**–15
  daylight saving time [dā/līt/ sā/vĭng tīm/] **19**–25
  every day [ĕv/rē dā/] **20**–21
  Independence Day [ĭn/də pĕn/dəns dā/] **22**–13
  Labor Day [lā/bər dā/] **22**–14
  Martin Luther King Jr. Day
    [mär/tən lōō/thər kĭng/ jōōn/yər-dā/] **22**–10
  Memorial Day [mə mör/ē əl dā/] **22**–12
  New Year's Day [nōō/ yïrz/ dā/] **22**–9
  Presidents' Day [prĕz/ə dənts dā/] **22**–11
  Veterans Day [vĕt/ər ənz dā/] **22**–16
Day [dā] **18**
DAY AT SCHOOL [dā/ ăt skōōl/] **11**
DAY AT WORK [dā/ ăt würk/] **186**–187
Days of the Week [dāz/ əv dhə wēk/] **20**
dead [dĕd]
  dead-bolt lock [dĕd/bōlt/ läk/] **51**–34
  dead end [dĕd/ĕnd/] **154**–6
deaf [dĕf] **32**–12
Dealer [dē/lər] **158**
dealership [dē/lər shĭp/] **126**–4
death certificate [dĕth/ sər tĭf/ə kət] **41**–11
debate [də bāt/] **139**–B
decaf coffee [dē/kăf/ kö/fē] **81**–38
decay [də kā/] **119**–7
December [dĭ sĕm/bər] **21**–36
decimal point [dĕ/sə məl poynt/] **17**–7
Decimals [dĕ/sə məlz] **17**
deck [dĕk] **240**–2
declaration [dĕk/lə rā/shən]
  declaration form [dĕk/lə rā/shən förm/] **161**–16
  Declaration of Independence
    [dĕk/lə rā/shən əv ĭn/də pĕn/dəns] **198**–5
decline [də klīn/] **12**–J
decorations [dĕk/ə rā/shənz] **240**–1
deductions [də dŭk/shənz] **165**–13
deed [dĕd] **41**–9
deer [dïr] **216**–14
defendant [dĭ fĕn/dənt] **141**–5
defense attorney [dĭ fĕns/ ə tür/nē] **141**–4
defroster [də frös/tər] **159**–41
degrees [də grēz/] **13**–8, **193**–26
delayed flight [də lād/ flīt/] **161**–30
delete [də lĕt/] **196**–C
DELI [dĕl/ē] **71**
deliver [də lĭv/ər] **11**–G, **135**–E
delivery person [də lĭv/ə rē pür/sən] **167**–21
dementia [də mĕn/shə] **111**–18
demonstration [dĕ/mən strā/shən] **122**–6
denim [dĕ/nəm] **99**–7

denominator [də nŏmə nā/tər] **192**–6
dental [dĕn/təl]
  dental assistant [dĕn/təl ə sĭs/tənt] **119**–2, **167**–22
  dental floss [dĕn/təl flös/, –fläs/] **109**–24
  dental hygienist [dĕn/təl hī jĕ/nĭst, –jē/nĭst] **119**–3
  dental instruments [dĕn/təl ĭn/strə mənts] **119**–4
DENTAL CARE [dĕn/təl kër/] **119**
Dental Problems [dĕn/təl präb/ləmz] **119**
dentist [dĕn/tĭst] **119**–1
Dentistry [dĕn/təs trē/] **119**
dentures [dĕn/chərz] **119**–10
deodorant [dē ō/dər ənt] **108**–5
department [dĭ pärt/mənt] **95**–7, **95**–8
  Department of Motor Vehicles
    [dĭ pärt/mənt əv mō/tər vē/ĭ kəlz] **124**–4
  department store [dĭ pärt/mənt stör/] **131**–13
DEPARTMENT OF MOTOR VEHICLES (DMV)
    [dĭ pärt/mənt əv mō/tər vē/ĭ kəlz] / [dē/ĕm/vē/]
    136–137
departure [dĭ pär/chər] **161**–5, **161**–7
deposit [dĭ päz/ət] **132**–3, **132**–7
  deposit slip [dĭ päz/ət slĭp/] **132**–4
depression [də prĕ/shən] **115**–5
depth [dĕpth] **17**–18
DESCRIBING CLOTHES [dĭ skrī/bĭng klōz/] **96**–97
DESCRIBING HAIR [dĭ skrī/bĭng hër/] **33**
DESCRIBING PEOPLE [dĭ skrī/bĭng pē/pəl] **32**
DESCRIBING THINGS [dĭ skrī/bĭng thĭngz/] **23**
desert [dĕz/ərt] **204**–4
design [dĭ zīn/] **175**–A
designated drivers [dĕz/ĭg nā/təd drī/vərz] **143** ✦
designer [dĭ zī/nər] **98** ✦, **167**–30, **175**–2, **176**–5
desk [dĕsk] **6**–7, **182**–9
  circulation desk [sür/kyə lā/shən dĕsk/] **133**–2
  desk clerk [dĕsk klürk/] **184**–11
  front desk [frŭnt/ dĕsk/] **184**–12
Desktop Computer [dĕsk/täp/ kəm pyōō/tər] **196**
Desserts [dĭ zürts/] **81**
dessert tray [dĭ zürt/ trā/] **83**–10
destination [dĕs/tə nā/shən] **161** ✦
detector [dĭ tĕk/tər] **51**–29
detergent [dĭ tür/jənt] **101**–8
device [də vīs/] **225**–20
diabetes [dī/ə bē/tēz, –təs] **111**–12
diagonal [dī ăg/ə nəl, –ăg/nəl] **193**–31
dial [dī/əl] **15**–A, **15**–E
diameter [dī ăm/ə tər] **193**–37
diamonds [dī/məndz] **233**–29
diaper [dī/pər] **37**–8, **37**–10
  diaper pail [dī/pər pāl/] **37**–7
diaphragm [dī/ə frăm] **194**–19
dice [dīs] **232**–6
dice [dīs] **77**–J
dictate [dĭk/tāt] **8**–N
dictator [dĭk/tā/tər] **199**–6
dictionary [dĭk/shə nër/ē] **7**–30, **7**–31
die [dī] **41**–R
dietician [dī/ə tĭsh/ən] **120**–15
difference [dĭf/rəns] **192**–8
different [dĭf/frənt, dĭ/fə rənt] **23**–16
DIFFERENT [dĭ/frənt, dĭ/fə rənt] **28**–29

DIFFERENT PLACES TO LIVE
    [dĭ/frənt plā/səz tə lĭv/, dĭ/fə rənt] **52**
difficult [dĭf/ĭ kŭlt/] **23**–24
digital [dĭ/jə təl]
  digital camera [dĭ/jə təl kăm/rə] **235**–19
  digital photo album [dĭ/jə təl fō/tō ăl/bəm] **235**–32
dime [dīm] **26**–3
Dimensions [də mĕn/shənz] **17**
diner [dī/nər] **82**–6, **185**–9
dining [dī/nĭng]
  dining area [dī/nĭng ër/ē ə] **46**–7
  dining room [dī/nĭng rōōm/] **82**–1
  dining room chair [dī/nĭng rōōm/ chër/] **55**–8
  dining room table [dī/nĭng rōōm/tā/bəl] **55**–9
Dining [dī/nĭng] **185**
DINING AREA [dī/nĭng ër/ē ə] **55**
dinner [dĭn/ər] **72**–28
  dinner fork [dĭn/ər förk/] **83**–28
  dinner plate [dĭn/ər plāt/] **83**–18
  dinner salad [dĭn/ər săl/əd] **80**–15
Dinner [dĭn/ər] **81**
diploma [də plō/mə] **40**–3
direct flight [də rĕkt/ flīt/, dī–] **161** ✦
Directions [də rĕk/shənz] **9**, **155**
DIRECTIONS AND MAPS
    [də rĕk/shənz ən măps/, dī–] **155**
directory [də rĕk/tə rē, dī–] **131**–24
  directory assistance
    [də rĕk/tə rē ə sĭs/təns, dī–] **14**–22
dirty [dür/tē] **101**–15
Disabilities [dĭ/sə bĭ/lə tēz] **32**
disagree [dĭ/sə grē/] **12**–L
disappointed [dĭ/sə poyn/təd] **28**–4
DISASTERS [dĭ/zăs tərz] **144**–145
disc [dĭsk] **231**–27
discipline [dĭs/ə plən] **36**–K
discuss [dĭ skŭs/] **8**–G
disease [dĭ zēz/] **111**–11, **111** ✦, **119**–11
Diseases [dĭ zē/zəz] **111**
disgusted [dĭ skŭs/təd] **42**–7
dish [dĭsh] **55**–1
  casserole dish [kăs/ə rōl dĭsh/] **78**–10
  dish rack [dĭsh/ răk/] **54**–5
  dish room [dĭsh/ rōōm/] **83**–13
  dish towel [dĭsh/ tow/əl] **61**–22
  dishwasher [dĭsh/wä/shər, –wö/–]
    54–8, **83**–14, **185**–2
  dishwashing liquid [dĭsh/wä/shĭng lĭk/wəd] **61**–21
  satellite dish [să/tə līt dĭsh/] **53**–6
  soap dish [sōp/ dĭsh/] **57**–25
disinfectant wipes [dĭs/ən fĕk/tənt wīps/] **61**–23
display case [dĭ splā/ kās/] **94**–5
disposable [dĭ spō/zə bəl]
  disposable diaper [dĭ spō/zə bəl dī/pər] **37**–10
  disposable gloves [dĭ spō/zə bəl glŭvz/] **93**–27
disposal [dĭ spō/zəl] **54**–7, **121**–31
dive [dīv] **230**–K
divide [də vīd/] **17**–A, **192**–D
diving [dī/vĭng] **227**–12
  diving mask [dī/vĭng măsk/] **225**–6
divorced couple [də vörst/ kŭ/pəl] **35**–21
DJ [dē/jā/] **64**–4

DMV [dē/ĕm/vē/]
DMV clerk [dē/ĕm/vē/ klürk/] **136**–3
DMV handbook [dē/ĕm/vē/ hănd/bŏŏk/] **136**–1
do [dōō] **39**–T
do an experiment [dōō ən ĭk spër/ə mənt] **195**–B
do crafts [dōō krăfts/] **232**–D
do errands [dōō ĕr/əndz] **128** ✦
do manual labor [dōō măn/yōō əl lā/bər] **170**–D
do not drink [dōō nät drĭnk/] **112**–F
do not enter [dōō nät/ ĕn/tər] **154**–2
do not operate [dōō nät/ äp/ə rāt/] **112**–E
do not take [dōō nät/ tāk/] **112**–F
don't be late [dōnt/ bē/ lāt/] **174**–E
don't litter [dōnt/ lĭ/tər] **219**–L
don't smoke [dōnt/ smōk/] **114**–G
dock [däk] **175**–15, **234**–3
dockworker [däk/wür/kər] **167**–23
doctor [däk/tər] **118**–5
DOCUMENTS [dä/kyə mənts] **40–41**
dog [dög] **79**–6, **215**–11, **215**–22
dogwood [dög/wŏŏd/] **210**–15
DOING THE LAUNDRY [dō/ĭng dhə lön/drē] **101**
doll [däl] **59**–21, **233**–28
dollhouse [däl/hows/] **59**–16
doll making kit [däl/ mā/kĭng kĭt/] **232**–13
dollar [däl/ər] **26**–7
dollar coin [däl/ər koyn/] **26**–6
fifty dollars [fĭf/tē däl/ərz] **26**–11
five dollars [fĭv/ däl/ərz] **26**–8
half dollar [hăf/ däl/ər] **26**–5
one hundred dollars
[wŭn/ hŭn/drəd däl/ərz] **26**–12
ten dollars [tĕn/ däl/ərz] **26**–9
twenty dollars [twĕn/tē däl/ərz] **26**–10
dolphin [däl/fən, döl/–] **213**–31
domesticated [də mĕs/tə kā/təd] **215** ✦
DOMESTIC ANIMALS AND RODENTS
[də mĕs/tĭk ăn/ə məlz ən rōd/nts] **215**
donkey [däng/kē, dŭng/–, döng/–] **215**–3
donut [dō/nŭt] **79**–15
donut shop [dō/nŭt shäp/] **129**–17
door [dör] **46**–3
doorbell [dör/bĕl/] **53**–14
door chain [dör/ chān/] **51**–33
doorknob [dör/näb/] **53**–12
doorman [dör/măn/] **184**–1
4-door car [för/ dör kär/] **156**–1
front door [frŭnt/ dör/] **53**–11
garage door [gə räj/ dör/] **53**–7
revolving door [rĭ väl/vĭng dör/] **184**–2
screen door [skrēn/ dör/] **53**–15
sliding glass door [slī/dĭng glăs/dör/] **53**–18
storm door [störm/ dör/] **53**–10
2-door car [tōō/dör kär/] **156**–2
dorm / dormitory [dörm] / [dör/mə tör/ē] **52**–8
dosage [dō/sĭj] **112**–6
double [dŭb/əl]
double bed [dŭb/əl bĕd/] **184**–14
double boiler [dŭb/əl boy/lər] **78**–8

down [down]
break down [brāk/ down/] **162**–D
downhill skiing [down/hĭl/ skē/ĭng] **227**–1
down jacket [down jăk/ət] **90**–16
down vest [down vĕst/] **90**–14
drop-down menu [dräp/ down/ mĕn/yōō/] **197**–8
put down [pŏŏt/ down/] **6**–J
sit down [sĭt down/] **6**–F
walk down [wäk down/] **153**–D
downstairs [down/stërz/] **51** ✦
DOWNTOWN [down/town/] **124–125**
drain [drān] **57**–5
drama [drä/mə] **236**–12
drapes [drāps] **56**–16
draw [drö] **8**–F, **118**–F, **195**–E
drawer [drör] **54**–23, **58**–2, **59**–6
dress [drĕs] **86**–3, **88**–5, **89**–20
dressmaker [drĕs/mā/kər] **100**–1
dressmaker's dummy [drĕs/mā/kərz dŭ/mē] **100**–2
dress socks [drĕs/ säks/] **91**–9
dress [drĕs] **36**–H, **174**–B
dressed [drĕst] **38**–D
dresser [drĕs/ər] **58**–1
Dressings [drĕs/ĭngz] **80**
dribble [drĭb/əl] **230**–J
drill [drĭl] **178**–9, **180**–8
drill bit [drĭl bĭt/] **180**–28
drill [drĭl] **119**–D
drink [drĭnk] **11**–J
do not drink alcohol
[dōō/ nät/ drĭnk/ ăl/kə höl/] **112**–F
don't drink and drive [dōnt/ drĭnk ən drīv/] **143**–G
drink fluids [drĭnk flōō/ədz] **114**–C
drip [drĭp] **121**–25
dripping [drĭp/ĭng] **63**–17
drive [drīv] **196**–6, **196**–8, **196**–9
drive-thru window [drīv/thrōō/ wĭn/dō] **128**–11
driveway [drīv/wā/] **53**–8
drive [drīv]
don't drink and drive [dōnt/drĭnk ən drīv/] **143**–G
drive a truck [drīv ə trŭk] **170**–E
drive through [drīv/ thrōō] **153**–K
drive to work [drīv/ tə würk/] **38**–I
driver [drī/vər] **152**–21, **169**–61
designated drivers [dĕz/ĭg nā/təd drī/vərz] **143** ✦
driver's license [drī/vərz lī/səns] **40**–4, **136**–9
driver's license number
[drī/vərz lī/səns nŭm/bər] **136**–11
Phillips screwdriver [fĭl/ĭps skrōō/drī/vər] **180**–31
screwdriver [skrōō/drī/vər] **180**–30
driving [drī/vĭng] **142**–5
drop [dräp]
drop cloth [dräp/ klöth/] **181**–54
drop-down menu [dräp/ down/ mĕn/yōō/] **197**–8
drop off [dräp/ öf/] **38**–G
dropper [dräp/ər] **195**–45
drops [dräps] **113**–31
drought [drowt] **145**–11
drown [drown] **116**–I
drugs [drŭgz] **116**–K, **142**–6
drums [drŭmz] **238**–16
drumsticks [drŭm/stĭks/] **70**–23
drunk driving [drŭngk/ drī/vĭng] **142**–5

dry [drī] **101**–18
dry cleaners [drī/ klē/nərz] **128**–2
dry erase marker [drī/ ĭ rās/ mär/kər] **7**–17
drywall [drī/wöl/] **178**–19
dry [drī] **60**–N, **108**–H
dryer [drī/ər] **50**–13, **101**–4
blow dryer [blō/ drī/ər] **33**–23, **108**–18
dryer sheets [drī/ər shēts/] **101**–5
Dry Measures [drī/ mĕzh/ərz] **75**
duck [dŭk] **70**–18, **214**–12
duct tape [dŭkt/ tāp/] **181**–49
dummy [dŭ/mē] **100**–2
dump truck [dŭmp/ trŭk/] **156**–19
dune [dōōn] **204**–5
duplex [dōō/plĕks/] **52** ✦
During an Emergency [dōō/rĭng ən ĭ mür/jən sē] **147**
dust [dŭst]
dustpan [dŭst/păn/] **61**–17
dust ruffle [dŭst/ rŭf/əl] **58**–17
dust storm [dŭst/ störm/] **13**–19
dust [dŭst] **60**–A
duster [dŭs/tər] **61**–1
DVD [dē/vē/dē/] **133**–19, **234**–11
DVD and CD-ROM drive
[dē/vē/dē/ ən sē/dē/räm/ drīv/] **196**–9
DVD player [dē/vē/dē/ plā/ ər] **56**–7, **234**–10
dye [dī] **33**–D
eagle [ē/gəl] **214**–9
ear [ïr] **32**–17, **105**–11
earache [ïr/āk/] **110**–3
ear infection [ïr/ ĭn fĕk/shən] **111**–3
earmuffs [ïr/mŭfs/] **90**–13, **179**–16
ear plugs [ïr/ plŭgz/] **179**–15
pierced earrings [pïrst/ ïr/ĭngz] **95**–36
early [ür/lē] **19**–22
Earth [ürth] **205**–3
earthquake [ürth/kwāk/] **144**–5
easel [ē/zəl] **233**–18
east [ēst] **155**–4
Eastern time [ē/stərn tīm/] **19**–32
easy [ē/zē] **23**–23, **76**–11
easy chair [ē/zē chër/] **56**–22
Easy Chicken Soup [ē/zē chĭk/ən sōōp/] **77**
eat [ēt] **11**–1
eat a healthy diet [ēt ə hĕl/thē dī/ət] **114**–F
eat breakfast [ēt brĕk/fəst] **38**–E
eat dinner [ēt dĭn/ər] **39**–S
eat out [ēt/ owt/] **82** ✦
eater [ē/tər] **176**–12
eclipse [ĭ klĭps/] **205**–16, **205** ✦
edit [ĕd/ət] **191**–I
education [ĕ jyōō/ kā/shən] **189**–17
eel [ēl] **212**–12
eggplants [ĕg/plănts/] **69**–23
eggs [ĕgz] **66**–7
eggbeater [ĕg/bē/tər] **78**–20
eggs over easy [ĕgz ō/vər ē/zē] **76**–11
eggs sunny-side up [ĕgz sŭn/ē sīd/ ŭp/] **76**–10
hardboiled eggs [härd/ boyld/ ĕgz/] **76**–8
poached eggs [pōcht/ ĕgz/] **76**–9
scrambled eggs [skrăm/bəld ĕgz/] **76**–7
Eggs [ĕgz] **76**

Index

eight [āt] **16**

eighteen [ā/tēn/] **16**

eighteenth [ā/tēnth/] **16**

eighth [ātth, āth] **16**

eightieth [ā/tē/əth] **16**

eighty [ā/tē] **16**

elastic bandage [ĭ lăs/tĭk băn/dĭj] **117**–12

elbow [ĕl/bō] **106**–12

elderly [ĕl/dər lē] **32**–3

elected [ĭ lĕk/təd] **139**–C

   elected official [ĭ lĕk/təd ə fĭ/shəl] **139**–32

Election [ĭ lĕk/shən] **139**

election results [ĭ lĕk/shən rĭ zŭltz/] **139**–31

elective [ĭ lĕk/tĭv] **189** ✦

electric [ĭ lĕk/trĭk] **116**–F

   electric can opener [ĭ lĕk/trĭk kăn/ ō/pə nər] **54**–14

   electric drill [ĭ lĕk/trĭk drĭl/] **180**–8

   electric keyboard [ĭ lĕk/trĭk kē/börd/] **238**–18

   electric mixer [ĭ lĕk/trĭk mĭk/sər] **54**–25

   electric pencil sharpener
      [ĭ lĕk/trĭk pĕn/səl shär/pə nər] **183**–26

   electric shaver [ĭ lĕk/trĭk shā/vər] **109**–26

electrical [ĭ lĕk/trĭ kəl] **116**–F

   electrical hazard [ĭ lĕk/trĭ kəl hăz/ərd] **186**–6

   electrical tape [ĭ lĕk/trĭ kəl tāp/] **181**–43

electrician [ĭ lĕk trĭsh/ən] **62**–9

electron [ĭ lĕk/trän] **195**–30

electronics [ĭ lĕk trän/ĭks]

   electronics repair person
      [ĭ lĕk trän/ĭks rĭ pĕr/ pür/sən] **167**–24

   electronics store [ĭ lĕk trän/ĭks stör/] **131**–20

ELECTRONICS AND PHOTOGRAPHY
   [ĭ lĕk trän/ĭks ən fə tä/grə fē] **234**–**235**

elementary school [ĕl/ə mĕn/trē skōōl/] **188**–2

elephant [ĕl/ə fənt] **217**–42

elevator [ĕl/ə vā/tər] **50**–9, **131**–21, **184**–9

eleven [ĭ lĕv/ən] **16**

eleventh [ĭ lĕv/ənth] **16**

elm [ĕlm] **210**–16

Email [ē/māl/] **197**

embarrassed [ĭm băr/əst] **43**–24

embroidery [ĭm broy/də rē] **233**–24

EMERGENCIES [ĭ mür/jən sēz] **116**

EMERGENCIES AND NATURAL DISASTERS
   [ĭ mür/jən sēz ən năch/rəl dĭ zăs/tərz,–năch/ə rəl–]
   144–**145**

emergency [ĭ mür/jən sē] **117**–3

   emergency card [ĭ mür/jən sē kärd/] **161**–26

   emergency exit
      [ĭ mür/jən sē ĕg/zət,–ĕk/sət] **51**–25, **161**–14

   emergency medical technician (EMT) [ĭ mür/jən sē
      mĕd/ĭ kəl tĕk nĭsh/ən] / [ē/ĕm/tē/] **121**–32

Emergency [ĭ mür/jən sē] **146**–**147**

Emergency Call [ĭ mür/jən sē köl/] **15**

EMERGENCY PROCEDURES
   [ĭ mür/jən sē prə sē/jərz] **146**–**147**

Emergency Room Entrance
   [ĭ mür/jən sē rōōm/ ĕn/trəns] **121**

Emergency Worker [ĭ mür/jən sē wür/kər] **93**

emery board [ĕm/ə rē börd/, ĕm/rē-] **109**–32

emperor [ĕm/pər ər] **199**–3

employee [ĕm ploy/ē] **165**–9

employer [ĕm ploy/ər] **164**–4

empty [ĕmp/tē] **23**–10

empty [ĕmp/tē] **60**–L

EMT (emergency medical technician) [ē/ĕm/tē/] /
   [ĭ mür/jən sē mĕd/ĭ kəl tĕk nish/ən] **121**–32

end [ĕnd] **154**–6

   endpoint [ĕnd/poynt/] **193**–21

   end table [ĕnd/ tā/bəl] **56**–14

energy [ĕn/ər jē] **218**–1, **218**–7, **218**–8

   bioenergy [bī/ō ĕn/ər jē] **218**–9

ENERGY AND CONSERVATION
   [ĕn/ər jē ən kän/sər vā/shən] **218**–**219**

Energy and Resources [ĕn/ər jē ən rē/sör/səz] **219**

Energy Sources [ĕn/ər jē sör/səz] **218**

engine [ĕn/jən] **158**–18, **197**–6

engineer [ĕn/jə nïr/] **167**–18, **167**–25

ENGLISH COMPOSITION
   [ĭng/glĭsh käm/pə zĭsh/ən] **190**–**191**

English muffin [ĭng/glĭsh mŭf/ən] **80**–5

enter [ĕn/tər]

   do not **enter** [dōō/ nät/ ĕn/tər] **154**–2

   enter data [ĕn/tər dā/tə] **171**–B

   enter the room [ĕn/tər dhe rōōm/] **11**–A

   enter your PIN [ĕn/tər yər pĭn/] **132**–E

ENTERTAINMENT [ĕn/tər tān/mənt] **236**–**237**

entrance [ĕn/trəns] **164**–1

Entrance [ĕn/trəns] **50, 121**

entry-level job [ĕn/trē lĕv/əl jäb/] **172**–1

Entryway [ĕn/trē wā/] **51**

envelope [ĕn/və lōp/] **134**–14, **183**–43

equation [ĭ kwā/zhən] **192**–13

equipment [ĭ kwĭp/mənt] **177**–12, **179**–4

Equipment [ĭ kwĭp/mənt] **179, 183**

EQUIPMENT [ĭ kwĭp/mənt] **231**

Equivalencies [ĭ kwĭv/və lən sēz/] **17, 75**

erase [ĭ rās/] **10**–M

eraser [ĭ rā/sər] **7**–19, **7**–21

errands [ĕr/əndz] **128** ✦

eruption [ĭ rŭp/shən] **145**–16

escalator [ĕs/kə lā/tər] **131**–23

escape [ĭs kāp/] **50**–2

   escape route [ĭs kāp/ rōōt/, rowt/] **146**–3

ESL [ē/ĕs/ĕl/] **189**–14

ESOL [ē/ĕs/ō/ĕl/] **189**–14

essay [ĕs/ā] **190**–4

Essay [ĕs/ā] **190**

e-ticket [ē/tĭ kət] **161**–19

evacuate [ĭ văk/yōō/ āt] **147**–K

evacuation route [ĭ văk/yōō/ā shən rōōt/, rowt/] **146**–5

evening [ĕv/nĭng] **18**–19

   evening gown [ĕv/nĭng gown/] **89**–18

even numbers [ē/vən nŭm/bərz] **192**–4

EVENTS [ĭ vĕnts/] **22, 40**–**41**

every day [ĕv/rē dā/] **20**–21

EVERYDAY CLOTHES [ĕv/rē dā/ klōz/] **86**–**87**

EVERDAY CONVERSATION
   [ĕv/rē dā/ kän/vər sā/shən] **12**

evidence [ĕv/ĭ dəns/] **141**–9

exam [ĭg zăm/] **122**–1, **136**–6

examination table [ĭg zăm/ə nā/shən tā/bəl] **118**–7

examine [ĭg zăm/ən] **118**–D, **118**–E

Examining Room [ĭg zăm/ə nĭng rōōm/] **118**

exchange [ĭks chānj/] **27**–I

excited [ĭk sī/təd] **43**–22

exclamation mark [ĕk/sklə mā/shən märk/] **190**–13

executive [ĭg zĕk/yə tĭv] **182**–5

   executive chef [ĭg zĕk/yə tĭv shĕf/] **185**–7

Executive Branch [ĭg zĕk/yə tĭv brănch/] **138**

exercise [ĕk/sər sīz/] **122**–4

exercise [ĕk/sər sīz/] **39**–P, **230**–N

Exercise Wear [ĕk/sər sīz/wër] **89**

exhausted [ĭg zö/stəd] **43** ✦

ex-husband [ĕks/ hŭz/bənd] **35** ✦

exit [eg/zət, ĕk/sət] **51**–25, **51** ✦, **161**–14

expensive [ĭk spĕn/sĭv] **23**–19, **97**–44

Experiment [ĭk spĕr/ə mənt] **195**

expiration date [ĕk/spə rā/shən dāt/] **112**–7, **136**–10

expire [ĕk/spīr/] **136** ✦

explain [ĭk splān/] **12**–M

exploration [ĕk/splə rā/shən] **199**–8

explorer [ĭk splör/ər] **199**–9

explosion [ĭk splō/zhən] **144**–4

exposed [ĭk spōzd/]

   overexposed [ō/vər ĭk spōzd/] **235**–34

   underexposed [ŭn/dər ĭk spōzd/] **235**–35

Express Mail® [ĭk sprĕs/ māl/] **134**–2

Extended Family [ĭk stĕn/dəd făm/lē, făm/ə lē] **34**

extension cord [ĭk stĕn/shən körd/] **181**–14

exterminate [ĭk stür/mə nāt/] **62** ✦

exterminator [ĭk stür/mə nā/tər] **63**–21

extinguisher [ĭk stĭn/gwə shər] **179**–21

extra [ĕk/strə]

   extra large [ĕk/strə lärj/] **96**–5

   extra small [ĕk/strə smöl/] **96**–1

ex-wife [ĕks/ wīf/] **35** ✦

eye [ī] **99**–27, **105**–11

   eyebrow [ī/brow/] **106**–9

   eyebrow pencil [ī/brow/ pĕn/səl] **109**–34

   eye drops [ī/dräps/] **113**–31

   eye hook [ī/hōōk/] **180**–40

   eyelashes [ī/lăsh/əz] **106**–11

   eyelid [ī/lĭd/] **106**–10

   eyeliner [ī/lī/nər] **109**–36

   eyepiece [ī/pēs/] **194**–14

   eye shadow [ī/shă/dō] **109**–35

Eye [ī] **106**

fabric [făb/rĭk] **98**–15

   fabric softener [făb/rĭk sö/fə nər] **101**–6

Fabric Store [făb/rĭk stör/] **99**

face [fās] **193**–44

   face mask [fās măsk/] **93**–32

   face powder [fās/ pow/dər] **109**–41

Face [fās] **106**

factory [făk/tə rē, –trē] **126**–3

   factory owner [făk/tə rē ō/nər] **175**–1

   factory worker [făk/tə rē wür/kər] **175**–3

Factory [făk/tə rē] **98**

FACTORY [făk/tə rē] **175**

Fahrenheit [făr/ən hīt/] **13**–1

fair [fër] **172**–13, **223**–13

   fair trial [fër/ trī/əl] **140**–5

FAIR [fër] **122**–**123**

fall [föl] **21**–39

fall [fôl] **40**–H, **116**–O
FAMILIES [făm/lēz, făm/ə lēz] **34**–**35**
Family [făm/lē, făm/ə lē] **34**
FAMILY REUNION
  [făm/lē rē yōōn/yən, făm/ə lē] **44**–**45**
famine [fă/mĭn] **145**–12
fan [făn] **55**–19, **229**–4
fancy [făn/sē] **97**–34
far from [fär/ frŭm/, –frəm/] **25** ✦
fare [fër] **152**–2
  fare card [fër kärd/] **152**–11
farm [färm] **52**–9
  farm equipment [färm ĭ kwĭp/mənt] **177**–12
  farmworker [färm/ wür/kər] **177**–8
Farm Animals [färm/ ăn/ə məlz] **215**
farmer [fär/mər] **177**–13
FARMERS' MARKET [fär/mərz mär/kət] **84**–**85**
FARMING AND RANCHING
  [fär/mĭng ən răn/chĭng] **177**
Farmworker [färm/ wür/kər] **92**
fashion [făsh/ən] **88** ✦
  fashion designer [făsh/ən dĭ zī/nər] **98** ✦
fast [făst] **23**–3
  fast food restaurant [făst/ fōōd/ rĕs/tə rənt, –ränt]
    128–10
fasten [făs/ən] **160**–H
fastener [făs/nər] **99**–29
FAST FOOD RESTAURANT
  [făst/ fōōd/ rĕs/tə rənt, –ränt] **79**
fast forward [făst/ för/wərd] **235**–D
fat [făt] **32**–7
father [fä/dhər] **34**–4, **35**–23
  father-in-law [fä/dhər ĭn lö/] **34**–11
  grandfather [grăn/fä/dhər, grănd/–] **34**–2
  stepfather [stĕp/fädhər] **35**–25
faucet [fö/sət] **57**–6
fax [făks] **171**–G
  fax machine [făks/ mə shēn/] **183**–21
feast [fēst] **239**–13
feather [fĕdh/ər] **214**–4
  feather duster [fĕdh/ər dŭs/tər] **61**–1
February [fĕb/yōō ër/ē, fĕb/rōō–] **21**–26
Federal Government
  [fĕ/də rəl gŭ/vərn mənt, fĕ/drəl] **138**
feed [fēd] **36**–C, **176**–D, **177**–D
feed dog / feed bar [fēd/dög/ / fēd/ bär/] **98**–20
feel [fēl] **110**–C, **110**–D
FEELINGS [fē/lĭngz] **42**–**43**
female [fē/māl/] **4**–18
fence [fĕns] **177**–19
fencing [fĕn/sĭng] **228**–7
ferry [fĕr/ē] **220**–4
fertilize [fürt/ əl īz/] **176**–D
fever [fē/vər] **110**–8
fiction [fĭk/shən] **237**–18
field [fēld] **5**–2, **177**–7
  ball field [böl/ fēld/] **224**–1
  track and field [trăk/ ən fēld/] **228**–18
fifteen [fĭf/tēn/] **16**
fifteenth [fĭf/tēnth/] **16**
fifth [fĭfth] **16**
fiftieth [fĭf/tē əth] **16**

fifty [fĭf/tē] **16**
  fifty dollars [fĭf/tē däl/ərz] **26**–11
  50 percent [fĭf/tē pər sĕnt/] **17**–10
fighter [fī/tər]
  firefighter [fīr/fī/tər] **144**–9, **167**–26
figs [fĭgz] **68**–27
figure [fĭg/yər] **233**–26
  figure skating [fĭg/yər skā/tĭng] **227**–5
figurine [fĭg/yə rēn/] **232**–1
file [fīl] **183**–44
  file cabinet [fīl kăb/ə nət] **182**–11
  file clerk [fīl klürk/] **182**–10
  file folder [fīl fōl/dər] **183**–50
fill [fĭl]
  fill a cavity [fĭl/ ə kăv/ə tē] **119**–E
  fill prescriptions [fĭl/ prĭ skrĭp/shənz] **112** ✦
  fill in [fĭl/ ĭn] **9**–O
  fill out [fĭl/ owt/] **173**–J
  fill the tank [fĭl/ dhe tănk/] **157**–G
  fill the tires [fĭl/ dhe tīrz/] **157**–L
filling [fĭl/ĭng] **119**–8
Filling Out a Form [fĭl/ĭng owt ə förm/] **4**
film [fĭlm] **235**–22
  film camera [fĭlm kăm/rə] **235**–21
find [fīnd] **160**–F
FINDING A HOME [fīn/dĭng ə hōm/] **48**–**49**
fine adjustment knob [fīn/ ə jŭst/mənt näb/] **194**–23
fingers [fĭng/gərz] **105**–16, **110**–16
  fingernail [fĭng/gər nāl/] **106**–18
  fingerprint [fĭng/gər prĭnt/] **136**–5
Fingers [fĭng/gərz] **106**
finish [fĭn/ĭsh] **112**–C, **230**–T
fins [fĭnz] **212**–1, **225**–7
fire [fīr] **144**–7, **144**–8
  campfire [kămp/fīr/] **226**–11
  fire escape [fīr ĭ skāp/] **50**–2
  fire exit [fīr/ ĕg/zət, –ĕk/sət] **51** ✦
  fire extinguisher [fīr ĭk stĭng/gwĭ shər] **179**–21
  firefighter [fīr/fī/tər] **144**–9, **167**–26
  fire hydrant [fīr hī/drənt] **129**–27
  fireplace [fīr/plās/] **56**–13
  fire screen [fīr skrēn/] **56**–12
  fire station [fīr stā/shən] **125**–12
  fire truck [fīr trŭk/] **144**–10
  fireworks [fīr/würks/] **239**–7
first [fürst] **16**
  first aid kit [fürst/ ād/ kĭt/] **117**–1, **146**–18
  first aid manual [fürst/ ād/ măn/yōō əl] **117**–2
  First Continental Congress
    [fürst/ kän/tə nĕnt/ əl käng/grəs] **198**–6
  first name [fürst/ nām/] **4**–2
  first president [fürst/ prĕz/ə dənt] **198**–11
First Aid [fürst/ ād/] **117**
FIRST AID [fürst/ ād/] **117**
First Aid Procedures [fürst/ ād/ prə sē/ jərz] **117**
First Floor [fürst/ flör/] **50**
First License [fürst/ lī/səns] **137**
fish [fĭsh] **66**–1, **81**–29, **209**–14
  catfish [kăt/fĭsh/] **71**–2
  goldfish [gōld/fĭsh/] **215**–16
  jellyfish [jĕ/lē fĭsh/] **212**–14
  starfish [stär/fĭsh/] **212**–16
  swordfish [sörd/fĭsh/] **71**–5

Fish [fĭsh] **71**, **212**
fisher [fĭsh/ər] **167**–17
fishing [fĭsh/ĭng] **226**–4
  fishing net [fĭsh/ĭng nĕt/] **226**–17
  fishing pole [fĭsh/ĭng pōl/] **226**–18
fitted sheet [fĭt/əd shēt/] **58**–12
fittings [fĭt/ĭngz] **181**–18
five [fīv] **16**
  five after one [fīv ăf/tər wŭn/] **18**–7
  five dollars [fīv däl/ərz] **26**–8
fix [fĭks] **62** ✦, **219**–F
fixture [fĭks/chər] **55**–18
flag [flăg] **239**–8
flammable liquids [flăm/ə bəl lĭk/wədz] **179**–8
flashlight [flăsh/līt/] **146**–14
flat [flăt]
  flat panel TV [flăt/ păn/əl tē/vē/] **234**–7
  flat screen TV [flăt/ skrēn/ tē/vē/] **234**–7
  flat sheet [flăt/ shēt/] **58**–13
  have a flat tire [hăv/ ə flăt/ tīr/] **162**–F
flats [flăts] **95**–27
fleas [flēz] **63**–25
  flea market [flē/ mär/kət] **222**–6
flight [flīt] **161**–30, **161** ✦
  flight attendant [flīt/ ə tĕn/dənt] **161**–12
Flight [flīt] **160**
float [flōt/] **239**–2
flood [flŭd] **145**–19
floor [flör] **46**–6, **58**–21, **179**–6
  floor lamp [flör lămp/] **56**–15
  floor plan [flör plăn/] **186**–4
Floor [flör] **50**
floral [flör/əl] **96**–25
florist [flör/ĭst] **130**–8, **167**–27
floss [flös, fläs] **109**–24
floss [flös, fläs] **109**–K
flounder [flown/dər] **212**–15
flour [flow/ər] **73**–29
Flower [flow/ər] **211**
flowers [flow/ərz] **208**–7
  flower bed [flow/ər bĕd/] **53**–20
FLOWERS [flow/ərz] **211**
flu [flōō] **111**–2
fluid [flōō/əd] **183**–36
  fluid ounce [flōō/əd owns/] **75**–1
flute [flōōt] **238**–1
fly [flī] **214**–28
fly [flī] **170**–F
flyer [flī/ər] **102**–1
flying disc [flī/ĭng dĭsk/] **231**–27
foam pad [fōm/ păd/] **226**–13
focus [fō/kəs] **235**–33
foggy [fö/gē, fäg/ē] **13**–20
foil [foyl] **72**–23
fold [fōld] **101**–F
folder [fōl/dər] **183**–50
folding [fōl/dĭng]
  folding card table [fōl/dĭng kärd/ tā/bəl] **102**–4
  folding chair [fōl/dĭng chër/] **102**–5
folk [fōk] **237**–29
follow [fäl/ō] **114**–J, **147**–F
Following Directions [fäl/ō də rek/shənz, –dī–] **9**

Index

food [food]
baby food [bā/bē food/] 37–4
canned food [kănd/ food/] 146–9
fast food restaurant [făst/ food/ rěs/tə ränt] 128–10
food court [food/kört] 131–15
food preparation worker
[food/ prě/pə rā/shən wür/kər] 185–4
food processor [food/ prä/sě sər] 54–26
packaged food [păk/ĭjd food/] 146–10
pet food [pět/ food/] 72–5
FOOD [food] 79
FOOD PREPARATION AND SAFETY
[food/ prě/pə rā/shən ən sāf/tē] 76–77
Food Processor [food/ prä/sě sər] 92
Foods [foodz] 72, 73
Food Safety [food/ sāf/tē] 76
FOOD SERVICE [food/sür/vəs] 185
foot [foot] 104–8
football [foot/böl/] 229–11, 231–21
football helmet [foot/böl/ hěl/mət] 231–19
footnote [foot/nōt/] 190–10
Foot [foot] 106
for [för] 128–B, 173–C
forceps [för/səps, –sěps] 195–43
forearm [för/ärm/] 106–13
forehead [för/əd/, –hěd/, fär/–] 106–2
forest [för/əst, fär/–] 204–1, 204–11
forest fire [för/əst fir/] 144–7
fork [förk] 55–3, 83–27, 83–28
forklift [förk/lĭft/] 175–12
Form [förm] 4
Formal Clothes [förm/əl klōz/] 89
former husband [för/mər hŭz/bənd] 35 ✦
former wife [för/mər wif/] 35 ✦
forms [förmz] 118–4, 134–19, 161–16
formula [för/myə lə] 37–3, 195–34
fortieth [för/tē əth] 16
forty [för/tē] 16
forward [för/wərd] 235–D
forward button [för/wərd bŭt/n] 197–3
foundation [fown dā/shən] 109–40
founders [fown/dərz] 198–7
fountain [fown/tn] 224–5, 224–9
four [för] 16
4-door car [för/dör kär/] 156–1
2 x 4 (two by four) [too/ bī för/] 181–19
fourteen [för/tēn/] 16
fourteenth [för/tēnth/] 16
fourth [förth] 16
Fourth Floor [förth flör/] 50
Fourth of July [förth əv joo li/] 22–13
fox [fäks] 216–15
Fractions [frăk/shənz] 192
Fractions and Decimals [frăk/shənz ən dě/sə məlz] 17
frame [frām] 58–4, 58–18
frayed cord [frād/ körd/] 179–5
free [frē] 122–7
free speech [frē/ spēch/] 140–2
freedom [frē/dəm]
freedom of religion [frē/dəm əv rĭ lĭ/jən] 140–3
freedom of the press [frē/dəm əv dhə prěs/] 140–4
freezer [frē/zər] 54–10, 185–3

freezing [frē/zĭng] 13–7
French [frěnch]
french fries [frěnch/ frīz/] 79–2
French horn [frěnch/ hörn/] 238–13
Frequency [frē/kwən sē/] 20
fresh [frěsh] 71–16
Friday [frī/dā, –dē] 20–13
fried [frīd] 76–6
fried chicken [frīd/ chĭk/ən] 76–1
fringe [frĭnj] 99–34
frog [frög, fräg] 212–25
front [frŭnt] 25–7
front desk [frŭnt/ děsk/] 184–12
front door [frŭnt/ dör/] 53–11
front seat [frŭnt/ sēt/] 159–51
front walk [frŭnt/ wök/] 53–2
Front Porch [frŭnt/ pörch/] 53
Font Yard and House [frŭnt/ yärd/ en hows/] 53
frostbite [fräst/bĭt/] 116–G
frozen [frō/zən] 63–16, 71–17
frozen dinner [frō/zən dĭn/ər] 72–28
frozen vegetables [frō/zən věj/tə bəlz] 72–27
Frozen Foods [frō/zən foodz/] 72
fruit [froot] 67–9
fruit salad [froot săl/əd] 80–21
FRUIT [froot] 68
frustrated [frŭs/trā/təd] 43–27
frying pan [frī/ĭng păn/] 78–5
fuel injection system
[fyoo/əl ĭn jěk/shən sĭs/təm] 158–17
full [fool] 23–9, 42–6
full-length mirror [fool/lěnth/ mĭr/ər] 58–6
full moon [fool/ moon/] 205–12
full slip [fool/ slĭp/] 91–22
fumes [fyoomz] 179–3
funnel [fŭn/əl] 195–40
funny photo [fŭn/ē fō/tō] 206–2
fur [für] 216–19
furious [fyoor/ē əs] 43 ✦
furnished apartment [für/nĭsht ə pärt/mənt] 48–3
furniture [für/nĭ chər] 53–19
furniture polish [für/nĭ chər päl/ĭsh] 61–8
furniture store [für/nĭ chər stör/] 126–8
Furniture and Accessories
[für/nĭ chər ən ĭk sěs/ə rēz] 59
fuse box [fyooz/ bäks/] 62–13
fusion [fyoo/zhən] 218–10
galaxy [găl/ək sē] 205–15
gallbladder [göl/blăd/ər] 107–44
gallon [găl/ən] 75–5
game [gām]
baseball game [bās/böl gām/] 44–2
board game [börd/ gām/] 232–5
game show [gām/ shō/] 236–8
video game console [vĭd/ē ō gām/ kän/sōl] 232–3
video game control [vĭd/ē ō gām kən trōl/] 232–4
Games [gāmz] 59
GAMES [gāmz] 232–233
gang violence [găng/ vĭ/ə ləns] 142–4
garage [gə räzh/, –räj/] 47–14, 124–1
garage door [gə räzh/ dör/] 53–7
Garage [gə räzh/, –räj/] 50

GARAGE SALE [gə räzh/ sāl/] 102–103
garbage [gär/bĭj]
garbage can [gär/bĭj kăn/] 53–24
garbage disposal [gär/bĭj dĭ spō/zəl] 54–7
garbage truck [gär/bĭj trŭk/] 127–22
garden [gär/dn]
botanical garden [bə tăn/ə kəl gär/dn] 222–3
roof garden [roof/gär/dn] 50–4
vegetable garden [věj/tə bəl gär/dn] 53–27, 177–14
garden [gär/dn] 53–B
gardener [gär/dn er, gärd/nər] 167–28
gardenia [gär děn/yə] 211–18
gardening [gärd/nĭng]
gardening crew [gärd/nĭng kroo/] 176–1
gardening crew leader
[gärd/nĭng kroo lēd/ər] 176–4
GARDENING [gärd/nĭng] 176
gargle [gär/gəl] 109–L
garlic [gär/lĭk] 69–30
garlic bread [gär/lĭk brěd/] 81–28
garlic press [gär/lĭk prěs/] 78–11
Garment Factory [gär/mənt făk/tə rē, făk/trē] 98
garment worker [gär/mənt wür/kər] 167–29
garter [gär/tər]
garter belt [gär/tər bělt/] 91–16
garter snake [gär/tər snāk/] 213–39
gas [găs] 218–3
gas gauge [găs/gāj/] 159–31
gas meter [găs mē/tər] 62–14
gas pedal [găs pěd/l] 159–46
gas shut-off valve [găs/ shŭt/öf vălv/] 146–4
gas station [găs stā/shən] 125–10
gas station attendant
[găs stā/shən ə těn/dənt] 162–3
gas tank [găs tăngk/] 158–10
gate [gāt] 50–16, 53–9, 161–8
Gate [gāt] 161
gauge [gāj]
blood pressure gauge [blŭd/ prěsh/ər gāj/] 118–9
gas gauge [găs/gāj/] 159–31
oil gauge [oyl/gāj/] 159–29
temperature gauge [těm/prə chər gāj/] 159–30
gauze [göz] 117–8
gear shift [gïr/ shĭft/] 159–47
gel [jěl] 108–2, 108–16
GEOGRAPHY AND HABITATS
[jē äg/rə fē ən hă/bə tăts/] 204
Geometric Solids [jē/ə mě/trĭk săl/ədz] 193
geometry [jē äm/ə trē] 192–17
geothermal energy [jē/ō thür/məl ěn/ər jē] 218–7
get [gět]
get a job [gět/ ə jäb/] 40–F
get a learner's permit
[gět/ ə lürn/ərz pür/mĭt] 137–F
get a library card [gět/ ə li/brĕr ē kärd/] 133–A
get a loan [gět/ ə lōn/] 49–J
get an electric shock [gět/ ən ĭ lěk/trĭk shäk/] 116–F
get a speeding ticket [gět/ ə spē/dĭng tĭk/ət] 162–C
get bed rest [gět/ běd/ rěst/] 114–B
get change [gět/ chānj/] 26–A
get dressed [gět/ drěst/] 38–D
get elected [gět/ ĭ lěk/təd] 139–C

get engaged [gĕt/ ĭn gājd/] **41**–J
get feedback [gĕt/ fēd/băk/] **191**–K
get frostbite [gĕt/ fröst/bīt/] **116**–G
get good grades [gĕt/ good/ grādz/] **10**–H
get hired [gĕt/ hīrd/] **173**–L
get home [gĕt/ hōm/] **39**–R
get immunized [gĕt/ ĭm/yə nīzd] **114**–I
get into [gĕt/ ĭn/tōō] **153**–E
get lost [gĕt/ löst/] **162**–B
get married [gĕt/ măr/ēd] **41**–K
get off [gĕt/ öf/] **153**–J
get on [gĕt/ än, ön/] **153**–I
get out of [gĕt/ owt/ əv] **153**–F
get the title [gĕt/ dhə tīt/l] **157**–E
get up [gĕt/ ŭp/] **38**–B
get your license [gĕt/ yər lī/səns] **137**–I
Getting Your First License
[gĕt/ĭng yər fürst/ lī/səns] **137**
Get Well [gĕt/ wĕl/] **114**
gift [gĭft/] **94** ✦, **240**–3
gift shop [gĭft/ shäp/] **130** ✦, **184**–5
gills [gĭlz/] **212**–2
giraffe [jə răf/] **217**–32
girder [gür/dər] **178**–3
girdle [gür/dl] **91**–15
girl [gürl/] **31**–10
give [gĭv] **15**–F, **122**–B, **148**–A,
glad [glăd] **44**–5
glass [glăs] **53**–18, **83**–22, **83**–23
glass cleaner [glăs klē/nər] **61**–14
glasses [glăs/əz] **92**–10, **115**–7, **179**–10
sunglasses [sŭn/glăs/əz] **90**–27
global positioning system (GPS) [glō/bəl
pə zĭ/shə nĭng sĭs/təm] / [jē/pē/ĕs/] **155**–11
gloves [glŭvz] **90**–6, **231**–17
disposable gloves [dĭ spō/ zə bəl glŭvz/] **93**–27
glove compartment [glŭv/ kəm pärt/mənt] **159**–44
latex gloves [lā/tĕks glŭvz/] **93**–34
rubber gloves [rŭb/ər glŭvz/] **61**–4
surgical gloves [sür/jĭ kəl glŭvz/] **121**–39
work gloves [würk/ glŭvz/] **92**–17, **179**–17
glue [glōō] **183**–33
glue stick [glōō/ stĭk] **232**–11
go [gō]
go back [gō/ băk/] **11**–M
go for [gō/ fər] **157**–J
go on [gō/ än] **173**–K
go over [gō/ ō/vər] **153**–B
go past [gō/ păst/] **155**–E
go straight [gō/ strāt/] **155**–A
go through [gō/ thrōō/] **160**–D
go to an employment agency
[gō/ tə ən ĭm ploy/mənt ā/jən sē] **173**–E
go to bed [gō/ tə bĕd/] **39**–Y
go to college [gō/ tə käl/ĭj] **41**–I
go to jail [gō/ tə jāl/] **141**–G
go to prison [gō/ tə prĭz/ən] **141**–G
go to school [gō/ tə skōōl/] **38**–J
go to sleep [gō/ tə slēp/] **39**–Z

go to the grocery store
[gō/ tə dhə grōs/rē stör/, grōsh/rē] **38**–L
go to the next line [gō/ tə dhə nĕkst/ līn] **196**–D
go to work [gō/ tə würk/] **38**–I
go under [gō/ ŭn/dər] **153**–A
to-go box [tə gō/ bäks/] **82**–5
GO [gō] **222**–223
goat [gōt] **215**–5
goggles [gäg/əlz] **179**–11
goldfish [gōld/fĭsh] **215**–16
golf [gälf, gölf] **228**–8
golf club [gälf/ klŭb/] **231**–1
good [good] **23**–17
Goods [goodz] **73**
goose [gōōs] **214**–13
gopher [gō/fər] **215**–19
gorilla [gə rĭl/ə] **217**–29
gospel [gäs/pəl] **237**–30
Government [gŭ/ vərn mənt] **138**–139
GOVERNMENT AND MILITARY SERVICE
[gŭ/ vərn mənt ən mĭ/ lə tër ē sür/vəs] **138**–139
governor [gŭ/ vər nər] **139**–20, **139**–21
gown [gown] **206**–8
evening gown [ēv/nĭng gown/] **89**–18
hospital gown [häs/pĭ tl gown/] **121**–19
nightgown [nīt/gown/] **91**–25
surgical gown [sür/jə kəl gown/] **93**–37, **121**–38
GPS (global positioning system) [jē/pē/ĕs/] /
[glō/bəl pə zĭ/shə nĭng sĭs/təm] **155**–11
grab bar [grăb/ bär/] **57**–9
grades [grādz] **10**–4
graduate [grăj/ōō āt/] **40**–D
graduated cylinder [grăj/ōō ā/təd sĭl/ən dər] **195**–38
GRADUATION [grăj/ōō ā/shən] **206**–207
graffiti [grə fēt/tē] **148**–1
grandchild [grăn/chīld, grănd–] **34** ✦
granddaughters [grăn/dö/tərz] **34** ✦
grandfather [grăn/fä/dhər, grănd–] **34**–2
grandmother [grăn/mŭdh/ər, grănd–] **34**–1
Grandparents [grăn/përʼənts, grănd–] **34**
grandson [grăn/sŭn/, grănd–] **34** ✦
grapefruit [grāp/frōōt/] **68**–6
grapes [grāps] **68**–3
graph [grăf] **192**–15
graphic designer [grăf/ĭk dĭ zī/nər] **167**–30
grasshopper [grăs/häp/ər] **214**–24
grate [grāt] **77**–G
grater [grā/tər] **78**–2
gray [grā] **24**–15
gray hair [grā hër] **33**–13
grease [grēs] **77**–B
green [grēn] **24**–5
green card [grēn/ kärd/] **40**–2
green onions [grēn/ ŭn/yənz] **69**–20
greet [grēt] **3**–G, **171**–M, **174**–H
GREETING [grē/tĭng] **2**–3
greeting card [grē/tĭng kärd/] **134**–15
grill [grĭl] **53**–17
grilled [grĭld/]
grilled cheese sandwich
[grĭld/ chēz/ săn/wĭch, –sănd/–] **80**–10

grilled fish [grĭld/ fĭsh/] **81**–29
grilled ribs [grĭld/ rĭbz/] **76**–2
grocery [grōs/rē, grōsh/rē]
grocery bag [grōs/rē băg/] **67**–13
grocery clerk [grōs/rē klürk/] **72**–4
Grocery Products [grōs/rē präd/ŭkts] **72**
GROCERY STORE [grōs/ rē stör/] **72**–73
ground [grownd]
ground beef [grownd/ bēf/] **70**–4
ground post [grownd/ pōst/] **134**–6
playground [plā/grownd/] **50**–3
group [grōōp] **115**–15
grower [grō/ər] **177**–13
guard [gärd] **141**–3
Coast Guard [kōst/ gärd/] **138**–18
lifeguard [līf/gärd] **225**–19
lifeguard station [līf/gärd/ stā/shən] **225**–21
National Guard [nă/shə nəl gärd/] **138**–19
security guard [sĭ kyōōr/ə tē gärd/] **132**–5, **169**–55
shin guards [shĭn/ gärdz/] **231**–13
guest [gĕst] **184**–10
guest room [gĕst/ rōōm] **184**–13
guest services [gĕst/ sür/vəs əs] **130**–12
guest speaker [gĕst/ spē/kər] **206**–4
guinea pig [gĭn/ē pĭg/] **215**–14
guitar [gĭ tär/] **238**–9
gums [gŭmz] **106**–6
gum disease [gŭm/ dĭ zēz/] **119**–11
gun [gŭn] **142**–13, **181**–21
gurney [gür/nē] **121**–33
gutter [gŭt/ər] **53**–4
gym [jĭm] **5**–19, **126**–10, **184**–24
gymnastics [jĭm năs/tĭks] **228**–9
gynecologists [gī/nə käl/ə jĭsts] **120** ✦
habitat [hă/bə tăt/] **194**–12
HABITATS [hă/bə tăts/] **204**
hacksaw [hăk/sö/] **180**–5
hail a taxi [hāl/ ə tăx/ē/]] **152** ✦
hailstorm [hāl/störm/] **13**–21
hair [hër] **104**–2
black hair [blăk/ hër/] **33**–16
blond hair [bländ/ hër/] **33**–17
brown hair [brown/ hër/] **33**–18
curly hair [kür/lē hër/] **33**–11
gray hair [grā/ hër] **33**–13
hair clip [hër klĭp/] **108**–19
hairdresser [hër/drĕs/ər] **167**–31
hair gel [hër jĕl/] **108**–16
hairnet [hër nĕt/] **93**–25
hair salon [hër sə län/] **131**–18
hair spray [hër sprā/] **108**–12
hair stylist [hër stī/lĭst] **167**–31
long hair [löng/ hër/] **33**–3
red hair [rĕd/ hër/] **33**–15
short hair [shört/hër/] **33**–1
shoulder-length hair [shōl/dər lĕnth/ hër/] **33**–2
straight hair [strāt/ hër/] **33**–9
wavy hair [wā/vē hër/] **33**–10
HAIR [hër] **33**

half [hăf]
  half bath [hăf/ băth/] **57** ✦
  half brother [hăf/ brŭdh/ər] **35**–28
  1/2 cup [hăf/ kŭp/] **75**–9
  half dollar [hăf/ däl/ər] **26**–5
  half past one [hăf/ păst/ wŭn/] **18**–11
  half sister [hăf/ sĭs/tər] **35**–27
  half slip [hăf/ slĭp/] **91**–23
halibut steak [hăl/ə bət stāk/] **71**–6
hall [höl] **124**–8
  hallway [höl/wā/] **5**–10, **184**–18
Hallway [höl/wā/] **51**
ham [hăm] **70**–9, **76**–5
hamburger [hăm/bür/gər] **79**–1
hammer [hăm/ər] **180**–1
  jackhammer [jăk/hăm/ər] **178**–9
  sledgehammer [slĕj/ hăm/ər] **178**–23
hammer [hăm/ər] **178**–D
hammock [hăm/ək] **53**–23
hamper [hăm/pər] **57**–1
hand [hănd] **105**–15, **177**–20
  DMV handbook [dē/ĕm/vē/ hănd/book] **136**–1
  handbag [hănd/băg/] **87**–9, **94**–2
  handbrake [hănd/ brāk/] **59**–48
  handcuffs [hănd/kŭfs/] **141**–2
  handsaw [hănd/sö/] **180**–4
  handset [hănd/sĕt/] **14**–1
  hand towel [hănd tow/əl] **57**–15
  hand truck [hănd trŭk/] **175**–11
Hand [hănd] **106**
handicapped parking [hăn/dē kăpt pär/kĭng]
  128–6, **154**–12
hand in [hănd/ ĭn/] **10**–O
hanger [hăng/gər] **101**–11
hang up [hăng/ ŭp/] **15**–D, **101**–H
happy [hăp/ē] **28**–6, **43**–31
hard [härd] **23**–5, **23**–24
  hardboiled eggs [härd/boyld/ ĕgz/] **76**–8
  hard drive [härd/ drīv/] **196**–6
  hard hat [härd/ hăt/] **92**–1, **179**–9
hardware store [härd/wër/stör/] **148**–4
harmonica [här mä/ nĭ kə] **238**–21
harvest [här/vəst] **177**–B
hash browns [hăsh/ brownz/] **80**–3
hats [hăts] **90**–1, **95**–11
  chef's hat [shĕfs/ hăt/] **93**–28
  cowboy hat [kow/boy/ hăt/] **92**–18
  hard hat [härd/ hăt/] **92**–1, **179**–9
  ski hat [skē/ hăt/] **90**–11
  straw hat [strö/ hăt/] **90**–23
have [hăv]
  have a baby [hăv/ ə bā/bē] **41**–L
  have a conversation [hăv/ ə kän/vər sā/shən] **11**–L
  have a heart attack [hăv/ ə härt/ ə tăk/] **116**–D
  have an allergic reaction
    [hăv/ ən ə lür/jĭk rē ăk/shən] **116**–E
  have a picnic [hăv/ ə pĭk/nĭk] **224**–D
  have dinner [hăv/ dĭn/ər] **39**–S
  have regular checkups
    [hăv/ rĕg/yə lər chĕk/ups] **114**–H
Hawaii-Aleutian time [hə wī/ē ə loo/shən tīm/] **19**–27

hay [hā] **177**–18
hazard [hăz/ərd] **186**–6
  hazard lights [hăz/ərd līts/] **159**–36
Hazardous Materials [hăz/ər dəs mə tïr/ē əlz] **179**
hazardous waste [hăz/ər dəs wāst/] **218**–12
Hazards [hăz/ərdz] **179**
head [hĕd] **69**–32, **104**–1
  headache [hĕd/āk/] **110**–1
  headband [hĕd/bănd/] **90**–3
  headboard [hĕd/börd/] **58**–10
  head chef [hĕd/ shĕf/] **185**–7
  headlight [hĕd/līt/] **158**–7
  headline [hĕd/līn] **133**–7
  headphones [hĕd/fōnz/] **6**–8, **234**–4
  headset [hĕd/sĕt] **14**–13
  headwaiter [hĕd/wā/tər] **185**–12
  headwrap [hĕd/răp/] **90**–7
  letterhead [lĕt/ər hĕd] **183**–42
  overhead compartment
    [ō/vər hĕd/ kəm pärt/mənt] **161**–13
  overhead projector [ō/vər hĕd/prə jĕk/tər] **7**–16
  wireless headset [wīr/ləs hĕd/sĕt] **14**–14
health [hĕlth] **167**–32
  health history form [hĕlth/ hĭs/tə rē förm/] **118**–4
  health insurance card
    [hĕlth/ ĭn shoor/əns kärd/] **118**–3
HEALTH [hĕlth] **114**–115
HEALTH FAIR [hĕlth/ fër/] **122**–123
Health Problems [hĕlth/ präb/ləmz] **115**
hear [hïr] **106**–B
hearing [hïr/ĭng]
  hearing aid [hïr/ĭng ād/] **115**–10
  hearing impaired [hïr/ĭng ĭm përd/] **32**–12
  hearing loss [hïr/ĭng lös/] **115**–2
heart [härt] **107**–38, **116**–D, **239**–6
  heart disease [härt/ dĭ zēz/] **111**–11
hearts [härts] **233**–31
heater [hē/tər] **159**–40
heating pad [hē/tĭng păd/] **113**–13
heat wave [hēt/ wāv/] **13**–13
heavy [hĕv/ē] **23**–13, **32**–7, **97**–27
hedge clippers [hĕj/ klĭp/ərz] **176**–11
heel [hēl] **94**–22, **106**–24
  high heels [hī/ hēlz/] **89**–21, **95**–25
height [hīt] **17**–16, **32**–5
Height [hīt] **32**
Heimlich maneuver [hīm/lĭk mə noo/vər] **117**–18
helicopter [hĕl/ə käp/tər] **151**–9
helmet [hĕl/mət] **93**–23, **231**–19
help [hĕlp] **8**–J, **147**–G
Help with Health Problems
  [hĕlp/ wĭth/ hĕlth/ präb/ləmz] **115**
hem [hĕm] **100**–8
hen [hĕn] **215**–8
herbal tea [ür/bəl tē/, hür/bəl–] **81**–40
herbs [ürbz, hürbz] **84**–9
hibiscus [hĭ bĭs/kəs, hī–] **211**–12
hide [hīd] **240**–D
high [hī] **91**–12, **97**–32, **188**–3
  high blood pressure [hī/ blŭd/ prĕsh/ər] **111**–14
  high chair [hī/ chër/] **37**–6, **82**–3
  high heels [hī/ hēlz/] **89**–21, **95**–25

  high-rise [hī/ rīz/] **127**–13
  high school [hī/ skool] **188**–4
highway [hī/wā] **155**–9
  highway marker [hī/wā mär/kər] **154**–17
hiking [hī/kĭng] **226**–7
  hiking boots [hī/kĭng boots/] **95**–31
hills [hĭlz] **204**–16
  downhill skiing [down/hĭl/ skē/ĭng] **227**–1
hip hop [hĭp/hăp] **237**–26
hippopotamus [hĭp/ə pät/ə məs] **217**–43
hire [hīr] **141**–B
  hired hand [hīrd/ hănd/] **177**–20
Historical Terms [hĭs/tör/ə kəl türmz/] **199**
history [hĭs/tə rē] **118**–4, **189**–12
HISTORY [hĭs/tə rē] **198**–199
hit [hĭt] **230**–B
HIV (human immunodeficiency virus)
  [āch/ī/vē/] / [hyoo/mən ĭm/yə nō
  dĭ fĭsh/ən sē vī/rəs] **111**–17
Hi-Visibility safety vest [hī/vĭ/zə bĭl/ə tē vĕst/] **92**–4
HOBBIES AND GAMES [häb/ēz ən gāmz/] **232**–233
hockey [häk/ē] **229**–13
  hockey stick [häk/ē stĭk/] **231**–11
hold [hōld] **36**–A
holder [hōl/dər]
  candle holder [kăn/dl hōl/dər] **56**–21
  cell phone holder [sĕl/ fōn/ hōld/ər] **94**–15
  magazine holder [măg/ə zēn/ hōld/ər] **56**–23
  pot holders [pät/ hōl/dərz] **78**–29
  toothbrush holder [tooth/brŭsh/ hōld/ər] **57**–22
holiday [häl/ə dā] **22**–7, **22**–8
Holidays [häl/ə dāz/] **22**
HOLIDAYS [häl/ə dāz/] **239**
holly [häl/ē] **210**–19
home [hōm] **52**–7, **52**–12
  home health care aide [hōm/ hĕlth/ kër ād/] **167**–32
  home improvement store
    [hōm/ ĭm proov/mənt stör/] **127**–20
  homemaker [hōm/mā/kər] **168**–33
  homesick [hōm/sĭk/] **43**–20
HOME [hōm] **46**–47, **48**–49
honeybee [hŭn/ē bē/] **214**–25
hood [hood] **158**–4
Hood [hood] **158**
hoof / hooves [hoof/] / [hoovz] **216**–17
hook [hook] **180**–39, **180**–40
  hook and eye [hook/ ən ī/] **99**–27
  hook and loop fastener
    [hook/ ən loop/ fă/sən ər] **99**–29
horn [hörn] **159**–32, **216**–21, **238**–11
  French horn [frĕnch/ hörn] **238**–13
horror story [hör/ər stör/ē, här/–] **237**–17
horse [hörs] **215**–4
  horseback riding [hörs/băk rī/dĭng] **226**–9
  horse racing [hörs/ rā/sĭng] **228**–19
  seahorse [sē/hörs/] **212**–13
hose [hōz] **53**–21, **91**–18
hospital [häs/pĭ tl] **125**–9, **154**–18
  hospital bed [häs/pĭ tl bĕd/] **121**–22
  hospital gown [häs/pĭ tl gown/] **121**–19
HOSPITAL [häs/pĭ tl] **120**–121
Hospital Room [häs/pĭ tl room/] **121**

Hospital Staff [häs/pĭ tl stäf/] **120**

hostess [hō/stəs] **82**–2

hot [hät] **13**–3, **42**–1

  hot cereal [hät sïr/ē əl] **80**–9

  hot dog [hät/ dög/] **79**–6

  hot water [hät/ wö/tər] **57**–8

  hot water bottle [hät/ wö/tər bät/l] **113**–15

hotel [hō tĕl/] **124**–3

A HOTEL [hō tĕl/] **184**

hour [ow/ər] **18**–1

house [hows]

  courthouse [kört/hows/] **125**–13

  dollhouse [däl/hows/] **59**–18

  housekeeper [hows/kē/pər] **168**–34, **184**–20

  housekeeping cart [hows/kē/pĭng kärt/] **184**–19

  House of Representatives

    [hows/ əv rĕp/rĭ zĕn/tə tĭvz] **138**–3

  house painter [hows/ pān/tər] **168**–46

  houseplant [hows/plănt/] **56**–4, **211**–27

  townhouse [town/hows/] **52**–6

  two-story house [tōō/stör/ē hows/] **52** ✦

  warehouse [wër/hows/] **175**–7

  White House [wīt/ hows/] **138**–7

House [hows] **49**, **53**

A HOUSE AND YARD [hows/ən yärd/] **53**

HOUSEHOLD PROBLEMS AND REPAIRS

  [hows/hōld/ präb/ləmz ən rĭ përz/] **62**–**63**

HOUSEWORK [hows/würk/] **60**

housing [how/zĭng] **52**–11

hubcap [hŭb/kăp/] **158**–9

hug [hŭg] **2**–E

human immunodeficiency virus (HIV)

  [hyōō/mən ĭm/yə nō dĭ fĭsh/ən sē vi/rəs] /

  [āch/ī/vē/] **111**–17

humid [hyōō/məd] **13**–15

humidifier [hyōō mĭd/ə fi/ər] **113**–11

humiliated [hyōō mĭl/ē ā/təd] **43** ✦

hummingbird [hŭm/ĭng bürd/] **214**–10

hump [hŭmp] **217**–51

hungry [hŭng/grē] **42**–5

hurricane [hür/ə kān/] **145**–14

hurt [hürt] **42**–16, **116**–C

husband [hŭz/bənd] **34**–13

  ex-husband [ĕks/ hŭz/bənd] **35** ✦

  former husband [för/mər hŭz/bənd] **35** ✦

hutch [hŭch] **55**–22

hybrid [hy/brĭd] **156**–3

hydrant [hī/drənt] **129**–27

hydroelectric power [hī/drō ĭ lĕk/trĭk pow/ər] **218**–5

hydrogen peroxide [hī/drə jən pə räk/sīd] **117**–9

hyena [hī ē/nə] **217**–30

HYGIENE [hy/jēn] **108**–**109**

hygienist [hī jē/nĭst, –jĕn/ĭst] **119**–3

hypertension [hī/pər tĕn/shən] **111**–14

hyphen [hy/fən] **190**–20

hypoallergenic [hī/pō ăl/ər jĕn/ĭk] **108** ✦

I beam [ī/ bēm/] **178**–3

ice [īs]

  ice cream [īs/ krēm/] **72**–26

  ice-cream cone [īs/ krēm/ kōn/] **79**–13

  ice cream shop [īs/ krēm/ shäp/] **131**–16

  ice hockey [īs/ häk/ē] **229**–13

ice pack [īs/ păk/] **117**–13

ice skates [īs/ skāts/] **231**–9

ice skating [īs/ skā/tĭng] **227**–4

iced tea [īst/ tē/] **79**–12

icy [ī/sē] **13**–22

ID [ī/dē/] **146**–19

identity theft [ī dĕn/tə tē thĕft/] **142**–9

ignition [ĭg nĭsh/ən] **159**–33

illegal drugs [ĭ lē/gəl drŭgz/] **142**–6

Illnesses and Childhood Diseases

  [ĭl/nə səz ən chĭld/hōōd dĭ zēz/ əz] **111**

ILLNESSES AND MEDICAL CONDITIONS

  [ĭl/nə səz ən mĕd/ĭ kəl kən dĭsh/ənz] **111**

Immediate Family

  [ĭ mē/ dē ət făm/lē, –fă/məlē] **34**

immigrant [ĭm/ə grənt] **199**–19

immigrate [ĭm/ə grāt/] **40**–C

immigration [ĭm/ə grā/shən] **199**–18

immunization [ĭm/yə nə zā/shən] **114** ✦

immunodeficiency [ĭm/yə nō dĭ fĭsh/ən sē] **111**–17

impaired [ĭm përd/] **32**–11, **32**–12

important [ĭm pört/ənt] **146**–19

improvement [ĭm prōōv/mənt] **127**–20

in [ĭn] **25**–6

  be in shock [bē/ ĭn shäk/] **116**–B

  bubble in [bŭb/l ĭn/] **10**–K

  call in [käl/ ĭn/] **186**–A

  check in [chĕk/ ĭn/] **160**–A

  check-in kiosk [chĕk/ĭn kē/äsk/] **160**–2

  fall in love [fäl/ ĭn lŭv/] **40**–H

  fill in [fĭl/ ĭn/] **9**–O

  hand in [hănd/ĭn/] **10**–O

  in fashion [ĭn făsh/ən] **88** ✦

  in front of [ĭn frŭnt/ əv] **24**–7

  in love [ĭn lŭv/] **42**–18

  in pain [ĭn pān/] **42**–11

  in style [ĭn stīl/] **88** ✦

  in the middle [ĭn dhə mĭd/l] **24**–2

  look in [lōōk/ ĭn] **173**–B

  move in [mōōv/ ĭn/] **48**–F

  send in [sĕnd/ ĭn/] **173**–H

  take in [tāk/ ĭn/] **100**–D

  turn in [türn/ ĭn/] **191**–M

  walk-in freezer [wäk/ĭn frē/zər] **185**–3

inch [ĭnch] **17**–15

indent [ĭn dĕnt/] **190**–D

independence [ĭn/də pĕn/dəns]

  Declaration of Independence

    [dĕk/lə rā/shən əv ĭn/də pĕn/dəns] **198**–5

  Independence Day [ĭn/də pĕn/dəns dā/] **22**–13

INDIVIDUAL SPORTS [ĭn/də vĭj/ōō əl spörts/] **228**

infant [ĭn/fənt] **31**–6

infection [ĭn fĕk/shən] **111**–3

infectious disease [ĭn fĕk/shəs dĭ zēz/] **111** ✦

influenza [ĭn/flōō ĕn/zə] **111** ✦

INFORMATION [ĭn/fər mā/shən] **4**

inhaler [ĭn hā/lər] **113**–33

injection [ĭn jək/shən] **114** ✦, **158**–17

injured [ĭn/ jərd] **116**–C

INJURIES [ĭn/jə rēz] **110**

ink [ĭnk]

  ink cartridge [ĭnk/ kär/trĭj] **183**–45

  inkjet printer [ĭnk/jĕt prin/tər] **183**–18

  ink pad [ĭnk/ păd/] **183**–46

inline [ĭn/lĭn/]

  inline skates [ĭn/lĭn/ skāts/] **231**–10

  inline skating [ĭn/lĭn/ skā/tĭng] **228**–10

inquire about benefits

  [ĭn kwīr/ ə bowt/bĕn/ə fĭts] **174** ✦

insects [ĭn/sĕkts] **209**–11

  insect bite [ĭn/sĕkt bīt/] **110**–11

  insect repellent [ĭn/sĕkt rĭ pĕl/ənt] **226**–23

Insects [ĭn/sĕkts] **214**

INSECTS [ĭn/sĕkts] **214**

insert [ĭn sürt/] **132**–D

INSIDE AND OUTSIDE THE BODY

  [ĭn/sīd/ ən owt/sīd/ dhə băd/ē] **106**–**107**

Inside the Car [ĭn/sīd/ dhə kär/] **159**

Inside the Kit [ĭn/sīd/ dhə kĭt/] **117**

Inside the Trunk [ĭn/sīd/ dhə trŭnk/] **158**

inspect [ĭn spĕkt/] **147**–N

install [ĭn stäl/] **176**–H, **178**–C

instructor [ĭn strŭk/tər] **6**–4

Instrument Panel [ĭn/strə mənt păn/əl] **159**

instruments [ĭn/strə mənts] **119**–4, **238**

insulation [ĭn/sə lā/shən] **178**–14

insurance [ĭn shōōr/əns] **118**–3, **136**–8

integers [ĭn/tə jərz] **192**–1, **192**–2

Integers [ĭn/tə jərz] **192**

intercom [ĭn/tər käm/] **50**–5

interest inventory [ĭn/trəst ĭn/vən tör/ ē] **172**–11

international call [ĭn/tər năsh/ə nəl köl/] **15**–35

Internet [ĭn/tər nĕt/]

  Internet listing [ĭn/tər nĕt/ lĭst/ĭng] **48**–1

  Internet map [ĭn/tər nĕt/ măp] **155**–12

  Internet phone call [ĭn/tər nĕt/ fōn/ käl] **14**–20

INTERNET [ĭn/tər nĕt/] **197**

internist [ĭn/tür/nĭst] **120**–1

internship [ĭn/türn shĭp/] **172**–6

interpreter [ĭn tür/prə tər] **168**–35

INTERSECTION [ĭn/tər sĕk/shən] **128**–**129**

INTERVIEW SKILLS [ĭn/tər vyōō/ skĭlz/] **174**

intestinal parasites [ĭn tĕs/tə nəl păr/ə sīts/] **111**–13

intestines [ĭn tĕs/tənz] **107**–42

In the Airline Terminal [ĭn dhə ër/lĭn tür/mə nəl] **160**

In the Examining Room

  [ĭn dhə ĭg zăm/ə nĭng rōōm/] **118**

In the Waiting Room [ĭn dhə wā/tĭng rōōm/] **118**

into [ĭn/tōō, –tə] **153**–E

intravenous drip (IV)

  [ĭn/trə vē/nəs drĭp/] / [ī/vē/] **121**–25

introduce [ĭn/trə dōōs/] **2**–C, **3**–I

introduction [ĭn/trə dŭk/shən] **190**–6

invention [ĭn vĕn/shən] **199**–12

inventor [ĭn vĕn/tər] **199**–13

inventory [ĭn/vən tör/ ē] **172**–11, **172**–12

invertebrates [ĭn vür/ tə brəts/] **194**–13

invitation [ĭn və tā/shən] **12**–I, **12**–J, **64**–9

invite [ĭn vīt/] **12**–H

iris [ī/rəs] **211**–16

iron [ī/ərn] **101**–13, **108**–17

iron [ī/ərn] **101**–G

Index

ironed [ī/ərnd] **101**–20
ironing board [ī/ər nĭng börd/] **101**–14
irritated [ĭr/ə tā/təd] **64**–6
island [ī/lənd] **204**–8
IV (intravenous drip)
    [ī/vē/] / [ĭn/trə vē/nəs drĭp/] **121**–25
ivory [ī/vər ē] **24**–16
ivy [ī/vē] **210**–25
jack [jăk] **158**–24
jacket [jăk/ət] **90**–8
    chef's jacket [shĕfs/ jăk/ət] **93**–29
    down jacket [down/ jăk/ət] **90**–16
    leather jacket [lĕdh/ər jăk/ət] **90**–4
    sports jacket [spörts/ jăk/ət] **89**–14
jackhammer [jăk/ hăm/ər] **178**–9
jack-o'-lantern [jăk/ə lăn/tərn] **239**–10
janitor [jăn/ĭ tər] **182**–3
January [jăn/yōō ër/ē] **21**–25
jar [jär] **74**–2, **74**–14
jasmine [jăz/mən] **211**–22
jaw [jö] **106**–4
jay [jā] **214**–6
jaywalk [jā/wäk] **128**–C
jazz [jăz] **237**–24
jeans [jēnz] **86**–2, **92**–19
jellyfish [jĕl/ē fĭsh/] **212**–14
jewelry [jōō/əl rē]
    jewelry department [jōō/əl rē dĭ pärt/mənt] **95**–8
    jewelry store [jōō/əl rē stör/] **130**–2
jigsaw [jĭg/sö/] **180**–10
job [jäb] **172**–1, **172**–3, **172**–7
    job fair [jäb/ fër] **172**–13
JOB SAFETY [jäb/ sāf/tē] **179**
JOBS AND OCCUPATIONS
    [jäbz/ ən äk/yə pā/shənz] **166**–**169**
JOB SEARCH [jäb/ sürch/] **173**
JOB SKILLS [jäb/ skĭlz/] **170**
Job Training [jäb/ trān/ĭng] **172**
jockstrap [jäk/străp/] **91**–6
join [joyn] **143**–L
judge [jŭj] **141**–6
Judicial Branch [jōō dĭ/shəl brănch/] **138**
juice [jōōs] **73**–32
July [jōō lī/] **21**–31
jump [jŭmp] **230**–I
jumper cables [jŭm/pər kā/bəlz] **158**–21
jump rope [jŭmp/ rōp] **224**–4
jumpsuit [jŭmp/sōōt/] **93**–24
June [jōōn] **21**–30
junior high school [jōōn/yər hī/ skōōl] **188**–3
junk mail [jŭnk/ māl/] **135** ✦
Jupiter [jōō/pə tər] **205**–5
jury [jŭr/ē] **141**–8
justices [jŭs/tə səz] **138**–12, **138**–13
kangaroo [kăng/gə rōō/] **217**–44
keep [kēp] **28**–B
ketchup [kĕch/əp, kăch/–] **79**–21
kettle [kĕt/l] **54**–21
key [kē] **51**–30, **155**–9
    key pad [kē/ păd/] **14**–5
    pound key [pownd/ kē/] **14**–7
    star key [stär/ kē/] **14**–6

keyboard [kē/börd/] **196**–14, **238**–18
Keyboarding [kē/börd/ĭng] **196**
kick [kĭk] **230**–E
kidney [kĭd/nē] **107**–43
kids' bedroom [kĭdz/ bĕd/rōōm/] **47**–9
KIDS' BEDROOM [kĭdz/ bĕd/rōōm/] **59**
king-size bed [kĭng/sīz/ bĕd/] **184**–15
kiosk [kē/äsk/] **131**–22, **160**–2
kiss [kĭs] **3**–K, **36**–P
kit [kĭt]
    doll making kit [däl/ mā/kĭng kĭt/] **232**–13
    first aid kit [fürst/ ād/ kĭt/] **117**–1, **146**–18
    model kit [mäd/l kĭt/] **232**–9
    woodworking kit [wŏŏd/wür/kĭng kĭt/] **232**–14
Kit [kĭt] **117**
kitchen [kĭch/ən] **46**–5, **83**–15
    kitchen timer [kĭch/ən tī/mər] **78**–18
A KITCHEN [ə kĭch/ən] **54**
Kitchen [kĭch/ən] **185**
KITCHEN UTENSILS [kĭch/ən yōō tĕn/səlz] **78**
kite [kīt] **225**–2
kitten [kĭt/n] **215**–10
kiwi [kē/wē] **68**–22
knee [nē] **106**–20
    knee highs [nē/hīz/] **91**–12
    knee pads [nē/pădz/] **179**–19
knife [nīf] **55**–4, **83**–30
    carving knife [kär/vĭng nīf/] **78**–12
    multi-use knife [mŭl/tē yōōs/nīf/, mŭl/tī–] **226**–20
    paring knife [për/ĭng nīf/] **78**–16
    steak knife [stāk/ nīf/] **83**–29
knit [nĭt] **233**–F
knitting needles [nĭt/ĭng nēd/lz] **233**–23
knit top [nĭt/ täp/] **88**–7
knob [näb] **194**–22, **194**–23
    doorknob [dör/näb/] **53**–12
knuckle [nŭk/l] **106**–17
koala [kō ä/lə] **217**–45
lab [lăb] **5**–15
    lab coat [lăb/ kōt/] **93**–33
Lab [lăb] **195**
label [lā/bəl]
    mailing label [mā/lĭng lā/bəl] **183**–41
    nutrition label [nōō trĭ/shən lā/bəl] **122**–8
    prescription label [prĭ skrĭp/shən lā/bəl] **112**–4
    warning label [wär/nĭng lā/bəl] **112**–8
label [lā/bəl] **9**–V
Labor Day [lā/bər dā/] **22**–14
lace [lās] **99**–9
    shoelaces [shōō/lā səz] **94**–24
ladder [lăd/ər] **178**–2
ladle [lā/dl] **78**–7
ladybug [lā/dē bŭg/] **214**–26
lake [lāk] **204**–13
lamb [lăm] **70**–14
    lamb chops [lăm/ chäps/] **70**–15
    lamb shanks [lăm/ shăngks/] **70**–13
Lamb [lăm] **70**
lamp [lămp] **56**–15, **58**–25
    lampshade [lămp/shād/] **56** ✦, **58**–26
land [lănd] **160**–K
landlord [lănd/lörd/] **51**–27

landmarks [lănd/märks/] **220**–1
landscape designer [lănd/skāp/ dĭ zī/nər] **176**–5
LANDSCAPING AND GARDENING
    [lănd/skā/pĭng ən gärd/nĭng] **176**
languages [lăng/gwĭ jəz] **189**–13
    language arts [lăng/gwĭj ärts/] **189**–9
lantern [lăn/tərn] **226**–22, **239**–10
laptop [lăp/täp/] **196**–16
large [lärj] **96**–4, **96**–5
laser printer [lā/zər prĭn/tər] **183**–19
lashes [lăsh/əz]
    eyelashes [ī/lăsh/əz] **106**–11
last [lăst]
    last name [lăst/ nām/] **4**–4
    last week [lăst/wēk/] **20**–18
late [lāt] **19**–24
latex gloves [lā/tĕks glŭvz/] **93**–34
laugh [lăf] **44**–A
laundromat [lön/drə măt/] **128**–1
laundry [lön/drē] **101**–1
    laundry basket [lön/drē băs/kət] **101**–2
    laundry detergent [lön/drē dĭ tür/jənt] **101**–8
LAUNDRY [lön/drē] **101**
Laundry Room [lön/drē rōōm/] **50**
lawn [lön] **53**–26
    lawn mower [lön/ mō/ər] **176**–6
lawyer [lö/yər] **168**–36
lay [lā] **178**–B
layer cake [lā/ər kāk] **81**–33
LCD projector [ĕl/sē/dē/ prə jĕk/tər] **6**–6, **235**–29
leader [lē/dər] **176**–4
leaf / leaves [lēf] / [lēvz] **210**–6, **211**–6
    leaf blower [lēf/ blō/ər] **176**–2
leaking [lē/kĭng] **62**–3
learn [lürn] **40**–E
Learning New Words [lür/nĭng nōō/ würdz/] **8**
lease [lēs] **48** ✦, **51**–28
leather [lĕdh/ər] **98**–6
    leather jacket [lĕdh/ər jăk/ət] **90**–4
leave [lēv] **11**–O, **38**–N, **82**–J, **160**–J, **171**–P
leaves / leaf [lēvz] / [lēf] **210**–6, **211**–6
    leaf blower [lēf/ blō/ər] **176**–2
lecture [lĕk/chər] **122**–9
left [lĕft] **25**–1, **154**–8, **155**–C
legal [lē/gəl]
    legal holiday [lē/gəl häl/ə dā/] **22**–8
    legal pad [lē/gəl păd/] **183**–38
Legal Holidays [lē/gəl häl/ə dāz/] **22**
LEGAL SYSTEM [lē/gəl sĭs/təm] **141**
Leg and Foot [lĕg/ ən fŏŏt/] **106**
leggings [lĕg/ĭngz] **90**–12
Legislature [lĕ/jəs lā/chər] **139**–23
legs [lĕgz] **70**–21, **105**–9
    leg of lamb [lĕg/ əv lăm/] **70**–14
lemonade [lĕm/ə nād/] **84**–2
lemons [lĕm/ənz] **68**–7
lend [lĕnd] **26**–C
length [lĕngkth] **17**–17, **96**–17
lengthen [lĕngk/thən] **100**–A
lens / lenses [lĕnz] / [lĕnz/əz] **115**–8, **235**–23
leopard [lĕp/ərd] **217**–34
let out [lĕt/ owt/] **100**–C

letter [lĕt/ər] **134**–13
   letter carrier [lĕt/ər kăr/ē ər] **134**–20
   letterhead [lĕt/ər hĕd/] **183**–42
lettuce [lĕt/əs] **69**–1
level [lĕv/əl] **172**–1, **180**–29
librarian [lī brër/ē ən] **133**–9
library [lī/brër ē] **5**–17, **125**–15
   library clerk [lī/brër ē klürk/] **133**–1
   library patron [lī/brër ē pā/trən] **133**–3
LIBRARY [lī/brër ē] **133**
license [lī/səns]
   driver's license [drī/vərz lī/səns] **40**–4, **136**–9
   driver's license number
      [drī/vərz lī/səns nŭm/bər] **136**–11
   license plate [lī/səns plāt/] **136**–12, **158**–12
   marriage license [măr/ĭj lī/səns] **41**–8
   renew a license [rĭ nōō/ ə lī/səns, –nyōō/–] **136** ✦
   taxi license [tăk/sē lī/səns] **152**–22
License [lī/səns] **137**
licensed practical nurse (LPN)
   [lī/sənst prăk/tə kəl nürs/] / [ĕl/pē/ĕn/] **120**–11
lid [lĭd] **78**–24
lieutenant governor [lōō tĕ/nənt gŭ/vər nər] **139**–21
life [līf]
   lifeguard [līf/gärd/] **225**–19
   lifeguard station [līf/gärd/ stā/shən] **225**–21
   lifesaving device [līf/sā/vĭng dĭ vīs/] **225**–20
   life vest [līf/ vĕst/] **161**–25, **226**–14
   wildlife [wīld/ līf/] **220**–3
LIFE [līf] **212**–**213**
LIFE EVENTS AND DOCUMENTS
   [līf/ ĭ vĕnts/ ən dä/kyə mənts] **40**–**41**
lift [lĭft] **11**–E
light [līt] **23**–14, **97**–28
   brake light [brāk/ līt/] **158**–14
   daylight saving time [dā/līt/ sā/vĭng tīm/] **19**–25
   flashlight [flăsh/līt/] **146**–14
   hazard lights [hăz/ərd līts/] **159**–36
   headlight [hĕd/ līt/] **158**–7
   light blue [līt/ blōō/] **24**–11
   light bulb [līt/ bŭlb/] **56** ✦
   light fixture [līt/ fĭks/chər] **55**–18
   light source [līt/ sörs/] **194**–21
   light switch [līt/ swĭch/] **58**–27
   night light [nīt/ līt/] **37**–27
   porch light [pörch/ līt/] **53**–13
   streetlight [strēt/līt/] **148**–3
   string lights [strĭng/ lītz/] **239**–18
   tail light [tāl/ līt/] **158**–13
   traffic light [trăf/ĭk līt/] **128**–8
   work light [würk/ līt/] **181**–44
lightning [līt/nĭng] **13**–17
lily [lĭl/ē] **211**–26
limbs [lĭmz] **106** ✦, **210**–3
limes [līmz] **68**–8
limit [lĭ/mət] **154**–4
limo / limousine [lĭ/mō] / [lĭ/mə zēn] **156**–11
line [līn] **73**–11
   assembly line [ə sĕm/blē līn] **175**–6
   clothesline [klōz/līn/] **101**–9
   curved line [kürvd/ līn/] **193**–23
   headline [hĕd/līn/] **133**–7

line cook [līn/ kŏŏk/] **93**, **185** ✦
line segment [līn/ sĕg/mənt] **193**–20
line supervisor [līn/ sōō/pər vi zər] **175**–4
   parallel lines [pă/rə lĕl līnz/] **193**–25
   perpendicular lines
      [pür/pən dĭk/yə lər līnz/] **193**–24
   straight line [strāt/ līn/] **193**–22
linen [lĭn/ən] **98**–2
   linen closet [lĭn/ən kläz/ət] **57** ✦
liner [lī/nər]
   eyeliner [ī/lī/nər] **109**–36
Lines [līnz] **193**
lingerie [län/zhə rā/, –jə–] **91** ✦
links [lĭnkz] **197**–10
lion [lī/ən] **213**–33, **216**–2, **217**–36
lip [lĭp] **106**–5
   lipstick [lĭp/stĭk/] **109**–38
Liquid Measures [lĭk/wəd mĕzh/ərz] **75**
liquids [lĭk/wədz] **61**–21, **179**–8
list [lĭst] **67**–14
listen [lĭs/ən] **6**–C, **118**–C, **174**–K
listing [lĭst/ĭng] **48**–1
litter [lĭ/tər] **148**–2
litter [lĭ/tər] **219**–L
little [lĭt/l] **23**–1
Little League [lĭt/l lēg/] **229** ✦
live [lĭv] **140**–H
LIVE [lĭv] **52**
live music [lĭv/ myōō/zĭk] **84**–1
liver [lĭv/ər] **70**–7, **107**–40
livestock [lĭv/stäk/] **177**–15
living room [lĭv/ĭng rōōm/] **47**–12
LIVING ROOM [lĭv/ĭng rōōm/] **56**
lizard [lĭz/ərd] **213**–40
llama [lä/mə] **217**–25
load [lōd] **101**–C
loading dock [lō/dĭng däk/] **175**–15
loaf [lōf] **74**–10, **74**–22
   meatloaf [mēt/lōf/] **81**–31
loafers [lō/fərz] **95**–30
Lobby [läb/ē] **50**
lobster [läb/stər] **71**–10
local call [lō/kəl köl/] **15**–31
lock [läk] **51**–34, **159**–25
   locksmith [läk/smĭth/] **62**–11
lock [läk] **143**–E
locker [lä/kər] **5**–11, **50**–17
locket [läk/ət] **95**–35
Logging on and Sending Email
   [lög/ĭng än/ ən sĕnd/ĭng ē/māl, –ön–] **197**
lonely [lōn/lē] **42**–17
long [löng] **96**–18
   long distance call [löng/dĭs/təns köl/] **15**–32
   long hair [löng/ hër/] **33**–3
   long-sleeved [löng/slēvd/] **96**–14
   long underwear [löng/ ŭn/dər wër/] **91**–3
look [lŏŏk]
   look at [lŏŏk/ ăt/, –ət] **49**–H, **157**–A
   look for [lŏŏk/ för/] / [lŏŏk/ fər] **133**–B, **173**–C
   look in [lŏŏk/ ĭn] **173**–B
   look up [lŏŏk/ ŭp] **8**–A
loop [lōōp] **99**–29

loose [lōōs] **97**–30
lose [lōōz] **229** ✦
loss [lös] **115**–2
lost child [löst/ chīld/] **144**–1
lotion [lō/shən] **37**–13, **108**–9
loud [lowd] **23**–11
loungewear [lownj/wër/] **91** ✦
love [lŭv] **40**–H, **42**–18
   love seat [lŭv sēt/] **56**–1
low [lō] **97**–31
   low-cost exam [lō/köst ĭg zăm/] **122**–1
   low-cut socks [lō/kŭt/ săks/] **91**–10
   low-fat milk [lō/făt/ mĭlk/] **81**–42
lower back [lō/ər băk/] **107**–29
lozenges [läz/ən jəz] **113**–30
LPN (licensed practical nurse) [ĕl/pē/ĕn/] /
   [lī/sənst präk/tə kəl nürs/] **120**–11
luggage [lŭg/ĭj] **161**–18
   luggage cart [lŭg/ĭj kärt/] **184**–8
lug wrench [lŭg/ rĕnch/] **158**–22
lumber [lŭm/bər] **178**–17
Lunch [lŭnch] **80**
lung [lŭng] **107**–39
machine [mə shēn/]
   answering machine [ăn/sər ĭng mə shēn/] **14**–17
   ATM (Automated Teller Machine) [ā/tē/ĕm/] /
      [ö/tə māt ĭd tĕ/lər mə shēn/] **132**
   fax machine [făks/ mə shēn/] **183**–21
   machine operator [mə shēn/ äp/ə rā tər] **168**–37
   machine screw [mə shēn/ skrōō/] **180**–32
   sewing machine [sō/ĭng mə shēn/] **98**–13
   sewing machine operator
      [sō/ĭng mə shēn/ äp/ə rā/tər] **98**–14
   stamp machine [stămp/ mə shēn/] **135**–11
   vending machine [vĕnd/ĭng mə shēn/] **152**–9
Machine [mə shēn/] **98**, **132**
magazine [măg/ə zēn/, măg/ə zēn/] **133**–5
   magazine holder [măg/ə zēn/ hōl/dər] **56**–23
magnet [măg/nət] **195**–36
magnolia [măg nōl/yə] **210**–8
mail
   airmail [ër/māl/] **134**–5
   Certified Mail® [sür/tə fīd māl/] **134**–4
   Express Mail® [ĭk sprĕs/ māl/] **134**–2
   junk mail [jŭnk/ māl/] **135** ✦
   mailboxes [māl/băk/səz] **50**–11, **53**–1, **128**–13,
      135–12
   media mail [mē/dē ə māl/] **134**–3
   overnight / next day mail
      [ō/vər nīt/ / nĕkst/ dā/ māl/] **135** ✦
   Priority Mail® [prī/ör ə tē māl/] **134**–1
mail [māl/] **135**–D
mailer [mā/lər] **183**–40
mailing [mā/lĭng]
   mailing address [mā/lĭng ə drĕs/, ă/drĕs/] **134**–22
   mailing label [mā/lĭng la/bəl] **183**–41
main office [mān/ ö/fəs] **5**–12
MAINTAINING A CAR [mān/tā nĭng ə kär/] **157**
maintenance [mān/tn əns] **184**–23
maitre d' [mā/trə dē/] **185**–11
make [māk] **156** ✦

make [māk]
  make a deposit [māk/ ə dĭ päz/ ət] **132**–B
  make a disaster kit [māk/ ə dĭz/ăs tər kĭt/] **146**–B
  make a mortgage payment
    [māk/ ə mör/gəj pā/mənt] **49**–L
  make an offer [māk/ ən ö/fər] **49**–I
  make a wish [māk/ ə wĭsh/] **240**–B
  make copies [māk/ käp/ēz] **171**–D
  make dinner [māk/ dĭn/ər] **39**–Q
  make eye contact [māk/ ī/ kän/tăkt] **174**–J
  make furniture [māk/ für/nĭ chər] **170**–G
  make lunch [māk/ lŭnch/] **38**–F
  make progress [māk/ prä/grəs] **10**–G
  make small talk [māk/ smöl/tök] **12**–B
  make the bed [māk/dhə bĕd/] **60**–F
maker [mā/kər]
  dressmaker [drĕs/mā/kər] **100**–1
  dressmaker's dummy [drĕs/mā/kərz dŭ/mē] **100**–2
  homemaker [hōm/mā/kər] **168**–33
Makeup [māk/ŭp] **109**
makeup remover [māk/ŭp rĭ mōōv/ər] **109**–42
making [mā/kĭng] **232**–13
MAKING ALTERATIONS [māk/ĭng öl/tə rā/shənz] **100**
MAKING CLOTHES [māk/ĭng klōz/] **98**–**99**
Making an Emergency Call
  [mā/kĭng ən ĭ mür/jən sē köl/] **15**
Making a Phone Call [mā/kĭng ə fōn/ köl/] **15**
male [māl] **4**–17
mall [möl] **126**–7
MALL [möl] **130**–**131**
mallet [măl/ət] **180**–2
mammals [măm/əlz] **209**–10
Mammals [măm/əlz] **213**
MAMMALS [măm/əlz] **216**–**217**
manager [măn/ĭ jər] **50**–8, **72**–8
  account manager [ə kownt/ măn/ĭ jər] **132**–9
  office manager [ö/fəs măn/ĭ jər] **182**–8
Manager [măn/ĭ jər] **92**
mane [mān] **217**–49
maneuver [mə nōō/vər] **117**–18
mangoes [măng/gōz] **68**–21
manicurist [măn/ə kyōō/rĭst] **168**–38
man / men [măn] / [mĕn] **30**–1, **30**–4
  doorman [dör/măn/] **184**–1
mantle [măn/təl] **56**–11
manual [măn/yōō əl] **117**–2
Manual Transmission [măn/yōō əl trănz mĭsh/ən] **159**
manufacture [măn/yə făk/chər] **175**–B
map [măp] **7**–12, **155**–12
Map [măp] **13**
maple [mā/pəl] **210**–12
Maps [măps] **155**
MAPS [măps] **155**
March [märch] **21**–27
margarine [mär/jər ən] **72**–20
marigold [măr/ə gōld/] **211**–13
MARINE LIFE, AMPHIBIANS, AND REPTILES
  [mə rēn/ līf/ ăm fĭb/ē ənz ən rĕp/tĭlz] **212**–**213**
Marines [mə rēnz/] **138**–17
mark [märk] **190**–12, **190**–13, **190**–15
  postmark [pōst/märk/] **134**–24

markers [mär/kərz] **7**–17, **7**–24, **154**–17
market [mär/kət] **222**–6
  supermarket [sōō/pər mar/kət] **127**–18
MARKET [mär/kət] **66**–**67**
marriage license [măr/ĭj lī/səns] **41**–8
married couple [măr/ēd kŭ/pəl] **35**–20
Mars [märz] **205**–4
martial arts [mär/shəl ärts/] **228**–11
Martin Luther King Jr. Day
  [mär/tən lōō/thər-kĭng/ jōōn/yər dā/] **22**–10
mascara [mă skăr/ə] **109**–39
mashed potatoes [măsht/ pə tā/tōz] **81**–23
mask [măsk] **239**–9
  catcher's mask [kăch/ərz măsk/] **231**–15
  diving mask [dī/vĭng măsk/] **225**–6
  face mask [fās/ măsk/] **93**–32
  oxygen mask [äk/sĭ jən măsk/] **161**–24
  particle mask [pär/tĭ kəl măsk/] **179**–14
  ski mask [skē/ măsk/] **90**–15
  surgical mask [sür/jĭ kəl măsk/] **93**–36
  ventilation mask [vĕnt/əl ā/shən măsk/] **92**–7
masking tape [măs/kĭng tāp/] **181**–53
mat [măt] **57**–3, **57**–28
  placemat [plās/măt] **55**–11
match [măch] **9**–T
matches [măch/əz] **146**–16, **226**–21
matching [mă/chĭng] **28**–3
Material [mə tïr/ē əl] **98**
materials [mə tïr/ē əlz] **98** ✦, **179**–7
Materials [mə tïr/ē əlz] **179**
maternity [mə tür/nə tē]
  maternity dress [mə tür/nə tē drĕs/] **88**–5
  maternity store [mə tür/nə tē stör/] **131**–19
math [măth] **189**–10
MATHEMATICS [măth/ə măt/ĭks] **192**–**193**
Math Operations [măth/ äp/ə rā/shənz] **192**
Math Problem [măth/ präb/ləmz] **192**
mattress [mă/trəs] **58**–20
May [mā] **21**–29
mayonnaise [mā/ə nāz/, mā/ə nāz/] **79**–23
mayor [mā/ər] **139**–26
meadow [mĕd/ō] **204**–20
measles [mē/zəlz] **111**–5
measure [mĕzh/ər] **100**–17, **181**–45
measure [mĕzh/ər] **17**–C
Measurement [mĕzh/ər mənt] **17**
MEASUREMENTS [mĕzh/ər mənts] **17**, **75**
Measures [mĕzh/ərz] **75**
Measuring Area and Volume
  [mē/zhər ĭng ër/ē ə ən văl/yəm, –yōōm] **193**
meat [mēt] **66**–2
  meatballs [mēt/bölz] **81**–27
  meatloaf [mēt/lōf/] **81**–31
Meat [mēt] **70**, **76**
MEAT AND POULTRY [mēt/ n pōl/trē] **70**
mechanic [mə kăn/ĭk] **166**–8
Mechanic [mə kăn/ĭk] **158**
media mail [mē/dē ə māl/] **134**–3
medical [mĕd/ĭ kəl] **121**–32
  medical chart [mĕd/ĭ kəl chärt/] **121**–24
  medical emergency bracelet
    [mĕd/ĭ kəl ĭ mür/jən sē brās/lət] **117**–3

medical records technician
  [mĕd/ĭ kəl rĕkərdz tĕk nĭsh/ən] **168**–39
medical waste disposal
  [mĕd/ĭ kəl wāst/ dĭ spō/zəl] **121**–31
MEDICAL CARE [mĕd/ĭ kəl kër/] **118**
MEDICAL CONDITIONS [mĕd/ĭ kəl kən dĭsh/ənz] **111**
MEDICAL EMERGENCIES [mĕd/ĭ kəl ĭ mür/jən sēz] **116**
Medical Procedures [mĕd/ĭ kəl prə se/jərz] **118**
Medical Specialists [mĕd/ĭ kəl spĕ/shə lĭsts] **120**
Medical Technician [mĕd/ĭ kəl tĕk nĭsh/ən] **93**
Medical Warnings [mĕd/ĭ kəl wör/nĭngz] **112**
medication [mĕd/ə kā/shən] **112**–3, **112** ✦,
  113–18, **121**–20
Medication [mĕd/ə kā/shən] **113**
medicine cabinet [mĕd/ə sən kăb/ə nət] **57**–20
medium [mē/dē əm] **96**–3
meet [mēt] **222**–6
meet [mēt] **49**–G, **49**–R
meeting [mē/tĭng]
  meeting place [mē/tĭng plās/] **146**–1
  meeting room [mē/tĭng rōōm/] **184**–25
MEETING AND GREETING [mē/tĭng ən grē/tĭng] **2**–**3**
melons [mĕl/ənz] **68**–19
  watermelons [wö/tər mĕl/ənz] **68**–18
membrane [mĕm/brān] **194**–6
Memorial Day [mə mör/ē əl dā/] **22**–12
memory card [mĕm/ə rē kärd/] **235**–20
men / man [mĕn] / [măn] **30**–1, **30**–4
  doorman [dör/măn/] **184**–1
  men's store [mĕnz/ stör/] **130** ✦
Men's Underwear [mĕnz/ un/dər wër/] **91**
menu [mĕn/yōō] **82**–7, **197**–8
  menu bar [mĕn/yōō bär/] **197**–1
MENU [mĕn/yōō] **80**–**81**
Mercury [mür/kyə rē] **205**–1
merge [mürj] **154**–10
mess [mĕs] **64**–8
message [mĕs/ĭj] **14**–18, **14**–19
messenger [mĕs/ən jər] **168**–40
meter [mē/tər] **62**–14, **129**–25, **152**–23
mice / mouse [mīs] / [mows] **63**–28, **196**–15, **215**–18
microphone [mī/krə fōn/] **234**–18
microprocessor [mī/krō prä/sĕ sər] **196**–4
Microscope [mī/krə skōp/] **194**
microwave [mī/krə wāv/] **77**–T
microwave oven [mī/krə wāv/ ŭv/ən] **54**–13
middle [mĭd/l] **25**–2
  middle-aged [mĭd/l ājd/] **32**–2
  middle initial [mĭd/l ĭ nĭsh/əl] **4**–3
  middle school [mĭd/l skōōl/] **188**–3
mid-length [mĭd/lĕnth] **96**–17
midnight [mĭd/nīt/] **18**–21
Military [mĭ/lə tër ē] **138**
MILITARY SERVICE [mĭ/lə tër ē sür/vəs] **138**–**139**
milk [mĭlk] **66**–5, **81**–42
  milkshake [mĭlk shāk/] **79**–14
milk [mĭlk] **177**–C
mini [mĭn/ē] **96**–15
  mini-blinds [mĭn/ē blĭndz/] **58**–8
  minivan [mĭn/ē văn/] **156**–8
minister [mĭ/nə stər] **199**–7

minutes [mĭn′əts] **18**–2
mirror [mĭr′ər] **57**–16
    full-length mirror [fŏŏl′lĕnth mĭr′ər] **58**–6
    rearview mirror [rĭr′vyŏŏ′ mĭr′ər] **159**–35
    sideview mirror [sīd′vyŏŏ′ mĭr′ər] **158**–3
misbehave [mĭs′bĭ hāv′] **44**–B
miss the bus [mĭs dhə bŭs′] **152** ✦
missing [mĭs′ĭng] **97**–40
mittens [mĭt′nz] **90**–10
mix [mĭks] **77**–R
mixed berries [mĭkst′ bĕr′ēz] **81**–36
mixer [mĭk′sər] **54**–25
mixing bowl [mĭk′sĭng bōl′] **54**–28, **78**–31
mobile [mō′bēl] **59**–5
    mobile home [mō′bəl hōm′] **52**–7
model [mäd′l] **156** ✦, **168**–41
    model kit [mäd′l kĭt′] **232**–9
    model trains [mäd′l trānz′] **233**–27
modern [mä′dərn] **199**–2
moist towelettes [moyst′ tow′əl ĕts] **146**–12
moisturizer [moys′chə rī′zər] **108**–9
mole [mōl] **32**–16
molecule [mäl′ĭ kyōōl′] **195**–27
monarch [mä′nərk, mä′närk′] **199**–4
Monday [mŭn′dā, –dē] **20**–9
MONEY [mŭn′ē] **26**
monitor [män′ə tər] **196**–11
    arrival and departure monitors
        [ə rī′vəl ən dĭ pär′chər män′ə tərz] **161**–7
    baby monitor [bā′bē män′ə tər] **59**–7
    vital signs monitor [vī′təl sīnz män′ə tər] **121**–26
monkey [mŭng′kē] **217**–26
month [mŭnth] **20**–3
Months of the Year [mŭnths′ əv dhə yĭr′] **21**
moon [mŏŏn]
    crescent moon [krĕs′ənt mŏŏn′] **205**–10
    full moon [fŏŏl′ mŏŏn′] **205**–12
    new moon [nŏŏ′ mŏŏn′] **205**–9
    quarter moon [kwŏr′tər mŏŏn′] **205**–11
Moon [mŏŏn] **205**
moose [mŏŏs] **216**–1
mop [mäp] **61**–6
mop [mäp] **60**–D
morning [mŏr′nĭng] **18**–15
mosque [mäsk] **126**–5
mosquito [mə skē′tō] **214**–22
motel [mō tĕl′] **126**–12
moth [mŏth] **214**–21
mother [mŭdh′ər] **34**–3, **35**–22
    grandmother [grăn′mŭdh′ər, grănd′–] **34**–1
    motherboard [mŭdh′ər bŏrd′] **196**–5
    mother-in-law [mŭdh′ər ĭn lö′] **34**–10
    stepmother [stĕp′mŭdh′ər] **35**–26
MOTION [mō′shən] **153**
motor [mō′tər] **124**–4
motorcycle [mō′tər sī′kəl] **150**–4
mountain [mown′tn]
    mountain biking [mown′tn bī′kĭng] **226**–8
    mountain lion [mown′tn lī′ən] **216**–2
    mountain peak [mown′tn pēk′] **204**–14
    mountain range [mown′tn rānj′] **204**–15
    Mountain time [mown′tn tīm′] **19**–30

mouse / mice [mows] / [mīs] **63**–28, **196**–15, **215**–18
mouth [mowth] **104**–7
    mouthwash [mowth′wäsh′, –wösh′] **109**–25
Mouth [mowth] **106**
move in [mŏŏv′ ĭn′] **48**–F
move out [mŏŏv′ owt′] **48** ✦
movement [mŏŏv′mənt] **199**–16
mover [mŏŏ′vər] **168**–42
movies [mŏŏ′vēz] **222**–2
    movie theater [mŏŏ′vē thē′ə tər] **126**–6
Movies [mŏŏ′vēz] **237**
Moving In [mŏŏ′vĭng ĭn] **49**
moving van [mŏŏ′vĭng văn′] **156**–18
mow [mō] **176**–A
mower [mō′ər] **176**–6
mozzarella cheese [möts′ə rĕ lə chēz′] **71**–29
MP3 player [ĕm′pē′thrē′ plā′ər] **234**–2
mudslide [mŭd′slīd′] **144**–6
muffin [mŭf′ən] **79**–16, **80**–5
muffler [mŭf′lər] **158**–16
muffs [mŭfs] **179**–16
mug [mŭg] **55**–7
mugging [mŭg′ĭng] **142**–11
multiply [mŭl′tə plī] **192**–C
multi-use knife [mŭl′tē yŏŏs′ nīf′, mŭl′tī–] **226**–20
mumps [mŭmps] **111**–7
murder [mŭr′dər] **142**–12
muscle [mŭs′əl] **107**–32
mushrooms [mŭsh′rŏŏmz′] **69**–27
music [myŏŏ′zĭk] **64**–3, **189**–15
    live music [līv′ myŏŏ′zĭk] **84**–1
    music store [myŏŏ′zĭk stör′] **130**–1
    world music [würld′ myŏŏ′zĭk] **237**–32
Music [myŏŏ′zĭk] **237**
MUSIC [myŏŏ′zĭk] **238**
musician [myŏŏ zĭsh′ən] **168**–43
mussels [mŭs′əlz] **71**–13, **212**–17
mustache [mŭs′tăsh] **33**–5
mustard [mŭs′tərd] **79**–22
mystery [mĭs′tə rē] **237**–20
nachos [nä′chōz] **79**–7
nail [nāl] **180**–34
    fingernail [fĭng′gər nāl′] **106**–18
    nail clipper [nāl klĭp′ər] **109**–31
    nail polish [nāl päl′ĭsh] **109**–33
    nail salon [nāl sə län′] **130**–3
    toenail [tō′nāl′] **106** ✦
name [nām] **4**–1, **4**–2, **4**–4
    name tag [nām′ tăg′] **92**–15
napkin [năp′kĭn] **55**–10, **83**–26
narrow [năr′ō] **97**–35
nasal [nā′zəl]
    nasal congestion [nā′zəl kən jĕs′chən] **110**–7
    nasal spray [nā′zəl sprā′] **113**–32
National Guard [nă′shə nəl gärd′] **138**–19
NATIONAL PARKS [nă′shə nəl pärks′] **220**–221
Native Americans [nā′tĭv ə mĕr′ə kənz] **198**–3
natural [năch′rəl, năch′ər əl′]
    natural gas [năch′rəl găs′] **218**–3
    natural materials [năch′rəl mə tĭr′ē əlz] **98** ✦
NATURE CENTER [nā′chər sĕn′tər] **208**–209
nature program [nā′chər prō′grăm] **236**–7

Navigating a Webpage [nă′və gā′tĭng ə wĕb′pāj] **197**
Navy [nā′vē] **138**–15
navy blue [nā′vē blŏŏ′] **28**–5
near [nĭr] **25** ✦
neck [nĕk] **96**–8, **96**–10, **104**–3
    crewneck [krŏŏ′nĕk] **96**–7
    necklaces [nĕk′lə sĕz] **95**–10
    turtleneck [tür′tl nĕk] **96**–9
needle [nēd′l] **98**–17, **100**–10, **210**–10, **233**–23
    needle plate [nēd′l plāt′] **98**–18
negative integers [nĕ′gə tĭv ĭn′tə jərz] **192**–1
negotiate [nĭ gō′shē āt′] **157**–D
neighborhood [nā′bər hŏŏd′] **128** ✦
nephew [nĕf′yŏŏ] **34**–19
Neptune [nĕp′tŏŏn] **205**–8
nervous [nür′vəs] **42**–10
nest [nĕst] **209**–12
net [nĕt] **226**–17
    hairnet [hĕr′nĕt′] **93**–25
network [nĕt′würk′] **173**–A
Neutral Colors [nŏŏ′trəl kŭl′ərz] **24**
neutron [nŏŏ′trän] **195**–32
new [nŏŏ]
    new job [nŏŏ′ jäb′] **172**–3
    new moon [nŏŏ′ mŏŏn′] **205**–9
    New Year's Day [nŏŏ′ yĭrz′ dā′] **22**–9
Newfoundland time [nŏŏ′fən lənd tīm′, –fənd–] **19**–34
news [nŏŏz]
    newspaper [nŏŏz′pā′pər] **133**–6
    news program [nŏŏz prō′grăm] **236**–1
    newsstand [nŏŏz′stănd′] **128**–12
newt [nŏŏt] **212**–26
New Words [nŏŏ′ würdz′] **8**
next [nĕkst]
    next day mail [nĕkst′ dā′ māl′] **135** ✦
    next to [nĕkst′ tŏŏ, –tə] **24**–9
    next week [nĕkst′ wēk′] **20**–20
nickel [nĭk′əl] **26**–2
niece [nēs] **34**–18
night [nīt] **18**–20
    nightclub [nīt′klŭb′] **223**–12
    nightgown [nīt′gown′] **91**–25
    night light [nīt′līt′] **37**–27
    nightshirt [nīt′shürt′] **91**–28
    nightstand [nīt′stănd′] **58**–23
    night table [nīt′ tā′bəl] **58**–23
nine [nīn] **16**
nineteen [nīn′tēn′] **16**
nineteenth [nīn′tēnth′] **16**
ninetieth [nīn′tē əth] **16**
ninety [nīn′tē] **16**
    90º angle [nīn′tē də grē′ ăng′gəl] **193**–26
ninth [nīnth] **16**
nipple [nĭp′əl] **37**–2
no [nō]
    no left turn [nō′ lĕft′ türn] **154**–8
    no outlet [nō′ owt′lĕt, –lət] **154**–6
    no parking [nō′ pär′kĭng] **154**–11
noise [noyz] **64**–5
noisy [noy′zē] **23**–11
noon [nŏŏn] **18**–16
    afternoon [ăf′tər nŏŏn′] **18**–17

Index

north [nörth] **155**–1

NORTH AMERICA AND CENTRAL AMERICA
[nörth/ ə mĕr/ə kə ən sĕn/trəl ə mĕr/ə kə] **200–201**

nose [nōz] **104**–6, **110**–17
  revolving nosepiece [rə väl/vĭng nōz/pēs] **194**–17

not [nät]
  can't breathe [kănt/ brēdh/] **116**–N
  do not drink [dōō/ nät/ drĭnk] **112**–F
  do not enter [dōō/ nät/ ĕn/tər] **154**–2
  do not operate [dōō/ nät/ äp/ər ät/] **112**–E
  do not take [dōō nät/ tāk/] **112**–D
  don't be late [dōnt/ bē/ lāt/] **174**–E
  don't litter [dōnt/ lĭt/ər] **219**–L
  don't smoke [dōnt/ smōk/] **114**–G
  not working [nät/ wür/kĭng] **62**–1

note [nōt] **183**–39
  footnote [fŏŏt/nōt/] **190**–10
  notebook [nōt/bŏŏk/] **7**–27
  notebook paper [nōt/bŏŏk/ pāp/ər] **7**–28
  spiral notebook [spī/rəl nōt/bŏŏk/] **7**–29

novel [nä/vəl] **133**–16
November [nō vĕm/bər] **21**–35
nuclear energy [nōō/klē ər ĕn/ər jē] **218**–8
nucleus [nōō/klē əs] **194**–7, **195**–29
numb [nŭm] **119**–C
number [nŭm/bər]
  access number [ăk/sĕs/ nŭm/bər] **14**–16
  apartment number [ə pärt/mənt nŭm/bər] **4**–6
  cell phone number [sĕl/ fōn/ nŭm/bər] **4**–12
  checking account number
    [chĕk/ĭng ə kownt/ nŭm/bər] **132**–14
  driver's license number
    [drī/vərz lī/səns nŭm/bər] **136**–11
  even numbers [ēv/ən nŭm/bərz] **192**–4
  odd numbers [öd/ nŭm/bərz] **192**–3
  phone number [fōn/ nŭm/bər] **4**–11, **15**–30
  prescription number
    [prĭ skrĭp/shən nŭm/bər] **112**–5
  savings account number
    [sā/vĭngz ə kownt/ nŭm/bər] **132**–11
  SKU number [ĕs/kā/yōō/ nŭm/bər] **27**–5
  Social Security number
    [sō/shəl sĭ kyŏŏr/ə tē nŭm/bər] **4**–15

Numbers [nŭm/bərz] **16**
NUMBERS [nŭm/bərz] **16**
Numerals [nōō/mər əlz] **16**
numerator [nōō/mər ā/ tər] **192**–5
nurse [nürs] **118**–8, **168**–44
  licensed practical nurse (LPN) [lī/sənst
    prăk/tə kəl nürs/] / [ĕl/pē/ĕn/] **120**–11
  nurse midwives [nürs/ mĭd/wīvz] **120** ✦
  nurse practitioners [nürs/ prăk tĭ/shən ərz] **120** ✦
  registered nurse (RN) [rĕj/ə stərd nürs/] / [är/ĕn/]
    120–10
  surgical nurse [sür/jĭ kəl nürs/] **120**–9
nurse [nürs] **36**–B
Nurse [nürs] **93**
nursery [nür/sə rē]
  nursery rhymes [nür/sə rē rīmz/] **37**–22
  nursery school [nür/sə rē skōōl/] **188**–1
nursing [nür/sĭng] **120**–12
  nursing home [nür/sĭng hōm/] **52**–12

Nursing Staff [nür/sĭng stăf/] **120**
nutrition label [nōō trĭ/shən lā/bəl] **122**–8
nuts [nŭts] **73**–36, **180**–36
nylon [nī/län] **99**–12
oak [ōk] **210**–17, **210**–24
obey [ō bā/] **140**–C
objective [əb jĕk/tĭv] **194**–18
oboe [ō/bō] **238**–3
observatory [əb zür/və tör/ē] **205**–21
observe [əb zürv/] **195**–C
obstetrician [äb/stə trĭsh/ən] **120**–2
obtuse angle [äb/tōōs ăng/gəl] **193**–27
occupational therapist
  [äk/yə pā/shən əl thĕr/ə pĭst] **168**–45
OCCUPATIONS [äk/yə pā/shənz] **166–169**
ocean [ō/shən] **204**–6, **225**–1
o'clock [ə kläk/] **18**–6
October [äk tō/bər] **21**–34
octopus [äk/tə pəs] **212**–9
odd numbers [öd/ nŭm/bərz] **192**–3
odometer [ō däm/ə tər] **159**–28
off [öf]
  clear off [klĭr/ öf/] **10**–I
  drop off [dräp/ öf/] **38**–G
  gas shut-off valve [găs/ shŭt/öf vălv/] **146**–4
  get off [gĕt/ öf/] **153**–J
  take off [tāk/ öf/] **109**–Q
  turn off [türn/ öf/] **11**–P, **160**–I, **174**–G, **219**–G
offer [ö/fər] **12**–D
office [ö/fəs] **164**–3
  main office [mān/ ö/fəs] **5**–12
  office building [ö/fəs bĭld/ĭng] **124**–2
  office manager [ö/fəs măn/ĭ jər] **182**–8
  office supply store [ö/fəs sə plī/ stör/] **127**–21
  post office [pōst/ ö/fəs] **125**–11
  post office box (PO box) [pōst/ ö/fəs bäks/] /
    [pē/ō bäks/] **135**–9
  run for office [rŭn/ fər ö/fəs] **139**–A
Office [ö/fəs] **51**
OFFICE [ö/fəs] **134–135, 182–183**
Office Equipment [ö/fəs ĭ kwĭp/mənt] **183**
officer [ö/fə sər] **161**–17, **168**–48
Office Skills [ö/fəs skĭlz/] **171**
OFFICE SKILLS [ö/fəs skĭlz/] **171**
Office Supplies [ö/fəs sə plīz/] **183**
Office Visit [ö/fəs vĭ/zət] **119**
official [ə fĭsh/əl] **139**–32, **229**–6
oil [oyl] **73**–31, **218**–6
  oil gauge [oyl/ gāj/] **159**–29
  oil paint [oyl/ pānt/] **233**–19
  oil spill [oyl/ spĭl/] **218**–17
ointment [oynt/mənt] **113**–24, **117**–10
OK [ō kā/] **154**–5
old [ōld] **31**–9, **31**–10
omelet [äm/lət, ä/mə lət] **76**–12
on [än, ön] **25**–11
  get on [gĕt/ än, –ön] **153**–I
  go on [gō/ än, –ön] **173**–K
  on-the-job training [än dhə jäb/ trā/nĭng, –ön]
    172–7
  on the left [än dhə lĕft/, –ön] **25**–1
  on the right [än dhə rīt/, –ön] **25**–3

on time [än tīm/, –ön] **19**–23, **16**–29
overdose on drugs [ō/vər dōs/ än drŭgz/] **116**–K
put on [pŏŏt/ än/, –ön/] **87**–B, **108**–D, **109**–P
try on [trī/ än/, –ön/] **95**–C
turn on [türn/ än/, –ön/] **11**–B
once a week [wŭns/ə wēk/] **20**–22
oncologist [än/kō lə jĭst/] **120**–5
one [wŭn] **16**
  five after one [fīv/ ăf/ tər wŭn/] **18**–7
  one billion [wŭn/ bĭl/yən] **16**
  one eighth [wŭn/ ätth/, –āth/] **17**–5
  one-fifteen [wŭn/fĭf/tēn/] **18**–9
  one-forty [wŭn/för/tē] **18**–12
  one-forty-five [wŭn/för/tē fīv/] **18**–13
  one fourth [wŭn/ förth/] **17**–4
  one half [wŭn/ hăf/] **17**–2
  one hundred [wŭn/ hŭn/drəd] **16**
  one hundred dollars
    [wŭn/ hŭn/drəd däl/ərz] **26**–12
  one hundred one [wŭn/ hŭn/drəd wŭn/] **16**
  100 percent [wŭn/ hŭn/drəd pər sĕnt/] **17**–8
  one hundredth [wŭn/ hŭn/drəth] **16**
  one hundred thousand
    [wŭn/ hŭn/drəd thow/zənd] **16**
  one million [wŭn/ mĭl/yən] **16**
  one o'clock [wŭn/ ə kläk/] **18**–6
  one-oh-five [wŭn/ō fīv/] **18**–7
  one-size-fits-all [wŭn/sīz fĭts/äl] **96**–6
  one-ten [wŭn/tĕn/] **18**–8
  one third [wŭn/ thürd/] **17**–3
  one-thirty [wŭn/thür/tē] **18**–11
  one thousand [wŭn/ thow/zənd] **16**
  one thousandth [wŭn/ thow/zənth] **16**
  one-twenty [wŭn/twĕn/tē] **18**–10
  one way [wŭn/ wā/] **154**–3
  one-way trip [wŭn/wā/ trĭp/] **152**–16
  one whole [wŭn/hōl/] **17**–1
  quarter after one [kwör/tər ăf/tər wŭn/] **18**–9
  ten after one [tĕn/ ăf/tər wŭn/] **18**–8
  twenty after one [twĕn/tē ăf/tər wŭn/] **18**–10
onions [ŭn/yənz] **69**–19, **69**–20
  onion rings [ŭn/yən rĭngz/] **79**–4
online [än/līn/, ön–]
  online catalog [än/līn/ kă/tə lög, ön–] **133**–11
  online course [än/līn/ körs/, ön–] **172**–8
only [ōn/lē] **154**–7
On the Airplane [än/ dhe ër/plān/] **161**
open [ō/pən] **6**–G, **143**–F
opener [ō/pən ər] **54**–8, **78**–1, **146**–8
Opening an Account [ō/pə nĭng ən ə kownt/] **132**
opera [äp/rə] **223**–11, **236**–5
operate [äp/ə rāt/] **112**–E, **170**–H
Operating Room [äp/ə rā/tĭng rōōm/] **121**
operating table [äp/ə rā/tĭng tā/bəl] **121**–40
Operations [äp/ə rā/shənz] **192**
operator [äp/ə rā/tər] **14**–21, **98**–14, **168**–37
ophthalmologist
  [äf/thəl mäl/ə jĭst, –thə mäl/–, äp/–] **120**–7
opinion [ə pĭn/yən] **44**–3
opossum [ə päs/əm, päs/əm] **216**–4
opponent [ə pō/nənt] **139**–30
optician [äp tĭsh/ən] **130**–9

optometrist [äp täm/ə trïst] **115**–6
orange [ör/ənj, är/–] **24**–4
oranges [ör/ən jəz, är/–] **68**–5
orangutan [ə răng/ə tăng/, –tăn/] **217**–39
orchard [ör/chərd] **177**–10
orchid [ör/kïd] **211**–19
order [ör/dər] **185**–1
    order puller [ör/dər pŏŏl/ər] **175**–10
order [ör/dər] **82**–D
orderly [ör/dər lē] **120**–16
Ordinal Numbers [ör/dn əl nŭm/bərz] **16**
organ [ör/gən] **238**–20
organic [ör gă/nïk] **84**–2
organisms [ör/gə nïzmz] **194**–1
organize [ör/gə nïz/] **171**–L, **191**–G
organizer [ör/gə nï/zər] **183**–49
ornament [ör/nə mənt] **239**–15
Orthodontics [ör/thə dän/tïks] **119**
orthodontist [ör/thə dän/tïst] **119**–5
orthopedists [ör/thə pē/dïsts] **120** ✦
Other Instruments [ŭdh/ər ïn/strə mənts] **238**
otter [ät/ər] **213**–35
ounce [owns] **75**–1, **75**–11
out [owt] **62**–2
    blow out [blō/ owt/] **240**–C
    check out [chĕk/ owt/] **133**–C
    cross out [krös/ owt/] **9**–R
    eat out [ēt/ owt/] **82** ✦
    fill out [fïl/ owt/] **173**–J
    get out of [gĕt/ owt/ əv] **153**–F
    let out [lĕt/ owt/] **100**–C
    move out [mōōv/ owt/] **48** ✦
    outfit [owt/fït] **88** ✦
    out of focus [owt/ əv fō/kəs] **235**–33
    out-of-state contact [owt/əv stāt/ kän/täkt] **146**–2
    run out of gas [rŭn/ owt/ əv găs/] **162**–E
    take out [tāk/ owt/] **9**–Y, **60**–Q, **82** ✦
    work out [würk/ owt/] **230**–N
OUTDOOR RECREATION [owt/dör rĕk/rē ā/shən] **226**
outlet [owt/lĕt, –lət] **58**–28, **154**–6, **159**–42
    outlet cover [owt/lĕt kŭv/ər] **181**–46
OUTSIDE THE BODY [owt/sïd/ dhe bä/dē] **106**–**107**
oven [ŭv/ən] **54**–15, **54**–20
    oven cleaner [ŭv/ən klē/nər] **61**–3
over [ō/vər] **76**–11, **153**–B
    overalls [ō/vər ölz/] **88**–6
    overcoat [ō/vər kōt/] **90**–2
    overexposed [ō/vər ïk spōzd/] **235**–34
    overflowing [ō/vər flō/ïng] **63**–17
    overhead compartment
        [ō/vər hĕd/ kəm pärt/mənt] **161**–13
    overhead projector [ō/vər hĕd/ prə jĕk/tər] **7**–16
    overjoyed [ō/vər joyd/] **43** ✦
    overnight mail [ō/vər nït/ māl/] **135** ✦
    over-the-counter medication
        [ō/vər dhə -kown/tər mĕd/ə kā/shən] **113**–18
overdose [ō/vər dōs/, ō/vər dōs/] **116**–K
Over-the-Counter Medication
    [ō/vər dhə kown/tər mĕd/ə kā/shən] **113**
owl [owl] **214**–5
owner [ō/nər] **166**–11, **175**–1
oxfords [äks/fərdz] **95**–29

oxygen mask [äk/sï jən mäsk/] **161**–24
oysters [oy/stərz] **71**–14
Pacific time [pə sïf/ïk tïm/] **19**–29
pacifier [păs/ə fï/ər] **37**–24
pack [păk] **74**–9, **117**–13, **235**–26
    backpack [băk/păk/] **94**–18, **226**–15
pack [păk] **49**–M, **162**–A
package [păk/ïj] **74**–8, **74**–20, **134**–17
packaged food [păk/ïjd fŏōd/] **146**–10
PACKAGING [păk/ə jïng] **74**
packer [păk/ər] **175**–18
packing tape [păk/ïng tāp/] **183**–32
pad [păd]
    bumper pad [bŭm/pər păd/] **59**–4
    changing pad [chānj/ïng păd/] **59**–2
    foam pad [fōm/ păd/] **226**–13
    heating pad [hē/tïng păd/] **113**–13
    ink pad [ïnk/ păd/] **183**–46
    knee pads [nē/ pădz/] **179**–19
    legal pad [lē/gəl păd/] **183**–38
    shoulder pads [shōl/dər pădz/] **231**–20
    steel-wool soap pads [stēl/wōōl/sōp/ pădz/] **61**–5
    sterile pad [stĕr/əl păd/] **117**–6
pail [pāl] **37**–7, **61**–7, **225**–8
pain [pān] **42**–11, **115**–3
    pain reliever [pān rï lē/vər] **113**–26
paint [pānt] **181**–25, **232**–10, **233**–19
    paintbrush [pānt/brŭsh/] **181**–22, **233**–20
    paint pan [pānt/ păn/] **181**–51
    paint roller [pānt/ rō/lər] **181**–23
paint [pānt] **49**–P, **178**–A, **233**–E
painter [pān/tər] **168**–46
Painter [pān/tər] **92**
painting [pān/tïng] **56**–9
pair of scissors [pĕr/ əv sïz/ərz] **100**–16
paisley [pāz/lē] **96**–26
pajamas [pə jä/məz, –jä/–] **91**–24
pallet [pă/lət] **175**–13
palm [päm] **106**–15, **210**–14
pan [păn] **54**–24
    bed pan [bĕd/ păn/] **121**–28
    cake pan [kāk/ păn/] **78**–26
    dustpan [dŭst/ păn/] **61**–17
    frying pan [frï/ïng păn/] **78**–5
    paint pan [pānt/ păn/] **181**–51
    pancakes [păn/kāks/] **80**–7
    pie pan [pï/ păn/] **78**–28
    roasting pan [rō/stïng păn/] **78**–13
    saucepan [sös/păn/] **78**–25
pancreas [păng/krē əs] **107**–45
panda [păn/də] **217**–41
pane [pān] **178**–16
panel [păn/əl] **234**–7
Panel [păn/əl] **159**
panther [păn/thər] **217**–40
panties [păn/tēz] **91**–13
pants [pănts] **87**–12
    security pants [sï kyŏŏr/ə tē pănts/] **93**–22
    training pants [trā/nïng pănts/] **37**–11
    work pants [würk/ pănts/] **92**–5
panty hose [păn/tē hōz/] **91**–18
papayas [pə pï/əz] **68**–20

paper [pā/pər]
    construction paper [kən strŭk/shən pā/pər] **232**–12
    copies of important papers
        [kä/pēz əv ïm pört/ənt pā/pərz] **146**–20
    newspaper [nōōz/pā/pər] **133**–6
    notebook paper [nōt/bŏōk/ pā/pər] **7**–28
    paper clip [pā/pər klïp/] **183**–31
    paper cutter [pā/pər kŭt/ər] **183**–22
    paper dolls [pā/pər dälz/] **233**–28
    paper shredder [pā/pər shrĕd/ər] **183**–24
    paper towels [pā/pər tow/əlz] **54**–3
    sandpaper [sănd/ pā/pər] **181**–56
    toilet paper [toy/lət pā/pər] **57**–17, **146**–13
    wallpaper [wäl/ pā/pər] **59**–8
parade [pə rād/] **239**–1
paragraph [păr/ə grăf/] **190**–3
parakeet [păr/ə kēt/] **215**–15
parallel lines [păr/ə lĕl/ līnz/] **193**–25
parallelogram [păr/ə lĕl/ə grăm/] **193**–33
paramedic [păr/ə mĕ/dïk] **116**–2
parasites [păr/ə sïts/] **111**–13
parcel post [pär/səl pōst/] **134**–6
parentheses [pə rĕn/thə sēz/] **190**–19
PARENTING [păr/ən tïng, pĕr/–] **36**–**37**
Parents [păr/ənts, pĕr/–] **34**
parent-teacher conference
    [păr/ənt tē/chər kän/frəns, pĕr/–] **22**–5
paring knife [pĕr/ïng nïf/] **78**–16
park [pärk] **223**–10
    park ranger [pärk/ rāng/jər] **220**–2
park [pärk] **129**–E
parka [pär/kə] **90**–9
PARK AND PLAYGROUND [pärk/ ən plā/grownd/] **224**
parking [pär/kïng] **128**–6, **154**–11, **154**–12
    parking attendant [pär/kïng ə tĕn/dənt] **184**–3
    parking garage [pär/kïng gə räzh/, –räj/] **124**–1
    parking meter [pär/kïng mē/tər] **129**–25
    parking space [pär/kïng spās/] **50**–18, **128**–5
PARKS [pärks] **220**–**221**
parochial school [pə rō/kē əl skōōl/] **5** ✦
parsley [pär/slē] **69**–28
part [pärt] **33**–4
participate [pär tï/sə pāt/] **10**–B
particle [pär/tï kəl]
    particle board [pär/tï kəl börd/] **181**–20
    particle mask [pär/tï kəl măsk/] **179**–14
Partner [pärt/nər] **8**
parts [pärts] **175**–5
Parts of a Bird [pärts/ əv ə bürd/] **214**
PARTS OF A CAR [pärts/ əv ə kär/] **158**–**159**
Parts of a Fish [pärts/ əv ə fïsh/] **212**
Parts of a Flower [pärts/ əv ə flow/ər] **211**
Parts of an Essay [pärts/ əv ən ĕs/ā] **190**
Parts of a Phone [pärts/ əv ə fōn/] **14**
Parts of a Sewing Machine
    [pärts/ əv ə sō/ïng mə shēn/] **98**
Parts of a Tree [pärts/ əv ə trē/] **210**
party [pär/tē] **64**–2
pass [păs] **161**–20
    passbook [păs/bŏōk/] **132**–10
    passport [păs/pört/] **41**–10
pass [păs] **10**–E, **137**–H, **230**–G

Index

passenger [păs/ən jər] **150**–2, **161**–15
past [păst] **155**–E
pasta [päs/tə] **67**–12
    pasta salad [päs/tə săl/əd] **80**–20
paste [pāst]
    toothpaste [tōōth/pāst/] **109**–23
pastrami [pə strä/mē] **71**–23
path [păth] **208**–3, **224**–3
Path [păth] **172**
patient [pā/shənt] **118**–6, **121**–18
patio [păt/ē ō] **53**–16
    patio furniture [păt/ē ō für/nǐ chər] **53**–19
patron [pā/trən] **82**–6, **133**–3
pattern [păt/ərn] **99**–22
PATTERNS [păt/ərnz] **96**
pause [pöz] **235**–E
paw [pö] **216**–20
pay [pā]
    paycheck [pā/chĕk/] **165**–14
    payroll clerk [pā/rōl klürk/] **165**–10
    pay stub [pā/ stŭb/] **165**–11
pay [pā]
    pay a late fine [pā/ ə lāt/ fīn/] **133**–E
    pay attention [pā/ ə tĕn/shən] **147**–D
    pay back [pā/ băk/] **26**–D
    pay cash [pā/ kăsh/] **27**–A
    pay for [pā/ för/, –fər] **27**–G
    pay phone [pā/ fōn/] **15**–25, **129**–23
    pay taxes [pā/ tăks/əz] **140**–B
    pay the application fee
        [pā/ dhe ăp/lə kā/shən fē/] **137**–D
    pay the check [pā/ dhe chĕk/] **82**–I
    pay the rent [pā/ dhe rĕnt/] **48**–E
Pay [pā] **27**
PBX [pē/ bē/ ĕks/] **182**–13
peaceful assembly [pēs/fəl ə sĕm/blē] **140**–1
peaches [pē/chəz] **68**–10
peacock [pē/käk/] **214**–14
peak [pēk] **204**–14
pearls [pürlz] **95**–39
pears [përz] **68**–4
peas [pēz] **69**–21
pedal [pĕd/əl] **159**–45, **159**–46
pedestrian [pə dĕs/trē ən] **128**–14
    pedestrian crossing [pə dĕs/trē ən krö/sǐng] **154**–13
pediatrician [pē/dē ə trǐsh/ən] **120**–4
peel [pēl] **77**–K
peeler [pē/lər] **78**–15
peephole [pēp/hōl/] **51**–32
pelvis [pĕl/vəs] **107**–50
pen [pĕn] **7**–22
pencil [pĕn/səl] **7**–20, **109**–34
    pencil eraser [pĕn/səl ǐ rā/sər] **7**–21
    pencil sharpener [pĕn/səl shär/pə nər] **7**–23, **183**–26
penguin [pĕng/wǐn] **214**–11
peninsula [pə nǐn/sə lə] **204**–7
penny [pĕn/ē] **26**–1
PEOPLE [pē/pəl] **32**
pepper [pĕp/ər] **55**–13, **69**–7, **69**–29
percent [pər sĕnt/]
    50 percent [fǐf/tē pər sĕnt/] **17**–10
    100 percent [wŭn/ hŭn/drəd pər sĕnt/] **17**–8

75 percent [sĕv/ən tē fīv/ pər sĕnt/] **17**–9
10 percent [tĕn/ pər sĕnt/] **17**–12
25 percent [twĕn/tē fīv/ pər sĕnt/] **17**–11
Percents [pər sĕnts/] **17**
Percussion [pər kŭsh/ən] **238**
perfume [pür/fyōōm/, pər fyōōm/] **108**–6
perimeter [pə rǐ/mə tər] **193**–43
period [pïr/ē əd] **190**–11
Period [pïr/ē əd] **198**
periodicals [pïr/ē äd/ǐ kəlz] **133**–4
periodic table [pïr/ē äd/ǐk tā/bəl] **195**–26
perm [pürm] **33**–B
peroxide [pə räk/ sīd] **117**–9
perpendicular lines [pür/pən dǐk/yə lər līnz/] **193**–24
person [pür/sən]
    appliance repair person
        [ə plī/əns rǐ pĕr/ pür/sən] **166**–4
    assemblyperson [ə sĕm/blē pür/sən] **139**–24
    businessperson [bǐz/nəs pür/sən] **166**–12
    bus person [bŭs/ pür/sən] **185**–13
    congressperson [kän/grəs pür/sən] **138**–4
    councilperson [kown/səl pür/sən] **139**–28
    counterperson [kown/tər pür/sən] **79**–17
    delivery person [də lǐv/ə rē pür/sən] **167**–21
    electronics repair person
        [ǐ lĕk trän/ǐks rǐ pĕr/ pür/sən] **167**–24
    repair person [rǐ pĕr/ pür/sən] **62**–10
personal CD player [pür/sə nəl sē/dē/ plā/ər] **234**–5
PERSONAL HYGIENE [pür/sə nəl hī/jēn] **108**–109
PERSONAL INFORMATION
    [pür/sə nəl ǐn/fər mā/shən] **4**
pesticide poisoning [pĕs/tə sīd poy/zə nǐng] **218**–16
pests [pĕsts] **62** ✦
pet [pĕt]
    pet food [pĕt fōōd/] **72**–5
    pet store [pĕt stör/] **130**–6
petals [pĕt/lz] **211**–8
petition [pə tǐ/shən] **148**–5
petroleum [pə trō/lē əm] **218**–6
Pets [pĕts] **215**
pharmacist [fär/mə sǐst] **112**–1
pharmacy [fär/mə sē] **128**–4
PHARMACY [fär/mə sē] **112**–113
Phase of the Moon [fāz/ əf dhə mōōn/] **205**
Phillips screwdriver [fǐl/ǐps skrōō/drī/vər] **180**–31
phlebotomist [flǐ bä/tə mǐst] **121**–29
phone [fōn]
    automated phone system
        [ö/tə māt ǐd fōn/ sǐs/təm] **14**–23
    cell phone holder [sĕl/ fōn/ hōl/dər] **94**–15
    cell phone kiosk [sĕl/ fōn/ kē/ösk] **131**–22
    cell phone number [sĕl/ fōn/ nŭm/bər] **4**–12
    cellular phone [sĕl/yə lər fōn/] **14**–8
    cordless phone [körd/ləs fōn/] **15**–24
    headphones [hĕd/ fōnz/] **6**–8, **234**–4
    Internet phone call [ǐn/tər nĕt/ fōn/ käl/] **14**–20
    microphone [mī/krə fōn/] **234**–18
    pay phone [pā/ fōn/] **15**–25, **129**–23
    phone bill [fōn/ bǐl/] **15**–28
    phone jack [fōn/ jăk/] **14**–3
    phone line [fōn/ līn/] **14**–4
    phone number [fōn/ nŭm/bər] **4**–11, **15**–30
    smart phone [smärt/ fōn/] **15**–27

Phone [fōn] **14**
Phone Bill [fōn/ bǐl/] **15**
Phone Call [fōn/ köl/] **15**
photo [fō/tō] **58**–3, **136**–4
    digital photo album [dǐ/jə təl fō/tō ăl/bəm] **235**–32
    funny photo [fŭn/ē fō/tō] **206**–2
    photo album [fō/tō ăl/bəm] **235**–31
    photocopier [fō/tə käp/ ər] **183**–23
    serious photo [sïr/ē əs fō/tō] **206**–3
photographer [fə täg/rə fər] **206**–1
PHOTOGRAPHY [fə täg/rə fē] **234**–235
photosynthesis [fō/tō sǐn/thə səs] **194**–10
physical [fǐz/ǐ kəl]
    physical education [fǐz/ǐ kəl ĕ jə kā/shən] **189**–17
    physical therapist [fǐz/ǐ kəl thĕr/ə pǐst] **115**–12
    physical therapy [fǐz/ǐ kəl thĕr/ə pē] **115**–11
physically challenged [fǐz/ǐ klē chăl/ənjd] **32**–10
physician assistant [fǐz/ǐ shən ə sǐs/tənt] **168**–47
physicist [fǐz/ǐ sǐst] **195**–33
Physics [fǐz/ǐks] **195**
pi (π) [pī] **193**–46
piano [pē ăn/ō] **238**–14
pick [pǐk] **108**–15
pickax [pǐk/ăks/] **178**–21
picker [pǐ/kər] **178**–5
pickle [pǐk/l] **80**–11
pick up [pǐk/ ŭp/] **6**–I, **11**–E, **38**–M, **112** ✦
pickup truck [pǐk/ŭp trŭk/] **156**–12
picnic [pǐk/nǐk] **224**–D
picnic table [pǐk/nǐk tā/bəl] **224**–8
picture [pǐk/chər]
    picture book [pǐk/chər bōōk/] **133**–12
    picture dictionary [pǐk/chər dǐk/shə nër ē] **7**–31
    picture frame [pǐk/chər frām/] **58**–4
pie [pī] **81**–35
    pie pan [pī/ păn/] **78**–28
pier [pïr] **225**–18
pierced [pïrst]
    pierced ear [pïrst/ ïr/] **32**–17
    pierced earrings [pïrst/ ïr/ǐngz] **95**–36
pig [pǐg] **215**–2, **215**–14
pigeon [pǐj/ən] **214**–15
pile [pīl] **53**–25
pill [pǐl] **113**–21
pillow [pǐl/ō] **56**–2, **58**–11
    pillowcase [pǐl/ō kās/] **58**–14
pilot [pī/lət] **161**–11
pin [pǐn] **95**–38
    bobby pins [bäb/ē pǐnz/] **108**–21
    clothespin [klōz/ pǐn/] **101**–10
    pin cushion [pǐn/ kōōsh/ən] **100**–13
    pushpin [pōōsh/pǐn/] **183**–35
    rolling pin [rō/lǐng pǐn/] **78**–30
    safety pin [sāf/tē pǐn/] **37**–9, **100**–14
    straight pin [strāt pǐn/] **100**–12
pine [pīn] **210**–9
    pinecone [pīn/kōn/] **210**–11
pineapples [pī/năp/əlz] **68**–23
pink [pǐnk] **24**–7
pint [pīnt] **75**–3
pipe [pīp] **158**–15, **181**–17
    pipe wrench [pīp rĕnch/] **181**–47

pitch [pĭch] **230**–A
pizza [pēt/sə] **79**–10
place [plās] **146**–1
    fireplace [fīr/plās/] **56**–13
    placemat [plās/ măt/] **55**–11
    place of birth [plās/ əv bürth/] **4**–14
    place setting [plās/ sĕt/ĭng] **83**–17
PLACES TO GO [plā/səz tə gō/] **222**–**223**
PLACES TO LIVE [plā/səz tə lĭv/] **52**
plaid [plăd] **96**–22
plain [plān] **97**–33
plains [plānz] **204**–19
plan [plăn] **186**–4
plan [plăn] **146**–A
plane [plān] **144**–3, **150**–8, **181**–57
Planets [plăn/əts] **205**
Planning a Career [plă/nĭng ə kə rēr/] **172**
plant [plănt] **176**–E, **177**–A, **219**–N
plants [plănts] **208**–5
    houseplant [hows/plănt/] **56**–4, **211**–27
Plants [plănts] **210**
PLANTS [plănts] **210**
plaque [plăk] **119**–12
plastic [plăs/tĭk]
    plastic storage bags [plăs/tĭk stör/ĭj băgz] **72**–25
    plastic storage container
        [plăs/tĭk stör/ĭj kən tā/nər] **78**–4
    plastic utensils [plăs/tĭk yōō tĕn/ səlz] **79**–19
    plastic wrap [plăs/tĭk răp/] **72**–24
plate [plāt] **55**–1
    bread-and-butter plate [brĕd/n bŭt/ər plāt/] **83**–19
    dinner plate [dĭn/ər plāt/] **83**–18
    license plate [lī/səns plāt/] **136**–12, **158**–12
    salad plate [săl/əd plāt/] **83**–20
    vanity plate [vă/nə tē plāt/] **136** ✦
platform [plăt/förm/] **152**–7
platter [plăt/ər] **55**–20
platypus [plăt/ĭ pəs, –pōōs/] **217**–46
play [plā] **223**–8
    play area [plā/ ër/ē ə] **130**–11
    playground [plā/grownd/] **50**–3
play [plā] **235**–B
    play an instrument [plā/ ən ĭn/strə mənt] **238**–A
    play cards [plā/ kärdz/] **233**–H
    play games [plā/ gāmz/] **232**–B
    play with [plā/ wĭth/] **36**–M
player [plā/ər] **229**–5
    CD player [sē/dē plā/ər] **159**–38
    DVD player [dē/vē/dē/ plā/ər] **56**–7, **234**–10
    MP3 player [ĕm/pē/thrē/ plā/ər] **234**–2
    personal CD player [pür/sə nəl sē/dē plā/ər] **234**–5
    portable cassette player
        [pör/tə bəl kə sĕt/ plā/ər] **234**–6
    portable DVD player
        [pör/tə bəl dē/vē/dē/ plā/ər] **234**–11
    video player [vĭd/ē ō plā/ər] **197**–11
PLAYGROUND [plā/grownd/] **224**
pliers [plī/ərz] **180**–7
plugs [plŭgz] **179**–15, **234**–16
plumber [plŭm/ər] **63**–20
plums [plŭmz] **68**–13
plunger [plŭn/jər] **181**–50

plywood [plī/wōōd/] **178**–18
p.m. [pē/ĕm/] **18**–5
pneumatic drill [nōō măt/ĭk drĭl/] **178**–9
poached eggs [pōcht/ ĕgz/] **76**–9
PO box (post office box) [pē/ō bäks/] /
    [pōst/ ö/fəs bäks/] **135**–9
pocket [päk/ət] **100**–7
podium [pō/dē əm] **206**–5
poinsettia [poyn sĕt/ē ə, –sĕt/ə] **211**–24
point [poynt] **17**–7,
    endpoint [ĕnd/poynt/] **193**–21
pointer [poyn/tər] **197**–12
poison [poy/zən] **116**–J
    poison ivy [poy/zən ī/vē] **210**–25
    poison oak [poy/zən ōk/] **210**–24
    poison sumac [poy/zən sōō/măk, –shōō/–] **210**–23
poisoning [poy/zən ĭng] **218**–16
poisonous fumes [poy/zən əs fyōōmz/] **179**–3
poles [pōlz] **226**–18, **231**–25
police [pə lēs/]
    police officer [pə lēs/ ö/fə sər] **141**–1, **168**–48
    police station [pə lēs/ stā/shən] **124**–6
polish [päl/ĭsh] **61**–8, **109**–33
polish [päl/ĭsh] **60**–E, **109**–O
political [pə lĭ/tĭ kəl]
    political campaign [pə lĭ/tĭ kəl kăm pān/] **139**–29
    political movement [pə lĭ/tĭ kəl mōōv/mənt] **199**–16
    political party [pə lĭ/tĭ kəl pär/tē] **139** ✦
polka-dotted [pō/kə dät/əd] **96**–21
pollution [pə lōō/shən] **218**–11, **218**–14
Pollution [pə lōō/shən] **218**
polo [pō/lō] **229**–15
    polo shirt [pō/lō shïrt/] **92**–14
poncho [pän/chō] **90**–19
pond [pänd] **204**–21
pool [pōōl] **51**–22, **184**–22, **228**–2
    pool service [pōōl/ sür/vəs] **184**–21
    pool table [pōōl/ tā/bəl] **50**–14
pop [päp] **73**–34, **237**–25
    pop-up ad [päp/ŭp/] **197**–9
porch light [pörch/ lĭt/] **53**–13
porcupine [pör/kyə pīn/] **216**–10
Pork [pörk] **70**
pork chops [pörk/ chäps/] **70**–10
porpoise [pör/pəs] **213**–30
port [pört] **196**–7
    airport [ër/pört/] **151**–10
portable [pör/tə bəl]
    portable cassette player
        [pör/tə bəl kə sĕt/ plā/ər] **234**–6
    portable DVD player
        [pör/tə bəl dē/vē/dē/ plā/ər] **234**–11
    portable TV [pör/tə bəl tē/ vē/] **234**–8
positive integers [pö/zə tĭv ĭn/tə jərz] **192**–2
post [pōst] **134**–6
    post card [pōst/kärd/] **134**–16
    postmark [pōst/märk/] **134**–24
    post office [pōst/ ö/fəs] **125**–11
    post office box (PO box) [pōst/ ö/fəs bäks/] /
        [pē/ō bäks/] **135**–9
postage [pō/stĭj] **135** ✦

postal [pō/stəl] **135**–10
    postal clerk [pō/stəl klürk/] **135**–7
    postal forms [pō/stəl förmz/] **134**–19
    postal scale [pō/stəl skāl/] **183**–27
    postal worker [pō/stəl wür/kər] **169**–49
POST OFFICE [pōst/ ö/fəs] **134**–**135**
pot [pät] **54**–16, **78**–6
    pot holders [pät hōl/dərz] **78**–29
    teapot [tē/pät/] **55**–16
potatoes [pə tā/tōz] **69**–17
    baked potato [bākt/ pə tā/tō] **81**–25
    mashed potatoes [măsht/ pə tā/tōz] **81**–23
    potato chips [pə tā/tō chĭps/] **73**–35
    potato salad [pə tā/tō săl/əd] **80**–19
    sweet potatoes [swēt/ pə tā/tōz] **69**–18
potty seat [pät/ē sēt/] **37**–12
pouch [powch] **217**–50
Poultry [pōl/trē] **70**, **76**
POULTRY [pōl/trē] **70**
pound [pownd] **75**–12
    pound key [pownd/ kē/] **14**–7
pour [pör] **82**–C
powder [pow/dər] **37**–14, **108**–4, **109**–41
power [pow/ər] **218**–2, **218**–5
    power cord [pow/ər körd/] **196**–2
    power outlet [pow/ər owt/lĕt] **159**–42
    power sander [pow/ər săn/dər] **180**–11
pox [pöks] **111**–6
practical [präk/tə kəl] **120**–11
prairie dog [prër/ē dög/] **215**–22
praise [prāz] **36**–J
pregnant [prĕg/nənt] **32**–15
preheat [prē/hēt/] **77**–A
preparation [prĕ/pə rā/shən] **185**–4
PREPARATION [prĕ/pə rā/shən] **76**–**77**
prepare [prĭ/pĕr/] **174**–A
PREPOSITIONS [prĕp/ə zĭsh/ənz] **25**
PREPOSITIONS OF MOTION
    [prĕp/ə zĭsh/ənz əv mō/shən] **153**
preschool [prē/skōōl/] **188**–1
prescribe medication [prĭ skrīb/ mĕd/ə kā/shən] **112** ✦
prescription [prĭ skrĭp/shən] **112**–2
    pick up a prescription
        [pĭk/ ŭp/ə prĭ skrĭp/shən] **112** ✦
    prescription label [prĭ skrĭp/shən lā/bəl] **112**–4
    prescription medication
        [prĭ skrĭp/shən mĕd/ə kā/shən] **112**–3
    prescription number [prĭ skrĭp/shən nŭm/bər]
        112–5
present [prĕz/ənt] **94** ✦, **240**–3
presentation [prĕ/zən tā/shən] **182**–6
president [prĕz/ə dənt] **138**–8, **199**–5
    first president [fürst/ prĕz/ə dənt] **198**–11
    Presidents' Day [prĕz/ə dənts dā/] **22**–11
    vice president [vīs/ prĕz/ə dənt] **138**–9
press [prĕs] **78**–11, **140**–4
press [prĕs] **15**–B, **15**–D
presser foot [prĕs/ər fōōt/] **98**–19
pressure [prĕsh/ər] **111**–14, **118**–9
pretend [prĭ tĕnd/] **233**–G
Prewriting [prē/rī/tĭng] **191**

Index

price [prīs] **27**–2, **27**–3, **27**–7
   price tag [prīs tăg/] **27**–1
prime minister [prīm/ mĭn/ə stər] **199**–7
principal [prĭn/sə pəl] **5**–4
print [prĭnt] **96**–23
   fingerprint [fĭng/gər prĭnt/] **136**–5
print [prĭnt] **4**–C, **171**–I
printer [prĭn/tər] **169**–50, **196**–17
   inkjet printer [ĭnk/jĕt prĭn/tər] **183**–18
   laser printer [lā/zər prĭn/tər] **183**–19
Priority Mail® [prī ör/ə tē māl/, –är/–] **134**–1
prism [prĭz/əm] **195**–35
prisoner [prĭz/nər] **141**–15
private school [prī/vət skool/] **5** ✦
Problem [präb/ləm] **192**
problems [präb/ləmz] **115**–1, **192**–11
Problems [präb/ləmz] **115**, **119**
PROBLEMS [präb/ləmz] **62**–63
Procedures [prə sē/jərz] **117**, **118**
PROCEDURES [prə sē/jərz] **146**–147
Process [prä/sĕs] **191**
processor [prä/sĕ sər] **54**–26
Processor [prä/sĕ sər] **92**
produce section [prō/dōōs sĕk/shən] **72**–2
product [präd/ŭkt] **192**–9
Products [präd/ŭkts] **72**, **73**
program [prō/grăm]
   children's program [chĭl/drənz prō/grăm] **236**–9
   nature program [nā/chər prō/grăm] **236**–7
   news program [nooz/ prō/grăm] **236**–1
   shopping program [shäp/ĭng prō/grăm] **236**–10
   sports program [spörtz/ prō/grăm] **236**–11
program [prō/grăm] **170**–I
Programs [prō/grămz] **236**
projector [prə jĕk/tər] **6**–6, **7**–16, **235**–29
promotion [prə mō/shən] **172**–4
proof of insurance [proof/ əv ĭn shoor/əns] **136**–8
proofread [proof/rēd/] **191**–I
prosecuting attorney
   [präs/ĭ kyoo/tĭng ə tür/nē] **141**–10
protect [prə tĕkt/] **143**–D
protector [prə tĕk/tər] **196**–1
proton [prō/tön] **195**–31
proud [prowd] **43**–21
prunes [proonz] **68**–26
pruning shears [proo/nĭng shïrz/] **176**–11
psychiatrist [sī kī/ə trĭst, sə–] **120**–8
PUBLIC SAFETY [pŭb/lĭk sāf/tē] **143**
public school [pŭb/lĭk skool/] **5** ✦
PUBLIC TRANSPORTATION
   [pŭb/lĭk trăns/pər tā/shən] **152**
pull [pool] **119**–F, **224**–A
puller [pool/ər] **175**–10
pullover sweater [pool/ō/vər swĕt/ər] **88**–3
pulse [pŭls] **122**–A
pumps [pŭmps] **95**–26
Punctuation [pŭngk/chōō ā/shən] **190**
puppy [pŭp/ē] **215**–12
purchase [pür/chəs] **94**–A
purifier [pyoo/rə fī/ ər] **113**–13
purple [pür/pəl] **24**–6
purses [pür/səz] **94**–2, **94**–14

push [poosh] **224**–B
pushpin [poosh/pĭn/] **183**–35
put [poot] **9**–X
put away
   [poot/ə wā/] **9**–Z, **60**–G
   put down [poot/ down/] **6**–J
   put in coolant [poot/ ĭn koo/lənt] **157**–I
   put on [poot/ än/, –ön/] **87**–B, **108**–D, **109**–P, **135**–C
   put on hold [poot/ än hōld/, –ön] **171**–N
   put the utilities in your name
      [poot/ dhe yoo tĭl/ə tēz ĭn yər nām/] **49**–O
puzzle [pŭz/əl] **59**–17
pyramid [pïr/ə mĭd] **193**–39
quad [kwäd] **5**–1
quart [kwört] **75**–4
quarter [kwör/tər] **26**–4
   quarter after one [kwör/tər ăf/tər wŭn/] **18**–9
   1/4 cup [kwör/tər kŭp/] **75**–8
   quarter moon [kwör/tər moon/] **205**–11
   quarter to two [kwör/tər tə too/] **18**–13
   3/4 sleeved [thrē/ kwör/tər slēvd/] **96**–13
question mark [kwĕs/chən märk/] **190**–12
Quick and Easy Cake [kwĭk/ ən ē/zē kāk/] **77**
quiet [kwī/ət] **23**–12
quill [kwĭl] **216**–23
quilt [kwĭlt] **58**–16
   quilt block [kwĭlt/ bläk/] **232**–15
quilt [kwĭlt] **232**–C
quotation [kwōt tā/shən] **190**–9
   quotation marks [kwō tā/shən märks/] **190**–15
quotient [kwō /shənt] **192**–10
rabbit [răb/ət] **215**–13
raccoon [ră koon/] **216**–13
race [rās] **230**–S
racing [rā/sĭng] **228**–19
rack [răk] **98**–16
   dish rack [dĭsh/ răk/] **54**–5
   roasting rack [rō/stĭng răk/] **78**–14
   towel rack [tow/əl răk/] **57**–13
racket [răk/ət] **231**–2
racquetball [răk/ət böl/] **228**–12
radiation [rā/dē ā/shən] **218**–15
radiator [rā/dē ā/tər] **158**–19
radio [rā/dē ō] **102**–6, **159**–37, **179**–22
radioactive materials
   [rā/dē ō ăk/tĭv mə tïr/ē əlz] **179**–7
radiologist [rā/dē äl/ə jĭst] **120**–6
radishes [răd/ĭ shəz] **69**–4
radius [rā/dē əs] **193**–35
rafting [răf/tĭng] **226**–2
rags [răgz] **61**–9
rail [rāl] **59**–10
railroad crossing [rāl/rōd krö/sĭng] **154**–14
rain [rān] **218**–13
   rain boots [rān/ boots/] **90**–20
   raincoat [rān/ köt/] **90**–18
   rain forest [rān/ för/əst, fär/–] **204**–1
raining [rā/nĭng] **13**–11
raise [rāz] **6**–A
raisins [rā/zənz] **68**–25
rake [rāk] **176**–8
rake [rāk] **176**–C

ranch [rănch] **52**–10
rancher [răn/chər] **177**–22
Ranch Hand [rănch hănd/] **92**
RANCHING [răn/chĭng] **177**
R&B [är/n bē/] **237**–28
range [rānj] **204**–15
ranger [rān/jər] **220**–2
rash [răsh] **110**–10
raspberries [răz/bĕr/ēz] **68**–15
rats [răts] **63**–27, **215**–17
rattle [răt/l] **37**–26
   rattlesnake [răt/l snāk/] **213**–38
raw [rö] **70**–24
ray [rā] **212**–11
razor [rā/zər] **109**–27
   razorblade [rā/zər blād/] **109**–28
reaction [rē/ăk shən] **116**–E
read [rēd]
   proofread [proof/rēd/] **191**–I
   read the card [rēd/ dhe kärd/] **135**–G
   read the definition [rēd/ dhe dĕ/fə nĭ/shən] **8**–B
   read the paper [rēd/ dhe pā/pər] **39**–V
   read to [rēd/ too] **36**–N
Reading a Phone Bill [rē/dĭng ə fōn/ bĭl/] **15**
reality show [rē ă lə tē shō/] **236**–6
rearview mirror [rïr/vyoo/ mïr/ər] **159**–35
receipt [rĭ sēt/] **27**–6
receive [rĭ sēv/] **135**–F
receiver [rĭ sē/vər] **14**–1
reception area [rĭ sĕp/shən ër/ē ə] **182**–15
receptionist [rĭ sĕp/shə nĭst] **118**–2, **164**–5,
   169–51, **182**–14
reclined seat [rĭ klīnd/ sēt/] **161**–27
record [rĭ körd/] **195**–D, **235**–A
records [rĕk/ərdz] **168**–39
RECREATION [rĕk/rē ā/shən] **226**
recreational vehicle (RV)
   [rĕk/rē ā/shən əl vē/ə kəl] / [är/vē/] **156**–10
Recreation Room [rĕk/rē ā/shən room/] **50**
recruiter [rə kroo/tər] **172**–14
rectangle [rĕk/tăng/gəl] **193**–29
recycle [rē sī/kəl] **60**–B, **219**–C
recycling bin [rē sī/klĭng bĭn/] **61**–2
red [rĕd] **24**–1
   red hair [rĕd/ hër/] **33**–15
   redwood [rĕd/wood/] **210**–18
redecorate [rē dĕk/ə rāt/] **48** ✦
reduce [rĭ doos/] **219**–A
referee [rĕf/ə rē/] **229**–6
reference librarian [rĕf/rəns lī brër/ē ən] **133**–9
refrigerator [rĭ frĭj/ə rā/tər] **54**–9
refund [rē/fŭnd] **97** ✦
reggae [rĕ gā/] **237**–31
register [rĕj/ə stər] **73**–15
register [rĕj/ə stər] **140**–D, **157**–F
registered nurse (RN)
   [rĕj/ə stərd nürs/] / [är/ĕn/] **120**–10
registration [rĕj/ə strā/shən]
   registration sticker
      [rĕj/ə strā/shən stĭk/ər] **136**–13
   registration tag [rĕj/ə strā/shən tăg/] **136**–13
regular price [rĕg/yə lər prīs/] **27**–2

regulations [rĕ gyə lā′shənz] **164**–6
relatives [rĕ lə tĭvz] **44**–6
relax [rĭ lăks′] **39**–U
relieved [rĭ lēvd′] **42**–15
reliever [rĭ lēv′ər] **113**–26
religious holiday [rĭ lĭj′əs hăl′ə dā′] **22**–7
remain [rē′mān′] **147**–E
remarried [rē măr′ēd] **35**–24
remote [rĭ mōt′] **234**–9
remove [rĭ mōōv′] **109**–Q, **132**–G
remover [rĭ mōō′vər] **109**–42
renew a license [rĭ nōō′ ə lī′səns, –nyōō′–] **136** ✦
rental agreement [rĕn′təl ə grē′mənt] **51**–28
Rental Office [rĕn′təl ö′fəs] **51**
Renting an Apartment [rĕn′tĭng ən ə pärt′mənt] **48**
repair [rĭ pĕr′] **166**–4, **167**–24
    repair person [rĭ pĕr′ pür′sən] **62**–10
repair [rĭ pĕr′] **170**–J
REPAIRS [rĭ pĕrz′] **62**–63
repellent [rĭ pĕl′ənt] **226**–23
replace [rĭ plās′] **157**–K
report [rĭ pört′] **143**–J, **143**–K
reporter [rĭ pör′tər] **169**–52
representative [rĕ′prĭ zĕn′tə tĭv] **138**–3, **167**–20
Reptiles [rĕp′tīlz] **213**
REPTILES [rĕp′tīlz] **212**–213
request [rĭ kwĕst′] **12** ✦
Requirements [rĭ kwīr′mənts] **140**
rescue [rĕs′kyōō] **145**–20
    rescue breathing [rĕs′kyōō brē′dhĭng] **117**–16
Resident Alien card [rĕz′ə dənt ā′lē ən kärd′] **40**–2
resource center [rē′sörs sĕn′tər] **172**–9
Resources [rē′sörs′səz, rĭ sör′səz] **219**
respirator [rĕs′pə rā′tər] **179**–13
Responding [rĭ spän′dĭng] **191**
Responsibilities [rĭ spän′sə bĭl′ə tēz] **140**
RESPONSIBILITIES [rĭ spän′sə bĭl′ə tēz] **140**
restaurant [rĕs′tə rənt, –ränt′] **125**–14, **128**–10
RESTAURANT [rĕs′tə rənt, –ränt′] **79, 82**–83
Restaurant Dining [rĕs′tə rənt dī′nĭng, –ränt′] **185**
Restaurant Kitchen [rĕs′tə rənt kĭ′chən, –ränt′] **185**
restrooms [rĕst′ rōōmz′] **5**–10
results [rĭ zŭltz′] **139**–31
resuscitation [rĭ sə sə tā′shən] **117**–17
retail clerk [rē′tāl′ klürk′] **169**–53
retire [rĭ tīr′] **41**–O
return [rĭ′türn′] **73**–16
    return address [rĭ türn′ ə drĕs′, –ă′drĕs] **134**–21
return [rĭ türn′] **27**–H, **133**–D
REUNION [rē yōōn′yən] **44**–45
reuse [rē yōōz′] **219**–B
revise [rĭ vīz′] **191**–J
Revising [rĭ vī′zĭng] **191**
Revolutionary War [rĕ′və lōō′shə nër ē wör′] **198**–8
revolving [rĭ väl′vĭng]
    revolving door [rĭ väl′vĭng dör′] **184**–2
    revolving nosepiece [rĭ väl′vĭng nōz′pēs′] **194**–17
rewind [rē wīnd′] **235**–C
rewrite [rē rīt′] **191**–J
rhinoceros [rī näs′ər əs] **217**–28
ribbon [rĭ′bən] **99**–30

ribs [rĭbz] **70**–5, **76**–2
rib cage [rĭb′ kāj′] **107**–48
rice [rīs] **67**–10, **81**–30, **177**–1
ride [rīd] **129**–D
rider [rī′dər] **152**–3
riding [rī′dĭng] **226**–9
right [rīt] **25**–3, **155**–B, **198**–10
    right angle [rīt′ ăng′gəl] **193**–26
    right turn only [rīt′ türn′ ōn′lē] **154**–7
Rights [rīts] **140**
RIGHTS AND RESPONSIBILITIES
    [rīts′ ən rĭ spän′sə bĭl′ə tēz] **140**
ring [rĭng] **37**–25, **79**–4, **95**–40
    clip-on earrings [klĭp′än ïr′ĭngz, –ön–] **95**–37
    pierced earrings [pïrst′ ïr′ĭngz] **95**–36
rinse [rĭns] **108**–F
ripe [rīp] **68**–30
ripped [rĭpt] **97**–41
ripper [rĭ′pər] **100**–18
rise [rīz] **127**–13
    sunrise [sŭn′rīz′] **18**–14
river [rĭv′ər] **155**–10, **204**–3
RN (registered nurse) [är′ĕn′] / [rĕj′ə stərd nürs′]
    120–10
road work [rōd′ würk′] **154**–16
Road Worker [rōd′ wür′kər] **92**
roast [rōst] **70**–1
    roast beef [rōst bēf′] **71**–21
    roast chicken [rōst chĭk′ən] **81**–22
    roasted turkey [rō′stəd tür′kē] **76**–4
    roasting pan [rō′stĭng păn′] **78**–13
    roasting rack [rō′stĭng răk′] **78**–14
robe [rōb] **91**–29
robin [räb′ən] **214**–16
rock [räk] **36**–D
rock concert [räk′ kän′sərt] **222**–5
rocking chair [räk′ĭng chër′] **37**–21
rocks [räks] **208**–6, **237**–23
Rodents [rōd′nts] **215**
RODENTS [rōd′nts] **215**
rollers [rō′lərz] **33**–19, **181**–23
rolling pin [rō′lĭng pĭn′] **78**–30
rolls [rōlz] **74**–11, **74**–23, **80**–17
romance [rō măns′, rō′măns] **237**–16
Roman Numerals [rō′mən nōō′mər əlz] **16**
roof [rōōf] **46**–1
roof garden [rōōf′ gär′dn] **50**–4
roofer [rōō′fər] **62**–8
room [rōōm]
    baby's room [bā′bēz rōōm′] **47**–10
    ballroom [böl′ rōōm′] **184**–26
    banquet room [băn′kwət rōōm′] **185**–14
    bathroom [băth′rōōm′] **46**–4
    bedroom [bĕd′rōōm′] **46**–2
    conference room [kän′frəns rōōm′] **182**–4
    dining room [dī′nĭng rōōm′] **82**–1
    dining room chair [dī′nĭng rōōm′ chër′] **55**–8
    dining room table [dī′nĭng rōōm′ tā′bəl] **55**–9
    dish room [dĭsh′ rōōm′] **83**–13
    guest room [gĕst′ rōōm′] **184**–13
    kids' bedroom [kĭdz′ bĕd′rōōm′] **47**–9

living room [lĭv′ĭng rōōm′] **47**–12
meeting room [mē′tĭng rōōm′] **184**–25
roommates [rōōm′māts′] **64**–1
room service [rōōm′ sür′vəs] **184**–17
storeroom [stör′rōōm′] **185**–5
Room [rōōm] **50, 118, 121**
ROOM [rōōm] **56**
rooster [rōō′stər] **215**–7
roots [rōōts] **210**–5, **211**–3
rope [rōp] **224**–4, **226**–19
rose [rōz] **211**–15
rotary [rō′tə rē]
    rotary card file [rō′tə rē kärd′ fil′] **183**–44
    rotary cutter [rō′tə rē kŭt′ər] **232**–16
rotten [rät′n] **68**–32
round trip [rownd′ trĭp′] **152**–17
route [rōōt] / [rowt]
    bus route [bŭs′ rōōt, –rowt] **152**–1
    escape route [ĕs′kāp rōōt, –rowt] **146**–3
    evacuation route
        [ĭ văk′yōō/ā shən rōōt, –rowt] **146**–5
    U.S. route [yōō′ĕs′ rōōt, –rowt] **154**–17
router [row′tər] **180**–12
ROUTINES [rōō tēnz′] **38**–39
rubber [rŭb′ər]
    rubber band [rŭb′ər bănd′] **183**–34
    rubber gloves [rŭb′ər glŭvz′] **61**–4
    rubber mat [rŭb′ər măt′] **57**–3
ruffle [rŭ′fəl] **58**–17
rug [rŭg] **58**–22
ruler [rōō′lər] **17**–13
rules [rōōlz] **64**–8
Rules [rōōlz] **190**
run [rŭn] **11**–D
    run across [rŭn′ə krös′] **153**–G
    run around [rŭn′ə rownd′] **153**–H
    run for office [rŭn′ fər ö′fəs] **139**–A
    run out [rŭn′owt′] **162**–E
runner [rŭ′nər] **185**–15
rural area [rōōr′əl ër′ē ə] **52**–4
RV (recreational vehicle)
    [är′vē′] / [rĕk′rē ā′shən əl vē′ə kəl] **156**–10
rye bread [rī′ brĕd′] **71**–20
sad [săd] **43**–19
safety [sāf′tē] **37**–19, **92**–4, **159**–53
    safety boots [sāf′tē bōōts′] **179**–20
    safety deposit box [sāf′tē dĭ păz′ət bäks′] **132**–7
    safety glasses [sāf′tē glăs′əz] **92**–10, **179**–10
    safety goggles [sāf′tē gäg′əlz] **179**–11
    safety pin [sāf′tē pĭn′] **37**–9, **100**–14
    safety rail [sāf′tē rāl′] **59**–10
    safety regulations [sāf′tē rĕ′gyə lā′shənz] **164**–6
    safety visor [sāf′tē vī′zər] **179**–12
Safety [sāf′tē] **76**
SAFETY [sāf′tē] **76**–77, **143, 179**
Safety Equipment [sāf′tē ĭ kwĭp′mənt] **179**
Safety Hazards and Hazardous Materials
    [sāf′tē hăz′ərdz ən hăz′ər dəs-mə tïr′ē əlz] **179**
sailboat [sāl′bōt′] **225**–3
sailing [sā′lĭng] **227**–8

Index

salad [săl/əd]
    chef's salad [shĕfs/ săl/əd] **80**–14
    dinner salad [dĭn/ər săl/əd] **80**–15
    fruit salad [frōōt/ săl/əd] **80**–21
    pasta salad [päs/tə săl/əd] **80**–20
    potato salad [pə tā/tō săl/əd] **80**–19
    salad bar [săl/əd bär/] **79**–24
    salad fork [săl/əd förk/] **83**–27
    salad plate [săl/əd plāt/] **83**–20
    spinach salad [spī/nĭch săl/əd] **80**–13
Salad Dressings [săl/əd drĕ/sĭngz] **80**
Salads [săl/ədz] **80**
salamander [săl/ə măn/dər] **212**–27
salami [sə lä/mē] **71**–24
SALE [sāl] **102**–**103**
sales [sālz]
    sale price [sāl/ prīs/] **27**–3
    salesclerk [sālz/klürk/] **94**–3
    sales tax [sālz/ tăks/] **27**–8
Salesperson [sālz/pür/sən] **92**
salmon [săm/ən] **71**–3
    salmon steak [săm/ən stāk/] **71**–4
salon [sə lön/] **130**–3, **131**–18
salt and pepper shakers
    [sölt/ n pĕp/ər shā/kərz] **55**–13
same [sām] **23**–15
SAME AND DIFFERENT
    [sām/ ən dĭ/frənt, –dĭ fə rənt] **28**–**29**
samples [săm/pəlz] **84**–5
sand [sănd] **225**–23
    sandbox [sănd/bäks/] **224**–15
    sand castle [sănd kăs/əl] **225**–12
    sand dune [sănd dōōn/] **204**–5
    sandpaper [sănd/pā/pər] **181**–56
sandals [săn/dlz] **88**–9
sander [săn/dər] **180**–11
sandwich [săn/wĭch, –sănd/–] **79**–5, **80**–10, **80**–12
sanitation worker [săn/ə tā/shən wür/kər] **169**–54
satellite [săt/əl īt/] **205**–20
    satellite dish [săt/əl līt/ dĭsh/] **53**–6
satisfied [săt/ĭs fīd/] **42**–6
Saturday [săt/ər dā/, –dē] **20**–14
Saturn [săt/ərn] **205**–6
saucepan [sös/păn/] **78**–25
saucer [sö/sər] **83**–25
sausage [sö/sĭj] **70**–12, **80**–2
sauté [sö tā/, sö –] **77**–E
save [sāv] **219**–E
saving [sā/vĭng] **19**–25, **225**–20
savings account number
    [sā/vĭngz ə kownt/ nŭm/bər] **132**–11
saw [sö] **180**–9
    hacksaw [hăk/sö/] **180**–5
    jigsaw [jĭg/sö/] **180**–10
saxophone [săk/sə fōn/] **238**–5
say [sā] **2**–A, **3**–L, **4**–A
scaffolding [skăf/əl dĭng] **178**–4
scales [skālz] **57**–27, **72**–3, **135**–8, **155**–7, **195**–41, **212**–3
    postal scale [pō/stəl skāl/] **183**–27
scallions [skăl/yənz] **69**–20
scallops [skăl/əps, skäl/–] **71**–12, **212**–19

scan [skăn] **171**–H
scanner [skăn/ər] **183**–20
scared [skërd] **43**–23
scarf / scarves [skärf] / [skärvz] **95**–12
    winter scarf [wĭn/tər skärf/] **90**–5
scenery [sē/ nə rē/ / sēn/rē] **162**–3
schedule [skĕj/ōōl, –ōō əl] **152**–4
schedule [skĕj/ōōl, –ōō əl] **171**–J
school [skōōl] **126**–9
    adult school [[ə dŭlt/–, ăd/ŭlt skōōl/] **188**–8
    elementary school [ĕl/ə mĕn/trē skōōl/] **188**–2
    high school [hī/ skōōl/] **188**–4
    junior high school [jōōn/yər hī/ skōōl/] **188**–3
    middle school [mĭd/l skōōl/] **188**–3
    nursery school [nür/sə rē skōōl/] **188**–1
    parochial school [pə rō/kē əl skōōl/] **5** ✦
    preschool [prē/skōōl/] **188**–1
    private school [prī/vət skōōl/] **5** ✦
    public school [pŭb/lĭk skōōl/] **5** ✦
    school bus [skōōl/ bŭs/] **156**–21
    school crossing [skōōl/ krö/sĭng] **154**–15
    technical school [tĕk/nĭ kəl skōōl/] **188**–5
    vocational school [vō kā/shə nəl skōōl/] **188**–5
SCHOOL [skōōl] **5, 10, 11**
School Registration Form
    [skōōl/ rĕj/ə strā/shən förm/] **4**
SCHOOLS AND SUBJECTS
    [sklōōz ən süb/jĭkts] **188**–**189**
science [sī/əns] **189**–11
SCIENCE [sī/əns] **194**–**195**
Science Lab [sī/əns lăb/] **195**
scissors [sĭz/ərz] **33**–20, **100**–16
scoop neck [skōōp/ nĕk/] **96**–10
score [skör] **10**–3, **229**–1
scorpion [skör/pē ən] **214**–30
scrambled eggs [skrăm/bəld ĕgz/] **76**–7
scraper [skrā/pər] **181**–52
screen [skrēn] **6**–2, **196**–11, **235**–30
    big-screen TV [bĭg/skrēn/ tē/ vē/] **50**–15
    fire screen [fīr/ skrēn/] **56**–12
    flat screen TV [flăt/ skrēn/ tē/vē/] **234**–7
    screen door [skrēn/ dör/] **53**–15
    sunscreen [sŭn/skrēn/] **108**–7, **225**–10
screener [skrēn/ər] **160**–5
screening area [skrē/nĭng ër/ē ə] **160**–4
screw [skrōō] **180**–32, **180**–33
    Phillips screwdriver [fĭl/ĭps skrōō/drī/vər] **180**–31
    screwdriver [skrōō/drī/vər] **180**–30
scroll bar [skrōl/bär/] **197**–15
scrub [skrŭb] **60**–K
scrubs [skrŭbz] **93**–31
    scrub brush [skrŭb/ brŭsh/] **61**–20
    surgical scrub cap [sür/jĭ kəl skrŭb/ kăp/] **93**–35
    surgical scrubs [sür/jĭ kəl skrŭbz/] **93**–38
scuba [skōō/bə]
    scuba diving [skōō/bə dī/vĭng] **227**–12
    scuba tank [skōō/bə tăngk/] **225**–5
sea [sē]
    sea anemone [sē/ ə nĕm/ə nē] **212**–24
    seahorse [sē/ hörs/] **212**–13
    sea lion [sē/ lī/ən] **213**–33
    sea otter [sē/ ät/ər] **213**–35

seashell [sē/shĕl/] **225**–24
sea urchin [sē/ ür/chən] **212**–21
seaweed [sē/ wēd/] **225** ✦
Sea Animals [sē/ ăn/ə məlz] **212**
SEAFOOD AND DELI [sē/fōōd/ ən dĕ/lī] **71**
seal [sēl] **213**–34
Sea Mammals [sē/ măm/əlz] **213**
seam ripper [sēm/ rĭp/ər] **100**–18
search [sürch]
    search and rescue team
        [sürch/ ən rĕs/kyōō tēm/] **145**–20
    search box [sürch/ bäks/] **197**–5
    search engine [sürch/ ĕn/jən] **197**–6
SEARCH [sürch] **173**
SEASONAL CLOTHING [sē/zə nəl klō/dhĭng] **90**
Seasons [sē/zənz] **21**
seat [sēt]
    backseat [băk/ sēt/] **159**–54
    car safety seat [kär/ săf/tē sēt/] **37**–19
    child safety seat [chīld/ săf/tē sēt/] **159**–53
    front seat [frŭnt/ sēt/] **159**–51
    love seat [lŭv/ sēt/] **56**–1
    potty seat [pät/ē sēt/] **37**–12
    reclined seat [rĭ klīnd/ sēt/] **161**–27
    seat belt [sēt/ bĕlt/] **159**–52
    upright seat [ŭp/rīt/ sēt/] **161**–28
seat [sēt] **82**–B
second [sĕk/ənd] **16**
Second Floor [sĕk/ənd flör/] **50**
seconds [sĕk/əndz] **18**–3
section [sĕk/shən] **72**–2
security [sĭ kyōōr/ə tē]
    security camera [sĭ kyōōr/ə tē kăm/rə] **50**–19
    security gate [sĭ kyōōr/ə tē gāt/] **50**–16
    security guard [sĭ kyōōr/ə tē gärd/] **132**–5, **169**–55
    security pants [sĭ kyōōr/ə tē pănts/] **93**–22
    security screener [sĭ kyōōr/ə tē skrē/nər] **160**–5
    security shirt [sĭ kyōōr/ə tē shürt/] **93**–20
Security Checkpoint [sĭ kyōōr/ə tē chĕk/poynt/] **160**
Security Guard [sĭ kyōōr/ə tē gärd/] **93**
sedan [sə dăn/] **156**–1
see [sē] **106**–A
seed [sēd] **211**–1
    seedling [sēd/lĭng] **211**–4
seek [sēk] **114**–A, **147**–H
seesaw [sē/sö/] **224**–16
select [sə lĕkt/] **196**–B
self-checkout [sĕlf/ chĕk/owt/] **73**–10, **133**–10
sell [sĕl] **170**–K
semi [sĕm/ī] **156**–15
semicolon [sĕm/ē kō/lən] **190**–18
Senate [sĕn/ət] **138**–5
senator [sĕn/ə tər] **138**–6
    state senator [stāt/ sĕn/ə tər] **139**–25
send [sĕnd] **197**–I
    send in [sĕnd/ ĭn] **173**–H
Sending a Card [sĕn/dĭng ə kärd/] **135**
Sending Email [sĕn/dĭng ē/māl/] **197**
senior [sēn/yər]
    senior citizen [sēn/yər sĭt/ə zən] **30**–5
    senior housing [sēn/yər howz/ĭng] **52**–11
Senses [sĕn/səz] **106**

sentence [sĕn/tns] **190**–2
sentence [sĕn/tns] **141**–E
separate [sĕ/pə rāt/] **76**–B
September [sĕp tĕm/bər] **21**–33
sequins [sē/kwĭnz/] **99**–33
Serious Medical Conditions
[sĭr/ē əs mĕd/ĭ kəl kən dĭsh/ənz] **111**
serious photo [sĭr/ē əs fō/tō] **206**–3
serve [sürv] **139**–D, **230**–P
serve on a jury [sürv/ än ə jŏŏr/ē, –ön–] **140**–E
serve the meal [sürv/ dhə mēl/] **82**–F
Serve [sürv] **76**
server [sür/vər] **82**–8, **83**–9, **169**–56, **185**–8
service [sür/vəs]
customer service [kŭs/tə mər sür/vəs] **97** ✦
customer service representative
[kŭs/tə mər-sür/vəs rĕ/prə zĕn/tə tĭv] **167**–20
guest services [gĕst/ sür/vəs əz] **130**–12
pool service [pōōl/ sür/vəs] **184**–21
room service [rōōm/ sür/vəs] **184**–17
SERVICE [sür/vəs] **138**–139, **185**
serving bowl [sür/vĭng bōl/] **55**–21
set [sĕt] **10**–A, **33**–C, **82**–A
set up [sĕt/ ŭp/] **173**–I
sunset [sŭn/sĕt/] **18**–18
setting [sĕ/tĭng] **83**–17
seven [sĕv/ən] **16**
seventeen [sĕv/ən tēn/] **16**
seventeenth [sĕv/ən tēnth/] **16**
seventh [sĕv/ənth] **16**
seventieth [sĕv/ən tē əth] **16**
seventy [sĕv/ən tē] **16**
75 percent [sĕv/ən tē fĭv/ pər sĕnt/] **17**–9
sew [sō] **98**–A, **98**–B, **170**–L
sewing [sō/ĭng]
sewing machine [sō/ĭng mə shēn/] **98**–13
sewing machine operator
[sō/ĭng mə shēn/ äp/ə rā/ tər] **98**–14
Sewing Machine [sō/ĭng mə shēn/] **98**
Sewing Supplies [sō/ĭng sə plīz/] **100**
sex [sĕks] **4**–16
shade [shād] **225**–13
lampshade [lămp/shād/] **56** ✦, **58**–26
shadow [shă/dō/] **109**–35
shake [shāk]
milkshake [mĭlk/shāk/] **79**–14
shake [shāk] **3**–J, **174**–I
shakers [shā/kərz] **55**–13
shampoo [shăm pōō/] **108**–10
shanks [shănks] **70**–13
shaper [shā/pər] **91**–15
Shapes [shāps] **193**
share [shĕr] **8**–M
Sharing and Responding
[shĕr/ĭng ən rĭ spän/dĭng] **191**
shark [shärk] **212**–4
sharpener [shär/pən ər] **183**–26
shave [shāv]
aftershave [ăf/tər shāv/] **109**–30
shave [shāv] **109**–M
shaver [shā/vər] **109**–26
shaving cream [shā/vĭng krēm/] **109**–29

shears [shĭrz] **176**–9
sheep [shēp] **215**–6
sheet [shēt]
cookie sheet [kŏŏk/ē shēt/] **78**–27
dryer sheets [drī/ər shēts/] **101**–5
fitted sheet [fĭt/əd shēt/] **58**–12
flat sheet [flăt/ shēt/] **58**–13
shelf [shĕlf] **54**–2
shell [shĕl]
seashell [sē/shĕl/] **225**–24
Shellfish [shĕl/fĭsh/] **71**
shelter [shĕl/tər] **52**–13
shield [shēld]
windshield [wĭnd/shēld/] **158**–1
windshield wipers [wĭnd/shēld wī/pərz] **158**–2
shift [shĭft] **159**–49, **159**–50
shin [shĭn] **106**–21
shin guards [shĭn/ gärdz/] **231**–13
shingles [shĭng/gəlz] **178**–20
ship [shĭp] **175**–D
shipping clerk [shĭp/ĭng klürk/] **175**–14
shirt [shürt] **86**–1
nightshirt [nīt/shürt/] **91**–28
polo shirt [pō/lō shürt/] **92**–14
security shirt [sĭ kyŏŏr/ə tē shürt/] **93**–20
sports shirt [spörts/ shürt/] **88**–4
T-shirt [tē/shürt/] **86**–4
work shirt [würk/ shürt/] **92**–2
shock [shäk] **116**–B, **116**–F
shoes [shōōz] **86**–7, **87**–13, **95**–32
shoe department [shōō/ dĭ pärt/mənt] **95**–7
shoelaces [shōō/lās əz] **94**–24
shoe store [shōō/ stör/] **130**–10
SHOES AND ACCESSORIES
[shōōz/ ən ĭk sĕs/ə rēz] **94**–95
shoot [shōōt] **211**–5
shoot [shōōt] **230**–H
shop [shäp]
barbershop [bär/bər shäp/] **129**–19
beauty shop [byōō/tē shäp/] **130** ✦
coffee shop [kö/fē shäp/] **126**–11
donut shop [dō/nŭt shäp/] **129**–17
gift shop [gĭft/ shäp/] **130** ✦, **184**–5
ice cream shop [īs/ krēm shäp/] **131**–16
shop [shäp] **28**–A, **143**–H
Shop [shäp] **100**
SHOP [shäp] **80**–81
shoplifting [shäp/lĭf/tĭng] **142**–8
shopping [shäp/ĭng]
shopping basket [shäp/ĭng băs/kət] **73**–9
shopping list [shäp/ĭng lĭst/] **67**–14
shopping mall [shäp/ĭng mäl/] **126**–7
shopping program [shäp/ĭng mäl/] **236**–10
SHOPPING [shäp/ĭng] **27**
shore [shör] **204**–12
short [shört] **32**–6, **96**–16
short hair [shört/ hĕr/] **33**–1
short-order cook [shört/ör/dər kŏŏk/] **185**–1
short-sleeved [shört/slēvd/] **96**–12
shorten [shört/ən] **100**–B
shorts [shörts] **89**–25, **91**–4

shoulder [shōl/dər] **105**–13
shoulder bag [shōl/dər băg/] **94**–17
shoulder blade [shōl/dər blād/] **107**–28
shoulder-length hair [shōl/dər lĕngkth/ hĕr/] **33**–2
shoulder pads [shōl/dər pădz/] **231**–20
shovel [shŭv/əl] **176**–7, **178**–22
show [shō] **236**–4, **236**–6, **236**–8
show [shō] **137**–C, **160**–C
shower [show/ər]
shower cap [show/ər kăp/] **108**–1
shower curtain [show/ər kür/tn] **57**–12
shower gel [show/ər jĕl/] **108**–2
showerhead [show/ər hĕd/] **57**–11
stall shower [stöl/ show/ər] **57** ✦
shredder [shrĕ/dər] **183**–24
shrimp [shrĭmp] **71**–11, **212**–18
shut [shŭt] **146**–4
shuttle [shŭt/l] **152**–19, **205**–19
sick [sĭk] **42**–12
homesick [hōm/sĭk/] **43**–20
side [sīd] **76**–10
sideburns [sīd/bürnz/] **33**–7
sideview mirror [sīd/vyōō/ mĭr/ər] **158**–3
Side Salads [sīd/ săl/ədz] **80**
sidewalk [sīd/wök/] **129**–24
sight impaired [sīt/ ĭm pĕrd/] **32**–11
sign [sīn] **4**–D
street sign [strēt/ sīn/] **129**–26
vacancy sign [vā/kən sē sīn/] **50**–7
vital signs monitor [vīt/l sīnz/ män/ə tər] **121**–26
sign [sīn] **48**–D
signal [sĭg/nəl]
strong signal [ströng/ sĭg/nəl] **14**–11
turn signal [türn/ sĭg/nəl] **158**–6, **159**–34
weak signal [wēk/ sĭg/nəl] **14**–12
signature [sĭg/nə chər] **4**–19
SIGNS [sīnz] **154**
silk [sĭlk] **98**–5
simmer [sĭm/ər] **77**–P
sing [sĭng] **36**–O, **238**–B
single [sĭng/gəl]
single father [sĭng/gəl fä/dhər] **35**–23
single mother [sĭng/gəl mŭdh/ər] **35**–22
sink [sĭnk] **54**–4, **57**–23
Sirius [sĭr/ē əs] **205** ✦
sister [sĭs/tər] **34**–5, **35**–27
sister-in-law [sĭs/tər ĭn lö/] **34**–16
stepsister [stĕp/sĭs/tər] **35**–29
sitcom (situation comedy)
[sĭt/käm/] / [sĭch/ōō ā/shən kăm/ə dē] **236**–2
sit down [sĭt/ down/] **6**–F
site [sīt] **126**–2
sitter [sĭt/ər] **166**–9
situation comedy (sitcom)
[sĭch/ōō ā/shən-kăm/ə dē] / [sĭt/käm/] **236**–2
six [sĭks] **16**
six-pack [sĭks/păk/] **74**–9, **74**–21
6-year-old boy [sĭks/yïr ōld/boy/] **31**–9
sixteen [sĭks/tēn] **16**
sixteenth [sĭks/tēnth/] **16**
sixth [sĭksth] **16**
sixtieth [sĭks/tē əth] **16**

Index

sixty [sĭks′tē] **16**

Sizes [sī′zəz] **96**

skate [skāt] **230**–U

skates [skāts] **231**–9, **231**–10

    skateboard [skāt′bōrd′] **224**–7

    skateboarding [skāt′bōr′dĭng] **228**–13

skating [skā′tĭng] **227**–4, **227**–5, **227** ✦, **228**–10

ski [skē] **230**–V

skiing [skē′ĭng] **227**–1, **227**–3

    waterskiing [wö′tər skē′ĭng] **227**–7

skill inventory [skĭl′ ĭn′vən tör′ē] **172**–12

Skills [skĭlz] **171**

SKILLS [skĭlz] **170, 171, 174**

skin [skĭn] **107**–31

    skinless [skĭn′ləs] **70** ✦

skirt [skürt] **87**–10

skis [skēz] **231**–24

    ski boots [skē′ bōōts] **231**–26

    ski hat [skē′ hăt′] **90**–11

    ski mask [skē′ măsk′] **90**–15

    ski poles [skē′ pōlz′] **231**–25

skull [skŭl] **107**–47

skunk [skŭngk] **216**–12

SKU number [ĕs′kā′yōō′ nŭm′bər, skyōō′] **27**–5

sky [skī] **209**–9

    skycap [skē′kăp′] **160**–1

    skyscraper [skī′skrā′pər] **127**–13

slacks [slăks] **87**–12

slaves [slāvz] **198**–4

sledding [slĕd′ĭng] **227**–6

sledgehammer [slĕj′hăm′ər] **178**–23

sleeper [slē′pər] **91**–27

sleeping bag [slē′pĭng băg′] **226**–12

Sleepwear [slēp′wër] **91**

SLEEPWEAR [slēp′wër] **91**

sleepy [slē′pē] **42**–3

sleeve [slēv] **100**–6

    long-sleeved [löng′slēvd′] **96**–14

    short-sleeved [shört′slēvd′] **96**–12

    sleeveless [slēv′ləs] **96**–11

    3/4 sleeved [thrē′kwör′tər slēvd′] **96**–13

slender [slĕn′dər] **32**–9

slice [slīs] **77**–C

slide [slīd] **194**–3, **224**–13

    mudslide [mŭd′slīd′] **144**–6

sliding glass door [slī′dĭng glăs′ dör′] **53**–18

sling [slĭng] **113**–19

slip [slĭp] **91**–22, **91**–23, **132**–4

slippers [slĭp′ərz] **91**–26

slippery floor [slĭ′pər ē flör′] **179**–6

slow [slō] **23**–4

small [smöl] **96**–1, **96**–2, **97**–37

    small town [smöl′ town′] **52**–3

smart phone [smärt′ fōn′] **15**–27

smell [smĕl] **106**–C

smile [smīl] **2**–D

smock [smŏk] **93**–26

smog [smäg, smög] **218**–11

smoggy [smä′gē, smö′–] **13**–14

smoke [smōk] **114**–G

    smoke detector [smōk′ dĭ tĕk′tər] **51**–29

    smoked turkey [smōkt′ tür′kē] **71**–25

Snack Foods [snăk′ fōōdz′] **73**

snail [snāl] **212**–22

snake [snāk] **213**–39

    rattlesnake [ră′təl snāk′] **213**–38

snap [snăp] **99**–26

sneeze [snēz] **110**–B

snorkeling [snör′kə lĭng] **227**–11

snow [snō]

    snowboard [snō′bōrd′] **231**–23

    snowboarding [snō′bör′dĭng] **227**–2

    snowstorm [snō′störm′] **13**–23

    snowing [snō′ĭng] **13**–12

soap [sōp] **57**–24, **61**–5, **108**–3

    soap dish [sōp′ dĭsh′] **57**–25

    soap opera [sōp′ äp′rə] **236**–5

sober [sō′bər] **143** ✦

soccer [säk′ər] **229**–12

    soccer ball [säk′ər böl′] **231**–12

social [sō′shəl]

    Social Security card

      [sō′shəl sĭ kyōor′ə tē kärd′] **40**–5

    Social Security number

      [sō′shəl sĭ kyōor′ə tē nŭm′bər] **4**–15

    social worker [sō′shəl wür′kər] **169**–57

socks [säks] **86**–6

    ankle socks [ang′kəl säks′] **91**–7

    crew socks [krōō′ säks′] **91**–8

    dress socks [drĕs′ säks′] **91**–9

    low-cut socks [lō′kŭt säks′] **91**–10

Socks [säks] **91**

soda [sō′də] **73**–34, **79**–11

sofa [sō′fə] **56**–18

    sofa cushions [sō′fə kōō′shənz] **56** ✦

soft [söft] **23**–6

    softball [söft′böl′] **229**–10

softener [sö′fən ər] **101**–6

software [söft′wër′] **167**–18, **196**–10

soil [soyl] **208**–2

solar [sō′lər]

    solar eclipse [sō′lər ĭ klĭps′] **205**–16, **205** ✦

    solar energy [sō′lər ĕn′ər jē] **218**–1

Solar System and the Planets

    [sō′lər sĭs′təm ən dhə plăn′əts] **205**

soldier [sōl′jər] **169**–58

sole [sōl] **94**–21

solid [säl′əd] **96**–19

Solids [säl′ədz] **193**

solution [sə lōō′shən] **192**–14

solve [sölv] **170**–M

son [sŭn] **34**–15

    grandson [grăn′sŭn′, grănd′–] **34** ✦

    son-in-law [sŭn′ĭn lö′] **34** ✦

sore throat [sör′ thrōt′] **110**–6

sort [sört] **101**–A

soul [sōl] **237**–28

soup [sōōp] **72**–18, **80**–16

    soup bowl [sōōp′ bōl′] **83**–21

    soupspoon [sōōp′spōōn′] **83**–32

Soup [sōōp] **77**

sour [söw′ər] **84**–4

    sour cream [sow′ər krēm′] **72**–21

Sources [sör′səz] **218**

sous chef [sōō′ shĕf′] **185**–6

south [sowth] **155**–3

soybeans [soy′bēnz′] **177**–3

space [spās] **50**–18, **128**–5

    space shuttle [spās′ shŭt′əl] **205**–19

    space station [spās′ stā′shən] **205**–18

Space [spās] **205**

Space Exploration [spās′ ĕk′splə rā′shən] **205**

spades [spādz] **233**–30

spaghetti [spə gĕt′ē] **81**–26

spare tire [spër′ tīr′] **158**–23

sparrow [spăr′ō] **214**–7

spatula [spăch′ə lə] **78**–19

speak [spēk] **170**–N

speakers [spē′kərz] **50**–5, **206**–4, **234**–14

Special [spĕ′shəl] **80**

Specialists [spĕsh′ə lĭsts′] **120**

speech [spēch] **140**–2

speed limit [spēd′ lĭm′ət] **154**–4

speedometer [spī däm′ə tər] **159**–27

speed skating [spēd′skā′tĭng] **227** ✦

spell [spĕl] **4**–B

sphere [sfîr] **193**–42

spider [spī′dər] **214**–29

spill [spĭl] **218**–17

spinach [spĭn′ĭch] **69**–11

    spinach salad [spĭn′ĭch săl′əd] **80**–13

spinal column [spī′nəl käl′əm] **107**–49

spiral notebook [spī′rəl nōt′bōōk′] **7**–29

splint [splĭnt] **117**–14

sponge [spŭnj] **61**–19

    sponge mop [spŭnj′ mäp′] **61**–6

spoon [spōōn] **55**–5, **78**–9

    soupspoon [sōōp′spōōn′] **83**–32

    tablespoon [tā′bəl spōōn′] **75**–7

    teaspoon [tē′spōōn′] **75**–6, **83**–31

spoon [spōōn] **77**–F

sports [spörts]

    sports car [spörts′ kär′] **156**–4

    sports coat [spörts′ kōt′] **89**–14

    sports jacket [spörts′ jăk′ət] **89**–14

    sports program [spörts′ prō′grăm] **236**–11

    sports shirt [spörts′ shürt′] **88**–4

    sport-utility vehicle (SUV) [spört′

      yōō tĭl′ə tē vē′ĭ kəl] / [ĕs′yōō′vē′] **156**–7

SPORTS [spörts] **228, 229, 230, 231**

SPORTS EQUIPMENT [spörts′ ĭ kwĭp′mənt] **231**

SPORTS VERBS [spörts′ vürbz′] **230**

sprained ankle [sprănd′ ăng′kəl] **110**–18

spray [sprā] **108**–12, **113**–32

    spray gun [sprā′ gŭn′] **181**–21

    spray starch [sprā′ stärch′] **101**–12

spread [sprĕd]

    bedspread [bĕd′sprĕd′] **59**–11

spring [sprĭng] **21**–37, **58**–19

sprinkler [sprĭng′klər] **53**–22

square [skwër] **193**–30

squash [skwäsh, skwösh] **69**–24

squeegee [skwē′jē] **61**–15

squid [skwĭd] **212**–7

squirrel [skwür′əl] **215**–21

stadium [stā′dē əm] **126**–1

staff [stăf] **185** ✦
Staff [stăf] **120**
stage [stāj] **194**–16
    stage clips [stāj/ klĭps/] **194**–24
stain [stān] **181**–24
stained [stānd] **97**–42
stairs [stërz] **50**–10
stairway [stër/wā/] **50**–10
stall shower [stöl/ show/ər] **57** ✦
stamps [stămps] **134**–18, **134**–23, **183**–47
    stamp machine [stămp/ mə shēn/] **135**–11
stand [stănd] **152**–18
    checkstand [chĕk/stănd/] **73**–12
    newsstand [nooz/stănd/] **128**–12
    nightstand [nīt/stănd/] **58**–23
stand [stănd] **141**–D
    stand up [stănd/ ŭp/] **6**–D
standard time [stăn/dərd tīm/] **19**–26
staple [stā/pəl] **171**–F
stapler [stā/plər] **183**–28
staples [stā/pəlz] **183**–29
star [stär] **205**–13
    starfish [stär/fĭsh/] **212**–16
    star key [stär/ kē/] **14**–6
starch [stärch] **101**–12
start [stärt] **12**–A, **40**–B, **230**–R
starting point [stär/tĭng poynt/] **162**–1
starving [stär/vĭng] **43** ✦
state [stāt] **4**–8, **146**–2
    state capital [stāt kă/pət əl] **139**–22
    state senator [stāt sĕn/ə tər] **139**–25
state [stāt] **15**–G, **195**–A
State Government [stāt gŭ/ vərn mənt] **139**
statement [stāt/mənt] **132**–16
station [stā/shən]
    bus station [bus/ stā/shən] **124**–7
    fire station [fīr/ stā/shən] **125**–12
    gas station [găs/ stā/shən] **125**–10
    gas station attendant
        [găs/ stā/shən ə tĕn/dənt] **162**–3
    lifeguard station [līf/gärd/ stā/shən] **225**–21
    police station [pə lēs/ stā/shən] **124**–6
    space station [spās/ stā/shən] **205**–18
    station wagon [stā/shən wăg/ən] **156**–6
    subway station [sŭb/wā/ stā/shən] **151**–11
Station [stā/shən] **152**
stationery [stā/shə nër/ ē] **183**–42
stay [stā]
    stay away [stā ə wā/] **147**–I
    stay fit [stā fĭt/] **114**–E
    stay on the line [stā ön dhə līn/] **15**–H
    stay on well-lit streets [stā ön wĕl lĭt/ strēts/] **143**–B
Stay Well [stā wĕl/] **114**
steak [stāk] **70**–2, **81**–24
    broiled steak [broyld/ stāk/] **76**–3
    halibut steak [hăl/ə bŭt stāk/] **71**–6
    salmon steak [săm/ən stāk/] **71**–4
    steak knife [stāk/ nīf/] **83**–29
steal [stēl] **142** ✦
steam [stēm] **77**–D
steamed vegetables [stēmd/ vĕj/tə bəlz] **81**–32
steamer [stē/mər] **78**–3

steel [stēl]
    steel toe boots [stēl/ tō/ boots/] **92**–6
    steel-wool soap pads [stēl/wool/ sōp/ pădz/] **61**–5
steering wheel [stïr/ĭng wēl/] **159**–26
stems [stĕmz] **211**–9
step [stĕp]
    stepbrother [stĕp/brŭdh/ər] **35**–30
    stepdaughter [stĕp/dö/tər] **35** ✦
    stepfather [stĕp/fä/dhər] **35**–25
    stepladder [stĕp/lăd/ər] **61**–13
    stepmother [stĕp/mŭdh/ər] **35**–26
    steps [stĕps] **53**–3
    stepsister [stĕp/sĭs/tər] **35**–29
stereo system [stĕr/ē ō sĭs/təm] **56**–8
sterile [stĕr/əl]
    sterile pad [stĕr/əl păd/] **117**–6
    sterile tape [stĕr/əl tāp/] **117**–7
stethoscope [stĕth/ə skōp/] **118**–10
stewing beef [stoo/ĭng bēf/] **70**–3
stick [stĭk] **231**–11, **232**–11
    drumsticks [drŭm/stĭks/] **70**–23
    lipstick [lĭp/stĭk/] **109**–38
    stick shift [stĭk/ shĭft/] **159**–50
    yardstick [yärd/stĭk/] **181**–16
sticker [stĭk/ər] **102**–3, **136**–13
sticky notes [stĭk/ē nōts/] **183**–39
stir [stür] **77**–O
    stir-fried beef [stür/frīd/ bēf/] **76**–6
stitches [stĭch/əz] **117**–15
stock clerk [stäk/ klürk/] **169**–59
stockings [stäk/ĭngz] **91**–17
stomach [stŭm/ək] **107**–41
    stomachache [stŭm/ək āk/] **110**–4
stop [stäp] **129**–16, **151**–13, **154**–1
    stopover [stäp/ō/vər] **161** ✦
stop [stäp] **155**–D
Stop [stäp] **152**
stopped up [stäpt/ ŭp/] **63**–19
storage [stör/ĭj] **72**–25, **78**–4
    storage locker [stör/ĭj läk/ər] **50**–17
store [stör]
    bookstore [book/stör/] **130**–4
    candy store [kăn/dē stör/] **131**–17
    card store [kärd/stör/] **130**–7
    convenience store [kən vēn/yəns stör/] **128**–3
    department store [dĭ pärt/mənt stör/] **131**–13
    electronics store [ē lĕk trän/ĭks stör/] **131**–20
    furniture store [für/nĭ chər stör/] **126**–8
    hardware store [härd/wër/ stör/] **148**–4
    home improvement store
        [hōm/ ĭm proov/mənt stör/] **127**–20
    jewelry store [joo/əl rē stör/] **130**–2
    maternity store [mə tür/nə tē stör/] **131**–19
    men's store [mĕnz/ stör/] **130** ✦
    music store [myoo/zĭk stör/] **130**–1
    office supply store [ö/fəs sə plī/ stör/] **127**–21
    pet store [pĕt/ stör/] **130**–6
    shoe store [shoo/ stör/] **130**–10
    toy store [toy/ stör/] **130**–5
    video store [vĭd/ē ō stör/] **129**–20
Store [stör] **99**
STORE [stör] **72**–**73**

storeroom [stör/room/] **185**–3
storm [störm] **13**–19
    hailstorm [hāl/störm/] **13**–21
    snowstorm [snō/störm/] **13**–23
    storm door [störm/ dör/] **53**–10
    thunderstorm [thŭn/dər störm/] **13**–16
story [stör/ē]
    action story [ăk/shən stör/ē] **237**–19
    adventure story [ăd vĕn/chər stör/ē] **237**–19
    horror story [hör/ər stör/ē, här/–] **237**–17
    science fiction story [sī/əns fĭk/shən stör/ē] **237**–18
    two-story house [too/stör/ē hows/] **52** ✦
stove [stōv] **54**–18, **226**–16
stow [stō] **160**–G
straight [strāt] **155**–A
    straight hair [strāt/ hër/] **33**–9
    straight line [strāt/ līn/] **193**–22
    straight pin [strāt/ pĭn/] **100**–12
strainer [strā/nər] **78**–22
straw [strö] **79**–18
    strawberries [strö/bër/ēz] **68**–14
    straw hat [strö/ hăt/] **90**–23
stream [strēm] **204** ✦
street [strēt] **150**–5, **155**–8
    streetlight [strēt/līt/] **148**–3
    street sign [strēt/ sīn/] **129**–26
    street vender [strēt/ vĕn/dər] **129**–29
STREETS [strēts] **126**–**127**
strep throat [strĕp/ thrōt/] **111**–4
stress [strĕs] **115**–4
stretch [strĕch] **230**–M
stretcher [strĕch/ər] **121**–33
string [strĭng]
    string beans [strĭng/ bēnz/] **69**–8
    string lights [strĭng/ līts/] **239**–18
    string of pearls [strĭng/ əv pürlz/] **95**–39
Strings [strĭngz] **238**
striped [strīpt] **96**–20
stripper [strĭ/pər] **181**–42
stroller [strō/lər] **37**–18
strong signal [ströng/ sĭg/nəl] **14**–11
stub [stŭb] **165**–11
stucco [stŭk/ō] **178**–15
student [stood/nt] **6**–5
study [stŭ/dē] **10**–D, **137**–A
STUDYING [stŭ/dē ĭng] **8**–**9**
stuffed animals [stŭft/ ăn/ə məlz] **59**–15
style [stīl] **88** ✦
Styles [stīlz] **96**
STYLES [stīlz] **96**
stylist [stī/lĭst] **167**–31
SUBJECTS [sŭb/jĭkts/] **188**–**189**
submit [səb mĭt/] **48**–C
substitute [sŭb/stə toot/] **79**–20
subtract [səb trăkt/] **192**–B
suburbs [sŭb/ürbz] **52**–2
subway [sŭb/wā/] **151**–12
    subway car [sŭb/wā/ kär/] **152**–6
    subway station [sŭb/wā/ stā/shən] **151**–11
Subway Station [sŭb/wā/ stā/shən] **152**
Succeed [sək sēd/] **10**
SUCCEEDING IN SCHOOL [sək sē/dĭng ən skool/] **10**

suede [swād] **99**–8
sugar [shŏŏg/ər] **73**–30
    sugar bowl [shŏŏg/ər bōl/] **55**–14
    sugar-free [shŏŏg/ər frē/] **122**–7
    sugar substitute [shŏŏg/ər sŭb/stə tōōt/] **79**–20
suit [sōōt] **87**–11
    bathing suit [bā/dhĭng sōōt/] **90**–26
    business suit [bĭz/nəs sōōt/] **88**–11
    jumpsuit [jŭmp/sōōt/] **93**–24
    three piece suit [thrē/pēs/ sōōt/] **88** ✦
    wet suit [wĕt/ sōōt/] **225**–4
suite [swēt] **184**–16
sum [sŭm] **192**–7
sumac [sōō/măk] **210**–23
summer [sŭm/ər] **21**–38
sun [sŭn] **209**–8
    sunblock [sŭn/blăk] **108**–8, **225**–0
    sunburn [sŭn/bürn] **110**–14
    sunflower [sŭn/flow/ər] **211**–10
    sunglasses [sŭn/glăs/əz] **90**–27
    sunrise [sŭn/ rīz] **18**–14
    sunscreen [sŭn/skrēn/] **108**–7, **225**–10
    sunset [sŭn/ sĕt] **18**–19
Sunday [sŭn/dā, –dē] **20**–8
sunny [sŭn/ē] **13**–9, **76**–10
superintendent [sōō/prĭn tĕn/dənt, sōō/pər ĭn–] **50**–8
supermarket [sōō/pər/ mär/kət] **127**–18
supervise [sōō/pər vīz/] **170**–O
supervisor [sōō/pər vī/zər] **165**–8, **175**–4
Supplies [sə plīz/] **100, 183**
SUPPLIES [sə plīz/] **61, 180–181**
supply [sə plī/] **127**–21
    supply cabinet [sə plī/ kăb/ə nət] **182**–1
support [sə pört/] **179**–18
    support group [sə pört/ grōōp/] **115**–15
supporter [sə pör/tər] **91**–6
Supreme Court [sə prēm/ kört/] **138**–11
surfboard [sürf/börd/] **225**–16
surfer [sür/fər] **225**–15
surfing [sür/fĭng] **227**–9, **227**–10, **227** ✦
surgeon [sür/jən] **121**–36
Surgeon [sür/jən] **93**
surge protector [sürj/ prə tĕk/tər] **196**–1
surgical [sür/jĭ kəl]
    surgical cap [sür/jĭ kəl kăp/] **121**–37
    surgical gloves [sür/jĭ kəl glŭvz/] **121**–39
    surgical gown [sür/jĭ kəl gown/] **93**–37, **121**–38
    surgical mask [sür/jĭ kəl măsk/] **93**–36
    surgical nurse [sür/jĭ kəl nürs/] **120**–9
    surgical scrub cap [sür/jĭ kəl skrŭb/ kăp/] **93**–35
    surgical scrubs [sür/jĭ kəl skrŭbz/] **93**–38
Surgical Assistant [sür/jĭ kəl ə sĭs/tənt] **93**
surprised [sər prīzd/, sə–] **43**–30
suspenders [sə spĕn/dərz] **94**–1
suspense [sŭs/pĕns] **237**–20
SUV (sport-utility vehicle) [ĕs/ yōō/ vē/] /
    [spört/ yōō tĭl/ə tē vē/ĭ kəl] **156**–7
swallow [swäl/ō] **116**–J
swap meet [swäp/ mēt/] **222**–6
sweat [swĕt]
    sweatpants [swĕt/pănts/] **89**–23
    sweatshirt [swĕt/shürt/] **89**–22

sweater [swĕt/ər] **28**–2, **87**–14
    cardigan sweater [kär/də gən swĕt/ər] **88**–2
    pullover sweater [pōōl/ō/vər swĕt/ər] **88**–3
sweep [swēp] **60**–J
sweet potatoes [swĕt pə tā/tōz] **69**–18
sweets [swĕts] **84**–9
swim [swĭm] **230**–L
    swimsuit [swĭm/sōōt/] **90**–26
swimming [swĭm/ĭng]
    swimming pool [swĭm/ĭng pōōl/] **51**–22
    swimming trunks [swĭm/ĭng trŭngks/] **90**–22
swing [swĭng] **230**–Q
swings [swĭngz] **224**–11
Swiss cheese [swĭs/ chēz/] **71**–27
switch [swĭch] **58**–27
swollen finger [swō/lən fĭng/gər] **110**–16
swordfish [sörd/fĭsh] **71**–5, **212**–10
symbol [sĭm/bəl] **155**–8
SYMPTOMS AND INJURIES
    [sĭmp/təmz ən ĭn/jə rēz] **110**
synagogue [sĭn/ə gäg/] **127**–16
synthetic materials [sĭn thĕ/tĭk mə tïr/ē əlz] **98** ✦
syringe [sə rĭnj/] **118**–12
syrup [sĭr/əp, sür/–] **113**–29
system [sĭs/təm]
    fuel injection system
        [fyōō/əl ĭn jĕk/shən sĭs/təm] **158**–17
    stereo system [stĕr/ē ō sĭs/təm] **56**–8
SYSTEM [sĭs/təm] **141**
tab [tăb] **197**–7
table [tā/bəl]
    bed table [bĕd/ tā/bəl] **121**–21
    changing table [chān/jĭng tā/bəl] **59**–1
    coffee table [kö/fē tā/bəl] **56**–19
    dining room table [dī/nĭng rōōm/ tā/bəl] **55**–9
    end table [ĕnd/ tā/bəl] **56**–14
    examination table [ĭg zăm/ə nā/shən tā/bəl] **118**–7
    folding card table [fōl/dĭng kärd/ tā/bəl] **102**–4
    night table [nīt/ tā/bəl] **58**–23
    operating table [äp/ə rā/tĭng tā/bəl] **121**–40
    periodic table [pïr/ē äd/ĭk tā/bəl] **195**–26
    picnic table [pĭk/nĭk tā/bəl] **224**–8
    pool table [pōōl/ tā/bəl] **50**–15
    tablecloth [tā/bəl klöth/] **55**–12
    tablespoon [tā/bəl spōōn/] **75**–7
    table tennis [tā/bəl tĕn/əs] **228**–14
    tray table [trā/ tā/bəl] **161**–21
    turntable [türn/tā/bəl] **234**–12
tablet [tăb/lət] **113**–22, **113**–27
tackle [tăk/əl] **230**–F
taco [tä/kō] **79**–8
tags [tăgz] **92**–15, **136**–13
tail [tāl] **216**–22
tail light [tāl/ līt/] **158**–13
tail pipe [tāl/ pīp/] **158**–15
tailor [tā/lər] **100**–3
take [tāk]
    do not take with dairy products
        [dōō nät/ tăk/ wĭth dër/ē prăd/ŭkts] **112**–A
    take a bath [tāk/ ə băth/] **108**–B
    take a break [tāk/ ə brāk/] **11**–H
    take a citizenship test
        [tāk/ ə sĭt/ə zən shĭp tĕst/] **140**–I

    take a driver education course
        [tāk/ ə drī/vərz ĕj/ə kā/shən körs/] **137**–B
    take a driver's training course
        [tāk/ ə drī/vərz trā/nĭng körs/] **137**–G
    take a message [tāk/ ə mĕs/ĭj] **171**–Q
    take a nap [tāk/ ə năp/] **53**–A
    take a picture [tāk/ ə pĭk/chər] **206**–B
    take a seat [tāk/ ə sēt/] **6**–F
    take a shower [tāk/ ə show/ər] **38**–C, **108**–A
    take a tour [tāk/ ə tōōr/] **220**–A
    take a written test [tāk/ ə rĭt/ən tĕst] **137**–E
    take care of children [tāk/ kër/ əv chĭl/drən] **170**–P
    take cover [tāk/ kŭv/ər] **147**–J
    take dictation [tāk/ dĭk/tā shən] **171**–K
    take in [tāk/ ĭn] **100**–D
    take medicine [tāk/ mĕd/ə sən] **114**–D
    take notes [tāk/ nōts/] **10**–C
    take off [tāk/ öf/] **109**–Q, **160**–J
    take one hour before eating
        [tāk/ wŭn/ ow/ər bĭ för/ ē/tĭng] **112**–B
    take out [tāk/ owt/] **9**–Y, **60**–Q, **82** ✦
    take ownership [tāk/ ō/nər shĭp/] **49**–K
    take temperature [tāk/ tĕm/prə chər] **118**–B
    take the bus to school
        [tāk/ dhə bŭs/ tə skōōl/] **38**–H
    take the car to a mechanic
        [tāk/ dhə kär/ tə dhə mə kăn/ĭk] **157**–C
    take the children to school
        [tāk/ dhə chĭl/drən tə skōōl/] **38**–G
    take the order [tāk/ dhē ör/dər] **82**–E
    take with food [tāk/ wĭth fōōd/] **112**–A
    take x-rays [tāk/ ĕks/rāz/] **119**–B
Taking a Flight [tā/kĭng ə flīt/] **160**
Taking a Test [tā/kĭng ə tĕst/] **10**
TAKING A TRIP [tā/kĭng ə trĭp/] **162–163**
Taking Care of Your Car [tā/kĭng kër/ əv yər kär/] **157**
TAKING CARE OF YOUR HEALTH
    [tā/kĭng kër əv yər hĕlth/] **114–115**
talk [tök]
    talk show [tök/ shō/] **236**–4
    talk therapy [tök/ thër/ ə pē] **115**–13
talk [tök]
    talk about [tök ə bowt/] **174**–L
    talk on the phone [tök/ ön dhə fōn/] **15**–C
    talk to friends [tök/ tə frĕndz/] **173**–A
    talk to the teacher [tök/ tə dhə tē/chər] **6**–B
tall [töl] **32**–4
tambourine [tăm/bə rēn/] **238**–17
tan [tăn] **24**–18
tangerines [tăn/jə rēnz/] **68**–9
tank [tăngk] **158**–10, **225**–5
    tank top [tăngk/ täp/] **89**–24
    tank truck [tăngk/ trŭk/] **156**–20
tape [tāp]
    clear tape [klēr/ tāp/] **183**–30
    correction tape [kə rĕk/shən tāp/] **183**–37
    duct tape [dŭkt/ tāp/] **181**–49
    electrical tape [ĭ lek/trĭ kəl tāp/] **181**–43
    masking tape [măs/kĭng tāp/] **181**–53
    packing tape [păk/ĭng tāp/] **183**–32
    sterile tape [stĕr/ əl tāp/] **117**–7
    tape measure [tāp mĕzh/ər] **100**–17, **181**–45

target [tär/gət] **231**–7
taste [tāst] **106**–D
tattoo [tă tōō/] **32**–18
tax / taxes [tăks] / [tăks/əz] **27**–8
taxi [tăk/sē] **150**–3
 hail a taxi [hāl/ ə tăk/sē] **152** ✦
 taxi driver [tăk/sē drī/vər] **152**–21
 taxi license [tăk/sē lī/səns] **152**–22
 taxi stand [tăk/sē stănd/] **152**–18
TB (tuberculosis) [tē/bē/] / [tōō bür/kyə lō/səs] **111**–15
TDD [tē/dē/dē/] **15**–26
tea [tē] **79**–12, **81**–39, **81**–40
 teacup [tē/kŭp] **55**–6
 tea kettle [tē/ kĕt/l] **54**–21
 teapot [tē/pät] **55**–16
 teaspoon [tē/spōōn/] **75**–6, **83**–31
teach [tēch] **170**–Q
teacher [tē/chər] **5**–8, **6**–4, **22**–5
 teacher's aide [tē/chərz ād/] **5**–16
team [tēm] **145**–20, **229**–3
TEAM SPORTS [tēm/ spörts/] **229**
technical school [tĕk/nĭ kəl skōōl/] **188**–5
technician [tĕk nĭsh/ən]
 computer technician
  [kəm pyōō/tər tĕk nĭsh/ən] **167**–19, **182**–12
 emergency medical technician (EMT)
  [ĭ mür/jən sē mĕd/ĭ kəl tĕk nish/ən] / [ē/ĕm/tē]
  121–32
 medical records technician
  [mĕd/ĭ kəl rĕk/ərdz tĕk nish/ən] **168**–39
Technician [tĕk nĭsh/ən] **93**
teddy bear [tĕd/ē bër/] **37**–23
teen / teenager [tēn] / [tē/nā/jər] **31**–11
teething ring [tē/dhĭng rĭng/] **37**–25
teeth / tooth [tēth] / [tōōth] **106**–7
 toothache [tōōth/āk/] **110**–2
 toothbrush [tōōth/brŭsh/] **57**–21, **109**–22
 toothbrush holder [tōōth/brŭsh/ hōl/dər] **57**–22
 toothpaste [tōōth/pāst/] **109**–23
telemarketer [tĕl/ə mär/kə tər] **169**–60
TELEPHONE [tĕl/ə fōn/] **14**–15
Telephone Skills [tĕl/ə fōn/ skĭlz/] **171**
telescope [tĕl/ə skōp/] **205**–23
television / TV [tĕl/ə vĭzh/ən] / [tē/vē/] **56**–6
 big-screen TV [bĭg/skrēn/ tē/vē/] **50**–14
 flat panel TV [flăt/ păn/əl tē/vē/] **234**–7
 flat screen TV [flăt/ skrēn/ tē/vē/] **234**–7
 portable TV [pör/tə bəl tē/vē/] **234**–8
teller [tĕl/ər] **132**–1
Teller [tĕl/ər] **132**
Telling Time [tĕl/ĭng tīm/] **18**
temperature [tĕm/prə chər] **110**–8
 temperature gauge [tĕm/prə chər gāj/] **159**–30
Temperature [tĕm/prə chər] **13**
ten [tĕn] **16**
 ten after one [tĕn/ ăf/tər wŭn/] **18**–8
 ten dollars [tĕn/ däl/ərz] **26**–9
 10 percent [tĕn/ pər sĕnt/] **17**–12
 ten thousand [tĕn/ thow/zənd] **16**
 10-year-old girl [tĕn/yïr ōld/ gürl/] **31**–10
tenant [tĕn/ənt] **50**–6
TENANT MEETING [tĕn/ənt mē/tĭng] **64**–65

tennis [tĕn/əs] **228**–15
 table tennis [tā/bəl tĕn/əs] **228**–14
 tennis court [tĕn/əs kört/] **224**–6
 tennis racket [tĕn/əs răk/ət] **231**–2
 tennis shoes [tĕn/əs shōōz/] **95**–32
tent [tĕnt] **226**–10
tenth [tĕnth] **16**
Terminal [tür/mə nəl] **160**
termites [tür/mīts] **63**–22
term [türm] **139** ✦
Terms [türmz] **199**
terrified [tĕr/ə fid/] **43** ✦
test [tĕst] **121**–30
 test booklet [tĕst/ bŏŏk/lət] **10**–1
 testing area [tĕs/tĭng ër/ē ə] **136**–2
 test tube [tĕst/ tōōb/] **195**–42
Test [tĕst] **10**
text [tĕkst]
 textbook [tĕkst/bŏŏk/, tĕks/-] **7**–25
 text box [tĕkst/ băks/, tĕks/-] **197**–13
 text message [tĕkst/ mĕs/ĭj, tĕks/-] **14**–19
thank [thăngk] **12**–E, **174**–N
Thanksgiving [thăngks gĭv/ĭng] **22**–17
theater [thē/ə tər] **126**–6, **127**–23
theft [thĕft] **142**–9
therapist [thĕr/ ə pĭst] **115**–12, **115**–14, **168**–45
therapy [thĕr/ ə pē] **115**–11, **115**–13
thermal undershirt [thür/məl ŭn/dər shürt/] **91**–2
thermometer [thər măm/ə tər] **118**–11
thick [thĭk] **23**–7
thighs [thīz] **70**–22, **106**–19
thimble [thĭm/bəl] **100**–15
thin [thĭn] **23**–8, **32**–9
THINGS [thĭngz] **23**
think [thĭnk] **191**–E
third [thürd] **16**
Third Floor [thürd/ flör/] **50**
thirsty [thür/stē] **42**–2
thirteen [thür/tēn/] **16**
 thirteen colonies [thür/tēn/ kä/lə nēz] **198**–1
thirteenth [thür/tēnth/] **16**
thirtieth [thür/tē əth] **16**
thirty [thür/tē] **16**
 35 mm camera
  [thür/tē fiv/ mĭl/ə mē/tər kăm/rə] **235**–21
this week [dhĭs/ wēk/] **20**–19
thorn [thörn] **211**–29
thread [thrĕd] **99**–23, **100**–11
three [thrē] **16**
 three piece suit [thrē/pēs/ sōōt/] **88** ✦
 3-ring binder [thrē/ rĭng/ bīn/dər] **7**–27
 3/4 sleeved [thrē/kwör/tər slēv/] **96**–13
 three times a week [thrē/ tīmz/ ə wēk/] **20**–24
throat [thrōt] **107**–35, **110**–6, **111**–4
 throat lozenges [thrōt/ läz/ən jəz] **113**–30
through [thrōō] **153**–K
throw [thrō] **230**–C
 throw away [thrō/ ə wā/] **11**–N
 throw up [thrō/ ŭp/] **110**–E
throw pillow [thrō/ pĭl/ō] **56**–2
thumb [thŭm] **106**–16
thunderstorm [thŭn/dər störm/] **13**–16

Thursday [thürz/dā, –dē] **20**–12
tick [tĭk] **214**–27
ticket [tĭk/ət] **152**–15, **161**–19
 ticket agent [tĭk/ət ā/jənt] **160**–3
 ticket window [tĭk/ət wĭn/dō/] **152**–12
tidal wave [tīd/l wāv/] **145**–17
tide [tīd] **225** ✦
tie [tī] **88**–12, **89**–16, **92**–13, **229** ✦
tie [tī] **86**–A
tiger [tī/gər] **217**–37
tight [tīt] **97**–29
tights [tīts] **91**–19
tile [tīl] **57**–10, **178**–11, **178**–D
time [tīm]
 Alaska time [ə lăs/kə tīm/] **19**–28
 arrival time [ə rī/vəl tīm/] **161** ✦
 Atlantic time [ət lăn/tĭk tīm/] **19**–33
 Central time [sĕn/trəl tīm/] **19**–31
 daylight saving time [dā/lĭt/ sā/vĭng tīm/] **19**–25
 departure time [dĭ pär/chər tīm/] **161** ✦
 Eastern time [ē/stərn tīm/] **19**–32
 Hawaii-Aleutian time
  [hə wī/ē ə lōō/shən tīm/] **19**–27
 Mountain time [mown/tn tīm/] **19**–30
 Newfoundland time
  [nōō/fən lənd tīm/, –fənd–] **19**–34
 on time [än/ tīm/, ön/ tīm/] **19**–23, **161**–29
 Pacific time [pə sĭf/ĭk tīm/] **19**–29
 standard time [stăn/dərd tīm/] **19**–26
 three times a week [thrē tīmz/ ə wēk/] **20**–24
 time clock [tīm/ kläk/] **165**–7
Time [tīm] **18**
TIME [tīm] **18**–19
timer [tī/mər] **78**–18
Times of Day [tīmz/ əv dā/] **18**
Time Zones [tīm/ zōnz/] **19**
tire [tīr] **158**–5, **158**–23, **162**–F
tired [tīrd] **43**–32
title [tīt/l] **133**–14, **190**–5
toad [tōd] **212**–28
toast [tōst] **80**–4
toaster [tō/stər] **54**–6
 toaster oven [tō/stər ŭv/ən] **54**–15
today [tə dā/] **20**–5
toddler [täd/lər] **31**–8
toe [tō] **92**–6, **94**–23, **105**–10
 toenail [tō/nāl/] **106** ✦
Tofu [tō/fōō/] **77**
toggle bolt [täg/əl bōlt/] **180**–38
to-go box [tə gō/ băks/] **82**–5
toilet [toy/lət] **57**–19
 toilet brush [toy/lət brŭsh/] **57**–18
 toilet paper [toy/lət pā/pər] **57**–17, **146**–13
token [tō/kən] **152**–10
tomatoes [tə mā/tōz] **69**–6
tomorrow [tə mär/ō, –mör/ō] **20**–6
tongs [tängz, töngz] **78**–23, **195**–44
tongue [tŭng] **106**–8
too [tōō]
 too big [tōō/ bĭg/] **97**–38
 too expensive [tōō/ ĭk spĕn/sĭv/] **97**–44
 too small [tōō/ smöl/] **97**–37

Index

tool belt [tool/ bĕlt/] 92–3
TOOLS AND BUILDING SUPPLIES
   [toolz/ ən bĭl/dĭng sə plīz/] 180–181
tooth / teeth [tooth] / [tēth] 106–7
   toothache [tooth/āk/] 110–2
   toothbrush [tooth/brŭsh/] 57–21, 109–22
   toothbrush holder [tooth/brŭsh/ hōl/dər] 57–22
   toothpaste [tooth/pāst/] 109–23
top [täp] 88–7, 89–24
torn [törn] 97–41
tornado [tör nā/dō] 145–15
torso [tör/sō/] 106 ✦
tortoise [tör/təs] 213–42
total [tōt/l] 27–9
totebag [tōt/ băg/] 94–19
touch [tŭch] 106–E
towel [tow/əl]
   bath towel [băth/ tow/əl] 57–14
   dish towel [dĭsh/ tow/əl] 61–22
   hand towel [hănd/ tow/əl] 57–15
   paper towels [pā/pər tow/əlz] 54–3
   towel rack [tow/əl răk/] 57–13
towelettes [tow/əl ĕts] 146–12
tower [tow/ər] 196–3
town [town] 52–3
   town car [town/ kär/] 152–20
   townhouse [town/hows/] 52–6
tow truck [tō/ trŭk/] 156–14
toy [toy]
   toy chest [toy/ chĕst/] 59–16
   toy store [toy/ stör/] 130–5
Toys and Games [toyz/ ən gāmz/] 59
track [trăk] 5–21, 152–14
   track and field [trăk/ ən fēld/] 228–18
tractor [trăk/tər] 177–9
   tractor trailer [trăk/tər trā/lər] 156–15
traffic light [trăf/ĭk līt/] 128–8
TRAFFIC SIGNS [trăf/ĭk sīnz/] 154
tragedy [trăj/ə dē] 237–14
trailer [trā/lər] 156–15, 156–17
train [trān] 150–7, 233–27
training [trā/nĭng] 172–2, 172–5, 172–7
   training pants [trā/nĭng pănts/] 37–11
Training [trā/nĭng] 172
Train Station [trān/ stā/shən] 152
transcribe [trăn skrīb/] 171–C
transfer [trăns für/, trăns/fər] 152–5
transfer [trăns für/, trăns/fər] 171–O
translate [trănz/lāt] 8–C
translator [trănz/lā/tər, trăns/–] 168–35
Transmission [trănz mĭsh/ən, trăns–] 159
Transportation [trăns/pər tā/shən] 152
TRANSPORTATION [trăns/pər tā/shən] 150–151, 152
trash [trăsh]
   trash bags [trăsh/ băgz/] 61–24
   trash bin [trăsh/ bĭn/] 51–23
   trash chute [trăsh/ shoot/] 51–26
travel [trăv/əl] 41–P
travel agency [trăv/əl ā/jən sē] 131–14
tray [trā] 55–17, 83–10
   tray table [trā tā/bəl] 161–21
Tree [trē] 210

trees [trēz] 208–1, 239–16
TREES AND PLANTS [trēz/ ən plănts/] 210
trench coat [trĕnch/ kōt/] 90–21
trial [trī/əl] 140–5
triangle [trī/ăng/gəl] 193–32
tricycle [trī/sĭ kəl] 224–12
trigonometry [trĭg/ə năm/ə trē] 192–18
trim [trĭm] 176–B
trip [trĭp] 152–16, 152–17
tripe [trīp] 70–8
tripod [trī/päd] 235–25
trombone [trăm bōn/] 238–10
trout [trowt] 71–1
trowel [trow/əl] 176–10, 178–13
truck [trŭk] 150–5
   dump truck [dŭmp/trŭk/] 156–19
   fire truck [fīr/ trŭk/] 144–10
   garbage truck [gär/bĭj trŭk/] 127–22
   hand truck [hănd/ trŭk/] 175–11
   pickup truck [pĭk/ŭp trŭk/] 156–12
   tank truck [tăngk/ trŭk/] 156–20
   tow truck [tō/ trŭk/] 156–14
   truck driver [trŭk/ drī/vər] 169–61
TRUCKS [trŭks] 156
trumpet [trŭm/pət] 238–11
Trunk [trŭngk] 158
trunks [trŭngks] 158–11, 210–4, 217–47
   swimming trunks [swĭm/ĭng trŭngks/] 90–22
try on [trī/ön] 95–C
TSA agent [tē/ĕs/ā/ ā/jənt] 160–5
T-shirt [tē/shürt/] 86–4
tsunami [soo nä/ mē/, tsoo–] 145–17
tub [tŭb]
   bathtub [băth/tŭb/] 57–2
tuba [too/bə] 238–12
tube [toob] 74–12, 74–24, 195–42
tuberculosis (TB)
   [too bür/kyə lō/səs] / [tē/bē/] 111–15
Tuesday [tooz/dā, –dē] 20–10
tulip [too/ləp] 211–11
tuna [too/nə] 71–7, 72–19, 212–8
tuner [too/nər] 234–13
turbulence [tür/byə ləns] 161–22
turkey [tür/kē] 70–17, 239–14
   roasted turkey [rōs/təd tür/kē] 76–4
   smoked turkey [smōkt/ tür/kē] 71–25
turn [türn] 154–5, 154–7, 154–8
   turn signal [türn/ sĭg/nəl] 158–6, 159–34
   turnstile [türn/stīl/] 152–8
   turntable [türn/tā/bəl] 234–12
turn [türn]
   turn in [türn/ ĭn/] 191–M
   turn left [türn/ lĕft/] 155–C
   turn off [türn/ öf/] 11–P, 160–I, 174–G, 219–G
   turn on [türn/ ön/, –än/] 11–B
   turn right [türn/ rīt/] 155–B
turnips [tür/nəps] 69–16
turquoise [tür/koyz, –kwoyz] 24–9
turtle [tür/tl] 213–43
   turtleneck [tür/tl nĕk/] 96–9
tusk [tŭsk] 217–48
tuxedo [tŭk sē/dō] 89–17

TV Programs [tē/vē/ prō/grămz] 236
TV / television [tē/vē/] / [tĕl/ə vĭzh/ən] 56–6
   big-screen TV [bĭg/skrēn/ tē/vē/] 50–14
   flat panel TV [flăt/ păn/əl tē/vē/] 234–7
   flat screen TV [flăt/ skrēn/ tē/ vē/] 234–7
   portable TV [por/tə bəl tē/vē/] 234–8
tweezers [twē/zərz] 117–4
twelfth [twĕlfth] 16
twelve [twĕlv] 16
twentieth [twĕn/tē əth] 16
twenty [twĕn/tē] 16
   twenty after one [twĕn/tē ăf/tər wŭn/] 18–10
   twenty dollars [twĕn/tē däl/ərz] 26–10
   twenty-first [twĕn/tē fürst/] 16
   twenty-five [twĕn/tē fīv/] 16
   25 percent [twĕn/fīv/ pər sĕnt/] 17–11
   twenty-four [twĕn/tē för/] 16
   twenty-one [twĕn/tē wŭn/] 16
   twenty-three [twĕn/tē thrē/] 16
   twenty to two [twĕn/tē tə too/] 18–12
   twenty-two [twĕn/tē too/] 16
twice a week [twīs/ ə wēk/] 20–23
twig [twĭg] 210–1
twins [twĭnz] 28–1
two [too]16
   2-door car [too/dör kär/] 156–2
   two-story house [too/stör/ē hows/] 52 ✦
   two-way radio [too/wā rā/dē ō] 179–22
   2 x 4 (two by four) [too/ bī/ för/] 181–19
type [tīp] 170–R, 196–A
   type a letter [tīp/ə lĕt/ər] 171–A
   type the message [tīp/ dhə mĕs/ĭj] 197–E
   type the subject [tīp/ dhə sŭb/jĭkt] 197–D
   type your password [tīp/ yər păs/würd/] 197–A
Types of Health Problems
   [tīps/ əv hĕlth/ prăb/ləmz] 115
Types of Job Training [tīps/ əv jäb/ trā/nĭng] 172
Types of Material [tīps/ əv mə tĭr/ē əl] 99
Types of Math [tīps/ əv măth/] 192
Types of Medication [tīps/ əv mĕd/ə kā/shən] 113
Types of Movies [tīps/ əv moo/vēz] 237
Types of Music [tīps/ əv myoo/zĭk] 237
Types of TV Programs [tīps/ əv tē/vē/ prō/grămz] 236
ugly [ŭg/lē] 23–22
umbrella [ŭm brĕl/ə] 90–17, 225–14
umpire [ŭm/pīr] 229 ✦
uncle [ŭng/kəl] 34–8
uncomfortable [ŭn kŭmf/tə bəl, –tər–] 42–9
unconscious [ŭn/kän/shəs] 116–A
under [ŭn/dər] 25–10, 153–A
   long underwear [löng/ ŭn/dər wër/] 91–3
   thermal undershirt [thür/məl ŭn/dər shürt/] 91–2
   underexposed [ŭn/dər ĭk spōzd/] 235–35
   underpants [ŭn/dər pănts/] 91–14
   undershirt [ŭn/dər shürt/] 91–1
underline [ŭn/dər līn/] 9–S
Under the Hood [ŭn/dər dhə hood/] 158
Underwear [ŭn/dər wër/] 91
UNDERWEAR AND SLEEPWEAR
   [ŭn/dər wër/ ən slēp/wër/] 91
undress [ən drĕs/] 36–E

278

unfurnished apartment
[ŭn/für nĭsht ə pärt/ mənt] **48**–4
uniform [yōō/nə förm/] **88**–10, **231**–16
Unisex Socks [yōō/nə sĕks/ säks/] **91**
Unisex Underwear [yōō/nə sĕks/ ŭn/dər wër] **91**
universal remote [yōō/nə vür/səl rĭ mōt/] **234**–9
UNIVERSE [yōō/nə vürs/] **205**
university [yōō/nə vür/sə tē] **188**–7
unload [ŭn lōd/] **101**–E
unpack [ŭn păk/] **49**–N
unraveling [ŭn răv/əl ĭng] **97**–43
unripe [ŭn rīp/] **68**–31
unscented [ŭn sĕn/təd] **108** ✦
unscramble [ŭn skrăm/bəl] **9**–W
up [ŭp]
buckle up [bŭk/əl ŭp/] **36**–L
clean up [klēn/ ŭp/] **147**–M
cut up [kŭt/ ŭp/] **77**–I
eggs sunny-side up [ĕgz/ sŭn/ē sīd ŭp/] **76**–10
get up [gĕt/ ŭp/] **38**–B
hang up [hăng/ ŭp/] **15**–D, **101**–H
look up [lŏŏk/ ŭp/] **8**–A
pick up [pĭk/ ŭp/] **6**–I, **11**–E, **38**–M
pop-up ad [päp/ ŭp ăd/] **197**–9
set up [sĕt/ ŭp/] **173**–I
stand up [stănd/ ŭp/] **6**–D
stopped up [stäpt/ ŭp/] **63**–19
throw up [thrō/ ŭp/] **110**–E
wake up [wāk/ ŭp/] **38**–A
walk up [wök/ ŭp/] **153**–C
upright seat [ŭp/rīt/ sēt/] **161**–28
upset [ŭp sĕt/] **43**–28
upstairs [ŭp/stërz/] **51** ✦
Uranus [yŏŏr/ə nəs, yŏŏ rā/nəs] **205**–7
urban area [ür/bən ër/ē ə] **52**–1
urchin [ür/chən] **212**–21
URL [yōō/är/ĕl/] **197**–4
U.S. [yōō/ĕs/]
U.S. Capitol [yōō/ĕs/ kă/pət əl] **138**–1
U.S. route [yōō/ĕs/ rōōt/, –rowt/] **154**–17
USB port [yōō/ĕs/ bē/ pört/] **196**–7
use [yōōz]
use a cash register [yōōz/ə kăsh/ rĕj/ə stər] **170**–S
use a credit card [yōōz/ə krĕ/dət kärd/] **27**–B
use a debit card [yōōz/ə dĕ/bət kärd/] **27**–C
use a gift card [yōōz/ ə gĭft/ kärd/] **27**–E
use deodorant [yōōz/dē ō/dər ənt] **108**–C
use energy-efficient bulbs
[yōōz/ ĕn/ər jē ĭ fĭ/shənt bŭlbz] **219**–H
use punctuation [yōōz/ pŭngk/chōō ā/shən] **190**–C
Used Car [yōōzd/ kär/] **157**
used clothing [yōōzd/ klō/dhĭng] **102**–2
U.S. HISTORY [yōō/ĕs/ hĭs/tə rē] **198**
U.S. NATIONAL PARKS
[yōō/ĕs nāsh/ə nəl pärks/] **220–221**
utensils [yōō tĕn/səlz] **79**–19
utility / utilities [yōō tĭl/ə tē] / [yōō tĭl/ə tēz]
48–5, **156**–7
U-turn [yōō/türn/] **154**–5
vacancy sign [vā/kən sē sīn/] **50**–7
vacation [vā kā/shən] **22**–6
vaccination [văk/sə nā/shən] **114** ✦

vacuum [văk/yōōm]
vacuum cleaner [văk/yōōm klē/nər] **61**–10
vacuum cleaner attachments
[văk/yōōm klē/nər ə tăch/mənts] **61**–11
vacuum cleaner bag
[văk/yōōm klē/nər băg/] **61**–12
vacuum [văk/yōōm] **60**–H
valley [văl/ē] **204**–17
valuables [văl/yə bəlz, –yə wə–] **132**–8
valve [vălv] **146**–4
van [văn] **156**–13, **156**–18
vandalism [văn/də lĭz/əm] **142**–1
vanity plate [vă/nə tē plāt/] **136** ✦
variable [vër/ē ə bəl] **192**–12
vase [vās, vāz, väz] **55**–23
vault [völt] **132**–6
VCR [vē/sē/är/] **102**–7
veal cutlets [vēl/ kŭt/ləts] **70**–6
Vegetable [vĕj/tə bəl] **77**
vegetables [vĕj/tə bəlz] **66**–8, **72**–27, **81**–32
vegetable garden [vĕj/tə bəl gär/dn] **53**–27, **177**–14
vegetable peeler [vĕj/tə bəl pē/lər] **78**–15
VEGETABLES [vĕj/tə bəlz] **69**
vegetarian [vĕj/ə tër/ē ən] **70** ✦
vehicles [vē/ĭ kəlz] **124**–4, **156**–7, **156**–10
vein [vān] **107**–37
velvet [vĕl/vət] **99**–10
vending machine [vĕn/dĭng mə shēn/] **152**–9
vendors [vĕn/dərz] **84**–7, **129**–29
ventilation mask [vĕnt/əl ā/shən măsk/] **92**–7
Venus [vē/nəs] **205**–2
verdict [vür/dĭkt] **141**–14
vertebrates [vür/ tə brəts] **194**–13
vest [vĕst] **89**–15
down vest [down/ vĕst] **90**–14
Hi-Visibility safety vest
[hī/vĭz/ə bĭl/ə tē săf/tē vĕst] **92**–6
life vest [līf/ vĕst/] **161**–25, **226**–14
Veterans Day [vĕt/ər ənz dā/] **22**–16
veterinarian [vĕt/ər ə nër/ē ən] **169**–62
vice president [vīs/ prĕz/ə dənt] **138**–9
victim [vĭk/təm] **142**–10
video [vĭd/ē ō]
videocassette [vĭd/ē ō kə sĕt/] **133**–18
video game console [vĭd/ē ō gām/ kän/sōl/] **232**–3
video game control [vĭd/ē ō gām/ kän trōl/] **232**–4
video player [vĭd/ē ō plā ər] **197**–11
video store [vĭd/ē ō stōr/] **129**–20
videotape [vĭd/ē ō tāp/] **240**–A
view [vyōō]
rearview mirror [rïr/vyōō/ mïr/ər] **159**–35
sideview mirror [sīd/vyōō/ mïr/ər] **158**–3
village [vĭ/lĭj] **52**–3
vine [vīn] **210**–22
vineyard [vĭn/yərd] **177**–16
violence [vī/ləns, vī/ə–] **142**–4
violet [vī/ə lət, vī/lət] **24**–8, **211**–23
violin [vī/ə lĭn/] **238**–6
virus [vī/rəs] **111**–17
vise [vīs] **180**–26
vision [vĭ/zhən]
vision exam [vĭ/zhən ĭg zăm/] **136**–6
vision problems [vĭ/zhən präb/ləmz] **115**–1

Visit [vĭ/zət] **119**
visor [vī/ zər] **179**–12
vital signs monitor [vīt/l sīnz/ män/ə tər] **121**–26
vitamins [vī/tə mənz] **113**–17
v-neck [vē/nĕk/] **96**–8
vocational [vō kā/shə nəl]
vocational school [vō kā/shə nəl skōōl/] **188**–5
vocational training [vō kā/shə nəl trā/nĭng] **172**–5
voice message [voys mĕs/ĭj] **14**–18
volcanic eruption [väl kăn/ĭk ĭ rŭp/shən] **145**–16
volleyball [väl/ē böl/] **229**–14, **231**–3
Volume [väl/yəm, –yōōm] **75, 193**
volunteer [väl/ən tïr/] **121**–17
volunteer [väl/ən tïr/] **41**–Q
vomit [väm/ət] **110**–E
vote [vōt] **140**–A
waffles [wä/fəlz, wö/–] **80**–8
wages [wā/jĭz] **165**–12
wagon [wä/gən] **156**–6
waist [wāst]
waist apron [wāst/ ā/prən] **93**–30
waistband [wāst/bănd/] **100**–5
wait [wāt] **94**–B, **128**–B, **170**–T
waiter [wā/tər] **82**–8
headwaiter [hĕd/wā/tər] **185**–12
waiting area [wā/tĭng ër/ē ə] **182**–16
Waiting Room [wā/tĭng rōōm/] **118**
waitress [wā/trəs] **83**–9
wait staff [wāt/ stăf/] **185** ✦
wake up [wāk/ ŭp/] **38**–A
walk [wök] **53**–2
crosswalk [krös/wök/] **128**–15
walk-in freezer [wök/ĭn frē/zər] **185**–3
walk [wök]
walk a dog [wök ə dög/] **129**–F
walk down [wök/ down/] **153**–D
walk to class [wök/ tə kläs/] **11**–C
walk up [wök/ ŭp/] **153**–C
walk with a friend [wök/ wĭth ə frĕnd/] **143**–A
walker [wö/kər] **113**–11
wall [wöl] **56**–10, **194**–5
drywall [drī/wöl/] **178**–19
wallpaper [wöl/pā/pər] **59**–8
wallet [wä/lət, wö/–] **94**–13
walrus [wöl/rəs] **213**–32
war [wör] **199**–10
Revolutionary War [rĕ/və lōō/shə nër/ē wör/] **198**–8
warehouse [wër/hows/] **175**–7
warm [wörm] **13**–4
warm clothes [wörm/ klōz/] **146**–6
warning label [wör/nĭng lā/bəl] **112**–8
Warnings [wör/nĭngz] **112**
wash [wäsh, wösh]
mouthwash [mowth/wäsh/, –wösh/–] **109**–25
washcloth [wäsh/klöth/, wösh/–] **57**–4
wash [wäsh, wösh]
wash clothes [wäsh/ klöz/, wösh/–] **219**–K
wash hair [wäsh/ här/, wösh/–] **108**–E
wash the dishes [wäsh/ dhə dĭsh/əz, wösh/–] **60**–M
wash the windows
[wäsh/ dhə wĭn/dōz, wösh/–] **60**–I
washer [wä/shər, wö/–] **50**–12, **101**–3, **180**–37
dishwasher [dĭsh/wäsh/ər, –wö/–] **54**–8, **185**–2

Index

washing [wä′shǐng, wö′–] **61**–21
wasp [wäsp, wösp] **214**–17
waste [wāst] **121**–31, **218**–12
    wastebasket [wāst′băs′kət] **57**–26
watch [wäch, wöch] **94**–16
watch [wäch, wöch] **39**–X, **147**–C
water [wö′tər] **209**–3, **225**–1
    body of water [bäd′ē əv wö′tər] **204** ✦
    bottled water [bät′ld wö′tər] **146**–11
    cold water [kōld′ wö′tər] **57**–7
    hot water [hät′ wö′tər] **57**–8
    hot water bottle [hät′ wö′tər böt′l] **113**–15
    watercolor [wö′tər kŭl′ər] **233**–21
    waterfall [wä′tər föl′] **204**–2
    water fountain [wö′tər fown′tn] **224**–9
    water glass [wö′tər glăs′] **83**–22
    watermelons [wö′tər mĕl′ənz] **68**–18
    water pollution [wö′tər pə lōō′shən] **218**–14
    water polo [wö′tər pō′lō] **229**–15
    waterskiing [wö′tər skē′ĭng] **227**–7
water [wö′tər] **176**–F
WATER SPORTS [wö′tər spörts′] **227**
wave [wāv] **145**–17, **225**–17
wave [wāv] **2**–F
wavy hair [wā′vē hër′] **33**–10
way [wā]
    hallway [häl′wā′] **184**–18
    one way [wŭn′ wā′] **154**–3
    one-way trip [wŭn′wā′ trǐp′] **152**–16
    two-way radio [tōō′wā′ rā′dē ō] **179**–22
    wrong way [röng′ wā′] **154**–2
Ways to Conserve Energy and Resources
    [wāz′ tə kən sürv′ ĕn′ər jē n rē′sör′səz,
    –rǐ sör′səz] **219**
Ways to Get Well [wāz′ tə gĕt′ wĕl′] **114**
Ways to Pay [wāz′ tə pā′] **27**
Ways to Serve Eggs [wāz′ tə sürv′ ĕgz′] **76**
Ways to Serve Meat and Poultry
    [wāz′ tə sürv′ mēt′ n pōl′trē′] **76**
Ways to Stay Well [wāz′ tə stā′ wĕl′] **114**
Ways to Succeed [wāz′tə sək sēd′] **10**
weak signal [wēk′ sǐg′nəl] **14**–12
WEATHER [wĕdh′ər] **13**
Weather Conditions [wĕdh′ər kən dǐsh′ənz] **13**
Weather Map [wĕdh′ər măp′] **13**
webcam [wĕb′kăm′] **196**–12
Webpage [wĕb′pāg′] **197**
website address [wĕb′sǐt ə drĕs′] **197**–4
wedding [wĕ′dǐng] **22**–2
Wednesday [wĕnz′dā, –dē] **20**–11
weed [wēd]
    seaweed [sē′ wēd′] **225** ✦
    weed eater [wēd′ ē′tər] **176**–12
    weed whacker [wēd′ wăk′ər] **176**–12
weed [wēd] **176**–G
week [wēk] **20**–15
    last week [lăst′ wēk′] **20**–18
    next week [nĕkst′ wēk′] **20**–20
    once a week [wŭns′ ə wēk′] **20**–22
    this week [dhǐs′ wēk′] **20**–19
    three times a week [thrē′ tǐmz′ ə wēk′] **20**–24
    twice a week [twǐs′ ə wēk′] **20**–23

weekdays [wēk′dāz′] **20**–16
weekend [wēk′ĕnd′] **20**–17
Week [wēk] **20**
weigh [wā] **75**–B
weight [wāt] **32**–8
Weight [wāt] **32, 75**
weightlifting [wāt′lǐf′tǐng] **228**–16
weights [wāts] **231**–22
WEIGHTS AND MEASUREMENTS
    [wāts′ ən mĕzh′ər mənts] **75**
welder [wĕl′dər] **169**–63
well [wĕl] **42**–14
Well [wĕl] **114**
west [wĕst] **155**–2
western [wĕs′tərn] **237**–15
wet [wĕt] **101**–17
    wet suit [wĕt′ sōōt′] **225**–4
whacker [wăk′ər] **176**–12
whale [wāl] **213**–29
wheat [wēt] **177**–2
wheat bread [wēt′ brĕd′] **71**–19
wheel [wēl] **159**–26
    wheelbarrow [wēl′băr′ō] **176**–3
    wheelchair [wēl′chër′] **113**–9
    wheel cover [wēl′ kŭv′ər] **158**–9
whisk [wǐsk] **78**–21
whiskers [wǐs′kərz] **216**–18
white [wǐt] **24**–14
    whiteboard [wǐt′börd′] **6**–3
    white bread [wǐt′ brĕd′] **71**–18
    White House [wǐt′ hows′] **138**–7
whole salmon [hōl′ săm′ən] **71**–3
wide [wǐd] **97**–36
widow [wǐd′ō] **41** ✦
widower [wǐd′ō ər] **41** ✦
width [wǐdth, wǐtth] **17**–19
wife [wǐf] **34**–12
    ex-wife [ĕks′ wǐf′] **35** ✦
    former wife [för′mər wǐf′] **35** ✦
wild [wǐld] **215** ✦
wildlife [wǐld′lǐf] **220**–3
willow [wǐl′ō] **210**–13
win [wǐn] **229** ✦
wind [wǐnd]
    windbreaker [wǐnd′brā′kər] **90**–24
    wind power [wǐnd′ pow′ər] **218**–2
    windshield [wǐnd′ shēld′] **158**–1
    windshield wipers [wǐnd′shēld′wǐ′pərz] **158**–2
    windsurfing [wǐnd′sür′fǐng] **227**–10, **227** ✦
window [wǐn′dō] **47**–11, **56**–17, **136**–7
    drive-thru window [drǐv′thrōō′ wǐn′dō] **128**–11
    ticket window [tǐk′ət wǐn′dō] **152**–12
    window pane [wǐn′dō pān′] **178**–16
windy [wǐn′dē] **13**–18
wine glass [wǐn′ glăs′] **83**–23
wing [wǐng] **70**–20, **214**–1
winter [wǐn′tər] **21**–40
    winter scarf [wǐn′tər′skärf′] **90**–5
WINTER AND WATER SPORTS
    [wǐn′tər ən wö′tər spörts′] **227**
wipe [wǐp] **60**–O
wipers [wǐ′pərz] **158**–2

wipes [wǐps] **37**–15, **61**–23
wire [wǐr] **181**–13
    wire stripper [wǐr′ strǐp′ər] **181**–42
wireless headset [wǐr′ləs hĕd′sĕt] **14**–14
wiring [wǐr′ǐng] **186**–7
withdraw [wǐdh drö′, wǐth–] **132**–F
witness [wǐt′nəs] **141**–11
wolf [wŏōlf] **216**–5
woman [wŏōm′ən] **30**–2
women [wǐ′mən] **30**–3
Women's Socks [wǐ′mənz säks′] **91**
Women's Underwear [wǐ′mənz ŭn′dər wër′] **91**
wood [wŏōd] **178**–18
    plywood [plī′wŏōd] **178**–17
    redwood [rĕd′wŏōd] **210**–18
    wood floor [wŏōd′ flör′] **58**–21
    woodpecker [wŏōd′pĕk′ər] **214**–8
    wood screw [wŏōd′ skrōō′] **180**–33
    wood stain [wŏōd′ stān′] **181**–24
    woodworking kit [wŏōd′wür′kǐng kǐt′] **232**–14
wooden spoon [wŏōd′n spōōn′] **78**–9
Woodwinds [wŏōd′wǐndz′] **238**
wool [wŏōl] **61**–5, **98**–3
word [würd] **190**–1
word problem [würd′ prä′bləm] **192**–11
Words [wördz] **8**
work [würk′] **121**–30, **154**–16
    workbook [würk′bŏōk′] **7**–26
    work gloves [würk′ glŭvz′] **92**–17, **179**–17
    work light [würk′ lǐt′] **181**–44
    work pants [würk′ pănts′] **92**–5
    work shirt [würk′ shürt′] **92**–2
work [würk′] **8**–I, **10**–J, **38**–K
WORK [würk′] **186**–187
Work Clothes [würk′ klōz′] **88**
worker [wür′kər]
    careful worker [kër′fəl wür′kər] **179**–2
    careless worker [kër′ləs wür′kər] **179**–1
    childcare worker [chǐld′kër wür′kər] **166**–16
    construction worker
        [kən strŭk′shən wür′kər] **178**–1
    dockworker [däk′wür′kər] **167**–23
    factory worker [făk′tə rē wür′kər, –trē] **175**–3
    farmworker [färm′wür′kər] **177**–8
    food preparation worker
        [fōōd′ prĕp ə rā′shən wür′kər] **185**–4
    garment worker [gär′mənt wür′kər] **167**–29
    postal worker [pō′stəl wür′kər] **169**–49
    sanitation worker [săn′ə tā′shən wür′kər] **169**–54
    social worker [sō′shəl wür′kər] **169**–57
Worker [wür′kər] **92, 93**
working [wür′kǐng]
    not working [nät′ wür′kǐng] **62**–1
    woodworking kit [wŏōd′wür′kǐng kǐt′] **232**–14
Working with a Partner [wür′kǐng wǐth ə pärt′nər] **8**
Working with Your Classmates
    [wür′kǐng wǐth yər klăs′māts′] **8**
work out [würk′ owt′] **230**–N
WORKPLACE [würk′ plās′] **164**–165
WORKPLACE CLOTHING
    [würk′ plās′ klō′dhǐng] **92**–93

world [würld]
    world languages [würld/ läng/gwĭ jəz] **189**–13
    world music [würld/ myōō/zĭk] **237**–32
WORLD MAP [würld/măp/] **202**–**203**
WORLD HISTORY [würld hĭs/tə rē] **199**
worm [würm] **212**–23
worried [wür/ēd] **42**–13
wrap [răp] **72**–24
wrap [răp] **240**–F
wrench [rĕnch] **158**–22, **181**–47, **181**–48
wrestling [rĕs/lĭng] **228**–17
wrinkled [rĭng/kəld] **101**–19
wrist [rĭst] **106**–14
    wristwatch [rĭst/wäch/, –wöch/] **94**–16
write [rīt]
    write a check [rīt/ ə chĕk/] **27**–D
    write a cover letter [rīt/ ə kŭv/ər lĕt/ər] **173**–G
    write a final draft [rīt/ ə fī/nəl drăft/] **191**–L
    write a first draft [rīt/ ə fürst/ drăft/] **191**–H
    write a note [rīt/ ə nōt/] **135**–A
    write a resume [rīt/ ə rĕ/zə mā/] **173**–F
    write a thank-you note
        [rīt/ ə thăngk/ yōō nōt/] **174**–O
    write back [rīt/ băk/] **135**–H
    write on the board [rīt/ ön dhə börd/] **6**–E
writer [rī/tər] **169**–64
Writing and Revising [rī/tĭng ən rĭ vī/ zĭng] **191**
Writing Process [rī/tĭng prä/sĕs] **191**
Writing Rules [rī/tĭng rōōlz] **190**
wrong way [röng/ wā/] **154**–2
xylophone [zī/lə fōn/] **238**–15
yard [yärd]
    courtyard [kört/ yärd/] **51**–21
    yardstick [yärd/stĭk/] **181**–16
YARD [yärd] **53**
yarn [yärn] **233**–22
year [yĭr] **20**–4, **31**–9, **31**–10
Year [yĭr] **21**
yellow [yĕl/ō] **24**–2
yesterday [yĕs/tər dā/, –dē] **20**–7
yield [yēld] **154**–9
yoga [yō/gə] **122**–4
yogurt [yō/gərt] **72**–22
young [yŭng] **32**–1
Your First License [yər fürst/ lī/səns] **137**
YOUR HEALTH [yər hĕlth/] **114**–**115**
zebra [zē/brə] **217**–33
zero [zĭr/ō] **16**
ZIP code [zĭp/ kōd/] **4**–9
zipper [zĭp/ər] **99**–25
Zones [zōnz] **19**
zoo [zōō] **222**–1
zoom lens [zōōm/ lĕnz/] **235**–23
zucchini [zōō kē/nē] **69**–25

Geographical Index

Continents

Africa [ăf/rĭ kə] **202–5**

Antarctica [ănt ärk/tĭ kə, –är/tĭ–] **202–7**

Asia [ā/zhə] **202–4**

Australia [ö strāl/yə] **202–6**

Europe [yŏŏr/əp] **202–3**

North America [nörth/ ə mĕr/ə kə] **200–201, 202–1**

South America [sowth/ ə mĕr/ə kə] **202–2**

Countries and other locations

Afghanistan [ăf găn/ə stän/] **203**

Albania [ăl bā/nē ə] **203**

Aleutian Islands [ə lōō/shən ī/ləndz] **200, 203**

Algeria [ăl jĭr/ē ə] **203**

American Samoa [ə mĕr/ə kən sə mō/ə] **202**

Andaman Islands [ăn/də mən ī/ləndz] **203**

Angola [ăng gō/lə] **203**

Argentina [är/jən tē/nə] **202**

Armenia [är mē/nē ə] **203**

Austria [ö/strē ə] **203**

Azerbaijan [ăz/ər bī jän/] **203**

Azores [ā/zörz] **202**

Baffin Island [băf/ən ī/lənd] **200**

Bahamas [bə hä/məz] **200, 202**

Bahrain [bä rān/] **203**

Bangladesh [băng/glə dĕsh/, bäng/–] **203**

Banks Island [bänks/ ī/lənd] **200**

Belarus [bē/lə rōōs/, byĕl/ə–] **203**

Belgium [bĕl/jəm] **203**

Belize [bə lēz/] **201, 202**

Benin [bə nĭn/, –nēn/] **203**

Bermuda Islands [bər myōō/də ī/ ləndz] **200, 202**

Bhutan [bōō tän/] **203**

Bolivia [bə lĭv/ē ə] **202**

Bosnia [bäz/nē ə] **203**

Botswana [bät swä/nə] **203**

Brazil [brə zĭl/] **202**

Brunei [brōō nī/] **203**

Bulgaria [bŭl gĕr/ē ə] **203**

Burkina Faso [bər kē/nə fä/sō] **203**

Burma [bür/mə] **203**

Burundi [bōō rōōn/dē] **203**

Cambodia [kăm bō/dē ə] **203**

Cameroon [kăm/ə rōōn/] **203**

Canada [kăn/ə də] **200, 202**

Canary Islands [kə nĕr/ē ī/ ləndz] **203**

Cape Verde [kāp/ vürd/] **202**

Central African Republic
    [sĕn/trəl ăf/rĭ kən rĭ pŭb/lĭk] **203**

Chad [chăd] **203**

Chile [chĭl/ē] **202**

China [chī/nə] **203**

Colombia [kə lŭm/bē ə] **202**

Comoros [kăm/ə rōz] **203**

Congo [käng/gō] **203**

Cook Islands [kŏŏk/ ī/ləndz] **202**

Corsica [kör/sĭ kə] **203**

Costa Rica [kōs/tə rē/kə, käs/–] **201, 202**

Croatia [krō ā/shə] **203**

Cuba [kyōō/bə] **201, 202**

Cyprus [sī/prəs] **203**

Czech Republic [chĕk/ rĭ pŭb/lĭk] **203**

Democratic Republic of the Congo
    [dĕm/ə krăt/ĭk rĭ pŭb/lĭk əv dhə käng/gō] **203**

Denmark [dĕn/märk] **203**

Devon Island [dĕv/ən ī/lənd] **200**

Djibouti [jĭ bōō/tē] **203**

Dominican Republic [də mĭn/ĭ kən rĭ pŭb/lĭk] **201, 202**

Ecuador [ĕk/wə dör/] **202**

Egypt [ē/jĭpt] **203**

Ellesmere Island [ĕl/əs mĭr/ ī/lənd] **200**

El Salvador [ĕl săl/və dör/] **201, 202**

Equatorial Guinea [ē/kwə tör/ē əl gĭn/ē, ĕk/wə–] **203**

Eritrea [ĕr/ə trē/ə] **203**

Estonia [ĕ stō/nē ə] **203**

Ethiopia [ē/thē ō/pē ə] **203**

Federated States of Micronesia
    [fĕd/ə rā/təd stāts/ əv mī/krə nē/zhə] **203**

Fiji [fē/jē] **203**

Finland [fĭn/lənd] **203**

France [frăns] **203**

Franz Josef Land [fränz/ yō/səf länd/] **203**

French Guiana [frĕnch/ gē ăn/ə, –ä/nə] **202**

French Polynesia [frĕnch/ päl/ə nē/zhə] **202**

Gabon [gä bôn/] **203**

Galápagos Islands [gə lä pə gōs ī/ləndz] **202**

Gambia [găm/bē ə] **203**

Georgia [jör/jə] **203**

Germany [jür/mə nē] **203**

Ghana [gä/nə] **203**

Greater Antilles [grā/tər ăn tĭl/ēz] **201**

Greece [grēs] **203**

Greenland [grēn/lənd, –länd/] **200, 202**

Guam [gwäm] **203**

Guatemala [gwä/tə mä/lə] **201, 202**

Guinea [gĭn/ē] **203**

Guinea-Bissau [gĭn/ē bĭ sow/] **203**

Guyana [gī ăn/ə] **202**

Haiti [hā/tē] **201, 202**

Hawaiian Islands [hə wī/ən ī/lənds] **200, 202**

Hispaniola [hĭs/pən yō/lə] **201**

Honduras [hän dŏŏr/əs] **201, 202**

Hong Kong [häng/ käng/] **203**

Hungary [hŭng/gə rē] **203**

Iceland [īs/lənd] **203**

India [ĭn/dē ə] **203**

Indonesia [ĭn/də nē/zhə] **203**

Iran [ĭ rän/, ĭ răn/] **203**

Iraq [ĭ räk/, ĭ răk/] **203**

Ireland [īr/lənd] **203**

Israel [ĭz/rē əl, –rā–] **203**

Italy [ĭt/l ē] **203**

Ivory Coast [īv/rē kōst/] **203**

Jamaica [jə mā/kə] **201, 202**

Japan [jə pän/] **203**

Jordan [jör/dn] **203**

Kazakhstan [kä/zäk stän/] **203**

Kenya [kĕn/yə, kēn/–] **203**

Kiribati [kĭr/ə bäs/] **203**

Kuwait [kōō wāt/] **203**

Kyrgyzstan [kĭr/gī stän/, –stän/] **203**

Laos [lows, lä/ōs] **203**

Latvia [lăt/vē ə] **203**

Lebanon [lĕb/ə nən, –nän/] **203**

Lesotho [lə sō/tō, –sōō/tōō] **203**

Lesser Antilles [lĕ/sər ăn tĭl/ēz] **201, 202**

Liberia [lī bĭr/ē ə] **203**

Libya [lĭb/ē ə] **203**

Lithuania [lĭth/ōō ā/nē ə] **203**

Luxembourg [lŭk/səm bürg/] **203**

Macedonia [măs/ə dō/nē ə] **203**

Madagascar [măd/ə găs/kər] **203**

Madeira Islands [mə dĭr/ə ī/ləndz] **203**

Malawi [mə lä/wē] **203**

Malaysia [mə lā/zhə] **203**

Maldives [möl/dēvz, mäl/–] **203**

Mali [mä/lē] **203**

Malta [möl/tə] **203**

Marshall Islands [mär/shəl ī/ləndz] **203**

Mauritania [mör/ə tā/nē ə] **203**

Mauritius [mö rĭsh/əs] **203**

Mexico [mĕk/sĭ kō/] **200, 201, 202**

Moldova [möl dō/və, mäl–] **203**

Monaco [män/ə kō/] **203**

Mongolia [mäng gō/lē ə] **203**

Montenegro [män/tə nē/grō, –nē/–] **203**

Morocco [mə räk/ō] **203**

Mozambique [mō/zəm bēk/] **203**

Namibia [nə mĭb/ē ə] **203**

Nepal [nə pöl/, –päl/] **203**

Netherlands [nĕdh/ər ləndz] **203**

New Caledonia [nōō/ kăl/ə dō/nē ə] **203**

New Zealand [nōō/ zē/lənd] **203**

Nicaragua [nĭk/ə rä/gwə] **201, 202**

Niger [nī/jər, nē zhër/] **203**

Nigeria [nī jĭr/ē ə] **203**

Northern Mariana Islands
    [nördh/ərn mä/rē ä/nə ī/ləndz] **203**

North Korea [nörth/ kə rē/ə] **203**

Norway [nör/wā] **203**

Oman [ō män/] **203**

Pakistan [păk/ə stän/] **203**

Palau [pə low/] **203**

Panama [păn/ə mä/] **201, 202**

Papua New Guinea [păp/yōō ə nōō/ gĭn/ē] **203**

Paraguay [păr/ə gwī/, –gwä/] **202**

Peru [pə rōō/] **202**

Philippines [fĭl/ə pēnz/, fĭl/ə pēnz/] **203**

Poland [pō/lənd] **203**

Portugal [pör/chə gəl] **203**

Puerto Rico [pwĕr/tə rē/kō, pör/tə–] **201, 202**

Qatar [kä/tär, kə tär/] **203**

Romania [rō mā/nē ə, rōō–] **203**

Russia [rŭsh/ə] **203**

Rwanda [rōō än/də] **203**

Samoa [sə mō/ə] **202**

Saudi Arabia [sow/dē ə rā/bē ə, sö/dē–] **203**

Senegal [sĕn/ə göl/, –gäl/] **203**

Serbia [sür/bē ə] **203**

Seychelles [sā shĕlz/, –shĕl/] **203**

Sierra Leone [sē ĕr/ə lē ōn/, –lē ō/nē] **203**

Singapore [sĭng/ə pör/] **203**

Slovakia [slō vä/kē ə] **203**

Slovenia [slō vē/nē ə] **203**

Society Islands [sə sī/ə tē ī/ləndz] **202**

Solomon Islands [säl/ə mən ī/ləndz] **203**

Somalia [sə mä/lē ə] **203**
South Africa [sowth/ ăf/rĭ kə] **203**
South Georgia [sowth/ jör/jə] **202**
South Korea [sowth/ kə rē/ə] **203**
Spain [spān] **203**
Sri Lanka [srē/ läng/kə, shrē/–] **203**
Sudan [so͞o dän/] **203**
Suriname [so͞or/ə nä/mə] **202**
Svalbard [sväl/bärd] **203**
Swaziland [swä/zē lănd/] **203**
Sweden [swēd/n] **203**
Switzerland [swĭt/sər lənd] **203**
Syria [sïr/ē ə] **203**
Tahiti [tə hē/tē] **202**
Taiwan [tī/wän/] **203**
Tajikistan [tä jĭk/ə stän/, –stän/] **203**
Tanzania [tăn/zə nē/ə] **203**
Tasmania [tăz mā/nē ə] **203**
Thailand [tī/lănd/, –lənd] **203**
Togo [tō/gō] **203**
Tonga [täng/gə] **202**
Tunisia [to͞o nē/zhə] **203**
Turkey [tür/kē] **203**
Turkmenistan [türk měn/ə stän/, –stän/] **203**
Uganda [yo͞o găn/də] **203**
Ukraine [yo͞o/krān, yo͞o krān/] **203**
United Arab Emirates [yo͞o nī/təd är/əb ĕm/ər əts] **203**
United Kingdom [yo͞o nī/təd kĭng/dəm] **203**
United States of America
    [yo͞o nī/təd stāts/ əv ə mĕr/ə kə] **200, 202**
Uruguay [yo͞or/ə gwī/, –gwä/] **202**
Uzbekistan [o͞oz bĕk/ə stän/, –stän/] **203**
Vanuatu [vä/no͞o ä/to͞o] **203**
Venezuela [vĕn/ə zwā/lə] **202**
Victoria Island [vĭk/tör ē ə ī/lənd] **200**
Vietnam [vē/ĕt näm/, –năm/] **203**
Wake Island [wāk/ ī/lənd] **203**
Western Sahara [wĕs/tərn sə här/ə] **203**
Yemen [yĕm/ən] **203**
Zambia [zăm/bē ə] **203**
Zanzibar [zăn/zə bär] **203**
Zimbabwe [zĭm bäb/wā] **203**

Bodies of water
Arctic Ocean [ärk/tĭk ō/shən] **200, 203**
Atlantic Ocean [ət lăn/ tĭk ō/shən] **200, 202–203**
Baffin Bay [băf/ən bā/] **200, 202**
Baltic Sea [böl/tĭk sē/] **203**
Beaufort Sea [bō/fərt sē/] **200**
Bering Sea [bër/ĭng sē/, bĭr/–] **200**
Black Sea [blăk/ sē/] **203**
Caribbean Sea [kăr/ə bē/ən sē/, kə rĭb/ē ən–] **201**
Caspian Sea [kăs/pē ən sē/] **203**
Coral Sea [kör/əl sē/] **203**
Gulf of Alaska [gŭlf/ əv ə lăs/kə] **200, 202**
Gulf of California [gŭlf/ əv kăl/ə förn/yə] **200**
Gulf of Mexico [gŭlf/ əv mĕk/sĭ kō/] **200, 202**
Hudson Bay [hŭd/sən bā/] **200, 202**
Indian Ocean [ĭn/dē ən ō/shən] **203**
Labrador Sea [lăb/rə dör/ sē/] **200**
Mediterranean Sea [mĕd/ə tə rā/nē ən sē/] **203**

North Atlantic Ocean [nörth/ ət lăn/tĭk ō/shən] **202**
North Pacific Ocean [nörth/ pə sĭf/ĭk ō/shən] **202, 203**
North Sea [nörth/ sē/] **203**
Pacific Ocean [pə sĭf/ĭk ō/shən] **200, 202, 203**
Philippine Sea [fĭl/ə pēn/ sē/] **203**
Red Sea [rĕd/ sē/] **203**
South Atlantic Ocean [sowth/ ət lăn/tĭk ō/shən] **203**
Southern Ocean [sŭdh/ərn ō/shən] **203**
South Pacific Ocean [sowth/ pə sĭf/ĭk ō/shən] **202, 203**

The United States of America
Capital: Washington, D.C. (District of Columbia)
    [wä/shĭng tən dē/sē/, wö/–] **200**

Regions of the United States
Mid-Atlantic States [mĭd/ət lăn/tĭk stāts/] **201–10**
Midwest [mĭd/wĕst/] **201–9**
New England [no͞o/ ĭng/glənd] **201–11**
Pacific States [pə sĭf/ĭk stāts/] **201–7**
Rocky Mountain States [räk/ē mown/tn stāts/] **201–8**
South [sowth] **201–13**
Southeast [sowth/ēst/] **201–13**
Southwest [sowth/wĕst/] **201–12**
West Coast [wĕst/ kōst/] **201–7**

States of the United States
Alabama [ăl/ə băm/ə] **200**
Alaska [ə lăs/kə] **200, 202**
Arizona [ăr/ə zō/nə] **200**
Arkansas [är/kən sö/] **200**
California [kăl/ə förn/yə] **200**
Colorado [kăl/ə răd/ō, –ra/dō] **200**
Connecticut [kə nĕt/ĭ kət] **200**
Delaware [dĕl/ə wër/] **200**
Florida [flör/ə də, flär/–] **200**
Georgia [jör/jə] **200**
Hawaii [hə wī/ē] **200**
Idaho [ī/də hō/] **200**
Illinois [ĭl/ə noy/] **200**
Indiana [ĭn/dē ăn/ə] **200**
Iowa [ī/ə wə] **200**
Kansas [kăn/zəs] **200**
Kentucky [kən tŭk/ē] **200**
Louisiana [lo͞o ē/zē ăn/ə] **200**
Maine [mān] **200**
Maryland [mĕr/ə lənd] **200**
Massachusetts [măs/ə cho͞o/səts] **200**
Michigan [mĭsh/ĭ gən] **200**
Minnesota [mĭn/ə sō/tə] **200**
Mississippi [mĭs/ə sĭp/ē] **200**
Missouri [mə zo͞or/ē, –zo͞or/ə] **200**
Montana [män tăn/ə] **200**
Nebraska [nə brăs/kə] **200**
Nevada [nə văd/ə, –vä/də] **200**
New Hampshire [no͞o/ hămp/shər] **200**
New Jersey [no͞o/ jür/zē] **200**
New Mexico [no͞o/ mĕk/sĭ kō/] **200**
New York [no͞o/ yörk/] **200**
North Carolina [nörth/ kăr/ə lī/nə] **200**
North Dakota [nörth/ də kō/tə] **200**
Ohio [ō hī/ō] **200**
Oklahoma [ō/klə hō/mə] **200**
Oregon [ör/ĭ gən, –găn/, är/–] **200**

Pennsylvania [pĕn/səl vān/yə] **200**
Rhode Island [rōd/ ī/lənd] **200**
South Carolina [sowth/ kăr/ə lī/nə] **200**
South Dakota [sowth/ də kō/tə] **200**
Tennessee [tĕn/ə sē/] **200**
Texas [tĕk/səs] **200**
Utah [yo͞o/tö, –tä] **200**
Vermont [vər mänt/] **200**
Virginia [vər jĭn/yə] **200**
Washington [wä/shĭng tən, wö/–] **200**
West Virginia [wĕst/ vər jĭn/yə] **200**
Wisconsin [wĭs kän/sən] **200**
Wyoming [wī ō/mĭng] **200**

Canada
Capital: Ottawa [ät/ə wə] **201**

Regions of Canada
British Columbia [brĭt/ĭsh kə lŭm/bē ə] **201–2**
Maritime Provinces [mër/ə tīm präv/ən səz] **201–6**
Northern Canada [nör/dhərn kăn/ə də] **201–1**
Ontario [än tër/ē ō/] **201–4**
Prairie Provinces [prër/ē präv/ən səz] **201–3**
Québec [kwĭ bĕk/] **201–5**

Provinces of Canada
Alberta [ăl bür/tə] **200**
British Columbia [brĭt/ĭsh kə lŭm/bē ə] **200**
Manitoba [măn/ə tō/bə] **200**
New Brunswick [no͞o/ brŭnz/wĭk] **200**
Newfoundland and Labrador
    [no͞o/fən lənd ən lă/brə dör/] **200**
Northwest Territories [nörth/wĕst/ tĕr/ə tör/ēz] **200**
Nova Scotia [nō/və skō/shə] **200**
Nunavut [no͞o/nə vo͞ot/] **200**
Ontario [än tër/ē ō/] **200**
Prince Edward Island [prĭns/ ĕd/wərd ī/lənd] **200**
Québec [kwĭ bĕk/] **200**
Saskatchewan [să skăch/ə wən, –wän/] **200**
Yukon [yo͞o/kän] **200**

Mexico
Capital: Mexico (City) [mĕk/sĭ kō/ (sĭt/ē)] **201**

Regions of Mexico
Chiapas Highlands [chē ä/pəs hī/ləndz] **201–18**
Gulf Coastal Plain [gŭlf/ kō/stəl plān/] **201–16**
Pacific Northwest [pə sĭf/ĭk nörth/wĕst] **201–14**
Plateau of Mexico [plă tō/ əv mĕk/sĭ kō/] **201–15**
Southern Uplands [sŭdh/ərn ŭp/ləndz] **201–17**
Yucatan Peninsula
    [yo͞o/kə tän/ pə nĭn/sə lə, yo͞o/kə tän/–] **201–19**

States of Mexico
Aguascalientes [ä/gwəs käl yĕn/täs] **201**
Baja California Norte [bä/hä käl/ə förn/yə nör/tä] **200**
Baja California Sur [bä/hä käl/ə förn/yə so͞or/] **200**
Campeche [käm pā/chä, käm pē/chē] **201**
Chiapas [chē ä/pəs] **201**
Chihuahua [chĭ wä/wä, –wə] **200**
Coahuila [kō/ə wē/lə] **200**
Colima Michoacán [kə lē/mə mē/chō ə kän/] **201**
Distrito Federal [dĭ strē/tō fĕd/ə räl/] **201**
Durango [do͞o räng/gō, –räng/–] **201**

Geographical Index

Index Índice

10 por ciento **17**–12
100 por ciento **17**–8
25 por ciento **17**–11
50 por ciento **17**–10
75 por ciento **17**–9
a cuadros **96**–24
a tiempo **19**–23, **161**–29
a.m. **18**–4
abadejo **212**–5
abalorios **95**–34
abdomen **107**–27
abedul **210**–7
abeja melífera **214**–25
abogado **168**–36
abogado defensor **141**–4
aborde el avión **160**–E
abra el libro **6**–G
abrace **2**–E
abrazadera en forma de C **180**–6
abrecosturas **100**–18
abrelatas **78**–1, **146**–8
abrelatas eléctrico **54**–14
abrigo **87**–14, **90**–2
abrigo cerrado **88**–3
abrigo de lana tejida **88**–2
abril **21**–28
abrocharle el cinturón **36**–L
abróchese el cinturón de
    seguridad **160**–H
abuela **34**–1
abuelo **34**–2
aburrido(a) **43**–25
acabe todo el medicamento **112**–C
acatar las leyes **140**–C
accesorios **181**–18
accesorios para aspiradora **61**–11
accidente aéreo **144**–3
accidente automovilístico **144**–2
acción **237**–19
acebo **210**–19
aceite **73**–31
acelerador **159**–46
acepte una disculpa **12**–G
acepte una invitación **12**–I
acera **129**–24
acolchar **232**–C
acomode los muebles **49**–Q
acondicionador **108**–11
acordeón **238**–19
acortar los pantalones **100**–B
acostarse **39**–Y
acta de nacimiento **40**–1
activista **199**–17
actor **166**–2
actriz **166**–2
actuar **233**–G
acuarelas **233**–21
acuario **222**–7
acupuntura **122**–2
acusado **141**–5

adaptador **234**–15
adjunte un archivo **197**–H
adjunte una foto **197**–G
administrador **50**–8, **120**–13
administradores **5**
admirador **229**–4
adolescente **31**–11
adorno **239**–15
adornos **99**
ADULTOS Y NIÑOS **30**–31
advertencias médicas **112**
aeromoza **161**–12
AEROPUERTO **160**–161
aeropuerto **151**–10
aerosol nasal **113**–32
afeitarse **109**–M
África **202**–5
afueras **52**–2
agallas **212**–2
agarraollas **78**–29
agarrar **230**–D
agencia de viajes **131**–14
agente de aduana **161**–17
agente de la TSA **160**–5
agente de pasajes **160**–3
agosto **21**–32
agradézcale a alguien **12**–E
agradézcale al entrevistador **174**–N
agresión **142**–3
agria **84**–4
agricultor **177**–13
AGRICULTURA Y LA GANADERÍA **177**
agua **209**–13, **225**–1
agua caliente **57**–9
agua en botella **146**–11
agua fría **57**–10
agua oxigenada **117**–9
águila **214**–9
aguja **98**–17, **100**–10, **210**–10
agujas de tejer **233**–23
ahogarse **116**–I
ahorrar agua **219**–E
aire acondicionado **159**–39
aislamiento **178**–14
ajedrez **232**–8
ajíes **69**–29
ajo **69**–30
ajustar el termostato **219**–J
ala **214**–1
alambre **181**–13
alargar los pantalones **100**–A
alas **70**–20
albañil **186**–8
albaricoques **68**–12
alberca **51**–22, **184**–22
albornoz **90**–25
álbum de fotos **235**–31
álbum de fotos digital **235**–32
alcachofas **69**–22
alcalde **139**–26

alcaldía **124**–8
alce **216**–1
aldea **52**–3
alegre **44**–5
alergias **111**–8
aleta **212**–1
aletas **225**–7
alfabeto **7**–13
alfalfa **177**–5
alfiler **100**–12
alfiler de seguridad **100**–14
alfiletero **100**–13
alfombra **56**–24, **58**–22
alfombra de goma **57**–5
alfombrilla para baño **57**–28
álgebra **192**–16
algodón **98**–1, **177**–6
alguacil **141**–13
alicates **180**–7
alicates pelacables **181**–42
alimentador **98**–20
alimentar **177**–D
alimentar las plantas **176**–D
alimentarlo **36**–C
alimento para bebé **37**–4
alimentos congelados **72**
alimentos envasados **72**
aliviado(a) **42**–15
aliviador de dolor **113**–26
almacén **175**–7, **185**–5
almacén-congelador **185**–3
almejas **71**–15
almidón para rociar **101**–12
almohada **58**–11
almohadilla **113**–13
almohadilla de tinta **183**–46
almohadilla para cambiar pañales **59**–2
alquiler a largo plazo **51**–28
alquiler de un apartamento **48**
alrededor del campus **5**
ALTERACIONES **100**
altiplano de México **201**–15
alto(a) **32**–4
altura **17**–16
ama de casa **168**–33
ama de llaves **168**–34, **184**–20
amalgama **119**–8
amamantarlo **36**–B
amanecer **18**–14
amarillo **24**–2
amarrar **86**–A
ambulancia **116**–1, **121**–34
americanos nativos **198**–3
ampolla **110**–15
añada las legumbres y hortalizas **77**–N
añadir el detergente **101**–B
analgésico **113**–26
anaranjado **24**–4
ancho **17**–19
anciana **30**–5

anciano(a) **32**–3
andador **113**–11
andamiaje **178**–4
andar en bicicleta **129**–D
anémona de mar **212**–24
anestesiar la boca **119**–C
anestesiólogo **121**–35
anfibios **212**
anfitriona **82**–2
anguila **212**–12
ángulo agudo **193**–28
ángulo de 90° **193**–26
ángulo obtuso **193**–27
ángulo recto **193**–26
ángulos **193**
anillo **95**–40
anillo barato **23**–20
anillo caro **23**–19
anillo de dentición **37**–25
anillos de cebolla **79**–4
animales de la granja **215**
animales de peluche **59**–15
ANIMALES DOMÉSTICOS
    Y ROEDORES **215**
aniversario **22**–3
año **20**–4
anochecer **18**–19
anote los resultados **195**–D
Antártica **202**–7
antebrazo **106**–13
antena **14**–9
antena parabólica **53**–6
anteojos **115**–7
anteojos de seguridad **92**–10
antes de una emergencia **146**
antiácido **113**–28
antifaz **239**–9
antiguas **199**–1
antílope **217**–35
antiparras **179**–10
antiperspirante **108**–5
anuncio de pancarta **44**–1
anuncios clasificados **48**–2
anuncios listados en Internet **48**–1
apagar las luces **219**–G
apague las luces **11**–P
apague su teléfono
    celular **160**–I, **174**–G
aparador **55**–24
aparador con vitrina **55**–22
aparato para trepar **224**–14
apartado postal (PO box) **135**–9
apartamento amueblado **48**–3
APARTAMENTOS **50**–51
apartamentos no amueblados **48**–4
apellido **4**–4
apertura de una cuenta **132**
apio **69**–9
aplaudir **148**–B
aplicarse **109**–P

apliques **99**–31
apósito estéril **117**–6
apóstrofe **190**–16
aprender a conducir **40**–E
aprender palabras nuevas **8**
araña **214**–29
arándanos **68**–16
arandela **180**–37
árbitro **229**–6
árbol de las pulgas **210**–24
árbol de Navidad **239**–16
árboles **208**–1
ÁRBOLES Y PLANTAS **210**
arce **210**–12
archivero **182**–11
archivista **182**–10
archivo de tarjetas giratorio **183**–44
arco **231**–6
ardilla **215**–21
ardilla listada **215**–20
área de control de seguridad **160**–4
área de espera **182**–16
área de examen **136**–2
área de juegos **130**–11
área de recepción **182**–15
área del comedor **46**–7
área rural **52**–4
área urbana **52**–1
arena **225**–23
aretes de colgar **95**–36
aretes de presilla **95**–37
armadillo **216**–8
armar **175**–C
armario **5**–11, **160**–1
armónica **238**–21
arquitecto(a) **166**–5
arranque **159**–33
arrastrar el cochecito **224**–A
arreglar una caries **119**–E
arreglo del cabello **33**
arrendador **51**–27
arrendajo azul **214**–6
arrendatario **50**–6
arrestar a un sospechoso **141**–A
arrojar **230**–C
arroz **67**–10, **81**–30, **177**–1
arteria **107**–36
artes **189**–15
artes del lenguaje **189**–9
artes marciales **228**–11
artículos de costura **100**
ARTÍCULOS DE LIMPIEZA **61**
artículos de oficina **183**
artista **166**–6
artritis **111**–16
asado **70**–1
asambleísta **139**–24
ascender los peldaños **153**–C
ascenso **172**–4
ascensor **50**–9, **131**–21, **184**–9

asesinato **142**–12
asfixiarse **116**–L, **116**–N
Asia **202**–4
asiente **12**–K
asiento de seguridad para
    el automóvil **37**–19
asiento delantero **159**–51
asiento en posición vertical **161**–28z
asiento para niños **159**–53
asiento reclinado **161**–27
asiento trasero **159**–54
asistenta de atención
    de la salud a domicilio **167**–32
asistente **120**–16
asistente administrativo(a) **166**–3
asistente certificada de
    enfermería **120**–12
asistente de director **5**–5
asistente del médico **168**–47
asistente del profesor o maestro **5**–16
asistente dental **119**–2, **167**–22
asistir a un cliente **95**–D
asma **111**–9
aspecto **32**
aspiradora **61**–10
aspirar la alfombra **60**–H
astronauta **205**–17
astrónomo **205**–22
asustado(a) **43**–23
atajar **230**–F
ataque **142**–11
atardecer **18**–18
ATENCIÓN DENTAL **119**
ATENCIÓN MÉDICA **118**
atender a los clientes **170**–T
atendiente en el mostrador **79**–17
aterriza **160**–K
atlas **133**–8
atletismo **228**–18
átomo **195**–28
atractivo(a) **32**–13
atragantarse **116**–L
atrapar **230**–D
atún **71**–7, **72**–19, **212**–8
audífono **14**–13, **115**–10
audífono inalámbrico **14**–14
audífonos **6**–8, **234**–4
audiolibro **133**–17
audiólogo **115**–9
auditorio **5**–18
auricular manual **14**–1
ausentarse por enfermedad **186**–A
Australia **202**–7
autobús **128**–9, **151**–14
autobús de servicio regular **152**–19
autobús puente **152**–19
automóvil **150**–1
automóvil de 2 puertas **156**–2
automóvil de 4 puertas **156**–1
automóvil deportivo **156**–4

automóvil urbano **152**–20
AUTOMÓVILES Y CAMIONES **156**
autopago **73**–10
autopista **155**–9
autor **133**–15, **169**–64
autora **169**–64
autoservicio **133**–10
auxiliar de estacionamiento **184**–3
avalancha **145**–18
avanzar rápido **235**–D
aventar **230**–C
aventarse **230**–K
aventuras **237**–19
avergonzado(a) **43**–24
avería del auto **162**–D
avión **150**–8
aviso **102**–1
aviso de "se alquila" **50**–7
aviso emergente **197**–9
avispa **214**–17
avocados **84**–6
ayer **20**–7
ayuda para los problemas de salud **115**
ayudante de la tienda **72**–4
ayudante de meseros **185**–13
ayudante del camarero **83**–12
ayudante del dentista **119**–2
ayudar a los pacientes **170**–B
ayude a las personas
    discapacitadas **147**–G
ayude a un compañero **8**–J
azadón de pico **178**–21
azafata **161**–12
azafrán **211**–17
azúcar **73**–30
azucarera **55**–14
azucena **211**–26
azul **24**–3
azul brillante **24**–12
azul claro **24**–11
azul marino **28**–5
azul oscuro **24**–10
azul turquesa **24**–9
azulejo **57**–12
babero **37**–5
bacalao **71**–8, **212**–5
bacinilla **37**–12, **121**–23
bádminton **228**–6
bagre **71**–2
bahía **204**–9
bailar **64**–A
baile **64**–A
bajarse del taxi **153**–F
bajo **238**–8
bajo cero **13**–7
bajo(a) **32**–6
balanza **57**–27, **72**–3, **195**–41
balcón **51**–20
balde **61**–7
baldosa **57**–12

baldosas **178**–11
ballena **213**–29
balompié **229**–12
balón de fútbol americano **231**–21
baloncesto **229**–8
bañarlo **36**–F
bañarse **108**–B
banca **224**–10
BANCO **132**
banco **124**–5
banda de cabeza **90**–3
bandeja **55**–17
bandeja de los postres **83**–10
bandeja de pintura **181**–51
bandeja para asar **78**–12
bandeja para galletas dulces **78**–27
bandera **239**–8
bañera **57**–2
BAÑO **57**
baño **46**–4
baños **5**–9
banqueta **129**–24
barba **33**–6
barbería **129**–19
barbilla **106**–1
barquillo de helado **79**–13
barra de avance **197**–15
barra de ensaladas **79**–24
barra de menús **197**–1
barra de sujeción **57**–11
barras de chocolate **73**–37
barrena **180**–28
barrer el piso **60**–J
base **109**–40, **193**–45, **194**–20
base conectora dock **234**–3
bastidor **98**–16
bastón **113**–16
bastones de esquí **231**–25
bastones dulces **239**–17
basura **148**–2
bata **91**–29
bata de hospital **121**–19
bata de playa **90**–25
bata la mezcla **77**–S
bata quirúrgica **121**–38
bate de béisbol **231**–14
batería **158**–20
batidor **78**–21
batidor de huevos **78**–20
batidora eléctrica **54**–25
baúl **158**–11
baúl para juguetes **59**–16
bayas **210**–20
bayas mixtas **81**–36
bazar **222**–6
beba **11**–J
beba líquidos **114**–C
bebé **31**–6
bebedero **224**–9
bebidas **73**

bebidas gaseosas **73**–34
beige **24**–18
béisbol **229**–9
berenjenas **69**–23
besarlo en la noche **36**–P
bese **3**–K
betabeles **69**–5
BIBLIOTECA **133**
biblioteca **5**–17, **125**–15
bibliotecario **133**–1
bibliotecario de información **133**–9
bicicleta **129**–22, **151**–15
bien **42**–14
bigote **33**–5
bigotes **216**–18
billar **228**–2
billete **152**–11, **152**–15
billete de abordaje **161**–20
billete de transbordo **152**–5
billetera **94**–13
billetes **26**
bioenergía **218**–9
biografía **133**–13
biología **194**
biólogo **194**–2
birrete **206**–7
bisonte **216**–6
bistec **70**–2, **81**–24
blanco **24**–14, **231**–7
blanqueador **101**–7
blazier **92**–12
bloque de colcha **232**–15
bloque de pilas secas **235**–26
bloqueador solar **108**–8
bloques **59**–19
blues **237**–22
blusa **87**–8
blusa bordada **88**–7
blusa lisa **97**–33
blusa vistosa **97**–34
blusón **93**–26
bobina **98**–21
boca **104**–7, **106**
boca de incendio **129**–27
bocina **159**–32
boda **22**–2
bodega **175**–7, **185**–5
bola **59**–12
bola de baloncesto **231**–4
bola de boliche **231**–5
bola de fútbol **231**–12
bola de voleibol **231**–3
bolas de carne **81**–27
boleto **152**–11, **152**–15
boliche **228**–3
bolígrafo **7**–22
bollo dulce **79**–16
bollo dulce Inglés **80**–5
bollos con forma de rosquilla **73**–40
bolsa **113**–13
bolsa **94**–19, **217**–50

bolsa bandolera **94**–17
bolsa de aire **159**–43
bolsa de comestibles **67**–13
bolsa de harina **74**–19
bolsa de hielo **117**–13
bolsa de lechuga **69**–31
bolsa para aspiradora **61**–12
bolsa para bebé **37**–16
bolsas **74**–7
bolsas de plástico
para almacenar **72**–25
bolsas para basura **61**–24
bolsillo **100**–7
bolso **87**–9
bolso de mano **89**–19
bombero **144**–9, **167**–26
bonito(a) **32**–14
bordado **233**–24
borde de la acera **129**–21
borde de la banqueta **129**–21
borrador **7**–19
borre **196**–C
borre el error **10**–M
bosque **204**–11
bosque húmedo **204**–1
botanas **73**
botas **95**–28
botas con punta de acero **92**–6
botas de esquí **231**–26
botas de seguridad **179**–20
botas para excursión **95**–31
botas para la lluvia **90**–20
botella **37**–1
botella de agua **74**–13
botella de agua caliente **113**–15
botellas **74**–1
botiquín **57**–22
botiquín de primeros
auxilios **117**–1, **146**–18
botón **99**–24
botón de avance **197**–3
botón de retroceso **197**–2
botón para llamar **121**–28
botones **184**–7
bóveda **132**–6
boxeo **228**–4
brazalete de emergencia médica **117**–3
brazaletes **95**–9
brazo **105**–14, **194**–23
brazo, la mano y los dedos **106**
brigadas de búsqueda y rescate **145**–20
broca **180**–28
brocha **181**–22
broche **108**–20
brócoli **69**–13
brote **211**–5
buceo con escafandra **227**–12
búfalo **216**–6
bufanda para el invierno **90**–5
bufandas **95**–12
buffet **185**–10

búho **214**–5
bulbo **211**–2
buldózer **178**–6
buriladora **180**–12
burrito **79**–9
burro **215**–3
buscando para comprar **28**–A
buscar avisos de
"se solicita ayuda" **173**–C
buscar en los anuncios
clasificados **173**–B
buscar en los sitios de empleos
de Internet **173**–D
buscar un libro **133**–B
busque la palabra **8**–A
busque refugio **147**–H
busque resguardo **147**–J
BÚSQUEDA DE CASA **48**–49
butaca **56**–22
buzón **53**–1, **128**–13, **135**–12
buzones **50**–11
caballete **233**–18
caballo **215**–4
caballo de mar **212**–13
cabecera **58**–10
cabello **104**–2
cabello a la altura de los hombros **33**–2
cabello castaño **33**–18
cabello corto **33**–1
cabello largo **33**–3
cabello liso **33**–9
cabello negro **33**–16
cabello ondulado **33**–10
cabello rizado **33**–11
cabello rubio **33**–17
cabestrillo **113**–19
cabeza **104**–1
cabeza de lechuga **69**–32
cabezal de la ducha **57**–13
cabina **156**–16
cabina del piloto **161**–10
cable **14**–2, **196**–13
cable desgastado **179**–5
cableado **186**–7
cables para pasar corriente **158**–21
cables puente **158**–21
cabra **215**–5
cacerola **54**–16, **78**–6
cacerola a vapor **78**–3
cacerola doble **78**–8
cachemir **98**–4
cachete **106**–3
cacillo **78**–25
cactus **210**–21
cadena **95**–33, **180**–41
cadena para puerta **51**–33
caerse **116**–O
café **24**–17, **73**–33, **81**–37
café descafeinado **81**–38
cafetera **54**–11
cafetería **5**–14, **126**–11

caimán **213**–36
caja **73**–12, **160**–6, **196**–3
caja de arena **224**–15
caja de cereal **74**–18
caja de fusibles **62**–13
caja de resortes **58**–19
caja de seguridad **132**–7
caja liviana **23**–14
caja para llevar **82**–5
caja pesada **23**–13
caja registradora **27**–10, **73**–15
caja torácica **107**–48
cajas **74**–6
cajas de cartón **74**–4
cajera **73**–13, **166**–15
cajero **73**–13, **132**–1, **166**–15
cajero automático **132**
cajón **54**–23, **58**–2
calabacín **69**–25
calabacita **69**–25
calabaza **69**–24
calamar **212**–7
calcetines **86**–6
calcetines al tobillo **91**–7
calcetines cortos **91**–11
calcetines de mujer **91**
calcetines de tobillo **91**–10
calcetines de trabajo **91**–8
calcetines de vestir **91**–9
calcetines hasta la rodilla **91**–12
calcetines unisex **91**
calculadora **17**–6, **183**–25
calcule **17**–B
cálculo **192**–19
caldera está estropeada **63**–15
CALENDARIO **20**–21
CALENDARIO DE EVENTOS **22**
calentador **159**–40
calentador de agua no funciona **62**–1
cálido **13**–3
caliente **13**–3
calificaciones **10**–4
calle **150**–5, **155**–8
calle sin salida **154**–6
callejón **51**–24
callejón sin salida **154**–6
CALLES DE LA CIUDAD **126**–127
calvo **33**–12
calzado atlético **86**–7
calzoncillos **91**–5
calzoncillos tipo bóxer **91**–4
calzoncitos de entrenamiento **37**–11
calzones **91**–14
cama **58**–9
cama de hospital **121**–22
cama doble amplia **184**–15
cámara congeladora **185**–3
cámara de 35 mm **235**–21
cámara de película **235**–21
Cámara de Representantes **138**–3
cámara de seguridad **50**–19

cámara de video y audio **235**–24
cámara digital **235**–19
cámara Web **196**–12
camarera **83**–9, **185**–8, **169**–56
camarero **82**–8
camarón **71**–11, **212**–18
cambiar **27**–I, **148**–C
cambiar las sábanas **60**–P
cambiar un cheque de viajero **27**–F
cambiarle el pañal **36**–G
cambie los servicios públicos a su
   nombre **49**–O
camello **217**–38
camilla **121**–33
camillero **120**–16
caminata **226**–7
camine a la clase **11**–C
camine con un amigo **143**–A
caminito **53**–2
camino para bicicletas **224**–3
camión **128**–9
camión de bomberos **144**–10
camión de la basura **127**–22
camión de mudanza **156**–18
camión semirremolque **156**–15
camión tanque **156**–20
camión volquete **156**–19
camionero **169**–61
camioneta **150**–6, **156**–6, **156**–12
camisa **86**–1
camisa arrugada **101**–19
camisa con mangas cortas **96**–12
camisa de dormir **91**–28
camisa de manga de 3/4 **96**–13
camisa de manga larga **96**–14
camisa de seguridad **93**–20
camisa de trabajo **92**–2
camisa deportiva **88**–4
camisa húmeda **101**–17
camisa planchada **101**–20
camisa seca **101**–18
camisa sin mangas **96**–11
camisa tipo polo **92**–14
camiseta **86**–4, **89**–24, **91**–1
camiseta limpia **101**–16
camiseta sucia **101**–15
camiseta térmica **91**–2
camisola **91**–21
camisón **91**–25, **93**–38
camisón de cirugía **93**–37
camotes **69**–18
campamento **226**–5
campaña política **139**–29
cámper **156**–9
campo **5**–2, **52**–4, **177**–7
campo de béisbol **224**–1
campo de búsqueda **197**–5
campo de texto **197**–13
campus **5**
caña **79**–18

caña de pescar **226**–18
Canadá del Norte **201**–1
canal **53**–4
canalón **53**–4
canas **33**–13
canasta **73**–9
cáncer **111**–10
cancha de baloncesto **229**–7
cancha de tenis **224**–6
canciones de cuna **37**–22
cangrejo **71**–9, **212**–20
canguro **217**–44
canilla **106**–21
cañón **204**–17
cansado(a) **43**–32
cantar una canción **238**–B
cantarle una canción de cuna **36**–O
cantimplora **226**–24
capacitación **172**–2
capacitación en el trabajo **172**–7
capacitación vocacional **172**–5
capital del estado **139**–22
capitalizar la primera letra de una
   oración **190**–B
capitalizar los nombres **190**–A
capitán de botones **184**–6
capitán de meseros **185**–12
capitolio de EE.UU. **138**–1.
capó **158**–4
capota **158**–4
cápsula **113**–23
capullo **211**–7
cara **106**, **193**–44
caracol **212**–22
carbón **218**–4
cardenal **110**–12
cardigan **88**–2
cardiólogo **120**–3
careta **239**–9
careta de buzo **225**–6
careta del receptor **231**–15
cargador **14**–10, **234**–17
cargador de pilas **235**–27
cargador para bebé **37**–17
cargar la lavadora **101**–C
caries **119**–7
carne **66**–2
carne de aves de corral **70**
carne de cerdo **70**
carne de cordero **70**
carne de res **70**
carne de res sofrita **76**–6
carne en conserva **71**–22
carne molida **70**–4
carne para guisar **70**–3
CARNE Y AVES DE CORRAL **70**
carnicero **166**–13
carpa **226**–10
carpa dorada **215**–16
carpeta de 3 anillos **7**–27

carpeta de archivo **183**–50
carpintero **62**–12, **166**–14
carrera de caballos **228**–19
carrera de fondo **227**–3
carretilla **176**–3
carretilla de mano **175**–11
carrito **37**–18, **72**–7, **129**–28
carrito de la limpieza **184**–19
carrito de maletas **184**–8
carroza **239**–2
carrusel de equipajes **161**–23
carta **134**–13
cartelera **7**–14
carteras **94**–2
cartero **134**–20
cartón de huevos **74**–16
cartucho de tinta **183**–45
Casa Blanca **138**–7
casa de muñecas **59**–18
casa móvil **52**–7
casa rodante **52**–7
CASA Y EL JARDÍN **53**
casaca roja **198**–9
casados nuevamente **35**–24
casarse **41**–K
cascada **204**–2
casco **93**–23
casco de fútbol americano **231**–19
casco de protección **92**–9
casco de protección para
   la cabeza **92**–1
casco protector **179**–9
castillo de arena **225**–12
castor **216**–9
catálogo en línea **133**–11
catarata **204**–2
catarinita **214**–26
catorce **16**
cavernas **220**–7
cazo **78**–7
cebollas **69**–19
cebollas verdes **69**–20
cebollitas **69**–20
cebra **217**–33
cecina **71**–22
ceder el paso **154**–9
ceja **106**–9
celebrar **206**–C
célula **194**–4
cementerio **127**–15
cemento **178**–10
cenar **39**–S
centavo **26**–1
centésimo **16**
centígrados **13**–2
centímetro [cm] **17**–14
centralita PBX **182**–13
CENTRO COMERCIAL **130–131**
centro comercial **126**–7
centro de convenciones **127**–24

centro de enseñanza preescolar **188**–1
centro de entretenimiento **56**–5
centro de fotocopiado **129**–18
CENTRO DE LA CIUDAD **124–125**
centro de recursos **172**–9
CENTRO ECOLÓGICO **208–209**
centro postal automático (CPA) **135**–10
cepillarse…el cabello **108**–I
cepillarse…los dientes **109**–J
cepillo **33**–22, **108**–14, **181**–57
cepillo de dientes **57**–23, **109**–22
cepillo de fregar **61**–20
cepillo de frotar **61**–20
cepillo para el inodoro **57**–20
cera para muebles **61**–8
cerca **177**–19
cerdo **215**–2
cereal caliente **80**–9
cerebro **107**–34
ceremonia **206**–6
cerezas **68**–11
cerezo silvestre **210**–15
cerillos **146**–16, **226**–21
cero **16**
cerradura está estropeada **62**–6
cerrajero **62**–11
cerrojo de seguridad **51**–34
certificado de defunción **41**–11
certificado de nacimiento **40**–1
certificado de naturalización **40**–6
Certified Mail™
   (el correo certificado) **134**–4
césped **53**–26
cesta **56**–3
cesta para el pan **83**–11
cesta para la ropa **57**–1
cesto para la ropa sucia **101**–2
cesto para pañales **37**–7
chaleco **89**–15
chaleco de seguridad de
   alta visibilidad **92**–4
chaleco relleno con plumas **90**–14
chaleco salvavidas **161**–25, **226**–14
champú **108**–10
chaqueta **90**–8
chaqueta de cuero **90**–4
chaqueta del chef **93**–29
chaqueta deportiva **89**–14
chaqueta gruesa **97**–27
chaqueta liviana **97**–28
chaqueta rellena con plumas **90**–16
charca **204**–21
charle **12**–B
charola **55**–17
chef **83**–16
chef de partida **185**–6
chef ejecutivo **185**–7
chef principal **185**–7
cheque **132**–13
cheque de pago **165**–14

chequera **132**–12
chícharos **69**–21
chiles **69**–29
chimenea **53**–5, **56**–13
chimpancé **217**–27
chinches **63**–24
chofer de taxi **152**–21
chofer lento **23**–4
chofer rápido **23**–3
choque **116**–B
chorrera **224**–13
chuletas de cerdo **70**–10
chuletas de cordero **70**–15
chuletas de ternera **70**–6
chupete **37**–24
chupón **37**–2, **37**–24, **181**–50
ciclismo **228**–5
ciclismo de montañas **226**–8
ciclista **224**–2
ciego(a) **32**–11
cielo **209**–9
cien **16**
cien dólares **26**–12
cien mil **16**
ciencia-ficción **237**–18
ciencias **189**–11
CIENCIAS **194–195**
ciento uno **16**
cierre **99**–25
cierre el libro **6**–H
cierre está estropeado **97**–39
cierre las puertas con llave **143**–E
cierres **99**
cilindro **193**–41
cilindro graduado **195**–38
cima de la montaña **204**–14
cincel **181**–55
cinco **16**
cinco centavos **26**–2
cinco dólares **26**–8
cincuenta **16**
cincuenta dólares **26**–11
cine **126**–6, **222**–2
cinta **99**–30
cinta adhesiva para conductos **181**–49
cinta adhesiva para empacar **183**–32
cinta adhesiva para proteger
    bordes **181**–53
cinta adhesiva transparente **183**–30
cinta aislante **181**–43
cinta correctora **183**–37
cinta de aislar **181**–43
cinta de enganche **99**–29
cinta de medir **100**–17, **181**–45
cinta de video **133**–18
cinta estéril **117**–7
cinta transportadora **175**–9
cinturón **100**–5
círculo **193**–34
circunferencia **193**–36

ciruelas **68**–13
ciruelas pasas **68**–26
cirujano **121**–36
cita **22**–4, **118**–1, **190**–9
citoplasma **194**–9
ciudad **4**–7, **52**–1
civilizaciones **199**
clarinete **238**–2
clásica **237**–21
clave **155**–6
clavel **211**–20
clavelón **211**–13
clavo **180**–34
claxon **159**–32
cliente **72**–1, **82**–6, **94**–4, **132**–2,
    164–2, **185**–9
clínica **186**–2
clip **183**–31
cloro **101**–7
clóset **58**–5
club nocturno **223**–12
cobija **58**–15, **91**–27
cobijas **146**–7
cobra **213**–41
cobre un cheque **132**–A
cochecito **37**–20
cochera **124**–1
cochino **215**–2
cociente **192**–10
cocina **46**–5, **54**–18, **83**–15
COCINA **54**
cocina de campamento **226**–16
cocina de restaurante **185**
cocinar **76**–C, **170**–C
cocine a fuego lento **77**–P
cocine el brócoli al vapor **77**–D
cocinero de platos rápidos **185**–1
cocodrilo **213**–37
cocos **68**–24
código de área **4**–10, **15**–29
código de barras **27**–4
código de la ciudad **15**–34
código del país **15**–33
código postal **4**–9
codo **106**–12
coja el lápiz **6**–I
cojín **56**–2
col **69**–2
cola **216**–22
coladera **78**–22
colcha **58**–16, **59**–11
colchón **58**–20
coleccionar objetos **232**–A
colgar la ropa **101**–H
colibrí **214**–10
coliflor **69**–14
colinas **204**–16
collar de perlas **95**–39
collares **95**–10
colmillo **217**–48

colocar ladrillos **178**–B
colonia **108**–6
colonos **198**–2
color crema **24**–16
color marfil **24**–16
colores **24**
colores básicos **24**
colores diferentes **23**–16
colores neutros **24**
Columbia Británica **201**–2
columna vertebral **107**–49
columpios **224**–11
coma **11**–I, **190**–14
coma una dieta saludable **114**–F
comedia **237**–13
comedia de situaciones **236**–2
COMEDOR **55**
comedor **82**–1
comejenes **63**–22
comenzar **230**–R
comer en un restaurante **185**
comer la cena **39**–S
cometa **205**–24, **225**–2
comida enlatada **146**–9
comida envasada **146**–10
comida para mascotas **72**–5
comidas congeladas **72**–28
comillas **190**–15
comisaría **124**–6
cómo abrir sesión y enviar un correo
    electrónico **197**
cómo llenar un formulario **4**
cómo navegar por una página Web **197**
CÓMO TENER ÉXITO EN LA ESCUELA **10**
cómo tomar una prueba **10**
cómoda **58**–1, **59**–6
compaginar papeles **171**–E
compañero(a)s de habitación **64**–1
comparación de la ropa **97**
comparecer ante el tribunal **141**–C
comparta un libro **8**–M
compartimiento **82**–4
compartimiento de guantes **159**–44
compartimiento para el equipaje de
    mano **161**–13
competir en una carrera **230**–S
comportarse mal **44**–B
composición **190**–4, **199**–15
COMPOSICIÓN EN INGLÉS **190–191**
compositor **199**–14
compra de un automóvil usado **157**
compra de una casa **49**
COMPRA Y MANTENIMIENTO DE UN
    AUTOMÓVIL **157**
comprar **27**–G, **94**–A
comprar productos reciclados **219**–D
comprar una casa **41**–M
cómprese un bocadito **11**–K
comprobante de depósito **132**–4
comprometerse para casarse **41**–J

computador **183**–17
computadora **7**–15
computadora portátil **196**–16
COMPUTADORAS **196**
computadores de escritorio **196**
con cuadros **96**–22
con flores **96**–25
con lunares **96**–21
con problemas auditivos **32**–12
con rayas **96**–20
con smog **13**–14
con trenzas tejidas en el cabello **33**–14
con viento **13**–18
concejal **139**–28
concertar una entrevista **173**–I
concesionaria de autos **126**–4
concha (de mar) **225**–24
concierto de música clásica **223**–14
concierto de música rock **222**–5
conclusión **190**–8
condenado **141**–15
condenar al acusado **141**–E
condiciones del tiempo **13**
condo **52**–5
condominio **52**–5
conducir a través del túnel **153**–K
conducir al trabajo **37**–24
conducir un camión **170**–E
conducir una orquesta **238**–C
conducto para basura **51**–26
conductor **152**–13
conejillo de Indias **215**–14
conejo **215**–13
CONFECCIÓN DE ROPA **98–99**
conferencia de padres y maestros **22**–5
confeti **239**–3
confundido(a) **43**–26
congelador **54**–10
congestión nasal **110**–7
congresista **138**–4
Congreso **138**–2
cono **193**–40, **210**–11
conozca a sus vecinos **49**–R
conseguir empleo **40**–F
consejero(a) **5**–6
consejo municipal **139**–27
conserje **184**–4
consolarlo **36**–I
constelación **205**–14
constitución **198**–12
CONSTRUCCIÓN **178**
contactos fuera del estado **146**–2
contador(a) **166**–1
contaminación **218**
contaminación del agua **218**–14
contaminación del aire **218**–11
contar **84**–A
contenedor de queso fresco **74**–17
contenedores **74**–5
CONTENEDORES Y ENVASES **74**

contento(a) **43**–31
contestadora **14**–17
conteste una pregunta **8**–L
continentes **202**
contorneador **180**–12
contrachapada **178**–18
contrapuerta **53**–10
contratar a un abogado **141**–B
contratista **186**–5
contrato de alquiler **51**–28
control de la cama **121**–27
control del juego de video **232**–4
control remoto universal **234**–9
convergir **154**–10
CONVERSACIÓN DIARIA **12**
converse con alguien **11**–L
convertible **156**–5
convertir en abono las sobras de
　　alimentos **219**–M
convertirse en abuelo(a) **41**–N
convertirse en ciudadano **40**–G
convierta **17**–D
convierta las medidas **75**–C
copa de vino **83**–23
copias de documentos
　　importantes **146**–20
copias de las tarjetas de identificación
　　y de crédito **146**–19
copie la palabra **8**–E
coral **220**–5
corazón **107**–38, **239**–6
corazones **233**–31
corbata **88**–12, **92**–13
corbata ancha **97**–36
corbata de moño **89**–16
corbata estrecha **97**–35
cordillera **204**–15
cordón de alimentación **196**–2
cordón del zapato **94**–24
cordón elástico **181**–15
cordón prolongador **181**–14
corduroy **99**–11
cornamenta del ciervo **216**–16
cornejo **210**–15
corno **238**–11
corno francés **238**–13
corona **119**–9
corra a la clase **11**–D
corral **177**–17
correa de herramientas **92**–3
correa de seguridad **159**–52
correa de soporte para
　　la espalda **179**–18
correas **94**–6
correo aéreo **134**–5
correo de otros medios
　　de información **134**–3
correr alrededor de la esquina **153**–H
corrija el error **10**–N
corríjalo **191**–I

cortador **176**–12
cortador rotatorio **232**–16
cortadora de césped **176**–6
cortadora de papel **183**–22
cortar el cabello **33**–A
cortar el césped **176**–A
cortarse…las uñas **109**–N
cortaúñas **109**–31
cortaviento **90**–24
corte **110**–13
corte el apio en trocitos **77**–J
corte el pollo **77**–I
corte las cebollas **77**–L
Corte Suprema **138**–11
cortina de la ducha **57**–14
cortinas **56**–16, **58**–7
cosechar **177**–B
coser a mano **98**–B
coser a máquina **98**–A
coser ropa **170**–L
costa oeste **201**–7
costillas a la parrilla **76**–2
costillas de res **70**–5
costo **27**–7
costurera **100**–1
country **237**–27
coupe **156**–2
coyote **216**–3
CPR (la resucitación
　　cardiopulmonar) **117**–17
CPU **196**–4
cráneo **107**–47
crema **81**–41, **113**–25
crema agria **72**–21
crema antihistamínica **117**–10
crema de afeitar **109**–29
crema para el cuerpo **108**–9
creyones **59**–14
CRIANZA Y CUIDADO DE
　　LOS NIÑOS **36**–**37**
crin **217**–49
crisantemo **211**–21
cromosoma **194**–8
cronómetro de cocina **78**–18
cruce del ferrocarril **154**–14
cruce escolar **154**–15
cruce peatonal **128**–15, **154**–13
cruzar corriendo la calle **153**–G
cruzar imprudentemente
　　una calle **128**–C
cruzar la calle **128**–A
cuaderno de papel de
　　tamaño legal **183**–38
cuaderno de trabajo **7**–26
cuadrado **193**–30
cuadragésimo **16**
cuadro **56**–9
cuarenta **16**
cuarto **16**, **17**–4
cuarto de galón de leche **75**–4

cuarto de lavado **83**–13
cuarto de taza de azúcar morena **75**–8
cuarto menguante **205**–11
cuarto para las dos **18**–13
cuatro **16**
cuatro de julio **22**–13
cubeta **61**–7
cubículo **182**–7
cubo **61**–7, **193**–38, **225**–8
cubrecama **58**–16, **59**–11
cucarachas **63**–26
cuchara **55**–5
cuchara de madera **78**–9
cuchara para sopa **83**–32
cucharada de azúcar **75**–7
cucharadita de sal **75**–6
cucharita **83**–31
cucharón **78**–7
cuchilla **180**–27
cuchilla de afeitar **109**–28
cuchillo **55**–4, **83**–30
cuchillo de pelar **78**–16
cuchillo de trinchar **78**–12
cuchillo multiusos **226**–20
cuchillo para carne **83**–29
cuelgue **15**–D
cuello **100**–4, **104**–3
cuentas **95**–34, **99**–32
cuerda **101**–9, **226**–19
cuerda para saltar **224**–4
cuerno **216**–21
cuero **98**–6
CUERPO **104**–**105**
cuerpo **190**–7
cueva **220**–6
cuidado de su automóvil **157**
CUIDADO DE SU SALUD **114**–**115**
cuidar niños **170**–P
culebra americana no venenosa **213**–39
cultivador **177**–13
cumpla con las indicaciones
　　médicas **114**–J
cumpleaños **22**–1
cuna **59**–3
cuna mecedora **59**–20
cuñada **34**–16
cuñado **34**–17
cupones **67**–15
curso en línea **172**–8
cursor **197**–14
cuy **215**–14
dados **232**–6
damas **232**–7
dar un discurso **148**–A
dar una clase **122**–B
darse una ducha **108**–A
dátiles **68**–28
dé su nombre **15**–F
dé un apretón de manos **3**–J
DE VUELTA DEL MERCADO **66**–**67**

debajo del capó **158**
debatir **139**–B
décimo **16**
decimocuarto **16**
decimonoveno **16**
decimooctavo **16**
decimoquinto **16**
decimoséptimo **16**
decimosexto **16**
decimotercero **16**
declaración de aduana **161**–16
declaración de derechos **198**–13
declaración de la independencia **198**–5
decoraciones **99**–31, **99**–33, **240**–1
dedal **100**–15
dedo **105**–16
dedo del pie **105**–10
dedo hinchado **110**–16
deducciones **165**–13
defensa **158**–8
dejar a los niños **38**–G
dejar un mensaje **171**–P
dejar una propina **82**–J
del oeste **237**–15
delantal **93**–38
delantal de laboratorio **93**–33
deletree su nombre **4**–B
delfín **213**–31
delgado(a) **32**–9
DELINCUENCIA **142**
delineador (de ojos) **109**–36
demencia **111**–18
demostración **122**–6
denominador **192**–6
dentadura postiza **119**–10
dentista **119**–1
dentro de la maletera **158**
dentro del automóvil **159**
dentro del botiquín **117**
DENTRO Y FUERA DEL
　　CUERPO **106**–**107**
denuncie los delitos a la policía **143**–K
denuncie los paquetes
　　sospechosos **143**–J
departamento de joyería **95**–8
DEPARTAMENTO DE VEHÍCULOS
　　MOTORIZADOS (DMV) **136**–**137**
Departamento de Vehículos
　　Motorizados **124**–4
departamento de zapatos **95**–7
dependiente de la gasolinera **162**–3
dependiente de la tienda
　　minorista **169**–53
dependiente encargado del despacho
　　de mercadería **175**–14
deporte de la patineta **228**–13
deporte de la tabla hawaiana **227**–9
DEPORTES DE INVIERNO
　　Y ACUÁTICOS **227**
DEPORTES EN EQUIPO **229**

DEPORTES INDIVIDUALES **228**
depósito **132**–3
depósito de almacenamiento **50**–17
depósito de basura **51**–23
depresión **115**–5
derechos **140**
DERECHOS Y RESPONSABILIDADES
    CÍVICAS **140**
derrame de petróleo **218**–17
derrumbe **144**–6
desagüe **57**–7
desatascador **181**–50
desayunar **38**–E
descansar **39**–U
descanse en la cama **114**–B
descargar la secadora **101**–E
descender los peldaños **153**–D
descifre las palabras **9**–W
descongelador **159**–41
DESCRIPCIÓN DE LA ROPA **96**–**97**
DESCRIPCIÓN DE LAS PERSONAS **32**
DESCRIPCIÓN DE LOS OBJETOS **23**
DESCRIPCIÓN DEL CABELLO **33**
desechos peligrosos **218**–12
desempaque **49**–N
desfile **239**–1
desierto **204**–4
desilusionada **28**–4
desmaquillador **109**–42
desodorante **108**–5
desorden **64**–8
despachar **175**–D
despega **160**–J
despejado **13**–9
despertarse **38**–A
desplantador **176**–10
destino **162**–5
destornillador **180**–30
destornillador de estrella **180**–31
destornillador Phillips **180**–31
DESTREZAS DE ENTREVISTA **174**
DESTREZAS DE OFICINA **171**
DESTREZAS LABORALES **170**
destrezas telefónicas **171**–L
desván **47**–8
desvestirlo **36**–E
detector de humo **51**–29
detenerse **154**–1
deténgase en la esquina **155**–D
detergente para ropa **101**–8
devolución de botellas **73**–16
devolver **27**–H
devolver un libro **133**–D
día **20**–2
día de acción de gracias **22**–17
día de año nuevo **22**–9
día de Colón **22**–15
día de la independencia **22**–13
día de la recordación **22**–12

día de los presidentes **22**–11
día de los veteranos **22**–16
día de Martin Luther King Jr. **22**–10
DÍA EN LA ESCUELA **11**
día feriado legal **22**–8
diabetes **111**–12
diafragma **194**–18
diagonal **193**–31
diamantes **233**–29
diámetro **193**–36
diariamente **20**–21
días de la semana **20**, **20**–16
DÍAS FERIADOS **239**
días feriados legales **22**
dibujo animado **236**–3
diccionario **7**–30
diccionario gráfico **7**–31
diciembre **21**–36
dictador **199**–6
dicte una oración **8**–N
diecinueve **16**
dieciocho **16**
dieciséis **16**
diecisiete **16**
dientes **106**–7
dietista **120**–15
diez **16**
diez centavos **26**–3
diez dólares **26**–9
diez mil **16**
diferencia **192**–8
diga cuál es la emergencia **15**–G
diga su nombre **4**–A
diga, "Hasta luego" **3**–L
diga, "Hola" **2**–A
dimensiones **17**
DINERO **26**
diploma **40**–3
diploma universitario **41**–7
dirección **4**–5
dirección de un sitio Web **197**–4
dirección del destinatario **134**–22
direcciones **155**
DIRECCIONES Y MAPAS **155**
director **5**–4
directora **5**–4
directorio **131**–24
discapacidades **32**
disciplinarlo **36**–K
disc-jockey **64**–4
disco duro **196**–6
disco volador **231**–27
discúlpese **12**–F
discuta un problema **8**–G
diseñador **175**–2
diseñador de paisajes **176**–5
diseñador gráfico **167**–30
diseñadora **175**–2
diseñar **175**–A

disfraz **239**–11
disiente **12**–L
disparar **230**–H
dispositivo salvavidas **225**–20
distribución de los cubiertos
    y vajillas **83**–17
divida **17**–A
dividir **192**–D
dobladillo **100**–8
doblar la ropa **101**–F
doblarse **230**–O
doble cama **184**–14
doce **16**
doctor(a) **118**–5
doctor(a) en veterinaria **169**–62
dólar **26**–7
dolor **115**–3
dolor de cabeza **110**–1
dolor de espalda **110**–5
dolor de estómago **110**–4
dolor de garganta **110**–6
dolor de muelas **110**–2
dolor de oído **110**–3
domingo **20**–8
dormirse **39**–Z
DORMITORIO **58**
dormitorio **46**–2
DORMITORIO DE LOS NIÑOS **59**
dormitorio de los niños **47**–9
dos **16**
dos puntos **190**–17
dos veces por semana **20**–23
dosis **112**–6
driblar **230**–J
drogas ilegales **142**–6
ducharse **108**–A
dúeña de negocios **166**–11
dueño **51**–27
dueño de la fábrica **175**–1
dueño de negocios **166**–11
dulcería **131**–17
dulces **84**–8, **239**–12
duna **204**–5
duodécimo **16**
durante una emergencia **147**
duraznos **68**–10
DVD (disco de video digital) **133**–19
échele salsa encima con
    una cuchara **77**–F
eclipse solar **205**–16
ecuación **192**–13
edad **32**
edificio de apartamentos **50**–1
edificio de oficinas **124**–2
edítelo **191**–I
educación física **189**–17
efectivo y las monedas **146**–17
ejercicio aeróbico **122**–5
ejército **138**–14, **199**–11

ejotes **69**–8
elabore respuestas **8**–H
elabore soluciones **8**–H
elección **139**
electricista **62**–9
electrón **195**–30
ELECTRÓNICA Y FOTOGRAFÍA **234**–**235**
elefante **217**–42
elevador **50**–9, **131**–21, **184**–9
elevador de carga **175**–12
elogiarlo **36**–J
elogie a alguien **12**–C
embarazada **32**–15
embrague **159**–49
embudo **195**–40
EMERGENCIAS MÉDICAS **116**
EMERGENCIAS Y DESASTRES
    NATURALES **144**–**145**
emocionado(a) **43**–22
empacador(a) **175**–8
empacar **162**–A
empaque **49**–M
empareje los objetos **9**–T
emperador **199**–3
empezar a ir al colegio **40**–B
empleada **5**–13
empleada de correos **169**–49
empleada de una fábrica
    de ropa **167**–29
empleado **5**–13, **165**–9, **182**–2
empleado de almacén **169**–59
empleado de correos **135**–7, **169**–49
empleado de servicios de la higiene
    pública **169**–54
empleado de una casa
    de mudanzas **168**–42
empleado de una fábrica
    de ropa **167**–29
empleado del DMV **136**–3
empleador **164**–4
EMPLEOS Y PROFESIONES **166**–**169**
empujar el columpio **224**–B
EN BUSCA DE TRABAJO **173**
en el avión **161**
en el lugar del concesionario **158**
en el punto de inspección
    de seguridad **160**
en el taller del mecánico **158**
en la aduana **161**
en la puerta **161**
en la sala de espera **118**
en la sala de examen **118**
en la terminal de la línea aérea **160**
en punto **18**–6
enagua entera **91**–22
enamorado(a) **42**–18
enamorarse **40**–H
encaje **99**–9
encargada del servicio de comida y
    bebidas **185**–16

encargado de admisiones **120**–14
encargado de nómina **165**–10
encargado de pedidos **175**–10
enchufe **58**–28, **234**–16
enchufe del teléfono **14**–3
encías **106**–6
encienda las luces **11**–B
encierre en un círculo la respuesta **9**–Q
encuentre su asiento **160**–F
endulzante artificial **79**–20
energía de biomasas **218**–9
energía de fusión **218**–10
energía eólica **218**–2
energía geotérmica **218**–7
energía hidroeléctrica **218**–5
energía nuclear **218**–8
energía solar **218**–1
ENERGÍA Y CONSERVACIÓN **218–219**
enero **21**–25
enfermedad de las encías **119**–11
enfermedades cardíacas **111**–11
enfermedades comunes y de la
    infancia **111**
ENFERMEDADES Y
    LOS PADECIMIENTOS **111**
enfermedades y padecimientos
    graves **111**
enfermera **118**–8, **168**–44
enfermera con licencia práctica **120**–11
enfermera quirúrgica **120**–9
enfermera registrada **120**–10
enfermero **118**–8
enfermero de urgencias **116**–2
enfermo(a) **42**–12
engrapadora **183**–28
engrapar **171**–F
engrase una cazuela para hornear **77**–B
enjuagarse…el cabello **108**–F
enjuague bucal **109**–25
enlaces **197**–10
ennegrezca el espacio correspondiente
    a la respuesta **10**–K
enojado(a) **43**–29
enredadera **210**–22
ensalada de cena **80**–15
ensalada de col **80**–18
ensalada de espinaca **80**–13
ensalada de frutas **80**–21
ensalada de papas **80**–19
ensalada de pasta **80**–20
ensalada del chef **80**–14
ensamblador(a) **166**–7
ensamblar **175**–C
ensamblar componentes **170**–A
ensayo **190**–4
enseñar **170**–Q
enterito **93**–24
entero **17**–1
entrada **164**–1
entrada **50**

entrada al apartamento **51**
entrada de la sala de emergencias **121**
entrada del garaje **53**–8
entrar en la autopista **153**–I
entregue la prueba **10**–O
entregue la tarjeta **135**–E
entregue los libros **11**–G
entregue su papel **191**–M
entrenador **5**–20, **229**–2
entrenar **230**–N
ENTRETENIMIENTO **236–237**
entusiasta **229**–4
envase especial para remitir objetos
    por correo **183**–40
envenenamiento con
    insecticidas **218**–16
envenenarse **116**–J
enviar su resumé y su carta de
    presentación **173**–H
enviar un documento por fax **171**–G
envíe el correo electrónico **197**–I
envíe la tarjeta **135**–D
envío de una tarjeta **135**
envío por vía terrestre **134**–6
envolver **240**–F
equipaje **161**–18
equipo **229**–3
equipo averiado o roto **179**–4
equipo de seguridad **179**
EQUIPO DEPORTIVO **231**
equipo para trabajar en
    el campo **177**–12
equipos de oficina **183**
equitación **226**–9
erizo de mar **212**–21
erupción **110**–10
erupción volcánica **145**–16
es demasiado caro **97**–55
es demasiado grande **97**–38
es demasiado pequeña **97**–37
escala **155**–7, **195**–41
escalera **178**–2
escalera automática **131**–23
escaleras **50**–10
escalerilla **61**–13
escalones **53**–3
escalones están rotos **62**–7
escalope **212**–19
escalopes **71**–12
escamas **212**–3
escanear un documento **171**–H
escáner **183**–20
escape **158**–15
escarabajo **214**–18
esclavo **198**–4
escoba **61**–16
escoja la respuesta correcta **9**–P
esconderse **240**–D
escorpión **214**–30

escriba con el teclado **196**–A
escriba el borrador final **191**–L
escriba el mensaje **197**–E
escriba el tema **197**–D
escriba en la pizarra **6**–E
escriba la dirección en el sobre **135**–B
escriba un mensaje en la tarjeta **135**–A
escriba un primer borrador **191**–H
escríbale una nota
    de agradecimiento **174**–O
escribiente **141**–12
escribir a máquina **170**–R
escribir un cheque (personal) **27**–D
escribir un resumé **173**–F
escribir una carta a máquina **171**–A
escribir una carta
    de presentación **173**–G
escritor(a) **169**–64
escritorio **6**–7, **182**–9
escritorio de distribución **133**–2
escritura del terreno **41**–9
escucharle el corazón **118**–C
escuche cuidadosamente **174**–K
escuche un CD **6**–C
ESCUELA **5**
escuela **126**–9
escuela de párvulos **188**–1
escuela intermedia **188**–3
escuela para adultos **188**–8
escuela primaria **188**–2
escuela secundaria **188**–4
escuela técnica **188**–5
escuela vocacional **188**–5
ESCUELAS Y MATERIAS **188–189**
escurridor **61**–15, **78**–17
esfera **193**–42
esgrima **228**–7
esmalte de uñas **109**–33
esmog **218**–11
esmoquin **89**–17
esnórquel **227**–11
espacio de estacionamiento **50**–18
espadas **233**–30
espalda **104**–5
espárragos **69**–26
espátula **78**–19, **181**–52
especialistas médicos **120**
espejo **57**–18
espejo largo **58**–6
espejo lateral **158**–3
espejo retrovisor **159**–35
esperar a que cambie
    el semáforo **128**–B
esperar en línea **94**–B
espina **211**–29
espinaca **69**–11
espinilla **106**–21
espinilleras **231**–13
esponja **61**–19
esponjas de lana de acero **61**–5

esposa **34**–12
esposas **141**–2
esposo **34**–13
esquí a campo traviesa **227**–3
esquí acuático **227**–7
esquí de descenso **227**–1
esquiar **230**–V
esquíes **231**–24
esquina **128**–7
está descosido **97**–41
está irritado **64**–6
está manchado **97**–42
está rasgado **97**–41
esta semana **20**–19
establezca una hipótesis **195**–A
estación de autobuses **124**–7
estación de bomberos **125**–12
estación de camiones **124**–7
estación de metro **152**
estación de policía **124**–6
estación de tren **152**
estación de tren subterráneo **152**
estación del metro **151**–11
estación del salvavidas **225**–21
estación espacial **205**–18
estacionamiento **124**–1
estacionamiento para
    minusválidos **128**–6, **154**–12
estacionar el auto **129**–E
estacionar el coche **129**–E
estaciones **21**
estadio **126**–1
estado **4**–8
estado de cuenta **132**–16
ESTADOS DE ÁNIMO
    Y SENTIMIENTOS **42–43**
estados de las
    Montañas Rocosas **201**–8
estados del centro del Atlántico **201**–10
estados del Pacífico **201**–7
estampado **96**–23
estampado búlgaro **96**–26
estampado de cachemira **96**–26
estampilla **134**–23
estanque **204**–21
estante **54**–2
estar en shock **116**–B
estar herido **116**–C
estar inconsciente **116**–A
estar informado **140**–F
estar lesionado **116**–C
estatura **32**
estatura promedio **32**–5
este **155**–4
esté bien arreglado **174**–C
esté pendiente de los informes del
    tiempo **147**–C
esté pendiente de sus
    alrededores **143**–I
estetoscopio **118**–10

estibador **167**–23

estilos **96**

estirarse **230**–M

estofado de verduras, hortalizas y tofú con queso **77**

estómago **107**–41

estornudar **110**–B

estréchense las manos **174**–I

estrella **205**–13

estrella de mar **212**–16

estrés **115**–4

estuche para la cámara **235**–28

estuco **178**–15

estudiante **6**–5

ESTUDIAR **8–9**

estudie el manual **137**–A

estudie en la casa **10**–D

estufa **54**–18

etiqueta **102**–3

etiqueta de advertencia **112**–8

etiqueta de identificación **92**–15

etiqueta de la receta **112**–4

etiqueta de nutrición **122**–8

etiqueta de registro **136**–13

etiqueta del precio **27**–1

etiqueta engomada de dirección postal **183**–41

Europa **202**–3

evacue el área **147**–K

evidencia **141**–9

examen de bajo costo **122**–1

examen de sangre **121**–30

examen de visión **136**–6

examen sanguíneo **121**–30

examinarle…la garganta **118**–E

examinarle…los ojos **118**–D

excursión **226**–7

expediente médico **121**–24

experimento **195**

explique algo **12**–M

exploración **199**–8

explorador **199**–9

explosión **144**–4

Express Mail® (el correo expreso) **134**–2

expuesta insuficientemente **235**–35

extender los pantalones **100**–C

extensión **181**–14

exterminador **63**–21

extinguidor de incendios **179**–21

extintor **179**–21

extra grande **96**–5

extra pequeño **96**–1

extraer un diente **119**–F

extraer una muela **119**–F

FÁBRICA **175**

fábrica **126**–3

fábrica de ropa **98**

fabricar **175**–B

factura telefónica **15**–28

fagot **238**–4

fahrenheit **13**–1

faja **91**–15

falda **87**–10

falda corta **96**–16

falda de media pierna **96**–17

falda larga **96**–18

falta un botón **97**–40

FAMILIAS **34–35**

farmaceuta **112**–1

farmacéutico **112**–1

FARMACIA **112–113**

farmacia **128**–4

fauna marina **212**

fauna y flora natural **220**–3

fax **183**–21

febrero **21**–26

fecha **20**–1

fecha de nacimiento **4**–13

fecha de vencimiento **112**–7, **136**–10

feliz **28**–6

femenino **4**–18

feria de comida rápida **131**–15

feria de empleos **172**–13

FERIA DE SALUD **122–123**

feria del condado **223**–13

ferretería **148**–4

fertilizar **176**–D

festividad **239**–13

ficha **152**–10

fichero **182**–11

fiebre **110**–8

fiesta **64**–2

FIESTA DE CUMPLEAÑOS **240–241**

fiesta religiosa **22**–7

figurilla **232**–1

fije metas **10**–A

filete **70**–2, **81**–24

filete de halibut **71**–6

filete de res asado a la brasa **76**–3

filete de salmón **71**–4

fin de semana **20**–17

firma **4**–19

firme el contrato de alquiler **48**–D

firme el contrato de renta **48**–D

firme su nombre **4**–D

fiscal **141**–10

física **195**

físico **195**–33

fisioterapeuta **115**–12

flaco(a) **32**–9

flauta **238**–1

flebótomo **121**–29

flecha **231**–8

fleco **33**–8, **99**–34

flequillo **33**–8

flor de Nochebuena **211**–24

florería **130**–8

florero **55**–23

flores **208**–7

FLORES **211**

florista **167**–27

floristería **130**–8

foca **213**–34

fogata **226**–11

folk **237**–29

folleto de prueba **10**–1

formas **193**

formas de conservar la energía y los recursos **219**

formas de pagar **27**

formas para tener éxito **10**

fórmese ideas **191**–F

fórmula **37**–3, **195**–34

formulario de historial médico **118**–4

formulario de inscripción escolar **4**

formularios de correo **134**–19

fósforos **146**–16, **226**–21

foto chistosa **206**–2

foto seria **206**–3

fotocopiadora **183**–23

fotografía **136**–4

fotografías **58**–3

fotógrafo **206**–1

fotos **58**–3

fotosíntesis **194**–10

fracciones **192**

fracciones y decimales **17**

fracturarse un hueso **116**–P

frambuesas **68**–15

frasco de mermelada **74**–14

frascos **74**–2

frecuencia **20**

fregadero **54**–4

fregar el fregadero **60**–K

fregona con esponja **61**–6

frenillos **119**–5

freno de mano **159**–48

frenos **119**–6

frente **106**–2

fresas **68**–14

fresco **13**–5

frijoles **72**–17

frijoles de soya **177**–3

frío **13**–6

frustrado(a) **43**–27

FRUTAS **68**

frutas **67**–9

frutos secos **73**–36

fuegos artificiales **239**–7

fuente **224**–5

fuente de agua para beber **224**–9

fuente de luz **194**–19

fuentes de energía **218**

fuera de foco **235**–33

Fuerza Aérea **138**–16

fumigador **63**–21

funcionario electo **139**–32

funda de la almohada **58**–14

fundadores **198**–7

fumigador **63**–21

furgón de carga **156**–13

fútbol **229**–12

fútbol americano **229**–11

gabardina **90**–18

gabinete **54**–1, **138**–10

gabinete de artículos de oficina **182**–1

gabinete de baño **57**–22

gafas **92**–10

gafas de seguridad **179**–10

gafas de sol **90**–27

gafas protectoras **179**–11

galaxia **205**–15

galletas dulces **73**–38

gallina **215**–8

gallo **215**–7

galón de agua **75**–5

gamuza **99**–8

ganadero **177**–22

ganado **177**–15, **177**–21

gancho **101**–11, **180**–39

gancho de ojo **180**–40

gancho para el cabello **108**–19

gancho y ojal **99**–27

ganso **214**–13

garaje **47**–14

gardenia **211**–18

garganta **107**–35

garra **214**–2, **216**–20

garrapata **214**–27

gas natural **218**–3

gasa **117**–8

gasolinera **125**–10

gatito **215**–10

gato **215**–9

gato hidráulico **158**–24

gaveta **54**–23, **58**–2

gavetero **59**–6

gel de cabello **108**–16

gel de ducha **108**–2

GEOGRAFÍA Y LOS HÁBITATS **204**

geometría **192**–17

gerente **72**–8

gerente de cuentas **132**–9

gerente de oficina **182**–8

gimnasia **228**–9

gimnasio **5**–19, **126**–10, **184**–24

girar **230**–Q

girasol **211**–10

gire a la derecha en Pine Street **155**–B

gire a la izquierda en Oak Street **155**–C

gis **7**–18

globos **44**–4

gobernador **139**–20

gobierno estatal **139**

gobierno federal **138**

gobierno municipal **139**

GOBIERNO Y EL SERVICIO MILITAR **138–139**

golf **228**–8

goma **183**–33

goma de borrar **7**–21

gorila **217**–29
gorra de baño **108**–1
gorra de béisbol **86**–5
gorra de cirugía **93**–35
gorrión **214**–7
gorrito **88**–1
gorro **90**–1
gorro de cirugía **93**–35
gorro de vaquero **92**–18
gorro del chef **93**–28
gorro para esquiar **90**–11
gorro quirúrgico **121**–37
gorros **95**–11
gotas para los ojos **113**–31
goteo intravenoso **121**–25
gotero **195**–45
GPS (sistema de posicionamiento global) **155**–11
grabar **235**–A
grabar en video **240**–A
gradas **5**–3
grados **13**–8
GRADUACIÓN **206**–207
graduarse **40**–D
graffiti **148**–1
gráfica **192**–15
grajo azul **214**–6
grande **96**–4
granizada **13**–21
granja **52**–9, **177**–11
grapadora **183**–28
grapas **183**–29
grifo **57**–8
grifo gotea **63**–17
grillo **214**–23
gripe **111**–2
gris **24**–15
grúa **156**–14, **178**–7
grúa alzacarro **178**–5
grupo de apoyo **115**–15
guajolote **239**–14
guante **231**–17
guantera **159**–44
guantes **90**–6
guantes de goma **61**–4
guantes de látex **93**–34
guantes de trabajo **179**–17
guantes de trabajo **92**–17
guantes desechables **93**–27
guantes quirúrgicos **121**–39
guardabosques de parque **220**–2
guardar los juguetes **60**–G
guarde su equipaje de mano **160**–G
guarde sus libros **9**–Z
guardería infantil **129**–30
guardia **132**–5, **141**–3
Guardia Costera **138**–18
guardia de seguridad **169**–55
Guardia Nacional **138**–19
guerra **199**–10
guerra revolucionaria **198**–8

guillotina **183**–22
guión **190**–20
guisantes **69**–21
guitarra **238**–9
gusano **212**–23
habichuelas **72**–17
habitación del bebé **47**–10
habitación en el hospital **121**
habitación para huésped **184**–13
hábitat **194**–11
hablar con los amigos **173**–A
hablar otro idioma **170**–N
hable con la maestra **6**–B
hable por teléfono **15**–C
hable sobre su experiencia **174**–L
hacer artesanías **232**–D
hacer copias **171**–D
hacer creer **233**–G
hacer ejercicios **230**–N
hacer ejercicios **39**–P
hacer gárgara **109**–L
hacer la cama **60**–F
hacer la cena **39**–Q
HACER LA COLADA **101**
hacer la permanente **33**–B
hacer la tarea **39**–T
hacer labores manuales **170**–D
hacer muebles **170**–G
HACER UN VIAJE **162**–163
hacer una comida campestre **224**–D
hacha **180**–3
hacienda **52**–10
haga clic en "registrar entrada" **197**–B
haga compras en sitios Web seguros **143**–H
haga contacto visual **174**–J
haga un depósito **132**–B
haga un dibujo **8**–F
haga un experimento **195**–B
haga un pago de hipoteca **49**–L
haga una gira **220**–A
haga una oferta **49**–I
haga una pregunta **8**–K
haga una reverencia **3**–H
haga una transacción bancaria en línea **132**–C
hágale preguntas **174**–M
hágase exámenes médicos regularmente **114**–H
hágase inmunizar **114**–I
hamaca **53**–23
hambre epidémica **145**–12
hamburguesa **79**–1
hamburguesa con queso **79**–3
harina **73**–29
hebilla **99**–28
hebilla del cinturón **94**–20
heladería **131**–16
helado **13**–22, **72**–26
helicóptero **151**–9
hemorragia nasal **110**–17

heno **177**–18
hermana **34**–5
hermanastra **35**–29
hermanastro **35**–30
hermano **34**–6
héroe de aventuras **233**–26
HERRAMIENTAS Y MATERIALES DE CONSTRUCCIÓN **180**–181
hibisco **211**–12
híbrido **156**–3
hiedra venenosa **210**–25
hielera **225**–9
hiena **217**–30
hierbas **84**–9
hierva el pollo **77**–M
hígado **70**–7, **107**–40
HIGIENE PERSONAL **108**–109
higienista dental **119**–3
higos **68**–27
hija **34**–14
hijo **34**–15
hilo **98**–2, **100**–11, **233**–22
hilo dental **109**–24
hilos **99**–23
hip hop **237**–26
hipertensión **111**–14
hipopótamo **217**–43
historia **189**–12
HISTORIA DE EE.UU. **198**
HISTORIA UNIVERSAL **199**
hockey sobre hielo **229**–13
HOGAR **46**–47
hogar **56**–13
hogar de ancianos **52**–12
hogaza de pan **74**–22
hogazas **74**–10
hoguera **226**–11
hoja **109**–28
hoja **210**–6
hoja de ingreso **132**–4
hoja de respuestas **10**–2
hoja de vidrio **178**–16
hojas **211**–6
hombre **30**–1
hombreras **231**–20
hombres **30**–4
hombro **105**–13
hongos **69**–27
hora **18**–1
HORA **18**–19
hora de Alaska **19**–28
hora de Hawai-Aleutianas **19**–27
hora de la montaña **19**–30
hora de Terranova **19**–34
hora de verano **19**–25
hora del Atlántico **19**–33
hora del centro **19**–31
hora del este **19**–32
hora del Pacífico **19**–29
hora estándar **19**–26
horario **152**–4

horas del día **18**
hormigas **63**–23
hornee **77**–H
hornee la mezcla en el horno microondas durante 5 minutos **77**–T
hornilla **54**–19
horno **54**–20
horno microondas **54**–13
horno tostador **54**–15
horquillas **108**–21
horror **237**–17
HOSPITAL **120**–121
hospital **125**–9, **154**–18
HOTEL **184**
hotel **124**–3
hoy **20**–5
huella digital **136**–5
huerta **53**–27, **177**–10
huerta de verduras y hortalizas **177**–14
huerto **53**–27
huerto de verduras y hortalizas **177**–14
hueso **107**–33
huésped **184**–10
huevos **66**–7
huevos duros **76**–8
huevos escalfados **76**–9
huevos fritos **76**–10
huevos fritos, con una vuelta **76**–11
huevos revueltos **76**–7
húmedo **13**–15
humidificador **113**–12
humos venenosos **179**–3
huracán **145**–14
hurtos en comercios **142**–8
identifique la imagen **9**–V
idiomas del mundo **189**–13
iglesia **127**–14
ignición **159**–33
IGUAL Y DIFERENTE **28**–29
iguales **28**–3
imán **195**–36
impedido(a) físico **32**–10
impedido(a) visual **32**–11
imperdible **100**–14
impermeable **90**–18
impresor **169**–50
impresora **196**–17
impresora de chorro de tinta **183**–18
impresora láser **183**–19
imprima su nombre **4**–C
imprimir un documento **171**–I
impuesto de ventas **27**–8
incendio **144**–8
incendio forestal **144**–7
incendio provocado **142**–7
incómodo(a) **42**–9
indentar la primera oración de un párrafo **190**–D
indicador de aceite **159**–29
indicador de gasolina **159**–31
indicador de temperatura **159**–30

Infantes de Marina **138**–17
infección de la garganta **111**–4
infección de oído **111**–3
infle los neumáticos **157**–L
INFORMACIÓN PERSONAL **4**
ingeniero **167**–25
ingeniero de software
   de computadoras **167**–18
inglés como segundo idioma
   (ESL) **189**–14
inglés para hablantes de otros idiomas
   (ESOL) **189**–14
ingrese al salón **11**–A
inhalador **113**–33
inicial del segundo nombre **4**–3
inicie una conversación **12**–A
inmigración **199**–12
inmigrante **199**–13
inmigrar **40**–C
inodoro **57**–21
inodoro está atorado **63**–19
inquilino **50**–6
inscribirse en el servicio selectivo del
   ejército **140**–D
insectos **209**–11
insectos y arácnidos **214**
inserte su tarjeta de cajero
   automático **132**–D
insignia **93**–21
inspector de seguridad **160**–5
instalar losas **178**–C
instalar un sistema de rociador **176**–H
instituto de enseñanza
   superior **127**–17, **188**–6
instructora **6**–4
instrumentos de bronce o metales **238**
instrumentos de cuerda **238**
instrumentos de percusión **238**
instrumentos de viento de madera **238**
instrumentos dentales **119**–4
intercomunicador **50**–5
internado **172**–6
internista **120**–1
intérprete **168**–35
interruptor de la luz **58**–27
INTERSECCIÓN **128**–**129**
intestinos **107**–42
introducción **190**–6
introducir datos **171**–B
introduzca su clave en el teclado **132**–E
introduzca su contraseña **197**–A
inundación **145**–19
invención **199**–19
inventario de destrezas **172**–12
inventario de interés **172**–11
inventor **199**–18
invertebrados **194**–13
invierno **21**–40
invitación **64**–9
invite a alguien **12**–H

ir a la cárcel **141**–G
ir a la clase **38**–J
ir a la tienda de comestibles **38**–L
ir a la universidad **41**–I
ir a prisión **141**–G
ir a una agencia de empleos **173**–E
ir a una entrevista **173**–K
ir al trabajo **37**–24
ir de campamento **226**–6
IR DE COMPRAS **27**
ir debajo del puente **153**–A
ir sobre el puente **153**–B
isla **204**–8
jabón **57**–4, **108**–3
jabonera **57**–3
jamón **70**–9
jamón hervido **76**–5
jarabe para la tos **113**–29
jardín aéreo **50**–4
jardín botánico **222**–3
jardín de verduras y hortalizas **53**–27
jardín delantero y la casa **53**
jardín posterior **53**
jardinero **167**–28
jarretes de cordero **70**–13
jazmín **211**–22
jazz **237**–24
jefe **164**–4
jefe de comedor **185**–11
jefe de comedor **82**–2
jefe del personal de jardinería **176**–4
jeringa **118**–12
jirafa **217**–32
joroba **217**–51
joven **32**–1
joyería **130**–2
jubilarse **41**–O
judías verdes **69**–8
jueces **138**–12
juego de artesanía en madera **232**–14
juego de béisbol **44**–2
juego de mesa **232**–5
juego de raqueta **228**–12
juego de video (el sistema) **232**–3
juego para construir modelos
   a escala **232**–9
juego para hacer muñecas **232**–13
jueves **20**–12
juez **141**–6
jugador **229**–5
jugar a los naipes **233**–H
jugar con él **36**–M
jugo de manzana **73**–32
juguetería **130**–5
juguetes y juegos **59**
juicio justo **140**–5
julio **21**–31
junio **21**–30
Júpiter **205**–5
jurado **141**–8

kiwis **68**–22
koala **217**–45
la crema humectante **108**–9
la tarjeta madre **196**–5
labio **106**–5
laboratorio **121**
laboratorio de ciencia **195**
laboratorio de computadoras **5**–15
laca **108**–12
ladrillos **178**–12
lagartija **213**–40
lago **204**–13
laguna **204**–21
lámpara **55**–18, **58**–25
lámpara de mano **146**–14
lámpara de pie **56**–15
lana **98**–3
langosta **71**–10
langostino **71**–11
lanzar **230**–A
lápiz **7**–20
lápiz de cejas **109**–34
lápiz de labios **109**–38
lastimado(a) **42**–16
lata de frijoles **74**–15
latas **74**–3
lavadora **50**–12, **101**–3
lavamanos **57**–25
lavamanos se desborda **63**–18
lavandería **128**–1
lavaplatos **54**–8, **83**–14, **185**–2
lavaplatos se desborda **63**–18
LAVAR LA ROPA **101**
lavar la ropa en agua fría **219**–K
lavar las ventanas **60**–I
lavar los platos **60**–M
lavarse…el cabello **108**–E
lazo **89**–16
lea la definición **8**–B
lea la tarjeta **135**–G
leche **66**–5
leche baja en grasa **81**–42
lechera **55**–15
lecho de flores **53**–20
lechuga **69**–1
lechuza **214**–5
lectura de la factura telefónica **15**
leer el periódico **39**–V
leerle **36**–N
leggings **90**–12
legislatura **139**–23
lejía **101**–7
lengua **106**–8
lenguado **212**–15
lente de zoom **235**–23
lentes de contacto **115**–8
león **217**–36
león marino **213**–33
leopardo **217**–34
letrero **129**–26

levantamiento de pesas **228**–16
levantarse **38**–B
levante la mano **6**–A
levante los libros **11**–E
libertad de expresión **140**–2
libertad de prensa **140**–4
libertad de religión **140**–3
libra de rosbif **75**–12
librería **130**–4
librero **7**–10
libreta **7**–27
libreta de banco **132**–10
libreta de citas **183**–48
libreta de espiral **7**–29
libro de dibujos **133**–12
libro de estampillas **134**–18
libro de pintar **59**–13
libro de texto **7**–25
libro delgado **23**–8
libro grueso **23**–7
libro hablado **133**–17
licencia de conducir **40**–4
licencia de manejar **136**–9
licencia de matrimonio **41**–8
licencia del taxi **152**–22
licuadora **54**–12
lienzo **233**–17
liga elástica **183**–34
liguero **91**–16
lijadora eléctrica **180**–11
lima **109**–32
limas **68**–8
límite de velocidad **154**–4
limonada **84**–3
limones **68**–7
limones verdes **68**–8
limpiador **61**–18, **182**–3
limpiador de hornos **61**–3
limpiador de vidrios **61**–14
limpiaparabrisas **158**–2
limpiar **76**–A
limpiar el filtro de pelusas **101**–D
limpiar el horno **60**–C
limpiar el mostrador **60**–O
limpiar el piso **60**–D
limpiar la barra **60**–O
limpiar la casa **39**–O
limpiar…los dientes **119**–A
limpiarse **109**–Q
limpie los escombros **147**–M
limpie su escritorio **10**–I
LIMPIEZA COMUNITARIA **148**–**149**
limusina **156**–11
línea **73**–11
línea curva **193**–23
línea de ensamblaje **175**–6
línea de montaje **175**–6
línea de teléfono **14**–4
línea recta **193**–22
líneas **193**

líneas paralelas **193**–25
líneas perpendiculares **193**–24
linterna **146**–14, **226**–22
linterna hecha de una calabaza **239**–10
líquido corrector **183**–36
líquido lavaplatos **61**–21
líquidos inflamables **179**–8
lirio **211**–16, **211**–26
lista de compra **67**–14
litera **59**–9
llama **217**–25
llamada a larga distancia **15**–32
llamada internacional **15**–35
llamada local **15**–31
llamada telefónica por Internet **14**–20
llame a sus contactos fuera
　del estado **147**–L
llame al administrador **48**–A
llana de albañil **178**–13
llano **204**–19
llanta **158**–5
llanta de repuesto **158**–23
llanura **204**–19
llave **51**–30, **57**–8
llave ajustable **181**–48
llave corrediza **181**–47
llave de tuerca **158**–22
llave gotea **63**–17
llave inglesa para tubos **181**–47
llega **160**–K
llegar a la casa **39**–R
llenar la lavadora **101**–C
llenar una solicitud **173**–J
llene el espacio en blanco **9**–O
llene el tanque con gasolina **157**–G
llevar a los niños al colegio **38**–G
llevar la bandeja **82**–H
lleve el automóvil a un mecánico **157**–C
lleve los libros **11**–F
lleve su resumé
　y su identificación **174**–D
llévelo para que le hagan una prueba
　de esmog **157**–J
llorar **206**–B
lluvia ácida **218**–13
lluvioso **13**–11
lobo **216**–5
loción para bebé **37**–13
loción para después
　de afeitarse **109**–30
lombriz **212**–23
longitud **17**–17
losa **57**–12
losa está rota **62**–4
losas **178**–11
lote de autos **126**–4
luces de peligro **159**–36
luces navideñas **239**–18
lucha **228**–17
luego de una emergencia **147**
lugar de encuentro **146**–1

lugar de nacimiento **4**–14
LUGAR DE TRABAJO **164**–**165**
lugar para estacionar **128**–5
LUGARES A DONDE IR **222**–**223**
LUGARES DIFERENTES PARA VIVIR **52**
lugares más famosos **220**–1
luna llena **205**–12
luna nueva **205**–9
lunar **32**–16
lunes **20**–9
luz de freno **158**–14
luz de la calle **148**–3
luz de noche **37**–27
luz de trabajo **181**–44
luz del porche **53**–13
luz delantera **158**–7
luz direccional **158**–6
luz trasera **158**–13
madera **178**–17
madera de 2 x 4
　(dos por cuatro) **181**–19
madera terciada **178**–18
madero **178**–17
madrastra **35**–26
madre **34**–3
madre soltera **35**–22
maestra **6**–4
maestro **5**–8
magnolia **210**–8
maíz **69**–12, **177**–4
MAL DÍA EN EL TRABAJO **186**–**187**
maletera **158**–11
maletero **50**–17
maletín **88**–13
malla para el cabello **93**–25
malteada **79**–14
mamadera **37**–2
mamíferos **209**–10
MAMÍFEROS **216**–**217**
mamíferos marinos **213**
mañana **18**–15, **20**–6
mandarinas **68**–9
mandil **92**–11
mandil de cintura **93**–30
mandril **217**–31
manejar en estado
　de embriaguez **142**–5
maneras de servir las carnes de res
　y de ave **76**
maneras de servir los huevos **76**
maneras para mantenerse sano **114**
maneras para sanarse **114**
manga **100**–6
mangos **68**–21
manguera **53**–21
manicurista **168**–38
maniobra de Heimlich **117**–18
maniquí de la costurera **100**–2
mano **105**–15
mano grande **23**–2
mano pequeña **23**–1

manta **58**–15
manta (o toalla) de playa **225**–11
mantas **146**–7
mantel **55**–12
mantel individual **55**–11
manténgase alejado
　de las ventanas **147**–1
manténgase en buena
　condición física **114**–E
mantenimiento **184**–23
mantequilla **66**–6
manual de primeros auxilios **117**–2
manual del DMV **136**–1
manzanas **68**–1
mapa **7**–12
MAPA DEL MUNDO **202**–**203**
mapa del tiempo **13**
mapa Internet **155**–12
mapache **216**–13
mapas **155**
maquillaje **109**
máquina de coser **98**–13
máquina de fax **183**–21
máquina expendedora **152**–9
máquina expendedora
　de estampillas **135**–11
máquina franqueadora **135**–8, **183**–27
maravilla **211**–13
marbete **136**–13
marcador **7**–24
marcador borrable en seco **7**–17
marcador de autopista **165**–7
marcador de tiempo **165**–7
marco de foto **58**–4
marco de la cama **58**–18
maremoto **145**–17
margarina **72**–20
margarita **211**–14
marina **138**–15
mariposa **214**–19
mariposa nocturna **214**–21
mariquita **214**–26
MARISCOS Y COMESTIBLES
　PREPARADOS **71**
marmota de las praderas **215**–22
marque 911 **15**–E
marque el número de teléfono **15**–A
marque las casillas correctas **9**–U
marrón **24**–17
marsopa **213**–30
marte **205**–4
martes **20**–10
martillar **178**–D
martillo **180**–1
martillo perforador **178**–9
marzo **21**–27
máscara **239**–9
máscara de cirugía **93**–36
máscara de esquí **90**–15
máscara de oxígeno **161**–24
máscara de ventilación **92**–7

máscara facial **93**–32
máscara para partículas **179**–14
mascotas **215**
masculino **4**–17
matasellos **134**–24
MATEMÁTICAS **192**–**193**
matemáticas **189**–10
materiales radioactivos **179**–7
mayo **21**–29
mayonesa **79**–23
mazo **178**–23, **180**–2
mecánico de automóviles **166**–8
mecerlo **36**–D
media docena de bebidas
　gaseosas **74**–21
media enagua **91**–23
media hermana **35**–27
media luna **205**–10
media taza de pasas **75**–9
mediana edad **32**–2
mediano **96**–3
medianoche **18**–21
medias **86**–6
medias de malla **91**–19
medias largas **91**–17
medias panti **91**–18
medicamento **121**–20
medicamento prescrito **112**–3
medicamento sin receta **113**–18
medicamentos sin receta **113**
medición de área y volumen **193**
médico **118**–5
MEDIDAS **17**
medidas para líquidos **75**
medidas secas **75**
medidor de aceite **159**–29
medidor de gas **62**–14
medidor de gasolina **159**–31
medidor de presión sanguínea **118**–9
medidor de temperatura **159**–30
medio **17**–2
medio dólar **26**–5
medio hermano **35**–28
medio oeste **201**–9
mediodía **18**–16
medusa **212**–14
mejilla **106**–3
mejillón **212**–17
mejillones **71**–13
melena **217**–49
mellizas **28**–1
melocotones **68**–10
melones **68**–19
membrana de la célula **194**–6
mensaje de texto **14**–19
mensaje de voz **14**–18
mensajero **168**–40
menú **82**–7
MENÚ DE UN CAFÉ **80**–**81**
menú desplegable **197**–8
MERCADO DE AGRICULTORES **84**–**85**

mercado de pulgas **222**–6
Mercurio **205**–1
meriendas **73**
mes **20**–3
mesa de billar **50**–15
mesa de cama **121**–21
mesa de centro **56**–19
mesa de examen **118**–7
mesa del comedor **55**–9
mesa para cambiar pañales **59**–1
mesa para comidas campestres **224**–8
mesa plegable **102**–4
mesa quirúrgica **121**–40
mesera **83**–9, **185**–8
mesero **82**–8
meses del año **21**
mesetas del sur **201**–17
mesita **56**–14, **161**–21
mesita de noche **58**–23
metro **151**–12
mezcle los ingredientes **77**–R
mezquita **126**–5
micrófono **234**–18
microprocesador **196**–4
microscopio **194**
mida **17**–C
mida los ingredientes **75**–A
miércoles **20**–11
mil **16**
mil millones **16**
milésimo **16**
milicianos **198**–10
millón **16**
mini-falda **96**–15
minipersianas **58**–8
miniván **156**–8
minutos **18**–2
mirar **102**–B
mire los anuncios
    de automóviles **157**–A
mirilla **51**–32
mismo color **23**–15
misterio **237**–20
mitones **90**–10
mocasines **95**–30
mochila **94**–18, **226**–15
modelo **99**–22, **168**–41
modernas **199**–2
módulo de información **130**–12
mofeta **216**–12
molde de carne **81**–31
molde para pastel **78**–28
molde para torta **78**–26
molde refractario **78**–10
molécula **195**–27
molesto(a) **43**–28
molinete **152**–8
mollete **79**–16
moluscos y crustáceos **71**
monarca **199**–4

mondongo **70**–8
moneda de un dólar **26**–6
monedas **26**
monedero **94**–14
monitor **196**–11
monitor de signos vitales **121**–26
monitor para bebés **59**–7
monitores de salidas y llegadas **161**–7
mono **93**–24, **217**–26
mono de trabajo **92**–8
monopatín **224**–7
monopatinador
    de nieve **227**–2, **231**–23
montar **175**–C
morado **24**–6, **110**–12
moras **68**–17
moreno **24**–18
moretón **110**–12
morir **41**–R
morsa **213**–32
mosca **214**–28
mosquito **214**–22
mostaza **79**–22
mostrador **54**–22
motel **126**–12
motocicleta **150**–4
motor **158**–18
motor de búsqueda **197**–6
móvil **59**–5
movimiento político **199**–16
mozo de campo **177**–20
mudanza **49**
múdese al apartamento **48**–F
mueblería **126**–8
muebles del patio **53**–19
muebles y accesorios **59**
muelle **58**–19, **225**–18
muelle de carga **175**–15
muestras **84**–5
muestre su billete de abordaje y su
    identificación **160**–C
muestre su identificación **137**–C
mujer **30**–2
mujeres **30**–3
muletas **113**–10
multiplicar **192**–C
muñeca **59**–21, **106**–14
muñecas de papel **233**–28
murciélago **216**–7
músculo **107**–32
museo de arte **223**–9
MÚSICA **238**
música **64**–3, **189**–16
música del mundo **237**–32
música en vivo **84**–1
músico **168**–43
muslo **106**–19
muslos **70**–22
muy frío **13**–7
nabos **69**–16

nacer **40**–A
nachos **79**–7
nadar **230**–L
nalgas **107**–30
naranjas **68**–5
narciso atrompetado **211**–25
nariz **104**–6
navaja **109**–28
Navidad **22**–18
neblinoso **13**–20
negocie un precio **157**–D
negro **24**–13
Neptuno **205**–8
nervioso(a) **42**–10
neumático **158**–23
neumático **158**–5
neutrón **195**–32
nevera **54**–9
nevera de playa **225**–9
nevoso **13**–12
nido **209**–12
nilón **99**–12
niña de 10 años **31**–10
niña pequeña **31**–8
niñera **166**–9
niño **31**–7
niño de 6 años **31**–9
niño perdido **144**–1
niños ruidosos **23**–11
niños tranquilos **23**–12
nivel **180**–29
no abra la puerta a extraños **143**–F
no beba alcohol **112**–F
no entrar **154**–2
no estacionarse **154**–11
no fume **114**–G
no hay electricidad **62**–2
no llegue tarde **174**–E
no maneje en estado
    de embriaguez **143**–G
no maneje ni opere maquinaria
    pesada **112**–E
no poder respirar **116**–N
no se debe tomar con productos
    lácteos **112**–D
no se permite girar a la izquierda **154**–8
no tirar basura **219**–L
noche **18**–20
nombre **4**–1
nonagésimo **16**
normas **64**–7
noroeste del Pacífico **201**–14
norte **155**–1
Norte América **202**–1
NORTE AMÉRICA Y CENTRO
    AMÉRICA **200**–**201**
nostálgico(a) **43**–20
nota al pie de la página **190**–10
novela **133**–16
noveno **16**

noventa **16**
noviembre **21**–35
nublado **13**–10
núcleo **194**–7, **195**–29
nudillo **106**–17
Nueva Inglaterra **201**–11
nueve **16**
numerador **192**–5
número de acceso **14**–16
número de apartamento **4**–6
número de cuenta corriente **132**–14
número de cuenta de ahorro **132**–11
número de la receta **112**–5
número de licencia
    de conductor **136**–11
número de Seguro Social **4**–15
número de teléfono **4**–11, **15**–30
número de teléfono celular **4**–12
número SKU **27**–5
NÚMEROS **16**
números cardinales **16**
números enteros **192**
números enteros negativos **192**–1
números enteros positivos **192**–2
números impares **192**–3
números ordinales **16**
números pares **192**–4
números romanos **16**
nutria marina **213**–35
obedecer las leyes **140**–C
obeso(a) **32**–7
objetivo **194**–16
objetos valiosos **132**–8
oboe **238**–3
obra **126**–2
obra teatral **223**–8
obrero **175**–3
obrero de construcción **178**–1
observatorio **205**–21
observe **195**–C
obstetra **120**–2
obtener cambio **26**–A
obtener una tarjeta para uso de la
    biblioteca **133**–A
obtenga atención médica **114**–A
obtenga buenas notas **10**–H
obtenga el título del vendedor **157**–E
obtenga su licencia **137**–I
obtenga un permiso de aprendiz **137**–F
obtenga un préstamo **49**–J
obteniendo su primera licencia **137**
océano **204**–6, **225**–1
ochenta **16**
ocho **16**
octavo **16**, **17**–5
octogésimo **16**
octubre **21**–34
ocular **194**–14
odómetro **159**–28
odontología **119**

oeste **155**–2
oficial **229**–6
oficial de la policía **168**–48
oficial de policía **141**–1
OFICINA **182**–183
oficina **164**–3
OFICINA DE CORREOS **134**–135
oficina de correos **125**–11
oficina principal **5**–12
ofrezca algo **12**–D
oftalmólogo **120**–7
oír **106**–B
ojo **105**–11, **106**
ojo mágico **51**–32
ola **225**–17
ola de calor **13**–13
oler **106**–C
olla **54**–16, **78**–3, **78**–6, **78**–25
olmo **210**–16
ómnibus escolar **156**–21
omóplato **107**–28
once **16**
oncólogo **120**–5
Ontario **201**–4
onza de queso **75**–11
onza líquida de leche **75**–1
ópera **223**–11
operaciones matemáticas **192**
operador **14**–21
operador de maquinaria **168**–37
operadora de la máquina
    de coser **98**–14
operadora de maquinaria **168**–37
operar maquinaria pesada **170**–H
opinión **44**–3
oponente **139**–30
oposum **216**–4
oprima "enviar" **15**–B
oprima "finalizar" **15**–D
óptica **130**–9
optómetra **115**–6
optometrista **115**–6
oración **190**–2
orador invitado **206**–4
orangután **217**–39
ordeñar **177**–C
oreja **105**–12
oreja perforada **32**–17
orejeras **90**–13, **179**–16
organice las ideas **191**–G
organismos **194**–1
organizador **183**–49
organizar materiales **171**–L
órgano **238**–20
orgulloso(a) **43**–21
orientador de carreras **172**–10
orilla **204**–12
ornitorrinco **217**–46
orquídea **211**–19

ortodoncia **119**
ortodoncista **119**–5
oruga **214**–20
osito de peluche **37**–23
oso **216**–11
oso hormiguero **217**–24
ostras **71**–14
otoño **21**–39
otros instrumentos **238**
otros productos **72**
oveja **215**–6
overol **88**–6, **92**–8
p.m. **18**–5
paciente **118**–6, **121**–18
padrastro **35**–25
padre **34**–4
padre soltero **35**–23
pagar **27**–G
pagar el dinero prestado **26**–D
pagar en efectivo **27**–A
pagar impuestos **140**–B
pagar la cuenta **82**–I
pagar una multa **133**–E
pague el alquiler del primer
    y del último mes **48**–E
pague la renta del primer
    y del último mes **48**–E
pague los costos de solicitud **137**–D
paisaje **162**–2
PAISAJISMO Y JARDINERÍA **176**
pájaro **208**–4
pájaro carpintero **214**–8
PÁJAROS, INSECTOS Y ARÁCNIDOS **214**
pala **61**–17, **176**–7, **178**–22, **225**–8
palabra **190**–1
palacio municipal **124**–8
palanca de cambio de
    velocidad **159**–47
palanca de luz direccional **159**–34
palanca de velocidades **159**–50
paleta **175**–13
palma **106**–15, **210**–14
palo de golf **231**–1
palo de hockey **231**–11
paloma **214**–15
paltas **84**–6
pan **67**–11
pan blanco **71**–18
pan con ajo **81**–28
pan de centeno **71**–20
pan de trigo **71**–19
pana **99**–11
panadera **166**–10
panadería **127**–19
panadero **166**–10
pañal de tela **37**–8
pañal desechable **37**–10
páncreas **107**–45
panda **217**–41
pandereta **238**–17

pandero **238**–17
pandillismo **142**–4
panecillos **80**–6, **80**–17
paño de calentamiento **113**–13
panqueques **80**–7
pantaletas **91**–14
pantalla **6**–2, **196**–11, **235**–30
pantalla de la lámpara **58**–26
pantalla de protección **56**–12
pantalón Capri **88**–8
pantalones **87**–12, **90**–12
pantalones apretados **97**–29
pantalones ceñidos **97**–29
pantalones cortos **89**–25
pantalones de ejercicio **89**–23
pantalones de seguridad **93**–22
pantalones de trabajo **92**–5
pantalones flojos **97**–30
pantalones holgados **97**–30
pantalones jeans **86**–2, **92**–19
pantera **217**–40
panties (bikinis) **91**–13
pantimedias **91**–18
pantorrilla **106**–22
pantuflas **91**–26
pañuelo de cabeza **90**–7, **92**–16
papa al horno **81**–25
papa asada **81**–25
papas **69**–17
papas fritas **79**–2
papas fritas de bolsa **73**–35
papayas **68**–20
papel de aluminio **72**–23
papel de construcción **232**–12
papel de escribir **183**–42
papel de lija **181**–56
papel de notas adhesivo **183**–39
papel higiénico **57**–19, **146**–13
papel membreteado **183**–42
papel para libreta **7**–28
papel tapiz **59**–8
papelera **57**–26
paperas **111**–7
papitas doradas **80**–3
paquete **134**–17
paquete de galletas dulces **74**–20
paquetes **74**–8
paquetes de seis **74**–9
par de tijeras **100**–16
para hacer una llamada
    de emergencia **15**
para llamar por teléfono **15**
para tomar un vuelo **160**
parabrisas **158**–1
parachoques **158**–8
parada de autobús **129**–16,
    151–13, **152**
parada de taxis **152**–18
paraguas **90**–17
paralelogramo **193**–33

paramédico **116**–2
pararse **154**–1
parásitos intestinales **111**–13
pared **56**–10
pared de la célula **194**–5
pared de yeso **178**–19
pareja **239**–4
pareja casada **35**–20
pareja divorciada **35**–21
paréntesis **190**–19
parientes **44**–6
parka **90**–9
parlantes **234**–14
párpado **106**–10
parque **50**–3
parque de atracciones **223**–10
PARQUE Y EL PATIO DE RECREO **224**
PARQUES NACIONALES
    DE EE.UU. **220**–221
parquímetro **129**–25
párrafo **190**–3
parrilla **53**–17, **54**–21
parrilla para asar **78**–14
parte inferior de la espalda **107**–29
PARTES DE UN AUTOMÓVIL **158**–159
partes de un ensayo **190**
partes de una flor **211**
partes de una máquina de coser **98**
participar en juegos **232**–B
participar en un plan de viaje
    compartido en auto (carpool) **219**–I
participe en la clase **10**–B
partida de nacimiento **40**–1
pasadores **108**–21
pasaje **152**–2
pasaje electrónico **161**–19
pasajero **150**–2, **152**–3, **161**–15
pasaporte **41**–10
pasar **230**–G
pasas **68**–25
PASATIEMPOS Y JUEGOS **232**–233
pascua **211**–24
pase a la siguiente línea **196**–D
pase Main Street **155**–E
pase por el área de seguridad **160**–D
pase una prueba **10**–E
pase una prueba de manejo **137**–H
pasear el perro **129**–F
paseo a caballo **226**–9
paseo en balsa **226**–2
paseo en bote **226**–1
pasillo **5**–10, **51**, **72**–6, **184**–18
pasta **67**–12
pasta de dientes **109**–23
pastel **81**–35
pastilla **113**–22
pastillas para el resfrío **113**–27
pastillas para la garganta **113**–30
pastrami **71**–23
pata **216**–20

pata de cordero **70**–14
patas **70**–21, **70**–23
patear **230**–E
patillas **33**–7
patinaje artístico de figuras **227**–5
patinaje sobre hielo **227**–4
patinaje sobre ruedas **228**–10
patinar **230**–U
patines de hielo **231**–9
patines de rueda **231**–10
patio **51**–21, **53**–16
patio interior **5**–1
pato **70**–18, **214**–12
patrón **99**–22
patrones **96**
pausar **235**–E
pavo **70**–17, **239**–14
pavo ahumado **71**–25
pavo al horno **76**–4
pavo real **214**–14
peatón **128**–14
peces **209**–14
pecho **104**–4, **107**–25, **107**–26
pechugas **70**–19
pedal de freno **159**–45
pedal de gasolina **159**–46
pediatra **120**–4
pedir del menú **82**–D
pedir un deseo **240**–B
pega **183**–33
pegamento **232**–11
pegar **230**–B
pegatina **102**–3
peinarse…el cabello **108**–G
peine **33**–21, **108**–13
peineta **108**–15
peinilla **33**–21, **108**–13
pelador de verduras y hortalizas **78**–15
pelaje **216**–19
peldaños **53**–3
pele las zanahorias **77**–K
peligro eléctrico **186**–6
peligros de seguridad y materiales
    peligrosos **179**
peligroso **186**–1
pelirrojo(a) **33**–15
pelo **104**–2
pelota de béisbol **231**–18
peluquera **167**–31
peluquería **131**–18
pelvis **107**–50
península **204**–7
península de Yucatán **201**–19
peón de labranza **177**–20
pepinillo en vinagre **80**–11
pepinos **69**–10
pequeño **96**–2
peras **68**–4
percha **101**–11, **212**–6
perderse **162**–B

pérdida de la audición **115**–2
perejil **69**–28
perfume **108**–6
perilla de ajuste fino **194**–22
perilla de ajuste grueso **194**–24
perilla de la puerta **53**–12
perímetro **193**–43
periódico **133**–6
período colonial **198**
periquito **215**–15
permanezca en calles bien
    iluminadas **143**–B
permanezca en la línea **15**–H
permanezca tranquilo **147**–E
perno **180**–35
peróxido de hidrógeno **117**–9
perrito **215**–12
perro **215**–11
perro bueno **23**–17
perro caliente **79**–6
perro malo **23**–18
persona de negocios **166**–12
persona que empaca la compra **73**–14
persona que realiza ventas por
    teléfono **169**–60
personal de enfermería **120**
personal de jardinería **176**–1
personal del hospital **120**
pesado(a) **32**–7
pesas **231**–22
pesca **226**–4
pescado **66**–1, **71**
pescado a la parrilla **81**–29
pescado congelado **71**–17
pescado fresco **71**–16
pescador comercial **167**–17
pese la comida **75**–B
peso **32**, **75**
peso promedio **32**–8
PESOS Y MEDIDAS **75**
pestaña **197**–7
pestañas **106**–11
pétalos **211**–8
petición **148**–5
petirrojo **214**–16
petróleo **218**–6
pez espada **71**–5, **212**–10
pezuñas **216**–17
pi **193**–46
piano **238**–14
picadura de insecto **110**–11
picaduras **119**–7
picaflor **214**–10
pickup **156**–12
pico **214**–3
pico de la montaña **204**–14
pida ayuda **10**–F
pie **104**–8
pie prensatelas **98**–19
piel **107**–31, **216**–19

piense sobre la tarea **191**–E
pierna **105**–9
pierna y el pie **106**
piezas **175**–5
pijama **91**–24
pila de abono **53**–25
pilas **146**–15
píldora **113**–21
piloto **161**–11
pimentones **69**–7
pimientos **69**–7
pimpollo **211**–4
piña **210**–11
piñas **68**–23
pincel **233**–20
pingüino **214**–11
pino **210**–9
pinta de yogurt congelado **75**–3
pintar **178**–A, **233**–E
pintarse las uñas **109**–O
pinte **49**–P
pintor (de casas) **168**–46
pintura **181**–25
pintura al óleo **233**–19
pintura de aceite **233**–19
pintura de acrílico **232**–10
pintura de uñas **109**–33
pinza para colgar la ropa **101**–10
pinza para el cabello **108**–19
pinzas **78**–23, **117**–4
piragüismo **226**–3
pirámide **193**–39
piscina **51**–22, **184**–22
piso **46**–6
piso de madera **58**–21
piso resbaloso **179**–6
pista **5**–21
pista de boliche **222**–4
pistola **142**–13
pistola rociadora **181**–21
pizarra **6**–1
pizarra para rotuladores **6**–3
pizza **79**–10
placa **136**–12, **158**–12
placa de la aguja **98**–18
plan del piso **186**–4
plancha **101**–13
planchar la ropa **101**–G
planicie de la costa del Golfo **201**–16
PLANIFICACIÓN DE CARRERAS **172**
planificación de la carrera **172**
planifique para una emergencia **146**–A
planta interior **56**–4
planta para interiores **211**–27
plantar un árbol **176**–E, **219**–N
plantas **208**–5, **210**
plántula **211**–4
plástico para envolver **72**–24
plátano maduro **68**–30

plátano pasado **68**–32
plátano podrido **68**–32
plátano verde **68**–31
plátanos **68**–2
platillo **83**–25
platina **194**–3
platito **83**–25
plato **55**–1, **83**–18
plato grande **55**–20
plato hondo **55**–2
plato hondo de servir **55**–21
plato para el pan
    y la mantequilla **83**–19
plato para ensalada **83**–20
platón **55**–20
playa **204**–10
PLAYA **225**
plomero **63**–20
pluma **7**–22, **214**–4
plumero **61**–1
podar los setos **176**–B
podio **206**–5
policía **141**–1
polilla **214**–21
pollo **66**–3, **70**–16
pollo asado **81**–22
pollo cocido **70**–25
pollo crudo **70**–24
pollo frito **76**–1
polo acuático **229**–14
polvo facial **109**–41
pomada **113**–24
poncho **90**–19
poner en espera al llamante **171**–N
poner la mesa **82**–A
ponerse **109**–P
ponerse protector solar **108**–D
ponérselo **87**–B
ponga las oraciones en orden **9**–X
ponga o escriba la dirección de correo
    electrónico del destinatario del
    correo electrónico **197**–C
póngale la estampilla **135**–C
póngale refrigerante **157**–I
póngase de pie **6**–D
pop **237**–25
porcentajes **17**
porche frontal **53**
portacelular **94**–15
portacepillos **57**–24
portaobjetivo rotatorio **194**–15
portaobjetos **194**–17
portavela **56**–21
portero **184**–1
postal **134**–16
postularse para un cargo **139**–A
pradera **204**–20
prado **204**–20
precaliente el horno **77**–A
precio **27**–7

precio de oferta **27**–3
precio normal **27**–2
pregunte, "¿Cómo está usted?" **2**–B
pregúntele al vendedor sobre el
    automóvil **157**–B
pregúntele sobre
    las características **48**–B
prendedor **95**–38
prendedores de seguridad **37**–9
prensa de tornillo **180**–26
prensa para ajo **78**–11
preocupado(a) **42**–13
PREPARACIÓN Y SEGURIDAD DE LOS
    ALIMENTOS **76**–77
preparador de comidas **185**–4
preparar el almuerzo **38**–F
preparar la cena **39**–Q
prepare un equipo de suministros en
    caso de desastres **146**–B
prepárese para la entrevista **174**–A
PREPOSICIONES **25**
PREPOSICIONES DE MOVIMIENTO **153**
prescripción **112**–2
presentación **182**–6
presente a un amigo **3**–I
presente su solicitud **48**–C
preséntese **2**–C
presidente **138**–8, **199**–5
presidente de la Corte Suprema **138**–13
presilla **99**–26
presillas del portaobjetos **194**–21
presión arterial alta **111**–14
preso **141**–15
prestar dinero **26**–C
prestarse dinero **26**–B
preste atención
    a las advertencias **147**–D
presupuesto **186**–3
pretina **100**–5
prima **34**–9
primavera **21**–37
primer congreso continental **198**–6
primer ministro **199**–7
primer nombre **4**–2
primer presidente **198**–11
primero **16**
PRIMEROS AUXILIOS **117**
primo **34**–9
Priority Mail®
    (el correo prioritario) **134**–1
prisma **195**–35
probarse zapatos **95**–C
problema difícil **23**–24
problema expresado
    con palabras **192**–11
problema fácil **23**–23
problema matemático **192**
problemas con la ropa **97**
problemas de visión **115**–1
problemas dentales **119**

PROBLEMAS Y REPARACIONES
    DOMÉSTICAS **62**–63
PROCEDIMIENTOS
    DE EMERGENCIA **146**–147
procedimientos de primeros
    auxilios **117**
procedimientos médicos **118**
procesador de alimentos **54**–26
proceso de escritura **191**
producto **192**–9
productos de pastelería **73**
productos lácteos **72**
productos orgánicos **84**–2
productos para pastelerías **73**
profesor **5**–8
profesora **6**–4
profundidad **17**–18
programar computadoras **170**–I
programar una reunión **171**–J
programas **196**–10
programas de drama **236**–12
programas de entrevistas **236**–4
programas de juegos **236**–8
programas de noticias **236**–1
programas de preguntas **236**–8
programas de realidad **236**–6
programas de ventas
    por televisión **236**–10
programas deportivos **236**–11
programas para niños **236**–9
programas sobre la naturaleza **236**–7
progrese **10**–G
protector **59**–4
protector de sobretensiones **196**–1
protector solar **108**–7, **225**–10
proteja el bolso o la cartera **143**–D
proteja la billetera **143**–D
protón **195**–31
provincias de las praderas **201**–3
provincias marítimas **201**–6
proyector LCD **6**–6, **235**–29
prueba de seguro **136**–8
pruebas **141**–9
púa **216**–23
publicaciones periódicas **133**–4
pueblo pequeño **52**–3
puerco **215**–2
puerco espín **216**–10
puerta **46**–3, **53**–9, **161**–8
puerta de seguridad **50**–16
puerta de vidrio deslizante **53**–18
puerta del garaje **53**–7
puerta giratoria **184**–2
puerta mosquitero **53**–15
puerta principal **53**–11
puesta del sol **18**–18
puesto de periódicos **128**–12
pulgada [pulg.] **17**–15
pulgar **106**–16

pulgas **63**–25
pulir los muebles **60**–E
pulirse las uñas **109**–O
pulmón **107**–39
pulóver **88**–3
pulpo **212**–9
pulsera de emergencia médica **117**–3
puma **216**–2
puño **100**–9
punta **94**–23
puntaje **10**–3
puntero **197**–12
punto **190**–11
punto de partida **162**–1
punto extremo **193**–21
punto o la coma decimal **17**–7
punto y coma **190**–18
puntos **117**–15
puntuación **190**, **229**–1
puré de papas **81**–23
purificador de aire **113**–14
Québec **201**–5
quedarse con **28**–B
quedarse sin gasolina **162**–E
QUEHACERES DOMÉSTICOS **60**
quemador Bunsen **195**–37
quemadura de sol **110**–14
quemar(se) **116**–H
quemarse por el frío **116**–G
queso **66**–4
queso americano **71**–26
queso cheddar **71**–28
queso mozzarella **71**–29
queso suizo **71**–27
quijada **106**–4
química **195**
químico **195**–25
quince **16**
quincuagésimo **16**
quinto **16**
quiosco **122**–3
quiosco de teléfonos celulares **131**–22
quiosco para registrarse **160**–2
quirófano **121**
quitar la maleza de las flores **176**–G
quitarse **109**–Q
R&B **237**–28
rábanos **69**–4
racimo de plátanos **68**–29
radiación **218**–15
radiador **158**–19
radio **159**–37, **193**–35
radio bidireccional **179**–22
radiólogo **120**–6
radio-reloj **102**–6
raíces **211**–3
raíz **210**–5
rallador **78**–2
ralle el queso **77**–G
rama **210**–2, **210**–3

rama ejecutiva **138**
rama judicial **138**
rama legislativa **138**
rama militar **138**
ramillete **211**–28
ramita **210**–1
ramo **211**–28
rana **212**–25
rancho **52**–10
raqueta de tenis **231**–2
rascacielos **127**–13
raspador **181**–52
rastrillar las hojas **176**–C
rastrillo **109**–27, **176**–8
rasuradora eléctrica **109**–26
rata **215**–17
ratas **63**–27
ratón **196**–15, **215**–18
ratones **63**–28
raya **33**–4, **212**–11
rebane el tofú **77**–C
rebobinar **235**–C
rebotar **230**–J
recepción **184**–12
recepcionista **118**–2, **164**–5, **169**–51,
    182–14, **184**–11
receptor **14**–1
receta **112**–2
rechace una invitación **12**–J
reciba comentarios **191**–K
reciba la tarjeta **135**–F
recibir una descarga eléctrica **116**–F
recibo **27**–6
reciclar **219**–C
reciclar los periódicos **60**–B
recipiente de plástico **78**–4
recipiente de reciclaje **61**–2
recipiente para desechos
    médicos **121**–31
recipiente refractario **78**–10
reclame su equipaje **160**–L
reclutador **172**–14
recogedor **61**–17
recoger a los niños **38**–M
recoger los pantalones **100**–D
recoger los platos **82**–G
recoja los libros **11**–E
recortador **176**–12
RECREACIÓN AL AIRE LIBRE **226**
rectángulo **193**–29
red de pescar **226**–17
RED INTERNET **197**
reducir la basura **219**–A
reemplace los limpiaparabrisas **157**–K
reescríbalo **191**–J
refregar **60**–K
refresco **79**–11
refrigerador **54**–9
refrigerar **76**–D
refugio **52**–13

regalos **240**–3
regar las plantas **176**–F
regatear **102**–A, **230**–J
reggae **237**–31
regiones de Canadá **201**
regiones de Estados Unidos **201**
regiones de México **201**
regiones montañosas
    de Chiapas **201**–18
registre el automóvil **157**–F
registre su equipaje **160**–B
regístrese electrónicamente **160**–A
regla **17**–13
reglamentos de seguridad **164**–6
reglas de escritura **190**
regrese a la clase **11**–M
reír **44**–A
reja de seguridad **50**–16
relacionarse con otros **173**–A
relámpagos **13**–17
relicario **95**–35
religiosa **237**–30
relleno de espuma **226**–13
reloj **7**–9
reloj (de pulsera) **94**–16
reloj de alarma **58**–24
reloj registrador **165**–7
remitente **134**–21
remolachas **69**–5
remolque **156**–17
reparador **62**–10
reparador de techos **62**–8
reparar electrodomésticos **170**–J
reparar los grifos goteantes **219**–F
repartidor **167**–21
repelente de insectos **226**–23
repisa de la chimenea **56**–11
repollo chino **69**–15
reportero(a) **169**–52
representante de servicio
    al cliente **167**–20
reproducir **235**–B
reproductor de cassette portátil **234**–6
reproductor de CD **159**–38
reproductor de CD boombox **234**–1
reproductor de DVD **56**–7, **234**–10
reproductor de DVD portátil **234**–11
reproductor de MP3 **234**–2
reproductor de video **197**–11
reproductor personal de CD **234**–5
reptiles **213**
requisitos de ciudadanía **140**
resbaladilla **224**–13
resfrío **111**–1
resguarde su clave **143**–C
residencia universitaria **52**–8
residencia urbana **52**–6
resolver problemas
    matemáticos **170**–M
respiración de boca a boca **117**–16

respirador **179**–13
responda **135**–H
responsabilidades **140**
restar **192**–B
RESTAURANTE **82**–83
restaurante **125**–14
RESTAURANTE DE COMIDA RÁPIDA **79**
restaurante de comida rápida **128**–10
resultados de las elecciones **139**–31
retire el efectivo **132**–F
retire la tarjeta **132**–G
retroexcavadora **178**–8
retroproyector **7**–16
reúnase con un agente
    inmobiliario **49**–G
REUNIÓN DE LOS INQUILINOS **64**–65
REUNIÓN FAMILIAR **44**–45
reunión pacífica **140**–1
REUNIRSE Y SALUDAR **2**–3
revisar los correos electrónicos **39**–W
revisar los mensajes **171**–R
revisarle…la presión sanguínea **118**–A
revise el aceite **157**–H
revise los servicios básicos **147**–N
revise su ortografía **197**–F
revise su trabajo **10**–L
revíselo **191**–J
revisor de seguridad **160**–5
revista **133**–5
revistero **56**–23
revuelva **77**–O
riel de seguridad **59**–10
rímel **109**–39
rinoceronte **217**–28
riñón **107**–43
río **155**–10, **204**–3
rizador **108**–17
rizadores **33**–19
rizar el cabello **33**–C
róbalo **212**–6
roble **210**–17
robo **142**–2
roca **208**–6
rociador **53**–22
rock **237**–23
rodilla **106**–20
rodilleras **179**–19
rodillo **78**–30
rodillo de pintar **181**–23
roedores **215**
rojo **24**–1
rollo de tela **98**–15
rollo de toallas de papel **74**–23
rollos **74**–11
rollos de película **235**–22
románticas **237**–16
rompa 2 huevos en un tazón
    para horno microonda **77**–Q
rompecabezas **59**–17
ropa casual **88**

ROPA CASUAL, DE TRABAJO
    Y FORMAL **88**–89
ropa de dormir **91**
ropa de la enfermera **93**–31
ROPA DE TEMPORADA **90**
ROPA DE TRABAJO **92**–93
ropa de trabajo **88**
ROPA DIARIA **86**–87
ropa formal **89**
ropa interior de hombre **91**
ropa interior de invierno **91**–3
ropa interior de mujer **91**
ropa interior unisex **91**
ROPA INTERIOR Y ROPA DE DORMIR **91**
ropa para hacer ejercicio **89**
ropa sucia **101**–1
ropa usada **102**–2
rosa **211**–15
rosado **24**–7
rosbif **70**–1, **71**–21
rosquilla **79**–15
rubor **109**–37
ruedo **100**–8
ruido **64**–5
ruta de autobús **152**–1
ruta de EE.UU. **165**–7
ruta de escape **146**–3
ruta de evacuación **146**–5
RUTINAS DIARIAS **38**–39
RV (vehículo recreacional) **156**–10
sábado **20**–14
sábana **58**–13
sábana esquinera **58**–12
saber la hora **18**
saborear **106**–D
sacapuntas **7**–23
sacapuntas eléctrico **183**–26
sacar la basura **60**–Q
sacar un diente **119**–F
sacar un libro en préstamo **133**–C
sacar una muela **119**–F
sacarle…sangre **118**–F
saco para dormir **226**–12
sacudir los muebles **60**–A
SALA **56**
sala **47**–12
sala de banquetes **185**–14
sala de conferencias **182**–4, **184**–25
sala de operaciones **121**
sala del tribunal **141**–7
salamandra **212**–27
salamandra acuática **212**–26
salami **71**–24
salchicha **70**–12, **79**–6, **80**–2
saldo **132**–17
salero y el pimentero **55**–13
salga del salón **11**–O
salida de emergencia **51**–25, **161**–14
salida de incendios **50**–2
salida del sol **18**–14

salir de la autopista **153**–J
salir del trabajo **38**–N
salir en libertad **141**–H
salmón entero **71**–3
salón de bailes **184**–26
SALÓN DE CLASE **6**–7
salón de clase **5**–7
salón de uñas **130**–3
salsa catsup **79**–21
saltamontes **214**–24
saltar **230**–I
saltee las setas **77**–E
saltee los hongos **77**–E
salto de agua **204**–2
saludar al que llama **171**–M
salude a la gente **3**–G
salude al entrevistador **174**–H
salude con la mano **2**–F
salvavidas **225**–19
sandalias **88**–9
sandías **68**–18
sándwich club **80**–12
sándwich de pollo **79**–5
sándwich de queso a la plancha **80**–10
sangrar **116**–M
sapo **212**–28
saque una conclusión **195**–E
saque una hoja de papel **9**–Y
sarampión **111**–5
sarpullido **110**–10
sarro **119**–12
sartén **54**–24, **78**–5
sastre **100**–3
satélite **205**–20
Saturno **205**–6
sauce **210**–13
saxofón **238**–5
se está descosiendo **97**–43
se va **160**–J
sea puntual **174**–F
secador **33**–23
secador de cabello **108**–18
secador de vajilla **54**–5
secadora **101**–4
secadora **50**–13
secaplatos **54**–5
secar los platos **60**–N
secarse…el cabello **108**–H
sección de verduras,
    hortalizas y frutas **72**–2
secoya **210**–18
secretario **141**–12
seda **98**–5
sedán **156**–1
segmento de línea **193**–20
seguir las instrucciones **9**
segundo **16**
segundos **18**–3
seguridad de los alimentos **76**

Index Índice

SEGURIDAD EN EL LUGAR
   DE TRABAJO **179**
SEGURIDAD PÚBLICA **143**
seguro de puerta **159**–25
seis **16**
seleccione **196**–B
sello **183**–47
selva tropical húmeda **204**–1
semáforo **128**–8
semana **20**–15
semana pasada **20**–18
semana próxima **20**–20
sembrar **177**–A
semilla **211**–1
Senado **138**–5
senador **138**–6
senador del estado **139**–25
señal débil **14**–12
señal fuerte **14**–11
SEÑALES DE TRÁFICO **154**
sendero **208**–3
seno **107**–26
sentar al cliente **82**–B
sentenciar al acusado **141**–F
sentido contrario **154**–2
sentidos **106**
sentir disgusto **42**–7
sentir dolor **42**–11
sentir náuseas **110**–D
sentirse mareado **110**–C
sentirse satisfecho(a) **42**–6
separar **76**–B
separar la ropa **101**–A
septiembre **21**–33
séptimo **16**
septuagésimo **16**
sequía **145**–11
ser contratado **173**–L
ser electo **139**–C
ser juzgado **141**–D
ser miembro de una banda
   de rock **238**–D
ser multado por exceso
   de velocidad **162**–C
serpiente de cascabel **213**–38
serrucho **180**–4
SERVICIO DE COMIDAS **185**
servicio de directorio **14**–22
servicio en la alberca **184**–21
servicio en la habitación **184**–17
servicio en la piscina **184**–21
servicio para automovilistas **128**–11
servicios públicos **48**–5
servidor de comida **185**–15
servilleta **55**–10, **83**–26
servir **139**–D, **230**–P
servir el agua **82**–C
servir en un jurado **140**–E
servir la comida **82**–F
sesenta **16**

setas **69**–27
setenta **16**
sexagésimo **16**
sexo **4**–16
sexto **16**
siembras **177**
siéntese **6**–F
sierra **204**–15
sierra alternativa vertical **180**–10
sierra circular **180**–9
sierra de arco **180**–5
siete **16**
siga las instrucciones **147**–F
signo de exclamación **190**–13
signo de interrogación **190**–12
silenciador **158**–16
silla **7**–11
silla alta **37**–6, **82**–3
silla blanda **23**–6
silla de playa **225**–22
silla de ruedas **113**–9
silla del comedor **55**–8
silla dura **23**–5
silla mecedora **37**–21
silla plegable **102**–5
sillón **56**–22
símbolo **155**–5
sin azúcar **122**–7
sinagoga **127**–16
SÍNTOMAS Y LAS LESIONES **110**
sintonizador **234**–13
siquiatra **120**–8
sistema estereofónico **56**–8
sistema inyector
   de combustible **158**–17
SISTEMA LEGAL **141**
sistema solar y los planetas **205**
sistema telefónico automatizado **14**–23
sobre **134**–14, **183**–43
sobreexpuesta **235**–34
sobrina **34**–18
sobrino **34**–19
sofá **56**–18
sofá para dos **56**–1
sófbol **229**–0
software **196**–10
sol **209**–8
soldado **169**–58
soldador **169**–63
soleado **13**–9
sólido **96**–19
sólidos geométricos **193**
sólo giro a la derecha **154**–7
solo sentido **154**–3
solo(a) **42**–17
solución **192**–14
sombra **109**–35, **225**–13
sombrero de paja **90**–23
sombrilla de playa **225**–14
sonaja **37**–26

sonajero **37**–26
sonría **2**–D
sopa **72**–18, **80**–16
sopa de pollo fácil **77**
soplador de hojas **176**–2
soplar las velas **240**–C
soporte atlético **91**–6
sorbeto **79**–18
sordo(a) **32**–12
sorprendido(a) **43**–30
sostén **91**–20
sostenerlo **36**–A
sótano **47**–13, **50**
soul **237**–28
spaghetti **81**–26
suavizador **101**–6
suavizante **101**–6
subchef **185**–6
subibaja **224**–16
subirse al taxi **153**–E
subraye la palabra **9**–S
suburbios **52**–2
SUCESOS DE LA VIDA
   Y DOCUMENTOS **40**–41
sudadera **89**–22
suegra **34**–10
suegro **34**–11
suela **94**–21
sueldos **165**–12
suelte el lápiz **6**–J
suéter **28**–2, **87**–14
suéter anaranjado está sobre
   el suéter gris **25**–9
suéter azul turquesa está dentro
   de la caja **25**–6
suéter blanco está en frente
   del suéter negro **25**–7
suéter con cuello de cisne **96**–7
suéter con cuello de tortuga **96**–9
suéter con cuello en V **96**–8
suéter con cuello redondo **96**–10
suéter gris está debajo del suéter
   anaranjado **25**–11
suéter negro está detrás del suéter
   blanco **25**–8
suéter verde está entre los suéteres
   rosados **25**–12
suéter violeta está al lado del suéter
   gris **25**–10
suéteres amarillos están a la
   izquierda **25**–1
suéteres azules están debajo de los
   suéteres rojos **25**–5
suéteres marrones están
   a la derecha **25**–3
suéteres morados están en medio **25**–2
suéteres rojos están encima de los
   suéteres azules **25**–4
suite **184**–16
sujetapapeles **183**–31

suma **192**–7
sumar **192**–A
superintendente **50**–8
supermercado **127**–18
supervisar a las personas **170**–O
supervisor **165**–8
supervisor de la cadena **175**–4
supervisor de línea **175**–4
sur **155**–3, **201**–13
Sur América **202**–2
sureste **201**–13
surfing **227**–9
surfing a vela **227**–10
suroeste **201**–12
suspenso **237**–20
suspensor **91**–6
sustancias ilegales **142**–6
SUV (vehículo deportivo
   utilitario) **156**–7
tabla de cortar **54**–27
tabla de partículas **181**–20
tabla de picar **54**–27
tabla hawaiana **225**–16
tabla para planchar **101**–14
tabla periódica **195**–26
tablero y el panel de instrumentos **159**
tablilla **117**–14, **136**–12, **158**–12
tablista **225**–15
tache la palabra **9**–R
tacho de basura **53**–24
tachuela **183**–35
taco **79**–8
tacón **94**–22
tacones **97**–31, **97**–32
tacones altos **89**–21, **95**–25
tacos altos **97**–32
tacos bajos **97**–31
taladrar un diente **119**–D
taladrar una muela **119**–D
taladro eléctrico **180**–8
taladro neumático **178**–9
talco **108**–4
talco para bebé **37**–14
talla universal **96**–6
tallas **96**
tallos **211**–9
talón **106**–24
talón de pago **165**–11
tambores **238**–16
tanque de buceo **225**–5
tanque de gasolina **158**–10
tanteo **229**–1
tapa **78**–24
tapa de rueda **158**–9
tapa del enchufe **181**–46
tapa del tomacorriente **181**–46
tapacubos **158**–9
tapete de hule **57**–5
tapones para el oído **179**–15

tarde 18–17, 19–24
tarjeta 239–5
tarjeta de cajero automático 132–15
tarjeta de emergencia 161–26
tarjeta de felicitación 134–15
tarjeta de llamada 14–15
tarjeta de memoria 235–20
tarjeta de residente permanente 40–2
tarjeta de seguro médico 118–3
tarjeta del club de conductores 162–4
tarjeta del seguro social 40–5
tarjeta principal 196–5
tarjetas de béisbol 232–2
tatuaje 32–18
taxi 150–3
taxímetro 152–23
taza 83–24
taza de aceite 75–2
taza de azúcar 55–14
taza de harina 75–10
taza de té 55–6
taza grande de café 55–7
tazón 55–2
tazón de sopa 83–21
tazón para batir 54–28
tazón para mezclar 54–28, 78–31
TDD 15–26
té 81–39
té de hierbas 81–40
té helado 79–12
teatro 127–23
techo 46–1
techo gotea 62–3
tecla estrella 14–6
tecla numérica 14–7
teclado 196–14
teclado del teléfono 14–5
teclado electrónico 238–18
técnica de registros médicos 168–39
técnico de
    computadoras 167–19, 182–12
técnico de reparación de aparatos
    electrodomésticos 166–4
técnico de reparación
    electrónica 167–24
técnico médico
    de emergencias 121–32
tejas de madera 178–20
tejer 233–F
tejido a gancho 233–25
tela de jeans 99–7
tela vaquera 99–7
TELÉFONO 14–15
teléfono celular 14–8
teléfono inalámbrico 15–24
teléfono inteligente 15–27
teléfono público 15–25, 129–23
telenovelas 236–5
teleobjetivo 235–23
telescopio 205–23

televisor 56–6
televisor de pantalla grande 50–14
televisor de pantalla plana 234–7
televisor portátil 234–8
temeroso(a) 43–23
temperatura 13
templado 13–5
temprano 19–22
tenazas 78–23, 195–43
tenazas para crisol 195–44
tendedero 101–9
tenedor 55–3, 83–28
tenedor para ensalada 83–27
tener 18 o más años de edad 140–G
tener calor 42–1
tener frío 42–4
tener hambre 42–5
tener náuseas 110–D
tener sed 42–2
tener sueño 42–3
tener un ataque al corazón 116–D
tener un bebé 41–L
tener un neumático reventado 162–F
tener una reacción alérgica 116–E
teñir el cabello 33–D
tenis 228–15
tenis de mesa 228–14
terapeuta 115–14
terapia del habla 115–13
terapia física 115–11
terapista ocupacional 168–45
tercero 16
tercio 17–3
terciopelo 99–10
terminar 230–T
términos históricos 199
termitas 63–22
termómetro 118–11
terno 87–11, 88–11
terraza 240–2
terremoto 144–5
testigo 141–11
tetera 54–17, 55–16
tía 34–7
tibio 13–4
tiburón 212–4
TIEMPO 13
tienda de alteraciones 100
tienda de aparatos electrónicos 131–20
tienda de artículos de oficina 127–21
tienda de campaña 226–10
TIENDA DE COMESTIBLES 72–73
tienda de conveniencia 128–3
tienda de donas 129–17
tienda de mascotas 130–6
tienda de mejoras para el hogar 127–20
tienda de música 130–1
tienda de regalos 184–5
tienda de ropa de maternidad 131–19
tienda de tarjetas 130–7

tienda de telas 99
tienda de videos 129–20
tienda por departamentos 131–13
tierra 205–3, 208–2
tigre 217–37
tijeras 33–20
tijeras de podar 176–9
tijeras para setos 176–11
timbre 51–31, 53–14
timón 159–26
tintorería 128–2
tintura para madera 181–24
tío 34–8
tipos de capacitación laboral 172
tipos de matemática 192
tipos de material 98–99
tipos de medicamento 113
tipos de música 237
tipos de películas 237
tipos de problemas de salud 115
tipos de programas de televisión 236
tirantes 94–1
tirar 230–H
tirarse 230–K
tire la basura 11–N
tiro con arco 228–1
titular 133–7
título 133–14, 190–5
tiza 7–18
toalla de baño 57–16
toalla de manos 57–17
toalla para frotarse 57–6
toalla para platos 61–22
toallas de papel 54–3
toallero 57–15
toallitas húmedas 37–15, 146–12
toallitas húmedas desinfectantes 61–23
toallitas para la secadora 101–5
tobillo 106–23
tobillo torcido 110–18
tocadiscos 234–12
tocar 106–E
tocar un instrumento 238–A
tocino 70–11, 80–1
todos los días 20–21
toga 206–8
toma de corriente 159–42
tomacorrientes 58–28
tomar dictado 171–K
tomar el autobús para
    ir al colegio 38–H
tomar la orden 82–E
tomar un baño 108–B
tomar un examen de ciudadanía 140–I
tomar un mensaje 171–Q
tomar una ducha 38–C
tomar una foto 206–A
tomar una radiografía 119–B
tomar una siesta 53–A
tomar una sobredosis de drogas 116–K

tomarle…la temperatura 118–B
tomates 69–6
tome asiento 6–F
tome notas 10–C
tome posesión 49–K
tome un curso de capacitación para
    conductores 137–G
tome un curso de manejo 137–B
tome un descanso 11–H
tome un medicamento 114–D
tome una prueba escrita 137–E
tómelo con alimentos o leche 112–A
tómelo una hora antes de comer 112–B
tope 54–22
tormenta 13–16, 13–23
tormenta de polvo 13–19
tornado 145–15
tornillo articulado 180–38
tornillo de banco 180–26
tornillo para madera 180–33
tornillo para máquina 180–32
toronjas 68–6
torre 196–3
torta 73–39
torta de capas 81–33
torta de queso 81–34
torta fácil y rápida 77
tortilla de huevos 76–12
tortuga 213–42, 213–43
toser 110–A
tostada 80–4
tostadora 54–6
total 27–9
trabajador agrícola 177–8
trabajador cuidadoso 179–2
trabajador descuidado 179–1
trabajador portuario 167–23
trabajadora de cuidado
    de niños 166–16
trabajadora social 169–57
trabajar 38–K
trabajar como voluntario 41–Q
trabajar con sus compañeros de clase 8
trabajar con un compañero 8
trabajar en el jardín 53–B
trabaje en grupo 8–I
trabaje por sí solo 10–J
trabajo de nivel de entrada 172–1
trabajo nuevo 172–3
trabajos en carretera 154–16
tractor 177–9
tractor nivelador 178–6
traductor 168–35
traduzca la palabra 8–C
traer 240–E
tragedia 237–14
trailer 156–15
traje 87–11, 88–11
traje de baño 90–22, 90–26
traje de buzo 225–4

tranquilo(a) **42**–8
transbordador **220**–4
transbordador espacial **205**–19
transcribir notas **171**–C
transferir la llamada **171**–O
transmisión automática **159**
transmisión manual **159**
transporte al o del aeropuerto **152**
TRANSPORTE BÁSICO **150–151**
TRANSPORTE PÚBLICO **152**
trapear **60**–D
trapo para cubrir **181**–54
trapos **61**–9
trayectoria de carrera **172**
tréboles **233**–32
trece **16**
trece colonias **198**–1
treinta **16**
tren **150**–7
tren subterráneo **151**–11, **151**–12
trenes a escala **233**–27
trepar las barras **224**–C
tres **16**
tres veces por semana **20**–24
triángulo **193**–32
tribunal **125**–13
triciclo **224**–12
trigésimo **16**
trigo **177**–2
trigonometría **192**–18
trinchera **90**–21
tripa **70**–8
trípode **235**–25
triste **43**–19
tritón **212**–26
triturador de desperdicios **54**–7
trituradora de papel **183**–24
trombón **238**–10
trompa **217**–47
trompeta **238**–11
trompón **211**–25
tronco **210**–4
trucha **71**–1
tuba **238**–12
tuberculosis **111**–15
tuberías están congeladas **63**–16
tubo **181**–17
tubo de pasta de dientes **74**–24
tubo de pruebas **195**–42
tubos **74**–12
tuerca **180**–36
tulipán **211**–11
tumbar **230**–F
turbulencia **161**–22
tuza **215**–19
TV **56**–6
uña **106**–18
una y cinco **18**–7
una y cuarenta **18**–12
una y cuarenta y cinco **18**–13
una y cuarto **18**–9

una y diez **18**–8
una y media **18**–11
una y quince **18**–9
una y treinta **18**–11
una y veinte **18**–10
únase al grupo de vigilancia del
    vecindario **143**–L
undécimo **16**
ungüento **113**–24
ungüento antibacteriano **117**–11
unidad flash **196**–8
unidad para discos DVD
    y CD-ROM **196**–9
uniforme **231**–16
uniforme **88**–10
universidad **188**–7
UNIVERSO **205**
uno **16**
Urano **205**–7
URL **197**–4
usar bulbos de bajo consumo
    energético **219**–H
usar desodorante **108**–C
usar hilo dental **109**–K
usar la puntuación **190**–C
usar una caja registradora **170**–S
usar una tarjeta de crédito **27**–B
usar una tarjeta de débito **27**–C
usar una tarjeta de regalo **27**–E
uso del teclado **196**
usuario de la biblioteca **133**–3
usurpación de identidad **142**–9
UTENSILIOS DE COCINA **78**
utensilios de plástico **79**–19
uvas **68**–3
vaca **215**–1
vacaciones **22**–6
vaciar la basura **60**–L
vaciar la secadora **101**–E
vagón del tren subterráneo **152**–6
vale **152**–10
vales **67**–15
valle **204**–18
válvula de cierre del gas **146**–4
vandalismo **142**–1
vaqueros **86**–2, **92**–19
variable **192**–12
varicela **111**–6
vaso de agua **83**–22
vaso de laboratorio **195**–39
vaso lleno **23**–9
vaso vacío **23**–10
vaya directo en Elm Street **155**–A
vaya una cuadra a First Street **155**–F
VCR **102**–7
vea casas **49**–H
vehículo de doble tracción **156**–7
veinte **16**
veinte dólares **26**–10
veinte para las dos **18**–12
veinticinco **16**

veinticinco centavos **26**–4
veinticuatro **16**
veintidós **16**
veintitrés **16**
veintiuno **16**
vejiga **107**–46
vela **56**–20
velerismo **227**–8
velero **225**–3
velocímetro **159**–27
vena **107**–37
venado **216**–14
venda adhesiva **117**–5
vendaje elástico **117**–12
vendedor **94**–3
vendedor ambulante **129**–29
vendedores **84**–7
vender automóviles **170**–K
venera **212**–19
venir a la casa **39**–R
VENTA DE GARAJE **102–103**
ventana **47**–11, **56**–17
ventana está rota **62**–5
ventanilla **136**–7
ventanilla de billetes **152**–12
ventanilla de boletos **152**–12
ventilador **55**–19
ventisca **145**–13
ventisca de nieve **13**–23
Venus **205**–2
ver **106**–A
ver televisión **39**–X
verano **21**–38
VERBOS UTILIZADOS EN LOS
    DEPORTES **230**
verde **24**–5
verduras congeladas **72**–27
VERDURAS Y HORTALIZAS **69**
verduras y hortalizas **66**–8
verduras y hortalizas al vapor **81**–32
vereda **53**–2
veredicto **141**–14
verificar…el pulso **122**–A
verifique la pronunciación **8**–D
verifique lo que oye **12**–N
vertebrados **194**–12
vesícula biliar **107**–44
vestíbulo **50**
vestido **86**–3
vestido de cóctel **89**–20
vestido de maternidad **88**–5
vestido de noche **89**–18
vestimentas calientes **146**–6
vestirlo **36**–H
vestirse **38**–D
vez por semana **20**–22
vía férrea **152**–14
viajar **41**–P
viajar en trineo **227**–6
viaje de ida **152**–16
viaje de ida y vuelta **152**–17

vicegobernador **139**–21
vicepresidente **138**–9
víctima **142**–10
VIDA MARINA, ANFIBIOS
    Y REPTILES **212–213**
video **133**–18
viernes **20**–13
viga I **178**–3
viga maestra **178**–3
vigésimo **16**
vigésimoprimero **16**
VIH **111**–17
viña **177**–16
violeta **24**–8, **211**–23
violín **238**–6
violoncelo **238**–7
virus de inmunodeficiencia
    humana **111**–17
visera de seguridad **179**–12
visita a la oficina del dentista **119**
vista fea **23**–22
vista hermosa **23**–21
vístase con ropa adecuada **174**–B
vitaminas **113**–17
vitrina **94**–5
viviendas para ancianos **52**–11
vivir en EE.UU. por cinco años **140**–H
volante **58**–17, **102**–1, **159**–26
volar un avión **170**–F
voleibol **229**–14
voluntaria **121**–17
voluntario **121**–17
volver a usar las bolsas
    de compra **219**–B
vomitar **110**–E
votar **140**–A
vuelo retrasado **161**–30
vuelta en U permitida **154**–5
wafles **80**–8
xilófono **238**–15
yarda **181**–16
yeso **113**–20
yoga **122**–4
yogurt **72**–22
zanahorias **69**–3
zapatería **130**–10
zapatillas **86**–7
zapatillas de tenis **95**–32
zapatos **87**–13
zapatos de salón **95**–26
zapatos de taco bajo **95**–27
zapatos Oxford **95**–29
ZAPATOS Y ACCESORIOS **94–95**
zarigüeya **216**–4
zarzamoras **68**–17
zona de abordaje **161**–9
zonas horarias **19**
zoológico **222**–1
zorrillo **216**–12
zorro **216**–15
zumaque venenoso **210**–23

Research Bibliography

The authors and publisher wish to acknowledge the contribution of the following educators for their research on vocabulary development, which has helped inform the principals underlying OPD.

Burt, M., J. K. Peyton, and R. Adams. *Reading and Adult English Language Learners: A Review of the Research.* Washington, D.C.: Center for Applied Linguistics, 2003.

Coady, J. "Research on ESL/EFL Vocabulary Acquisition: Putting it in Context." In *Second Language Reading and Vocabulary Learning*, edited by T. Huckin, M. Haynes, and J. Coady. Norwood, NJ: Ablex, 1993.

de la Fuente, M. J. "Negotiation and Oral Acquisition of L2 Vocabulary: The Roles of Input and Output in the Receptive and Productive Acquisition of Words." *Studies in Second Language Acquisition* 24 (2002): 81–112.

DeCarrico, J. "Vocabulary learning and teaching." In *Teaching English as a Second or Foreign Language,* edited by M. Celcia-Murcia. 3rd ed. Boston: Heinle & Heinle, 2001.

Ellis, R. *The Study of Second Language Acquisition.* Oxford: Oxford University Press, 1994.

Folse, K. *Vocabulary Myths: Applying Second Language Research to Classroom Teaching.* Ann Arbor, MI: University of Michigan Press, 2004.

Gairns, R. and S. Redman. *Working with Words: A Guide to Teaching and Learning Vocabulary.* Cambridge: Cambridge University Press, 1986.

Gass, S. M. and M.J.A. Torres. "Attention When?: An Investigation Of The Ordering Effect Of Input And Interaction." *Studies in Second Language Acquisition* 27 (Mar 2005): 1–31.

Henriksen, Birgit. "Three Dimensions of Vocabulary Development." *Studies in Second Language Acquisition* 21 (1999): 303–317.

Koprowski, Mark. "Investigating the Usefulness of Lexical Phrases in Contemporary Coursebooks." *Oxford ELT Journal* 59(4) (2005): 322–32.

McCrostie, James. "Examining Learner Vocabulary Notebooks." *Oxford ELT Journal* 61 (July 2007): 246–55.

Nation, P. *Learning Vocabulary in Another Language.* Cambridge: Cambridge University Press, 2001.

National Center for ESL Literacy Education Staff. *Adult English Language Instruction in the 21st Century.* Washington, D.C.: Center for Applied Linguistics, 2003.

National Reading Panel. *Teaching Children to Read: An Evidenced-Based Assessment of the Scientific Research Literature on Reading and its Implications on Reading Instruction.* 2000. http://www.nationalreadingpanel.org/Publications/summary.htm/.

Newton, J. "Options for Vocabulary Learning Through Communication Tasks." *Oxford ELT Journal* 55(1) (2001): 30–37.

Prince, P. "Second Language Vocabulary Learning: The Role of Context Versus Translations as a Function of Proficiency." *Modern Language Journal* 80(4) (1996): 478-93.

Savage, K. L., ed. *Teacher Training Through Video - ESL Techniques: Early Production.* White Plains, NY: Longman Publishing Group, 1992.

Schmitt, N. *Vocabulary in Language Teaching.* Cambridge: Cambridge University Press, 2000.

Smith, C. B. *Vocabulary Instruction and Reading Comprehension.* Bloomington, IN: ERIC Clearinghouse on Reading English and Communication, 1997.

Wood, K. and J. Josefina Tinajero. "Using Pictures to Teach Content to Second Language Learners." *Middle School Journal* 33 (2002): 47–51.